STUDIES
IN LEADERSHIP

Leadership and Democratic Action

STUDIES
IN LEADERSHIP

Leadership and Democratic Action

EDITED BY

ALVIN W. GOULDNER

NEW YORK

RUSSELL & RUSSELL · INC

1965

TO THE MEMORY OF
Jeremiah F. Wolpert

A great man is great not because his personal qualities give individual features to great historical events, but because he possesses qualities which make him most capable of serving the great social needs of his time, needs which arose as a result of general and particular causes. Carlyle, in his well-known book on heroes and hero-worship, calls great men *beginners*. This is a very apt description. A great man is precisely a beginner because he sees *further* than others, and desires things *more strongly* than others. He solves the scientific problems brought up by the preceding process of intellectual development of society; he points to the new social needs created by the preceding development of social relationships; he takes the initiative in satisfying these needs. He is a hero. But he is not a hero in the sense that he can stop, or change, the natural course of things, but in the sense that his activities are the conscious and free expression of this inevitable and unconscious course. Herein lies all his significance; herein lies his whole power. But this significance is colossal, and the power is terrible . . . And it is not only for "beginners," not only for "great" men that a broad field of activity is open. It is open for all those who have eyes to see, ears to hear and hearts to love their neighbors. The concept *great* is a relative concept. In the ethical sense every man is great who, to use the Biblical phrase, "lays down his life for his friend."

—George Plekhanov, *The Role of the Individual in History*, International Publishers, 1940.

Politics is a strong and slow boring of hard boards. It takes both passion and perspective. Certainly all historical experience confirms the truth—that man would not have attained the possible unless time and again he would have reached out for the impossible. But to do that a man must be a leader, and not only a leader but a hero as well, in a very sober sense of the word. And even those who are neither leaders nor heroes must arm themselves with that steadfastness of heart which brave even the crumbling of all hopes. This is necessary right now, or else men will not be able to attain even that which is possible today. Only he has the calling for politics who is sure that he shall not crumble when the world from his point of view is too stupid or too base for what he wants to offer. Only he who in the face of all this can say, "In spite of all!" has the calling for politics.

—Max Weber, "Politics as a Vocation," from H. H. Gerth and C. Wright Mills, *From Max Weber: Essays in Sociology*, Oxford University Press, 1946.

To put the choice with the crudest possible emphasis, the problem for the creative mind was how to avoid the gangster without turning into the spinster.

—Lewis Mumford, *City Development*, Harcourt, Brace & Co., 1945.

Contributors

T. W. ADORNO, Institute of Social Research

JOHN W. ALEXANDER, Columbia University

BERNARD BARBER, Department of Sociology, Smith College

DANIEL BELL, *Fortune* Magazine, on leave from the Division of Social Sciences, University of Chicago

REINHARD BENDIX, Department of Sociology and Social Institutions, University of California, Berkeley

BERNARD BERELSON, University of Chicago

MORROE BERGER, Commission on Law and Social Action, The American Jewish Committee

ELI CHINOY, Department of Political Economy, University of Toronto

OLIVER C. COX, School of Education, Tuskegee Institute

LEWIS A. DEXTER, Department of Sociology, Park College

LEONARD W. DOOB, Department of Psychology, Yale University

JOSEPH W. EATON, Department of Sociology, Wayne University

LEWIS S. FEUER, Department of Philosophy, Vassar College

HAZEL GAUDET, Bureau of Applied Social Research, Columbia University

NATHAN GLAZER, *Commentary* Magazine and Institute of Human Relations, Yale University

ARNOLD W. GREEN, School of Social Sciences and Public Affairs, The American University

NORBERT GUTERMAN, Institute of Social Research

BERNARD KUTNER, Sarah Lawrence College

PAUL F. LAZARSFELD, Department of Sociology, Columbia University

ALFRED MCCLUNG LEE, Department of Sociology, Brooklyn College

ALEXANDER H. LEIGHTON, New York State School of Industrial and Labor Relations, Cornell University

KURT LEWIN

SEYMOUR M. LIPSET, Department of Sociology and Social Institution, University of California, Berkeley

J. O. LOW, University of Chicago

LEO LOWENTHAL, Columbia University and Institute of Social Research

ELEANOR MELNICK, School of Social Science and Public Affairs, The American University

ROBERT K. MERTON, Department of Sociology, Columbia University

NORMAN MILLER, Department of Sociology and Anthropology, University of Buffalo

ROBERT A. NISBET, Department of Sociology and Social Institutions, University of California, Berkeley

DAVID RIESMAN, Law School and Institute of Human Relations, Yale University

PHILIP SELZNICK, Project RAND, on leave from the Department of Sociology, University of California, Los Angeles

W. LLOYD WARNER, Departments of Anthropology and Sociology, University of Chicago

WILLIAM FOOTE WHYTE, New York State School of Industrial and Labor Relations, Cornell University

JEREMIAH F. WOLPERT

Contents

PART THREE: AUTHORITARIAN AND DEMOCRATIC LEADERS

PART FOUR: THE ETHICS AND TECHNICS OF LEADERSHIP

PART FIVE: AFFIRMATIONS AND RESOLUTIONS

Preface

THERE is unfortunately no clear-cut prescription as to what an "editor" is or should be. Anyone who dares to set foot in this no man's land and presumes to "edit" his colleagues' work can hope only to establish and delineate his role to the perfect satisfaction of at most one man: himself. This is hardly a mean accomplishment (where it can be realized) for a volume of this coöperative sort seems to get possessed by an inner dynamic of its own which may diverge from an editor's original intentions. Every editor, I am fairly certain after this experience, always finishes his task with something at least a bit different from what was initially conceived.

Happily, the present volume is as near to my original conception of it as I could hope. This anthology was born of a variety of experiences which I have had in democratic-action groups and in which I found that my professional training as a sociologist seemed to throw considerable light on what was taking place. I found, too, that most people in such groups, whether or not they possessed a formulated "ideology," did not have adequate conceptual tools with which to think about their own group and its internal functioning. They were quite astute when they analyzed the operations of "government," the tactics of "lobbies," the connections between "interest groups"; when, however, they sought to evaluate their own group, they were uncertain as to where to begin and of what to take hold.

It occurred to me to reëxamine a range of social science concepts and propositions with a view to sifting out those which might prove useful to democratic-action groups. This volume constitutes a partial report of what I have found. It deals primarily with analyses of leadership, made by social scientists of many kinds, which promise some help to people engaged in democratic action. Without doubt there are many lacunae here—even when judged in terms of the special orientation which we possessed. Some of these derive from an absence of research or reasoned expressions of opinion about the problems that were of interest. Other omissions occur because limitations of space often imposed an either—or choice.

An effort has been made to minimize the presentation of chopped-up excerpts from previously published works. When use was made of articles or books already published, we sought to use these in divisions that their authors themselves had established, without excerpting a paragraph here and there and pinning them together. A similar courtesy was of course extended to the contributors of the articles which are published here for the first time.

As nearly as I can state, without coaching by my psychoanalytical friends, I have conceived of my role as editor in the following way: My first responsibility, I believed, was to secure materials, whether original or previously published, which would implement the underlying design. Articles which, because they were oriented to a limited range of related problems, would possess some degree of organic integration.

I have not expected that each article would adopt an approach congenial to my own. There are, in fact, expressions of attitude, orientations to problems, and illustrations used here which I myself might not have chosen to employ and some few to which I take vigorous exception. Similarly, the contributors occasionally disagree among themselves. Short of an artificially imposed uniformity, this was both inevitable and healthy, considering the diversity of orientations to be found in modern social science.

In neither case, however, have I accented these inner tensions. This could have been permissible only if rebuttals were invited and the latter would have made an already sizable book unwieldy. Where I have thought the differences among contributors involved important issues, I have—out of a responsibility to the reader—suggested the contrast in their points of view. The discerning reader will observe these and can draw his own conclusions.

If I have dwelt on the diversities that may be found, it is because they occasionally encompass significant questions and also because they have been treated quietly and without fuss. I believe, however, that the volume is marked by a higher degree of consensus in the choice of concepts, the evaluation of problem areas, the orientation to common sources such as Weber, Freud, Marx, Mannheim, and Durkheim, and similarity of attitude nuance, than I had a right to expect.

In my own introductions to each section of this work, I considered it superfluous to present more than the merest summary of what each contributor has written. The place of each article in the volume, its title, and my brief digests indicate the contents of the articles in a general way. I was persuaded that my function could be best performed if some political and scientific frameworks into which the articles could be placed were accentuated. This is why I have called my introductions "contexts."

Please note: I have sometimes proposed contexts other than those which the authors themselves have used. Occasionally I have noted the relevance of articles for problems with which they were not originally intended to deal. *The authors, of course, bear no responsibility for my interpretations.* Moreover, I have felt free to voice opinions and express value-judgments in these introductions. This is mentioned as a warning to the reader so that he will not confuse these with statements of fact. If they stimulate thought and provoke independent examination, they will have accomplished precisely what was intended.

Though an editor's contribution to a coöperative volume is a comparatively small one, he still has the pleasurable responsibility of acknowledging the sources from which his work springs and the assistance he has received. My major debt remains, as it must for a long time to come, to my teacher, Robert K. Merton. As much by example as by lecture, Merton has provided his students—five of whom besides myself are represented in this work—with a viable conception of social science. Of all the things which a student needs of a teacher, none is more important, nor more frequently denied, than that which we freely received from Robert Merton, namely, the right to pursue our own "demons."

Without Gardner Murphy's warm encouragement this volume certainly would never have made its appearance. I should like also to express my appreciation to Daniel Bell for allowing me to read a stimulating unpublished manuscript which he has written on leadership. Nathaniel Cantor, Llewellyn Z. Gross, Milton Albrecht, Victor Barnouw, Norman Miller, and Jeremiah Wolpert, my colleagues at the University of Buffalo, have all taken a lively interest in the progress of this book and have given freely of their time and talents. The latter two, Jeremiah Wolpert and Norman Miller, have been very helpful with their suggestions and criticisms, allowing me to explore many problems with them. My students have been a continual source of encouragement, enlightenment, and occasional wonderment. I hope they will permit me to assure them, *en bloc*, of my enduring appreciation and affection. In particular, Maurice R. Stein, a graduate student, was a source of sustained stimulation. Miss Patricia Walker provided interested and alert secretarial assistance, ably seconded by Miss Clara Mroz. Harold J. Bershady was of much help in the laborious task of checking and arranging footnotes and, together with George Hartman, prepared the indexes. My wife, Helen Sattler Gouldner, though of considerable help in many ways, especially problems of style, made her major contribution to this volume simply by being the nice person that she is.

The University of Buffalo   ALVIN W. GOULDNER
September, 1950

INTRODUCTION

Introduction

THAT THE forms, the problems, the techniques and goals of leadership are a matter of public interest in our society is a proposition few will challenge. Customarily this interest is given expression by recurrent calls for "wiser," "firmer," more "flexible," and other kinds of leadership. Businessmen and trade unionists, professors and Boy Scouts, social workers and generals, all have on many occasions in the recent past voiced a desire for more and better leadership in their respective spheres. During the last depression urgent demands for "capable" leadership, some of which had unmistakably fascist overtones,[1] were widely heard. These were still a live echo in the ears of those who, only a short while later, began to develop ingenious tests to select leadership for war. Today, it is still not entirely clear whether the voices that speak loudest are those seeking a leadership for peace or whether they call, once again, for martial guidance. Time will clarify this painful ambiguity.

This book itself is but one of many current efforts to provide some understanding of leadership behavior. These efforts can be interpreted as being in part a *response* to popular interest. Pedestrian as recognition of the widespread attention to leadership is, it nevertheless has implications which should seriously affect the character of self-conscious investigation.

LEADERSHIP AS A SOCIAL PROBLEM

One of the most important of these implications is this: since scientific study of leadership derives *in part* from the pressures and tensions experienced by plain people, it behooves us to ask questions about the current concern with leadership. An answer to these ques-

[1] Robert S. Lynd and Helen M. Lynd, *Middletown in Transition* (New York, 1937), cf. chap. 13.

3

tions, however proximate and tentative it must now be, may serve to sensitize us to certain of the *specific* compulsions guiding the social scientist's study of leadership, and thereby enhance understanding of the directions it has taken. It is not suggested, however, that these considerations will provide criteria whereby the *validity* of scientific work about leadership may be assayed. This must be gauged with a different set of measures.

Instead, what may be secured is some insight into the social conditions which have impelled modern social science to define leadership in one way rather than in another; to emphasize certain of its facets but to neglect some; to employ particular concepts, hypotheses, and assumptions while leaving alternative possibilities unexplored. Such knowledge may provide us with some *clues* explaining the emphases or the lacunae in scientific work on leadership. It is useful because it tentatively maps out the pitfalls by which this investigation may be impeded. Finally, and very importantly, it suggests some of the concrete *social responsibilities* which a social scientist who studies leadership may wish to take into account. Alternatively formulated, specification of what people mean when they speak of leadership may serve to provide one guide-line in evaluating the specifications of leadership made by other social scientists and in selecting our own specification of this concept.

Why, then, are people in our society and in our time interested in leadership? First, it may be noted that *extensive* and *articulate* concern with leadership is a phenomenon *conditioned* by modern democratic values. Typically, men and women of Western European society believe that leadership behavior *may be learned*, that one does not have to be "born to the purple" in order to lead. This, in contradiction to the feudal conception of leadership which held that leadership skills were the distilled product of generations of rule. While potentially sharpened by study or experience, the feudal approach held that leaders "must possess the *inborn instinct*. . . ." Regarding political forces as fundamentally irrational, the feudal conception of leadership maintained, as Karl Mannheim has pointed out,[2] that ". . . only a traditionally inherited instinct . . . can be of aid in moulding the future." This ideology of leadership served to legitimate and thereby

[2] Karl Mannheim, *Ideology and Utopia* (New York, 1946), pp. 107-108.

reinforce the dominant status of a hereditary aristocracy, fortifying it against new contenders for power and position.

Those who finally supplanted this aristocracy throughout Western Europe, the ascending middle class, had to confront and take account of the existent justification of the old aristocratic leadership. As part of their conflict with the feudal nobility, the bourgeoisie supported a conception of leadership as learnable behavior which, through thought, discussion, and rational organization, could master the social process. In this sense, then, leadership was accessible to all men of will and intellect—the "natural aristoi" of Thomas Jefferson. This new conception of leadership also had its social functions: simultaneously it served as an ideological weapon against the established elite and as a justification stabilizing the power to which the middle class had newly succeeded.

This belief in the possibility and legitimacy of a "learned" leadership is a necessary condition for current concern and demands for new and better leaders. Unless it was believed that leadership skill could be acquired, leadership could not have become what it is today, a social problem—a matter of rightful concern and intended remedy, explicitly articulated by wide social strata. Leadership, in short, is as much a social problem as unemployment, housing, or race relations. Like other social problems, it is conditioned by and formulated in terms of specific values, one of which has already been discussed. But social problems become such, not alone because they impair some social entity or disrupt some settled routine, but also because they challenge or transgress an important value.[3] Which of our values has the present-day world so affronted as to evoke the clamor for leadership?

ALIENATION AND MASTERY

The most relevant of these would seem to be the drive to mastery and control over the environment, a value stimulated by the rise of the triumvirate: Protestantism, modern science, and capitalism. Since

[3] For development of this conception of social problems see Richard C. Fuller and Richard R. Myers, "The Natural History of a Social Problem," pp. 780-787, in Sociological Analysis by Logan Wilson and William L. Kolb (New York, 1949).

the Renaissance, each of these has oriented men to the mastery of events. Calvinism enjoined men to labor and build an earthly monument to the glory of God.[4] Science, demanding "an active interest in the simple occurrences of life for their own sake," rewarded men with an inconceivable control over nature.[5] Capitalism, with its destruction of traditional ties, heightened men's sense of individuality and imparted, at least to the middle classes, the sense that they were captains not only of industry but also of their own souls. Recently writing of North Americans, Clyde Kluckhohn has remarked that "they like to think of the world as man-controlled."[6]

But in a multitude of spheres, the expanding phenomenon of "alienation"[7] challenges and undermines this value. By "alienation" is meant that men pursue goals, and use means in their pursuit, determined either by social entities with which they do not feel intimately identified or by forces which they may be unable to recognize at all. Thus no man "wants" war, yet two are fought on a world-wide scale within a quarter-century. Practically everyone desires economic security, yet our society encountered its most devastating depression during the thirties, and fears still another. These are but two dramatic indications that social forces are abroad which most men little understand, to say nothing of master.

The growth of alienation implies that the range of choices open to the ordinary individual, the area of discretion available to him, is declining. The work of contemporaries such as C. Wright Mills, William F. Whyte, Lloyd Warner, to speak of only a few, has convincingly documented the growth of alienation in our economic, political, and civic life.[8] The sociology of masters such as Weber, Marx, and Mannheim was nucleated with the problem of alienation.

As Robert Nisbet quotes, "It is not new for men to be cogs in the machine; it is new for them to be frustrated by the fact." That men

[4] Cf. Max Weber, *The Protestant Ethic and The Spirit of Capitalism*, tr. by Talcott Parsons (London, 1930).

[5] Alfred North Whitehead, *Science and the Modern World* (New American Library, 1948), p. 14.

[6] Clyde Kluckhohn, *Mirror for Man* (New York, 1949), p. 234.

[7] For a competent discussion of the concept of alienation see Herbert Marcuse, *Reason and Revolution* (New York, 1941).

[8] The relevant studies of the last two of these authors are presented in this volume.

are thus *frustrated* by the experience of alienation is in great part a consequence of the value they place upon mastery.

It is in large measure out of the challenge to this fundamental value that much of the present emphasis on leadership derives, and by which it is given a distinctive stamp. When leadership is invoked today, often what is being asked for implicitly are men who can accomplish what the alienated individual, overcome by a sense of his powerlessness, feels he cannot. The leader becomes the symbol of control and mastery, of knowledge and insight, denied the masses. One may well remember a pre-Nazi song of German workers which went: "We are like marbles rolled against the wall." The anxiety-motored drive for security, evoked by a mass sense of powerlessness, finds outlets in a quest for dependence upon leadership.

The modern man is thus disposed to "escape from freedom" to the authoritarian solicitude of the "magic helper"—that "impossible He" who presumably can satisfy all our wants and needs and, as Horney and Fromm have shown, through identification with whom we can vicariously escape our frustrating limitations.[9] Here, then, is a crucial source of much recent interest in leadership.

An attempted interpretation of the spreading concern about leadership must meet certain further conditions. As a minimum demand, some of the factors in terms of which the rising curve of leadership-attention is explained must be covariant with the curve. For example, while the democratic creed is a necessary condition for the general attention to leadership behavior, it cannot explain the recent quickening of this attention. For similar reasons, the universality of leadership, the fact that it is apparently found at all times and in all places—though tremendously varied in structure and function—is an inadequate account of the enlivened interest in leadership. As constants, neither of the above two elements can explain the variation in intensity of the modern concern about leadership.

RISE OF THE DICTATORS

Sidney Hook has suggested that the arrogation of tremendous power by recent dictators abroad, and the gradual enlargement of the area of executive discretion in our own country, is one element focusing

[9] Cf., especially, Erich Fromm, *Escape From Freedom* (New York, 1941).

attention on leadership behavior.[10] This is a factor partially correlated with the phenomena it seeks to explain, and may be of some importance. Nevertheless, it does not seem altogether satisfactory. The widespread acceptance of modern dictators would appear to imply prior existence of the very attitudes and situations conducing to the growth of attention to leadership.

Moreover, it was at least a logical possibility that the rise of modern dictators could have been viewed as a symptom, as signifying a larger malaise of which the dictator was but a first indication. Instead, however, of being understood as a clue to deeper-going social problems, the emergence of the authoritarian leader was widely accepted as the crucial development, in and of itself.

It became, and still is, fashionable to characterize whole societies solely on the basis of whether they possessed authoritarian leaders. It is, however, more than doubtful whether the resultant division of the world into "authoritarian" states on the one side and "democratic" on the other can impart the depth of discrimination to a public opinion and foreign policy requisite for a stable peace.

But why, in their attitude toward the dictatorships, do so many mistake the rash for the germ? In great degree because the ideological or theoretical tools disseminated among the masses of people either ignored or were incompetent to deal with the institutional sources of the crisis. While this may seem applicable to a country such as the United States, it may, offhand, appear inappropriate for nations such as Germany and Italy whose class-conscious masses did have some understanding of social structure via Marxism.

There were, however, more things in modern heaven and earth than those with which Marxist philosophy was prepared to cope. One of the tragedies of Marxist theory is that it failed to grow and grapple with these problems. In the grip of political pundits, who used it more to legitimate than to guide policies, it failed to articulate in an organic way with modern psychology.[11] Moreover, Marxism was unable to handle, with any show of skill, the phenomena referred to by such basic concepts of modern sociology as "values," "social function," "in-

[10] Sidney Hook, The Hero in History (New York, 1943), pp. 5-6.

[11] This is not to deny that orthodox Marxists have made keen analyses of psychoanalysis and, as the pages of Science and Society testify, have written extensively about it. These writings, however, in no way manifest an effort to determine what supplementations or modifications of Marxism are implied by psychoanalysis.

formal group," and "informal solidarity." Oriented by their theory to secondary groups—such as the State, economic enterprises, and political parties—the Marxists knew and know nothing of primary and informal groups, concepts so necessary for understanding of the atomized and uprooted masses who were the foot soldiers of fascism. The coming of the fascist dictators was as traumatic to the Marxists as it was to most others.

It may be suggested tentatively, therefore, that popular concern about leadership arises when existent social problems become urgent but when prevalent conceptual tools, the leading ideas of the time, fail to make intelligible the institutional roots of the problems. These tensions are then defined as possible of solution by changes in leading personnel. Institutional changes, or modifications of the social structure, are not accounted desirable or possible, if thought about at all, as crisis-remedies. Ignorance of social structure and social processes, in the face of crises, is one element disposing people to seek aid from individual leaders and, in general, to become concerned about the problem of leadership. The disposition to such remedies is of course furthered by an individualistic bias.

Such ignorance of social structure is not, to be sure, equally distributed throughout all social strata, nor is it entirely or equally injurious to all. It may be expected that tendencies to define social problems as solvable by "throwing the rascals out" is functional to groups which possess at least two characteristics: (1) institutionally preëmpted benefits—i.e., groups whose privileged position, whose wealth, power, or prestige is contingent upon continuance of the institutional status quo, and (2) positions that are not defined as subject to routine or purposive replacement. In short, the plea for leadership may serve to divert energies, both scientific and political, from a study and modification of institutional realities that would impair existent vested interests.

The classical middle-class emphasis on the potentialities of leadership within all, epitomized by the American commonplace "any boy can become President," while very far from dead, has at least become a subject for cynical comment. The social conditions in which this ideology can grow unchallenged were those of a mobile open-class society for some members of which a Horatio Alger hero could be a plausible and inspiring model of morality.

But the self-subsistent agricultural economy of the American past is by now altered beyond recognition. In its place sprang up a nation of industry, mechanized, standardized, machine-tooled, brilliant in its technological perfection. The modern factory, concentrated in urban agglomerations and largely organized in corporate form, became the dominant purchaser of labor power, from the sale of which the largest group of Americans now secure their livelihoods.

As the factories pyramided into tremendous edifices, in terms of both capitalization and number of workers employed, the possibilities of an independent livelihood grew progressively dim for most Americans. The proportion of *self-employed* farmers, professionals, and independent businessmen declines, giving way to a burgeoning group of *employed* white-collar workers, professionals, and managers. With the disappearance of apprenticeship, the initial steps up the socio-economic ladder are made more difficult for the worker. Conversely, the substitution of semiskilled machine jobs for tasks of higher skills flattens the peak to which ascent is possible for most factory laborers. Supervision, moreover, tends to be recruited increasingly from groups other than operating personnel, thus further impeding the latter's ascendancy.

If the worker wishes to escape by way of establishing his own business, he finds that capital is difficult to obtain, or, when found, is placed in jeopardy by competition from chains, department stores, and large, nationally organized enterprises.[12] Seeing the conventional individualized avenues of ascendancy bottlenecked, workers employed new implements—the trade unions—to realize their goals and provide themselves with a measure of security. The existent business elite engages in a variety of conflicts with these new interest-groups and, feeling itself on the defensive, gropes about for new ways of legitimating its leadership. The conception of leadership as accessible to all is no longer quite so satisfactory to the embattled business strata as it was to their antecedents. As their prestige declined in the American community, greater emphases began to be placed on the businessman as the "natural leader" of American society, as a man whose

[12] The above discussion of elements inhibiting socio-economic mobility is in large part derived from *Economic Concentration and World War II*, Report of the Smaller War Plants Corporation to the Special Committee to Study Problems of American Small Business, United States Senate (United States Government Printing Office, No. 206 [1946]).

unusual endowments justified his leadership.[13] Conceptions of leadership tending to endow those who already possess it with an indefinable, almost mystical prowess begin to swell the currents of opinion.

In this way the status anxiety of the dominant elite fuses with the alienation of the masses to dilate the interest in leadership.

In sum: leadership appears to have emerged as a social problem when individuals possessing a specific frame of reference confront crisis situations with which they feel themselves impotent to deal. This frame of reference emphasizes democracy, individualism, and mastery of the environment.

IMPLICATIONS FOR THIS VOLUME

If this diagnosis of the circumstances under which leadership emerges as a social problem has made contact with reality, then certain implications of relevance to this book would seem to follow.

Should this work wish to articulate with the social tendencies giving impetus to interest in leadership, it must take cognizance of the antidemocratic direction latent and overt in these tendencies. The forms, techniques, the social and psychological conditions evoking authoritarian leadership, and possible ways of containing it, should come under consideration. This seems as justifiable and vital an undertaking as medical science's study and efforts to control the pathogenic agents impairing the human organism. Needless to say, however, our efforts can bear nothing like the degree of precision or reliability attained by medical science.

Social scientists disagree among themselves as to the possibility of a scientific ethic; some believe, while others vigorously deny, that science can determine values or decide what is good and bad. All scientists agree, though, that they are legitimately entitled to use their methods and knowledge to realize a value. In this volume, we choose to support democratic values, implementing them with whatever scientific competence can be mustered. In short, this is a frankly partisan book. It may be worthy of note that this value-decision does not, when made by social scientists, rest on "pure" or selfless motivation. Instead, if it is believed that contemporary history documents the conclusion that democratic values and institutions are a necessary condition for the fullest development of social science, then reasoned but energetic

13 Robert and Helen Lynd, op. cit.

support of democratic patterns is helpful to the vested professional interests of social scientists.

Beyond maintaining that democratic patterns are ethically good for our society, no further value-choices are insisted upon. It is not, for example, necessary to entertain here propositions asserting that any one organization of the economy is, now, necessary for the retention of democratic values. Concretely, it is not postulated that what some have called, euphemistically, the "free enterprise system" or what certain Marxists have alleged with equivalent fervor to be "socialism" must be either maintained or created in order to further democracy. The only commitment herein is to *democratic* values and forms.

It is, of course, evident that there is the closest connection between democratic or authoritarian patterns on the one side, and the mode of organizing subsistence-getting and distribution on the other. Recognition of this interrelationship would not seem reason to hold that either the economic or the political alternatives embodied in the dominant nations of today have exhausted men's ingenuity. New ways of balancing the need for economic security with the desire for freedom are even now in the process of development. (It is, in part, because of its alertness to this problem that the chapter on *Leadership In Israel* appears most instructive.)

Approaching leadership in the context of this value-choice, we have therefore sought in Part III of this book to elaborate certain of the consequences of democratic or authoritarian leadership, the personality and social conditions fostering them, a description of some methods employed by authoritarian leaders and of proposed counteragents.

In Part IV further attention is accorded problems which are the special concern of those who seek to have leadership both effective and democratic. In certain intellectual quarters the growing and realistic fear of authoritarian leadership is sometimes transformed into an irrational anxiety and hostility toward all leadership. But the social crises which attend the growth of authoritarianism can no more be eluded or solved without leadership than can any other human problem. Irrational hostility toward leadership in general easily disposes to political quiescence, to an abortion of democratic action, which inescapably contributes to the victory of antidemocratic movements.

The problem confronting democrats is how to use leadership for realizing their goals, rather than how to get along without leadership.

Put differently, the problem is the old one of combining democratic with effective social organization. This would seem to be advanced by enlarging the understanding which rank-and-file members of any group have of their leadership. Such an understanding would entail analytic thinking about leadership and encourage an emotional objectivity that would sap the *mystique* of leadership. Simultaneously, it would be required that the leadership's understanding of their problems, and themselves, also be encouraged. An ineffectual leadership is of no use to adherents of any set of values, let alone to hard-pressed democrats. It is for these reasons that the problems devolving about apathy, innovation, propaganda, succession, and leadership selection have been treated. If the intention is to communicate thinking about leadership which is culturally relevant and capable of translation into democratic action, it must to some extent be formulated in terms of problems already familiar to those engaged in it.

Nor is this enough. The group contexts of leadership must be specified if a formalism sterile of action utility is to be avoided. Leadership must be examined in specific kinds of situations, facing distinctive problems. The opposite shortcoming must also be detoured; in other words, the similarities among some leadership situations or problems must be emphasized. Failure to do so would enmesh our investigation in an infinite analysis of unique situations as devoid of practical potentiality as the formalist approach.

Many eminent and competent social scientists today eschew work with relevance for social problems, looking forward to an unspecified time when the careful cumulation of reliable, delimited studies will enable them to assume social responsibilities. Two questionable assumptions seem implicit in this point of view:

1. That the analysis of delimited leadership problems will some day facilitate the handling of the macroscopic problems faced on the action level. It appears no more certain that this will be the result than will continuous practice at lifting a growing calf enable a farmer to carry the grown cow. It seems likely that a different, probably more gross, conceptual level, continually alert to differences of group, culture, situation, and time, is required for a social science oriented to the needs of practice in a dynamic democracy.

2. There seems to be an untested and optimistic premise that social scientists have an *indefinite time* at their disposal in which to perfect

their researches and bring them, when fully formed, to practical uses. No doubt the full period of gestation is most comfortable for mother and child alike—but there are times when Caesareans, induced artificial labor, or forceps must be used to safeguard both. It does not appear alarmist to maintain that this is the situation of present-day social science. It must either attempt to fructify democratic action with whatever imperfect concepts and generalizations are now available, or risk delivery of a fully developed discipline, which, if not dead at birth, will be born orphaned. Bereft of the democratic culture which conceived it, this social science will be unable to mature. Certainly there are risks aplenty in a premature delivery of the *action implications* of social science. Nevertheless, it would seem presently necessary for social scientists to assume the calculated risks involved in accepting and developing roles as sociological "consultants" or "experts."

Pressed by the conviction that practical application of current knowledge about leadership requires consideration of typical contexts in which it operates, we have devoted a major section of this book (Part II) to this approach. Leadership is examined at work in ethnic groups, in different class strata, among a sexually differentiated group —women, in the arena of the community, and on a variety of different levels within the realm of politics. In each of these specific areas an effort has been made to focus on those problems of leadership which seem specifically helpful as guides to democratic action or which, more generally, round out the perspective of the individual and promise aid in making him a more informed *participant* of a democracy.

The approach employed would also seem especially useful as a counteragent to popular tendencies to divorce leadership from institutional structure. Far from bending to pressures to view leadership in isolation, the intention throughout, and particularly in this section, is to view leadership behavior in its interconnections with particular institutions or groups and their specific problems.

APPROACHES TO LEADERSHIP

Before proceeding further, it will be necessary to make more explicit the sense in which this book employs the terms "leader" or "leadership." Current literature refers to a variety of different things when the term *leader* is used. In general, Mapheus Smith's classification of the meanings of leadership appears to have sifted out the essential distinctions that have been made. Smith found that three formulations include the most typical usages of leadership.[14] These are:

1. The leaders as those whose *attainments*, in terms of a set of goals, are considered "high."
2. The leaders as those whose *status* is recognized as superior to others engaged in the same activities.
3. The leaders as those who emit stimuli that are "responded to integratively by other people."

In the first of these conceptions, individuals characterized as "geniuses" or "extremely competent" would sometimes be referred to as "leaders." In this notion the index of leadership is neither the deference extended the person, nor his ability to integrate social action in the pursuit of some goal. They may perhaps be thought of as being "ahead" rather than "higher" than others, in respect to the attainment of some group-approved end.

Quite commonly, in our society, such accomplishments will enable the individual to assume leadership in the two other senses. Nevertheless, it is clear that people defined as leaders in terms of their status or social position, or because their behavior channels or patterns the behavior of others, need not be noted for outstanding, objectively determinable attainments. Their leadership may rest on, or derive from, totally different sources.

However justifiable it may be to use attainments as an index of leadership for some purposes, this conception will not be central to the chapters that follow. Oriented as this volume is to the needs of democratic action, the notion of leadership by attainment would remove us far from the varied modes of ascendancy of leaders, their techniques and problems, and encourage undue attention to what is at best simply part of the leadership configuration. Insofar as leadership has emerged as a social problem growing out of persisting crises, it would seem that what social scientists are being asked for is data bearing upon the role of leadership in the integration of social action.

The other conceptions, those centering on leadership in terms of status, or on its integration-function, therefore seem more appropriate to the goals of this volume. Some social scientists, however, appear

[14] Mapheus Smith, "Leadership: the Management of Social Differentials," *Journal of Abnormal and Social Psychology*, 1935-1936, p. 348.

desirous of limiting the *kinds* of social status which are to be used as a measure of leadership. The nature of their limitations on the use of status as an index of leadership may be illustrated by the comments of Cecil Gibb: "When once the group activity has become dominated by an established and accepted organization, leadership tends to disappear . . . any continuance of the organization as such . . . represents a transition to a process of domination or headship."[15]

Reference to "established organization" presumably means *formal* organization, and exclusion of "leadership" from formal groups implicitly locates it in *informal* groups. Thus only informally recognized statuses would tend to be acknowledged as criteria of leadership. It is our contention, however, that an approach to leadership *suitable for use on the action level* must include those characteristics of leaders such as power, prestige, and authority which in large degree accrue to and are reinforced by formal statuses.

The exclusion of "leadership" from formal groups—those with explicit rules of procedure and specific, delimited ends—presumes, among other things, too sharp a *dichotomy* between *informal* and *formal* organization. The concepts of formal and informal organization are useful for analytically distinguishing different kinds of social action and relationships, both of which most often exist together in any one *concrete* group. In certain instances a specific group may be so clearly typified by formal or informal social relations that designation of it as a formal or informal group is meaningful. Most groups, however, are coöperative enterprises which manifest both formal and informal procedures, even if to unequal degrees.

The bureaucracy, which may be conceived of as an ideal type of formal organization, is far from devoid of informal groups and relationships. In actuality, by virtue of its formalized division of labor and delimitation of roles, the bureaucracy *fosters* the growth of informal cliques, networks, and procedures. It is in these that the personality finds more spontaneous, less purpose-oriented participation.

Conversely, many informal groups sponsor various forms of formal procedures and regulations. The boys' club with its heatedly wrought "constitution" is a familiar illustration. It is, moreover, doubtful whether the informal norms, values, or ends of an informal group

---

[15] Cecil A. Gibb, "The Principles and Traits of Leadership," *Journal of Abnormal and Social Psychology,* 1947, p. 272.

function in a manner radically different from those which are formalized, *insofar as leadership patterns are concerned.* For example, the informal prohibitions which limit leadership roles permissible for women in our society are no less effective than the formal rules demanding that a candidate for President of the United States be thirty-five years old. Formal and informal norms alike operate to sift out individuals with certain characteristics, permitting some access to leadership while denying it to others.

In Gibb's viewpoint, moreover, the term leadership implicitly means *democratic* leadership. According to Gibb, leadership is a form of "authority" *not* determined by "factors other than popular selection."[16] (There would, incidentally, appear to be justifiable doubts whether *accurate* determination of *who* the "popular selection" is, is possible without the *formal* mechanisms of democratic procedure.) The "dominator," antithesis of a "leader," is held to be one who by forcible assumption of authority, and accumulation of prestige, "regulates the activities of others for purposes of his own choosing."[17] Aside from other difficulties of this formulation, most of the dictators of the modern world—"dominators" of unmistakable cut—cannot be spoken of meaningfully as pursuing "purposes of their own choosing." Committed as they were to alliances with interest-groups in their own nations and limited by the popular, albeit inarticulate, sentiments of the masses, their goals were far from being as arbitrary or self-determined as Gibb's formulation implies.

If this analysis is to be oriented to the problems of leadership as it is *socially* defined, then we cannot reserve the term "leader" for informal and democratic groups or behavior. To the extent that leadership has become a social problem, it is not conceived of as being limited to those groups which are devoid of "established" modes of organization. The social scientist who limits his conception of leadership to the "natural leader" may be increasing the rigor of his analysis; he is, however, enhancing the reliability of his work at the expense of its social relevance.

A leader will, then, here be considered as any individual whose behavior stimulates patterning of the behavior in some group. By emitting some stimuli, he facilitates group action toward a goal or

16 *Ibid.*
17 *Ibid.*

goals, whether the stimuli are verbal, written, or gestural. Whether they are rational, nonrational, or irrational in content is also irrelevant in this context. Whether these stimuli pertain to goals or to means, cluster about executive or perceptive operations, is a secondary consideration, so long as they result in the structuring of group behavior.

This is somewhat different from saying that a leader "integrates" group behavior. More realistically, he integrates (at least) part of the group, for not infrequently a leader's stimulus may evoke opposition or apathy from some in the group. This opposition is nevertheless part of the group patterns, and is often as much oriented to the leader's stimulus as the pattern which is favorably oriented to it. The opposition may be transitional, and those opposed to any one stimulus issued by a leader may react positively to others he issues. If the opposition is extended, however, and becomes a major source of cleavage, those opposed may soon orient themselves to other leaders and possibly separate from the group. It seems more accurate to state, therefore, that a leader's stimuli integrate some of the group but pattern the behavior of the whole group.

Far from incisive, this definition has its own difficulties. For example, the behavior of a group is of course structured by elements other than leadership. Group behavior is never random because members share common sentiments, values, means and ends, conceptions of legitimate roles, and scales of stratification. These, internalized by the individuals comprising the group, conduce to recurrent or persistent patterns of behavior. What, then, may be said of the *differences* between leadership and other elements patterning group behavior?

Leadership appears to involve an *implementation* of the other structural elements. The latter are always generalized and can never be spelled out, so that their application to concrete problems or situations becomes a mechanical matter. Moreover, structural elements other than leadership, sentiments, or values, for example, may be in conflict. This conflict may be internalized within the same individual, or conflicting elements may be held by different individuals. As our later references to the work of Fritz Redl illustrate, what leadership appears to do is to *resolve* such conflicts in the norms, or *apply* an existent set of norms to a *concrete* situation.

To varying degrees, however, every individual in a group contributes to the resolution of such conflicts and the application of existent norms to specific cases. Where, now, is the difference between leaders and followers? If a *dichotomized* difference is sought between leaders and followers, then there is none. The difference is most probably a matter of degree, regardless of which definition of leadership is employed. This by no means impairs our ability to use such a definition. For in many cases the difference of degree seems sufficiently sharp to make possible a workable distinction among a group of individuals. In other words, given a group of one hundred people, we could probably be sure that those who were at one extreme in their ability to structure behavior were leaders, while those at the other extreme were followers. We would undoubtedly have difficulty with the people in the "middle." This inability to dichotomize leaders and followers should also serve to emphasize that no unbridgeable gulf exists between leaders and followers, such as is sometimes implied in certain stereotypes.

But difficulties remain. What of the gangster who at the point of a gun herds a group of people to the back of a room? The group is unmistakably responding to the stimuli which the gunman emits. Perhaps one final consideration may help to sharpen a distinction between leaders and followers. Within a group, patterns of expectations concerning the behavior of individual members tend to crystallize. A configuration of expectations regarding the behavior of each individual is established, and some of these expectations become group-approved rights and group-demanded obligations. In this sense a leader would be an individual in a group who, in some situations, has the *right* to issue *certain* kinds of stimuli which tend to be accepted by others in the group as obligations.

It is *not*, therefore, the individual who first develops an idea or makes a suggestion (not the man "ahead of his time") who is necessarily a leader, in the sense proposed. The leader would be, rather, that individual who is able by his support or espousement of the proposal to legitimate it. He transforms it into something to which group members are obliged to orient themselves. He is, to use one of Kurt Lewin's terms, the "gatekeeper." For this reason, while the gunman emits group-integrating stimuli, he is not a leader. People respond to his stimuli not because they feel the least spark of moral obligation to him but because they are afraid. Leaders may of course have means at their disposal to instill fear in their followers, but that is not the *sole* motive which individuals have in orienting themselves to a leader's stimuli. The leader is one who may legitimately, or "rightfully," structure the group's behavior.

Those individuals, then, whose behavior results in the channeling of the behavior of others because it is viewed, at least to some degree, as invoking a moral obligation, will be regarded as leaders. The reasons why a leader's stimuli may be held as legitimate are varied. The leader might be viewed as being a person with unusual endowments; perhaps his stimuli are legitimated by virtue of the legal or traditional system of norms governing his appointment or election, perhaps because of his knowledge or expertise, or because he exemplifies other qualities valued by the group.

Individuals, therefore, emitting legitimate, group-patterning stimuli, whether "orders," "commands," "instructions," or "suggestions," will be considered leaders regardless of their degree of attainments or their social status. In this conception, leaders may be democratic or authoritarian, formally or informally recognized, and operating within a group which may or may not have an "established" organization.

Leadership is in this sense a *role* which an individual occupies at a given time in a given group. A leader is not a total personality, but a person who in certain situations emits legitimate group-patterning stimuli. Clearly, the same individual can be both follower and leader in two different "segments" of his life, or in the same segment at different times.

It has been emphasized here that "leaders" *emit* stimuli to which "followers" respond. But as the above discussion implies, leaders also receive, while followers may emit, stimuli. This interaction between leaders and followers has long been recognized, and finds one formulation in Georg Simmel's comment, "All leaders are also led as in countless cases the master is the slave of his slaves." The norms the leader applies, the conflicts he resolves, the proposals he legitimates, involve his continual adaptation to and organization of stimuli which are issued by the behavior of group members. There is, though, a difference between a stimulus issued by a follower and one from a leader: this is in the probability that the stimulus structures the group behavior. A leader's stimulus has a higher probability of structuring a group's behavior—because of a group-endowed quality, the follow-ers' belief that he is a legitimate source of stimuli.

In the succeeding sections this conception of leadership will be examined in greater detail. How it emerged in the work of some social scientists, what its implications are, and some of the problems con-nected with it which are yet to be solved will be discussed. Particular attention will be given to the work of certain social psychologists, especially the "trait" analysts and the "situationists." The approaches developed by sociologists and other schools of psychology, notably the psychoanalytical, will be enlarged upon in later chapters.

LEADERSHIP TRAITS

The above account, accenting as it does relations between leaders and followers and the situational or group context of leadership, involves an approach which was not always entertained in studies of leadership. In the past, the conditions which permitted an individual to become or remain a leader were often assumed to be qualities of the individual. These were in some way believed to be located in the leader. It was postulated that leadership could be explained in terms of the "traits" possessed by the leader. Thus a multitude of studies were made which purported to characterize leaders' traits—i.e., those of their distinctive ways of acting, or personality characteristics, which tended to recur.

Since the trait approach has in many ways exercised an important influence on thinking about leadership, examination of some of its findings and assumptions will further serve to orient this work. Trait studies of leadership can be classified in many ways. Two that seem most useful from the present point of view are: (1) classification of trait analyses of leadership in terms of the method of study used; and (2) the relationship that is assumed to exist between the traits of leaders and the group or situational context.

In terms of the first method of classifying trait studies, two major categories may be found: first, the impressionistic accounts and, second, the experimental studies employing forms of controlled ob-servation. Both kinds of studies were alike, of course, in that they were guided by their use of this concept. Each author tended to conclude his work with a list of adjectives (or trait-names) of varying length and content. Charles Bird, for example, studying some twenty trait-analyses of leadership, found about seventy-nine traits mentioned altogether.[18]

Typical of the early impressionistic analyses of leadership traits are the lists proposed by two military men, Munson and Miller. Miller[19] maintained that the outstanding military leaders were typified by a personality structure manifesting self-control, assiduity, common sense, judgment, justice, enthusiasm, perseverance, tact, courage, faith, loyalty, and other traits. Among the general leadership traits mentioned by Munson were: personality, manner, use of language, tact, cheerfulness, courtesy, justice, and discipline.[20] E. S. Bogordus proposed five traits allegedly universal to leadership: imagination, foresight, flexibility, versatility, and inhibition.[21]

Bertrand Russell, adding his list to the many already existing, commented: "To acquire the position of leader he (the individual) must excel in the qualities that confer authority: self-confidence, quick decision and skill in deciding the right measures."[22] Robert Michels has suggested the following traits: force of will, relatively wide knowledge, Catonian strength of conviction, self-sufficiency, and others.[23]

The *impressionistic* surveys of leadership traits were, in some respects, far surpassed by the more careful studies of Terman, Reaney, Nutting, Rohrbach, Bellingrath, Marion Brown, Bennett, Jones, and T. L. McCuen.[24] But they have been superseded mainly in the rigor of the investigational techniques by which the traits were isolated or determined. That is, they too assumed that leadership hinged on, and could be best described in terms of, the trait-qualities of individuals. Recently commenting on this, Lindesmith and Strauss have stated: "Leadership is commonly thought of in terms of leadership quali-

---

[18] Charles Bird, *Social Psychology* (New York, 1940).

[19] Arthur Harrison Miller, *Leadership* (New York, 1920).

[20] Edward L. Munson, *The Management of Men* (New York, 1921).

[21] E. S. Bogardus, *Fundamentals of Social Psychology* (New York, 1942), chap. 12.

[22] Bertrand Russell, *Power, A New Social Analysis* (New York, 1938).

[23] Robert Michels, *Political Parties* (Hearst International Library, 1915), p. 64ff.

[24] E. DeAlton Partridge, *Leadership Among Adolescent Boys* (Teachers College, Columbia University, No. 608 [1934]); this contains a very able summary of the work of these men up to that date.

ties. . . . In taking over this common-sense notion, social psychologists have been led to seek those traits of personality that are most usually associated with being a leader."[25]

Thus, as Lindesmith and Strauss suggest, many of the trait analyses of leadership have apparently been influenced by current popular conceptions of leaders as being in some way unusual beings possessed of extraordinary powers alien to the common run of mankind. As such, they are objects capable of being transformed into the "magical helpers" sought by those whose need for security is resolved by finding some powerful authority upon whom they can become dependent. Moreover, these trait analyses also conform to the popular conceptions of leadership in that, by divorcing the leader from his group and institutional setting, they do not challenge the assumption that social crises may be met without institutional changes.

INADEQUACIES OF THE TRAIT APPROACH

The inadequacies of the above type of trait studies can be only briefly summarized here. Leaving aside questions concerning their investigational technique, the following points may be raised:

1. Those proposing trait lists usually do not suggest which of the traits are most important and which least. Not uncommonly, lists of more than ten traits are presented. In most such lists it seems very unlikely that each of the traits is equally important and deserves the same weighting. Bearing in mind that practical application of leadership studies (as, for example, in leadership selection or training) requires compromises due to time limitations and the number of candidates available, the failure to indicate the rank order of importance of the traits makes it difficult to know at what points compromises may be made. It is only within very recent years that the work of trait-analysts, like Raymond Cattell, gives promise of coping with this problem.

2. It is evident, too, that some of the traits mentioned in a single list are not mutually exclusive. For example, Miller lists tact, judgment, and common sense as leadership traits. It would seem, ordinarily, that the first two would be included in the last.[26]

[25] Alfred R. Lindesmith and Anselm L. Strauss, Social Psychology (New York, 1949), p. 274.
[26] I have derived this illustration from E. Partridge, op. cit.

3. Trait studies usually do not discriminate between traits facilitating ascent to leadership and those enabling it to be maintained. It seems to be assumed that all the traits which differentiate leaders from followers are functional to ongoing leadership. It appears entirely possible, however, that certain of the traits of leaders were necessary conditions for success in the competition to become a leader but are not needed by an established leadership.

4. Typically, most trait studies, and those of leadership are no exception, raise questions concerning the organization of behavior, the range of recurring behavior patterns manifested by individuals. They are largely descriptive. Usually they do not ask how these traits develop, or how the behavior became organized.[27] Thus, in so many of the trait studies there is the tacit assumption that the leaders' traits existed prior to their ascendance to leadership. It is therefore inferred that the leaders' possession of these traits are to help explain how he became a leader.

Even in some of the trait studies which maintain that leadership traits are specific to the situation, that the situation makes them useful, it appears to be assumed that the individual already possesses the useful traits when he enters into leadership. The possibility that the reverse is true, namely, that it is the leadership position which fosters the original emergence of distinctive traits, is hardly ever systematically explored. In sum, one usually is not informed whether, and which, leadership traits exist before and which develop after leadership is assumed.

5. Finally, the study of the personalities of leaders, as of any other group of individuals, in terms of traits involves certain debatable assumptions regarding the nature of personality. It seems to be believed that the leader's personality can be, or is, described if all the traits by which it is composed are determined. Implicit is the notion that a personality is the sum of its component traits. This would seem, however, to ignore one of the fundamental properties of personality, its possession of organization. The same "trait" will function differently in personalities which are organized differently. To characterize the component elements of an entity such as personality

---

[27] Anne Anastasi, "The Nature of Psychological Traits," *Psychological Review*, May, 1948, pp. 127-138.

is an insufficient description in that it omits consideration of the fact that these elements have varying *positions* or *arrangements*. It is only when attention is paid to arrangement or position that organization, as such, can be brought into account.

Most trait studies, flowing from the empiricist tradition, have approached the study of personality atomistically, and with little regard for personality as an organized whole. Not being oriented to any systematic theory of personality, they have pursued the "facts" of personality only to find that empiricism can be just as treacherous a guide as the most speculative of theoretical systems. It is, in part, because of the lack of any theoretical guide lines that the trait studies of leadership have produced relatively little convergence. Some scholars, for example, speak of two, ten, nineteen, and some of thirty, traits of leadership. Charles Bird's analysis of trait studies of leadership found that only 5 percent of the traits mentioned were common to four or more investigations.[28]

SITUATIONS AND GROUPS: THE SITUATIONIST CRITIQUE

As already indicated, traits studies may be subdivided according to the manner in which they relate traits to the leadership *situation*. In general, a twofold subdivision may be made: (1) those implying or stating that the traits of leaders are universal: in other words, that the traits of leaders do not depend upon the situation, that leaders in any situation will possess the same traits; (2) the trait study which suggests that it is impossible to talk about leadership traits in general, but only about the traits manifested in concrete, particular situations. Leadership traits are conceived of as varying from situation to situation and group to group.

In order to understand the reasons which have fostered the emergence of the situational studies of traits, it is necessary to consider some of the implications of the proposition that leadership traits are universal and will not vary with the situation.

If this proposition were to be demonstrated, then several things should follow: (a) the traits or personal qualities which made an individual a leader in one group should also be useful for leadership in

[28] Bird, *op. cit.*

other groups; (b) a man who is a leader in one group should tend
to be a leader in others.

That a leader is *involved in a network of relationships* with other
individuals who, together with him, comprise a group, is a consideration the full implications of which elude these trait-analysts. No
matter how spontaneous and informal the group, its members never
engage in random, continually unpatterned activities. There is a
certain degree of persistence or patterning in the activities which a
group undertakes, be it bowling, playing bridge, engaging in warfare,
or shoplifting. These persisting or habitual group-activities, among
other things, set *limitations* on the kind of individuals who become
group members and, no less so, upon the kind of individuals who
come to lead the group.

If by nothing else, the traits of a group's leaders are limited by the
traits of the individuals who comprise the universe from which
leaders are drawn. Any group functions as an attracting, repelling,
and selecting mechanism. Not all individuals would wish, nor could
they if they so desired, to become members of any group. As obvious
examples: modern trade unions practically always exclude employers
from membership; Girl Scouts exclude boys; armies, those physically
or mentally ill. Similarly, pacifists would not be *interested* in joining
the National Guard, nor would political conservatives be interested
in obtaining membership in radical parties.

Trait studies themselves inform us that psychological traits are not
distributed uniformly through all social strata. The distribution of
traits differs with age, education, occupation, and sex.[29] From this it
follows that members of particular groups will tend to possess certain traits both more and less than others. Since leaders tend to be
members either of the group which they lead or of other limited
groups, one may expect that the traits of leaders will vary with those
of their group. Jenkins, in a recent summary[30] of leadership studies,
concludes that "Leaders tend to exhibit certain characteristics in
common with the members of their group. Two of the more obvious
of these characteristics are interests and social background." The

[29] Anastasi, *op. cit.*

[30] William O. Jenkins, "Review of Leadership Studies with Particular Reference to Military Problems," *Psychological Bulletin*, January, 1947, pp. 54-79.

probability seems great, therefore, that the leaders of some groups possess some traits different from the leaders of other groups, and that "leadership traits" are not universal.

Not only are the traits of leaders limited by the traits of the individuals from which leadership is drawn, but they are further limited by the character of the group's specific activities. Even one of the earlier studies, made by Caldwell and Wellman, found that while certain traits—physical prowess, for example—were influential in the selection of school *athletic* leaders, these traits were not characteristic of leaders in *other* school activities. While height may be helpful to basketball players, its absence did not deter three rather short men— Mussolini, Hitler, and Lenin—from assuming the leadership of nations. In this vein, Cecil Gibb writes: "There is no one leadership type of personality. One man might achieve leadership status because he has superior intellectual endowments which force him consistently upon the notice of others and make them dependent upon him. A second achieves leadership because he has a quiet helpful interest in fellow group-members and because what British psychiatrists call his 'contact' is good. Leadership resides not exclusively in the individual but in his functional relationship with other members of his group."[31]

A. J. Murphy,[32] emphasizing the relative fluidity of leadership traits, points out that the "self-confidence" of a work leader may disappear if his group is placed in a parlor situation. Or that a leader noted for his "dominance" may become "shy" when placed in a situation in which his *skills* are not useful. Thus not only must the group in which the leader operates be considered, but also the *situation* which the group encounters. Both of these elements seem to affect the character of leadership traits. Jenkins' first conclusion of his summary of leadership studies emphasizes this: "Leadership is specific to the particular situation under investigation. Who becomes a leader of a given group engaging in a particular activity and what the leadership characteristics are in the given case are a function of the specific situation including the measuring instruments employed."[33]

31 Gibb, *op. cit.*, p. 231.
32 Albert J. Murphy, "A Study of Leadership Process," *American Sociological Review*, 1941, pp. 675-676.
33 Jenkins, *op. cit.*, p. 75.

SKILLS AND SITUATIONS: THE SITUATIONIST
CRITIQUE CONTINUED

The interaction between skills and situations, noted by Murphy above, has recently received cogent amplification by the OSS assessment staff:

A member of an organization who cannot do what is expected of him is immediately confronted by the stress of self-criticism and of criticism, implicit or explicit, from his supervisor and from his co-workers. His self-confidence will diminish, and feelings of inferiority emerge; he is likely to become hypersensitive and defensive in his social relations, and blame others for his own shortcomings. . . . Thus, as soon as the strength of one component—in this case that of specific ability—drops below a certain minimum, other components are similarly affected. . . . Contrariwise, a man whose talents are exactly suited to the job assigned to him and who, therefore, attains or surpasses the level of social expectation for him, will be continually encouraged by signs of approval and of respect from his associates, and under these conditions, his energy and initiative, motivation, effective intelligence, emotional stability, and social relations are likely to reach their maximum.[34]

The intricate relations between the psychological aspects or traits (skill, self-confidence, etc.) and the group aspects (respect, approval), so clearly described above, seem most likely to operate in the manner described in a culture such as our own. That is, in our culture great value is placed on specialized skills as the basis of legitimating occupancy of a great variety of roles, often including leadership roles. In consequence, the presence or absence of required skills may elicit a stronger group response in our society than it might in more traditional societies where skill was not such a primary basis of legitimation.

This suggests that skill may not be an open-sesame to leadership, universally facilitating ascent to or success in it. The situationists' emphasis on the role of skills may require trimming to more modest implications; in particular, limiting its operation to groups or societies outside the traditionalistic orbit. Formulated positively, the boundary conditions tacitly assumed by the situationists—and in terms of which their proposed interrelationship between situationally-functional

---

[34] The OSS Assessment Staff, *The Assessment of Men* (New York, 1948), p. 456.

skills and leadership appears probable—include a relatively high division of labor and degree of specialization, an emphasis on achievement rather than ascription of certain statuses, and the use of skills as a basis of achieving and legitimating these statuses.

A second way in which the role of skills may be culturally bounded can be suggested. The OSS analysis of the *consequences* of skill-deficiencies or skill-competencies, their extraction of group deference, approval or respect, or their opposites, and their effects on the individual's traits (self-confidence, initiative, etc.) involve certain assumptions about *personality*.

Specifically, what must be assumed is that the individual has some motive or need for the high degree of responsiveness which he manifests to group judgments. The problem rests in the character of the motive or need. To find individuals responding to their groups, adapting, learning, modifying and being changed is not, in the light of modern psychology and sociology, in the least startling. Some degree of responsiveness and behavior modification must be accepted as "normal." But to find, or allege, individuals to be adaptable to the extent suggested by the situationists—that is, almost infinitely plastic —can be anticipated only under very limited psychological and, therefore, cultural conditions.

It may be hypothesized that the personality which would react as responsively or immediately to current group pressures is, perhaps, likely to manifest a weak or insecure ego and is in some measure, because of this, extremely dependent upon group judgments. Too, one might look for a heavy emotional investment in "success." Given these two psychological conditions, group judgments of individual worth may be *swiftly* responded to by the individual. Particularly so, if these judgments explicitly or implicitly involve assessments of the individual's "success," for it is with this that, in our culture, the individual's sense of worthiness is so intimately tied.

If such psychological conditions are pervasive, they must be presumed to be institutionally compelled. Possibly they emerge with the weakening of the stable traditional relations of family, neighborhood or church, and their substitution by the shifting, calculating ties of a market society. But the intent here is not to define the specific cultural boundaries yielding validity to the situationist propositions about the fluidity of traits, but only to suggest that these are *definable*.

To return to the situationist position:

"In practically every study reviewed," writes Jenkins, "leaders showed some superiority over the members of their group, in at least one of a wide variety of abilities. The only common factor appeared to be that leaders in a particular field tend to possess superior general or technical competence or knowledge in that area."[35]

Thus distinctive situations make specifically different demands for skill, and individuals failing to possess these will be limited in their chances for leadership. It is in this context that William F. Whyte's comment in a later chapter, to the effect that street-corner gang leaders tend to initiate group activities in which they excel, may be placed.

The unique experiences of the OSS assessment staff underscore the role of the situation still further. Directed to provide the OSS with personnel capable of performing *secret* missions, the assessment staff therefore only had a *general idea* of the assignment each man was to undertake. Consequently the assessment men could rate candidates only "according to their conception of *all-round men in a given field of activity*." (Our emphasis—A. W. G.) In attempting to explain why many of the men to whom they gave "high" ratings received "low" appraisals from the units to which they were assigned, the assessment staff writes: ". . . actually, the assessed man who went overseas was not called upon to deal fairly well with a multiplicity of rather general situations, but to deal very well with a limited number of specific situations . . . these men were appraised in the theater according to how effectively they performed a particular role in a particular location."[36]

Though not intended to refer to leadership alone, these conclusions of the OSS staff strongly suggest the limitations which concrete situations place upon the utility of leadership traits. It was clearly not enough to know the candidate's *general* field of activity to successfully predict his performance; a man *generally* competent in a field often would be judged incompetent to handle the *specific situation* in which he found himself. It is significant, too, that the assessment staff's prediction about the performance of the candidates was much more successful for those who "undertook the mis-

[35] Jenkins, *op. cit.*
[36] OSS Assessment Staff, *op. cit.*, p. 374.

sions originally proposed for them than it was in the case of men who were given entirely different missions on arriving overseas."[37]

These, then, are some of the major lines of argument which those who consider, as Gibb states, that "leadership is relative always to the situation," have used in refutation of that branch of the trait school which held leadership qualities to be the same in all situations. By and large, the former school, characterizable as "situationists," have won the day. By now it is probably true that most social scientists would sympathize with A. H. Lloyd when he spoke even of great individual leadership as a "noble fiction." But uneasy rests the head that wears the crown of science.

UNIVERSAL TRAITS?

For even among the situationists themselves, one might say among the very situationists who have done some of the most original and distinguished thinking about leadership, certain incongruous notes are heard. The hypothesis that there are indeed *certain* traits found among all leaders occasionally peers out of the cracks of situationist paragraphs, jarring us out of our complacency. Even a field social-psychologist, such as J. F. Brown, oriented to the determining role of the situation and its structure, has implied this. "It would be absurd," he writes, "to deny that two factors of a semibiological nature are important in leadership, intelligence and psychosexual appeal. Of these, probably the most important is intelligence."[38]

It is significant, also, that the sociometrist, Helen H. Jennings, emphasizing as she does that leadership is the product of "interpersonal interaction and not of the attributes residing within persons," nevertheless concludes that while leadership roles differ greatly, certain *constant* characteristics of leaders were found in her own studies. Her comments seem to be of such crucial theoretical importance as to deserve extensive quotation:

In a population so large as that of the test-community, the varieties of leadership are manifold. Nevertheless, *in personality a number of characteristics of leaders stand out as common attributes.* Each leader 'improves' from the point of view of the membership, through one method or the other, the social milieu. Each widens the social field for participation of

37 *Ibid.*
38 J. F. Brown, *Psychology in the Social Order* (New York, 1936), p. 347.

others (and indirectly her own social space) by ingratiating them into activities, introducing new activities, and by fostering tolerance on the part of one member towards another. Each leader shows a feeling for when to censure and when to praise. . . . No leader is invariably a 'pleasant' person . . . instead each is definite in her stand and will fight for what she considers 'right' . . . each leader appears to succeed in controlling her own moods at least to the extent of not inflicting negative feelings of depression or anxiety upon others. Each appears to hold her own counsel and not to confide her personal worries except to a selected friend or two. . . . Each appears able to establish rapport quickly and effectively with a wide range of other personalities. . . . Each appears to possess to a greater or less degree unusual capacity to identify with others. . . .[39]

Gibb makes a similar comment: "There do seem to be, however, certain general characteristics of personality, the possession of which does not necessarily cause a man to have leadership status conferred upon him, but which does place him higher than he would otherwise be on the scale of choice in any group."[40] (Our emphasis—A.W.G.)

The hypothesis that there are some traits common to all leaders is presently unfashionable. Recognition that this is so should serve as a warning signal, cautioning scientist and layman alike to "go slow." For without the utmost care we may too easily shrug aside the potentialities of this hypothesis. Several questions devolve about the problem:

1. Do social scientists today have any reliable evidence concerning allegedly universal leadership traits?
2. Whether or not such evidence exists, what reasons may be advanced for expecting that some traits common to all leaders might be found?
3. Finally, and this is the most crucial question of all, how is it that some traits have not been discovered which—while not universal—are at least common to leaders in more than one or two situations or groups? Jenkins' study found, for example, "wide variations in the characteristics of individuals who become leaders in similar situations, and even greater divergence in leadership behavior in different situations."

To consider the first question, is there any reliable evidence demon-

---

[39] Helen Hall Jennings, *Leadership and Isolation* (New York, 1943), pp. 203-204.

[40] Gibb, *op. cit.*, p. 281.

strating the existence of traits common to all leaders? The answer is plainly no. Jenkins notes that a "number of studies suggest superiority of leaders over those in their groups in physique, age, education, and socio-economic background. . . ." He is perhaps enjoying an understatement when he adds: ". . . but the need for further research in this connection is evident."[41]

INTELLIGENCE AS A LEADERSHIP TRAIT

"Psychosexual appeal" aside, Brown's reference to intelligence would seem a more formidable candidate for status as a universal trait. The work of Caldwell, Wellman, Partridge, Wetzel, Hollingworth, Fence, Carroll,[42] and others has long suggested certain definite relationships between the leaders' intelligence and the average intelligence in their groups. These relationships appear to be twofold: (a) The leader tends to have an intelligence higher than the average in his group, and (b) there is a limit to the superiority of intelligence which a leader may possess. That is, superiority of intelligence beyond a certain degree, relative to the group, may prevent an individual from obtaining or holding onto leadership.

Regarding this last point, Murphy, Murphy, and Newcomb comment: "Children who are too superior in age and abilities are not accepted as leaders. For instance, children with intelligence quotients of 150 are more likely to be leaders in a group of children with intelligence quotients in the neighborhood of 130 to 140 than in a group of children with average intelligence."[43]

The evidence is, however, by no means definitive. Perhaps the most which may be said is that lower than (group) average intelligence inhibits access to leadership, but higher than average intelligence is no guarantee of leadership. It should be emphasized, in passing, that those who would attribute to intelligence a role in leadership usually insist that the *specific level* of intelligence, either aiding or impeding leadership, is a function of the average of the group. So much of the evidence on this problem derives also from studies of children's groups that its applicability to adult situations is doubtful. Moreover,

---

41 William Jenkins, *op. cit.*, p. 75.
42 Cf. Partridge, *op. cit.*
43 Gardner Murphy, Lois Barclay Murphy, and Theodore M. Newcomb, *Experimental Social Psychology* (New York, 1937), p. 525.

Krout relates, "The great men of the civilized world have been analyzed for us by competent psychologists on the basis of materials sufficient to determine brightness or intelligence. The results seem to show that 'great men,' including outstanding leaders in the public life of Europe and America, range all the way from dull normal to genius."[44]

At this time there is no reliable evidence concerning the existence of universal leadership traits. Murphy, Murphy, and Newcomb suggest that "If there is such a thing as a psychology of leadership in the abstract, it will arise from studies in which behavior resemblances of leaders in varying life situations are investigated. . . ."[45] In other words, the conduct of situationally oriented studies, far from impeding, may be the only basis for determining which of the traits of leaders are universal. This is a sound injunction, and deserves some amplification.

The crucial problem seems to be one of the *direction* in which leadership traits universal to all situations might be sought. It may well be that no universal traits have been found because those which might exist are very different from those conventionally anticipated, e.g., intelligence, superior height, etc. The mere study of leadership traits in different situations, and the comparison of these findings, however indispensable, will only *fortuitously* lead to the discovery of universal leadership traits unless each study is guided by theoretically rooted hypotheses.

The second question asked above now becomes relevant; on what grounds may we suspect the existence of universal traits? Why should any traits be *universal* to leadership? Whether traits are universal, or only specific to concrete situations, it is necessary to explain *why* they are manifested by the leadership and found useful to them.

Consideration of this problem may be opened by noting the popular formulation: "Leadership, or leadership traits, are relative to the situation." This means that a person's traits either develop out of his experience in playing a leadership role or that given types of leadership roles will attract individuals who already possess traits useful in the performance of the role. The diversity of leadership traits men-

[44] Maurice H. Krout, *Introduction to Social Psychology* (New York, 1942), p. 644.
[45] Murphy, Murphy and Newcomb, *op. cit.*, p. 313.

tioned is presumed to be, in one of the two ways mentioned, a response to the diversity of the situation and the group.

Suppose, however, it were demonstrated that all human groups contained some elements in common, and that these could be spelled out. It should therefore be expected that there would be some leadership traits manifested commonly by all leaders. In short, there is no reason why leadership traits should constitute adaptations only to the *diversities* of groups; they should, too, involve adaptations to the *similarities* of groups. Thus some leadership traits should be unique, specific to concrete groups and situations, while some could be common to all leaders.

GROUP NEEDS

The notion that all social groups are in certain respects similar has, in fact, recently been developed by an emerging school of American sociologists, the "structural-functionalists." The structural-functionalists postulate that any empirical system, any concrete social system or group, has a number of "functional prerequisites" which must exist in order for the group to continue. These functional prerequisites comprise "needs" which, if the group is not to be disorganized and sooner or later discontinued, must be satisfied. In the words of Philip Selznick, the most basic of all these needs "is the maintenance of the integrity and continuity of the system itself."[46]

This implies that any group has stability-maintaining elements so that changes in one aspect of the group organization induce "compensating changes in others," thereby maintaining the group's integrity. These stability-maintaining elements constitute "secondary" or "derivative" needs which provide the matrix from which techniques of defense develop. Among the derivative needs which Selznick tentatively suggests as common to coöperative human groups are:

1. Guarding the organization against all possible encroachments, aggressions or threats from the environing actions of others.
2. Stability of lines of authority and communication. Leaders must continue to have access to the rank and file.
3. Stability of informal relations, since these tie an individual

[46] Philip Selznick, "Foundations of the Theory of Organization," *American Sociological Review*, February, 1948, pp. 25-35.

to an organization and widen opportunities for effective communication.

4. Continuity of policy and the sources of its determination.
5. Homogeneity of outlook with respect to the meaning and role of the organization—agreement on means and ends.

These, emphasizes Selznick, are at best a beginning list of the derivative needs which must be satisfied, to insure survival or self-maintenance of coöperative systems of organized action.

Talcott Parsons, with whose name structural-functional theory is widely associated, has also suggested a number of functional prerequisites, not for smaller groups but for the social system as a whole. Parsons lists the following functional prerequisites:

a. A social system must somehow provide for the minimum biological and psychological needs of a sufficient proportion of its component members.
b. ". . . the coordination of the activities of the various members (must be accomplished) in such a way that they are prevented from mutually blocking each other's action or destroying one another by actual physical destruction. . . ." The social action of members of a society must be "sufficiently geared in with each other so that they do mutually contribute to the functioning of the system as a whole."
c. The system can only function if a sufficient proportion of its members perform the essential roles with an adequate degree of effectiveness.[47]

These, Parsons believes, may constitute starting points from which a variety of further elaborations of the problem of functional prerequisites can be worked out.

It is impossible here to indicate more than briefly some of the key problems and present inadequacies of structural-functional theory. Robert K. Merton, in a critique of Parson's article,[48] touches upon the most crucial of these. Merton notes that the concept of "needs" is "at present one of the cloudiest and least articulated concepts in the entire panorama of functional-conceptions." Moreover, present structural-functional theory emphasizes the "needs" for *maintenance* or *survival* of any given social system. "All intent aside," writes Merton, "emphasis on the need for survival tends to focus attention

---

[47] Talcott Parsons, *Essays in Sociological Theory Pure and Applied* (Glencoe, Ill., 1949), chap. 2.

[48] Robert K. Merton, "Discussion," *American Sociological Review*, April, 1948, pp. 164-167.

of observers on statics rather than on change and to direct attention away from the functional needs for determinate types of changes." To this, one further point of relevance might be added: the structural-functionalists tend to focus on those threats to the stability of a group that spring from sources external to the group involved. Selznick, for example, writes of the need to safeguard the group from the "environing actions of others." Those sources of group instability which are *internally compelled* are treated by the structural-functionalists, if at all, in an *ad hoc* manner.

While probably the most theoretically astute school of American sociology, despite these considerable shortcomings, structural-functionalism is still too undeveloped to estimate accurately the potentialities it has for the study of leadership. Should the structural-functionalists' belief that there are such things as needs common to social systems or groups be validated, then a specific *direction* may be indicated for a further search into common leadership traits. Structural-functional theory might, if some common leadership traits were discovered, be able to provide an explanation for the specific universals unearthed. Such universals would not be attributes of individual personality any more than the leadership traits claimed to be specific to situations. They would be functional responses to group needs, albeit needs which are constant.

It is precisely because the proposition that there are some leadership traits common to leaders is so at variance with current social-science thinking that it has been emphasized here. If nothing else, the clash of antithetical propositions may serve to awaken some fruitful doubts about prevalent conceptions of the matter.

The possibility that there are some traits common to all leaders is not interpretable as meaning that "all leaders are the same" everywhere. There seems no a priori reason that leaders, like people in general, should not be *both similar to and different from* others.

SITUATIONS, CONCRETE AND ABSTRACT

From a scientific point of view, it is doubtful whether the proposition that "leadership traits are relative to the situation" is more readily demonstrable than the proposition "leaders have *certain* traits in common." A "situation" is a *unique* constellation of events and processes which is unduplicable. No two scientists could ever study exactly the same situation and, consequently, the discovery of traits specific to a concrete situation could not be verified.

What the situationists mean (and their looseness of phrase is not a straw man deliberately concocted as a basis of criticism) is that some traits are specific to certain aspects, facets, or dimensions, which they must of necessity *abstract* from the situation. (Once this is recognized, the next legitimate question becomes: Which aspects or facets of the situation shall be abstracted, and kept in view?)

Scientifically, situations can only be treated as *abstractions*, never in terms of their inexhaustible, concrete reality. Relative to *what aspects* of a situation are leadership traits specific? If certain aspects of a situation conduce to certain leadership traits in one case, then, other things even roughly held constant, there is no reason why they should be unable to do so in another.

If the situationists had specified which *aspects* of situations were held to determine leadership traits, they would have been compelled to distinguish between the ephemeral or unique features and the more persistent and relatively enduring ones. The relevant point here, however, is that there are some aspects of situations which are relatively more persistent than others. (A "functional prerequisite" is, in one respect, simply a response-provoking feature of a situation with maximal persistence.)

If this is granted, then several things follow. There is sound reason for expecting that the persisting elements of situations will produce persisting consequences; that some traits of leadership which derive from "long-tenure" features of a situation will continue. (A situation is as enduring as the elements we choose to define it.) In other words, certain leadership traits may be expected to be evoked over a period of time. Thus the possibility of historically extensive, or limited, types of leadership emerges. Some traits of leadership should, in brief, be common to a group, or social system, over a historical span.

Moreover, facets of a situation which are historically extensive, which last for periods of time, are not likely to be culturally isolated, or manifested by only one subgroup or association in a society. Their ability to persist suggests favorable social conditions and, consequently, their probable existence in varied subgroups or associations. Different groups and situations may, then, be seen as possessing certain (abstracted) characteristics in common, at any one time. There should therefore be certain traits held in common by leaders in different situations or groups, even if not all.

For example, it seems *possible* that most leaders in contemporary American society, and over our history, have manifested a higher degree of "aggression" than most leaders of Indian culture. Again, ours may be a historical period in which increasing leadership opportunities are available to individuals with "anal-compulsive" traits, readily integrated as they seem to be in bureaucratic situations. People with "receptive," "withdrawing," or "contemplative" traits have comparatively little chance for leadership in our society.

Leaders of modern industry seem also to possess different personality traits from those which may be said to have typified their antecedents. No "rugged individualist," the present-day industrialist appears to have left behind the traits of "forthrightness," "drive," "strength" which the popular image, at least, attributes to a Rockefeller, a Carnegie, Hill or Harriman. None of these are genuine types; they are merely *speculations* about types intended only to suggest the probability that certain traits are *common* to some leaders, of some groups, during certain periods.

For these reasons, then, the failure to find some characteristics which some leaders, in a number of different situations, have in common would seem most unexpected.

What are the possible reasons for this failure? We have already implicitly suggested one: namely, their inadequate specification of the *aspects* of the situation eliciting specific leadership traits. Without properly sifting out different dimensions of situations, it is impossible to determine whether two situations are either significantly different or similar. Unless the particular ways in which two concrete situations may be different or the same are specified, *types* of situations cannot be determined. One cannot, therefore, test whether or not these will evoke similar leadership traits. This appears to be one reason for the failure to find common leadership traits among some leaders, for these could be common only to leaders in the same type of situation. No traits common to a number of leaders were perceived because the common elements in the situations, which might have engendered them, were not adequately established. Where formerly some psychologists tended to focus on the individual and his uniqueness, this tendency seems to have been transferred to the group and situational level, with *differences* between groups or situations becoming *emphasized* and *similarities obliterated.*

CHARACTER TRAITS AND BEHAVIORAL TRAITS

There appears to be another major reason why traits common to different leaders have not emerged. This seems to reside in the concept of "traits" which has been employed. The early trait analyses of leadership tended to speak of psychological traits as if they were similar to physical traits, as stable patterns of concrete behavior, "relatively permanent features of the organism."[49] They suggested that leadership was determined by the individual's traits, that if an individual possessed certain traits he would tend to become a leader.

The situationists pointed out that these concrete behavior patterns were not stable and varied with the situation. (A man could be "mercenary," "competitive," and "intolerant" in his business role, yet "generous," "friendly," and "understanding" as a father.) In one way or another, the situation or role determined the traits manifested by leadership: either by selecting for leadership individuals with useful traits, or by fostering the required traits after the individual had become a leader.

There is, however, the possibility that the search for common traits of leadership, conceived as concrete behavior patterns, maximizes differences between the "traits" of leaders. Though the situationists emphasized the *instability* of behavioral traits, they still tend to think of them as relatively concrete entities, failing to note that apparently contradictory behaviors might still be part of a single "larger" trait.

It is at this point that the psychoanalytical concept of "character trait" may be helpful. By a character trait is meant a deep-going, persisting motivation—to some degree unconscious—which may produce variable behavior, but variable within limits. Traits so conceived are not so likely to undergo significant modification due to role or group needs in adult groups. According to Erich Fromm, character traits "underlie behavior and must be inferred from it."[50] They are thus not identical with behavior. Moreover, ". . . the fundamental entity in character is not the single character trait but the total organization from which a number of single character traits follow. These

---

[49] Alfred R. Lindesmith and Anselm L. Strauss, *op. cit.,* p. 275.
[50] Erich Fromm, *Man For Himself* (New York, 1947), p. 57.

character traits are to be understood as a syndrome which results from a particular organization or . . . orientation of character."[51] Fromm then goes on to formulate types of syndromes which are in certain respects very similar to those proposed by other neo-Freudians.

With the Freudian analytical tools, then, a fairly extensive number of concrete behavioral traits is conceptually supplanted by a more delimited number of character traits, and an even more limited number of types of "character structures" or syndromes. If for no reason other than the comparative simplicity of these analytic tools, and possibly even their relative lack of precision, it seems probable that psychological characteristics common to numbers of leaders would be easier to isolate. The close approximation of actual behavior involved in the use of the conventional concept of traits probably tended to expand the number of traits, impeding their incorporation into types and making it difficult to perceive similarities of personality among leaders.

GROUP INTEGRATION

One study of leadership may serve to suggest the potentialities of the psychoanalytical approach to personality for leadership study. This is the work of Fritz Redl,[52] which is particularly interesting in that it also combines consideration of a group need with a situational emphasis.

One of the functional prerequisites of groups (at least) implicit in the work of the structural-functionalists is that a group must possess a degree of "integration." Thus, when Selznick speaks of a need for a "homogeneous outlook," or when Parsons refers to the need for group mechanisms which control the mutually inhibitory actions of individuals, both imply the existence of some empathy or mutual understanding among group members—an understanding that permits members to know, within limits, what kinds of behavior may be expected from other individuals filling different roles in the group. Concomitantly they develop a feeling of common membership in a social entity, and sense to some extent that their behavior affects and is affected by others in this unit. Integration also involves

[51] *Ibid.*
[52] Fritz Redl, "Group Emotion and Leadership," *Psychiatry,* 1942, cf. pp. 576-583.

a system of reciprocal roles, with certain of the obligations of one role being the rightful privileges of another. It is in this complex sense that some degree of integration is spoken of here as a functional prerequisite or need of any group.

Redl's work, going far beyond its initial Freudian impulse, suggests a personality attribute of leaders, functional for the attainment of group integration. It is not the men with "strong" personalities who are the effective leaders, he states, but rather, those with "group psychological flexibility." Such flexibility enables a leader to issue integrating psychic stimuli in varying situations and to a diversity of individuals. Redl's emphasis on "flexibility" is also implicit, but unmistakable in the comments of Jennings quoted above. (For example, the leader knows when to censure and when to praise, is not invariably pleasant, etc.)

Redl feels that the term "leader" is no longer in step with a situationally-sensitive psychology. This term, he believes, conceals the multiplicity of groups, the variety of ways in which they are integrated, and the different ways in which a leader's behavior results in group integration. In place of "leader," Redl proposes the terms "central" or "focal" person, the central person being the one "around whom" group formative processes take place. That is, central persons are those whose actions in specific ways reinforce or bring about group integration.

Ten types of central persons and group-integrative situations are proposed, only one of which Redl calls "the leader." These are:

1. The "Patriarchical Sovereign": here the group is integrated because they incorporate the super-ego, or conscience, of the central person into their own. Wanting his approval, they adopt his standards of right and wrong. They thereby come to hold similar values and are able to orient themselves to each other.

2. The "Leader": In this situation the group is integrated because the individuals want to be like the central person, rather than because they accept the values for which he stands. They accept his authority because he sympathizes with their urges, or possibly illicit goals. Wanting to be like him establishes a common bond among the members, which furthers integration.

3. The "Tyrant": Here, too, as in the "patriarch," the group is integrated because they accept the values of the central person. Unlike the first type, however, they do so out of fear, rather than love. The ends are similar, but the individual's motivation is different.

4. The "Love Object": The central person is not idealized; the members do not accept his values, nor do they aspire to be like him. The group is integrated because they love the same person.

5. The "Object of Aggression": The situation is similar to number 4, except that the central person integrates the group because he is the common object of their aggression, rather than their love.

6. The "Organizer": Neither love, hatred nor fear of the central person is the basis of group integration in this case. By facilitating the members' satisfaction of "forbidden pleasures" the central person minimizes their inner conflicts and guilt feelings. Because the organizer "services" those of the group's common ends which are non-legitimate, he becomes a focus for integration.

7. The "Seducer": Integration is enhanced when the central person commits an "initiatory act," satisfying the socially disapproved ends of the individuals around him. These individuals ordinarily may be inhibited from pursuing these ends by their super-ego. By doing it first, the "Seducer" enables the others to engage in the forbidden action openly by providing them with some justification for their own behavior and thereby minimizing their guilt feelings. (As later indicated, some of the success of the fascist agitator is understandable in that light.)

8. The "Hero": Contrary to the "Seducer," the "Hero" integrates the group by encouraging the manifestation of socially approved action. The "Hero's" initiatory act is courageous, enabling other individuals to cast off their anxieties, and permitting them to take a stand in favor of approved values.

9. The "Bad Influence": While similar to the "Seducer," there is in this case no initiatory act integrating the group. The "bad influence" is one not inhibited or blocked by his con-

science, in the same way that others are. Those of his drives which are socially forbidden do not meet the resistance of a formidable super-ego. He simply pursues these ends without conflict and "infects" the others so that they may do likewise without guilt. Since they have a common mode of solving their internal conflict, the individual's relationships with each other may be integrated.

10. The "Good Example": Similar to the "bad influence," this central person integrates the group by encouraging the opposite kind of solution to their conflicts. The "good example's" lack of conflict leads him in the direction of the socially approved ends. The conscience of the others is reinforced by his actions.

The ten types of leaders and modes of group integration are not, of course, mutually exclusive. Any one individual may play a combination of these roles. (There are, however, some roles to which the term "leader" could not be extended—for example, the "object of aggression.") Since these typically tend to be transitory, Redl suggests that the effective or successful leader will tend to be "group psychologically flexible." Clearly, Redl's orientation to a group need like integration has led him to focus on a psychological characteristic very different from those conventionally proposed as common to leaders. Group psychological flexibility would seem to be either a character trait or an aspect of personality organization as a whole.

Flexibility is not, as such, held to foster integration of the group. Instead, it is the varied modes of behavior that resolve common individual conflicts and satisfy common individual needs, which this trait makes possible, and through which it results in group integration. Thus Redl's analysis does not organismically reify the group. Rather, it indicates the source of those relations among individuals which enable them to comprise a group.

PERSONALITY CHARACTERISTICS AND THE LEADERSHIP CORPS

One final comment concerning the measurement of the personality characteristics of leaders: when the personality characteristics of leaders are considered, the unit attended to is always the individual leader. There seems to be another unit whose personality characteristics deserve some consideration, that is, the leadership corps of the group. In other words, when investigating the personalities of leaders, we are perhaps overly influenced by an individualistic bias. It may be that for certain purposes a useful unit of examination would be all the leaders of the group, treated as an entity, rather than the individual leader.

In employing the leadership corps as the unit of study, it is possible that a minimum "core" of personality characteristics of leadership could be isolated. The "core" would not contain psychological characteristics necessarily found in each leader of the group but would, in a sense, be a composite of some of their personality features. This core could be established by comparing the range of character traits manifested in a group with those evidenced in like groups. Different personality cores might thus be established for different kinds of groups.

Once determined and validated, such group personality cores may be useful for leadership selection. For example, suppose a certain group's leaders manifest personality characteristics A, B, C, F, G. These might be contrasted with the core typical of their kind of groups, which might contain elements A, B, C, D, E, F, G. One diagnostic hypothesis might be that the group is in need of leaders with personality elements D and E; this diagnosis might then serve to govern their leadership recruitment (presuming it could be purposively controlled).

Put in a more general way, the point involved is that the traits of leaders should be evaluated not only in relation to their own roles (potential or existent), but also in relation to the traits of other leaders, as well as the needs of the group as a whole, rather than solely the particular segment in which they operate. Instead of seeking personality characteristics common to leaders, it may be fruitful to look for traits common to leadership corps. That leaders have important relations with other leaders, not merely with their followers, is a fact often neglected in the researches of social psychologists. Focus on the leadership corps, the groups' leaders treated as an entity, may also serve to highlight this crucial area.

THE IDEOLOGICAL ROLE OF SITUATIONISM

In an earlier section we raised the question of why it was that the situationists had found few or no traits common to numbers of leaders. In general, our answer up to this point has noted the role which inadequate concepts of "situations" and "traits" have probably played in bringing this about. But other reasons, of an entirely different nature, must also be brought into view.

Social scientists, like members of other professions and people in general, are moved to employ certain concepts and hypotheses for other than purely professional or scientific reasons. In large measure this may be understood as a consequence of the fact that they play roles other than that of "scientist," and that today they operate as scientists in some relation to particular kinds of structures—publics or bureaucracies, for example.

It is proposed here that certain of the emphases in the work of the situationists—insofar as they are determined by other than scientific factors—may be derivatives of their own peculiar "work situation." (The situationists' work is, in a sense, being examined with their own tools.) In particular, the situationists' focus on the uniqueness of a leader's traits, their specificity to his situation, seem to be, in part, consequences of social scientists' relations with the great bureaucracies such as the Army, Navy, Civil Service, and big industry.

A peculiar development appears to have taken place. The situationist approach apparently first emerged out of a polemic with the "Great Man" theory of leadership. This theory stated that it was men of a distinctive stamp, predestined by their possession of unusual traits, who led events and molded situations. The situationists developed the antithetical position—that it was the situation that determined the leader's traits. The situationists' antithetical position was largely influenced by their adherence to democratic values, the belief that leaders were not born, but made.

Gradually, however, these social scientists, engaged in the empirical study of leadership, were drawn into the orbit of those who could supply financial and other assistance—the bureaucracies. The research needs of bureaucracies are, however, distinctive. They limit the scope of problems and hypotheses which students of leadership, subject to their pressures, are encouraged to investigate. Most importantly, by virtue of their very organization, the bureaucracies were principally concerned about filling highly specific roles, which had delimited areas of authority and responsibility. Typically, bureaucracies are composed of highly specialized offices demanding, in turn, highly specialized individuals.

When the problem of leadership becomes articulate in a bureaucracy, it is formulated precisely in terms of the needs of highly limited, and specific, situations. In industry, for example, current practice dictates formulation of a "job-analysis"—what does a particular job entail, what skills are required of its occupants? In addition to modeling part of their procedure after that of the job-analysts, it is noteworthy that some students of leadership have explicitly adopted the term "job-analysis."[53] In short, what originally began as a revolt against an aristocratic social theory, the "Great Man" philosophy, may now serve as an all too comfortable rationalization for research cut to fit bureaucratic needs. This is not so remarkable if it is remembered that bureaucrats, no less than democrats, have little prejudice in favor of "great men." The bureaucracy is after all a form of social organization whose efficiency derives in part from the circumscription and inhibition of personalities, ordinary and extraordinary.

The foregoing is not intended to constitute an indictment of the situationists, or a charge of improper scientific behavior. Nor is it intended as a refutation of the findings or hunches proposed by them. The question of the *validity* of the situationists' work is not to be decided by analysis of its ideological functions, or the social pressures which it reflects. Truth, as well as error, is conceived in the womb of social pressures.

What is intended, however, is a caution—one, it hardly need be said, which does not apply to all situationists equally. A caution to the effect that much of present-day leadership research is operating in a social vortex having its own lines of developments, its own needs, not all of which provide a favorable context for the advancement of leadership research.

The tendency of leadership studies grown in the shadow of bureaucratic walls is, for example, to concentrate on limited aspects of the leader-follower relationship: principally, to *ascertain methods of enhancing the control of leaders over their followers*. Studies which culminate in knowledge that facilitates the *control of leadership by followers* find no nourishment in a bureaucratic setting. There is a certain truth in Thomas Jefferson's belief that "the tree of liberty is watered by the blood of tyrants." It seems as important for us to

53 T. Coffin, "A Three-Component Theory of Leadership," *Journal of Abnormal and Social Psychology*, 1944.

know how to get rid of a leader as how to get one. Such knowledge is a life-and-death matter for a people determined to remain democratic. Bureaucracies, authoritarian organizations controlled from a remote top, are unlikely to foster studies of this import.

For similar reasons there are relatively few studies of the highest leadership in bureaucracies. The focus of most studies is on the intermediary layers of leadership, foremen or junior officers. But the scientific study of top leadership is at very least as crucial as that of lower levels. Certainly it is vital to study those who make and formulate the policies which lower echelons implement. These nerve centers of power are sensitive, however, and most often prefer investigation of those beneath them.

Industrial job-analysts seek to determine the requirements of personnel needed for an established task; they seek to fit the man to the job, not the job to the man. In like fashion, bureaucratically oriented studies of leadership strive to analyze the requirements of personnel who can fill given leadership roles. Questions as to how modifications of the authority system would effect the operation of leadership are left unasked.

It is noteworthy that the situationists emphasize the role of a leader in satisfying the needs of his group, almost to the complete exclusion of the leader's role in frustrating the needs of his group. Thus one writer compares the leader to a dentist in that both satisfy existent needs. Popularly acknowledged problems such as oligarchy, distortion of group goals, apathy, manipulation, and many others, all involve some implication of the group-frustrating operations of leadership. These problems, however, find little reflection in the work of the situationists. It may be expected that the group-frustrating, as well as the group-satisfying, operations of leadership are also attributable to aspects of the situation in which the leader finds himself. Both forms of behavior must be considered as equally compelled. Analysis of the group-frustrating behavior of the leader would, however, necessarily lead to questions about the aspects of the situation which provoke them. Ultimately, this would evoke analysis of the system of authority which defines and channels the leader's behavior. But the problem of bureaucracies is to obtain conformance to the established system of authority; modification of the system in any substantial respect is a possibility scarcely entertained.

In general, social psychologists have paid little attention to the authority system within which leaders operate, except to suggest, as some do, that where established authority exists, "true leadership" disappears. A dichotomy is established between "authority" and "leadership," thereby relegating studies to leadership types with relatively little power.

A radical emphasis on leadership traits in relation to concrete situations and roles, narrowly conceived, while useful to bureaucratic organization, is not of equal value to democratic organization. Democratic leadership rarely operates in a situation whose contours can be stated with the precision of bureaucratic situations. Nor is the situation as stable for democratic as it is for bureaucratic leadership. The possibilities of crisis continually enlarge. The problem of how, for example, to retain democratic patterns among leadership, in the midst of crisis, is exceedingly remote from the knowledge derived from bureaucratically oriented studies.

Unless social scientists become sensitive to the social consequences, or lack of consequences, which their work has, there is no guarantee that they will be able to make a significant contribution to the defense and development of democratic values.

Part One: TYPES OF LEADERS

Contexts: Bureaucrats and Agitators

As OUR preceding discussion indicates, social psychologists have had great difficulty in sifting out traits common to a number of leaders. This, in conjunction with their failure to provide dimensions in terms of which "situations" could be compared, has impeded their ability to establish *types* of leaders. In consequence, this section which deals with types of leaders must be based principally upon the work of sociologists.

Their comparative success in establishing types rests in the main on the distinctions which they have made between different types of situations—or that part of situations to which they have devoted considerable study, social structures. Like the situationist psychologists, the sociologists believe that the structures in which leaders operate compel different forms of leadership behavior. The sociologists have succeeded, however, in abstracting from the variety of unique, concrete social structures, certain aspects by which some structures tend to be characterized when contrasted with others. On the basis of these distinctions they have constructed *typical* structures and have attempted to analyze aspects of the behavior of leaders within these as responses to the structure.

Any such structure, for example, the "bureaucracy," is not intended to represent a concrete organization. It is instead an *ideal* type, in which certain tendencies of concrete structures are highlighted by emphasis. Not every formal association will possess all the characteristics incorporated into the ideal-type bureaucracy. The ideal type may be used as a yardstick enabling us to determine in which particular respects an actual organization is bureaucratized. It may also enable us to state which of two concrete organizations is most bureaucratized. The ideal-type bureaucracy may be used much as a twelve-inch ruler is employed. We would not expect, for example, that all objects measured by the ruler be exactly twelve inches—some would be more or some less.

In like manner the bureaucratic ideal-type operates as a "bench mark" in terms of which comparisons and distinctions among concrete groups may be made. It provides a criterion by which we may orient ourselves without getting lost in the infinite complexity of each unique group. Ultimately, perhaps, the work of sociologists may enable us to formulate propositions something like the following: given such and such a structure, with stated typical characteristics, the following leadership behaviors (A,B,C, . . .) will tend to occur.

Not all of the proposals concerning types of leaders have detailed the relationship between leadership behavior and the structures which have fostered it. It may be useful to indicate briefly some types of leadership which have been proposed that are only very loosely related to delimited aspects of social structures—if at all.

William Cowley,[1] for example, has made a distinction between "headmen" and "leaders." The "leaders" were those who had a definite program and group objective; the "headmen," in contrast, had no program and were merely "officeholders" who received their positions on bases other than "leadership" abilities. F. C. Bartlett[2] has suggested a threefold classification. The first type of leader maintains his position through the prestige accruing to his office and is more successful if he deals impersonally with his followers. The second maintains his position by dominating his followers, while the third does so by persuading them. Sanderson and Nafe[3] suggest a fourfold typology of "static," "executive," "professional," and "group" leaders. The static leaders are "men of distinction," having prestige but relatively little power. The executive, by contrast, is a leader with power and force at his disposal. The professionals—perhaps clergymen, teachers, or social workers—are not members of the group they supposedly

---

[1] William H. Cowley, "Three Distinctions in the Studies of Leaders," *Journal of Abnormal and Social Psychology*, July-September, 1928, pp. 147-157. Also, "Traits of Face-to-Face Leaders," *Journal of Abnormal and Social Psychology*, Oct.-Dec., 1931, pp. 304-313.

[2] F. C. Bartlett, "The Social Psychology of Leadership," *Journal of the National Institute of Industrial Psychology*, October, 1926, pp. 188-193.

[3] Dwight Sanderson and Robert W. Nafe, "Studies in Rural Leadership," *Publications of the American Sociological Society*, October, 1929, pp. 163-175.

lead. The "group" leader is a member of the group, a planner and spokesman for it.

Nafe[4] has suggested a further distinction between "static" and "infusive" leaders. The latter elicits highly emotionalized types of activity from his followers and, suggests Nafe, while motivating them to work actively for the group goals, emphasizes principles and ideational content. Sir Martin Conway[5] has formulated a threefold classification: the crowd compeller, the crowd exponent, and the crowd representative. The "compeller" is an orator of unusual persuasiveness who sometimes lays claim to divine inspiration. The "exponent" articulates what the crowd feels and wants; unlike the "compellers" who mold the crowd, the "exponent" is its product. The crowd "representative" gives expression to established folkways and occupies some institutionalized office, even more hedged in by existent opinion than the "exponent."

Though inadequately articulated with group structures, these briefly sketched leadership typologies are useful in two ways:

1. They suggest several of the dimensions which some of those concerned about leadership typologies have emphasized: principally (a) the modes of leadership ascent, the techniques employed to rise in the structure; (b) the techniques employed to maintain leadership.

It would seem that these are useful dimensions to keep in mind in establishing leadership typologies. They appear to be, moreover, facets which become somewhat obscured in the more complex typologies sometimes used by sociologists. Nevertheless, the above-mentioned typologies are decidedly incomplete in that explanation is rarely tendered analyzing why one, rather than another, technique of obtaining or maintaining leadership is employed. The structural elements conducing to distinctive techniques are neglected. Again, the consequences of the use of different leadership techniques, particularly for the group in which people act as leaders, are also rarely treated in any systematic fashion. For example: in what specific ways does the leader's situationally-determined, typical behavior satisfy the group's needs? Specifically which needs are being satisfied? Equally important, but

---

[4] Robert W. Nafe, "A Psychological Description of Leadership," *Journal of Social Psychology*, May, 1930, pp. 248-266.

[5] Martin Conway, *The Crowd in Peace and War* (New York, 1915).

often neglected, are the ways in which a leader's behavior *impairs* the group's operation and *inhibits* the satisfaction of its needs.

2. A further observation perhaps more important than that mentioned, may be drawn from the above leadership typologies. That is, the extent to which they *converge* and *overlap*. Thus, when Cowley speaks of "headmen" as mere administrators, Bartlett of those who maintain leadership due to the prestige of their position, Sanderson and Nafe of the "executive," and Conway of the "crowd representative"—there seems to be suggested a central core of social characteristics which they commonly share. In part this involves the leaders' dependence upon some officially designated rights and privileges, their occupancy of a formal office. This convergence assumes all the more significance when notice is taken of the typologies of Harold D. Lasswell and Max Weber. Comparable types are found in each of these, Lasswell[6] referring to the "Administrator" and Weber[7] making a major contribution to social science in his analysis of the "Bureaucrat."

Another nuclear cluster also seems observable: the "dominators" and "persuaders" of Bartlett, Nafe's dynamic "infusive" leaders, and Conway's spellbinding "crowd-compeller." Again, like the above, these appear to overlap, manifesting an area of central tendency. Their similarity to a type referred to by Lasswell[8] as the "agitator" seems evident. Closely akin to all of these is Max Weber's[9] "charismatic" leader, the man "called" to fulfill a mission and a "persuader" of unequalled magnitude.

Several further "satellite" types are discernible in the literature— "satellite" because they tend to play roles of a secondary character both in the public arena and in scientific literature. One of these is recognizable by references to the "natural," "spontaneous," or "informal" "group" leaders.

In sum, three clusters of leadership types have been noted; these are given constant reinterpretation and varied emphases in current discussions of leadership typologies. We shall refer to these as (1) the Agitators, (2) the Bureaucrats, and (3) the Informal leaders. The con-

---

[6] Harold D. Lasswell, *Psychopathology and Politics* (Chicago, 1930), chap. 8.

[7] Max Weber, *The Theory of Social and Economic Organization*, tr. A. M. Henderson and Talcott Parsons, ed. with an introduction by Talcott Parsons (New York, 1947), pp. 329-340.

[8] Harold D. Lasswell, op. cit., chaps. 6-7.

[9] Max Weber, op. cit., pp. 358-372.

tributions in this section deal with an elaboration of some of the characteristics of these types.

Each of these will be discussed as an "ideal type." The concrete, individual leader, it need hardly be mentioned, will only approximate in varying degrees the characteristics indicated for each. He may, moreover, possess combinations of the characteristics of two or more of the types to be presented.

THE BUREAUCRAT

A few preliminary warnings are always in order when the terms "bureaucrat" and "bureaucracy" are used. If the full implications of the article on bureaucrats is to be grasped, it is imperative that the popular stereotypes of bureaucracy be separated from the scholarly analyses. In the popular view, for example, bureaucracy is synonymous with governmental inefficiency. This connotation was, however, farthest from the intentions of Max Weber, the sociologist who formulated the ideal-type concept of bureaucracy. To Weber the opposite was true. As he saw it in the perspective of his remarkable fund of historical knowledge, bureaucracy was the most efficient form of social organization ever developed. It signified the decline of the undependable amateur and his supercession by the qualified specialist.

It is, in fact, impossible to understand Robert K. Merton's "Bureaucratic Structure and Personality" unless this is appreciated. For Merton's article is in part an effort to balance Weber's one-sided analysis by examining the ways in which bureaucracy's negative aspects come about. Unlike the situationists, Merton is concerned with the "group-frustrating" aspects of leadership. Most significantly, he interprets these as being derived from certain features of the bureaucratic structure; features which are often the same as those which contribute to its efficiency.

Not only does Weber's view of bureaucracy differ radically from the popular estimate of its efficiency, but it differs also regarding the institutions in which it is held to be found. The popular stereotype stamps "bureaucracy" onto government agencies only, while the bureaucrat is thought of only as a civil service employee. Weber's analysis was entirely different. He maintained that bureaucracy was one of the characteristic forms of organization of modern society finding wide expression in industry, science, religion, as well as government. The essence of Weber's argument is missed unless this distinction between the popular conception and his own view is clarified. (That there is this gap between Weber's conception of bureaucracy, and bureaucracy when defined as a social problem, is, from the general orientation used here, grounds for its reëxamination rather than its ritualistic employment.)

Central to Weber's concept of bureaucracy is the polemic which (to borrow a phrase from Albert Salomon) he was conducting against Karl Marx's ghost. Marx had maintained that ours was a society characterized by the workers' alienation from the means of production, a capitalist society doomed to ultimate overthrow by the proletariat which it had disinherited. Weber moved to counter this thesis with the following clever gambit: Marx, suggested Weber, misinterprets the significance of the workers' separation from the means of production; he interprets it—continues Weber—as an *isolated* phenomenon whereas, in reality, the same process takes place in many other modern institutions. In science, for example, the scientist no longer has control over the means of research, which are now controlled by research foundations. Whereas in certain feudal armies soldiers armed and outfitted themselves, controlling their own means of warfare, today the soldier is separated from the means of violence. Similarly in other spheres and, of course, in industry. In other words, said Weber, "For the time being, the dictatorship of the official and not that of the worker is on the march."[10]

For this original reply to the Marxists, Weber came to be called the "Marx of the Bourgeoisie." It is noteworthy and unfortunate that no American Marxist intellectual has yet seen fit to rebut Weber's challenge; some, like the scholarly *Science and Society* group, barely acknowledge Weber's existence, while others, like the penetrating William Blake, consider him the only "bourgeois" social scientist worth reading, but fail to present their criticisms.[11]

At any rate, just as Marxism has an ideological function, so, too, does Weber's theory of bureaucracy. This, however, no more *invalidates* it than the ideological role which Darwin's theory of natural

---

[10] H. H. Gerth and C. Wright Mills, *From Max Weber: Essays in Sociology* (New York, 1946), quoted on p. 50 of the Introduction.

[11] William J. Blake, *An American Looks at Karl Marx* (New York, 1939), cf. p. 704.

selection came to have invalidated evolutionary theory. Nevertheless, recognition of this ideological component should serve notice that certain rigidities may be induced in the theory, preventing its full scientific development.

For example: Weber's theory fulfills an ideological function by minimizing differences between capitalism and socialism. The choice between them may no longer seem so significant since both are subsumed under a single concept, bureaucracy. If Marx said that the workers of the world had nothing to lose but their chains by revolting, Weber contended that they really had nothing to gain. Weber did indicate that a bureaucratic caste might harden and arrogate to itself special prerogatives in a socialist state. It was, though, a major tendency of Weber's theory to cast into shadow differences between one type of bureaucracy and another, between one type of bureaucrat and another.

If, however, we are indeed living in an epoch of "the bureaucratization of the world," then it may be that we have all the more need for theoretical tools which will point up distinctions among bureaucracies and bureaucrats. A single type of bureaucracy is not adequate, either for scientific purposes or practical political action, in a bureaucratized world. A type which includes within itself as much as Weber's does leaves no room for the discriminations without which choice is impossible, scientific advance difficult, and pessimism probable. It seems possible that social scientists, autistically, have a need not to see differences in bureaucracies. In this way, perhaps, we can take a "plague-on-both-your-houses" attitude, thereby rationalizing our political inaction and preserving our energies for personal career efforts, with a clear conscience.

It is in this context that the recent research of Leonard Reissman, "A Study of Role Conceptions in Bureaucracy" (Social Forces, March, 1949) may be fitted. Reissman suggests that there are four types of bureaucrats, the "functional," "specialist," "service," and "job" bureaucrats. The functional bureaucrat seeks recognition from and is oriented to a professional group outside the bureaucracy and avoids identification with the office group. The specialist bureaucrat, while professionally oriented, seeks his recognition from within his department and advancement through the bureaucracy. The service bureaucrat seeks recognition from a group outside the bureaucracy, while the *job* bureaucrat is totally immersed within the bureaucratic structure.

The main distinction between *types* of bureaucrats which emerges clearly in Reissman's research has to do with whether the bureaucrat is seeking recognition from some group outside the bureaucracy or not. It seems especially significant that Reissman found that the two types of bureaucrats who were not seeking outside recognition (the specialist and job bureaucrats) conformed rigorously to bureaucratic rules and procedures, that is, have a high probability of red-tape behavior. One hypothesis which this work therefore suggests is that extra-bureaucratic identifications and memberships may serve to minimize red-tape behavior. It may be that in times of social cleavage and ideological conflicts, pressures, for example, in the form of loyalty investigations may loosen the bureaucrats' outside ties in general and increase their red-tape susceptibilities.

THE AGITATOR

To the extent that Max Weber held a theory of historical change, it seemed to imply a rotation of bureaucratic or traditional leadership, on the one side, with charismatic (or, as it has been called here, agitational) leadership on the other. Since "traditional" leadership involves problems remote from those of democratic, Western European culture, it will not be considered here. In our discussion, then, the polar types are the bureaucratic and the charismatic (or agitator) leaders.

The rotations of leadership type referred to were believed by Weber to take place against a background of increasing rationalization in society. The process may be conceived of as a (bureaucratic-charismatic) cycle fluctuating around a rising curve (social rationalization). Charismatic leadership, based on the acceptance of a leader because of his presumed, unusual personal attributes, was held to disrupt the process of rationalization. The conditions under which it occurs are only barely sketched by Weber. In general, Weber held that it came about when existent *routines* proved unable to cope with growing social problems. The charismatic leader announces himself amidst the agony of class conflicts or civil wars, invasions or threats of invasions, economic deprivation and mass frustration. Usually attendant are cleavages which fracture the society into multiple factions, destruction of the individual's customary ties to many of his groups, the dissolution of moral norms which oriented him, and the mushrooming of psychological anxiety on a mass scale: the fragmentation of a society, the atomization of the individual. This is the social setting in which the full-blown charismatic leader declares his mission.

Hitherto, the behavior of specific charismatic leaders has been studied at far remove, with the most impressionistic of methods and little theoretical relevance. Leo Lowenthal and Norbert Gutterman's "Self-Portrait of a Fascist Agitator" deals with those of the present, that batch of fledgling charismatic leaders who operate in the United States today, awaiting and contributing to the full development of the chaotic social situation in which they can take wing. In the richness of its detail, the extensivity of the group it surveys, and the penetration of its insight, Lowenthal and Gutterman's study is one of the most remarkable analyses of charismatic leadership in the literature.

Conventionally, many Americans presume that the fascist agitator is a carbon copy of a German or Italian model. This is a crucial assumption, and dangerous if false, for it guides the strategy of those seeking to combat them. Lowenthal and Gutterman believe it an erroneous assumption, and stress that the fascist agitator has roots deep in the American social and character structures. As such, he is unlikely to be uprooted either by the "hush-hush" method of surrounding him with silence, or with the usual glib techniques of exposure.

Their analysis is based upon examination of common elements extracted from a tremendous mass of speeches and articles produced by the agitators themselves. The agitators who have been selected for study were, as Lowenthal and Gutterman state elsewhere, "those who have openly and conspicuously expressed their sympathy with and admiration for Naziism and Fascism, or who have openly and conspicuously expressed anti-Semitic opinions, and who have tried publicly to persuade others to support such views."

The charismatic agitators discussed by them are therefore exponents of a very specific brand of ideology. In consequence, it may be expected that certain of the characteristics which they possess would not be manifested by different kinds of agitators or charismatic leaders. Nevertheless, certain of their traits stamp them as unmistakably charismatic in the sense of Weber's ideal type.

For example, an emphasis on their predestination as leaders is typical of the charismatic leader who presents himself to others, not as an elected leader or in any way expressing their will, but as one whom they have a duty to follow. He is, too, the spokesman of doom and the apocalypse who, while occasionally muting his attack on established institutions, is explicitly and implicitly hostile to them, declaring in effect, "It is written, but I say unto you." Thrusting his own personality to the center of the stage, the agitator intimates that he is the "special chosen" of God and sometimes likens himself to Jesus Christ.

Hostile both to routine and formalized organization, the charismatic leader surrounds himself with followers loyal to his *person* and his mission. He prefers to maintain direct personal contact with his staff of disciples, and establishes little or no hierarchy. This insistence on face-to-face relations with his disciples, particularly his administrative staff, and his hostility to routine have been among the chief weaknesses of the American fascist agitator.

Living largely by booty and the gifts of followers, hostile to routine, to formal organization and, *typically*, to the obligations of family life, charismatic leadership is ephemeral in the extreme. Almost from its very inception it is subject to pressures which ultimately cause its transformation, either into bureaucratic or traditional types of social organization. This transformation is catalyzed when the disciples, seeking to secure both the movement and their status in it, are confronted with the problem of succession upon the death of the charismatic leader.

The analysis of the agitator which H. D. Lasswell delineated corresponds with Weber's charismatic leader to a great degree. In Lasswell's terms, the agitator is a leader who places a high value on an emotional response from his audience and is able to communicate his excitement about public policy to them. As someone once described Huey Long, "He had a kindlin' power." Contentious, undisciplined, given to appeals in terms of general principles, frustrated by masses of technical detail, Lasswell's agitator looks to single acts of innovation to bring much good.[12]

If Weber neglected systematic discussion of the *negative* aspects of bureaucratic leadership, it may be said that the corresponding shortcoming in his treatment of the charismatic leader is *underemphasis* on the *positive* aspects of charismatic leadership. It is true that Weber

12 Harold D. Lasswell, *op. cit.*

attributed enormous historical significance to charismatic leadership, considering it, in one of its forms, as the only means of undermining magical practices and establishing a rational conduct of life. Nevertheless, he contributes little systematic analysis of the group needs satisfied by the charismatic leader.

Weber's gross, single type of charismatic leader somewhat obscures the functioning of various possible related types of agitators whose operations may take place in a more stable context, and who do not lay claim to a special "call." We may perhaps tentatively distinguish two types of agitators, the "sacred" and the "secular." The "sacred" type of agitator would be Weber's charismatic leader; the "secular" agitator might be conceived of as an individual who feels no special call to impress new duties upon a following, nor to impose upon them obligations of personal loyalty to himself as the personification of a new value system. In other respects he may be similar to Weber's charismatic leader and Lasswell's agitator.

This, or some similar distinction between types of agitators—the secularization of Weber's charismatic type—seems useful for analysis of leadership behavior in contemporary associations. For while ours is an age of deep-going social disorganization, it is also an age of disenchantment in which relatively few agitators can with real conviction even hint at their divine inspiration. Conversely, others who feel no such genuine "call"—as seems likely for some of the fascist agitators—may pretend to hear it.

It is perhaps easier to see the group needs which are satisfied by the "secular" agitator than the "sacred." For example, the secular agitator seems to be particularly useful to certain groups in their recruiting efforts. Functioning as a "salesman," he can readily establish a face-to-face nexus with an audience from which his group would like to enlist membership or other assistance. In contrast, the bureaucrat seems most adept at arranging "deals" with the leaders of other groups and for the coördination of the organization's internal affairs. The agitator, the literature suggests, seems most satisfied when expounding group ends; the bureaucrat is perhaps most satisfied in ordering the means. If the bureaucrat is the master of the daily routine, the agitator seems oriented to crisis and the unusual event or unexpected happening—and crisis is a social fact as significant in an organization's history as daily occurrences.

From the point of view of democratic values, both types of leaders may represent a potential threat. The agitator by his Caesaristic possibilities (aspects of which are analyzed by Jeremiah Wolpert in his essay in the last section of this volume) and, perhaps, by a certain "crisis-tropism" which may dispose him to adventuristic policies. The bureaucrat, on the other hand, may impair the democratic values of his organization through his tendency to establish cliques, which, by their familiarity with membership lists, sources of finance, office procedure, and filing systems, may enable them to become a controlling oligarchy. In addition, the bureaucrat, as Merton notes, may have a "rule-tropism" which disposes him to fit new problems into old categories. In the process, unique aspects of the problems may be lost sight of, significant changes may be left unattended, and may therefore adversely affect the group.

In the modern association the needs which both agitator and bureaucrat serve may be neglected only at the risk of probable impairment of the association. Both, or functional equivalents of them, seem necessary to the modern democratic group. If, however, a reading of the trade union movement's history may serve as an impressionistic guide in the absence of careful investigations, the secular agitator is as transitional a type of leader in the association as the charismatic leader is on a larger scale. He seems to be replaced, with varying degrees of speed, by leaders approximating the bureaucratic type.

Studies of trade union leadership suggest that the "hothead" (i.e., the agitator) is replaced by the more "coöperative" and "calm" leader (i.e., the bureaucrat) as the union is accepted by management and conflict abates. In a general way, then, the "situation" seems to be determining the kind of leaders who emerge; leaders who can serve the group's new needs are *apparently* being brought forth. This view of the picture obscures two important problems:

1. The replacement of "agitators" by "bureaucrats" is not an automatic or mechanical phenomenon. The process is "given a hand" by the bureaucratic leaders; history, like God, helps those who help themselves. What seems to ensue in many associations which this writer has had occasion to observe is a *conflict* between the agitational and bureaucratic leadership. The precipitants, or the forms which this conflict takes, vary with the occasion. Some of the more general conditions of this conflict may be: (a) the different power bases of the

two kinds of leaders. The agitator's power rests with the mass following he is able to arouse; the bureaucrat's, with his control over the organizational machinery. Each may wish to expand the organizational practices which enhance his power; this, however, requires development of the organization along two different channels. (b) There may, too, be characterological differences between agitators and bureaucrats which reinforce the above divergence by adding personal animosities. Fritz Wittels has suggested the importance of conflicts between the "obsessional" and the "hysterical" character types. Wittels states, "The obsessional type hates the hysteric wherever he finds him. The hysteric type spoils all his ideas . . . they represent two worlds that do not understand each other."[13]

2. The implicit assumption that the dispossession of the agitators by the bureaucrats serves group needs also requires closer analysis. Once established, it may be that a group no longer has a need for agitators to act as "salesmen." In trade unions, for example, the "check-off," the "closed shop," and the union security clause may operate as functional equivalents to some extent. The other needs which agitators may serve are not so readily institutionalized. A sensitivity to changing situations, fluid public sentiments, or a capacity in crisis or in situations in which old routine methods collapse, these are skills which are difficult to provide for purposively. In such circumstances the agitator may serve to bridge a gap. He is useful, it would appear, precisely for potential or unpredictable needs. Unless in some way apprehended by the group, these needs exist only as "futures." They are easily neglected by a group under the pressure of solving daily problems.

With the onset of crisis an established group may find itself in one of two difficult situations. Either it has by now decimated its ranks of agitator material and will flounder and possibly be destroyed, or it "scrapes the barrel" and comes up with new agitational leadership. Aside from their technical inexperience, these new agitators are not fully "socialized." The institutionalized patterns of leadership are not internalized within them, and they may move in a Caesarist direction.

In the conventional associations of our relatively stable society, the bureaucrats will only rarely lose out to the agitators. The long-term

[13] Fritz Wittels, "Economic and Psychological Historiography," American Journal of Sociology, May, 1946, pp. 527-532.

social processes seem to be on their side. This, however, unbalances the leadership corps, probably diminishing its sensitivity to change and its ability to satisfy the potential needs of future crises. Special "cultivation" and socialization of secular, agitational material may safeguard group stability. The tendencies to conflict between agitator and bureaucrat, which their coleadership might entail, may—if carefully set within normative limits—result in mutual inhibition of the anti-democratic potential of each.

Bureaucratic Structure and Personality[1]

BY ROBERT K. MERTON

A FORMAL, rationally organized social structure involves clearly defined patterns of activity in which, ideally, every series of actions is functionally related to the purposes of the organization.[2] In such an organization there is integrated a series of offices, of hierarchized statuses, in which inhere a number of obligations and privileges closely defined by limited and specific rules. Each of these offices contains an area of imputed competence and responsibility. Authority, the power of control which derives from an acknowledged status, inheres in the office and not in the particular person who performs the official role. Official action ordinarily occurs within the framework of pre-existing rules of the organization. The system of prescribed relations between the various offices involves a considerable degree of formality and clearly defined social distance between the occupants of these positions. Formality is manifested by means of a more or less complicated social ritual which symbolizes and supports the "pecking order" of the various offices. Such formality, which is integrated with the distribution of authority within the system, serves to minimize friction by largely restricting (official) contact to modes which are previously defined by the rules of the organization. Ready calculability of others' behavior and a stable set of mutual expectations is thus

[1] Reprinted from *Social Forces*, 1940, by permission of the editors. Copyright, 1940, by the Williams and Wilkins Co.
[2] For a development of the concept of "rational organization," see Karl Mannheim, *Mensch und Gesellschaft in Zeitalter des Umbaus* (Leiden, 1935), esp. pp. 28 ff.

built up. Moreover, formality facilitates the interaction of the occupants of offices despite their (possibly hostile) private attitudes toward one another. In this way, the subordinate is protected from the arbitrary action of his superior, since the actions of both are constrained by a mutually recognized set of rules. Specific procedural devices foster objectivity and restrain the "quick passage of impulse into action."[3]

The ideal type of such formal organization is bureaucracy and, in many respects, the classical analysis of bureaucracy is that by Max Weber.[4] As Weber indicates, bureaucracy involves a clear-cut division of integrated activities which are regarded as duties inherent in the office. A system of differentiated controls and sanctions are stated in the regulations. The assignment of roles occurs on the basis of technical qualifications which are ascertained through formalized, impersonal procedures (e.g., examinations). Within the structure of hierarchically arranged authority, the activities of "trained and salaried experts" are governed by general, abstract, clearly defined rules which preclude the necessity for the issuance of specific instructions for each specific case. The generality of the rules required the constant use of *categorization*, whereby individual problems and cases are classified on the basis of designated criteria and are treated accordingly. The pure type of bureaucratic official is appointed, either by a superior or through the exercise of impersonal competition; he is not elected. A measure of flexibility in the bureaucracy is attained by electing higher functionaries who presumably express the will of the electorate (e.g., a body of citizens or a board of directors). The election of higher officials is designed to affect the purposes of the organization, but the technical procedures for attaining these ends are performed by a continuous bureaucratic personnel.[5]

The bulk of bureaucratic offices involve the expectation of life-long tenure, in the absence of disturbing factors which may decrease the

[3] H. D. Lasswell, *Politics* (New York, 1936), pp. 120-121.

[4] Max Weber, *Wirtschaft und Gesellschaft* (Tubingen, 1922), Pt. III, chap. 6, pp. 650-678. For a brief summary of Weber's discussion, see Talcott Parsons, *The Structure of Social Action* (New York, 1937), esp. pp. 506 ff. For a description, which is not a caricature, of the bureaucrat as a personality type, see C. Rabany, "Les types sociaux: le fonctionnaire," *Revue generale d'administration*, LXXXVIII (1907), 5-28.

[5] Karl Mannheim, *Ideology and Utopia* (New York, 1936), pp. 18n., 105 ff. See also Ramsay Muir, *Peers and Bureaucrats* (London, 1910), pp. 12-13.

size of the organization. Bureaucracy maximizes vocational security.[6] The function of security of tenure, pensions, incremental salaries and regularized procedures for promotion is to ensure the devoted performance of official duties, without regard for extraneous pressures.[7] The chief merit of bureaucracy is its technical efficiency, with a premium placed on precision, speed, expert control, continuity, discretion, and optimal returns on input. The structure is one which approaches the complete elimination of personalized relationships and of nonrational considerations (hostility, anxiety, affectual involvements, etc.).

Bureaucratization is accompanied by the centralization of means of production, as in modern capitalistic enterprise, or, as in the case of the post-feudal army, complete separation from the means of destruction. Even the bureaucratically organized scientific laboratory is characterized by the separation of the scientist from his technical equipment.

Bureaucracy is administration which almost completely avoids public discussion of its techniques, although there may occur public discussion of its policies.[8] This "bureaucratic secrecy" is held to be necessary in order to keep valuable information from economic competitors or from foreign and potentially hostile political groups.

In these bold outlines, the positive attainments and functions of bureaucratic organization are emphasized and the internal stresses and strains of such structures are almost wholly neglected. The community at large, however, evidently emphasizes the imperfections of bureaucracy, as is suggested by the fact that the "horrid hybrid," bureaucrat, has become a *Schimpfwort*. The transition to a study of the negative aspects of bureaucracy is afforded by the application of Veblen's concept of "trained incapacity," Dewey's notion of "occupational psychosis" or Warnotte's view of "professional deformation." Trained incapacity refers to that state of affairs in which one's abilities function as inadequacies or blind spots. Actions based upon training and skills

---

[6] E. G. Cahen-Salvador suggests that the personnel of bureaucracies is largely constituted of those who value security above all else. See his "La situation materielle et morale des functionnaires," *Revue politique et parlementaire* (1926), p. 319.

[7] H. J. Laski, "Bureaucracy," *Encyclopedia of the Social Sciences*. This article is written primarily from the standpoint of the political scientist rather than that of the sociologist.

[8] Weber, *op. cit.*, p. 671.

which have been successfully applied in the past may result in inappropriate responses under changed conditions. An inadequate flexibility in the application of skills will, in changing milieu, result in more or less serious maladjustments.[9] Thus, to adopt a barnyard illustration used in this connection by Burke, chickens may be readily conditioned to interpret the sound of a bell as a signal for food. The same bell may now be used to summon the "trained chickens" to their doom as they are assembled to suffer decapitation. In general, one adopts measures in keeping with his past training and, under new conditions which are not recognized as significantly different, the very soundness of this training may lead to the adoption of the wrong procedures. Again, in Burke's almost echolalic phrase, "people may be unfitted by being fit in an unfit fitness"; their training may become an incapacity.

Dewey's concept of occupational psychosis rests upon much the same observations. As a result of their day to day routines, people develop special preferences, antipathies, discriminations and emphases.[10] (The term psychosis is used by Dewey to denote a "pronounced character of the mind.") These psychoses develop through demands put upon the individual by the particular organization of his occupational role.

The concepts of both Veblen and Dewey refer to a fundamental ambivalence. Any action can be considered in terms of what it attains or what it fails to attain. "A way of seeing is also a way of not seeing—a focus upon object A involves a neglect of object B."[11] In his discussion, Weber is almost exclusively concerned with what the bureaucratic structure attains: precision, reliability, efficiency. This same structure may be examined from another perspective provided by the ambivalence. What are the limitations of the organization designed to attain these goals?

THE BUREAUCRATIC DILEMMA

For reasons which we have already noted, the bureaucratic structure exerts a constant pressure upon the official to be "methodical, prudent, disciplined." If the bureaucracy is to operate successfully, it must

[9] For a stimulating discussion and application of these concepts, see Kenneth Burke, Permanence and Change (New York, 1935), pp. 50 ff.; Daniel Warnotte, "Bureaucratic et Fonctionnarisme," Revue de l'Institut de Sociologie, XVII (1937), 245.

[10] Ibid., pp. 58-59.

[11] Ibid., p. 70.

attain a high degree of reliability of behavior, an unusual degree of conformity with prescribed patterns of action. Hence, the fundamental importance of discipline which may be as highly developed in a religious or economic bureaucracy as in the army. Discipline can be effective only if the ideal patterns are buttressed by strong sentiments which entail devotion to one's duties, a keen sense of the limitation of one's authority and competence, and methodical performance of routine activities. The efficacy of social structure depends ultimately upon infusing group participants with appropriate attitudes and sentiments. As we shall see, there are definite arrangements in the bureaucracy for inculcating and reinforcing these sentiments.

At the moment it suffices to observe that, in order to ensure discipline (the necessary reliability of response), these sentiments are often more intense than is technically necessary. There is a margin of safety, so to speak, in the pressure exerted by these sentiments upon the bureaucrat to conform to his patterned obligations, in much the same sense that added allowances (precautionary overestimations) are made by the engineer in designing the supports for a bridge. But this very emphasis leads to a transference of the sentiments from the *aims* of the organization onto the particular details of behavior required by the rules. Adherence to the rules, originally conceived as a means, becomes transformed into an end-in-itself; there occurs the familiar process of *displacement* of goals whereby "an instrument value becomes a terminal value."[12]

Discipline, readily interpreted as conformance with regulations,

12 This process has often been observed in various connections. Wundt's *heterogony of ends* is a case in point; Max Weber's *Paradoxie der Folgen* is another. See also MacIver's observations on the transformation of civilization into culture and Lasswell's remark that "the human animal distinguishes himself by his infinite capacity for making ends of his means." See R. K. Merton, "The Unanticipated Consequences of Purposive Social Action," *American Sociological Review*, I (1936), 894-904. In terms of the psychological mechanisms involved, this process has been analyzed most fully by Gordon W. Allport, in his discussion of what he calls "the functional autonomy of motives." Allport emends the earlier formulations of Woodworth, Tolman, and William Stern, and arrives at a statement of the process from the standpoint of individual motivation. He does not consider those phases of the social structure which conduce toward the "transformation of motives." The formulation adopted in this paper is thus complementary to Allport's analysis; the one stressing the psychological mechanisms involved, the other considering the constraints of the social structure. The convergence of psychology and sociology toward this central concept suggests that it may well constitute one of the conceptual bridges between the two disciplines. See Gordon W. Allport, *Personality* (New York, 1937), chap. 7.

whatever the situation, is seen not as a measure designed for specific purposes but becomes an immediate value in the life-organization of the bureaucrat. This emphasis, resulting from the displacement of the original goals, develops into rigidities and an inability to adjust readily. Formalism, even ritualism, ensues with an unchallenged insistence upon punctilious adherence to formalized procedures.[13] This may be exaggerated to the point where primary concern with conformity to the rules interferes with the achievement of the purposes of the organization, in which case we have the familiar phenomenon of the technicism or red tape of the official. An extreme product of this process of displacement of goals is the bureaucratic virtuoso, who never forgets a single rule binding his action and hence is unable to assist many of his clients.[14] A case in point, where strict recognition of the limits of authority and literal adherence to rules produced this result, is the pathetic plight of Bernt Balchen, Admiral Byrd's pilot in the flight over the South Pole.

According to a ruling of the department of labor Bernt Balchen . . . cannot receive his citizenship papers. Balchen, a native of Norway, declared his intention in 1927. It is held that he has failed to meet the condition of five years' continuous residence in the United States. The Byrd Antarctic voyage took him out of the country, although he was on a ship flying the American flag, was an invaluable member of an American expedition, and in a region to which there is an American claim because of the exploration and occupation of it by Americans, this region being Little America.

The bureau of naturalization explains that it cannot proceed on the assumption that Little America is American soil. That would be *trespass on international questions* where it has no sanction. So far as the bureau is concerned, Balchen was out of the country and *technically* has not complied with the law of naturalization.[15]

Such inadequacies in orientation which involve trained incapacity clearly derive from structural sources. The process may be briefly

---

[13] See E. C. Hughes, "Institutional Office and the Person," *American Journal of Sociology*, XLIII (1937), 404-413; R. K. Merton, "Social Structure and Anomie," *American Sociological Review*, III (1938), 672-682; E. T. Hiller, "Social Structure in Relation to the Person," *Social Forces*, XVI (1937), 34-44.

[14] Mannheim, *op. cit.*, p. 106.

[15] Quoted from the Chicago Tribune (June 24, 1931), p. 10, by Thurman Arnold, *The Symbols of Government* (New Haven, 1935), pp. 201-2. (My italics.)

recapitulated. (1) An effective bureaucracy demands reliability of response and strict devotion to regulations. (2) Such devotion to the rules leads to their transformation into absolutes; they are no longer conceived as relative to a given set of purposes. (3) This interferes with ready adaptation under special conditions not clearly envisaged by those who drew up the general rules. (4) Thus, the very elements which conduce toward efficiency in general produce inefficiency in specific instances. Full realization of the inadequacy is seldom attained by members of the group who have not divorced themselves from the "meanings" which the rules have for them. These rules in time become symbolic in cast, rather than strictly utilitarian.

Thus far, we have treated the ingrained sentiments making for rigorous discipline simply as data, as given. However, definite features of the bureaucratic structure may be seen to conduce to these sentiments. The bureaucrat's official life is planned for him in terms of a graded career, through the organizational devices of promotion by seniority, pensions, incremental salaries, etc., all of which are designed to provide incentives for disciplined action and conformity to the official regulations.[16] The official is tacitly expected to and largely does adapt his thoughts, feelings and actions to the prospect of this career. But *these very devices* which increase the probability of conformance also lead to an over-concern with strict adherence to regulations which induces timidity, conservatism, and technicism. Displacement of sentiments from goals onto means is fostered by the tremendous symbolic significance of the means (rules).

BUREAUCRATIC CLIQUES

Another feature of the bureaucratic structure tends to produce much the same result. Functionaries have the sense of a common destiny for all those who work together. They share the same interests, especially since there is relatively little competition insofar as promotion is in terms of seniority. In-group aggression is thus minimized and this arrangement is therefore conceived to be positively functional for the bureaucracy. However, the esprit de corps and informal social organization which typically develops in such situations often leads

16 Mannheim, *Mensch und Gesellschaft*, pp. 32-33. Mannheim stresses the importance of the "Lebensplan" and the "Amtskarriere." See the comments by Hughes, *op. cit.*, p. 413.

the personnel to defend their entrenched interests rather than to assist their clientele and elected higher officials. As President Lowell reports, if the bureaucrats believe that their status is not adequately recognized by an incoming elected official, detailed information will be withheld from him, leading him to errors for which he is held responsible. Or, if he seeks to dominate fully, and thus violates the sentiment of self-integrity of the bureaucrats, he may have documents brought to him in such numbers that he cannot manage to sign them all, let alone read them.[17] This illustrates the defensive informal organization which tends to arise whenever there is an apparent threat to the integrity of the group.[18]

It would be much too facile and partly erroneous to attribute such resistance by bureaucrats simply to vested interests. Vested interests oppose any new order which either eliminates or at least makes uncertain their differential advantage deriving from the current arrangements. This is undoubtedly involved, in part, in bureaucratic resistance to change but another process is perhaps more significant. As we have seen, bureaucratic officials affectively identify themselves with their way of life. They have a pride of craft which leads them to resist change in established routines; at least, those changes which are felt to be imposed by persons outside the inner circle of co-workers. This nonlogical pride of craft is a familiar pattern found even, to judge from Sutherland's *Professional Thief*, among pickpockets who, despite the risk, delight in mastering the prestige-bearing feat of "beating a left breech" (picking the left front trousers pocket).

In a stimulating paper, Hughes has applied the concepts of "secular" and "sacred" to various types of division of labor; "the sacredness" of caste and *Stände* prerogatives contrasts sharply with the increasing secularism of occupational differentiation in our mobile society.[19] However, as our discussion suggests, there may ensue, in particular vocations and in particular types of organization, the *process*

[17] A. L. Lowell, *The Government of England* (New York, 1908), I, 189 ff.

[18] For an instructive description of the development of such a defensive organization in a group of workers, see F. J. Roethlisberger and W. J. Dickson, *Management and the Worker* (Boston, 1934).

[19] E. C. Hughes, "Personality Types and the Division of Labor," *American Journal of Sociology*, XXXIII (1928), 754-768. Much the same distinction is drawn by Leopold von Wiese and Howard Becker, *Systematic Sociology* (New York, 1932), pp. 222-25 *et passim*.

of *sanctification* (viewed as the counterpart of the process of secularization). This is to say that through sentiment-formation, emotional dependence upon bureaucratic symbols and status, and affective involvement in spheres of competence and authority, there develop prerogatives involving attitudes of moral legitimacy which are established as values in their own right, and are no longer viewed as merely technical means for expediting administration. One may note a tendency for certain bureaucratic norms, originally introduced for technical reasons, to become rigidified and sacred, although, as Durkheim would say, they are *laique en apparence*.[20] Durkheim has touched on this general process in his description of the attitudes and values which persist in the organic solidarity of a highly differentiated society.

THE IMPERSONALITY OF BUREAUCRATS

Another feature of the bureaucratic structure, the stress on depersonalization of relationships, also plays its part in the bureaucrat's trained incapacity. The personality pattern of the bureaucrat is nucleated about this norm of impersonality. Both this and the categorizing tendency, which develops from the dominant role of general, abstract rules, tend to produce conflict in the bureaucrat's contacts with the public or clientele. Since functionaries minimize personal relations and resort to categorization, the peculiarities of individual cases are often ignored. But the client who, quite understandably, is convinced of the "special features" of *his* own problem often objects to such categorical treatment. Stereotyped behavior is not adapted to the exigencies of individual problems. The impersonal treatment of affairs which are at times of great personal significance to the client gives rise to the charge of "arrogance" and "haughtiness" of the bureaucrat. Thus, at the Greenwich Employment Exchange, the unemployed worker who is securing his insurance payment resents what he deems to be "the impersonality and, at times, the apparent

---

[20] Hughes recognizes one phase of this process of sanctification when he writes that professional training "carries with it as a by-product assimilation of the candidate to a set of professional attitudes and controls, a *professional conscience and solidarity. The profession* claims and aims to become a moral unit." Hughes, *op. cit.*, p. 762 (italics inserted). In this same connection, Sumner's concept of pathos, as the halo of sentiment which protects a social value from criticism, is particularly relevant, inasmuch as it affords a clue to the mechanisms involved in the process of santification. See his *Folkways* (Boston, 1906), pp. 180-181.

abruptness and even harshness of his treatment by the clerks. . . .
Some men complain of the superior attitude which the clerks have."[21]

Still another source of conflict with the public derives from the
bureaucratic structure. The bureaucrat, in part irrespective of his
position within the hierarchy, acts as a representative of the power
and prestige of the entire structure. In his official role he is vested
with definite authority. This often leads to an actual or apparent
domineering attitude, which may only be exaggerated by a discrepancy between his position within the hierarchy and his position with
reference to the public.[22] Protest and recourse to other officials on the
part of the client are often ineffective or largely precluded by the
previously mentioned esprit de corps which joins the officials into a
more or less solidary in-group. This source of conflict may be minimized in private enterprise since the client can register an effective
protest by transferring his trade to another organization within the
competitive system. But with the monopolistic nature of the public

21 " 'They treat you like a lump of dirt they do. I see a navvy reach across
the counter and shake one of them by the collar the other day. The rest of us
felt like cheering. Of course he lost his benefit over it. . . . But the clerk deserved
it for his sassy way.' " (E. W. Bakke, The Unemployed Man [New York, 1934],
pp. 79-80.) Note that the domineering attitude was imputed by the unemployed
client who is in a state of tension due to his loss of status and self-esteem in a
society where the ideology is still current that an "able man" can always find a
job. That the imputation of arrogance stems largely from the client's state of
mind is seen from Bakke's own observation that "the clerks were rushed, and
had no time for pleasantries, but there was little sign of harshness or a superiority
feeling in their treatment of the men." Insofar as there is an objective basis for
the imputation of arrogant behavior to bureaucrats, it may possibly be explained
by the following juxtaposed statements. "Auch der moderne, sei es offentcliche,
sei es private, Beamte erstrebt immer und geniesst meist den Beherrschten
gegenuber eine spezifisch gehobene, 'standische' soziale Schatzung." (Weber, op.
cit., p. 652.) "In persons in whom the craving for prestige is uppermost, hostility
usually takes the form of a desire to humiliate others." (K. Horney, The Neurotic
Personality of Our Time [New York: Norton, 1937], pp. 278-79.)

22 In this connection, note the relevance of Koffka's comments on certain
features of the pecking order of birds. "If one compares the behavior of the bird
at the top of the pecking list, the despot, with that of one very far down, the
second or third from the last, then one finds the latter much more cruel to the
few others over whom he lords it than the former in his treatment of all members.
As soon as one removes from the group all members above the penultimate, his
behavior becomes milder and may even become very friendly. . . . It is not difficult
to find analogies to this in human societies, and therefore one side of such
behavior must be primarily the effects of the social groupings, and not of individual
characteristics." K. Koffka, Principles of Gestalt Psychology (New York, 1935),
pp. 668-9.

organization, no such alternative is possible. Moreover, in this case, tension is increased because of a discrepancy between ideology and fact: the governmental personnel are held to be "servants of the people," but in fact they are usually superordinate, and release of tension can seldom be afforded by turning to other agencies for the necessary service.[23]

This tension is in part attributable to the confusion of status of bureaucrat and client; the client may consider himself socially superior to the official who is at the moment dominant.[24]

Thus, with respect to the relations between officials and clientele, one structural source of conflict is the pressure for formal and impersonal treatment when individual, personalized consideration is desired by the client. The conflict may be viewed, then, as deriving from the introduction of inappropriate attitudes and relationships. Conflict within the bureaucratic structure arises from the converse situation, namely, when personalized relationships are substituted for the structurally required impersonal relationships. This type of conflict may be characterized as follows:

The bureaucracy, as we have seen, is organized as a secondary, formal group. The normal responses involved in this organized network of social expectations are supported by affective attitudes of members of the group. Since the group is oriented toward secondary norms of impersonality, any failure to conform to these norms will arouse antagonism from those who have identified themselves with the legitimacy of these rules. Hence, the substitution of personal for impersonal treatment within the structure is met with widespread disapproval and is characterized by such epithets as "graft," "favoritism," "nepotism," "apple-polishing," etc. These epithets are clearly manifestations of injured sentiments.[25] The function of such "automatic

[23] At this point the political machine often becomes functionally significant. As Steffens and others have shown, highly personalized relations and the abrogation of formal rules (red tape) by the machine often satisfy the needs of individual "clients" more fully than the formalized mechanism of governmental bureaucracy.

[24] As one of the unemployed men remarked about the clerks at the Greenwich Employment Exchange: " 'And the bloody blokes wouldn't have their jobs if it wasn't for us men out of a job either. That's what gets me about their holding their noses up.' " Bakke, op. cit., p. 80.

[25] The diagnostic significance of such linguistic indices as epithets has scarcely been explored by the sociologist. Sumner properly observes that epithets produce "summary criticisms" and definitions of social situations. Dollard also notes that

resentment" can be clearly seen in terms of the requirements of bureaucratic structure.

Bureaucracy is a secondary group mechanism designed to carry on certain activities which cannot be satisfactorily performed on the basis of primary group criteria.[26] Hence behavior which runs counter to these formalized norms becomes the object of emotionalized disapproval. This constitutes a functionally significant defense set up against tendencies which jeopardize the performance of socially necessary activities. To be sure, these reactions are not rationally determined practices explicitly designed for the fulfillment of this function. Rather, viewed in terms of the individual's interpretation of the situation, such resentment is simply an immediate response opposing the "dishonesty" of those who violate the rules of the game. However, this subjective frame of reference notwithstanding, these reactions serve the function of maintaining the essential structural elements of bureaucracy by reaffirming the necessity for formalized, secondary relations and by helping to prevent the disintegration of the bureaucratic structure which would occur should these be supplanted by personalized relations. This type of conflict may be generically described as the intrusion of primary group attitudes when secondary group attitudes are institutionally demanded, just as the bureaucratic-client conflict often derives from interaction on impersonal terms when personal treatment is individually demanded.[27]

The trend toward increasing bureaucratization in Western society, which Weber had long since foreseen, is not the sole reason for sociologists to turn their attention to this field. Empirical studies of the

---

"epithets frequently define the central issues in a society," and Sapir has rightly emphasized the importance of context of situations in appraising the significance of epithets. Of equal relevance is Linton's observation that "in case histories the way in which the community felt about a particular episode is, if anything, more important to our study than the actual behavior. . . ." A sociological study of "vocabularies of encomium and opprobrium" should lead to valuable findings.

[26] Cf. Ellsworth Faris, *The Nature of Human Nature* (New York, 1937), pp. 41 ff.

[27] Community disapproval of many forms of behavior may be analyzed in terms of one or the other of these patterns of substitution of culturally inappropriate types of relationship. Thus, prostitution constitutes a type-case where coitus, a form of intimacy which is institutionally defined as symbolic of the most "sacred" primary group relationship, is placed within a contractual context, symbolized by the exchange of that most impersonal of all symbols, money. See Kingsley Davis, "The Sociology of Prostitution," *American Sociological Review*, II (1937), 744-55.

interaction of bureaucracy and personality should especially increase our understanding of social structure. A large number of specific questions invite our attention. To what extent are particular personality types selected and modified by the various bureaucracies (private enterprise, public service, the quasi-legal political machine, religious orders)? Inasmuch as ascendancy and submission are held to be traits of personality, despite their variability in different stimulus-situations, do bureaucracies select personalities of particularly submissive or ascendant tendencies? And since various studies have shown that these traits can be modified, does participation in bureaucratic office tend to increase ascendant tendencies? Do various systems of recruitment (e.g., patronage, open competition involving specialized knowledge or "general mental capacity," practical experience) select different personality types? Does promotion through seniority lessen competitive anxieties and enhance administrative efficiency? A detailed examination of mechanisms for imbuing the bureaucratic codes with affect would be instructive both sociologically and psychologically. Does the general anonymity of civil service decisions tend to restrict the area of prestige-symbols to a narrowly defined inner circle? Is there a tendency for differential association to be especially marked among bureaucrats?

The range of theoretically significant and practically important questions would seem to be limited only by the accessibility of the concrete data. Studies of religious, educational, military, economic, and political bureaucracies dealing with the interdependence of social organization and personality formation should constitute an avenue for fruitful research. On that avenue, the functional analysis of concrete structures may yet build a Solomon's House for sociologists.

Self-Portrait of the Fascist Agitator[1]

BY LEO LOWENTHAL AND NORBERT GUTERMAN

THE DEMOCRATIC leader usually tries to present himself as both similar to and different from his followers—similar in that he has common interests with them, different in that he has special talents for representing those interests. The agitator tries to maintain the same sort of relationship to his audiences, but instead of emphasizing the identity of his interests with those of his followers, he depicts himself as one of the plain folk, who thinks, lives and feels like them. In agitation this suggestion of proximity and intimacy takes the place of identification of interests.

The nature of the difference between leader and follower is similarly changed. Although the agitator intimates that he is intellectually and morally superior to his audience, he rests his claim to leadership primarily on the suggestion of his innate predestination. He does resort to such traditional American symbols of leadership as the indefatigable businessman and the rugged frontiersman, but these are overshadowed by the image he constructs of himself as a suffering martyr who, as a reward for his sacrifices, deserves special privileges and unlimited ascendancy over his followers. The agitator is not chosen by his followers but presents himself as their pre-chosen leader—pre-chosen by himself on the basis of a mysterious inner call, and pre-chosen as well by the enemy as a favorite target of persecu-

[1] Reprinted from *The Prophets of Deceit*, by Leo Lowenthal and Norbert Guterman, Harper & Brothers, 1949. Used by permission of the publishers.

tion. One of the plain folk, he is yet far above them; reassuringly close, he is yet infinitely aloof.

While spokesmen for liberal and radical causes refrain, for a variety of reasons, from thrusting their own personalities into the foreground of their public appeals, the agitator does not hesitate to advertise himself. He does not depend on a "build-up" manufactured by subordinates and press agents, but does the job himself. He could hardly trust anyone else to paint his self-image in such glowing colors. As the good fellow who has nothing to hide, whose effusiveness and garrulousness know no limit, he does not seem to be inhibited by considerations of good taste from openly displaying his private life and his opinions about himself.

This directness of self-expression is particularly suitable for one who aspires to be the spokesman for those suffering from social malaise. He seems to realize almost intuitively that objective argumentation and impersonal discourse would only intensify the feelings of despair, isolation, and distrust from which his listeners suffer and from which they long to escape. Such a gleeful display of his personality serves as an *ersatz* assertion of individuality. Part of the secret of his charisma as leader is that he presents the image of a self-sufficient personality to his followers. If they are deprived of such a blessing, then at least they can enjoy it at second remove in their leader.

Those who suffer from malaise always want to pour their hearts out, but because of their inhibitions and lack of opportunities they seldom succeed. Conceiving of their troubles as individual and inner maladjustments, they want only a chance to be "understood," to clear up the "misunderstandings" which others have about them. On this need the agitator bases his own outpouring of personal troubles. When he talks about himself the agitator vicariously gratifies his followers' wish to tell the world of their troubles. He lends an aura of sanction and validity to the desire of his followers endlessly to complain, and thus his seemingly sincere loquacity strengthens his rapport with them. His trials are theirs, his successes also theirs. Through him they live.

By seemingly taking his listeners into his confidence and talking "man to man" to them, the agitator achieves still another purpose: he dispels any fear they may have that he is talking above their heads or against their institutionalized ways of life. He is the elder brother

straightening things out for them, not a subversive who would destroy
the basic patterns of their lives. The enemy of all established values,
the spokesman of the apocalypse, and the carrier of disaffection creates the atmosphere of a family party in order to spread his doctrine
the more effectively. Blending protestations of his weakness with intimations of his strength, he whines and boasts at the same time. Cannot one who is so frank about his humility also afford to be equally
frank about his superiority?

The agitator's references to himself thus fall into two groups or
themes: one covering his familiarity and the other his aloofness, one
in a minor key establishing him as a "great little man," and the other
in a major key as a bullet-proof martyr who despite his extraordinary
sufferings always emerges victorious over his enemies.

THE GREAT LITTLE MAN

Unlike those idealists who, sacrificing their comfort in behalf of a
lofty social goal, "go to the people," the agitator is always eager to
show that socially he is almost indistinguishable from the great mass
of American citizens. "I am an underdog who has suffered through
the depression like most of the people."[2] Like millions of other
Americans, he is "one of [those] plain old time, stump grubbing,
liberty loving, apple cider men and women."[3] Yet he is always careful
to make it clear that he is one of the endogamic élite, "an American-
born citizen whose parents were American born and whose parents'
parents were American born. I think that's far enough back."[4] There
is no danger that anyone will discover he had an impure grandmother.

Not only is he one of the people, but his most ardent wish is always
to remain one and enjoy the pleasures of private existence. He hates
to be in the limelight, for he is "an old-fashioned American" who,
he cheerfully admits, does not even know his "way round in the circles
of high society at Washington."[5] If it were really up to him, and if
his conscience didn't tell him otherwise, he'd spend all his time on his
favorite hobby: "If we had a free press in America I doubt if Gerald
Smith would publish The Cross and the Flag. I am sure I wouldn't

[2] Phelps, Los Angeles, Sep. 26, 1940, radio.
[3] Smith, New York, Oct. 20, 1936, meeting.
[4] Phelps, Los Angeles, Aug. 7, 1941.
[5] Smith, The Hoop of Steel, p. 24.

publish AMERICA PREFERRED. In my spare time I'd play golf."[6] Even when he finally does seek office, it is only after a heart-rending conflict and after he has received the permission of his parents: ". . . first, I would have to get the consent of my Christian mother and father because years ago I had promised them that I would not seek office."[7] And on those rare occasions when he can escape from his duties for a few minutes of relaxation, he proudly tells his listeners about it: "Well, friends, Lulu and I managed to get time out to attend the annual carnival and bazaar of the Huntington Park Chapter of the Indoor Sports Club."[8]

Even at this rather uncomplicated level of identification the agitator is ambiguous. By his very protestations that he is quite the same as the mass of Americans he smuggles in hints of his exceptional status. Public life, he intimates, is a bother, and whoever deserts his private pleasures in its behalf must have some good reason for doing so. By constantly apologizing for his abandonment of private life and his absorption in public life, the agitator suggests that there are special provinces and unusual responsibilities that are limited to the uniquely endowed. If one of the plain people, such as he, gains access to such privileges and burdens, then it must surely be because of his unusual talents. He has embarked on a difficult task for which he is specially qualified, and therefore his followers owe him gratitude, admiration, and obedience.

A GENTLE SOUL. Although he is, by virtue of his special talents, a man who has risen out of the common people, the agitator remains a kindly, gentle soul—folksy, good-natured, golden-hearted. Far be it from him to hold any malice against any fellow human being, for "if we must hate, let us hate hate."[9] Nor is he "the kind of person who carries hatred or bitterness for any length of time. . . . In spite of all I have gone through . . . I have never lost my sense of humor, my ability to laugh, even right into the face of seeming disaster."[10]

Like all other Americans, he is a good and solicitous father to his children, and in a moment of difficulty appeals touchingly to his friends for help: "My son, 9½ years old, is pestering me, wanting a

6 America Preferred (Mote), May, 1945.
7 The Cross and The Flag (Smith), May, 1942.
8 Phelps, Los Angeles, July 28, 1941, radio.
9 Coughlin, Speech on Jan. 29, 1939, reprinted in Why Leave Our Own.
10 Phelps, Los Angeles, July 21, 1941, radio.

bicycle. Get in touch with me, please, if anyone knows where I could obtain a second-hand bicycle very cheap."[11] But his virtues come out most clearly in his role as model husband. He regales his audience with bits of intimate family dialogue: "I said one day to my sweet wife."[12] And even he, the would-be dictator, does not hesitate to admit that the little, or not so little, wife is the boss at home: "If I don't look out I'll be looking for a boss' lap on which to sit and chew gum. Well, Lulu's the boss and, having gained about 25 pounds during the past six months, she has plenty of lap on which to sit."[13]

As he makes the rounds of his meetings, his faithful wife accompanies him: "A few weeks ago found Mrs. Winrod and me spending Sunday at Sioux City, Iowa, holding meetings in the Billy Sunday Memorial Tabernacle."[14] And when he wishes to express his gratitude to his followers, it is again as the gentle soul, the faithful family man: "The wife and I are very grateful for the prayerful letters, kind words, and sums remitted so far . . ."[15] So sweet and lovable are both his personality and his family life that he offers family pictures for sale: "How many have received (1) Calendar of Mrs. Smith, me and Jerry? (2) A copy of my 'undelivered speech'?"[16]

TROUBLES SHARED. One of the agitator's favorite themes is his economic troubles, about which he speaks to complete strangers with perfect ease:

I must confide to you without reservation . . . I have spent everything I have; I have surrendered every possession I had in this world in order to carry on this fight. I will not be able to borrow any more money; I have nothing left to sell.[17]

Another agitator complains that by engaging in political activity he has embarked on "a gamble with the security of my wife and children at stake."[18] And still another offers the audience a detailed financial statement:

[11] Phelps, Los Angeles, Sept. 19, 1940, radio.
[12] Smith, New York, Oct. 20, 1936, meeting.
[13] Ibid.
[14] The Defender (Winrod), Feb., 1943.
[15] Hudson, letter to subscribers of his Bulletin, July, 1942.
[16] Smith, Detroit, Apr. 9, 1942, meeting.
[17] Smith, Why Is America Afraid?
[18] Phelps, Los Angeles, Aug. 18, 1940, radio.

The taxes in my Kenilworth home are unpaid and there are some $1800 in outstanding bills accrued since I stopped depleting my few remaining securities, although I have paid light, phone and groceries . . . his [her husband's] refusal to give us any of the milk check income from my farm, his continuing to spend this income while associating with the women he brought to sleep in my own bed at my farm, finally made it necessary to take some legal steps to protect the family.[19]

The agitator is just as frank about the condition of his health as about his financial or marital contretemps, and his extraordinary sacrifices that cause him to commiserate with himself: "I come home and say to Mrs. Smith, 'How does this old heart of mine keep up?' . . . But I know how men like that go—they go all of a sudden."[20] And even when his heart doesn't bother him, his teeth do: "The last time I saw Charlie Hudson, he still had been unable to afford to get needed dental work done. His wife takes roomers."[21] His afflictions threaten to handicap his political work:

My dentist informed me I must have four teeth removed at once. I don't mind that so much as I do the fact that I may come on the air tomorrow, after the teeth have been extracted, and sound like a dear old gentleman who has been drawing old-age pension for forty years or more.[22]

By multiplying such references to his family, his health, and his finances, the agitator tries to create an atmosphere of homey intimacy. This device has immediate, gratifying implications. The personal touch, the similarity between agitator and audience and the intimate revelations of "human interest" provide emotional compensation for those whose life is cold and dreary, especially for those who must live a routinized and atomized existence.

Equally gratifying to the listeners is the fact that such revelations help satisfy their curiosity—a universal feature of contemporary mass culture. It may be due to the prevalent feeling that one has to have "inside information" that comes "from the horse's mouth" in order to get along in modern society. Perhaps, too, this curiosity is derived from an unconscious infantile desire to glimpse the forbidden life of

19 Round Table Letter (Dilling), Feb. 28, 1942.
20 Smith, Detroit, Mar. 19, 1943, meeting.
21 Round Table Letter (Dilling), Apr. 8, 1942.
22 Phelps, Los Angeles, Jan. 14, 1941, radio.

the grownups—a desire closely related to that of revealing and enjoying scandals. When the listener is treated as an insider, his libido is gratified, and it matters little to him whether he hears revelations about crimes and orgies supposedly indulged in by the enemy or about the increase in weight of the agitator's wife. He has been allowed to become one of those "in the know."

PUBLIC PRIVACY. When the agitator indulges in his uninhibited displays of domesticity and intimacy, he does so not as a private person but as a public figure. This fact endows his behavior with considerable ambivalence. His lyrical paeans in praise of the pleasures of private existence imply *ipso facto* a degrading of this privacy when he exposes it to public inspection. This gesture has the double meaning of an invasion of the agitator's private life by his public life and of his public life by his private life. In this way the traditional liberal differentiation between the two is made to seem obsolete and in any case untenable. Privacy is no longer possible in this harsh social world —except as a topic of public discussion.

Finally, these revelations of private life serve to enhance the agitator's stature as a public figure, who, as has already been suggested, vicariously symbolizes the repressed individualities of his adherents. He establishes his identity with the audience by telling it of his financial troubles and other kinds of failures, but he also underlines the fact of his success. He has risen from the depths in which the followers still find themselves; in contrast to them, he has managed to integrate his public and private personalities. The proof of this is simple enough —is he not talking to the followers and are they not listening to him? As a symbol of his followers' longings, the agitator centers all attention on himself, and soon his listeners may forget that he is discussing, not public issues, but his qualifications for leadership.

That the agitator simultaneously stresses his own weakness, that he pictures himself as all too human, does not impair the effectiveness of his attempt at self-exaltation. By the very fact that he admits his weaknesses while stressing his powers, he implies that the followers too can, if to a lesser extent, become strong once they surrender their private existence to the public movement. They need but follow the path of the great little man.

BULLET-PROOF MARTYR

Aside from his remarkable readiness to share his troubles with his fellow men, what are the qualities that distinguish the great little man from the rest of the plain folk and make him fit to be one of "those . . . who lead"?[23] Here again the agitator is ready to answer the question. Although the agitator calls himself an old-fashioned Christian American, Christian humility is hardly one of his outstanding virtues. For all his insistence that he is one of the common folk, he does not hesitate to simultaneously declare that he is an exceptionally gifted man who knows and even admires his own talent.

That he has no difficulty in overcoming conventional reticence about such matters is due not merely to his quite human readiness to talk about himself but also to the fact that his prominence is not merely his own doing. As he has emphasized, his natural inclination is not to lead humanity: he would rather play golf. But he cannot help it—forces stronger and more imperious than his own will push him to leadership. Both because of his innate dynamism and because he has been singled out by the enemy, the mantle of leadership, like it or not, falls on his shoulders.

The Inner Call. Suggesting that his activity is prompted by sacred command, the agitator speaks of himself as a "voice of the great unorganized and helpless masses."[24] He is "giving vocal expression to the thoughts that you have been talking about around your family tables."[25] But it also comes from holier regions: "Like John the Baptist," the agitator is "living just for the sweet privilege of being a voice in the wilderness."[26] As such, the agitator does not hesitate to compare himself to Christ: "Put down the Crown of Thorns on me."[27] He sees himself continuing the work of the "Divine Savior."[28]

But for all his suggestions that he has a divine responsibility the agitator does not pretend to bring any startlingly new revelation. He does not claim to make his audience aware of a reality that they see only partially; he does not claim to raise the level of their conscious-

23 *The Cross and The Flag* (Smith), July, 1945.
24 *The Cross and The Flag* (Smith), May, 1942.
25 Stewart, New York, July 13, 1940, street corner.
26 Smith, Cleveland, May 11, 1943, meeting.
27 Smith, Detroit, Apr. 9, 1942, meeting.
28 *The Defender* (Winrod), Oct., 1942.

ness. All he does is to "say what you all want to say and haven't got the guts to say it."[29] What "others think . . . privately," the agitator says "publicly."[30] And for this purpose he is specially talented: as one agitator says of himself, he delivered what was "perhaps the greatest address we have ever had on Christian statesmanship."[31]

Like a new Luther, he bellows defiance of established powers without regard to consequences: "I am going to say some things this afternoon that some people won't like, but I cannot help it, I must speak the truth."[32] Nothing can "halt and undo the innermost convictions of stalwart sons of Aryan blood,"[33] not even the ingratitude of those who spurn him: "Nevertheless, there I will stand demanding social justice for all even though some of the ill-advised whom I am endeavoring to defend will take a pot shot at me from the rear."[34]

Nor is the agitator's courage purely spiritual:

If the Gentiles of the nation back up Pelley now in his challenge to the usurpers of American liberties, they are going to get a "break" that they have never dreamed possible till Pelley showed the spunk to defy the nepotists.[35]

The agitator, aware of both his qualifications and his courage, knows that

When the history of America is written . . . concerning the preservation of the American way of life, I am going to be thankful that in the day when men were cowardly and overcautious and crawled under the bed and allowed themselves to be bulldozed by a bunch of wire-whiskered Communists and atheists and anti-God politicians, that there was one man by the name of Gerald L. K. Smith that had the courage to be an old-fashioned, honest to God, Christian American![36]

And the agitator knows too that his courage extends to somewhat smaller matters as well:

When I went to the Auditorium, although it was very cold, probably

[29] Smith, St. Louis, Mar. 25, 1944, meeting.
[30] Social Justice (Coughlin), July 7, 1941.
[31] The Cross and The Flag (Smith), Aug., 1943.
[32] Smith, Why Is America Afraid?
[33] Liberation (Pelley), Sept. 21, 1939.
[34] Social Justice (Coughlin), June 5, 1938.
[35] Roll Call (Pelley), Oct. 20, 1941.
[36] Smith, Detroit, Mar. 19, 1943, meeting.

five degrees below zero—twenty degrees the first time, five degrees the second time—the place was packed and every inch of standing room was taken. I had to pass through a picket line, one of those vicious picket lines organized by Reds and enemies of our meeting there.[37]

It is this blending of seriousness and unseriousness, of the sublime Crown of Thorns and the toothache, that characterizes the agitator's approach to composing his self-portrait as well as to the other themes of his speeches and writings. He is both the little man suffering the usual hardships and the prophet of truth: Walter Mitty and Jeremiah rolled up into one.

Such an indiscriminate mixture of trivial and sublime symbols might appear blasphemous or simply disgusting, but the agitator seems to count on a different kind of reaction. Instead of imposing on his listeners the difficult task of following a saint, a task which might after all cause them to feel that they too must assume some of the traits of sainthood, the agitator gratifies them by dragging the lofty notions of sainthood down to a humdrum, *kleinburgerlich* level. The followers thereby are offered an object of admiration, the image of the desanctified saint, that is closer to their own level of feeling and perception. The agitator imposes no strain on them.

There is still another gratification for the audience in the agitator's narcissistic outbursts of self-praise. A courageous and self-reliant man might be disgusted with the spectacle of someone celebrating himself as the repository of all the manly virtues, but people who are acclimated to self-denial and self-hatred are paradoxically attracted by the selfish narcissist. As a leading psychoanalyst puts it: "This narcissistic behavior which gives the dependent persons no hope for any real love arouses their readiness for identification."[38] Accordingly, the agitator does not count on the support of people capable of self-criticism or self-reliance; he turns to those who constantly yearn for magical aids to buttress their personalities.

PERSECUTED INNOCENCE. Like any advocate of social change the agitator appeals to social frustration and suffering, but in his output there is a striking contrast between the vagueness with which he refers to the sufferings of his listeners as a social group and the vividness

[37] Smith, *ibid.*

[38] Fenichel, *The Psychoanalytical Theory of Neurosis* (Norton, New York, 1945), p. 510.

with which he documents his personal trials. He speaks as though the malaise resulted in tangible hardship in him and him alone. His trials and ordeals are truly extraordinary, almost superhuman, and by comparison the complaints of his followers seem merely to refer to minor nuisances, insignificant reflections of his glorious misfortunes. He is the chosen martyr of a great cause—himself. As they compare their lot to his, the followers cannot but feel that they are almost like safe spectators watching a battle between the forces of evil and their benighted champion of virtue.

In building up this image of persecuted innocence, the agitator uses some religious symbols. He "has come through the most heart-rending Gethsemane, I believe, of any living man in America today,"[39] and he does not hesitate to compare himself to the early Christian martyrs: "Many leaders . . . sneered at Father Coughlin and turned thumbs down on the Christian Fronters, as did the Patrician population of Rome turn their thumbs down on the Christian slave martyrs."[40]

But these religious associations are only decorations for ordeals that are strictly secular; the agitator's sufferings are of this world. Yet here he runs into a difficulty. In actual fact, he has met with little interference from the public authorities.[41] Yet he realizes that as a man with a mission, he must be persecuted. If the past will yield no evidence, perhaps the future will, for who is to deny him the right to premonitions:

I don't know what is going to happen to me. All I ask you to do is, don't be surprised at anything. If I am thrown in jail, if I am indicted, if I am smeared, if I am hurt physically, no matter what it might be, don't be surprised at anything, because everything in the calendar is now being attempted. . . . I am glad to make that sacrifice.[42]

One reason why the agitator has difficulty in specifying the persecutions to which he is subjected is that his enemies work in secret. They force him to the most surreptitious behavior: "I, an American, must sneak in darkness to the printer to have him print my booklet

---

[39] The Defender (Winrod), Nov., 1940.
[40] Social Justice (Coughlin), July 7, 1941.
[41] Except for those involved in the wartime sedition trial and one agitator convicted as an enemy agent, the American agitators have suffered only from exposures and criticism.
[42] Smith, Detroit, Mar. 19, 1943, meeting.

and to get it out to the people like a bootlegger."[43] He is beset by vague dangers that are difficult to pin down: "One of these newspapermen, according to another newspaperman, is said to have predicted somewhat as follows: 'Two Jews from England were over here to see that Hudson does not get home alive.' "[44]

But when the agitator gets down to bedrock, it becomes clear that what he most resents is public criticism, which he describes as "smearing" and "intimidation." He complains that "Jewish New Dealers in the Congress . . . started a mighty ball rolling to smear Pelley from the scene."[45] And "because I dare to raise my voice foreigners are intimidating me and trying to get me off the air."[46] Nor does he feel happy that "frequently we have heard it prophesied over the radio by such noble patriots as Walter Winchell and others, that we were about to be incarcerated in concentration camps."[47]

A SLIGHT CASE OF MURDER. However insubstantial the evidence, he can summon for his martyrdom, the agitator, it must be admitted, works it for all it is worth. He continually suggests that he has embarked on a dangerous career and that he is actually risking his life. The threat never abates, as we shall see in tracing it during the course of one agitator's statements over a period of twelve years.

As early as October, 1936, he realized that his death warrant had been signed. Like his political boss, who was assassinated, ". . . it may cost my life."[48] And not without reason: "Ten threats came to me within twenty-four hours here in New York City."[49]

Three years later these threats of murder were still harassing him: "I continue to receive all sorts of threats against my life."[50]

By 1942 the rather slow-working murderers had a definite objective: to keep him out of the Senate. "I am convinced that there are men in America who would rather commit murder than see me in the United States Senate."[51] Other murderers, or perhaps the same ones, found his literary output more objectionable than the possibility of

[43] Phelps, Los Angeles, Nov. 20, 1940, radio.
[44] America in Danger (Hudson), June 23, 1942.
[45] Pelley, What You Should Know About The Pelley Publications, pp. 4-5.
[46] Phelps, Los Angeles, Sept. 29, 1940, radio.
[47] Smith, Detroit, Mar. 22, 1943, meeting.
[48] Smith, New York, Oct. 20, 1936, meeting.
[49] Smith, Ibid.
[50] Smith, Reds On The Run.
[51] The Cross and The Flag (Smith), May, 1942.

his becoming a Senator: "I have been warned that I will not live to complete this series of articles."[52]

Half a year passes, and the enemy is still intent on murder. "A certain set of ruthless men in this nation have actually called for my assassination."[53] The murderers seem finally to have worked up enough energy or courage to come within striking distance:

I held a meeting down in Akron, Ohio, one time and my Committee resigned the afternoon of the meeting. . . . I had to walk into that armory alone. . . . I walked from the hotel over to this place which seated about 6,000 people alone, and when I got over there, the place was packed. . . . I walked down the center aisle, walked right up to the microphone and the first thing I said was this, "There are men in this room who would like to see me killed tonight". . .[54]

Yet even then there is no record of the murderers doing anything. Two more years went by and by the spring of 1945 the still healthy agitator noted that the threat to his life had become so real that it was even confirmed by police authorities: "Shortly before the end of the meeting I received a message from the police detectives to the effect that they were convinced that there was a definite plot to do me great injury, perhaps kill me."[55] Nothing seems to have come of that danger, but by the summer of the same year the agitator reported that "people who know what is going on are convinced that a plan is on foot to actually get me killed at the earliest possible moment."[56] As of the moment of writing, the agitator remains alive and unharmed, never having once been the victim of assault or assassination. As late as April 29, 1948, he still maintained that he was the object of an attempt on his life, this time by means of "arsenic poisoning."[57]

That he has no genuine factual data to support his charges does not seem to disturb the agitator: he persists in believing that an evil force is out to get him. His recital of fears, smearing, premonitions, anonymous letters—all this adds up to the familiar picture of paranoia.

[52] The Cross and The Flag (Smith), Oct.-Nov., 1942.
[53] The Cross and The Flag (Smith), Feb., 1943.
[54] Smith, Detroit, Feb. 7, 1943, meeting.
[55] The Cross and The Flag (Smith), Apr., 1945.
[56] Smith, Letter, July, 1945.
[57] Smith, St. Louis, Apr. 29, 1948, meeting.

The paranoiac's conviction that he is persecuted cannot be logically refuted since it is itself extralogical. In agitation the leader acts out, as it were, a complete case history of persecution mania before his listeners, whose own inclinations to regard themselves as the target of persecution by mysterious forces is thus sanctioned and encouraged. Nevertheless it is the agitator who remains at the center of the stage; it is on him that all the imaginary enemy blows fall. By symbolically taking upon himself all the burdens of social suffering, he thus creates unconscious guilt feelings among his followers, which he can later exploit by demanding their absolute devotion as recompense for his self-sacrifice. And since the enemy exacts the heaviest penalty from him, he has the implicit right to claim the highest benefits once the enemy is defeated. Similarly, since the enemy singles him out for persecution, he has the right to engage in terroristic reprisals. All of these consequences follow from the agitator's self-portrait as martyr.

But simultaneously the agitator, for all the dangers to which he is exposed, does manage to survive and continue his work. He is not merely the martyr but also the remarkably efficient leader, and on both counts he deserves special obedience. Since he is both more exposed and better equipped than his followers, his claims to leadership are doubly vindicated.

THE MONEY-MINDED MARTYR. There are many indications that, at its present stage at least, American agitation is a racket as well as a political movement. To what extent the agitator actually depends on his followers' financial contributions it is difficult to say with any degree of certainty. In any event he does not account for the use of the money he collects. It seems probable that at least some agitators have been heavily subsidized by anonymous wealthy donors, while it is known that some of the smaller fry make a living by selling their literature.

When the agitator appeals to his followers for money, he strengthens their devotion to the cause by leading them to make financial sacrifices. In agitation such psychological factors are probably of greater importance than in other movements. For it must be remembered that in agitation the follower has no precise idea what his cause is, that the whole background of the agitator's appeal is one of destruction and violence, with a meager minimum of positive stimuli.

What remains then is the agitator himself—his inflated personality and his pressing needs. The agitator does not hesitate to act the insistent beggar. He begs meekly: "Oh, I'm just a common American citizen, friends, poor in the world's gifts, depending on the quarters and dollars of friends and radio listeners."[58] But he also begs for himself as the agent of history: "It is a long grind to get the thousands of dollars absolutely necessary as a minimum in this way. But it must be done if the fight is to go on."[59] "Why hold back your financial aid NOW—when revolution itself is being shouted from our public rostrums?"[60]

He begs for aid, but he also warns that those who do not come through now may live to regret it: "If any of you don't agree with the principles of America First and don't care to contribute to our cause, this is the time for you to get up and walk out."[61] Those who do not comply face the dreaded penalty of exclusion—they have to walk out and be alone with themselves.

MAGIC OF SURVIVAL. That he managed to survive under terrible financial handicaps and political persecution arouses the agitator's self-admiration. ". . . How could he emerge unscathed with such colossal forces arrayed to smash him?"[62] His invulnerability is remarkable and is only slightly short of miraculous. His safety is, in fact, adduced as proof that he has gone through dangers, and as he concludes his report of the plot hatched against him by English Jews, he remarks with a note of defiance in his voice: "I arrived safely Sunday night."[63] His life seems to him protected by an anonymous providence: "Pelley is an absolute fatalist . . . he believes that nothing can harm him until he has done the work which he came into life at this particular period to do."[64] And he always returns to the fight: "I intend to . . . toss off the shackles that have been thrown around me . . . to spread my wings again . . . and to soar to new heights to carry on the battle."[65] For his powers of exertion are tremendous: "I

[58] Phelps, Los Angeles, Sept. 8, 1940, radio.
[59] Dilling, Letter, Aug. 10, 1942.
[60] Social Justice (Coughlin), Nov. 27, 1939.
[61] Smith, St. Louis, Mar. 25, 1944, meeting.
[62] Pelley, What You Should Know About The Pelley Publications, pp. 4-5.
[63] America in Danger (Hudson), June 23, 1942.
[64] Pelley, Official Despatch, p. 4.
[65] Phelps, Los Angeles, Dec. 31, 1940, radio.

speak two hours here and two hours there, and write all night and talk all day to people and write letters and work and . . . and everything else, and still I always seem to have the strength to do what lies before me."[66]

Seen from one perspective, all this bragging is rather harmless. A narcissist naturally believes himself invulnerable and omnipotent, and his slightly ridiculous posturings only endear him to his audience. He is reduced to a level that is within their vision. Like the extraordinary exploits of the hero of a movie or a cheap novel, the agitator's adventure ends on an ultimately happy note—the hero is saved. From this harmless relapse into an adolescent atmosphere, the followers, together with the agitator himself, draw a certain simple gratification. They have been in the company of a hero who is not too heroic to be akin to them.

And yet somewhere in the interstices of this harmless braggadocio there lurk the grimmer notes of violence and destruction. The agitator's self-portrait of miraculous survival has a solid reality basis; he really does enjoy a high degree of impunity. He is safe and sound, magically immune, secretly protected—and this despite his verbal violence and scurrilous denunciations of the powers that be or of some of the powers that be. If his enemies do not carry out their threats of murder, it is not because they would not want to but because they do not dare. Their power, the agitator thereby suggests, is rather less impressive than it appears; they have only the façade of power. Real power is on his side.

Behind this defiance of the enemy's threats lurks another suggestion: when the hour strikes and the seemingly strong enemy is revealed in his true weakness, the agitator will take revenge for the torments of fear that have been imposed on him. Perhaps it is not too bold to conjecture that as the agitator continually stresses his own bodily vigor, he is implicitly developing a complementary image to his leading metaphor of the enemy as a Low Animal. His own body is indestructible, but the helpless bodies of the enemy—those parasitical and disease-breeding low animals—are doomed to destruction. Behind the whining complaints and the triumphant self-admiration of this indestructible martyr looms the vision of the eugenic storm troops. The agitator is a good little guy, to be sure; he is a martyr who

66 Smith, Detroit, Mar. 19, 1943, meeting.

suffers endlessly; he survives by virtue of superior destinies; but in the long run he makes sure to protect himself.

TOUGH GUY. The agitator knows that sometimes he must bare his teeth. Often he does it with the air of a youthful gangleader testing his hoodlums:

> I am going to test my people. I am going to see if the fathers that left their bones on the desert had real sons. I am going to find out if the children of the men that rebuilt San Francisco after the earthquake are real men.[67]

Such vague anticipations of the agitator's future role are supplemented with more direct hints about his present strength. He means business, even if he is a great little man. "I am a tough guy. I am tough because I have got the goods on them."[68] The easy-going braggart is also a brutal swashbuckler. "They can threaten me all they want to. I am not a damned bit afraid to walk the streets of New York all by myself. I don't have to. I have the toughest men in New York with me."[69] Nor does he always have to sneak in the dark to his printer: "Huskies of my 'American Group' protect me when I take my printed booklets from the printer's plant."[70]

The bodyguard, however, is used not merely against the enemy. The same bodyguard that protects the leader from the enemy also protects him from any interference from his listeners: their role is to listen, not to participate. When he speaks, you had better listen—or else. In this way the agitator already establishes himself as a constituted authority. The agitator brags about this:

> So as we moved down through the middle of the meeting I said, "Now, we are not going to have any disturbance, we are not going to be heckled and the first man who attempts that, we will throw him out through the nearest window." So one fellow like this boy, way up in the balcony said something and somebody didn't understand what he said, he was almost pitched out of the window.[71]

It is in this atmosphere, in which even the followers are threatened with manhandling if they step out of line, that the agitator tests out a

[67] Smith, New York, Oct. 20, 1936, meeting.
[68] Phelps, Los Angeles, Oct. 8, 1940, radio.
[69] McWilliams, New York, July 29, 1940, street corner.
[70] Phelps, Los Angeles, Nov. 12, 1940, radio.
[71] Smith, Detroit, Feb. 7, 1943, meeting.

future device: the totalitarian plebiscite. "Do you authorize me to send a telegram to Senator Reynolds . . . put up your hands. . . . All right, that is number one."[72] He feeds them cues: "I bid for the American vote under that flag. Give that a hand."[73] Such presentiments of the plebiscite are in themselves trivial enough, but they serve to emphasize the agitator's role as the sole legitimate voice to which everyone must listen in silence except when told to speak up in unison.

INSIDE KNOWLEDGE. Not only is the agitator physically powerful and something of a terrorist to boot, but he also has access to secret and highly important information, the source of which he is most careful not to reveal. He quotes mysterious "sources" that enabled him "to correctly diagnose 3 years ago that the 1940 presidential election would not be bona fide."[74] He claims that "there has fallen into my hands a copy of these confidential instructions which came out from New York City concerning the underground science."[75] By miraculous but unspecified means he manages to penetrate into the heart of the enemy fortress where his sharp ears hear the confidences that "Zionists in America whispered within secret circles."[76]

On other occasions the agitator can offer only promises of revelations to come: "I shall try to keep you posted concerning the diabolical conspiracy."[77] Or his information is too horrible to disclose: "I personally have had some experiences in the last year that would make your blood run cold, if I could tell you what they were."[78] Or he is bound by professional secrecy:

Two contacts, best unnamed on account of nature of information divulged, inform: ". . . believes that he has discovered the hdqtrs. of what seems to be Grand Orient Masonry . . . uptown in New York City. A building in the middle of a large block, surrounded by apartment houses; in a sort of courtyard, with a high barbed wire fence around it. No one is ever seen to enter this place, altho access could be had underground from one or more of the surrounding houses. A large telephone cable,

[72] Smith, Detroit, Mar. 19, 1943, meeting.
[73] Smith, New York, Oct. 20, 1938, meeting.
[74] America in Danger (Hudson), Jan. 19, 1942.
[75] Smith, Dictatorship Comes With War.
[76] Social Justice (Coughlin), July 14, 1941.
[77] Smith, Letter, Mar., 1943.
[78] The Cross and The Flag (Smith), Feb., 1943.

sufficient for over 100 lines, goes to the place which is guarded night and day by armed guards . . ."[79]

The agitator uses the language of an adolescent gang leader. He seeks to ingratiate himself with his listeners by promising them some highly important information. Someday the listeners will be "let in." But the agitator uses this technique of innuendo in ways other than the relatively harmless promise to divulge secrets. He withholds information in the very gesture by which he seems to give it out. He reveals not secrets but the existence of secrets; the secrets themselves are another variety of "forbidden fruit." Those affected by the promise to be "let in" are even more affected by the fact that the agitator has access to information inaccessible to them. To listen to innuendo and to rely on deliberately vague statements requires a certain readiness to believe, which the agitator directs toward his own person. So long as he does not reveal the "sources" of his knowledge, the agitator can continue to command the dependence of his followers. Unlike the educator, he never makes himself superfluous by revealing his methods of gaining knowledge. He remains the magical master.

This secret knowledge, like his toughness, is a two-edged weapon. It implies an ever present threat from which no one is quite safe: "Some day that thing is really going to come out, and when it comes out it is going to smell so high that any man that is connected with them, with that outfit, will be ashamed to say that he ever knew them."[80] or: "I have written a letter containing some mighty important information which I have placed in the hands of attorneys in this city. . . . The letter will not be printed . . . if we arrive home safely at the end of our campaign."[81]

Behind such statements there is the suggestion that he knows more than he says, and that nothing can ultimately remain hidden from him. If his self-portrait as a tough guy anticipates the storm trooper, then his insistence on his "inside knowledge" anticipates the secret files of the totalitarian police, which are used less against the political enemy, known in any case, than as a means to keep the followers in line. Sternly the agitator indicates this to his followers: get used to

[79] America in Danger (Hudson), Nov. 26, 1941.
[80] Smith, New York, Oct. 20, 1936, meeting.
[81] Phelps, Los Angeles, Feb. 7, 1941, radio.

the idea now, if you want a share in this racket, you have to obey its rules—and I make the rules.

THE CHARISMATIC LEADER. To the unseduced, the self-portrait of the agitator may seem a little ridiculous. Such an absurd creature—at once one of the plain folk and the sanctified leader; the head of a bedraggled family and a man above all material considerations; a helpless victim of persecution and a dreaded avenger with fists of iron! Yet contemporary history teaches us that this apparently ridiculous braggart cannot be merely laughed away.

In establishing this ambivalent image of himself the agitator achieves an extremely effective psychological result. In him, the martyr ultimately triumphant over his detractors and persecutors, the adherents see all their own frustrations magically metamorphosed into grandiose gratifications. They who are marginal suddenly have a prospect of sharing in the exceptional; their suffering now can appear to them as a glorious trial, their anonymity and servitude as stations on the road to fame and mastery. The agitator finds the promise of all these glories in that humdrum existence of his followers which had driven them to listen sympathetically to his appeals; he shows them how all the accumulated stuff of repression and frustration can be lit up into a magnificent fireworks, how the refuse of daily drudgery can be converted into a high explosive of pervasive destruction.

The self-portrait of the agitator is thus a culmination of all his other themes, which prepare the audience for the spectacle of the great little man acting as leader. Taking advantage of all the weaknesses of the present social order, the agitator intensifies his listeners' sense of bewilderment and helplessness, terrifies them with the specter of innumerable dangerous enemies and reduces their already crumbling individualities to bundles of reactive responses. He drives them into a moral void in which their inner voice of conscience is replaced by an externalized conscience: the agitator himself. He becomes the indispensable guide in a confused world, the center around which the faithful can gather and find safety. He comforts the sufferers of malaise, takes over the responsibility of history and becomes the exterior replacement of their disintegrated individuality. They live through him.

Contexts: Informal Leaders

DURING the past two decades social scientists have begun to emphasize the role of the "informal group" and "informal leader." Studies of the community and of industry have, in particular, pointed up the utility of these concepts. Broadly, what is referred to as an "informal group" consists of a number of individuals who spontaneously come together, under certain circumstances, for the pursuit of multiple ends, most of which are vaguely defined. (Put in this way, the similarity between the concepts of "informal group" and Ferdinand Tönnies' "gemeinschaft" is evident.)

Informal groups may be found within different social settings. They may exist either within the confines of a formal organization, such as a bureaucracy, or apart from it, in the manner of the street corner gang. The bases on which informal groups may be established are many: people who live or work near each other, people who are in the same ethnic, age, sex or occupational group may, without plan or intention, come together and establish informal groups. The existence of these groups may be observed in several ways. Among these are: noting which people—perhaps in an office or factory—eat lunch together with a fair degree of regularity, which people tend to go bowling together, to the movies or, perhaps, those who exchange turns at "baby-sitting" for each other. Similarly, their presence may be detected by observing those individuals who use the same technical jargon or vernacular. While far from infallible, attention to such mundane behavior will often reveal the extent, character, and number of informal groups with a surprising degree of accuracy.

Like the formally organized group, the informal group has a structure. The behavior of its members is not random but is instead patterned by normative elements and by its leadership. William Foote Whyte's "Informal Leadership and Group Structure" is a close-up account of these two phenomena and their intricate interlacing. The groups studied were "corner-gangs," young men who habitually frequented the same corners, in an Italian-American community of a large New England city. Whyte's study focuses, in particular, on the internal structure of the informal group and its leadership and on the relations between different informal groups and informal leaders. Whyte notes the relatively high social mobility of the informal leader and his role in integrating his group with others.

The leaders of informal groups function also as bridges between informal and formal structures. Thus the corner boy leader may relate his group to the local political machine. It should be emphasized, however, that the traffic across the bridge provided by the informal leader goes two ways.

In one respect, leaders of informal groups provide a vehicle through which formal structures and leadership come to influence the informal group members. This particular type of relationship is at the center of attention in the article on "Informal Opinion Leaders and A National Election," by Lazarsfeld, Berelson, and Gaudet. The specific ways in which informal leadership may be more effective than formal communication media are spelled out in convincing detail. This article is part of a larger study of how and why people voted as they did during the national election of 1940. Conducted in Erie County, Ohio, the study examined changing attitudes toward Franklin D. Roosevelt and Wendell Willkie, from the beginning of the campaign to the election.

A second way in which informal leaders articulate their groups with formal structures is by the upward transmission of their groups' sentiments and values to formal leaders. Since the (ideal-type) informal leader possesses no official status, he is only imperceptibly set off from other members and has a high degree of face-to-face interaction with them. There is no desk, no office, few symbolic marks of superiority or material advantage, which would inhibit full interchange between leader and follower. Consequently the informal leader knows the intimate feelings of his members, either because there is relatively little to restrain their expression or because the leader can easily empathize with them. Expressions of group sentiment by the informal leader, when they occur in the context of a formal organization, are often viewed by the formal leaders as manifestations of aggression. In bureaucracies, with their sharply defined ends, established and formulated at the top, such voicings of group feelings may be interpreted as "insubordination," "trouble making," "lack of understanding of the party line."

To the extent that informal leaders function as a two-way transmission belt, they do so in unanticipated and planless ways. Much of their effectiveness derives from the casualness of their methods. Typically, they are people who have no "ax to grind." Very often they are not conceived of as "leaders" either by themselves, their followers, or even outside observers. Being the antithesis of the "Great Man," without "a cause," devoid of the conventional appurtenances of power, they shade off into the coloring of their immediate social circle.

In part, because of this difficulty in observing informal groups and informal leaders, the formal leaders of groups often operate on the assumption that their followers are atomized individuals. In actuality, the formal leader of any sizable group never leads isolated individuals but, rather, subgroups of individuals each having their own informal leadership. Recognition of informal leadership can extend the range of effective group action and participation by broadening the channels of communication between formal leaders and followers. The mutual interstimulation of formal leaders and members may be intensified through the medium of informal leaders. In this respect, then, the accent currently placed on "informal" leaders may be a part of a growing emphasis on grass-roots participation.

Very possibly, however, the growing emphasis upon informal leadership also represents an intensification of dissatisfaction with the formal leadership in our society. When it is part of a democratic belief-system, emphasis on informal leadership may be made by those with an antipathy for ensconced bureaucrats, but with a fear of potential, antidemocratic, charismatic leaders.

The focus on informal leadership in the context of authoritarian or manipulative motives has, however, quite a different meaning. Groups which are "on the rise," but as yet divorced from positions of formal leadership, may come to view informal leadership as a means through which new power may be obtained. Similarly, formal leaders whose prestige and legitimacy are being challenged may see informal leadership as a way in which their crumbling techniques of control may be reinforced and extended. Certain studies in industrial sociology strongly suggest that this is the use to which knowledge of informal leadership may be put.

One crude, rule-of-thumb yardstick may be employed to ascertain the syndrome in which "informal leadership" is being used, and to judge whether it is manipulative or democratic. This is the way in which the communication function of informal leadership is treated. If the communication problem is *separated* from the *power* structure of the formal organization, informal leadership is probably being used in a manipulative way. For example: some analyses stress the upward flow of sentiment and information which the informal leader may provide, and insist upon the use to which this may be put by formal leaders. As far as it goes, this proposition is correct.

Usually, however, such analyses are incomplete, neglecting the question of why the informal leader's expression of group sentiment may be disregarded, or why the informal leader may not wish to make such expressions to formal leaders, or how, apart from informal leadership, upward communication may be enlarged. Much of the answer to these questions resides in the power structure and its potential modification. Where the power structure is authoritarian, informal leaders may not wish to give expression to group sentiment at variance with the goals of the formal leadership. The formal leadership may, in its turn, disregard these manifestations of group feeling, reinforcing the short-circuit of upward communication. Solution of this problem, in the context of a democratic belief-system, would not neglect the possible modification of the authoritarian power structure.

Whether operating as part of a democratic or authoritarian syndrome, recognition of and emphasis on "informal leadership" is—as Robert Merton once suggested—probably a derivative of a larger cultural imperative which strives to see "*underlying*" motives, causes, and patterns. It bears the mark of a society which, with growing mass suspicion, seeks "the news behind the news," the "boss" behind the politician, the structures within the structure. That such forces provide the social context in which the concepts of "informal leadership" and "informal structure" emerge, and foster interest in them, in no way vitiates their practical or scientific utility.

Informal Leadership and Group Structure[1]

BY WILLIAM FOOTE WHYTE

THE CORNER-GANG structure arises out of the habitual association of the members over a long period of time. The nuclei of most gangs can be traced back to early boyhood, when living close together provided the first opportunities for social contacts. School years modified the original pattern somewhat, but I know of no corner gangs which arose through classroom or school-playground association. The gangs grew up on the corner and remained there with remarkable persistence from early boyhood until the members reached their late twenties or early thirties. In the course of years some groups were broken up by the movement of families away from Cornerville, and the remaining members merged with gangs on near-by corners; but frequently movement out of the district does not take the corner boy away from his corner. On any evening on almost any corner one finds corner boys who have come in from other parts of the city or from suburbs to be with their old friends. The residence of the corner boy may also change within the district, but nearly always he retains his allegiance to his original corner.

Home plays a very small role in the group activities of the corner boy. Except when he eats, sleeps, or is sick, he is rarely at home, and his friends always go to his corner first when they want to find him. Even the corner boy's name indicates the dominant importance of the gang in his activities. It is possible to associate with a group of

[1] Reprinted from *Street Corner Society*, by William F. Whyte, The University of Chicago Press, 1937. Used by permission of the publishers.

men for months and never discover the family names of more than a few of them. Most are known by nicknames attached to them by the group. Furthermore, it is easy to overlook the distinction between married and single men. The married man regularly sets aside one evening a week to take out his wife. There are other occasions when they go out together and entertain together, and some corner boys devote more attention to their wives than others, but, married or single, the corner boy can be found on his corner almost every night of the week.

His social activities away from the corner are organized with similar regularity. Many corner gangs set aside the same night each week for some special activity, such as bowling. With the Nortons [one of the corner-boy groups] this habit was so strong that it persisted for some of the members long after the original group had broken up.

Most groups have a regular evening meeting-place aside from the corner. Nearly every night at about the same time the gang gathers for "coffee-and" in its favorite cafeteria or for beer in the corner tavern. When some other activity occupies the evening, the boys meet at the cafeteria or tavern before returning to the corner or going home. Positions at the tables are fixed by custom. Night after night each group gathers around the same tables. The right to these positions is recognized by other Cornerville groups. When strangers are found at the accustomed places, the necessity of finding other chairs is a matter of some annoyance, especially if no near-by location is available. However, most groups gather after nine in the evening when few are present except the regular customers who are familiar with the established procedure.

The life of the corner boy proceeds along regular and narrowly circumscribed channels. As Doc said to me:

Fellows around here don't know what to do except within a radius of about three hundred yards. That's the truth, Bill. They come home from work, hang on the corner, go up to eat, back on the corner, up a show, and they come back to hang on the corner. If they're not on the corner, it's likely the boys there will know where you can find them. Most of them stick to one corner. It's only rarely that a fellow will change his corner.

The stable composition of the group and the lack of social assurance on the part of its members contribute toward producing a very high rate of social interaction within the group. The group structure is a product of these interactions.

Out of such interaction these arises a system of mutual obligations which is fundamental to group cohesion. If the men are to carry on their activities as a unit, there are many occasions when they must do favors for one another. The code of the corner boy requires him to help his friends when he can and to refrain from doing anything to harm them. When life in the group runs smoothly, the obligations binding members to one another are not explicitly recognized. Once Doc asked me to do something for him, and I said that he had done so much for me that I welcomed the chance to reciprocate. He objected: "I don't want it that way. I want you to do this for me because you're my friend. That's all."

It is only when the relationship breaks down that the underlying obligations are brought to light. While Alec and Frank were friends, I never heard either one of them discuss the services he was performing for the other, but when they had a falling-out over the group activities with the Aphrodite Club, each man complained to Doc that the other was not acting as he should in view of the services that had been done him. In other words, actions which were performed explicitly for the sake of friendship were revealed as being part of a system of mutual obligations.

Not all the corner boys live up to their obligations equally well, and this factor partly accounts for the differentiation in status among them. The man with a low status may violate his obligations without much change in his position. His fellows know that he has failed to discharge certain obligations in the past, and his position reflects his past performances. On the other hand, the leader is depended upon by all the members to meet his personal obligations. He cannot fail to do so without causing confusion and endangering his position.

The relationship of status to the system of mutual obligations is most clearly revealed when one observes the use of money. During the time that I knew a corner gang called the Millers, Sam Franco, the leader, was out of work except for an occasional odd job; yet, whenever he had a little money, he spent it on Joe and Chichi, his closest friends, who were next to him in the structure of the group. When Joe or Chichi had money, which was less frequent, they reciprocated. Sam frequently paid for two members who stood close to the bottom of his group and occasionally for others. The two men who held positions immediately below Joe and Chichi were considered very well off according to Cornerville standards. Sam said that he occasionally borrowed money from them, but never more than fifty cents at a time. Such loans he repaid at the earliest possible moment. There were four other members with lower positions in the group, who nearly always had more money than Sam. He did not recall ever having borrowed from them. He said that the only time he had obtained a substantial sum from anyone around his corner was when he borrowed eleven dollars from a friend who was the leader of another corner gang.

The situation was the same among the Nortons. Doc did not hesitate to accept money from Danny [one of his lieutenants], but he avoided taking any from the followers.

The leader spends more money on his followers than they on him. The farther down in the structure one looks, the fewer are the financial relations which tend to obligate the leader to a follower. This does not mean that the leader has more money than others or even that he necessarily spends more—though he must always be a free spender. It means that the financial relations must be explained in social terms. Unconsciously, and in some cases consciously, the leader refrains from putting himself under obligations to those with low status in the group.

The leader is the focal point for the organization of his group. In his absence, the members of the gang are divided into a number of small groups. There is no common activity or general conversation. When the leader appears, the situation changes strikingly. The small units form into one large group. The conversation becomes general, and unified action frequently follows. The leader becomes the central point in the discussion. A follower starts to say something, pauses when he notices that the leader is not listening, and begins again when he has the leader's attention. When the leader leaves the group, unity gives way to the divisions that existed before his appearance.

TECHNIQUES OF INFORMAL LEADERSHIP

The members do not feel that the gang is really gathered until the leader appears. They recognize an obligation to wait for him before beginning any group activity, and when he is present they expect him to make their decisions. One night when the Nortons had a bowling match, Long John had no money to put up as his side bet, and he agreed that Chick Morelli should bowl in his place. After the match Danny said to Doc, "You should never have put Chick in there."

Doc replied with some annoyance, "Listen, Danny, you yourself suggested that Chick should bowl instead of Long John."

Danny said, "I know, but you shouldn't have let it go."

The leader is the man who acts when the situation requires action. He is more resourceful than his followers. Past events have shown that his ideas were right. In this sense "right" simply means satisfactory to the members. He is the most independent in judgment. While his followers are undecided as to a course of action or upon the character of a newcomer, the leader makes up his mind.

When he gives his word to one of his boys, he keeps it. The followers look to him for advice and encouragement, and he receives more of their confidences than any other man. Consequently, he knows more about what is going on in the group than anyone else. Whenever there is a quarrel among the boys, he hears of it almost as soon as it happens. Each party to the quarrel may appeal to him to work out a solution; and, even when the men do not want to compose their differences, each one takes his side of the story to the leader at the first opportunity. A man's standing depends partly upon the leader's belief that he has been conducting himself properly.

The leader is respected for his fair-mindedness. Whereas there may be hard feelings among some of the followers, the leader cannot bear a grudge against any man in the group. He has close friends (men who stand next to him in position), and he is indifferent to some of the members; but, if he is to retain his reputation for impartiality, he cannot allow personal animus to override his judgment.

The leader need not be the best baseball player, bowler, or fighter, but he must have some skill in whatever pursuits are of particular interest to the group. It is natural for him to promote activities in which he excels and to discourage those in which he is not skillful; and, in so far as he is thus able to influence the group, his competent performance is a natural consequence of his position. At the same time his performance supports his position.

The leader is better known and more respected outside his group than are any of his followers. His capacity for social movement is greater. One of the most important functions he performs is that of relating his group to other groups in the district. Whether the relationship is one of conflict, competition, or coöperation, he is expected to represent the interests of his fellows. The politician and the racketeer must deal with the leader in order to win the support of his followers. The leader's reputation outside the group tends to support his standing within the group, and his position in the group supports his reputation among outsiders.

The leader does not deal with his followers as an undifferentiated group. Doc explained:

On any corner you would find not only a leader but probably a couple of lieutenants. They could be leaders themselves, but they let the man lead them. You would say, "They let him lead because they like the way he does things." Sure, but he leans upon them for his authority. Many times you find fellows on a corner that stay in the background until some situation comes up, and then they will take over and call the shots. Things like that can change fast sometimes.

The leader mobilizes the group by dealing first with his lieutenants. It was customary for the Millers to go bowling every Saturday night. One Saturday Sam had no money, so he set out to persuade the boys to do something else. Later he explained to me how he had been able to change the established social routine of the group. He said:

I had to show the boys that it would be in their own interests to come with me—that each one of them would benefit. But I knew I only had to convince two of the fellows. If they start to do something, the other boys will say to themselves, "If Joe does it—or if Chichi does it— it must be a good thing for us too." I told Joe and Chichi what the idea was, and I got them to come with me. I didn't pay no attention to the others. When Joe and Chichi came, all the other boys came along too.

Another example from the Millers indicates what happens when the leader and his lieutenant disagree upon group policy. This is Sam talking again:

One time we had a raffle to raise money to build a camp on Lake Blank (on property lent them by a local businessman). We had collected $54, and Joe and I were holding the money. That week I knew Joe was playing pool, and he lost three or four dollars gambling. When Saturday came, I says to the boys, "Come on, we go out to Lake Blank. We're gonna build that camp on the hill."

Right away, Joe said, "If yuz are gonna build that camp on the hill, I don't come. I want it on the other side."

All the time I knew he had lost the money, and he was only making up excuses so he wouldn't have to let anybody know. Now the hill was really the place to build that camp. On the other side, the ground was swampy. That would have been a stupid place. But I knew that if I tried to make them go through with it now, the group would split up into two cliques. Some would come with me, and some would go with Joe. So I let the whole thing drop for a while. After, I got Joe alone, and I says to him, "Joe, I know you lost some of that money, but that's all right. You can pay up when you have it and nobody will say nothin'. But, Joe, you know we shouldn't have the camp on the other side of the hill because the land is not good there. We should build it on the hill."

So he said, "All right," and we got all the boys together, and we went out to build the camp.

Disagreements are not always worked out so amicably. I once asked Doc and Sam to tell me who was the leader of a corner gang that was familiar to both of them. Sam commented:

Doc picked out Carmen. He picked out the wrong man. I told him why he was wrong—that Dominic was the leader. But that very same night, there was almost a fight between the two of them, Dominic and Carmen. And now the group is split up into two gangs.

Doc said:

Sometimes you can't pick out one leader. The leadership may be in doubt. Maybe there are a couple of boys vying for the honors. But you can find that out.

The leadership is changed not through an uprising of the bottom men but by a shift in the relations between men at the top of the structure. When a gang breaks into two parts, the explanation is to be found in a conflict between the leader and one of his former lieutenants.

This discussion should not give the impression that the leader is the only man who proposes a course of action. Other men frequently have ideas, but their suggestions must go through the proper channels if they are to go into effect.

In one meeting of the Cornerville S. and A., Dodo, who held a bottom ranking, proposed that he be allowed to handle the sale of beer in the clubrooms in return for 75 percent of the profits. Tony spoke in favor of Dodo's suggestion but proposed giving him a somewhat smaller percentage. Dodo agreed. Then Carlo proposed to have Dodo handle the beer in quite a different way, and Tony agreed. Tony made the motion, and it was carried unanimously. In this case Dodo's proposal was carried through, after substantial modifications upon the actions of Tony and Carlo.

In another meeting Dodo said that he had two motions to make: that the club's funds be deposited in a bank and that no officer be allowed to serve two consecutive terms. Tony was not present at this time. Dom, the president, said that only one motion should be made at a time and that, furthermore, Dodo should not make any motions until there had been opportunity for discussion. Dodo agreed. Dom then commented that it would be foolish to deposit the funds when the club had so little to deposit. Carlo expressed his agreement. The meeting passed on to other things without action upon the first motion and without even a word of discussion on the second one. In the same meeting, Chris, who held a middle position, moved that a member must be in the club for a year before being allowed to hold office. Carlo said that it was a good idea, he seconded the motion, and it carried unanimously.

The actions of the leader can be characterized in terms of the origination of action in pair and set events. A pair event is one which takes place between two people. A set event is one in which one man originates action for two or more others. The leader frequently originates action for the group without waiting for the suggestions of his followers. A follower may originate action for the leader in a pair event, but he does not originate action for the leader and other followers at the same time—that is, he does not originate action in a set event which includes the leader. Of course, when the leader is not present, parts of the group are mobilized when men lower in the structure originate action in set events. It is through observation of such set events when the top men are not present that it is possible to

determine the relative positions of the men who are neither leaders
nor lieutenants.

Each member of the corner gang has his own position in the gang
structure. Although the positions may remain unchanged over long
periods of time, they should not be conceived in static terms. To
have a position means that the individual has a customary way of
interacting with other members of the group. When the pattern of
interactions changes, the positions change. The positions of the members are interdependent, and one position cannot change without
causing some adjustments in the other positions. Since the group is
organized around the men with the top positions, some of the men
with low standing may change positions or drop out without upsetting
the balance of the group. For example, when Lou Danaro and Fred
Mackey stopped participating in the activities of the Nortons, those
activities continued to be organized in much the same manner as
before, but when Doc and Danny dropped out, the Nortons disintegrated, and the patterns of interaction had to be reorganized along
different lines.

One may generalize upon these processes in terms of group equilibrium. The group may be said to be in equilibrium when the interactions of its members fall into the customary pattern through which
group activities are and have been organized. The pattern of interactions may undergo certain modifications without upsetting the
group equilibrium, but abrupt and drastic changes destroy the
equilibrium.

The actions of the individual member may also be conceived in
terms of equilibrium. Each individual has his own characteristic way
of interacting with other individuals. This is probably fixed within
wide limits by his native endowment, but it develops and takes its
individual form through the experiences of the individual in interacting with others throughout the course of his life. Twentieth-
century American life demands a high degree of flexibility or action
from the individual, and the normal person learns to adjust within
certain limits to changes in the frequency and type of his interactions
with others. This flexibility can be developed only through experiencing a wide variety of situations which require adjustment to different patterns of interaction. The more limited the individual's

experience, the more rigid his manner of interacting, and the more difficult his adjustment when changes are forced upon him.

This conclusion has important implications for the understanding of the problems of the corner boy. As we have seen, gang activities proceed from day to day in a remarkably fixed pattern. The members come together every day and interact with a very high frequency. Whether he is at the top and originates action for the group in set events, is in the middle and follows the origination of the leader and originates for those below him, or is at the bottom of the group and always follows in set events, the individual member has a way of interaction which remains stable and fixed through continual group activity over a long period of time. His mental well-being requires continuance of his way of interacting. He needs the customary channels for his activity, and, when they are lacking, he is disturbed.

Doc told me this story:

One night Angelo and Phil went to the Tivoli to see a picture. They didn't have enough money for Frank, so they had to leave him behind. You should have seen him. It's a terrible thing to be left behind by the boys. You would have thought Frank was in a cage. I sat next to him by the playground. Danny was holding the crap game in the playground. Frank said to me, "Do you think Danny would have a quarter for me?"

I said, "I don't know. Ask him if you want to."

But Frank didn't want to ask him. He asked me, "Do you think Long John has a quarter?"

I said, "No, I know that Long John is clean." Frank didn't know what to do. If he had got the nerve up to ask Danny for the quarter right away, he could have run after the boys and caught up with them before they reached the theater. I knew that he would run if he had the money. But he waited too long so he wouldn't be able to catch up with them. It was nine-thirty when the crap game broke up. Frank went into the playground with me. He wanted me to ask Danny for something, but I told him to ask himself. He didn't want to. He said he thought he would go home, and he started, but then he came back. He asked us when we were going down to Jennings. I told him ten o'clock. We always go at ten now. He said that was too long to wait so he went home. Danny, Long John, and I went down to Jennings. We had been there about fifteen minutes when in walks Frank, and he sits down at a table next to us and starts reading the paper. Danny says, "What's the matter, Frank, no coffee?"

Frank says, "That's all right. I don't feel like it."

Danny says, "Go ahead, get your coffee." So Frank got coffee. We were ready to go before Angelo and Phil had come in. I could see that Frank didn't want to leave, but he had to because you're supposed to go out with the man that takes care of your check. He walked home with us, and then I guess he went back to Jennings to meet Angelo and Phil.

Frank had a very high regard for Danny and Doc, and at an earlier period he would have been perfectly happy in their company, but since Angelo had become the leader of the group he had seldom interacted wth them and he had been interacting regularly and frequently with Angelo and Phil. When he was deprived of their company, the resulting disturbance was strikingly apparent.

A man with a low position in the group is less flexible in his adjustments than the leader, who customarily deals with groups outside of his own. This may explain why Frank was so upset by events of only a few hours' duration. However, no matter what the corner boy's position, he suffers when the manner of his interaction must undergo drastic changes. This is clearly illustrated in the cases of Long John's nightmares and Doc's dizzy spells.

Long John had had this trouble on certain previous occasions, but then the fear of death had gone, and he had been able to sleep without difficulty. He had not been troubled for a long period up to the time that he experienced his latest attack. I do not know the circumstances surrounding the earlier attacks, but on this occasion Long John's social situation seemed clearly to explain his plight. He had become adjusted to a very high rate of interaction with Doc and Danny. While he did not have great influence among the followers in the Nortons, they did not originate action for him in set events, and he occasionally originated action for them. When the Nortons broke up and Doc and Danny went into Spongi's inner circle, Long John was left stranded. He could no longer interact with Doc and Danny with the same frequency. When he went over to Norton Street, he found the followers building up their own organization under the leadership of Angelo. If he was to participate in their activities, he had to become a follower in set events originated by Angelo. The members who had been below him in the Nortons were constantly trying to originate action for him. When his relationship with Doc and Danny broke down, he had no defense against these aggressions.

Doc brought about the cure by changing Long John's social situation. By bringing him into Spongi's inner circle, Doc reëstablished the close relationship between Long John, Danny, and himself. In so doing, he protected Long John from the aggressions of the former followers. When Long John was once more interacting with Doc and Danny with great frequency, his mental difficulties disappeared, and he began acting with the same assurance that had previously characterized his behavior.

Doc's dizzy spells came upon him when he was unemployed and had no spending money. He considered his unemployment the cause of his difficulties, and, in a sense, it was, but in order to understand the case it is necessary to inquire into the changes which unemployment necessitated in the activity of the individual. While no one enjoys being unemployed and without money, there are many Cornerville men who could adjust themselves to that situation without serious difficulties. Why was Doc so different? To say that he was a particularly sensitive person simply gives a name to the phenomenon and provides no answer. The observation of interactions provides the answer. Doc was accustomed to a high frequency of interaction with the members of his group and to frequent contacts with members of other groups. While he sometimes directly originated action in set events for the group, it was customary for one of the other members to originate action for him in a pair event, and then he would originate action in a set event. That is, someone would suggest a course of action, and then Doc would get the boys together and organize group activity. The events of Doc's political campaign indicate that this pattern had broken down. Mike was continually telling Doc what to do about the campaign, and I was telling him what to do about seeing Mr. Smith and others to get a job. While we originated action for him with increasing frequency, he was not able to originate action in set events. Lacking money, he could not participate in group activities without accepting the support of others and letting them determine his course of action. Therefore, on many occasions he avoided associating with his friends—that is, his frequency of interaction was drastically reduced. At a time when he should have been going out to make contacts with other groups, he was unable to act according to the political pattern even with the groups that he knew, and he saw less and less of those outside his circle of closest friends. When he was alone, he did not get dizzy,

but, when he was with a group of people and was unable to act in
his customary manner, he fell prey to the dizzy spells.

When Doc began his recreation-center job, the spells disappeared.
He was once again able to originate action, first for the boys in his
center, but also for his own corner boys. Since he now had money,
he could again associate with his friends and could also broaden his
contacts. When the job and the money ran out, the manner of interaction to which Doc was adjusted was once more upset. He was
unemployed from the time that the center closed in the winter of
1939-40 until he got a W.P.A. job in the spring of 1941. The dizzy
spells came back, and shortly before he got his job he had what his
friends called a nervous breakdown. A doctor who had an excellent
reputation in Eastern City examined him and was unable to find any
organic causes to account for his condition. When I visited Cornerville in May, 1941, he was once again beginning to overcome the dizzy
spells. He discussed his difficulties with me:

When I'm batted out, I'm not on the corner so much. And when I
am on the corner, I just stay there. I can't do what I want to do. If the
boys want to go to a show or to Jennings or bowling, I have to count
my pennies to see if I have enough. If I'm batted out, I have to make
some excuse. I tell the boys I don't want to go, and I take a walk by
myself. I get bored sometimes hanging in Spongi's but where can I go?
I have to stay there. Danny offers me money, and that's all right, but
he's been getting tough breaks. Last week he was complaining he was
batted out and a couple of days later he offered me two dollars. I refused.
I don't want to ask anybody for anything. Sometimes I say to Danny or
Spongi, "Do you want a cigarette?" They say, "No, we've got some,"
and then I say, "All right, I'll have one of yours." I make a joke out of
it, but still it is humiliating. I never do that except when I'm desperate
for a cigarette. Danny is the only one that ever gives me money.

Before I got this W.P.A. job, I looked terrible. I eat here at home,
but I can't expect them to buy clothes for me. I had one suit, and that
was through at the elbow, and the cuffs had more shreds than a chry-
santhemum. When I had to go places, I kept my overcoat on, or else I
carried it over my arm to hide the hole in the elbow. And I was literally
walking on the soles of my feet. You think I like to go around like that?

Lou Danaro has been after me to go out with him. He's got a new
Buick—a brand-new Buick. That's pretty nice, you know. He wants me
to get a girl, and we'll go out together. But I won't go. I'd have to play

a secondary role. No, that's what you want me to say. I mean, I wouldn't be able to do what I want to do.

Last summer, they asked me to be chairman of the Norton Street Settlement outing. I worked with the committee, and all that, but the night before the outing the whole committee was supposed to go out to the camp and spend the night there. That was a big time. But I didn't go. I didn't have any money. Next morning I saw them off on the bus, and I said I would be out later. I went around and bummed a couple of bucks and drove up with one of the boys. I stayed a couple of hours, and then I came home. The chairman is expected to be active at one of those affairs. He is supposed to treat people—things like that. They think I'm shirking my responsibilities, but it isn't true. It's the money.

I have thought it all over, and I know I only have these spells when I'm batted out. I'm sorry you didn't know me when I was really active around here. I was a different man then. I was always taking the girls out. I lent plenty of money. I spent my money. I was always thinking of things to do and places to go.

Doc showed that he was well aware of the nature of his difficulties, but understanding was not enough to cure him. He needed an opportunity to act in the manner to which he had grown accustomed. When that was lacking, he was socially maladjusted. If he had been a man with low standing in the group and had customarily been dependent upon others to originate action for him in set events, the dependence which resulted from having no money would have fitted in with the pattern of his behavior in the group. Since he had held the leading position among his corner boys, there was an unavoidable conflict between the behavior required by that position and the behavior necessitated by his penniless condition.

The type of explanation suggested to account for the difficulties of Long John and Doc has the advantage that it rests upon the objective study of actions. A man's attitudes cannot be observed but instead must be inferred from his behavior. Since actions are directly subject to observation and may be recorded like other scientific data, it seems wise to try to understand man through studying his actions. This approach not only provides information upon the nature of informal group relations but it also offers a framework for the understanding of the individual's adjustment to his society.

Informal Opinion Leaders and a National Election[1]

BY PAUL F. LAZARSFELD, BERNARD BERELSON, AND HAZEL GAUDET

THE NON-VOTERS represent the low point in political participation. The high point is illustrated by the people most active in a presidential campaign—the "opinion leaders." Common observation and many community studies show that in every area and for every public issue there are certain people who are most concerned about the issue as well as most articulate about it. We call them the "opinion leaders."

The opinion leaders of a community could best be identified and studied by asking people to whom they turn for advice on the issue at hand and then investigating the interaction between the advisers and the advisees. It is obvious that in a study involving a sample, like the present one, that procedure would be extremely difficult if not impossible since few of the related leaders and "followers" would happen to be included within the sample. As a substitute device, however, we can identify the opinion leaders and the followers within our panel, without relating them directly to one another.

At about the middle of the campaign, the respondents were asked these two questions:

"Have you tried to convince anyone of your political ideas recently?"

"Has anyone asked your advice on a political question recently?"

All those people who answered "Yes" to either or both of these

[1] Reprinted from *The People's Choice*, by Paul F. Lazarsfeld, Bernard Berelson, and Hazel Gaudet, Duell, Sloan & Pearce, 1944. Copyright, 1944, by Paul F. Lazarsfeld. Used by permission of the author.

questions—21% of the entire group—were designated as opinion leaders. Their responses to other questions during the series of interviews as well as subsequent check-ups on their objective roles within certain groups established the validity of the identification. In short, the opinion leaders are substantially representative of that aggressive section of the community—or rather, the aggressive sections of the several sub-communities—which tried to influence the rest of the community.

In connection with this last, one important matter must be emphasized: the opinion leaders are not identical with the socially prominent people in the community or the richest people or the civic leaders. They are found in all occupational groups (Table 1).

TABLE 1.   Proportion of Opinion Leaders and Others in Various Occupations

Occupation	Cases	Opinion Leaders %	Others %
Professional	17	35	65
Proprietary, managerial	28	25	75
Clerical	21	33	67
Commercial, sales	16	44	56
Skilled workers	37	35	65
Semiskilled workers	31	32	68
Unskilled workers	47	23	77
Farmers	46	15	85
Housewives	230	13	87
Unemployed	13	15	85
Retired	23	35	65

In all respects, the opinion leaders demonstrated greater political alertness. Whereas only 24% of the "followers" professed a great deal of interest in the election, fully 61% of the opinion leaders rated themselves thus. Similarly in exposure to political communications: on each level of interest, the opinion leaders read and listened to campaign material much more than the non-opinion leaders (Table 2). What is more, the opinion leaders who considered their interest only "moderate" or "mild" still managed to read and listen more than the non-opinion leaders who thought they were "greatly interested." In addition, they talked politics more than the others. Fully

90% of the opinion leaders (OLs) conversed about the campaign with their associates just before our October interview whereas only 58% of the others had done so.

TABLE 2. Index of Exposure of Opinion Leaders and Others to the
Formal Media of Communication

	Great Interest		Less Interest	
	OLs	Others	OLs	Others
Newspaper	15.8	12.3	14.8	6.6
Radio	14.6	12.3	13.0	7.6
Magazine	20.6	14.1	15.8	4.6

In all important respects, then, the opinion leaders were the most responsive to campaign events.

PERSONAL CONTACTS REACH THE UNDECIDED

In comparison with the formal media of communication, personal relationships are potentially more influential for two reasons: their coverage is greater and they have certain psychological advantages over the formal media.

Whenever the respondents were asked to report on their recent exposure to campaign communications of all kinds, political discussions were mentioned more frequently than exposure to radio or print. On any average day, at least 10% more people participated in discussions about the election—either actively or passively—than listened to a major speech or read about campaign items in a newspaper. And this coverage "bonus" came from just those people who had not yet made a final decision as to how they would vote. Political conversations, then, were more likely to reach those people who were still open to influence.

For example, people who made up their minds later in the campaign were more likely to mention personal influences in explaining how they formed their final vote decision. Similarly, we found that the less interested people relied more on conversations and less on the formal media as sources of information. Three-fourths of the respondents who at one time had not expected to vote but were then finally "dragged in" mentioned personal influence. After the election, the voters were given a check list of "sources from which they got most of the information or impressions that caused them to form their judgment on how to vote." Those who had made some change during the campaign mentioned friends or members of their family relatively more frequently than did the respondents who kept a constant vote intention all through the campaign.

THE TWO-STEP FLOW OF COMMUNICATIONS

A special role in the network of personal relationships is played by the "opinion leaders." We noted that they engaged in political discussion much more than the rest of the respondents. But they reported that the formal media were more effective as sources of influence than personal relationships. This suggests *that ideas often flow from radio and print to the opinion leaders and from them to the less active sections of the population.*

Occasionally, the more articulate people even pass on an article or point out the importance of a radio speech. Repeatedly, "changers" referred to reading or listening done under some personal influence. Take the case of a retired school teacher who decided for the Republicans: "The country is ripe for a change. . . . Willkie is a religious man. *A friend read and highly recommended* Dr. Poling's article in the October issue of the *Christian Herald* called 'The Religion of Wendell Willkie'."

So much for the "coverage of personal contacts." *The person-to-person influence reaches the ones who are more susceptible to change, and serves as a bridge over which formal media of communications extend their influence.* But in addition, personal relationships have certain psychological advantages which make them especially effective in the exercise of the "molecular pressures" finally leading to the political homogeneity of social groups. We turn now to a discussion of five such characteristics.

NON-PURPOSIVENESS OF PERSONAL CONTACTS

The weight of personal contacts upon opinion lies, paradoxically, in their greater casualness and non-purposiveness in political matters. If we read or tune in a speech, we usually do so purposefully, and in doing so we have a definite mental set which tinges our receptiveness. Such purposive behavior is part of the broad area of our political experiences, to which we bring our convictions with a desire to test them and strengthen them by what is said. This mental set is armor against influence. The extent to which people, and particularly those with strong partisan views, listen to speakers and read articles with which they agree in advance is evidence on this point.

On the other hand, people we meet for reasons other than political discussion are more likely to catch us unprepared, so to speak, if they make politics the topic. One can avoid newspaper stories and radio speeches simply by making a slight effort, but as the campaign mounts and discussion intensifies, it is hard to avoid some talk of politics. Personal influence is more pervasive and less self-selective than the formal media. In short, politics gets through, especially to the indifferent, much more easily through personal contacts than in any other way, simply because it comes up unexpectedly as a sideline or marginal topic in a casual conversation. For example, there was the restaurant waitress who decided that Willkie would make a poor president after first thinking he would be good. Said she: "I had done a little newspaper reading against Willkie, but the real reason I changed my mind was from *hearsay*. So many people don't like Willkie. Many customers in the restaurant said Willkie would be no good." Notice that she was in a position to overhear bits of conversation that were not intended for her. There are many such instances. *Talk that is "forbidden fruit" is particularly effective because one need not be suspicious as to the persuasive intentions of the speakers; as a result one's defenses are down.* Furthermore, one may feel that he is getting the viewpoint of "people generally," that he is learning how "different people" think about the election.

Such passive participation in conversation is paralleled in the case of the formal media by accidental exposure, e.g., when a political speech is heard because it follows a favorite program. In both conversation and the formal media, such chance communication is particularly effective. And the testimony to such influence is much more frequent in the case of personal contacts. The respondents mentioned it time and again: "I've heard fellows talk at the plant. . . . I hear men talk at the shop . . . My husband heard that talked about at work. . . ."

FLEXIBILITY WHEN COUNTERING RESISTANCE

But suppose we do meet people who want to influence us and suppose they arouse our resistance. Then personal contact still has one great advantage compared with other media: the face-to-face contact can counter and dislodge such resistance, for it is much more flexible. The clever campaign worker, professional or amateur, can make use of a large number of cues to achieve his end. He can choose the occasion at which to speak to the other fellow. He can adapt his story to what he presumes to be the other's interests and his ability to understand. If he notices the other is bored, he can change the subject. If he sees that he has aroused resistance, he can retreat, giving the other the satisfaction of a victory, and come back to his point later. If in the course of the discussion he discovers some pet convictions, he can try to tie up his argument with them. He can spot the moments when the other is yielding and so time his best punches.

Neither radio nor the printed page can do anything of the kind. They must aim their propaganda shots at the whole target instead of just at the center, which represents any particular individual. In propaganda as much as in other things, one man's meat is another man's poison. This may lead to boomerang effects, when arguments aimed at "average" audiences with "average" reactions fail with Mr. X. The formal media produced several boomerangs upon people who resented what they read or heard and moved in the opposite direction from that intended. But among 58 respondents who mentioned personal contacts as concretely influential, there was only one boomerang. The flexibility of the face-to-face situation undoubtedly accounted for their absence.

REWARDS OF COMPLIANCE

When someone yields to a personal influence in making a vote decision, the reward is immediate and personal. This is not the case in yielding to an argument via print or radio. If a pamphlet argues that voting for the opposite party would be un-American or will jeopardize the future, its warning may sound too remote or improbable. But if a neighbor says the same things, he can "punish" one immediately for being unimpressed or unyielding: he can look angry or sad, he can leave the room and make his fellow feel isolated. The pamphlet can only intimate or describe future deprivations; the living person can create them at once.

Of course all this makes personal contacts a powerful influence only for people who do not like to be out of line. There are certainly some people who gain pleasure from being non-conformists, but under normal circumstances they are probably very much in the minority. Whenever propaganda by another person is experienced as an expression of the prevailing group tendencies, it has greater chances of being successful than the formal media because of social rewards. For example, here is a woman who was for Roosevelt until the middle of the campaign: "I have always been a Democrat and I think Roosevelt has been all right. But my family are all for Willkie. They think he would make the best president and they have been putting the pressure on me." She finally voted for Willkie. This aspect of personal contacts was especially important for women.

The rewards of compliance to other people are learned in early childhood. The easiest way for most children to avoid discomfort is to do what others tell them to do. Someone who holds no strong opinions on politics and hence makes up his mind late in the campaign may very well be susceptible to personal influences because he has learned as a child to take them as useful guides in unknown territory. The young man who was going to vote for Roosevelt because "my grandfather will skin me if I don't" is a case in point.

TRUST IN AN INTIMATE SOURCE

More people put reliance upon their personal contacts to help them pick out the arguments which are relevant for their own good in political affairs than they do in the more remote and impersonal newspaper and radio. The doubtful voter may feel that the evaluations he reads or hears in a broadcast are plausible, for the expert writer can probably spell out the consequences of voting more clearly than the average citizen. But the voter still wonders whether these are the issues which are really going to affect *his own* future welfare. Perhaps these sources see the problem from a viewpoint entirely different from his own. But he can trust the judgment and evaluation of the respected people among his associates. Most of them are people with the same status and interests as himself. Their attitudes are more relevant for him than the judgments of an unknown editorial writer. In a formal communication the content can be at its best; but in a face to face contact the transference is most readily achieved. For example, here is the case of a young laborer who professed little or no interest in the campaign and who did not even expect to vote until late October: "I've been discussing the election with *the fellows*

at the shop and I believe I'll vote, but I haven't decided yet who for."
His constant exposure to the views of his fellow-workers not only
brought him to the ballot booth but also brought out his final Democratic vote in line with his colleagues.

A middle-aged woman who showed great interest in the campaign
was undecided until late October and then voted for Willkie: "*I was
talking politics just this morning with a friend, a businessman.* He
says business will improve if Willkie is elected and that Willkie
promises to keep us out of the war. FDR is getting too much power.
He shouldn't have a third term." Her friend had apparently run out
for her what amounted to a small catalogue of Republican arguments
and he was impressive enough to clinch her vote, which had been in
the balance throughout the campaign. Her trust in his judgment
settled her mind.

Trust in another person's point of view may be due to his prestige
as well as to the plausibility of what he has to say or its relevancy to
one's interests. It is obvious that in all influences prestige plays a
considerable role. The degree of conformity is greater the higher the
prestige of the person in our group who seeks to influence us. The
plausibility of the consequences he presents will seem greater if he is
important. (Of course, the formal media are also important in this
respect.) The heightening of trust through the prestige of certain
personal contacts was clear in the case of the driver of a bread truck
who changed to Willkie because the prominent president of a business firm had done him the honor of persuading him in that direction.
Then, too, there is the case of a middle-aged housewife with little
education who was for Willkie from May through September, became undecided in October, and finally voted for Roosevelt. She left
Willkie because of the statements of people whom she considered
authorities: "I talked with a *college student* from Case, in Cleveland,
and students are for Roosevelt because he has helped recreation. I
talked, too, with a *man from Chicago who is very interested in politics,*
and he doesn't seem to think that Willkie is a big enough man to
handle international affairs."

PERSUASION WITHOUT CONVICTION

Finally, personal contacts can get a voter to the polls without
affecting at all his comprehension of the issues of the election—
something the formal media can rarely do. The newspaper or maga-

zine or radio must first be effective in changing attitudes related to the action. There were several clear cases of votes cast not on the issues or even the personalities of the candidates. In fact, they were not really cast for the candidates at all. They were cast, so to speak, for the voters' friends.

"I was taken to the polls by a worker who insisted that I go."

"The lady where I work wanted me to vote. She took me to the polls and they all voted Republican so I did too."

In short, personal influence, with all its overtones of personal affection and loyalty, can bring to the polls votes that would otherwise not be cast or would be cast for the opposing party just as readily if some other friend had insisted. They differ from the formal media by persuading uninterested people to vote in a certain way without giving them a substantive reason for their vote. Fully 25% of those who mentioned a personal contact in connection with change of mind failed to give a real issue of the campaign as a reason for the change, but only 5% of those who mentioned the formal media omitted such a reason. When personal influence is paramount in this way, the voter is voting mainly for the personal friend, not the candidate.

PRACTICAL IMPLICATIONS

In a way the outcome of the election in Erie County is the best evidence for the success of face-to-face contacts. It so happened that for some time the Republican machine in that area worked much more vigorously than its Democratic opponent. When asked whether they knew people who had good ideas about politics, our respondents mentioned considerably more Republican than Democratic local politicians. A few people who did not expect to vote but finally went to the polls mentioned Republican canvassers as the main influence, but we could not trace a similar success for the Democratic machine.

However, one should not identify the personal contacts discussed in this chapter with the efforts of the *professional* political machines. These personal contacts are what one might call *amateur machines* which spring up during elections—individuals who become quite enthusiastic or special groups that try to activate people within their reach. One might almost say that the most successful form of propaganda—especially last-minute propaganda—is to "surround" the people whose vote decision is still dubious so that the only path left to them is the way to the polling booth. We do not know how the budget of the political parties is distributed among different channels of propaganda but we suspect that the largest part of any propaganda budget is spent on pamphlets, radio time, etc. But our findings suggest the task of finding the best ratio between money spent on formal media and money spent on organizing the face-to-face influences, the local "molecular pressures" which vitalize the formal media by more personal interpretation and the full richness of personal relationships into the promotion of the causes which are decided upon in the course of an election.

In the last analysis, more than anything else people can move other people. From an ethical point of view this is a hopeful aspect in the serious social problem of propaganda. The side which has the more enthusiastic supporters and which can mobilize grass-root support in an expert way has great chances of success.

Part Two: LEADERSHIP AND
ITS GROUP SETTINGS

Contexts: Leadership Among Social Classes

IN THE last section we have considered three types of leadership, some of their characteristics, and the kinds of situations which foster these. The three types, bureaucrats, agitators, and informal leaders—or approximations of them—are to be found in a great number of actual organizations and groups. This does not, of course, mean that the configuration of leadership types will be the same for each specific group. Some groups may have a preponderance of leadership tending toward the bureaucratic type, others toward the informal, and so on. Each concrete group, moreover, has special objectives, values, techniques which further differentiate it from others of its type. For example, a big business and a government agency may both be bureaucracies—and for certain problems it is indispensable to see them as such —but the specific ends which they prosecute, the social functions which they perform, are different.

The intention of this section is therefore to see leadership at work in structures or situations that are defined in ways cutting across our previous formulations. These will be situations that are somewhat more familiar, involving as they will more conventional definitions of social structures. People may readily recognize themselves as being members of the groups on which we will now focus. The types of situations and structures to be considered in the following section are: (1) social classes, (2) minority groups, and (3) political groups. Each of these have problems and patterns of leadership which are not adequately taken cognizance of simply by an interpretation of the roles of bureaucrats, agitators, and informal leaders.

Consideration of leadership in these groups is useful also because

131

people become conscious of leadership problems in frameworks such as these. Unless social scientists can demonstrate the reliability of their knowledge on these levels—and at least answer some questions as laymen ask them—it is probable that we will not be given a chance to "show our stuff" regarding the problems laymen now only dimly perceive.

Like soldiers who encounter only a small segment of a battlefront, most human beings never have contact with more than a relatively small part of the total social structure. The social scientists' contribution will be assessed in terms of its ability to clarify experiences and problems with which laymen are *familiar*. The layman will use his experiences with a relatively small part of the social structure to "test" and evaluate the social scientist's analysis—and from the viewpoint of democratic values this seems eminently appropriate.

It is in part for this reason that the analyses of leadership presented in this section emphasize the *local* as well as the more remote, or national, aspects of leadership among different groups. (This, of course, is subject to the limitations which available research establishes.) In addition, the problem of democratic action is largely one of participation on the level and in the area in which the individual finds himself. This warrants emphasis on the grass-roots level, for it is here that the power of consent fitfully stirs, it is here that paper plans are implemented and built into the culture, and it is here, only, that the cadres for defense and extension of democratic institutions and values will be found, or found wanting.

The kind of specific situations in which leadership is to be studied first is that of social classes. The importance which social scientists attribute to social classes is often at great variance with that of the popular estimate. Social scientists, for example, have found that an infant's chance to live a year or more is affected by the social class to which his parents belong, that different social classes have distinctive child-rearing practices, that attitudes toward education vary with one's social class, as does the amount of education youths receive. The courting, marital and family patterns; how liquor is consumed (to say nothing of what kind!); what type of organizations the individual has membership in; how active he is in these; his sexual behavior; which newspapers, magazines, books and radio programs he prefers; even the manner in which breakfast is eaten—all these are influenced by the social class in which individuals are born or belong.

In the articles which follow, three social classes will be singled out for attention:

1. The "business class," including the owners and top management of production and distribution enterprises; that is, individuals who own or who are the agents of those who own these enterprises and who purchase the services of

2. the "working class," whose indispensable source of income derives from the sale of its labor power to the business class, and

3. the "middle class" which may be divided in to two sections: (a) the "old" middle class, consisting of independent, self-employed, entrepreneurs whose entrepreneurial units are small and in which they play an active part, and, also, self-employed professionals; (b) the "new" middle class (often recruited from the children of the "old" middle class), consisting of white-collar, professional, and lower managerial employees. While in many respects arbitrary, these definitions seem adequate as orientations to the articles which follow.

Class leaders, it may be noted in concluding this general introduction, operate in one or both of two general kinds of situations: (1) informal groups which tend to be composed of members of one class only, or of two "adjacent" classes; for example, in working-class taverns or upper-class country clubs, or, perhaps, in status-segregated neighborhoods; (2) in formal, possibly bureaucratized, associations organized either for (a) the satisfaction of the needs, interests, or wants distinctive of a class or segments of it, e.g., trade unions, manufacturers' associations, trade associations or certain kinds of political parties, or (b) those engaged in the distribution or production of commodities, as in factories and stores. Insofar as a social class can be said to engage in social action, what is referred to is the operation of formal, class-oriented associations (2a). Social classes as a whole never engage in social action; segments of the class are organized and led by associations which identify themselves with the interest of the class.

POWER IN SEARCH OF PRESTIGE

Traditionally, the business-class leader has not only led members of his own social class but has, also, been accepted as a leader by members of social classes other than his own. In this sense he has for a long period of time been accepted and played a role as a "community" leader. As Wilbert Moore has written, "The community leadership of high-ranking businessmen was throughout the nineteenth century rarely challenged in theory and even more rarely challenged in fact." During the last half-century or so, however, an extremely significant change took place: the business-class leader began to lose his multi-class leadership and became more and more restricted to members of his own class. In other words: the probability that a business-class individual would be found to lead individuals in classes other than his own has declined.

This, however, does not mean that the business class has lost its *power*, or that this has declined. The business class' power—the probability that its decisions will result in actions on the part of others, that they are in a position to carry out their decisions despite the resistance of others—this, if anything, has increased. All that the above reference to the declining *multi*-class leadership role of businessmen implies is that their decisions are more often conformed with by middle- or working-class people for reasons other than a sense of moral obligation. Obedience is rendered business-class decisions, but now not so much because the latter is thought to have a *right* to issue orders. Much of the behavior of business-class leaders is explicable as a response to the tension between their relatively high power and their declining legitimacy and prestige. Power without legitimacy is not leadership and is insecure. Attitudes of expediency are developed by those subject to nonlegitimized power; these lessen the probability that any given order will be obeyed. In the last analysis such power must rest on force.

One of the most interesting (if somewhat oblique) evidences of the decline of the business class' leadership role is derivable from a study (worthy of greater attention) by Leo Lowenthal.[1] This investigation consists of a content-analysis of biographies in popular magazines published between 1901 and 1941. Lowenthal came to the following conclusions which are relevant to our problem:

1. "*The first quarter of the century* cherishes biography in terms of an open-minded liberal society which really wants to know something about its own leading figures on the social, commercial, and cultural fronts. . . .

[1] Leo Lowenthal, "Biographies in Popular Magazines," *Radio Research* 1942-43, Paul F. Lazarsfeld and Frank Stanton, eds. 1944, pp. 507-548.

Their biographies are written almost exclusively to supplement the reader's knowledge of the technical accomplishments of their respective fields. . . . Unbroken confidence in the opportunities open to every individual serves as the leitmotiv of the biographies. To a very great extent they are to be looked upon as examples of success which can be imitated. (The subjects of the biographies of this period are aptly dubbed by Lowenthal as the "idols of production.")

2. "If a student in some very distant future should use popular magazines in 1941 as a source of information as to what figures the American public looked to in the first stages of the greatest crisis since the birth of the Union, he would come to a grotesque result. While the industrial and professional endeavors are geared to a maximum of speed and efficiency, the idols of the masses are not, as they were in the past, the leading names in the battle of production, but the headliners of the movies, the ball parks, and the night clubs."

In short, the "idols of production" are being superseded by the "idols of consumption." This is a process strongly suggestive of a decline in the legitimacy and prestige of the business class among other social classes. Other partial evidences of this declining public prestige might include: (a) increased governmental regulation of certain economic affairs, in opposition to the desires of segments of the business class, but with the support of large numbers of people in other social classes; (b) establishment and growth of a labor movement, beginning with the rise of the A.F. of L., which did not formally identify its interests with those of employers.

What are some of the factors which have narrowed down the range of business-class leadership by undermining its legitimacy and impairing its public prestige?

To begin with, it will be useful to examine the ways in which leadership of the business class was historically and may at the present be legitimated. In other words, what are the grounds on which the power of the business class has been considered rightful, and to that extent transformed into leadership? There seem to be three such bases[2] which, it will be seen, parallel Max Weber's more general types of leadership:

1. "Traditional Entrepreneur": The businessman's power may be

[2] The following formulations are heavily indebted to Fritz Redlich, History of American Business Leaders (Ann Arbor, 1940), pp. 16-17, although divergent in several respects.

legitimized because of the way in which he acquired his *ownership* of the business. In this type the method of acquisition is inheritance, usually from either father or father-in-law. Usually, also, this type of entrepreneur further legitimates his position by assumption of community obligations. In a sense, the orientation is toward the *past* and it is in part because the entrepreneur is identified with it that he is legitimated.

2. *"Creative Entrepreneur"*: This businessman is held legitimate by reason of his promise of a better *future*, the fact that he established the enterprise, possibly his invention of new techniques or introduction of new products. There seems to be considerable similarity between this type—exemplified by a Henry Ford—and Weber's charismatic leader.

3. The *"Manager"*: This businessman legitimates his role neither in terms of loyalty to the past nor promise for the future. He is legitimated by virtue of his accomplishments in the *present*, because of the legal guarantees of his position, because he enables current expectations of living standards to be met. His leadership is "rightful" because "he gets things done" in the here—now. The similarity of this type to Weber's "bureaucrat" is evident.

Two developments, relating to the sources of legitimacy, contribute to the decline of the business class' prestige and legitimacy.

1. The standards in terms of which legitimacy is accorded businessmen by workers and others have not kept pace with changing forms of business organization. The prevalent images of businessmen are still very much influenced by conceptions of the "traditional" and "creative" entrepreneurs. In reality, however, the modern businessman is increasingly a *hired manager*. Instead of having built up his own business, or having inherited it, the present-day business head is, with ever growing likelihood, *appointed* to his job on the basis of his technical qualifications.

The much-commented-on "separation of ownership and management" is one facet of the bureaucratization of business. (In a sense, capitalists—or some of them, at any rate—become separated from their capital.) W. Lloyd Warner and J. O. Low's article in this section, "Managers and Owners, Then and Now," is a striking depiction of the consequences which result when the public images of business leaders ("managers") do not accord with their actual status—"They were not the men their fathers were." It is, too, a careful analysis of the growing bureaucratization of one industry, and the problems thwarting the industrial form of the bureaucrat—the "manager." Warner and Low's study is an analysis of a strike which took place in a shoe-manufacturing town, "Yankee City," an old New England community. Like John Alexander and Morroe Berger's sketch of a local union leader in this same section, it suggests another of the conditions which subvert the businessman's legitimacy and prestige.

2. This second element has to do with the consequences of depressions, in particular that of 1929-1941. The "manager," it will be remembered, is legitimized in terms of his performance in the "here-now." His legitimacy is far more vulnerable than that of the "traditional" and "creative" entrepreneurs. It is difficult to challenge the "traditional" legitimation of the businessman because the attitudes it invokes are sentimental and nonrational; so, too, is the "creative entrepreneur's" legitimacy relatively difficult to impugn—for it rests on a success or failure reposing in an unspecified future, which is also seen through the wrappings of nonrational sentiments. The "manager," however, is legitimated in exceedingly rational terms; in terms of "what he gives me now for what I give him—now." The evidence in terms of which a manager's legitimacy may be judged is not buried in an idealized past or an unforeseeable future. For this reason the managerial legitimation of business leadership is most susceptible to critical attack.

With the coming of a depression, the "manager" cannot easily invoke nonrational sentiment to bolster his position. He is most often neither the "worthy son of a wise father," nor the author of great happenings. His legitimacy easily melts under the pressure of economic crisis. One needs only to read Robert and Helen Lynd's Middletown In Transition to get a clear picture of the scorching attack on the business class which the last depression precipitated.

As the scope of business operations becomes wider and finally dependent on a world market, as the bureaucratization of business piles echelon on echelon, the current businessman can no longer be squeezed into the mold of the creative, individual entrepreneur. He is not so easily thought of, nor can he so conceive of himself, as the shaper of events and the master-maker of decisions. Any individual's estimation of himself reflects the estimations which those around him have made. It may well be wondered how businessmen react to their declining social prestige and their loss of multi-class leadership. Hypothetically, we might anticipate the sapping of moral conviction about their social and personal worth, and an increase of internal conflict and anxiety. John P. Marquand's recent novel, *Point of No Return*, is a somewhat saddening representation of the apparent, barely subsurface anxieties of a rising young banker. (Compare this with Dreiser's powerful study of "The Financier" and an impressionistic but brilliantly insightful history of a changing type can be found.) While it is part of our *zeitgeist* to entertain psychoanalytical speculations, it may be that current journalistic analyses of businessmen in government, which emphasize their psychological ills, contain some core of truth.

Much of the behavior of business leaders today may be viewed as a response to the threatening gap between their great power and their dwindling prestige. Among these efforts at adaptation the most important seem to be:

1. *Ideological:* In part, these take the form of recurring, if somewhat desperate, reassertions of the businessman as a "natural" leader, possessed of unusual, charismatic powers. This is perhaps more successful as a form of self-assurance among businessmen than as an effective technique of public persuasion.

2. *Increased Reliance on Formal Controls:* This has two aspects: (a) *growing bureaucratization of business:* For men with the anxieties we have hypothesized, bureaucratized business is not only an "efficient" form of enterprise, but could also function as a source of psychological security, patterning actions in detail, delimiting responsibilities, facilitating decisions, as it does; (b) *closer and more formalized relations with the State;* for example, businessmen assuming official State positions, and also greater reliance on the State in relations with workers, e.g., the Taft-Hartley and other labor laws. This does not restore business-class prestige or legitimacy, but invokes the use of an agency, the State, with relatively high legitimacy.

3. *"Formal Coöptation" of Labor Leaders:* Taking the leaders of labor "into the business," recognizing their legitimacy and, in turn, securing from them recognition of the legitimacy of business-class leadership. This has many forms: joint labor-management committees, joint community chest drives, etc. The "sophisticated conservatives,"

as C. Wright Mills calls a section of the business-class leadership, stop fighting labor in a rough and tumble way and put forth a "harmony" ideology.

There are many dangers to democratic values which may be spawned by the present disequilibrium between the business class' power and prestige. One of these has already been implied: namely, potential and gradual transition to a "Garrison State" which would consist of an alliance between business, governmental (including military), and labor bureaucrats, with the latter operating in a framework rigidly delimited by the first two. Failing this, we might then observe promiscuous "flirtations" with fledgling fascist agitators which, given appropriate financing, may blossom into the "real thing." The business-class leaders may, in their efforts to compensate for their declining prestige and endangered status, find themselves being drawn to either or both of these solutions in a somnambulistic fashion, following one "small" commitment with another until there is at last reached a "Point of No Return."

TRADE UNION LEADERSHIP. To a great extent, those who are hostile to the American labor movement focus these attitudes on trade union leaders. People commonly remark: "Unions are all right but the rackets aren't. Such as Lewis and the big shots who are out for all they can get." "Unions are all right but sometimes the fellows who run them are too unreasonable with the employers." "Unions are mismanaged now." "Unions are good, if honest men are at the head of them." This direction of hostility toward union leaders is in part a consequence of labor's growing power. Millions of Americans now belong to unions. An antiunion viewpoint, held by many having access to communication media, cannot, therefore, be as sweeping and uncompromising as it was formerly. Expressions of criticism must take into account the possible responses of union membership; fear of offending them may temper and channelize criticism. The focus of antiunion criticisms upon leadership functions to separate them from their membership, if it is successful.

These continuing criticisms of trade union leaders should not, however, be allowed to obscure the fact that after the organization of the A.F. of L. the labor leader attained social recognition and prestige which had previously been denied him. Looking back somewhat nostalgically, labor leaders whose careers had bridged this transformation have commented on it. Eugene Debs, for example, claimed: "The labor agitator of the early days held no office, had no title, drew no salary, saw no footlights, heard no applause, never saw his name in print, and fills an unknown grave."

More acid in the tone of her comments was "Mother" Jones: "Many of our modern leaders have wandered far from the thorny path of the early crusaders. Never in the early days of the early struggle would you find leaders wining and dining with the aristocracy; nor did their wives strut about like diamond-bedecked peacocks."

This change in the community status of union leadership has important consequences for the relations between union leaders and followers. For to the extent that union leadership becomes a recognized social role, it now becomes a legitimate aspiration for some of the more career-minded members of the working and middle classes who may come to view it as an avenue of social mobility, all the more useful as others are impeded. These conceptions of labor leadership easily dispose a leader to a loss of identification with his membership and consequently to the use of manipulative controls and oligarchical techniques. This tendency, then, provides the labor movement with one of its most crucial problems: namely, that of securing leadership that has motivations which are congruent with its formally democratic goals and structure.

The two studies of labor leadership included in this section—Eli Chinoy's "Local Union Leadership" and John W. Alexander and Morroe Berger's "Grass Roots Labor Leader"—are both concerned with the problem of the motivation of labor leadership. Both seek answers to the question: why is it that people wish to become labor leaders? Both studies indicate that a labor leader's motivations are extremely complex and encompass much more than displaced career expectations. The latter, however, deserves emphasis because, unless it can in some way be contained, it may do injury to group goals and democratic functioning. Both articles reveal that students of labor leadership have come a long way from the time when the principal object of study was the union's formal organization, as outlined in its constitution. While it should be emphasized that a democratic union constitution is an indispensable component of democratic trade unionism, it is not, however, a foolproof safe that gives warning when tampered with by those possessed of careerist intentions.

Chinoy, also points his analysis at the problem of why individuals may refuse leadership, indicating the manner in which institutionally derived pressures from family and occupation may deter workers from seeking union leadership and create a leadership shortage. (This last is a theme to which Bernard Barber will return in his paper on "Apathy" in *The Ethics and Technics of Leadership*.) Both of these problems, careerist or potentially undemocratic leaders and insufficient leadership cadres, are interconnected. For to the extent that the latter exists, even unions alert to the dangers of careerism may be forced to compromise their standards in order to meet their minimum leadership needs.

Two of the leadership problems of a trade union, to whom democratic values and internal functioning are a serious matter, may therefore be summarized as follows:

1. How can leadership be obtained which will be emotionally identified with the rank-and-file members so that formal, democratic decisions will not be warped by the action of the leader's personal interests, disguised as "necessary administrative discretion"?

2. How can such leaders, once obtained, be kept identified with the rank-and-file members?

To repeat: a full and adequate answer to these questions will include formulation of constitutional safeguards, but it will involve much more than these. Above all, what seems to be required are certain normative attitudes which—if internalized in leaders and members—may enhance the leaders' identification with their membership. Many trade unions have quite spontaneously established a number of such normative practices. Usually, however, each of these also has potential dangers to democratic and efficient operations. Studies of these "natural" institutions, so that their functional and dysfunctional consequences may be separated, would be most useful.

Some of the trade union practices which heighten or reinforce leaders' identification with their membership are:

1. *Salary Limitations:* Relating the leaders' salaries in some way to the prevailing wage patterns paid to the union membership; for example, paying leaders no more than the average wage received by union members in the upper-third income bracket. This might serve to keep union leaders at a standard of living similar

to their members thereby reinforcing identification with them and, perhaps, providing an additional incentive to obtain pay raises for their membership. Salary-conscious, middle-class career-ists might thus be sifted out. The *danger* here is that pressures may be set up which could conduce to grafting or a possible shortage of aspirants to leadership.

2. *Inner-Union Leadership:* Having either appointed or elected leadership positions open only to unionists who have been rank-and-file members of the union subdivision which they are to lead for a specified period of time. The leader's identification with his membership is presumably furthered by the fact that he has gone through similar occupational experiences. When inner-union leadership becomes a normative practice, it also serves to hold the union's ideological allies at arm's length. For example, if a union is known to be a left-wing organization, it may obtain a certain prominence in radical circles. It is consequently beset by nonunion job-hunters who trade upon their ideological affinity with the union's leadership. The norm of inner-union leadership serves to ward off the infiltration of ideological allies by making available a *traditional* explanation for their ineligibility. The re-jection is thereby softened. If these friends succeeded in obtain-ing leadership positions because of their ideological affinity with the union, this would obligate the successful candidate to his ideological group and, in turn, diminish his identification with union members. The norm of inner-union leadership also in-creases the possibility of the rank and file's advancement to union office, thereby increasing the devotion and activity of those rank and filers who may be seeking leadership. The *danger* here is that a "localistic" ideology may begin to flourish in such a union, that its orientation becomes narrow and "inbred," and that it may lose its identification with the trade union movement as a whole. This norm may also become one of the bulwarks which an oligarchy uses to defend its prerogatives.

These are only two practices which give promise of obtaining leaders who identify with their membership and of retaining such identifica-tion. Others worthy of examination in this context might be (1) the encouragement of marriages among union members; (2) periodic re-turns by union leaders to ordinary shop and factory work; this, however, must not come to be defined as a "punishment" if it is to bring about the desired attitudes. Undoubtedly, careful study of existent trade unions would bring to light many other practices which function to strengthen leaders' identification with the rank and file.

Trade unions have played a major role in nourishing the roots of freedom. From 1770, when Philadelphia mechanics demanded a place in the Colonial government ("Have we not an equal right of electing or being elected"), up until the present movement against segregation and discrimination, trade unions have had a dynamic part in the unfolding of American democracy. That they have done so primarily when they defined it is as being in their "self-interest" will be occasion for disenchantment only by those who believe that freedom—like little girls—is compounded solely of "sugar, and spice, and all things nice." The trade union movement, however, will be able to enlarge its contribution only if it becomes acutely aware that democracy is not only a problem someplace "out there," in society at large, but also right at home in its own associations.

Managers and Owners, Then and Now[1]

BY W. LLOYD WARNER AND J. O. LOW

THREE DEAD men played powerful, important, and, at times, decisive roles in the outcome of the strike. Paradoxically, although they were former owners and managers of the factories, their influence materially aided the strikers and helped defeat management. Throughout the struggle, the owners,[2] workers, and most of Yankee City continued to recognize the great wisdom of these dead owners and managers and always bowed to their judgments. The authority of these men accordingly was constantly quoted by each side to gain approval for what it said and did and to stigmatize the words and actions of its antagonists. The peacemakers quoted the deeds and sayings of the three as parables and precepts to force the warring parties to come to agreement. It is unlikely that the actual behavior of these three men corresponded to the symbols into which they had been fabricated by those who remembered them after their deaths. But it is

[1] Reprinted from *The Social System of the Modern Factory*, by W. Lloyd Warner and J. O. Low, Yale University Press, 1947. Used by permission of the publishers.

[2] Each person, each institution, and each incident is a composite drawing. No one actual individual or family in Yankee City is depicted, rather the lives of *several individuals* are compressed into that of one fictive person. . . . The justification for these changes lies in our attempt to protect our subjects and to tell our story economically. We have not hesitated to exclude all material which might identify specific persons in the community; and we have included generalized material wherever necessary to prevent recognition. The people and situations in some of the sketches are entirely imaginary. In all cases where changes were introduced in the reworking of our field notes, we first satisfied ourselves that they would not destroy the essential social reality of the points of the original interview. Only then were such materials included in our text.

certain that the values inherent in them as collective representations ordered and controlled much of the thinking of everyone and greatly contributed to the workers' winning the strike.

THE MANAGERS OF MEN WERE GODS

The three—Caleb Choate, Godfrey Weatherby, and William Pierce —were constantly quoted; episodes from their exploits, as brilliant Yankee City industrialists and wise and generous employers of Yankee City men, were frequently spoken of and applied to present conditions in the shoe industry to the detriment of the contemporary managers and owners. Since the sagacity of the three verged on the supernatural, no flesh and blood owner living in Yankee City at the time of the strike could hope to measure up to the standards of these demigods. It is small wonder that managers felt weak and inadequate when they compared themselves with the great men of the past, and it is certain from their utterances and deeds that they shared feelings of guilt in the presence of their accusing employees. Their private knowledge of themselves and faith in the great managers of the past made them weak, for now that myth-making had done its work and mortals were translated into gods, the prosaic men of the present could never hope to compete with these heroes and demigods who plagued them from the past.

We will examine the evidence to see what these men were in real life but only briefly since it was what the men and women of the strike believed them to have been that made them important for this study. In the section which follows we will discuss the social personalities of the contemporary managers; then we will compare the evidence from the past and present to learn why the three dead owners were still powerful when their successors, with all the recognized glory of modern technology to support them, were considered weak and inadequate.

Caleb Choate was a pioneer in large-scale shoe manufacturing in Yankee City; both Godfrey Weatherby and William Pierce received their training under him.

Mr. Choate's success is indicated by the fact that from a capital of $100 (in 1866) he had built up a business with annual gross sales of a million dollars. By 1877, at the age of thirty, he was the "head of a large and successful manufacturing business and was one of the solid and respected citizens of Yankee City. . . . A large factor in the early success of the business was the prompt adoption of the McKay stitching machine while other shoe manufacturers were considering whether it would pay. Mr. Choate was one of the first to combine the many parts of shoe manufacturing under one roof and to successfully operate a large establishment where from the raw materials shoes were made up complete from start to finish under the management and care of one man. By 1892 annual sales totalled $1,440,250."

Before Godfrey Weatherby died he said: "There was almost entire absence of bitter feeling between Mr. Choate and his employees. . . . There were no strikes by reason of dissatisfaction with wages. He commanded respect rather than won popularity. He was a kindly man and just, intolerant of inefficiency and dishonesty, always master in his own sphere, a good judge of men. Leaders among the workmen were satisfied that they were justly and fairly treated."

Another decided factor in Caleb Choate's business success was the financial help given him by Mr. Davis Cole, a member of an "old Yankee City family." Mr. Cole was in business in Boston and retired at the age of forty-four with a fortune. He owned a home in Yankee City and planned to live on the income from his savings, placed in the bank at 5 percent interest. Mr. Choate, with much ambition and very little money, started his shoe concern and asked Mr. Cole to endorse some notes. Mr. Cole agreed to this several times, so the story goes, without paying much attention to the amounts. Three years later, Mr. Cole was called over to the bank and learned that he had endorsed $100,000 worth of paper. Caleb Choate said "if Cole put him into bankruptcy he wouldn't get ten cents on a dollar but if he was allowed to continue he would get one hundred cents." Mr. Cole, who had complete confidence in Mr. Choate, was put in active charge by the bank and the business was successful.

Reference is made to this venture in Mr. Choate's memorial volume: "To Mr. Cole he (Caleb Choate) always expressed a grateful sense of obligation for the courage which he manifested and confidence he placed in the ability and integrity of the managing partner."

According to an elderly Yankee City businessman (upper-upper), who at one time was in partnership with him, Caleb Choate employed ten salesmen who visited the "whole of the United States from the

Atlantic to the Pacific. Up to 1900 he manufactured many times more than all the other Yankee City manufacturers put together."

"His business methods were exceptionally fair and praiseworthy," another said. "The fact that he was in any way connected with an enterprise was all that was needed to inspire complete confidence. His name stood for quality, honest value, fair treatment and good service in almost every city in the United States."

Caleb Choate started Godfrey Weatherby in business. According to Godfrey Weatherby's friends, they were very different. Mr. Choate was decided and abrupt, while Godfrey was more gentle and kindly. "He wouldn't be taken in by anyone," an old lady from Hill Street said, "but if a man showed he wanted to do what was right Godfrey always stood ready to help him. He became very successful and always showed a great interest in community affairs. Everyone trusted him and he never had any labor troubles of any kind. He had been to the local school with a good many of his employees and they knew his word was as good as his bond."

According to the most important and respected opinion-maker in the city, "if he (Weatherby) had been in business today he wouldn't have had any strike because his employees believed in him and he would have put all his cards on the table."

One of the partners of a large firm which still bore the name of Weatherby said: "Mr. Weatherby has been dead a good many years but we kept his name because he was such a fine man and his name meant so much. He did more for Yankee City than anyone else. If it hadn't been for Mr. Weatherby many big Yankee City companies would have been on the rocks."

At the time of the strike another upper-class informant said: "Mr. Weatherby was highly revered and respected and there's scarcely a meeting during this strike where his name isn't mentioned. He was a real leader."

Both Caleb Choate and Godfrey Weatherby died in their early fifties, Mr. Choate at fifty-five and Mr. Weatherby at fifty-three. The same remark was applied to the lives of both men—"sad that it should be cut off ere it was fully rounded out." Godfrey Weatherby made this comment at the memorial service for Caleb Choate, and Frederick Choate, son of Caleb Choate, repeated it in his address at the memorial service for Godfrey Weatherby eighteen years later. A close friend, in commenting on his early death, said: "If Godfrey had lived he undoubtedly would have trained one of his sons to succeed him in company with William Pierce's son. But the children were so young when he died that his brother felt he would not have wanted his sons trained by the sort of managers that are in the shoe factories today. So he placed them in banks or bond houses where they would come under the influence of worthy, upright men, the type of men who used to be in the shoe business."

William Pierce started in the shoe business selling shoe laces for Caleb Choate and later became a shoe salesman. Following Mr. Choate's death, Mr. Pierce and Mr. Weatherby went into partnership and continued business under the firm name of Weatherby and Pierce for over thirty years, Mr. Weatherby responsible for the manufacturing end and Mr. Pierce for selling. Following the death of Mr. Weatherby, the firm liquidated.

Fred Jackson, of Jones and Jackson, in speaking about Mr. Pierce, of Weatherby and Pierce, said "what a good man he was. The firm liquidated because one partner (Weatherby) died and another had a bad heart. Mr. Pierce always felt responsible, for all his employees thought he was perfect, and he was worth half a million when he died."

A Greek shoe worker said: "I used to work for his father (Cabot Pierce) before he died. His father was a fine man. He was always a gentleman and would treat you right. He always paid more than anyone else."

The firm of Weatherby and Pierce shared this reputation, too. Among the items appearing in the *Herald* during the shoe strike and signed by the shoe workers, one observed: "The factory under William Pierce and Godfrey Weatherby's management was known the country over as a factory with ideal conditions between employer and employee. They (the employees) were always met more than half way and it was a privilege to work for them."

"The shoe business has changed considerably now," said a member of the upper-upper class. "Weatherby and Pierce was a fine concern. They made a very high-grade shoe, had the best workers in Yankee City and paid high wages. Both Godfrey and William were born and raised in Yankee City, and a lot of the shoe workers had been to school with them. Consequently they never treated the workers as employees but as friends."

This last statement was embodied in a story told over and over again during the strike: "Once Mr. Pierce met a shoe cutter named Sam Taylor on the stairs. Taylor said, 'Good morning, Mr. Pierce.' Mr. Pierce said, 'Good morning.' After he got back to his office he sent for Taylor and said, 'Sam, you went to school with me,' and Taylor said, 'Yes, Mr. Pierce.' 'Well,' said Mr. Pierce, 'you called me Mr. Pierce on the stairs just now. You always used to call me William, and I want you to continue to call me William just as you always did.' That was just a little thing, but subsequently whenever there was any dissatisfaction in the cutting room Sam would come down to the office and he and William would sit down at the table and settle the thing, each side giving in a little, and everyone would be satisfied. So there never was even the slightest hint of any labor trouble."

This parable was frequently told during the strike when all relationships between the owners and workers had been severed, the conclusion of the story serving as an eloquent moral lesson which the workers used to attack management.

"Every year they would shut down the plant," our interviewers were often told, in another story, "and the company would pay all the expenses of the employees for a day at the shore or in the country and everyone would have a share of chicken dinner costing two or three thousand dollars. The company had insurance for its employees, a benefit association, a hospital and trained nurse. . . . Of course all this cost a lot of money and added to the expense of making shoes."

In brief, the old owners were gods and not men. They had become heroes to labor as well as management. Where truth ends and idealization begins cannot be learned, but, fact or fiction, these memories stalked through the events of the strike like the ghost of Hamlet's father and motivated their sociological sons, their successors in the shoe business, to make decisions which were disastrous to them.

STRUCTURAL ANALYSIS OF THE STATUS OF THE OLD AND NEW MANAGERS

Shortly after Caleb Choate's death, a number of prominent Yankee City men published a memorial volume which contained the usual words of high praise for a great man. Since these same words, unlike those of many memorial volumes, were said about him by ordinary men of the street, and, as we have said earlier, were used during the strike, it is important to examine them. Mr. Perkins Cantridge of Hill Street, a member of one of the oldest families of Yankee City, wrote: "Caleb Choate was one of the most remarkable men ever connected with Yankee City; a business man of liberal culture, of fine literary taste, gifted as an orator, in music and theatricals. . . . He was an acquisition to any society. He honored any public station, however high. . . . He achieved more in his fifty years of life than most men can point to after marking a very old age. . . .

"He was identified with the public health of this city and was a conspicuous figure in all its great social functions as long as his health permitted it. He was a leading financier and a man who at once took and ever afterwards occupied a prominent position in this community. For years, by common consent, he was the leading man of the city. . . . Forcefulness of character made him the commanding spirit in every undertaking in which he shared and in every circle in which he moved."

Our analysis of Mr. Choate's participation in the community provides the crucial evidence on why Mr. Choate became the powerful symbol and collective representation which were used against the contemporary managers during the strike. We will briefly review some of the memberships that he had in the more powerful institutions of Yankee City.

In the business and financial sphere he was: (1) owner and head of his million-dollar shoe company; (2) president of one of the most powerful banks in the city; (3) member of the Board of Trustees of the Financial Institute, a firm of the utmost prestige and power in the community; (4) director of the Security Trust Company, another powerful financial institution; (5) director of the Yankee City Gas and Electric Company. He was involved in a large number of civic enterprises and was a member of many civic institutions: (6) director and one of the founders of the city's most important hospital; (7) director of the Public Library; (8) member of the School Committee; (9) trustee of the Revere Free School; (10) president of the City Improvement Society. He also took an important part in politics. He was: (11) chairman of the Republican City Committee; (12) member of the City Council; (13) delegate to the National Republican Convention; (14) mayor of the city. Mr. Choate was also prominent in church and religious affairs. He was: (15) president of the Yankee County Unitarian Club; (16) president of the Yankee County Unitarian Conference. He was a leader in fraternal affairs and was: (17) Past Master of St. John's Lodge; (18) member of several important fraternal orders. Mr. Choate was an active member of some of the most exclusive clubs of the city including: (19) The Drama Club; (20) the Thursday Night Club; (21) the January Club; (22) the February Club; (23) the Lowell Club; (24) the Country Club.

The evidence demonstrates that in all these organizations he was active and powerful. This brief survey of some of his participation in the community demonstrates that his activities ramified throughout the city and that much of the life of the city was centered in him. It also demonstrates that he accepted responsibility for the larger affairs of the community and helped integrate its activities, for he provided responsible leadership for the whole life of the community. "He was a man you could depend on."

Very much the same could be said about Mr. William Pierce and Mr. Godfrey Weatherby. They, too, were responsible elders of the city. Their factories provided jobs and wages. They were citizens of the town and men who felt obligated to it. Their membership in local institutions compares very favorably with that of Mr. Choate.

The essential point to remember about all three of these men is that they were subject to local control, because, first, they were dominated by local sentiments which motivated them "to take care of their own people"; second, they were under the powerful influence of the numerous organizations to which they belonged; and, third, their personal contacts with the local citizens directly related them to influences from every part of the city.

Mr. Cohen, Mr. Shulberg, Mr. Bronstein, and Mr. Luntski [present owners or controllers of the shoe factories] did not even live in the city. The workers knew or felt that the forces which controlled the local men did not control these "outsiders." The vast network of relations and memberships which made Choate, Weatherby, and Pierce local leaders, as well as local manufacturers, was reduced to a purely economic relation of employer and employee. It was that and nothing more. It is small wonder that the workers "gave the horse laugh when the managers talked about being good fellows."

Mr. Cohen and his group belonged to the last period in the economic evolution of Yankee City, that of Big City capitalism, which had superseded the small town capitalism in the vertical structure of corporate enterprise and had extended on beyond Yankee City to the great metropolises. At the time of the strike the local men, although born and reared in Yankee City, were little more than the factory managers for Big City capitalists since they occupied inferior positions in this vastly extended vertical structure. They were not in a position to take leadership; they were not in a position of great power where they were free to make the decisions which always characterized the lives of Choate, Weatherby, and Pierce.

Each of these local men felt what had happened very deeply, and some of them were explicit enough about it to say so. We knew some of them well. They were not weak men or unscrupulous persons as their opponents made them out to be. They had good personal reputations in the business world. Some of them had been trained by their own fathers to be community leaders, but their place in the new socio-economic structure of Yankee City prevented them from playing this role, and each in his own way contributed directly to the defeat of the managerial group. Part of their ineptness was due to their inability to measure up in their own minds to the great men of the past. This was a dead past, glorious and safe, when men knew themselves to be free men and Yankee City was "the hub of the universe." Clinging to the traditions of Choate, Weatherby, and Pierce, both workers and management longed to return to those days when it was possible for William Pierce, with all his power and prestige, to stop and gently chide Sam Taylor, the cutter, and he and Sam could talk about "the trouble in the cutting room." Power was under control and security was present then; manager and worker were part of a self-contained system in which each knew his part.

In these days of Big City capitalism, when Yankee City has lost control of its own destinies, few workers go up to the "Big Boss" to tell him about "what's wrong in the cutting room," and those who do are not considered respected friends at court of the workers but "stool pigeons who are getting theirs from management."

During the strike the local men cut poor figures as fighters for management's side. Tim Jones and "Big Mike" Rafferty openly lined up with the strikers. Local sentiment and the feeling against "the foreigners" were too much for them. They materially contributed to the workers' victory.

Jackson damaged the cause of management when he tried to (physically) fight the head of the union. Everyone said he blustered, and everyone said he acted badly when he challenged union leadership. Jackson was under the control of higher management and occupied an inferior managerial position where he had little freedom to assume command and take leadership. Yet he had learned from William Pierce when he worked for him how his kind of man should act, and he knew that an owner and manager should assume control. It seems a reasonable hypothesis that the conflict between his beliefs about how a man should act (how Mr. Pierce would do it) and what he was permitted to do by his status greatly contributed to causing his unfortunate act, an act which materially aided the union. He tried to take command in a situation where it was impossible, and he could only "bluster."

His antagonist, on the other hand, was "top manager" of the union. He did have power and he could make decisions. His beliefs about what should be done and his status were commensurate, and he used them to the greatest effect for the cause of the union.

To the workers, Mr. Land was everything that an owner should not be. His letters to the workers only embittered them. "His high and mighty attitude," was ridiculed because they believed he wasn't free and that he had to take orders even as an owner from his one big customer, Mr. Cohen. Cabot Pierce refused to take any action. He felt defeated before the strike began and acted accordingly, and thus gave no strength to the managers' side.

All of these local men knew somehow they were "not the men their fathers were," and the three dead men, symbolizing the glorious past, overawed and helped defeat them.

In the days before Big City capitalism took control, the local enterpriser was financed by Yankee City banks. These banks and other investment houses possessed more autonomy and prestige than they do now. In the development of Mr. Choate's shoe empire, local financiers played important and necessary roles, and, at least part of the time, were silent partners in the business. Much of the wealth they derived from their investments was re-invested in Yankee City. The money was put into new enterprises, their own living, or in civic activities. Their white Georgian houses on Hill Street, whose gardens bordered those of the manufacturers, were majestic symbols of their power and prestige and forever reminded, and often reassured, everyone of the visible presence of these powerful and protecting men in Yankee City.

The Yankee City financiers, too, were men of responsibility, dominated by sentiments of local pride. They did well for themselves, but they also did well for the city. Perhaps the price was high, but the product bought by the rest of the community was substantial and of high quality. Their philanthropies, combined with their power and leadership, contributed enormously to the city's development and provided a firm foundation for the larger civic life of the community. Parks, libraries, hospitals, societies to help the unfortunate and aged, foundations to send young men to college, endowments of schools, churches, and many other worthy civic and public enterprises were granted and maintained by the money and leadership of the local financiers and manager-owners.

The ABC chain store with all its satellite factories, scattered through many cities and financed by several New York investment houses, is but one of many enterprises that these New York financial houses control. Their body of investment included Yankee City because it is one of the tens of thousands of living areas which make up the world. The flow of wealth from Yankee City's banks and factories, once a great local arterial system giving life and strength to the town, now has shrunk to an infinitesimal part of Big City, worldwide capitalism, where it has no vital significance.

The following account about the finances of the ABC Company, taken verbatim from a June 1945 issue of a large New York newspaper, supplies clear evidence for every statement which has been made here about the extension of the vertical hierarchy and the submergence of Yankee City into a very minor role in a world-wide financial-industrial structure:

A group headed by Oppenheimer and Co. and Brandeis and Son, and including the Stultz Co., has concluded an agreement for purchase of the majority of Lion Shoe Corp. stock, it was announced today.
Lion Shoe will be merged into its wholly-owned retail subsidiary, the A.B.C. Shoe Corp., with subsequent public issue of securities of the latter company.

Abraham Cohen, associated with the companies in an executive capacity
for more than 20 years, will be elected president and general manager.
Frederick Stultz, president of the Stultz Co., will be made chairman of
the board.
The A.B.C. Shoe Corp. owns a number of factories equipped to manu-
facture 20,000 pairs of shoes daily and operates a chain of 110 stores in
56 cities.

Decisions on these high levels of national and international
finances, which vitally influence Yankee City and its chances of
survival, can be, and are being, made, which totally disregard all
Yankee City's needs and vital interests. It is certain that decisions
charged with ruin or success for the economy of Yankee City and the
stability of the lives of its people are made by men at the policy level
of such international financial houses who do not so much as know
the name of Yankee City and who, beyond all doubt, do not care
what happens to the town or its people.

The men of yesterday are dead; but their "souls go marching on"
in the memories of the living, and Mr. Choate, Mr. Weatherby, and
Mr. Pierce are collective symbols of that lost age when the prestige
and power of local financiers and local producers "took care of our
own people." Admittedly, these men did it for a high price, but at
least the workers and ordinary town people were more highly rewarded
by Mr. Choate than by the banking houses of New York and London.
Today even the name of Yankee City is not known to those whose
financial power often controls decisions of the utmost importance
for the town. It is not difficult to understand why the symbols of
Mr. Choate, Mr. Weatherby, and Mr. Pierce collectively represented
small city finance and its lost rewards and satisfactions, as well as the
one-time security of local ownership of the factories. Given the significance of the symbols, it is obvious why they became powerful
allies of the strikers and helped force management into submission.

From this analysis, several important propositions can be offered
which contribute to our understanding of why the strike happened
and why it took the course it did. The vertical extension of the
corporate structure of the shoe manufacturing enterprises had pushed
the top of the hierarchy into the great metropolises and, in so doing,
had brought in "outsiders" who were "foreigners" in culture and

lacking in understanding, feeling, and prestige for the local workers and for the town itself.

This extension of the industrial hierarchy reduced the local men to inferior positions in the hierarchy where they were incapable of making decisions and could not initiate actions which would give them the power of leadership for the workers and for the rest of the town. Reducing the local managers to inferior statuses in the factory contributed to their lower social-class ranking in the community and thereby greatly reduced their strength as leaders and men who could form community opinion in times of crisis when the position of management was threatened. They could no longer lead the workers or the community. Because of the inferior position of the managers, those men in the community who would have once been their natural allies and who enjoyed top social-class position were now above them and shared none of their interests, were hostile to them and friendly to the workers. The vertical extension of the corporate structure of the shoe business introduced owners into the community who had only economic memberships, whereas in the previous period of local control an owner had power and leadership in all of the important institutions.

The longing for the idealized past when men had self-respect and security was symbolized in the three dead owners; and these symbols materially aided the workers in defeating management since the workers and management felt that the present men could not match the "gods" of the past. The workers and managers in the shoe industry had lost their sense of worth and mutual loyalty. No longer were they men who had a common way of life in which each did what he had to do and, in so doing, worked for himself and for the well-being of all.

Local Union Leadership[1]

BY ELI CHINOY

As UNIONS have anchored themselves solidly in the American scene, labor leadership has apparently become a new avenue of social mobility.[2] Unions have given men and women who otherwise would have been condemned to a narrow range of opportunity a chance to do more challenging work, to secure a higher income, and to achieve social power. As the union's existence has been recognized by industry, the pressure has been removed from it and the status of its leaders has changed. Instead of being an outcast from respectable society and a threat to the established order, the labor leader is increasingly a sought-after person in civic life, although it would be easy to overestimate the degree of acceptance among the public at large.

Although in the eyes of the public, labor leadership is such men as Walter Reuther, John L. Lewis, and Harry Bridges, a large share of the effective work of directing union activities remains in the hands of local leadership. Overall policy may be set by the national executive board, and a single figure such as Lewis may dominate a union's program, but the day-to-day job of marshaling workers' energies into coöperative action, of guiding further local organization and setting local policy, and of representing labor in the community rests with the local officers, the shop committee, and in part even with the shop

[1] The data for this previously unpublished paper were secured on a Social Science Research Council Pre-doctoral Field Fellowship in 1946-1947.

[2] "Another important contribution of the labor movement . . . is the provision of a new ladder by which the average boy or girl can rise to a position of influence. . . . Some twenty thousand men and women have risen to full time positions in leading their fellow workers." Goodwin Watson, "Labor Unions and Morale," in *Civilian Morale*, Second Yearbook of the Society for the Psychological Study of Social Issues, 1942, p. 379.

stewards. Labor representatives are to be found on school boards, as officers of the local community chest, and in various other public and semipublic bodies. It has even become a problem in some communities to find enough men who are both willing to serve and capable enough to represent effectively the interests and the viewpoint of organized labor.

These lower echelons are also of considerable importance as a major source of future national union leadership. On the basis of a statistical analysis of labor leaders, C. Wright Mills concluded that: "The great majority of the labor leaders began their union career on the local level, as shop stewards and then local officers, or simply as elected local officers."[3] Though there is an increasing demand for men with special knowledge and skill, the great bulk of leadership will probably continue to come up from the ranks.

The kind of policies that can be enunciated and carried through by a national union depends in large measure on what men hold local offices and what kind of leadership they provide. In spite of the apparent new status of labor leadership, a major problem for the top union executives is the development of a competent group of local officials. The fact that office in the union can be a new avenue for achieving "success" means that there is a constant problem of reconciling private interests and group purposes. These problems may be illuminated by an analysis of the characteristics of local union office and local leaders. What features of union office deter men from assuming positions of leadership and responsibility? What features attract them? How do men achieve positions of leadership? What motivations do they have? How do they view themselves as leaders?

The findings that are presented here are based upon a year's close observation of leadership in five locals of the United Automobile Workers-CIO in a middle-sized Midwestern city. The locals ranged in size from several hundred to several thousand. We are including as leaders all elected officials: local union officers, members of bargaining committees, and department committeemen and stewards, as well as the few international representatives appointed to service the city's locals. The latter were officially appointed through the international, but they were all graduates of locals in the city, had formerly held local office, and were to some extent selected by the dominant political group in their particular shop.

[3] C. W. Mills, *The New Men of Power* (New York, 1948), p. 97.

OBSTACLES TO LEADERSHIP RECRUITMENT

Although most of the rank-and-file members of the union are intensely loyal to it, only a few of them feel called upon to accept any sort of responsible position. No tradition of personal responsibility for the welfare of the union exists to corral the energies of the members. In addition, a number of major obstacles stand in the way of active pursuit of leadership or even a willing acceptance of duties and responsibilities.

Acceptance of union office involves certain social demands and obligations that in the eyes of many workers make it undesirable and a task to be avoided. Active participation can entail an enormous investment of time, even though it may only be necessary because too few members volunteer their services and a relative handful must carry the burden. Outside interests such as painting one's house, playing with one's children, digging in one's garden, or merely "having a good time" must be set aside or neglected in favor of attending meetings or doing other tasks. The union often becomes a man's second wife, and the first one may object strongly to bigamy. Alvin Gouldner has shown how family demands may conflict with the demands of union office, even among leaders who are dedicated to their cause and whose wives are in sympathy with their husband's ideals.[4] In the occasional case, this family disagreement may even be part of a situation which leads to divorce. (In these occasional cases, it is difficult to ascertain whether the husband's activities helped produce the family conflict, or whether family troubles provided one reason for the husband's pursuit of activities outside the home.)

Myrdal has pointed out the passivity that seems to characterize the working classes in America and produces what union leaders call the "let George do it" attitude.[5] In the early days of organization of the UAW, however, a high degree of active participation and assumption of responsibility occurred, and a crisis situation still arouses a strong response from the membership. The emphasis of the total culture

[4] A. W. Gouldner, "The Attitudes of 'Progressive' Trade Union Leaders," *American Journal of Sociology*, 52:5:389 (March, 1947).

[5] "The observer is struck by the importance played by salaried 'organizers' and the relative unimportance of, or often the lack of, a spontaneous drive from the workers themselves." Gunnar Myrdal, *An American Dilemma* (New York, 1944), p. 713.

upon the personal and private, rather than upon the social, means that only unusual circumstances can drive many men into accepting responsibility and assuming leadership. In a crisis situation in one local, an obvious spokesman for an aggrieved group of members exclaimed: "I wouldn't be down here if things were running smoothly. I don't have to spend an evening here if things are going all right. I've never been down here before, but something has to be done." As the permanent crisis that attended the union's early struggles ceased, many workers have withdrawn from active participation in order to pursue their own personal interests. One ex-official commented: "I used to be active, but not lately so much. When we first got started I held a couple of offices. They wanted me to run for committeeman this year too, but I turned it down. I've got too much work to do on my house."

Collective bargaining and union politics, even on the lowest shop level, may also demand personality traits which will keep otherwise capable workers from accepting any position. The kind of personalities which the collective bargaining process selects out may vary from time to time, depending upon specific circumstances. Golden and Ruttenberg have suggested, for example, that a militant anti-union management precipitates aggressive workers into union leadership, and that a coöperative management produces coöperative union leaders.[6] Similarly, a bitter internal battle in the union may drive away the man who prefers to avoid conflict situations.

Although union leadership has given opportunities to many people, it is not yet generally accepted as an alternate avenue of mobility. To the rank-and-file member, a career in the union is hardly more than an inadequate substitute for other preferred goals. If a worker has any ambitions at all, they are primarily the traditional ones of a small business, a farm, or ascent in the management hierarchy in the factory. The following comment by a local official is probably the minority view, even though it may become more frequent in the future: "I know what I'd tell a young fellow to do these days. Somebody wrote in a newspaper column a few years ago that if he was going to start all over again, he'd start in the union and work his way up there. If a fellow went through high school and then took a year

[6] C. Golden and H. J. Ruttenberg, *The Dynamics of Industrial Democracy* (New York, 1942), Chap. 3.

of law, and got some labor history and stuff like that, and then got onto the union payroll, he'd be set." One further reason for the failure of many rank-and-file members to see in the union a new means of rising in the world is their ignorance of what union office entails. The advantages and gratifications to be found in leadership positions are hardly visible until a member begins to participate actively in the union's affairs.

PATTERNS OF ASCENT

Given the liabilities in union office, the obstacles to active participation, and the lack of knowledge about the perquisites of leadership, how do men come to assume positions as leaders? Some men, whom we may call "accidental" leaders, are elected to a union position as a result of pressure from their fellows to take on a job that someone has to fill and that no one wants. An election occasionally finds no candidates for a steward's or a committeeman's job. In this situation, the informal leader or spokesman for a group of workers is socially pressured by his co-workers into accepting the position. The choice usually falls upon someone who has shown an ability to talk and who has some definite ideas which he has expressed and with which his fellow workers are in general agreement. As one of the most experienced leaders in the city put it: "The men are always looking for someone who has a definite opinion and offers leadership." One newcomer to active participation described his election: "They just elected me one day. I didn't want it but the old committeeman dropped out and I used to talk about the union and things with them and they just elected me."

Once elected the "accidental" leader may find considerable intrinsic satisfaction in his job. Participation in collective bargaining can give a worker a sense of increased power and an exciting new range of experience. Once he has been elected as a steward or a department committeeman, his relations with his superiors on the job change. When a grievance is brought to him, he becomes the momentary equal of his supervisor and is no longer his inferior. He can take on the foreman with the knowledge that his arguments cannot be arbitrarily dismissed and that he runs no personal risk by disagreeing with him. It becomes a test of bargaining and negotiating skill rather than a power contest. A number of department committeemen who were candidates for election to the shop committee in one plant explained their desire for the higher position by the fact that they "got a kick out of arguing with the bosses." One four-term local president observed that "There are some men who get into leadership because they like to bargain with the management. It inflates their egos, sort of, and they get a kick out of it, and then they really get interested in it." In addition to the ego-gratification it thus provides, the task of handling grievances and of dealing with supervision opens up a new range of ideas and viewpoints. One shop steward remarked that "I like to argue with the stuffed shirts there. Sometimes I show them they're wrong. Sometimes I'm wrong. We've always got squabbles up there. That's interesting."

Gradually, as the "accidental" leader continues to carry on his duties, new possibilities of union office may unfold before him. The demands of even a steward's job, on the very bottom of the union structure, force him to learn a great deal about the contract with the employer and about the union machinery. Attendance at local meetings and at educational sessions is stressed. He is encouraged to take special courses in public speaking, in collective bargaining, economics, and labor history. His name is placed on the mailing list of the international for literature aimed at thousands like himself. Contact with higher union officers is increased. If he is willing to accept additional responsibility, the newcomer to active leadership is placed on some sort of committee, where there is always room for another willing worker. On occasion he is given time off from his work for union business, and the union pays him the wages he loses. He may be sent as a delegate to one of the numerous conferences the union sponsors, or to one of the union's summer schools for a week's study, all at the local's expense.

LEADERSHIP GRATIFICATIONS

As he acquires new skills in bargaining and parliamentary discussion, and greater organizational savoir-faire, the growing leader begins to see higher union posts as legitimate objectives for himself. Each upward step entails new responsibilities and new opportunities to learn, and widens his perception of the satisfactions and rewards to be secured in union office. He can see that the shop chairman and the local president are on occasion the equals of top management. In the bargaining situation the $1.55-an-hour shop chairman can talk on a par with the $10,000-a-year executive. With the knowledge and skills he has acquired, the aspiring leader may feel that he too could handle such situations as well as the incumbent officer, or even better. The rewards of higher status and prestige which also follow from top union office are more difficult to ascertain, though one may be fairly sure that they exist as important elements in the unionist's appraisal of the advantages inherent in high office.

Active participation and union office also involve the worker in a round of social activities and a network of social relationships which may in themselves be intrinsically rewarding. In an increasingly impersonal urban society the union often comes to serve as an institutional center where members can find satisfying social relationships. This is particularly so in the case of those men who hold office. Their duties bring them together regularly with a number of other people with whom more or less intimate interpersonal relationships develop. The extreme illustration of such circumstances is found in the socially isolated individual for whom the union becomes the focus for his social existence. "I wouldn't know what to do with myself if there wasn't the union," said one single man in his late thirties. "I don't like to hang around beer parlors or anything like that, and so I keep busy in the union during the week—except for Thursday, when I like to go to the wrestling."

These social and psychological gratifications are the things that keep many officeholders in their posts without any thought of personal economic advantage. To these men, who do the "Jimmy Higgins" work, the thankless duties without which the union cannot function adequately, the union becomes more than an institutional device for securing protection in the shop and for bettering their economic circumstances. It is a place where they can find a kind of personal and social experience it would be difficult to secure any place else. There are, of course, men who hold office for a year or two, and find these and other rewards inadequate to balance the things they may have had to give up. Which factors tip the scales toward withdrawal from active leadership or toward continued participation will shift from case to case. To spell them out goes beyond the confines of this analysis.

In addition to the perhaps intangible personal gratifications provided by office in the union, there are a number of more concrete advantages. If the local union is large enough, the president may be relieved of his perhaps unpleasant job in the shop. He receives a leave of absence for his term of office without any loss of seniority. His salary, paid by the union, is at least equal to his factory wage and is usually more; he is provided with an expense account. He need not punch a time clock and may escape the necessity to change shifts every few weeks, though he may actually put in far longer hours than he would in the shop. He wears a shirt and tie and business suit, instead of overalls and a blue denim shirt.

The practical advantages for stewards and committeemen are not as great as those secured by the full-time official, but they are still substantial. When one local executive was asked why men ran for election as stewards and committeemen, he answered:

They get more money; in fact they make more money than the president. [This is probably untrue.] Whenever there is any overtime they get that, because if any one works, the committeeman has to be there. They are the last ones fired, if there is a layoff, and the first ones called back. And the top [shop] committee doesn't even work. The chairman of the top committee is supposed to have seven hours a day for bargaining; the rest of the members five hours. But you can't use a man for one hour or three hours in lots of jobs in the shop; so it means that they don't work at all, lots of times, and the foreman just assumes that he has to get along without the top committeeman doing any work—unless the company decides to tie them up for a while and keep them at work as much as they can.

This statement describes only one shop, but many of its particulars apply rather widely. The chairman of the shop committee may not avoid work completely, but he does escape it for those hours when he is freed from his job to carry on his duties in the bargaining process. Top seniority for elected bargaining representatives is frequently written into union contracts in order to protect them from possible temporary layoff during their term of office because of low seniority. In this way the union maintains the stability of its leadership and avoids midyear elections. The presence of a steward or committeeman when any one works overtime is provided in some contracts as a guarantee that a worker will have recourse to union protection at all times.

"AMBITIOUS" AND "IDEOLOGICAL" LEADERS

Unlike those who do not see the advantages of union office until they are pushed into it, there are those whom we may call the "ambitious" leaders. They see clearly the advantages to be had by acquiring a position in the union, and they view it as a means for satisfying ambitions that had been frustrated or were out of reach. The middle-class person who was forced into the shop by economic necessity, the working-class person who was never able to afford the education he wanted, or who was never able to save the capital needed to buy a farm or to start a business of his own, may see in union work an outlet for his abilities and an escape from a blind-alley job. One official explicitly described his entry into union affairs as an alternative to an economically inadequate teaching career. "I was a school teacher for a while, and I couldn't make enough money at it, so I went into the shop. When the CIO got started I asked somebody how I could get a job with them and he told me I had to start in the local union. So I got active in the local, held a couple of offices, and finally got on the payroll."

Accident and ambition may work together to start a man on his way in the union. One of the few stewards who explicitly admitted that he had ambitions for a paid union post had graduated from college and had been a bank clerk until the depression cost him his job and forced him into an automobile plant. During the war he had been frozen to his job; after the war he felt that his family obligations and the security he had acquired through his seniority made it unwise for him to take any chances and strike out on his own in a new direction. He had been talked into accepting a steward's post by his co-workers and after some experience in it had finally come to look at the union as a possible source of a better kind of work for himself.

At the opposite pole from the "ambitious" leaders are those for whom the possible advantages of union office are largely irrelevant. These, whom we may call "ideological" leaders, embark upon active union work and accept responsibility on the basis of a strongly held set of social and economic beliefs. To them the union is an instrument for achieving broad social and economic purposes. They may be socialists or communists, with an eye to reforming the entire society, or they may merely have strong personal feelings about the treatment they feel workingmen should have on the job.

These "ideological" leaders come from various backgrounds. A strain of socialist thought and native radicalism in Midwestern America has produced some of the active leaders. One candidate for a local presidency had come to the auto industry after years of participation in the United Mine Workers in Illinois. Here and there one can pick out a man who has come from a family with a strong socialist and trade union tradition. On the national level the Reuther brothers probably provide the outstanding example of this background, but similar cases are frequent. An executive in a large local explained that socialist beliefs acquired from his father had directed him into union work. He had begun his career by actively helping to organize the large plant where he worked on the assembly line. Fortified by his beliefs, he had fought the strong company opposition to the union and had risked the dangers to which the early leaders were exposed.

A socially oriented Christianity brought a number of Christian Socialists and lay preachers from working-class churches into union leadership. The Christian ideal of social justice provided a religious justification for union work. Although some of the lay preachers initially found the Bible and the union to be incompatible, once they were converted to the union cause their religious positions facilitated their rise to union leadership.

Although no large group of foreign-born radicals was found in the city's predominantly native-born population (92.3 percent native-born white in 1940), a dash of foreign radical flavoring was present in a few class-conscious British workers. For example, organization of the skilled trades in one of the city's larger plants was accomplished primarily under the guidance of an English socialist toolmaker. A similar class-conscious radicalism was produced in a few men by the impact of the depression. Seeking for an explanation for poverty and their inability to secure steady work, these men had found an answer in an aggressive trade unionism, which was occasionally coupled with a radical political ideology.

As the "ideological" leader becomes part of the union hierarchy, however, and secures the gratifications and rewards it provides, his orientation toward his position may change. Michels and others[7] have

---

[7] See R. Michels, *Political Parties* (Hearst's International Library, 1913); S. Kopald, *Rebellion in Labor Unions* (New York, 1924), Chap. 1.

traced out in detail the process by which the security of the leader's position is eventually equated with the best means of achieving the union's goals, and the personal ends of the leader come to supplant those of the organization. Ideology is replaced by self-interest where the two conflict, though any decisions that are made are justified in terms of organizational necessity. Although the question of the inevitability of this process, labeled the "iron law of oligarchy" by Michels, remains an open one, the fact that it can and does occur must be taken into account in any analysis of union leadership.

In spite of the obvious importance of personal rewards as a factor in union leadership, they are the "unmentionables" among those in office. This soft-pedaling of personal ambition and advantage is part of a set of ideas about leadership that seems to be widely, almost universally, held by local union officials in the city. Labor leadership is viewed by them as a selfless calling which demands a strong sense of responsibility to those whom they represent, and an awareness of the leader's importance in guiding the thinking and behavior of the rank and file.

LEADERSHIP ATTITUDES TOWARD THEIR ROLE

Gouldner has found that the idea of a selfless calling, the deprecation of personal advantage, and a sense of responsibility are part of a constellation of attitudes characteristic of the "progressive" trade union leader.[8] In these UAW locals all leaders, "ambitious," "ideological," and "accidental," subscribed, at least outwardly, to these tenets. There appears to be a dynamic tradition of leadership in the UAW to which all men are expected to adhere. As they move up in the hierarchy, growing leaders must give verbal allegiance to this tradition and their behavior must at least appear to conform to it. Undoubtedly it becomes a significant directing force for many men in determining their behavior in relations to their followers.

The selflessness of their calling is evidenced in the reasons leaders give for embarking upon active union work. According to one, whom we could classify as "ambitious": "I'm in this because I want to do a job for the union and I think I'm qualified to do it." One "ideological" leader asserted that he had become active because: "I hate to see a fellow get kicked around and not get what's coming to him."

[8] Gouldner, op. cit.

And an "accidental" leader started because: "I like to see a fellow get what's coming to him, 'specially from the management." However these men may have actually begun their union careers, once they have achieved positions of responsibility they are caught up in the tradition of selflessness.

Leadership consequently assumes an almost sacred quality, and anyone who profanes his role by evidencing personal ambition is an object of strong disapproval. The worst that can be said of a union leader is that he is an "opportunist," or that he is "ambitious." This was clearly illustrated in the behavior of the delegates from the city's locals to the 1947 UAW convention. The international representatives in the city had backed the losing slate in the election and were obviously going to lose their staff positions. Their friends felt that as good union men they would return to their regular factory jobs and continue to be active in union affairs. Their opponents uniformly thought that they would never return to their factory jobs because they were only "out for themselves," and with their union experience they could probably find better positions. (Four of these international representatives are back in the shop and active in the local unions. The fifth quit shortly after returning and is now on a farm bought during the war.)

The sense of responsibility and the awareness of their role as leaders appears in the constant discussion of union problems among local officers. Their followers are constantly referred to as "our people." "We have responsibilities to our people," they say. The need for a solidified support from the union membership, in dealing with management, forces leaders to try constantly to keep the rank and file alert to current problems and issues. "We've got to get our people to see what's going on; they have to be told what management is trying to do," said the chairman of a shop committee to a meeting of shop stewards.

Although the tradition of leadership as a selfless calling developed in a period of bitter struggles to organize the union, it continues to have a real meaning in present circumstances. Personal dangers have been eliminated, but the demands on time and effort, as we have already pointed out, are strenuous enough to prevent the individual from pursuing any private interests. This "sacrifice," as many label the inability to satisfy personal interests, is evidence of the devotion to a cause greater than oneself. The political nature of union office keeps the leader responsive and responsible to his constituents. Thus the normal circumstances in which the union official acts continue to give concrete significance to the ideas of selflessness, responsibility, and leadership.

These facts, the attractions and liabilities of union office, the kind of men who become leaders, the paths upward in the union, the status of leadership, and the ideas that surround it, are in part known to the more perceptive union executives in the higher levels of the organization and enter into their calculations of program and tactics.

Two major obstacles stand in the way of developing new leadership from interested rank-and-file members: their outside interests and the objections of their wives. Efforts are being made to deal with both of them. Through such varied activities as athletics, movies, parties, and outings, an attempt is made to bind members more closely to the union, to provide them with an opportunity to satisfy their interests directly through the organization and at the same time to bring the rest of the family closer to it. When the whole family becomes involved in such activities, it is easier for the member to participate and to accept office and responsibility. The development of women's auxiliaries with independent activities is designed to catch the interest of the wives directly. These ventures may have some success, but there are difficulties in their way which have yet to be overcome: the problem of distance from the union center, and the competing demands and attractions of kin, personal friends, and other organizations.

Perhaps the major staff problem of top leadership is to keep the union hierarchy from becoming a nesting place for the ambitious and opportunistic, whose major concern is with personal advancement rather than with the welfare of the union. Since all international staff members except the regional directors are appointive, the motivations that lead men into union work are to some extent recognized and taken into account by top officers. The men responsible for the appointment of the five international representatives in the city commented:

Only certain kinds of guys go into union leadership. There's the fellow with a radical background. His father or uncle or somebody was in the old labor movement. Sometimes that's good and sometimes that's bad. It depends on how smart and flexible the guy is. Then there's the guy like Al. Mentally he would have liked to be a big shot and never could. The union offered him an opportunity to express himself. The union took up his time and gave him a chance to become important. Then there are a lot of green guys who look to the union to improve their lot. They get into it and they go in deeper and deeper, learning more and more about it. Like Bill. He's smart, and the crusader type.

The effect of active participation upon a man's plans for himself is also recognized. One local officer, commenting on his colleagues in the union and on himself, went so far as to remark: "I think that everybody who gets active thinks that some day he might get a union job. Of all the people on the top committee, there's only one who probably doesn't think of it. I know I myself have thought of it. I've thought I might try to make a career out of working for the union. I could possibly get a job and then if I had the stuff I could probably stay. They won't admit it, most of them, but they would like to be on the union payroll." Even though men may thus come to think of the union as a possible career, the fiction of "pure" motives must be maintained, as the last sentence above suggests.

An evaluation of a man's motives may be a significant factor in the election of staff, but ability and political weight and complexion are of major importance, and in some situations one or the other may have overriding weight. Appointive staff members find political skills useful aids to advancement, and candidates for elective office must obviously have vote-catching talents. Increasing demands for definite knowledge and skills in union officials do weed out some aspiring leaders as they try to move upwards, even when they have acceptable motives and a wide range of political abilities. The astute "politician" may achieve office beyond the limits of his abilities, but a failure to serve the membership adequately leads to political defeat.

PRIVATE AMBITIONS VS. GROUP PURPOSES

The rewards, economic, social, and psychic, of union office make even the most devoted official unwilling to give it up. Once on the union payroll, the official looks at a return to the shop as a most undesirable possibility. He must give up highly valued social relationships on the job, interesting activity, and considerable social prestige and power when he returns to the factory. In this situation staff members may easily shift their energies from union duties to efforts to secure their own positions, thus creating a major problem for the union. If he does lose his position, the ex-staff member can usually manage to assume leadership within his local union, if he desires, because of the experience and knowledge he has acquired while on the union payroll. If this were to occur to any appreciable extent, it would obviously strengthen the hand of the union in dealing with local managements. The four former international representatives who returned to their factory jobs in the city were quickly elected to office in their locals. (A major political error was made prior to the 1947 UAW convention by one regional director. Just before local elections were held he fired several members of his staff who were on the other side of the union's political fence. They immediately returned to their locals, were elected to local office, and successfully spearheaded the political campaign to unseat the regional director.)

The turnover of officers and staff members also creates the problem of keeping ex-officials, who are frequently bitter and resentful, as active and valuable members of the union. This problem occurs more frequently on the local level, where annual elections are held, than on the international level, where staff members are appointed for an indefinite tenure. If the pattern of other unions is repeated in the UAW this difficulty may diminish in the future, only to be replaced by new problems. The history of organized labor in the United States has usually seen a solidification of leadership after the initial thrust of organization has thrown new figures to the top. Whether or not this will be the case with the UAW remains to be seen. It may be that the union provided opportunities for those men who were blocked by the collapse of the 1930's, and that there will be little room at the top for a fairly long time to come. This would create pressure and dissatisfaction from below among ambitious local leaders. An increase in the number of positions on the international staff as the union increases its functions, and new full-time positions created by local unions as they expand their activities, may stave off this closing down of opportunities in the organization.

Several factors would appear to be on the side of the top union executive as he endeavors to create an efficient and loyal staff. The path of the rising leader includes a number of places where the

union's educational apparatus has an excellent opportunity to influence him. (According to the UAW constitution, two cents of each
member's monthly dues go to the International Educational Fund,
and two and one-half cents a month go to the local union's Educational and Recreational Fund. With about 1,000,000 members, this
provides a sizable fund for educational purposes.) Because the growing union leader has frequently been thrown into office by accident
and knows relatively little about union organization, economics, and
politics, the union's educational program has almost virgin soil in
which to operate. The need for knowledge and skill in union office
also forces the "ambitious" leader to take courses and to attend
summer schools. Not only can an educational program provide
knowledge and skills, it can also build understanding and create
loyalties. If the international leadership is a progressive one, the
lower levels can easily be directed toward a broad conception of the
role of organized labor instead of a limited bread-and-butter unionism.

The fact that the advantages of union office and the possibilities
of advancement may attract the ambitious worker is also a potential
source of strength. Myrdal has pointed out the extent to which the
working class has lost its leadership as the more capable men rose in
the economic scale.[9] As union leadership achieves status as a respectable avenue of mobility, these capable men may well remain within
their class and provide effective leadership for it. Myrdal expected
a growing rigidity of class lines to keep capable workers in their own
class, but the evidence for the narrowing range of opportunity for
workers is by no means conclusive. Many capable working men who
have risen in the union may yet have to choose between remaining as
active union leaders and moving up into the lower rungs of management as foremen.

The existence of a tradition of leadership which stresses devotion
to the union and imposes responsibilities is also of considerable value
in maintaining a loyal staff, concerned primarily with problems of
union welfare. In the course of his work the union official builds up
social ties with other active unionists, to whom he consequently looks

---

[9] ". . . social mobility drained the masses in every generation of most of their
organizational catalysts. Few potential 'leaders' remained in the lower classes to
stimulate their loyalty and to organize their resistance against pressure." Myrdal,
op. cit., p. 714.

for social approval. Since their approval is largely granted on the basis of the tradition which stresses devotion to the union, the leader is steered away from actions which would brand him as a bad unionist. Although this may produce an in-group feeling among the leaders, vis-à-vis the rank and file, it may also produce a strong sense of loyalty to the interests of the union.

As in any mass organization which requires a staff to organize and carry out its program, the union faces the problem of gearing private ambitions to group purposes. In its days of bitter struggles it demanded devotion and sacrifice from its leaders. Now that it has achieved a certain maturity it still needs the devotion and loyalty, but it must create and organize them. It cannot assume that they are automatically present among those who acquire positions of leadership. Nor can the union overlook the fact that it can now satisfy private interests and will attract and hold men because of it. Upon its ability to create and corral the devoted energies of its leadership, and to harness the ambitions of capable men to the union's machinery, rests in good measure its future well being.

Grass-Roots Labor Leader[1]

BY JOHN W. ALEXANDER AND MORROE BERGER

TOM COBURN, a semiskilled worker in the Acme Brass Mill in a New England town of five thousand people, was in the vice-president's office negotiating for a wage increase for the three hundred production workers he represents as head of the Acme local of the International Union of Mine, Mill and Smelters Workers. Tom remarked that prices had gone up so high that a man's weekly pay envelope didn't contain enough to support his family decently any more. The vice-president turned to Tom and said, slowly:

"Well now, Tom, you're not doing so badly. You just paid off the mortgage on the house a couple of months back."

This is how trade unionism sometimes looks at the grass-roots level: collective bargaining takes on a personal tone since management can obtain through local connections information that would be irrelevant in bargaining on the regional or national level. But what of the union leader's relation to his members? How does this situation look at the grass-roots level? What does it mean to be the head of the union local at no salary plus headaches? How does a grass-roots labor leader, working in the plant alongside the men he represents, exercise and maintain his leadership?

To get one set of answers to these questions we studied the career of Tom Coburn at first hand. We found that Tom's story could illuminate still another set of questions because his parent union, the International Union of Mine, Mill and Smelter Workers, is said to be led by Communists and fellow travelers—two years ago locals began to secede on this very issue—and Tom is in full sympathy with

[1] This is a previously unpublished paper.

174

this leadership. So we must ask now, how does the small-town local of such an international union reflect the program and policies of the bigwigs at national headquarters? Is the ideology of the leaders transmitted to the working men in small towns that hear but a faint rumble of the leftist storms and squalls in the great urban centers of radicalism such as New York, Chicago, Detroit and San Francisco. What role does the leader of the grass-roots local play as the link between the rank and file and the union hierarchy, especially where the latter is selling ideology along with traditional business unionism?

Tom is at the point where the pressure applied from above by the ideological aims of the union hierarchy meets the pressure applied from below by the bread-and-butter aims of the Acme Brass Mill workers. We found that Tom tries to get the ideological message down to his rank and file, but that what he can communicate to them is primarily a general feeling of dissatisfaction with events rather than a specific course of political action. Tom talks radicalism, but his style of life and his goals are traditionally middle-class. The middle-class motif in this double pattern of belief and behavior actually reinforces rather than weakens his apparent radicalism: it enables him, as we shall see in a moment, to express his radicalism freely and without regard to the organizational discipline of the Communist party, the leadership of the Mine, Mill and Smelter Workers, or the Progressive party, on whose ticket Tom ran for Congress last fall.

CAREER PATTERN

Tom, now forty-five years old, was born in a rural New England community. His forebears came from Sheffield, England, where they were cutters and grinders of knives. Tom's father, following the knife shops around New England, never managed to raise himself and his family of eight children out of the poverty into which all of them had been born. At the age of forty Tom's father died of illness brought on by the constant inbreathing of metal particles produced in the grinding process, and by the cramped position he had to assume at the workbench.

Even before his father's death Tom had already quit school after completing the sixth grade and had started to work in local shops. His mother took in washing to help support the eight Coburns now left fatherless. His aims unfocused, Tom took and left a series of factory jobs that required little or no skill. Then in 1925, at the age of twenty-two, he started a new career pattern by joining a construction gang building a tunnel under a nearby lake for the water line to a large city in the area. At first Tom fired the boilers in the engine room; later he ran the engines.

This job impressed Tom a great deal. In the first place, it was his first sustained contact with Negroes, who lived in a Jim Crow camp on the construction site. With no set attitude toward Negroes as yet, Tom was able to find them interesting friends and "real sports." Secondly, his ideas about workers and bosses crystallized. This was Tom's first experience in a large-scale enterprise where his relationship to the employer was impersonal. He says that it was on this job that he learned how the bosses "pit worker against worker, black against white." Finally, he liked the rough camaraderie he found among the workers, and his sense of loyalty to them was sharpened. There were other ways in which this job was decisive for Tom. At twenty-three he married Martha Wilson, a local girl who had just quit her job in a clock factory. Tom bought a farm and a home, hoping eventually to make a living at full-time farming. But the depression of the 1930's shattered his hopes, and Tom had to keep working for other men. His farm failed, he had mortgage payments to meet, and he now had two young sons to support. In 1937 he found it necessary to return to factory work and took a night-shift job at the Acme Brass Mill about ten miles from his home. This is the plant in which he still works and where he is president of the union. On the job he now has, Tom draws twenty-foot unfinished brass rods through a machine that readies them for cutting by finishing them and making them longer and narrower.

RISE TO LEADERSHIP

Tom's rise to leadership, unlike that of many other union heads, was not the result of a long hard inter-union struggle. Tom got his card in 1941, about a year after the local was organized. At this time it suffered from a lack of willing and capable leadership, perhaps because there were no other unions in town to help out, and because many of the workers in the plant were first- and second-generation Poles who weren't confident of their ability to meet with the more socially polished representatives of management.[2] One day a couple of the active union men asked Tom if he would take over the leadership in order to help the union obtain a majority in the imminent NLRB election. They felt that Tom could deal more confidently with the company officials. He was pleasant to talk to, was liked by the men in the plant, and was certainly loyal to "the boys." But Tom wasn't immediately convinced that he ought to accept the offer. He had his house to take care of, and some farm land around it that he was working in his spare time. Besides, he was pretty busy in the plant, too, selling milk to the workers during lunch hours to pick up extra money. Finally, becoming the union head would in a way deeply commit him to factory work, and he didn't like that. His friends won out, though, and Tom became chairman of the organizing committee. When the union won the NLRB election in 1942 the workers made Tom president.

Tom's personality, of course, had much to do with his rise to leadership. He is easy-going, patient, willing to listen, not given to outbursts of temper. Though he is only a little above average in height, everything else about him is big—his hands, his body, his face and head; yet he is good-looking in a rough, hardy way. Tom often says of himself: "I'm an easy son-of-a-bitch to get along with— you know, hiya boy and a slap on the back." Though he is what most people would call a modest man, Tom likes to impress listeners with the delicacy of his position as representative of the workers both to management and the international union. "You know," he is sure to remark when he talks about his union work, "you got to be careful—you got 'em shoving and pressing from all sides and you got to watch your step."

Though he insists that as a leader he merely does what the union members instruct him to do, Tom actually leads by deliberate attempts to bring the men around to his point of view on political as well as local union matters. His technique is to ask apparently innocent questions in a discussion, and to pursue a line directly to the

[2] Though they might not have made good negotiators, the Poles, Tom told us, made pretty good union members. They sent their children to school as a way of raising their status, and the educated sons and daughters would point out the value of unionism to their fathers and older brothers.

outcome he seeks. In playing this game Tom puts himself on the
same intellectual level as the workers; he does not pose as one who
is better-informed than they, though he truly is. Tom is essentially
a moderate and careful leader, yet he combines this moderation with
a verbal toughness and militancy that are appropriate to the frequently profane, bantering manner of the men he works with. Since
he has a genuine sympathy for the working class, he is willing to work
hard at being a union man. The Acme workers know and appreciate
Tom's concern for their welfare. He is so popular with them that
there is no opposition to him at all; only once since 1942 has there
been a candidate to oppose him for the presidency, and that con-
testant withdrew before the election.

Acme officials, too, respect Tom's ability. David Peters, the retired
superintendent of the plant with whom Tom had much contact, says
that he is probably the best man to defend the Acme workers' interests. Peters, a cautious Scotsman who plays his hand close to his chest,
told us: "Tom's a good man for the workers—he reads up on the
contract and all that." Yet Peters is not uncritical of Tom. When
we asked if he thought Tom was pretty intelligent, he said, "Yes, I
suppose so. But he wasn't deep. He did his thinking afterwards."
Tom's ex-boss gave us the impression that he believed Tom has
ambitious motives for his union activity. We asked what Peters
thought Tom was looking for, and the old man paused, then raised
his eyebrows. "Power and money," he said, looking straight at us.[3]

THE "MIDDLE-CLASS" PROLETARIAN

Born into a working-class family, Tom's aspirations and the outward
aspects of his style of life, we have said, are essentially middle-class.
Yet, unlike many other union heads whose outlook is much the same,
Tom's middle-class thinking is not the result of any rise in income

[3] Peters himself is an interesting example of the older type of plant supervisor.
He is reputed in town to have been the one man who made the Acme plant a
paying enterprise by his enormous knowledge of machines. He struck us as somewhat paternalistic toward the workers and resentful toward the present Acme
management. We caught a hint of Peters' feeling that men like himself were being
edged out these days by the professional managerial class. We asked him if he
considered Tom smart enough to be a foreman or supervisor. When he answered,
"Not in this generation," there was the clear implication that supervisors now come
in at the top level, and neither the David Peters nor the Tom Coburns have the
future they once had.

or any change in living patterns owing to his position as a union leader. He still works in the plant, where he earns one dollar and thirty-nine cents an hour. All he gets from the union is twenty-five dollars every three months for expenses. Tom's middle-class qualities, then, developed in him even before he joined the union. They not only remained with him, but now they actually condition the nature of his leadership by reinforcing his strong working-class sympathies and by preparing him for his role as the transmitter of the union hierarchy's ideology to his rank and file. This is the influence of the double pattern which we have already mentioned. Before we can show its precise effects, however, we must analyze its character more closely.

Tom's acute sense of class cleavage, his working-class sympathies and his radicalism are all separate aspects of his verbal and ideological identification with the workers. Although his father was no radical, the "old gent," as Tom calls him, did impart to his son some notion of what it meant to be one of the underprivileged. Tom's feeling of outrage at the circumstances of his father's death has probably been intensified by his growing conscious leftism, but undoubtedly that sharp event, occurring when he was only fourteen, had a terrific impact upon him. Tom often repeats a remark his mother made to him after she had begun to take in washing. "Tom," she said, "some day there's going to be a war between the rich and the poor." Tom's mother, still alive, seems to have had the realism, resentment and grinding anguish of the poor that is not necessarily translated into political radicalism. Tom can recall no militant class-consciousness in his home, no labor or radical literature, only the spiritless talk of the poor. One of the few bits of workers' lore he remembers is a ditty his father taught him:

> Don't ever let them put your old man on the pan.
> He's worked for you and done the best he can,
> So don't ever let them put your old man on the pan.

There is no cynicism in Tom's sympathy for the working class. He likes its informality, the taunting friendliness of men doing a physically tough job. His working-class feeling is so strong that he tries to avoid making remarks that he thinks are not appropriate for a class-conscious worker. When we first asked him what were his ambitions for the future, he shrugged his shoulders at the implication that he might aspire to something beyond the ken of a worker. "Who knows what's going to happen?" he remarked. "I guess I'll just stay on in the plant." Yet further questioning revealed that Tom has for at least twenty years been actively planning to farm for a living. "I want to get the hell away from the goddamned whistle," he told us. He vigorously denied the possibility that he might rise in the plant, basing his objection not on the ground that his road to higher income and status might come via the union rather than through the business hierarchy, but upon the ground of loyalty to the men he has worked with. "How would it look," he asked, "if I was to go up and take a management job after being with the workers all these years? Fellows'd be asking, 'Say, Tom, who the hell've you been working for all this time?' " Everything about Tom, except his fellow-travelerism, suggests the class-conscious militant American Wobbly—in fact, the old Western Federation of Miners, out of which the present mine, mill union grew, was the moving spirit in the organization of the I.W.W. in 1905.

RADICALIZATION PROCESS

What is it that makes Tom a radical, an appropriate medium for the transmission of the International's political ideas to the workers in the Acme plant? The sources of his radicalism cannot be readily identified. Tom was not brought up in a radical home, nor did he get radical ideas from his reading or from any identifiable person he knew before joining the union. We think his leftism, evoked by his contacts as union leader with management, the Acme workers, and the union hierarchy, comes from his experiences as a worker and from his personality. Tom had to go to work at menial jobs while still a boy. He saw others going to high school and college and into their fathers' or their uncles' businesses, but he had to scratch around on jobs without a future. At the same time he has always had a strong sense of loyalty to those he associates with, seeks their approbation, and tends to look at situations without romantically interpreting them.

Tom is unable to say when it was that this general feeling for the workers became a special brand of political radicalism. In 1924, for example, he voted for Coolidge, in 1928 for Hoover, and for Roosevelt in the next four elections. The depression years apparently had much to do with Tom's leftward drift. He clearly recalls the months he worked at the water reservoir, talking over "bad times" with other workers around the brush fire on winter days. He remembers the flow of job-seekers past his house—beaten men who had lost confidence in themselves. The depression years pushed Tom into factory work, something he had been able to avoid ever since he could choose between jobs. And he now realized that farming for a living was out of the question. The depression was but one step in his development. The next one came with his acceptance of the leadership of the local union. Already class-conscious, as the president of the Acme local Tom came into frequent contact with higher-echelon union men who talked his language and the language of leftism. It was this contact that translated Tom's general sympathy for the working class into the more conscious political radicalism of the fellow traveler.

Despite this ideology, Tom's way of living and his aims are middle-class. Early in his adulthood he attached importance to home ownership. He bought his present home in 1926 and by 1944 he had paid off the mortgage. Though small, it is an attractive house, with a sizable, well-kept lawn, a flower garden, and comfortable lawn furniture. The house furnishings are respectable but worn—Tom says he won't buy new furniture (or an inside privy, for that matter) until a dollar will get him what he put into earning it. Tom calls his property Shelter Farm; not many places in the area have names. When we first went to call on him we stopped at a crossroads filling station and asked the way to Shelter Farm. The attendant thought for a moment, then answered, "Well, I guess that's what he calls the place—it's a mile down this road."

Even today, despite his leadership of the union, Tom is not fully committed to factory labor. To him the factory has always been a place to work only when he couldn't make a living in other ways. Tom's working-class qualities are not urban qualities; they are rural in character, and this gives them a middle-class rather than a proletarian tone. If Tom is a proletarian at all, he is a *rurban* proletarian: he lives on a farm that he owns and works, and is employed in a large factory as a semiskilled laborer. This combination is made possible by the rapid, private, and cheap means of transportation, the automobile. Tom, then, is neatly balanced between two poles: his status as a factory worker and union leader, and as a farm-owner and prospective full-time farm operator.

On most domestic issues Tom is in agreement with either the Democratic or the Progressive party, but his special combination of opinions on these questions, on American foreign policy and on the Soviet Union identify him as a fellow traveler. Yet this is an oversimplification. When all the evidence is considered, it is clear that Tom is an unsophisticated radical who has not had enough contact with leftists to be able to distinguish among the various labels. When we told Tom that he talks like a fellow traveler he answered calmly that he is neither a Communist party member nor a supporter, but that he refuses to be a "red-baiter." To label a man a fellow traveler, Tom feels, is to take part in what he calls "the Red smear." Though he does not accept such socialist principles as government ownership of most of industry, agriculture, and other forms of property, Tom consciously avoids criticizing persons as Communists or fellow travelers. He would not like to see political questions in the United States settled in the violent manner of eastern Europe, he said, yet he offered the common C.P. rationalizations of Soviet foreign policy. When pressed for clear answers, however, Tom said things he usually identifies with "the Red smear." For example, he thought long and hard when we asked him if he considers Russia a free and democratic country. "I don't know," he finally said, "but maybe with this school teacher (Oksana Kasenkina) jumping out of the window, maybe it isn't too pleasant in Russia."

On the conscious ideological level, then, Tom talks like a fellow traveler. In two important respects, nevertheless, he deviates from that pattern. In the first place, because he lacks experience in interleftist affairs, he doesn't have the Communist's and fellow traveler's intense hatred of the anti-Communist left. Second, in his speculation about a successor to the presidency of the Acme local he doesn't apply the criterion of adherence to the C.P. line or to that of the International's leadership, or the Wallace movement. The worker Tom would like to see as the next head of the Acme local, Steve Konski, is a vigorous man in his thirties, a loyal Catholic of Polish descent who unhesitatingly expresses his distrust of the Soviet Union and American Communists. Tom's intense loyalty in his personal relations, and his deep concern for the Acme union and its members, dictate that in local matters he must make his decisions without regard to, and even in violation of, the ideology he himself accepts.

LOYALTY TO THE LOCAL UNION

We are now in a position to see how the double pattern, Tom's combination of radical politics and middle-class aspirations, conditions the way in which he functions as the link between the three hundred union men at Acme and the leadership of the International Union of Mine, Mill and Smelter Workers. This double pattern, first of all, reinforces his loyalty to the local, since he aims to advance his welfare not through the union hierarchy but through his part-time and eventually his full-time farming. As a consequence, he owes neither his present power nor his future to the leadership above him.[4] Tom sincerely believes in the fellow-traveling politics of the union hierarchy, and is therefore a willing carrier of its message to the Acme workers. But this willingness is simply the result of the coincidence of Tom's politics and the hierarchy's. Because Tom's aspirations lie entirely outside the realm of unionism and the factory, he adheres to the International's politics by ideological choice rather than economic necessity. Hence Tom is not so reliable a transmitter of the top leadership's politics as, say, a local union head who is dependent upon the hierarchy's good will for his own power and for his future in the labor movement, or the local union head whose membership includes a powerful Communist faction. Tom's double pattern, then, reinforces his loyalty to his local rather than to his ideological mentors, and makes him an uncontrollable transmitter of the International's political line. This situation can be illustrated by the diagram on page 184.

Although he owes his position in the local to no one at International headquarters, Tom has always stood well with the top leadership. He shares their political faith. He regularly attends the conventions, personally knows and likes many of the International bigwigs, including Reid Robinson, a fellow-traveling ex-president who fell into disfavor because he had tried to borrow money from

---

4 In the early days of his leadership Tom was considerably dependent upon Jim Gallagher, the International representative assigned to the local. Tom learned leadership techniques through Jim, but is now entirely independent of him. In fact, Tom now patronizes Jim, who, because of his pretentiousness, is often the butt of jokes among the Acme workers.

an employer with whom the union was negotiating a new contract. Several years ago Tom showed his loyalty to the International in concrete fashion by resisting a strong movement to take many New England locals out of the Mine, Mill and Smelter Workers Union and into the CIO Marine and Shipbuilding Workers of America. Backed by CIO national and state heads, George Bartlett, a former district official in the mine, mill union, led a secession drive over the

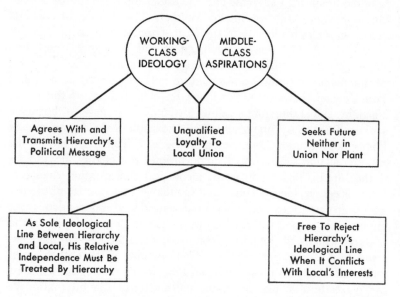

Communist issue that seriously weakened the International's power and prestige. Tom stood by the International, and his stock with the leaders shot up accordingly. He held his predominantly Catholic local in line even though Bartlett had the support of the Church.

Aside from agreeing with the International on specific political issues, Tom agrees with the hierarchy on the general proposition that trade unions must be alert to politics if they are fully to serve the interests of their members. Tom feels that a union should provide the worker not only with leadership in the old "business union" sense but also in broader matters which, in his view, are equally essential for the security of the workers as a group. Yet it is not this broader conception that keeps the Acme workers loyal both to Tom and the

International, but precisely their faith in the leadership's ability to supply the "business" services of unionism, its ability to deal with management in a manner the workers consider satisfactory. Tom, especially, is judged *only* on this ability to settle the bread-and-butter issues satisfactorily. By their ability to perform this utilitarian function for the workers, Tom and the International leaders are able also to serve them what an Englishman once called the pot of message. The political ideology is presented to the Acme workers because Tom wants it presented to them. We have no doubt that he can effectively close the door of the local to the International's ideological salesmen if he wants to; and we have no doubt that if the message interfered with the attainment of the Acme workers' bread-and-butter aims Tom would not hesitate to exclude it.

THE WALLACE CAMPAIGN

In unions that hold democratic elections it is possible to check the membership's opinion of the leadership's handling of the main business of unionism. It is not so easy, however, to check the membership's reaction to the political program of its leaders. Fortunately the election campaign of 1948 provides such a test in the case of Acme workers and Tom Coburn. Tom was an early supporter of Henry Wallace for president, attended the nominating convention of the Progressive party, and ran for Congress on its ticket. Tom's candidacy was a real test of his ability to get across an ideological message to the membership, a message which the International was also pushing on higher levels. How did he fare? Very poorly.

One hundred and twenty-five Acme workers signed Tom's petitions to get him on the ballot. In our bull sessions with them they told us they were voting for Wallace and for Tom. Though in private conversations some workers said they would vote for Truman, not a single one we talked to said he would vote against Tom. But Tom's total vote in the two towns where most Acme workers live was only 74 out of 5140 votes cast for the office he sought. He couldn't even get the votes of all those who had petitioned to get him on the ballot. In his own town he got only 8 out of more than 400. In the entire Congressional district the Republican won with almost 63,000 votes, the Democrat got over 58,000 and Tom mustered only 1191.

In one respect this showing surprised us. We had expected that

Wallace would do poorly, but we expected that Tom would draw many more votes than he did, especially in the towns near the Acme plant. It turned out that Tom could not transmit the ideological message in this case either for himself or for the head of his ticket. Like the pollsters, we were misled by the verbal responses of Tom's union boys. When approached by Tom or a friend of his to sign the petition to get him on the ballot, the Acme workers willingly did so. When we asked them in a group or individually whether they would vote for Tom, they said you're damned right they would. But when they closed the curtain in the voting booth they acted differently. Tom has their loyalty and support in bread-and-butter union business, but he obviously failed to get across his own and the International's politics.

Business unionism is the vessel on which the ideology of the leadership is carried to the rank and file, but the cargo doesn't always get there with the vessel itself. Leadership can communicate a general approach to larger political issues, but its specific program is something else again, as Tom's campaign experience shows. The union hierarchy gets resolutions passed and runs the conventions, but how far do they influence their members on issues that divide the labor movement itself? The evidence in this case study gives one answer: not very deeply. The union looks one way at the top and another way at the grass roots. The International Union of Mine, Mill and Smelter Workers is a Communist-influenced union, but it has an entirely different aspect at the local level where trade unionism is the reality for most workers. Because he has their respect for his ability to face management in their behalf, Tom gets the unanimous support of the Acme workers; but he can't get them to think his way in the political game. He tries to get a political idea to them because he believes in it; this idea happens also to bind the International leadership. It is Tom, not the International, who stands high with the Acme men; hence it is through him that the message must pass. He lets it pass and gets behind it to give it a shove, but it doesn't get as far as he would like. The Acme workers respond to other loyalties in many situations they face, not merely to their loyalty to Tom and the union.

Contexts: Leadership Among Minority Groups

To THOSE alert to the problems involved in the defense and extension of democratic values, the position of minority groups in the United States provides a perpetual challenge—and a promise that there is a long, hard row yet to hoe. Just as some Americans once believed that social classes would wither and disappear, so, too, there are those who believe that the presence of ethnic minorities is merely an ungainly expression of our nation's adolescence. In due time, the proponents of the "melting pot" theory urge, and especially with the maturation of second and third generations, America will settle down into a stable and homogeneous society.

The ultimate status of the Negro people was never settled by the "melting pot" theorists; what their final disposition was to be was far from clear. Today, students of intercultural relations have growing doubts about this prognosis; doubts not only in regard to the ultimate status of the Negro people, but for other ethnic minorities as well. And at present, when students of minority problems dare to raise questions of values, some of them begin to wonder whether this was a good idea in the first place. While this problem cannot be resolved here, it is probable that a new outbreak of mass prejudice and bigotry would engrave American society with enduring ethnic cleavages.

Certainly there can be no doubt that a significant and distinctive aspect of the American social structure consists of the polyglot, many-hued minority groups making us, as few other countries, "a nation of nations." These minority groups have already and can in the future make potent contributions to the expansion of democratic vistas. To the extent that American minorities are forced to suffer discriminations, it is probable that their own vested interests—even if nothing else—will motivate them to play important roles in continuing efforts to implement democratic values.

In this section, problems of leadership relating to four types of minority groups are analyzed. Kurt Lewin's "A Problem of Minority Leadership" and Norman Miller's study of "The Jewish Leaders of Lakeport" analyze certain of the leadership processes among people of the Jewish religion. Oliver C. Cox's unequivocating article deals with "Leadership Among Negroes in the United States," while, once again, we turn to William F. Whyte's Street Corner Society for an analysis of "Leadership in an Italian-American Community." As the final chapter in this section, Arnold W. Green and Elinore Melnick estimate the position of the woman leaders in our culture and attempt to find out "What Has Happened to the Feminist Movement?"

A word of explanation may be necessary concerning this last-mentioned article: Why, it may be asked, have women been characterized as a minority group? The term "minority" is a somewhat deceptive one. Legal rights cannot be the touchstone of the definition of a minority, for, while constitutionally equal, Negroes undergo countless discriminations which make them the minority par excellence. Nor can non-American birth be the key to minority status—witness the plight of our antecedents, the American Indian. Finally, the size of the group has never been a reliable clue to minority status, as the experience of colonial countries indicate. Essentially the problem is one of the distribution of power; above all else, minority groups are those subordinated to others. Both groups, subordinate and dominant, explicitly and implicitly recognize their relative positions and develop attitudes which reflect a conception of their status.

In this sense, then, characterization of women as a "minority group" seems amply justified, for there is no question of the subordination of women in the decisive institutions of contemporary life—political, economic, and familial.

The group processes and patterns of leadership among women, by their similarity with those of other minorities, further justify their inclusion in this section. As Kurt Lewin emphasizes, the situation in which members of minorities find themselves encourages a desire to leave the group. It further disposes minority members to assume characteristics of the dominant group; in a sense, to leave the group symbolically. Thus some Jewish people change their names, some Negroes may strive to "pass," while some women may, consciously or unconsciously, adopt the behavior patterns typical of men.

The American minority group is, in the main, oriented to the norms of the dominant group. It seeks their recognition and acceptance. In this way, pressures internal and external to the minority group may bring about the emergence of a leadership which possesses characteristics acceptable to the dominant group. As we shall mention below, this is sometimes a self-defeating process, for such leadership may quickly become nominal. At any rate, the situation which disposes to the development of different modes of leadership involves the interrelations between groups, and not merely the internal group structure.

Stereotyped images of minority groups obliterate a fact of utmost significance for study of their leadership patterns—the fact of stratification within the minority groups. Lewin claims that those who achieve leadership of the minority group tend to be upper-class people, the more economically advantaged members. Those in minority group leadership are therefore conceived of by Lewin as being at the periphery of their group, and within the orbit of the dominant group's influence.

In this way the minority group leader may be responding to needs other than those of his own group. In fact, it is Oliver Cox's contention that the "conservative" Negro leader is more functional to the needs of the dominant group than to those of his own. The upper-class minority leader is placed in a cross-pressures situation in which conflicting demands may be exerted upon him. Which of his statuses has a prior claim upon his loyalties, time, and energy—class or minority-group status? Very often a decision in favor of the class status is rationalized by a minority member by saying that he is "first of all an American." The tensions between minority-group status and class status are clearly presented by Green and Melnick, whose work indicates the extent to which class interests have brought about cleavages in the feminist movement.

The orientation of "leaders on the periphery" toward the dominant groups apparently has its effects on the range of strategies which minority group leaders propose. Most particularly, the notion of tactical alliances with other minority groups—to say nothing of organic federation—seems to play little part in the political thinking of American minority leaders. Each instead seeks to relate itself, in one-to-one fashion, with the dominant group. This, in turn, reinforces the minority group's disposition to accept as its own the prejudices which the dominant group has toward other minorities. Negroes may therefore become anti-Semitic, while Jewish people may be anti-Negro. In this way cleavages among minority groups flourish, each attempting to make a separate "deal" with the dominant group.

From the point of view of their potential for effective democratic action, the minority group's ability to coördinate its social action, not only with other minorities, but also with other kinds of groups, is a significant consideration. When, however, the initiative for such coördinated action rests with individuals from dominant groups, say, of Protestant, Anglo-Saxon descent, their tendency is to establish liaison with members of the minority group who are most like themselves. These, though, are often people who possess little or no leadership role among the minority group. In consequence no coördination among the groups actually takes place. William Whyte's article develops some of the specific conditions which bring this process to its frustrating conclusion.

There seem to be other factors contributing to the failure of coördinated social action in such situations. These may be detected if the question is raised as to why some individuals, who are actually leaders in their own minority group, lose their positions of leadership there after they begin to work with leaders of dominant groups. Part of the answer seems to reside in the previously mentioned motivation of some minority leaders, their desire to leave their own group and become like the members of the dominant group. In this way they lose or muffle the characteristics of their own group and therefore much of the conditions of leadership. Another factor seems pertinent: this has to do with their *status* in presumably coördinated inter-group efforts. Very often leaders of the minority group will be given positions of only *nominal* power by the dominant group. They will have the symbols, not the reality, of power. The notion of the "token Negro" implies recognition and rejection of this process which Philip Selznick has labeled "formal coöptation." Lacking the substance of power in the inter-group relationship, the formally coöpted minority-leader is unable to use his status in the inter-group situation to repay obligations which he has incurred during his ascent in the minority group. He is, moreover, unable to satisfy his group's expectation that he will in some way substantially remedy its position. For these reasons he tends to lose his leadership of the minority group. Simultaneously he loses much of his function for the dominant group, whether it was seriously concerned about genuinely united inter-group efforts or had merely sought to use him as a "bellwether."

This whole problem seems of utmost importance to those who recognize that the scope of democratic liberties will not be enlarged for minority groups by their own action alone. Unfortunately, however, it has not yet received the intensive study which it deserves.

The Problem of Minority Leadership[1]

BY KURT LEWIN

MEMBERS OF the majority are accustomed to think of a minority as a homogenous group which they can characterize by a stereotype like "the Jew" or "the Negro." It has been shown that this stereotype is created in the growing child by the social atmosphere in which he grows up, and that the degree of prejudice is practically independent of the amount and kind of actual experience which the individual has had with members of the minority group.

Actually, every group, including every economically or otherwise underprivileged group, contains a number of social strata. There exists, however, the following difference between the typical structure of a privileged and an underprivileged group. The forces acting on an individual member of a privileged group are directed toward the central layers of that group. The forces acting on a member of an underprivileged group are directed away from the central area, toward the periphery of the group and, if possible, toward the still higher status of the majority. The member would leave if the barrier set up by the majority did not prevent him. This picture represents the psychological situation of those members of the underprivileged group who have a basically negative balance. It is the structure of a group of people who are fundamentally turned against themselves.

It is clear that an effective organization of a group becomes more difficult the more it contains members having a negative balance, and

[1] Reprinted from *Resolving Social Conflicts*, by Kurt Lewin (edited by Gertrud Weiss), Harper & Brothers, 1948. Used by permission of the publishers.

the stronger this negative balance is. It is a well-known fact that the task of organizing a group which is economically or otherwise under-privileged is seriously hampered by those members whose real goal is to leave the group rather than to promote it. This deep-seated conflict of goals within an underprivileged group is not always clear to the members themselves. But it is one reason why even a large under-privileged group which would be able to obtain equal rights if it were united for action can be kept rather easily in an inferior position.

It is particularly damaging for the organization and action of a minority group that certain types of leaders are bound to arise in it. In any group, those sections are apt to gain leadership which are more generally successful. In a minority group, individual members who are economically successful, or who have distinguished themselves in their professions, usually gain a higher degree of acceptance by the majority group. This places them culturally on the periphery of the underprivileged group and makes them more likely to be "marginal" persons. They frequently have a negative balance and are particularly eager to have their "good connections" not endangered by too close a contact with those sections of the underprivileged group which are not acceptable to the majority. Nevertheless, they are frequently called for leadership by the underprivileged group because of their status and power. They themselves are usually eager to accept the leading role in the minority, partly as a substitute for gaining status in the majority, partly because such leadership makes it possible for them to have and maintain additional contact with the majority.

As a result, we find the rather paradoxical phenomenon of what one might call "the leader from the periphery." Instead of having a group led by people who are proud of the group, who wish to stay in it and to promote it, we see minority leaders who are lukewarm toward the group, who may, under a thin cover of loyalty, be funda-mentally eager to leave the group, or who try to use their power out-right for acts of negative chauvinism. Having achieved a relatively satisfactory status among non-Jews, these individuals are chiefly con-cerned with maintaining the status quo and so try to soft-pedal any action which might arouse the attention of the non-Jew. These Jews would never think of accusing Knudsen of "double loyalty" for pre-siding at an American Danish rally, but they are so accustomed to viewing Jewish events with eyes of the anti-Semite that they are afraid of the accusation of double loyalty in the case of any outspoken Jewish action. If there is "danger" of a Jew's being appointed to the Supreme Court, they will not hesitate to warn the President against such an action.

As stated in the beginning, it may be difficult to determine in a given case exactly where the boundary between Jewish chauvinism, normal loyalty, and negative chauvinism may lie. However, our analysis should make it clear that an unmanly and unwise (because unrealistic) hush-hush policy springs from the same forces of negative chauvinism or fear as Jewish self-hatred does. In fact, it is one of the most damaging varieties of Jewish self-hatred.

There are indications that the percentage of such people among leading members of the American Jewish community has increased since the First World War. In spite of the disastrous consequences which this policy had for the Jews of Germany, there are probably more Jews in America today who have a negative balance than there were in 1910.

On the other hand, the development of Palestine, the recent history of the European Jews, and the threat of Hitlerism have made the issues more clear. A few Jews, such as the infamous Captain Naumann in Germany, have become Fascistic themselves under the threat of Fascism. However, many Jews who had lost contact with Judaism have come back under the threat of Nazism in Europe. The history of revolutions teaches us that the most active and efficient leadership of the underprivileged has come from certain individuals who left the privileged groups and voluntarily linked their fate with that of the minority. These people must have had, for one reason or another, a particularly strong positive balance of the forces toward and away from the group. It would be in agreement with historical experience if there were found to be efficient leaders among those who have re-entered the ranks of the conscious Jew.

The Jewish Leadership of Lakeport[1]

BY NORMAN MILLER

In 1948-1949, the Jewish residents of Lakeport contributed an estimated $350,000[2] to the Community Chest, $1,700,000 to the Allied Jewish Fund, and an estimated $60,000 to miscellaneous Jewish organizations. Yet the average Jew knows almost nothing about what is done with this money except that in some general way it "goes to help people who need it." It should be clear that the raising and distribution of such funds involves a tremendous amount of responsibility and requires a rather large network of organizations charged with the job.

This study is about the people who run the show. It does not deal with all Jewish leaders, only with those who may be considered as exercising a crucial influence in the groups in which they play a part. The purpose of this study is to determine who these individuals are, how they got that way, why they do it. An attempt will also be made to examine the consequences of this leadership situation. The method employed here is largely that of the case study, including such specific techniques as depth-interviewing and participant-observation. In addition, the author has drawn briefly upon the findings of a pilot study conducted among the Jewish population.[3] Certain conclusions are

---

[1] This is a previously unpublished paper.

[2] This is an estimated figure, since the Community Chest does not have information pertaining to the ethnic origins of its contributors.

[3] The present essay is related to a larger study of social organization among the Jews of Lakeport, in which it is hoped to explore further some of the problems only hinted at here. The author wishes to express his sincere thanks to Messrs.

admittedly tentative. For decisive results, more detailed and refined analytic techniques must be brought to bear upon the problem. This essay, however, is more than a *descriptive* account of a power machine. On the contrary, the analysis has proceeded in terms of a conceptual scheme which, it is hoped, will be of general, as well as specific, theoretical relevance.

First, however, a few words about Lakeport:[4]

THE JEWISH POPULATION

Lakeport is a thriving industrial and shipping center situated in the North Central region of the United States. Its population numbers 700,000, of whom approximately 20,000 are Jews. Of these, more than two-thirds were born in the United States, and about 96 percent are American citizens.

According to Engelman,[5] about 12 percent of the "economically active" population can be classified as owners, but over 45 percent are engaged—either as owners or employees—in business. Skilled workers account for 16 percent, professionals (physicians, lawyers, teachers, etc.) comprise 15 percent, and white-collar workers 10 percent. The remaining 7 percent were semi-skilled or unskilled workers, while 7 percent were unemployed.

Karl Girshman, William Greene, S. Richard Maisel, and Jacob Wayne for their invaluable assistance.

[4] The material in the following section is drawn largely from a comparable study of a "typical Jewish community," U. Z. Engelman's "Medurbia," *Contemporary Jewish Record*, 4:339-348, 511-521 (1941). Subsequent quotations from this article are reproduced with the permission of the publishers. Other examples of this sort of research can be found in S. Robison, "Jewish Population Studies" (New York, 1943), and in a host of community studies. Although many of these analyses, such as Engelman's, are based upon accurate research, the level of insight is typically rather low. The emphasis on gathering "facts," the lack of fruitful theoretical schemes, the failure to formulate or test hypotheses are all indices of the sad state of writing about Jews in America. One of the reasons for this situation is the frank hostility on the part of the "recordkeepers" to impart information to "unauthorized" individuals—a difficulty encountered by the present writer which accounts for the absence of much important data. This distrust is a feature of most bureaucratic structures, but involves another dimension in the case of Jewish organizations: the fear that such information might become grist for the anti-Semitic mill. The writer takes the position that "hush-hush" tactics are palpably ridiculous, and that anti-Semites do not need "evidence" to confirm or exacerbate the notions of their diseased minds. Rather, the author hopes that this piece of "pre-action research" will interest and be of use to those who are genuinely concerned with organizational and "community" democracy.

[5] U. Z. Engelman, *op. cit.*, pp. 341-342.

The Jewish population is largely concentrated in three areas of the city, but with considerable scatter in other areas. According to Engelman:

> Only three decades ago, most Jews lived in one area, the East Side, not far from the water front. When they first came to the city as immigrants, they built their homes and synagogues there, organized landsmanshaften, and established numerous charitable and social institutions. Today, the East Side still harbors the old Jewish Community Building, the Community Talmud Torah, the offices of the Jewish Welfare Society, the Mother's Club, the Benevolent Credit Association (Gemilath Hasodim), the Sheltering Home, and seven orthodox synagogues.
>
> These synagogues, however, are in reality stranded institutions, for many of the older immigrants who worshipped there have died since. Their children, having climbed a rung or two on the social and financial ladder, have moved into other districts which reflect more adequately their improved status. Newer institutions, which similarly reflect the more modern trends in [Lakeport], have also moved away from this first zone of Jewish settlement.
>
> But moving into new residential areas meant more than a mere physical change of habitat for [Lakeporters]. They actually underwent a deep psychological transformation, abandoning old loyalties and assuming new ones. In the newer sections they established a modernized version of the old shul, the temple, which, both in appearance and in ritual, reflected their new standards.[6]

In the intervening decade, even more has changed. The Jewish Community Building, the Community Talmud Torah, the Jewish Welfare Society (which has also changed its name), all have moved to other areas. The number of orthodox synagogues has dwindled to two or three.

In dealing with religious organizations, Engelman writes:

> One reason for the many synagogues in the old [Lakeport], no longer operative today, was that men who originally emigrated from the same European districts, as they organized their own landsmanshaften, also banded together for worship. Thus in [Lakeport] only a short time ago there were the Russian, "Slobotker," Warsaw, Galician, Hungarian, and Lubavitch congregations. Each of these usually owned a burial ground for both its own members and those of the landsmanshaft.

---

[6] U. Z. Engelman, op. cit., p. 511.

To maintain a modern [Lakeport] temple, however, is expensive, the cost often running into tens of thousands of dollars. Hence, in place of numerous Jewish houses of worship which old [Lakeport] possessed, there are only four temples of which Temple "Beth Aleph" is the oldest. This congregation traces its origin back ninety-four years to a little shul formed by East European immigrants and located in a second story loft of an industrial building, a strange contrast with the present magnificent structure. Its first cantor was also the shohet, Hebrew school teacher, collector, sexton, and secretary—all at the munificent salary of $250 a year.

This one-man staff is a far cry from the highly specialized personnel which serves the congregation today and which consists of a seminary-ordained rabbi, a cantor who is a graduate of one of America's finest schools of music, a choir director who is also a composer, Hebrew and Sunday school teachers, a sexton, and a full-time secretary.

For four decades the congregation was orthodox, conforming in every detail to the pattern set by the East European synagogue, including the Yiddish sermon. In 1885 the first change was made: the English sermon replaced the Yiddish droshe. In the following years, as the sons and daughters of the early settlers grew up, responsive readings in English were made a part of the service. By 1910, when the congregation moved to its present site, it had ceased to be a shul. It had become a Conservative temple.

Temple "Beth Beth," the only Reform congregation in [Lakeport], was organized in the middle sixties when a number of German Jewish immigrants settled in the community. By 1890, when they had achieved a measure of prosperity, they proudly dedicated the first domed temple in [Lakeport]. While it was being constructed, it is interesting to note, the congregation held its services in two neighboring Christian churches. It has since grown very rapidly and now claims the largest membership in [Lakeport], almost 700 families. Its rapid growth is due in no small measure to the high social prestige its members enjoy in the community.

For years this temple was [Lakeport's] citadel of anti-Zionism and assimilation. During the last decade, however, it has developed a distinct trend toward traditional Judaism. Hebrew reading has become part of the Sunday school curriculum, and provision has even been made for a more intensive study of the ancient language by the fifty children who attend the weekday classes. A modified Bar Mitzvah ceremony was also introduced, and children of the religious school are offered special credit for making the kiddush (blessing) and the prayer over the candles at home on Friday nights. These changes have been introduced because of the increased number of East European Jews and their descendants in the temple's membership, and the influence of the rabbi. A small but influential group within the temple, however, is still very strongly opposed to all these innovations.[7]

So much for Lakeport.

THE LEAGUE OF JEWISH CHARITIES

Beginning in the 1850's, Lakeport's Jews formed organizations for the relief of "needy coreligionists." These were the "West-Side" societies with such titles as: "Daughterhood of Israel," "Ladies Knitting and Philanthropic Society," "Young Men's Alms-Verein," etc. With the influx, beginning in the 1880's, of Polish and Russian Jews, other relief organizations emerged, the "East-Side" societies. These were characterized by a totally different conception of charity, a conception which persists among the counterparts of these organizations to this day. Perhaps the best distinction between the West- and East-side societies is that the former regarded their work as *philanthropic*. The latter, however, viewed *chesed* as a personal religious responsibility, and the recipient not as an object of benevolence but as an individual with a definite *right* to assistance.[8] There was even present an element of *fear* of the poor, lest mistreatment of them incur the wrath of God.[9]

[7] U. Z. Engelman, op. cit., pp. 512-514.

[8] Although both "philanthropy" and *chesed* signify love of man, the first remains a nonimperative ethical concept and the second involves the notion of duty. The Old Testament and Talmud are replete with references to the prescriptive right of the stranger, the levite, the orphan, and the widow to be cared for. See, for example, the classic work by G. F. Moore, *Judaism* (Cambridge, 1927), II, 162-179.

[9] An amusing example of the latter principle is found in the famous story by Israel Zangwill, "The King of the Schnorrers." The theme of "ingratitude" and "arrogance" on the part of clients of Jewish social agencies is one of the few points that may be said to have been adequately covered in the literature. The records of the early years of all West-Side agencies everywhere bear eloquent testimony to the almost total lack of understanding of the problems of the East-European immigrants. Thus, both in its early period and since the period of professionalization—with its attendant emphasis on "scientific" case-work—the work of the League has been primarily that of a *gesellschaft* nature.

Related to the above is what might be described as a positive dislike of local charity on the part of the League. Instead, it tends to concentrate more and more upon "community-wide" services such as recreation, group work, and camping. This is partly due to the decline in the number of eligible charity clients. What is important, however, is the positive *enthusiasm* with which most leaders endorse and finance expensive building projects, an enthusiasm unthinkable in the case of the charity agency.

Around the turn of the century, the "West-Side" societies, largely run by the wealthier "German" Jews, consolidated into a single fund-raising organization, henceforth to be called the League of Jewish Charities. It is this organization and its constituent agencies which will be the chief focus-point of this study.

The League, from its very inception, considered itself as the "accredited representative of the Lakeport Jewish Community." This claim was based on the fact that it was the largest single Jewish fund-raising organization in the city. Most of the funds came from private subscribers. In 1905 there were 128, who contributed a total of $9000. In 1928, 2717 contributed $129,000. Reflected in these figures is an increase in the number and kind of services offered, and the increasing professionalization of the League and its agencies.

In 1933, largely due to the increased needs of German-Jewish refugees, the Allied Jewish Appeal was founded. In 1933, it raised less than $20,000. In 1940, the amount collected was about $112,000. In 1949, the Appeal raised about $1,700,000. This fantastic increase in giving has had far-reaching consequences for the leadership structure, as we shall see later.

The League itself derives its funds from the Lakeport Community Chest. Its budget in 1949 was approximately $310,000.

The League, for almost twenty years, was headed by a Mr. S. Metro-Mayer, who had married into one of the largest Jewish fortunes in Lakeport. His wife was by far the largest single contributor to the League. A man of independent means, he served as unpaid executive director of the League. Until his death in 1943, he ran the organization single-handed. He stoutly resisted the insurgence of the "wrong kind" of leaders, an attitude which led to a good bit of ill-feeling on the part of certain ambitious individuals who were eager to become active in the councils of the League. The few East-European Jews who managed to enter the machine were firmly oriented to the German-Jewish pattern.

Mr. Metro-Mayer's death in 1943 occurred at a rather critical time. The war had brought about an enormously increased problem of over-seas aid, which reached its peak in the period since 1947. The 1946 Allied Jewish Appeal quota for Lakeport was $500,000; in 1947, $1,253,750; in 1948, $1,771,525; and in 1949, $1,800,600. Such sums could only be raised by recruiting "new blood." The absence of Mr. Metro-Mayer greatly facilitated this process.

Mr. Metro-Mayer was eventually succeeded by a professional social worker, a man who specialized in fund-campaigning. His role will be discussed at a later point.

Engelman's account of the relations between the League of Jewish Charities and other Jewish relief societies in Lakeport is of some interest to the present discussion:

> The old division between German and Russian Jews, which was quite sharp in [Lakeport] in the early part of the century, still survives in the differences between the officials of these charitable institutions and those of the League, which is controlled largely by descendants of German immigrants. Efforts to incorporate the independent institutions with the League have been spurned by both sides. The League objects to the unscientific way the organizations are run, while the institutions counter with the criticism that the scientific probing of the League's leaders should be tempered with more of the traditional Jewish rahmonus (mercy). 'When a mother brings in a child and asks us to care for it,' said an active worker in the Mothers' Club to this writer, 'we do not treat her as a "case." We simple take the child.'[10]

THE DIMENSIONS OF LEADERSHIP

In a recent discussion of the writings on Jewish history in America, Dr. Oscar Handlin[11] points out that one of the major difficulties in the area is the defensive-polemical atmosphere in which it presently thrives. The same situation is unfortunately true in the case of socio-logical analysis of Jewish life in America. Despite the annual outpour-ing of theses, dissertations, and "community studies," the best sources remain—whatever their literary merit—such fictional studies as *The Old Bunch, Focus,* or *Wasteland.* In the twenty-odd years since Wirth's eulogy on quaintness, the *Ghetto,*[12] no sociological literature about Jews in America has appeared which equals Drake and Cayton's study of urban Negro life.[13] Non-Jewish social scientists, on the other

10 U. Z. Engelman, *op. cit.,* p. 519.
11 O. Handlin, "New Paths in American Jewish History," *Commentary,* 7:388-394 (1949).
12 L. Wirth, *The Ghetto* (Chicago, 1929).
13 St. C. Drake and H. R. Cayton, *Black Metropolis* (New York, 1945).

hand, seem to regard this area as a private domain of their Jewish colleagues: the Jews will probably never have a Myrdal.[14]

One of the major reasons for this situation is the fact that much research on Jews is sponsored by organizations whose interests are often narrow, if not frankly sectarian. The emphasis is on "facts," but only such facts as may be useful for purposes of apologetics or administration. The search for facts is made in terms of an implicit conceptual scheme, including unstated value-premises, which actually hampers the development of fruitful and theoretically relevant research. There must be no unsavory facts. For example, widely used concepts, such as "community," function as a red herring, leading the sociologist into a rather one-sided and ineffectual search for the indices of "integration," "cohesiveness," and other notions emphasizing the degree of solidarity, while ignoring other important dimensions of social organization. Ethnic unity should be a *subject*, not a *guide* for study.

Several preliminary considerations must be discussed before the analysis of leadership is undertaken. For this study, the notion of leadership is limited to those individuals[15] who occupy an "influential" position, either formally or informally, in one or more of a selected number of organizations, the "most important" Jewish organizations in Lakeport. It will not be possible to consider the relations between this leadership stratum and any others. There will, however, be some mention of the relationships between this stratum and those of equal rank among non-Jews.

A word is necessary concerning the analysis of leadership in a group context. It is especially through *organized* group channels that an individual is able to manifest *regular* and *systematic* influences over other members in the group. This is not to deny the importance of informal groupings as they affect formal organization. The problem is precisely to examine the manner in which informal influences permeate and find expression in formal organization.

Another important problem is the conceptualization of the relevant

---

[14] G. Myrdal, *An American Dilemma* (New York, 1944).

[15] In the ensuing discussion, the terms "individual," "actor," "prestige-candidate," etc. will always refer to the leadership personnel. Terms such as "rater," "prestige-bestower," etc. involve the relevant "other person(s)," although in other contexts they may themselves be leaders. The terms "ranking" and "rating" will be considered synonymous in this essay.

facets of leadership. The following presentation is offered as a useful analytic tool for our purposes. The legitimation of leadership involves three distinct stages: awareness, judgment in terms of some normative system, and the conferment of recognition.

The initial stage, awareness, deserves most consideration. It is seen as involving two major dimensions which must be considered separately. The first, a *prominence-notoriety salient*, may be defined as the degree to which an individual is "known" without reference to any specific role or status. It is characterized by vagueness. The second, a *power salient*, may be defined as the degree to which the specific *relevant* role and status of the individual are "known." It is actually possible to find limiting cases of both types of awareness. For example, many people are quite familiar with the *name* of an important government official without being able to specify anything whatever *about* him. Conversely, the power salient is reflected in talk about the "power behind the throne," the "real brains," etc., where the *identity* of the individual involved may be unknown. We shall, however, concern ourselves in this discussion with only the great majority of cases which typically receive both prominence and power ratings.

A characteristic of prominence is its tendency to become generalized, a phenomenon closely related to what is sometimes called the "halo effect."[16] The limits to which prominence can become generalized depend upon a number of factors, including the relevant roles and statuses of the individual, the relationship between the individual and the rater, and the normative system which may be employed in ranking. Actually, of course, most raters do know something of the individual who is being rated. Thus one speaks of a "prominent attorney" or of one who is "well-known in the younger social set." The important element in both these situations is that there is no concern with the particular power position that the individual may have as an attorney or as a member of the social set—this despite the fact that such power positions may be the original reasons for the prominence of the individuals involved. Awareness of power, on the other hand, involves a recognition of the specific roles played by the individual, an appreciation of the functional importance of such roles

[16] See R. T. LaPiere and P. R. Farnsworth, *Social Psychology* (New York, 1936), pp. 308-309.

for any given organization, and offers the rating individual a better criterion for the invidious ranking of any one individual with others.

One implication which flows from this analysis is that the concept of leadership must always be considered in terms of the group or groups involved in the legitimating process. Depending upon the relationship between the leader and the individuals in the group, there will be different degrees of awareness of the prominence and/or power of the leader. Such a relativistic position is not without its difficulties. It is, however, useful for our purposes, and is in keeping with our general position that greater specificity is needed before one can handle in a meaningful manner such terms as leadership or prestige.

Several consequences result from the above distinctions. Individuals are likely to be rated as prominent when the "social distance" or action-gap between the individual and the rater is great. Conversely, the power rating granted depends upon the action-bonds between the individual and the rater.[17] Thus a passive or apathetic community will generally be aware of its leaders only as prominent individuals, and will be unaware and relatively unconcerned with the power salient of the leaders' positions. (See Gouldner's previous reference to Lowenthal's study of popular biographies.) Such lack of concern with the tangible aspects of leadership makes it possible for the leaders in such a situation to indulge in a considerable amount of autocratic and manipulative action. Conversely, an active group, through its awareness of the power aspects of leadership, makes it less likely that an oligarchy might develop which is not, at crucial points, highly responsive to the needs and demands of the membership.

An example of the first situation is furnished by a pilot study done in Lakeport in which a representative sample was asked to choose the most important Jewish people in the community and to give the reasons for their choice. The results indicated:

1. A tendency to choose people who are actually prominent without in any way being powerful.

2. A tendency to justify choices even of those who actually have power only in terms of the prominence of the individuals chosen.

A somewhat similar test was given to a small group of individuals

[17] This of course applies only in those cases where the rater is part of the same group as the leader. It is always possible for individuals outside of the group context to do ratings of their own. This will be considered later.

who are close to those rated as "most important." Here, as might be expected, there was remarkable unanimity with regard to the identity of the foremost leaders, and the reasons given all tended to refer to specific power positions of the leaders involved.

This same confusion of prominence and power ratings is probably even more marked when the ratings are made by non-Jews.[18]

The consequences of such a situation are to bring about the coöptation of individuals who are thought to be Jewish leaders but who may be actually only prominent figures without real power. This in turn, by a reverse process, makes it possible for the individual thus honored by the non-Jewish world to attain a position of greater prominence and/or power, or at least to slow up his decline from a previous position. This is not, however, the only possible consequence. Manipulative individuals in the dominant group who are aware of the situation might choose only such individuals who have "sufficient" prominence, but no real power. This makes it difficult for any critics of the scheme to raise objections that this is only a formal or token coöptation, and insures that no real danger will ensue to the coöptive organization from this procedure. It has a further consequence in that it fills some of the top positions, toward which the broad mass of people will look for leadership, with individuals who actually have little power.

[18] This analysis sheds light upon another related problem. Myrdal, in his discussion of Negro leaders, describes as one of their major "functions" that of go-betweens, since Negroes and Whites are separated by a "glass plate," able to see each other but unable to work together. In describing the way in which Negro leaders are coöpted, Myrdal writes of the "common assumption among Whites that upper-class Negroes are leaders of their people. . . ." and of the "expectation on the part of white community leaders who happen to know about them (upper-class Negroes), observe their superiority in education, manners, standards, and wealth, and take their influence among the common Negroes for granted." (Op. cit., p. 731.) Myrdal, by not considering the problem in terms of the preceding analysis, is unable to further explore the dynamics of the situation. The coöptation of Negro leaders is a case in point of the confusion of prominence with power. But such a situation arises most often where the relations between the two groups are not of a highly interactive character. The relations between Jews and non-Jews are certainly not the same as those between Negroes and Whites. Nevertheless, to the extent that there is some vagueness on the part of non-Jews as to the structure of the Jewish group, it becomes likely that the ranking of individuals will, as in the case of the Negro, be characterized by prominence references rather than by power references. For a discussion of the concept of coöptation, see P. Selznick, "Foundations of the Theory of Organization," American Sociological Review, 13:25-35 (1948).

Up to this point we have discussed the awareness of prominence and power in relation to the observer. The problem is now to specify a position somewhere along the continuum in order to deal "objectively" with what follows. The position that we shall take is that of an observer who is sufficiently close to the front office to know something of the "real" situation, and who has confirmed his impressions with other individuals who are as close, or even closer, to the power setup. At the same time, he has neither membership nor leadership in the organizations involved.

Another conceptual tool employed in this study is that of prestige as an object of leadership-striving. Prestige is here employed in the sense used by Davis,[19] with the qualification that the invidious rankings do not flow from a unitary normative system. Most treatments of the concept of prestige seem to follow this latter course. Actually a non-solidary society, such as the one in the United States, might be better characterized as a society employing different and often mutually contradictory normative systems. Proponents of a theory of prestige which presumes a solidary society have often been embarrassed when trying to describe some of the invidious rankings accorded men like Dillinger or Al Capone, and have been forced into conferring low prestige upon such individuals.[20] It is suggested here that a more realistic interpretation is that those actions which are in conflict with certain norms of our society (honesty, etc.), but in agreement with other norms (e.g., pecuniary success), are accorded an ambivalent kind of prestige which distinguishes them greatly from the actions of the common or garden-variety criminal.[21]

There is at least one important relationship between the dimen-

[19] Prestige is used to denote "the invidious value attached to any given status or office, or combination of them." See K. Davis, "A Conceptual Analysis of Stratification," *American Sociological Review*, 7:309-321 (1942).

[20] See, for example, F. H. Giddings, *Principles of Sociology* (New York, 1896), pp. 127-128. For a more recent example of this type of treatment, see the modification of Warner's famous "discovery" of class by A. C. Kinsey, W. B. Pomeroy, and C. E. Martin, *Sexual Behavior in the Human Male* (Philadelphia, 1948), pp. 77-79. Without specifically making the ranking referred to above, this reasoning is implicit in the Yankee City Series. See W. L. Warner and P. S. Lunt *The Social Life of a Modern Community* (New Haven, 1941), pp. 81-91.

[21] Graham Greene, in his *Brighton Rock*, ably portrays the gangster-as-businessman, and shows how a mixed respect accrues to him because he "keeps the racetrack quiet." See also T. Veblen, *The Theory of the Leisure Class* (New York, 1934), pp. 117-118.

sions of leadership and the mechanism of prestige-ranking. Prestige, according to Davis, is related to the "structural personality."[22] In our terms, prominent individuals possess by definition a very vague structural personality. The consequence of such vagueness for purposes of esteem-rating is that there are few if any ways by which the rater can award esteem in accordance with what the individual actually "does" to deserve it. Esteem in such cases tends to be more or less automatic.

On the other hand, the individual whose claim for prestige is based primarily upon his power position must strive to maintain and strengthen his position in order to insure the continued flow of high-prestige rankings. Although there is a notable tendency for power to flow over into prominence, it is nevertheless probable that the power leader cannot rest upon his laurels.[23]

In order to expand upon the concept of prestige as an object of leadership-striving, the following four questions must be answered:

1. From which prestige-bestowing groups is the individual seeking recognition?

2. What are the typical attitudes of the members of the groups with respect to prestige-worthy action?

3. How does the prestige-candidate satisfy (a) the general, (b) the specific role requirements?

4. How are the validation-efforts of the individual related to, and limited by, his "objective" economic, occupational, ethnic, and religious positions?

[22] Structural personality means "the person in so far as he is a product of the sum-total of positions which he occupies." K. Davis, op. cit., p. 311.

[23] This treatment ignores the affective attitudes toward leadership types among the members of the group involved. Llewellyn Z. Gross has suggested a possible relationship between "reluctant legitimation" and the compulsive need on the part of power-holders to consolidate and strengthen their positions: "mere" power is a very insecure situation. On the other hand, it is also possible to speak of a tendency on the part of various members within a group to encourage attainment of power by certain other individuals. This happens in the case of leaders "known" for their "life-long devotion," "selflessness," and "retiring, modest service to the people." They are the subjects of frequent manifestations of "spontaneous and unanimous" choice for some important office. The presence of a number of "sincere" leaders is functional for the organization in that it minimizes internecine squabbles to the extent that others bury their differences in rallying behind a truly or pseudocharismatic type. It also enables individual members of the organization to fulfill their idealized self-images vicariously as public servants and men-of-good-will.

The author is not at all satisfied that he has complied with the criteria set forth above. He feels, however, that as a research model it is a valid and useful one.

Before leaving this general discussion, a comment is in order on the work of the late Kurt Lewin, who was greatly interested in some of the problems facing Jews in the modern world.[24] According to Lewin, those Jews who, as members of an underprivileged minority, are attracted away from the center of their own group to that of the more highly privileged non-Jewish group find it difficult to win more than partial acceptance in the latter, and may thus be driven back to activity within the Jewish group. This is involved in the situation which Lewin terms "leadership from the periphery."[25] Although such an initial formulation is highly useful, it is not considered adequate for the analysis of more than a small part of any empirically observable leadership constellation. There are several reasons for this.

1. Assuming a situation in which periphery leaders actually have control of the power machine within the Jewish community, it follows that the activities of the organization, as well as the attitudes and values expressed both formally and informally, will emulate very closely those of the non-Jewish counterparts of the organization involved. To this extent, therefore, the tendency for future generations of Jews to seek escape via assimilation into the non-Jewish world should be lessened, since it is now possible for them to share vicariously many features of the style of life of those whom they wish to emulate, namely upper-class non-Jews. The organization, therefore, although it may be peripheral in many of its orientations, nevertheless also serves as a desirable *goal* for many potential Jewish assimilants.

2. Depending upon the formal goals of the organization (in this case the rendering of services to the Jewish community, raising money for refugees, etc.), it is to be expected that there will be some internalization of these formally held values.

3. It is not justifiable to assume that all who are in a position to escape will wish to do so. It is also completely unjustified to assume that all those who buck the barrier remain peripheral leaders. One

---

[24] See, for example, the selected papers in the posthumous volume, K. Lewin, *Resolving Social Conflicts* (New York, 1948).

[25] K. Lewin, *op. cit.*, "Self-Hatred Among Jews," pp. 195-197.

possible reaction-formation, for example, is that of "overdoing" one's Jewishness, of becoming a "200 percent Jew."[26]

4. Due to the awareness on the part of a large number of Jews that they are "unwanted," many leaders never attempt to cross the barrier and may orient themselves only to the specific Jewish group which emulates in many ways its counterpart in the non-Jewish community. Nevertheless, there will be significant ways in which the ideological content will differ from that of a non-Jewish group, especially with regard to formally held "Jewish values."

THE STRUGGLE FOR POWER

The social stratification of a Jewish community is very often explained in terms of the split between German Jews and East-European Jews. Although it is true that the *manifest* content of the principles of stratification is often so formulated, it is more reasonable to view the terms mentioned above as epithets rather than as accurate labels for the groups involved. It has been pointed out by others that many East-European Jews came to America at the same time as, and even earlier than, many German Jews.[27] Haym Salomon of Poland, a financier of the American Revolution, is a case in point.

Upon close examination of so-called German families in Lakeport, one finds that, in the case of many, their predecessors came from Poland, Hungary, Galicia, etc. Furthermore, the presence of such non-German Germans within the League's structure is by no means a new phenomenon. As a matter of fact, the reverse is true. The first president of the League was East-European, and Mr. Metro-Mayer, who reigned supreme for many years thereafter, was the son of an orthodox Hungarian Jew. In short, it is incorrect and unwise to say that *ethnic origin* as such determines the social stratification of the Jewish community; it is rather the *ethnic orientation* of an individual plus his ability—financial, educational, etc.—to make good his claim for new ethnic identity. Stratification among Jews, like stratification elsewhere, is a social class phenomenon, not merely ethnic or confessional.

[26] For an interesting discussion of this problem, see D. Riesman, "A Philosophy for 'Minority' Living," *Commentary*, 7:388-394 (1949).

[27] See, for example, M. M. Margolis and A. Marx, *A History of the Jewish People* (Philadelphia, 1927), p. 648.

There is a close relationship between *social* and *power* stratification. Within the power structure, the struggle goes on between the "Old Guard" and the "New Group" whom we shall call the "Insurgents." The Old Guard consists of those individuals who came into power with Metro-Mayer. It consists of the charmed circle of individuals who represent "all that is best" in Lakeport Jewry. They might be impressionistically described as well-educated, reasonably wealthy, completely Americanized, and probably of German extraction. They also tend to be rather older than the Insurgents. The Insurgents, on the other hand, are typically of East-European origin, *nouveaux riches*, more oriented toward "vulgar" middle-class American values than the upper-class values of the Old Guard. They wear loud ties, know little about wines, and their automobiles are rarely black in color.

On the organizational level, the members of the Old Guard tend to retain what power they have by virtue of their past performances, and because they are typically the more prominent individuals in the League: not in the eyes of the general Jewish population, but rather with upper-class non-Jews. Many of the active Old Guard leaders are important leaders in city-wide (hence "non-Jewish") organizations like the Red Cross, the S.P.C.A., and various civic groups. Among the Old Guard one finds the few Jews who are allowed to join the exclusive clubs. Within the League they tend to occupy honorific posts, although some are still extremely powerful.

The Insurgents, on the other hand, have actually a great deal of power but little *relevant* prominence; that is, they are prominent only among the Jewish population and are unknown without. The hardest workers, the largest money-givers among them, are nonentities—vulgar pushers—in the world of "family" and gracious living. We shall examine at a later point the precise ways by which the climb to power is achieved.

To some extent the social class distinction between Old Guards and Insurgents tend to break down among the younger set; although there is still some awareness of social distance among members of this age group, it is nevertheless true that there is much more social intercourse among them than was the case for their fathers. Some of the reasons involved in this shift are the rise in educational standards among the younger Insurgents, a greater familiarity and feeling of ease with such American patterns as drinking, golf, etc.

Somewhere between these two groups is a fairly large number of "floaters," individuals who have almost, but not quite, succeeded in gaining complete acceptance by the Old Guard. By education, style of life, value orientations, they approximate the Old Guard pattern almost perfectly. Nevertheless, the friends with whom they feel most at ease are likely to be Insurgents; this leads to a good deal of ambivalence. In some cases, an added boost in the direction of acceptance by the Old Guard comes through marriage with members of elite families or with non-Jews.

The floater is a man in a dilemma: on the one hand he seeks to avoid embarrassing or endangering his position by fighting against the Old Guard; on the other hand he owes a good deal of loyalty to the Insurgents, since he was probably helped into power through their influence, and because their general mobility has made his own easier.

The conflict between the Old Guard and the Insurgents is often quite sharp, especially in the League, although it sometimes takes other forms, such as the conflict in Temple Beth-Beth referred to earlier by Engelman. This conflict is typically played down by the floaters. They speak of the "so-called old group" and the "so-called new group." On closer questioning, however, it becomes clear that the phrase "so-called" is inserted for polemical purposes only, and that the speaker is perfectly aware of the conflict. Thus one floater says: "This business of two groups is sheer nonsense. I don't believe there are such groups, and there shouldn't be any. I would like to see less bickering about it. . . . The members of the so-called 'Old Group' have a lot to say in their favor. For years they carried the ball by themselves, and now they see themselves being gently forced out. . . . As a matter of fact [heatedly], I have seen the looks in some of their eyes [the Insurgents] when they win a point. . . ."

There is a brisk trade in genealogical information. Usually, if little is known about the origins of an individual, it is tacitly assumed that he is a Russian Jew. A typical comment with reference to any one of a number of high League officials is: "Joe Strauss? I'll tell you something about that guy. His father came over from Poland with ten cents in his pocket. Why, my father and he used to belong to the same shul. A junkman. And now look at him!" A favorite joke in certain League circles is: "There is no German Jew like the one whose father comes from Minsk." It is hardly necessary to point out the *ressentiment* reflected by such remarks.

PRESTIGE STRIVING

Two types of action are given high ratings by Jewish prestige-bestowing groups. First, nonspecifically Jewish actions outside the group leading to a generalized high-prestige position, recognized by the total society or by some relevant portion of it, and tending to reflect favorably on the Jews as a whole: judges, scholars, scientists, soldiers, athletes. Second, action within the group, or dealing with the group, which is seen as "useful" or "beneficial" to it; service in nonsectarian or Jewish agencies, financial contributions, especially those entailing some sacrifice on the part of the giver.

In line with the more general propositions suggested earlier in this discussion, it is possible to examine more concretely the various patterns of prestige-striving. To the extent that the prestige-bestowing group is in close social contact with the prestige-candidate, the number and specificity of (claim-validating) demands made upon him will increase. Thus it is sufficient for an individual to occupy a judgeship in order for him to become prominent and to be accorded high prestige by those groups with which he has little personal or social contact. A judgeship, conversely, is only the *base* position from which a whole new series of actions must ensue before the candidate can be accorded prestige and esteem in those groups with which he is in *close* social contact.

Thus a lower-class Jew, when asked to name someone important in the Jewish community, answers: "Rabbi Hirsch, because he has done so much to make the others like us," or: "Irving Gutmann, because he is a big giver." An active upper-middle-class Jew, on the other hand, answers: "James Singleton, because he has been on a lot of boards and committees, and was active in Temple C." When the proximity between the leader and the person rating him is close, the leader's activities will be more carefully and accurately observed.

Lest it be supposed that there is a one-to-one correspondence between the class level of the rater and the type of reply to be expected of him, it must be stated at once that this is not the case. The correspondence is rather between the number and type of organizational affiliations of the respondent and his evaluation of the individual. Finally, there is some correlation between class level and organizational affiliations. However, those who are on the same class level as the candidate may have a rather detailed knowledge of his activities and prestige without being very organized themselves, this knowledge stemming from the increased number of informal channels of information open to them.

In cases where the prestige-candidate is seeking recognition from individuals in his own social stratum, where consequently most of his actions are readily observed and reviewed, there is a constant demand for specific prestige-validating actions. Where the immediate group involved has amazingly accurate information as to the income, organizational activities, clique associations, etc. of the candidate, it is not possible to press a claim for prestige by relying on one's past accomplishments or by engaging spasmodically in activities. On the contrary, the candidate *is forced to engage more or less intensively and regularly in a highly stylized pattern of action.* The extent to which this pattern is actually carried out by any individual depends upon (1) the intensity of his motivations, (2) the "objective" limitations of his station, (3) the degree of acceptance of the candidate as "legitimate."[28]

Functionally, the organization serves for the prestige-candidate as a stage from which he can make a regular and conspicuous show of his efforts. In this connection, the *visible* aspects of the organization must not be overlooked. The League publishes its own newsletter, thus assuring its active members an amount of publicity which might not otherwise be forthcoming if it were to rely solely upon the general city dailies or the local Jewish newspaper. The functional significance of the newsletter becomes even more striking when we realize that few but the "interested" people read it, and that even fewer are particularly concerned with the identities of the stylishly-dressed women, smiling self-consciously at the plans for a luncheon which the chairlady, Mrs. *Herman* Stromberg (seated), is holding in her hand.

In former years, there was an even more effective "claim recorder," which was regretfully discontinued when the League became affiliated with the Community Chest in 1942. This consisted of a yearbook, the greatest portion of the contents being devoted to the League subscribers. Three types of information were presented: the amount

---

[28] See, for example, T. Veblen, *op. cit.*, pp. 85-89.

of money pledged the preceding year, the amount of money paid on that pledge, and the amount pledged for the current year. This made it possible for interested persons to judge the amount of "sacrifice" entailed, whether the individual carried through or was only bluffing, and whether the prestige-candidate was "moving ahead" or "coasting along." There is talk of reviving the yearbook, but the anguished cries of the "coasters" will probably effectively block this plan.[29] The discontinuance of the yearbook meant an end to this particular kind of display *within the Jewish group*. Since the contributions to the Community Chest are *not publicized*, the prestige-candidate finds it difficult to impress his fellow Jews. On the other hand, the A.J.A. provides an audience for the candidate which the Community Chest took away; an audience, moreover, which is much more sympathetic to overseas aid than to welfare on the local scene.

In contrast with the high dignity of a Community Chest campaign, that of the A.J.A. is charged with emotion and drama, culminating in the "kick-off" dinner. (The campaign has actually begun two months previously.) At this dinner, after an exciting speech by "a man who has been on the scene," the floor is open for pledges (nothing below $500 accepted). The dinner is almost entirely unnecessary, since approximately 98 percent of the money to be pledged that evening has already been solicited by hard-working teams of volunteer fund-raisers. The pledging ritual proceeds nonetheless. The audience, which is quite aware of the purely ceremonial nature of the dinner, nevertheless becomes rather tense when the chairman calls out: "And who will give the first pledge over $50,000?" No one does. Finally, after having reduced the amount to $30,000, someone responds. The chairman, consulting a list, nods approval and there is perfunctory anticlimatic applause.[30] Occasionally the following incident occurs: a donor rises to give his pledge, only to be abruptly stopped by the chairman, who says: "Wait a minute, I've got some-

[29] Informants have indicated that the Los Angeles Jewish community still maintains this system. According to one report: "When that Blue Book comes out, you can find every Jewish family in Los Angeles sitting home reading it." In view of the rapid growth of the Jewish population in that city, it is readily understandable how important such a sheep-separating operation is.

[30] Frequently, pledges are made for entire families. Since these families usually consist of several well-to-do parents and siblings, the total is quite impressive. This redounds to the honor of the family name, from which every single member derives an honorific increment.

one before you," and then calls off from his list the name of someone whose contribution is higher. There must be no illicit crowding of the ladder.

Another feature of the dinner is the periodic outbreak of planned spontaneity. An individual who has already given his pledge rises and declares that he has been so moved by the address of the principal speaker that he wishes to pledge an additional sum. Since this tactic rarely produces "new" money, it serves mainly to give the individual an extra shot at the prestige-basket.

In addition to giving, hard work is an extremely important type of prestige-gaining activity. It would be misleading to state that only hard work *within* the organization is important. Frequently the individual may do most of his hard work elsewhere. If the locus happens to be a high-prestige organization (a "non-Jewish" agency, for instance), the prestige already accorded him by the members of the latter organization might serve in lieu of prestige-validating efforts in the Jewish organization, although he is required to maintain a minimum number of commitments and obligations. These may approach the point of paper chairmanships, etc. Although there may be some resentment by the Jewish group of this climbing, the individual rarely leaves the League, first of all because his position in it is one of the reasons for his presence on the board of the "non-Jewish" organization; secondly, because he must continue to maintain some position in the organization which is most visible and accessible to the group with which he is in closest social contact.

There are three main areas of organizational work: membership on various boards, trouble-shooting, and fund-raising. Although the first serves as a further boost to prestige, it is generally a reward for services already rendered; since the era of professionalization, the board has been generally little more than a rubber stamp for the "tradition" of the agency and the "suggestions" of the executive. Nevertheless, board-membership is *interpreted* as work.

Fund-raising, on the other hand, is actually hard work, and represents a tremendous outlay of time and energy. The fund drive is carried out by divisions and teams; the major amount of money is brought in by the men's division. Most of this money is gathered by business and professional teams, each profession and industry being approached by colleagues. The masses are independently approached by the Histadruth (the Labor-Zionist organization) in house-to-house canvassing. The number of dinners, conferences, phone-calls during this period are incalculable. This is often a nerve-racking experience for the workers concerned, an experience tempered by the knowledge that they are working for a "good cause," and by the pleasure they receive from manipulating, pulling strings, handling very large sums of money—all without the stigma of gathering it for private or selfish purposes. The higher-level fund campaigner has an exciting and ego-gratifying role, what with the Hollywood-style battery of telephones (not likely to be found in his own office), the corps of lieutenants, the feverish conferences within conferences, and the enduring satisfaction of being able to say: "Did you see Dave Silva? The cheapskate is ashamed to look me in the eye!" This of a man who could have been in the prestige race, but has certainly lost this lap.

There is an element in the structure of the fund drive which is of some interest. The lowest ranks in the hierarchy are simply called workers. The next highest ranks are called lieutenants, captains, majors, and colonels. At the point, however, where the next rank logically calls for general, there is an abrupt, self-conscious switch to the more democratic, less invidious chairman.

The third major type of activity, trouble-shooting, represents behind-the-scenes manipulation par excellence. Included in this category are the individuals active in "coördinating," members of survey-committees, study commissions—the self-appointed guardians of the public weal who jealously maintain watch for actions which may be against the "best" interests of the community. Some of the trouble-shooting occurs in such open situations as committee meetings, but most of it takes place at lunches, via telephone calls, etc. The pattern is something like this: an unaffiliated organization is planning a capital-fund drive. The trouble-shooter gets wind of it, calls together a few "interested persons," who discuss the matter at some length and make appropriate plans. These plans may include more formal action by one of the League agencies, or they may be effected solely through further informal meetings. The trouble-shooter and his group will try to convince representatives of the deviating organization that a capital-fund drive at this time would conflict with the overseas needs of Jewish D.P.'s. If this is not a sufficient argument, a deal may be made, with the organization being offered a certain amount of money in return for canceling the campaign, but with an added rider calling for closer ties between the two organizations in the future.

It is important to note that the trouble-shooter may or may not be a board member of the agency or agencies involved. He derives his strength *not* from formal office-holding but from his powerful ties in the community. In order to play this role successfully, he must possess certain attributes not necessarily held by other individuals; he must have a reputation for detached honesty which places him (like the early DeGaulle) *au dessus des partis;* he must not be too closely associated with a single organization; he must have a reputation for "principled" rather than "expedient" conduct; etc. Clearly, the building up of such a reputation does not happen in a day, but the nature of the job makes it possible for the individual to advance his claims at a regular pace; trouble-shooting is a year-round activity. (The fact that a fund drive is seasonal work is one of the reasons why this type of organizational activity is rarely sufficient for ambitious prestige-candidates.)

THE MACHINERY OF LEADERSHIP

We turn now to the question: how do they get there, and how do they stay? For this, a brief statement of the formal structure of the League is necessary.

The League consists at present of four agencies: a community center, a multiple-function case-work agency, a Jewish education body, and a summer camp. The latter is run completely by women, and does not figure very much in the running of the League. In addition, the League has its own board of regents.

There is a special historic connection between the League and the case-work agency, since until 1930 they were one and the same. In the intervening generation, the case-work agency has managed to retain the aura of being *the* League agency. (As far as most people are concerned, "going to the League" still means going to the case-work agency for help, although the League has been nothing but a fund-raising body for almost twenty years.)

The League board consists at present of eighty-six members, most of whom represent the constituent agencies, some of whom are directly elected; ten representatives from various local Jewish organizations; and five representing the Temples. A preliminary analysis of the board memberships and Temple affiliations of all individuals who have belonged to a League-affiliated board since 1930 indicates that a significantly larger number of members of Beth Beth (the reformed Temple) have occupied board positions on the case-work agency than members of any other Temple.

The rules governing selection of board members are roughly as follows:

1. Officers are elected on a "single-slate" ticket, having been chosen by a nominating committee of each board.

2. All Jews who have contributed $10.00 in the preceding year are entitled to vote.

3. No individual can remain a board member of any agency for more than three years.

In the section that follows, each of these formal elements will be considered more carefully.

RECRUITMENT CHANNELS

Any formally organized leadership is required to provide certain channels whereby new leadership personnel can be recruited into the organization and trained. Several problems face the leadership at any moment: (1) how to insure that the new leaders are acceptable; (2) how to involve new people in the work of the organization.

The first problem is in part taken care of by the single slate, discussed below. The second problem is worthy of some detailed consideration. There are three initiatory sources for recruitment: the executive, the board member, the individual himself. Each source has special criteria and values, not always shared by the other two. The executive values two types of individuals: (a) an interested person, but not too strong: one whom he can "educate"; (b) someone with connections, whose favor he wants. The board member is more likely to be interested in individuals who are: (a) socially acceptable; (b) wealthy; (c) interested. The individual wants to become a board member for reasons outlined earlier.

The executive develops, the board brings in, the individual gets himself on.

The many organizational channels for board appointments are: committee, surveys, studies, and fund-drive activities. Occasionally the individual does not have to go through channels but is imme-

.

diately appointed to a board due to extremely high prestige elsewhere, money, personnel shortages, etc. The committee assignment is usually handled through the executive, with occasional nominations from the board.

Fund-drive activity is radically different. Because of the ideological factors involved, everyone who wants to work is welcome—if only at a very low level. In this situation individuals have a chance to prove their mettle and to make their weight felt. The volunteer on other levels is more shunned than anything else. Of course, an already active person can indicate his desire to get on a board, but an unknown has to be asked. There are ways by which a self-instigated candidate can indicate his willingness to serve other than by directly volunteering. For instance, he can put in an appearance at one of the few public meetings, and by such means as asking "intelligent" questions establish himself. The unsponsored candidate must refrain from asking too many questions, from showing himself too eager, from being in short, a "loud-mouth."

A note is in order concerning the actual election of board members. This takes place at the annual dinner, a gala affair held in the city's leading hotel. The 400-odd persons attending find at their places an attractively printed program setting forth the names of the nominees for the various boards. At an appropriate point in the evening's entertainment, formal motions are made to pass on the recommendations of the nominating committees. They are seconded, a mild chorus of "ayes" fills the room, and the boards are elected. That is all there is to it.

During one recent election, a group of young men afterward characterized as "radicals" and "hotheads" sought to make a test-case of the single-slate principle. When motions were in order, one of them rose and stated that he wished to make some nominations from the floor. He was blandly informed by the chairman that this was not the proper time to make such nominations and that he was therefore out of order. The chairman, an eminent attorney, and personally known to the author as a man of the highest integrity, remarked after the vote: "Well, now that we have democratically chosen the board members for the coming year. . . ." He was drowned out by the laughter of the assembled guests.

THE SINGLE SLATE

It is noteworthy with what unanimity the single-slate system is defended by League circles, even by those who are critical of much that goes on. The most popular defense of it seems to be that a multiple slate leads to the election of "bad elements." An informant relates: "A few years ago, when we still had a double slate, some of the best men we had refused to campaign; they just wouldn't lower themselves to ask favors. But some other men, loud-mouths, men who had never done anything for the community, put up a disgraceful campaign. They buttonholed people and urged them to vote. It was very undignified."

Another informant reports: "I'm not against the double slate in principle, but in this particular case, we have to be very careful. Our agency is just starting out, and if we had a board made up of just anyone, we could never steer through the first year successfully."

There are two dominant strains in the single-slate concept: (1) it is the only way of choosing "deserving" individuals; and (2) it is the only way of choosing "safe" individuals. The first is echoed by the board members, the second by the executive. Let us examine each in turn.

Why should "deserving" individuals not campaign for board election? For an answer to this we must turn to the previous analysis defining board membership as a reward for services rendered. However, since the claims for recognition are never made in a competitive context ("See what I have done, and see what my opponent has done"), rewards must flow from a clear recognition on the part of the prestige-bestowers of the honorable nature of the actor's work. To demand prestige[31] is to negate the whole tenor of the action, since in terms of the formal structure the individual's actions are selfless. He is giving time and money, deserting his family and television set, in order to serve the community. To claim prestige is to admit that one's activity is neither selfless nor so transparently prestige-serving

[31] The author is aware of the valid distinction made by Davis, *op. cit.*, p. 312, between prestige and esteem. He feels, however, that for purposes of this paper such a distinction is not particularly pertinent, and will consider both words as synonymous.

that honor accrues automatically. Needless to say, the fear of humiliation attendant upon defeat also militates against the multiple slate.

This contradiction involved in getting "good men" becomes more clear when it is recognized that board actions depend very little upon the specific individuals involved. The board "tradition" and the far-reaching power of the executive have rendered boards into rubber stamps on many points. It should therefore make little or no "real" difference who is elected.

A tentative explanation for the widespread acceptance of the single-slate principle is in order. If the board election serves as a prestige-bestowing device for the candidate, it is no less a means whereby the "public" can recognize and defer to honorable men.

Up to now, we have considered the single slate as it functions for the actor in the situation. The single slate also functions for the group by insuring a closer degree of control, a control approaching monopoly, over its candidates for leadership. By making certain that the prestige-level of its members does not sink below a given point, the other members of a group can be certain that their own membership in it will continue to reflect a given amount of glory upon them. A popularly chosen multiple slate will almost completely deprive the board of its present kind of prestige-bestowing function.

Furthermore, through the single slate, the professional executive is virtually assured of a board which will not substantially interfere with his policy suggestions; something which might not be true in the case of an opportunist buttonholer, out to make something of his position.

THE ROLE OF THE PROFESSIONAL

Of great importance in discussing the changes in leadership patterns is the growth of a professional bureaucracy within the League. It is unnecessary to give details here of the reasons for the shift, a shift which is not limited to this agency, nor to Jewish agencies, but is part of the increasing rationalization of certain social forms. (It does stand in sharp contrast, however, to the mode of operation of the non-affiliated, East-Side agencies. The latter continue to be run almost entirely by the agencies' board members. In one case, members of the agency bring food and gifts, and visit with their clients. There is manifested not only a great deal of loyalty to the organization, but a spirit of intimate camaraderie extending all the way down to the clerical workers.)

The League, since its professionalization, has become more and more of a *gesellschaft* organization. It has raised its standards of work considerably, and with the aid of professional fund-raisers has also substantially increased its "take." These high standards and smooth operating procedures render it less necessary for the board members to do any administrative work. This situation enables board members to concentrate on fund-raising and allocations, on starting new projects, etc. Thus a professionally-run organization functions for the lay leadership by providing a prestigeful front for the individuals who are formally responsible for its work.

The top professional is also a leader. Although he is technically a paid employee of the League, he is rarely thought of as such. Instead, his social status is in a sense *artificially* raised to approximate that of his employers. He receives a high salary, but one not nearly large enough to fully account for his social status. A reasonable hypothesis is that the salary of the top executive is pegged to match his social status. The executive has an important job and he must receive a salary sufficiently large to enable him to maintain an adequate style of life. The $15,000-a-year giver cannot see himself receiving direction from a man in a shabby suit, nor will he feel comfortable in the latter's home. The professional must be in a position to sustain the polite fiction that all men (that is, the League hierarchy) are equal and can call one another by their first names. At the same time, the top professional does not strive for prestige in the same way as do the leaders. His prestige derives purely from his job; he is therefore not in competition with the leaders.

The professional executive is thus in a *formally* crucial position. To the extent that he successfully retains this neutrality, he functions for the organization in the following important ways:

1. He serves as a shock absorber for the conflicts among leaders.
2. He is able to effect action compromises which more ego-involved individuals would not be able to bring about.
3. He influences the selection of new board members.

We cannot stop with a delineation of the professional's *formal* role. The professional is not only concerned with cementing his power position, but to the extent that he is aware of and concerned with his power position he is likely to become considerably ego-involved himself. In addition, the professional may have a given "ideological" stand which if brought too far into the open would vitiate his pose of neutrality.

He must carefully steer his course between the formal demands for neutrality and the power needs for informal alliances. He becomes a man who talks out of both sides of his mouth at once, and while doing so, somehow manages to get what he wants.

By virtue of his ability to influence the selection of new board members, the professional is able to build a personal apparatus, a group of individuals who are primarily beholden to him for their positions. In order to insure a maximum of personal loyalty, the individuals chosen should be, ideally, strangers to the organization, unbound to any of the existing vested interests. The presence on a board of such individuals enables the professional to have others represent him while he sits back and plays the public part of an impartial executive.

Since, typically, the Insurgents are less likely to be related to any of the existing vested interests, it is to the advantage of the professional to promote such individuals. This has an important bearing upon the actual influx of Insurgents into the League.

THE CRUCIAL LEADERSHIP

Aside from the executive, the League of Jewish Charities is completely dominated by a small group of individuals commonly known as the "Unholy Ten." The measure of crucial leadership is not necessarily reflected in the prominence of the individual, but should be sought in the power ratings by those who are close to the League hierarchy.

As mentioned above, a group of the latter were actually asked to make such ratings. A list of twenty names was presented them, and they were asked to choose the top ten men of power, and the top three financial controllers. Although there was not complete agreement as to the identity of the individuals, eight crystallized out as men of power, two as financial controllers. One individual was rated as having more financial than organizational power. It was explained by the raters that he could have organizational power whenever he wanted it.

Financial power is not synonymous with great wealth. Some of the wealthiest Jews contribute little or nothing to the Fund drive. A safe generalization is that although financial contributions are not *automatic* guarantees of organizational power, they are the *surest* way of achieving it.

It is one of the goals of social science to locate the *specific* dynamics of social interaction, but the goal is not always within reach. It is possible to isolate several of the most important factors involved, but it is precisely in studying their interrelationships that the researcher is often stymied. Of course there is no reason to expect an exact, unfixed order in the situation. One of the notable features of the social system under discussion is that of *vagueness.* In the last analysis, membership in the power structure is often decided by reference to such residual categories as: length of residence, personal qualities (sic), amount of work, etc. The function of vagueness seems to be the rendering of an amount of elasticity within the system.[32] It also accounts for the relative ease with which certain individuals (despite many strikes against them) can sometimes work themselves into important leadership positions.

A striking manifestation of the importance of money for the acquisition of top leadership positions is found in the fund campaign. Since it is the aim of the organization to maximize the amount of money received, the choice of individuals who can head the drive is strictly delimited. The rationale involved is that big contributors will only respond to requests (and threats) from their peers. A fund-raiser, who is otherwise opposed to the lack of democracy in the organization, says: "After all, in this you can't blame them. If a poor guy who can't give more than $100 approaches a really rich man, the rich one can donate $5000 and the solicitor is impressed. After all, he only gave $100. But in reality, the other can easily afford to give $10,000 or $15,000. This means a loss of $5000 or $10,000. That's why the rich guys have got to control the organization."

Implied in the above statement is the suggestion that giving is not simply a matter of contributing to a *cause,* but contributing *through,* or *in front of,* the *right people.*

[32] For a discussion of this point, see T. Parsons, "An Analytical Approach to the Theory of Social Stratification," *American Journal of Sociology,* 45:841-862 (1940).

There are certain further consequences of this situation. For one, the fact that fund-raising activities are so thoroughly controlled by large contributors affects the allocation of the funds received. It is to be remembered that the vast bulk of net receipts goes to overseas relief and largely to Israel. Israel is controlled by a labor government, and many of the leading Zionist and pro-Israeli organizations in this country have been sympathetic to labor. Formerly, when these organizations raised their own funds, there was no problem as to allocation. Now, however, that these funds are allocated to them by the Allied Jewish Fund of the several cities, their former autonomy has been replaced by the control of wealthy individuals, many of them non-Zionists, who have no democratic or popular mandate for their power and who are likely to be antilabor.

Another consequence, related to the above, and bearing out a point made earlier, is that fund-drive activity, unlike the Community Chest campaign, is a really *big* venture. The prestige-bearing possibilities of fund-raising are enormous. Not only does the big giver derive prestige from being known as such *locally*; in addition, he might *control* funds (a pseudo-business activity), which offers much vicarious satisfaction; and he is made to feel that he is a power on a national, even international, level. This is done through such media as autographed photos of Chaim Weizmann, national conferences without end, personal calls from the great and near great. Consider the magnate who can say in an offhand fashion: "Ben-Gurion told me a wonderful story . . . ," or: "When I was in New York, I had a short chat with Eban, who is just back from Israel. . . ." There is also the more formal publicity in the press which announces that: "Mr. Rice has just returned from an international conference in Geneva, where he represented the Lakeport Allied Jewish Appeal. He was chairman of the International Affairs Committee at the conference." Another local boy has made good.

CONCLUSIONS

This has been an attempt to describe an important segment of the Jewish leadership in a typical American city.[33] It has not concerned

---

[33] At least two very important features were not treated: the role of wives in the leadership structure and the recruitment of youth for future leadership positions.

itself with all levels of leadership, such as those found in small local Jewish organizations. Neither did it treat "national" Jewish leadership, that is, those whose prominence and power are not limited to any specific city. The author warns against application to the latter two types of any of the conclusions found in this article.

The conceptual device employed was that of prestige as a goal of leadership activity. Viewing leadership as inseparable from some organized group context, it was shown how the goal-strivings of individuals are routed through the structures in which they operate. Some of the elements involved in this process are: the groups from which the individual seeks prestige-conferment, the normative systems employed in ranking, the available organizational channels, and the ways in which all of the above are articulated with the functional needs of the organization.

The observer, when first confronted with the slogans of the League, is apt to be struck with the democratic spirit of the organization. Watchwords such as: "We need fresh blood," "Broaden the base," "We have to have total community participation," give the impression of a grass-roots ideology. The truth is that the slogans are ideological, but the ideology is a false one. It serves as camouflage for a class-rooted power clique which makes little or no effort to render itself democratic.

The Lakeport Jewish community is not so much led as controlled by a moneyed oligarchy which is only vaguely responsive to the "needs" and the "interests" of the individuals supposedly being "served." The prospects for a change in the basic situation are rather dim. We have already shown that most leaders are recruited in such a way as to insure the social homogeneity of the power centers and to minimize the danger of including elements hostile to it.

On the other hand, there are the ordinary people. In recent years they have been deeply stirred by the extermination of six million Jews in Europe and by the subsequent establishment of the state of Israel. Generally, however, they can only be described as an apathetic mass, people who have no real interest in the problems of Jewishness beyond occasionally attending religious services, and—often reluctantly—contributing to the fund drives. Although it is not our purpose here to examine this general apathy, it must at least be recognized that the problem goes much deeper than the present leadership system.

Rather, both are probably due to factors equally rooted in the general social structure. However, the League leadership is undoubtedly to some extent responsible.

One further conclusion seems safe: as long as the Jewish people of Lakeport continue to be "led" by the League, there will be no democratic community. In view of the fact that such a community cuts across social class lines, it is difficult to see how it could be otherwise.

Leadership Among Negroes in the United States [1]

BY OLIVER C. COX

NEGROES, PROBABLY more than any other group of Americans, have had an abiding common cause. We shall consider as leaders of the Negro people those who, through their energy and insight, have become advocates of means and methods of dealing with this common cause and whose advocacy has been significantly accepted by the group. These leaders have invariably thought of themselves as way-showers and as having responsibility for determining the destiny of the people. For example, Frederick Douglass once remarked: "I never rise to speak before an American audience without something of the feeling that my failure or success will bring blame or benefit to my whole race." [2]

The common cause of Negroes is an all-pervasive social phenomenon, affecting and determining the individual's existence. Says W. E. B. Du Bois: "We cannot do our daily work, sing a song or write a book or carry on a university and act as though these things were not." [3] Sometimes this cause of the Negro becomes more important to him than any other thing in life. "What to me," exclaims Frederick Douglass, "are questions of silver and gold, of tariffs and currency, while my people are torn from their little cabins, snatched

---

[1] Without any intimation of responsibility the writer would like to thank his colleagues, Mr. Lewis Jones and Dr. Alonzo J. Davis, for discussion and criticism of the content of this previously unpublished article.

[2] Frederick Douglass, *Life and Times of Frederick Douglass* (New York, 1941), p. 415.

[3] "The Negro College," *The Crisis*, Aug., 1933, p. 175.

from jails by furious mobs with no chance to prove their innocence of the crime imputed to them, shot down, hanged and burned to death?"[4]

But the common cause of Negroes in the United States is not fundamentally limited to Negroes. It is in fact an aspect of the wider phenomenon of political-class antagonism inseparably associated with capitalist culture. A principle involved in the process of democratic development is at the basis of the Negro's cause; and for this reason leadership among Negroes is likely to be as effectively white as black. Our discussion, then, is not one essentially of Negro leaders, but rather of leadership in the common cause as it affects Negroes specifically.

Since the social situation in which leadership develops is one of inter-group conflict and antagonism, it becomes necessary to define the antagonists. At the outset, therefore, we shall postulate, with the hope of demonstrating the point later, that in the United States racial conflict has never been between white people and black people as such; rather it has been between a particular class of white people and Negroes virtually as a whole. During slavery the core of the antagonism involved the master class and the slaves.[5] Since slavery, however, the struggle has been centered in the conflicting aims and interests of the antidemocratic, white capitalist class and black workers in general. Thus the Negro's cause has taken form within the social context of the larger democratic process.

These, then, are the antagonists. In this essay we shall consider (a) the structure or descriptive aspects of Negro leadership, (b) the dynamics or interrelational phases, and (c) the vectors or lines of force and directional phases of Negro leadership.

THE STRUCTURE OF NEGRO LEADERSHIP

For the purpose of this description we may adopt the usual division of history: slavery, reconstruction, and post-reconstruction. However, we shall think of reconstruction as ending with 1915, which marks the year Booker T. Washington died and which approximates the beginning of World War I.

---

[4] Benjamin Quarles, *Frederick Douglass* (Washington, D. C., 1948), p. 318.

[5] One Negro leader points out the antagonists as follows: "Slaveholders I held to be individually and collectively responsible for all the evils which grew out of the horrid relation, and I believe they would be so held in the sight of God." Douglass, *op. cit.*, p. 119.

SLAVERY. There seem to have been four general opportunities for the emergence of leaders among Negroes during slavery, namely, those provided for the insurrectionists, for the favorite slaves, for the underground workers, and for the abolitionists.

The insurrectionists were leaders who secretly planned the organization of slaves for the purpose of violently attacking the master class and thus the entire system of slavery. Although slaves had achieved a degree of accommodation, there was always a prepotent drive to revolt against the system. Of some two hundred attempts at insurrection, however, only about four reached mass proportions; and none, of course, ever succeeded in overthrowing the institution. The outstanding leaders of these movements were Gabriel Prosser in Virginia in 1800, Denmark Vesey in South Carolina in 1822, Nat Turner in Virginia in 1831, and John Brown at Harpers Ferry, Virginia, in 1859.[6] All these leaders and their accomplices were executed; but the effect of the insurrections was to increase the social unrest not only in the slave states but also in the nation as a whole. It should be noted that John Brown, one of the most desperate and effective of these leaders, was a white man.

The favorite slave was the very opposite type of leader to the insurrectionists. He may be thought of as a bellwether whose powers of leadership were derived solely from the authority of the master and whose function was chiefly that of directing and accommodating the slaves to the system. Ordinarily he held the position of a driver in the field, of a skilled workman, or of house slave. These were trusted men who could sometimes be depended upon to put down personally acts of insubordination among the slaves and to betray plots for insurrection. Because of his preferred status among the bondsmen, the ordinary slave looked to this type of leader for advice and for intercession with the master in times of need and stress.

Slave plots for revolt were almost invariably broken up or reported by favorite slaves; and frequently the reward of these slaves was money and freedom. The leaders of the Denmark Vesey insurrection knew the proclivities of the favorite slave; and, in spite of great care to keep the secret from "those waiting-men who receive presents of old coats,

---

[6] For accounts of slave revolts see: Joseph C. Carroll, *Slave Insurrections in the United States 1800-1865* (Boston, 1938) and Herbert Aptheker, *American Negro Slave Revolts* (New York, 1943).

etc., from their masters,"[7] a slave cook betrayed them. These persons could assume the status of leadership among Negroes because in the slaveocracy the common cause of the slaves was made to appear not only illegal but also sinful. Therefore the gifted slave, who identified himself with the purpose of the master, might, according to the degree of accommodation of the mass of slaves and the symbolic distinction derived from the master's favors to him, rise to relatively great estimation among the slaves themselves.

The underground-railroad leader helped to provide the means of escape from slavery to freedom. Although only a very small fraction of the slaves ever escaped from the South to hide away, particularly in the North and Canada, the fate and exploits of the runaway contributed greatly to the final abolition of slavery. There were many leaders in this illegal traffic. These persons gave direction, encouragement, food, and sanctuary to the fugitive; and the most active of them were sometimes white men such as Daniel Drayton and the Reverend Calvin N. Fairbank. Among the distinguished Negroes in this activity were William Still in Philadelphia, Charles L. Redmond in Massachusetts, James McCune Smith and Daniel Ruggles in New York, and Levi Coffin in Cincinnati.

One of the most daring of all was Harriet Tubman, the unfailing North Star of her people. Harriet, herself an escaped slave, went into the South repeatedly and brought out little bands of fugitives. Says Earl Conrad: "Harriet was the unquestioned leader of her escaping patrols. The attitude was martial and severe. She could not read or write but she had military genius."[8] Ordinarily the hardships and obstacles in the way of escape were so formidable that quite frequently the slave preferred bondage to the attempt. Frederick Douglass, who should know, explains that ". . . in a slave state an unsuccessful runaway was not only subjected to cruel torture, and sold away to the far South, but he was frequently execrated by the other slaves. He was charged with making the condition of the other slaves intolerable

[7] Carroll, op. cit., p. 91. "Percell, the free Negro, who advised the slave [Devany] to report the plot, received a reward of one thousand dollars. Devany, the slave of Colonel Prioleau, who informed his master about the plot, was given his freedom, and established in business as a drayman. He lived long in Charleston, thriving greatly in his vocation and enjoying the special distinction of being the only man in that state whose property was exempted from taxation." Ibid., p. 102.
[8] Earl Conrad, Harriet Tubman (Washington, D. C., 1943), p. 63.

by laying them all under the suspicion of their masters—subjecting them to greater vigilance, and imposing greater limitations on their privileges."[9]

The abolitionists, who might be thought of as intellectual leaders, developed and led public opinion against slavery. These leaders, by innumerable public speeches, group discussions, writings, and political debates, kept the antislavery issue constantly before the American people. Probably the role of the white leader in the Negro's cause may be observed most clearly in this movement; indeed the greatest of the abolitionists were white men. In the field there were such champions as Elijah P. Lovejoy, William Lloyd Garrison, Wendell Phillips, and Abby Kelly Foster. A most effective group of these white leaders were in the Congress. Says Frederick Douglass: "Without Adams, Giddings, Hale, Chase, Wade, Seward, Wilson and Sumner to plead our cause in the councils of the nation, the taskmasters would have remained the contented and undisturbed rulers of the union. . . ."[10]

And yet the Negro was the natural abolitionist. He was most immediately affected by the institution of bondage, and his leaders never lacked determination. Representatives of these would include Charles L. Redmond, James McCune Smith, John M. Langston, Sojourner Truth, Henry H. Garnet, Frederick Douglass, and Samuel R. Ward. These Negroes had to make their appeal particularly to a white public and exclusively in the North. But even in the North only a fraction—though an increasingly large one—of the white people were ever open to abolitionist suggestion; hence these leaders, white and black, were constantly menaced by mob action. Some of the abolitionists, the Garrisonians particularly, charged that the Constitution was a slave-masters' instrument and consequently should not be honored, while others, including Frederick Douglass, thought that freedom could be achieved within its sanctions. In spite of certain disagreements, however, the criticism of the abolitionists kept the slaveocracy continually agitated. Says one of these agitators: "If a slave made good his escape from slavery, it was generally alleged that he had been persuaded and assisted to do so by the abolitionists. If a slave killed his master, or struck down his overseer, or set fire to his master's dwelling, or committed any violence or crime, out of the

9 Douglass, op. cit., pp. 184-185.
10 Ibid., p. 536.

common way, it was certain to be said that such a crime was the legitimate fruits of the abolition movement."[11]

RECONSTRUCTION. Reconstruction may be thought of as that period following the Civil War in which the white ruling class of the South regained a new position of exploitation over the masses, so as to preclude any significant political interference from the latter. Thus leadership among Negroes was fashioned in resistance to the counter-revolution and restoration of the southern oligarchy. Moreover, during this period the outstanding leaders of the Negroes were white men and women, the missionaries, who followed the Federal armies into the South and began the systematic education of the Negroes.

The missionaries felt that the only power capable of transforming the slave to the citizen was education—education directed toward the instilling of literary confidence in the freedmen. This was the means of accomplishing a *de facto* freedom of the slaves. In the old system the slave's learning to read, to decipher the lettered page, was almost always the most dangerous threat to the peace of the community. And now, if he was to be made independent of his old master's will, he had to be taught to think for himself, a process practically impossible without some significant command of book knowledge. To be sure, this aim of the missionaries was diametrically opposed to the plans of the ruling class. For, although the war abolished slavery, the mass of docile black workers were still available. To educate these workers as the masters themselves were educated presaged to the latter the real consummation of their social calamity.

The battle of the leaders, therefore, centered about the education of the freedmen, which was thought of as a continuation of the Civil War hostilities. Although there were undoubtedly a variety of motives leading the northern teachers to adventure in the old slave states, the dominant motives seem to have been humanitarian, religious, and abolitionist. The enthusiasm of some of these workers may be indicated by the following appeal to the American Missionary Association:

We need teachers, men of the right stamp; actuated by pure philan-thropic motives—working men—men who hate slavery—ABOLITIONISTS! dyed with pure dye—men who dare face this miserable, wheedling con-servatism, and do something to merit at least the prevalent epithet 'nigger on the brain'—men who can feel that they are in this work elevating in

11 *Ibid.*, p. 98.

the scale of being and manhood those who, like themselves, were created in the likeness of God, free and equal—men who can see in the slave, blinded with ignorance . . . the future intelligent Christian citizen. . . .[12]

Many of these teachers believed that they were participating directly in the process of planning a new society, and they advocated fundamental principles of equality between the races. Most of the associations formed in the North to sponsor education among the Negroes were against segregation in the schools.

In the beginning the teachers had to be endured, but as the ruling class began to reassert its power, open antagonism against them mounted. Many schoolhouses were burned, teachers ostracized or mobbed and persecuted generally. And yet a significant number of them remained to lay an imperishable foundation of Negro education in the South. The American Missionary Association alone established such schools as Hampton Institute, Fisk University, Talladega College, Straight University, and Tougaloo College—all before 1870. The Freedmen's Bureau established Howard University in 1867. The heads of all the early institutions of higher learning for Negroes were white. Among the most distinguished of these leaders were General O. O. Howard of Howard, Erastus M. Cravath of Fisk, Edmund A. Ware and Horace Bumstead of Atlanta, Henry S. De Forrest, of Talladega, General S. C. Armstrong of Hampton, and Laura M. Towne of Penn School. It is particularly from this missionary and humanitarian movement that the new generations of Negro leaders were produced.

THE POLITICIANS.   The schools were symbolic of the vital area of struggle between the commonality, represented particularly by the Negroes, and the ruling class, but the black reconstruction politicians actually established a bridgehead on the power monopoly of the oligarchy. Therefore, the elimination of this incursion upon traditional rights became a responsibility to be achieved at virtually any cost. The effective means to this end was of course the disfranchisement of the Negro. However, the disfranchisement of the Negroes did not conclude the struggle, it merely shifted again the relative position of the antagonists to their pre-Civil War status. The Negroes and their white allies now began a new offensive against the en-

[12] Captain H. R. Pease, Port Hudson, Louisiana, *American Missionary*, VIII, 6 (June, 1864), 150, quoted in Henry L. Swint, *The Northern Teacher in the South 1862-1870* (Nashville, 1941), p. 51.

trenched power, and the right to vote and campaign for political office in the South became the pith of their common cause. Thus the ruling class has been continually in a defensive position.

In this situation also, white men have been outstanding leaders in the Negroes' struggle for political freedom. They aided the latter immeasurably in their local campaigns. In the Congress, Charles Sumner and Thaddeus Stevens were at the forefront of leadership for civil rights. However, it was the spectacular emergence and political articulation of the black statesmen which was most meaningful. For the first time in the history of the United States, Negroes had an opportunity to be heard and to meet face to face the representatives of their exploiters in the great parliaments of the nation. To a considerable extent this was the significant fruition of their leadership, the crucial culmination of responsible citizenship.

Between 1869 and 1901, when the last of the reconstruction Negro politicians ended his term, twenty-two Negroes served in the Congress: twenty in the House of Representatives and two in the Senate. A much larger number served in the state legislatures. The two senators, H. R. Revels and B. K. Bruce, were sent from Mississippi, while the twenty representatives came from eight different states. Although these leaders were greatly outnumbered, they fought continually for the primary rights of citizens and made it considerably more difficult for the southern ruling class, with the assistance of northern interests, to disfranchise the black and white masses of the South. Moreover, they established for the Negro people an unalterable claim to the primary right of political representation, and demonstrated to them not only its basic social value but also the possibilities of its immediate attainment. The withholding of civil rights now became an *unjust deprivation* rather than a limitation of aspirations to new freedoms.

THE RISE OF BOOKER T. WASHINGTON, 1895-1915. By 1895 the southern oligarchy seemed assured that it had eliminated the Negro from its political life, and therefore continued to consolidate its monopoly of political power. To do this, it was necessary to gain control not only of the Negro's educational institutions but also of his leadership. And to establish this control, an understanding had to be reached with the real power in the North, the great capitalists and businessmen. The Civil War had virtually eliminated the old planter aristocracy as the dominant class and a new class of southern business-men came into prominence. It was therefore a relatively easy matter for the ruling class of the new South to come to terms with that of the North, and as a consequence the Republican and the Democratic parties became factions of a single political class[13] with interests opposed fundamentally to those of workers with whom the Negroes were almost wholly included.

The admitted ideologist and spokesman of the New South was Henry W. Grady, who reached the height of his fame in the late eighties. He pointed the way to industrial coöperation between the two areas and explained the conditions under which the Negroes were to live in the South. Thus he observed: "In her industrial growth the South is daily making new friends. Every dollar of Northern money invested in the South gives us a new friend in that section. . . . We shall secure from the North more friendliness and sympathy, more champions and friends through the influence of our industrial growth, than through political aspiration. . . ."[14]

In other words, Grady was attempting to show that politics depended upon the economic-class interest of the group. He was explaining and encouraging the already rapid flow of northern capital into the South. However, he had to take into consideration the public sentiment on the Negro question among other groups in the North. His procedure in doing this has become the standard for other advocates of the interests of the southern ruling class. Grady asserted that the white people of the South, the Negro's neighbors, are the Negro's best friends; that the Negro realizes this and that he is as much opposed to outside interference as whites are.

Grady pleaded, therefore, that the South should be left alone because "Interference simply irritates, and outside opinion simply misjudges. The Negroes are prospering and are contented."[15] Moreover, "the problem should be left with the two races at interest."[16] This, then, was—and still is—the great desideratum of the southern oli-

---

[13] For a discussion of the nature of the political class see Oliver C. Cox, *Caste, Class and Race* (New York, 1947).

[14] Henry W. Grady, *The New South, with a Character Sketch of Henry W. Grady by Oliver Dyer* (New York, 1890), p. 138.

[15] *Ibid.*, p. 251.

[16] *Ibid.*, p. 235.

garchy. Having monopolized the power it was confident that it was able to deal effectively with the Negroes if left alone.

But the South did not only desire to be secure in its control of the Negroes; it also felt that it was able to make positive and generous economic concessions to them. For "realizing that on his prosperity ours depends,"[17] it was only "enlightened self-interest" to give the Negro "every right" to advancement. Grady pointed out that in the South the economic fate of Negroes and whites is inseparably associated, and that the whites welcome this association. And yet he made it emphatically clear that this economic interdependence does not imply social integration. He argued that the South favors economic coöperation between the races but insists upon social separation. "Behind the laws of man and the decrees of war, stands the law of God. What God hath separated let no man join together."[18] But Grady explained also the intent of the ruling class in carrying out the will of God; it is in essence the insistence upon the political impotence of the Negroes. Hence he postulated: "That the whites shall have clear and unmistakable control of public affairs. They own the property. They have the intelligence. Theirs is the responsibility. For these reasons they are entitled to control. Beyond these reasons is a racial one. They are the superior race, and will not and cannot submit to the domination of an inferior race."[19]

Grady showed that the oligarchy planned to preserve racial superiority, and one vital means was to secure the inferiority of the Negro's intellect—to gain control of his schools and the content of his instruction. As Henry L. Swint observed: "Gradually the white people . . . became convinced that the best defense against the yankee teacher was active participation in Negro education."[20] Therefore, Grady confidently asserted: "We hear much of the intimidation of the colored vote in the South. There is intimidation, but it is the menace of the compact and solid wealth and intelligence of a great social system . . . that is why the Negro fails to vote in the South. He will not vote except under persistent and systematic and inspiring organization, this organization cannot be effected or maintained

[17] *Ibid.*, pp. 112-113.
[18] Henry W. Grady, *The New South and Other Addresses* (New York, 1904), pp. 53-54.
[19] *Ibid.*, p. 239.
[20] *Ibid.*, p. 123.

against a powerful . . . social system that embraces the wealth and intelligence of the community."[21]

Accordingly, the powerful ruling class which controls the wealth and intelligence of the community will see that there is no "systematic and inspiring organization" among Negroes to produce their vote. And this brings us to a crucial point in leadership among Negroes. *The oligarchy proposed to use the "best" Negroes, the most gifted of them, to forestall the political aspirations of their own people.* "We have no fear of [the Negro's gaining control in the South]; already we are attaching to us the best elements of that race, and as we proceed our alliance will broaden."[22]

In this setting, then, we approach the year 1895. Frederick Douglass, the great patriarch of Negro leadership, died in this year, and B. K. Bruce and John M. Langston had already passed from the scene. Negroes, then, were rather destitute of aggressive leadership. In this year also, a distinguished, but relatively unknown, Negro, Booker T. Washington, was invited to Henry Grady's home town, Atlanta, Georgia, as the colored speaker at the Atlanta Cotton States and International Exposition. Booker T. Washington had been already recognized as a developer of industrial education among Negroes at Tuskegee Institute, in Alabama, but this speech brought him into the serious consideration of the ruling class as a trusted leader. The following may be thought of as its great oath of allegiance:

As we have proved our loyalty to you in the past, in nursing your children, watching by the sick-bed of your mothers and fathers, and often following them with tear-dimmed eyes to their graves, so in the future, in our humble way, we shall stand by you with a devotion that no foreigner can approach, ready to lay down our lives if need be, in defense of yours, interlacing our industrial, commercial, civil and religious life with yours in a way that shall make the interests of both races one. In all things that are purely social we can be as separate as the fingers, yet one as the hand in all things essential to mutual progress . . .[23]

In this way, six years after Grady's death, a Negro leader put the latter's determined conditions for peace between the races, economic interdependence but social separation, into an effective metaphor. The

---

[21] *Ibid.*, p. 243.
[22] *Ibid.*, pp. 103-104.
[23] Booker T. Washington, *Up From Slavery* (New York, 1901), p. 160ff.

editor of the *Atlanta Constitution*, the paper on which Grady had worked as an editor, remarked that "The whole speech is a platform upon which blacks and whites can stand with full justice to each other."[24] Moreover, Washington insisted in this speech that "the wisest among my race understand that the agitation of questions of social equality is the extremist folly. . . ." Washington was immediately accepted by the southern and northern press as the outstanding Negro leader, and from this time until his death in 1915 he was so completely depended upon by the ruling class as the authority on questions of race relations in the United States that historians of Negro life have referred to this period as the "age of Booker T. Washington." *From the very day of the speech, however, as Washington himself recognized, a certain group of Negroes opposed him.* This group has constantly increased in size and importance.

POST-RECONSTRUCTION 1915-. We may think of this period beginning with the World War I as the post-reconstruction period in race relations. By this time, the white leaders of the "New South" were well established. The Republican party, the party of the capitalist interests, had established a working relationship of conservatism with the southern oligarchy, while lynching and Washingtonian leadership had apparently subdued the political aspirations of Negroes.

But under this superficial view of victory for the reactionary forces of the nation, there were vigorous sprouts of militant, democratic leadership among Negroes. Year after year, in spite of great limitations, the colleges for Negroes in the South had been sending out their little armies of trained Negroes. The war stimulated an extraordinary migratory movement of Negroes to the North and a new base of aggressive leadership and politics was established. Beginning with Oscar DePriest in 1928, four Negro representatives have been sent to Congress. Moreover, the ideological pressure of World War I developed the concept of democracy into a social stereotype of positive value.

Probably the most significant nucleus about which the new leadership took its rise was the National Association for the Advancement of Colored People. And here again white leaders played a dominant role; indeed, the organization was not only initiated but also mainly supported for a long time by white people. Of the five incorporators

24 *Ibid.*, p. 163.

of the organization in New York in 1910, Mary White Ovington, Oswald Garrison Villard, Walter E. Sachs, John H. Holmes, and W. E. B. Du Bois, only one, Du Bois, is colored. The efforts of the NAACP have been directed toward the stimulation among Negroes of a conception of themselves as full American citizens by right; and the contesting in the courts, as far as its limited means permit, of the abrogation of the civil rights of Negroes all over the nation.

Yet, although the effectiveness of the NAACP derived from its organization, the work of W. E. B. Du Bois as editor of its organ, the *Crisis*, was so outstanding that for a long time the Association had been almost identified with his ideas and principles. Du Bois was a contemporary and antagonist of Washington. His claim to leadership was based particularly on his insistent demand for unlimited civil rights for Negroes *here and now*.

Soon after the War, a new Negro leader, Marcus Garvey, came into prominence. In 1916 Marcus Garvey had come from Jamaica to the United States with a diffused idea for uplift of Negroes, particularly in Jamaica. His coming to the United States, after he had gone to England and other European countries, was mainly inspired by his reading Booker T. Washington's *Up From Slavery*. Although Garvey was encouraged by some high-status white people in Jamaica, he developed an organization and movement in the United States almost entirely by support from his black followers.

Garvey, a tireless advocate and promoter, met the popular stereotype of Negro inferiority frontally. Being himself a black man, he insisted by every means at his contrivance that not only the black skin but also the native intelligence of the African was superior to those of white people. He glorified and exalted the physical features of Negroes. His great audiences in New York and in other cities, even in the South, were inspired and raised to unexpected levels of racial elation and self-appreciation. However, he insisted that the black man should be charitable and not despise the mulatto, because the dilution of the latter's superior black blood was not his responsibility. "We desire to have every shade of color, even those with one drop of African blood, in our fold; because we believe that none of us . . . is responsible for our birth. . . ."[25] The goal of his movement was the

[25] Amy Jacques-Garvey, *Philosophy and Opinions of Marcus Garvey or Africa for the Africans*, II (New York, 1925), 55.

recapture of all Africa as the national homeland for all the Negro people in the world; and to do this he asked the assistance of the United States particularly. This aid, Garvey thought, should be gladly given since he offered, as compensation, to rid the white world of its race problems by inducing all the Negro people outside Africa to return to that continent.

In 1925 Garvey was convicted in the federal courts on a charge of using the mails to sell fraudulent stock in his Black Star Line, a commercial steamship enterprise; he was jailed and finally deported in 1927. He died in London in 1940.

A rather small but potentially powerful group of white and black leaders, the Communists, have had an indirect appeal to Negroes in general. In the United States Communist principles and ideology decided in the Party councils have been more determining than the personality of any of the leaders. Moreover, these leaders have associated the problems of race conflict so closely with the general aims of Communism that they may be thought of as Communist first and then as leaders among Negroes. The race problem, though important, has been subordinated to the larger national and international class struggle.

James W. Ford, who was the Communist candidate for Vice-President in three elections, 1932 to 1940, Benjamin J. Davis, Jr., a councilman in New York City, and Doxey A. Wilkerson, former Professor at Howard University, are three outstanding Negro Communists. Ordinarily the Communists have been vigorous champions of civil rights for Negroes. Frequently, when the citizen rights of Negroes have been infringed, they have gone into the field of action to beseech, coerce, or resist the authorities. And yet organized Communism in the United States has probably made no greater impression upon Negroes than it has upon the general population. The Communist theory that the Negroes in the United States constitute a separate nation will be discussed in the following section.

THE DYNAMICS OF NEGRO LEADERSHIP

While it is necessary to have a historical picture of leadership among Negroes, an analysis of the system of attitudes which develops in the various areas of leadership seems to constitute the major challenge of the problem. These dominant social attitudes are the dynamic drives behind the leader's advocacy. These attitudes have been broken down into five typical patterns: protest, conservatism, compromise, nationalism, and revolt.

PROTEST.   The leadership which employs protest as its main line of action seeks to influence public opinion through propaganda and juridical devices to the point where effective pressure in favor of civil rights for Negroes would be brought to bear upon the political institution. "We shall not be satisfied," says W. E. B. Du Bois, "to take one jot or tittle less than our full manhood rights. We claim for ourselves every right that belongs to a free-born American: political, civil, and social; and until we get these rights, we shall never cease to protest and assail the ears of America."[26]

Protest has been the most prolonged and significant line of action of Negro leadership. Indeed, protest was the instrument of the abolitionists, and since the Civil War almost all the Negro newspapers and magazines have been protest organs. Probably the greatest of these post-Civil War protest leaders was Frederick Douglass. He saw that although slavery was abolished, the ruling class still sought to submerge the will of the Negroes. "Though slavery was abolished, the wrongs of my people were not ended. Though they were not slaves, they were not yet quite free. No man can be truly free whose liberty is dependent upon the thought, feeling, and action of others, and who has himself no means in his own hands for guarding, protecting, defending, and maintaining that liberty. Yet the Negro, after his emancipation, was precisely in this state of destitution. The law on the side of freedom is of great advantage only where there is power to make that law respected."[27]

Moreover, Douglass recognized not only the crucial importance of the franchise but also the power of public sentiment in the North to coerce the southern oligarchy. "A government that can give liberty in its constitution," he said, "ought to have the power in its administration to protect and defend that liberty."[28] Thus he concentrated his leadership on the problem of securing political rights for Negroes.[29]

[26] W. E. Burghardt Du Bois, *Dusk of Dawn* (New York, 1940), p. 90; from the resolutions of the Niagara Movement.

[27] Douglass, *op. cit.*, p. 415.

[28] *Ibid.*, p. 620.

[29] *Ibid.*, pp. 417-418. In another context Douglass declared, ". . . I looked upon suffrage to the Negro as the only measure which could prevent him from being thrust back into slavery." *Ibid.*, p. 437.

Perhaps one of the most penetrating bits of insight in Douglass' protest was his recognition that the ruling class in the South, the "best white people," are directly responsible for the racial antagonism existing between the black and the white masses. In fact, Douglass' argument in favor of civil rights for Negroes is so important in giving perspective to the problem of leadership among Negroes that it should be quoted at length.

The enfranchisement of the freedmen was resisted on many grounds, but mainly on these two: first, the tendency of the measure to bring the freedmen into conflict with the old master class and the white people of the South generally; secondly, their unfitness, by reason of their ignorance, servility and degradation, to exercise over the destinies of this great nation so great a power as the ballot.

These reasons against the measure which were supposed to be unanswerable, were in some sense the most powerful arguments in its favor. The argument that the possession of suffrage would be likely to bring the Negro into conflict with the old master class in the South, had its main force in the admission that the interests of the two classes antagonized each other and that the maintenance of the one would prove inimical to the other. It resolved itself into this, that, if the Negro had the means of protecting his civil rights, those who had formerly denied him these rights would be offended and make war upon him.

Experience has shown in a measure the correctness of this position. The old master was offended to find the Negro whom he lately possessed the right to enslave and flog to toil, casting a ballot equal to his own, and resorted to all sorts of meanness, violence, and crime, to dispossess him of the enjoyment of this point of equality. In this respect the exercise of the right of suffrage by the Negro has been attended with the evil, which the opponents of the measure predicted, and they could say "I've told you so," but immeasurably and intolerably greater would have been the evil consequences resulting from the denial to one class of this natural means of protection, and granting it to the other, and hostile class. It would have been, to have committed the lamb to the care of the wolf— the arming of one class and the disarming of the other—protecting one interest, and destroying the other, making the rich strong, and the poor weak—the white man a tyrant, and the black man a slave. The very fact, therefore, that the old master classes of the South felt that their interests were opposed to those of the freedman, instead of being a reason against their enfranchisement, was the most powerful one in its favor.

Until it shall be safe to leave the lamb in the hold of the lion, the laborer in the power of the capitalist, the poor in the hands of the rich, it will not be safe to leave a newly emancipated people completely in the power of their former masters, especially when such masters have not ceased to be such from enlightened moral convictions but by irresistible force.

As to the second point, namely, the Negro's ignorance and degradation, there was no disputing either. It was the nature of slavery, from whose depths he had arisen to keep him both ignorant and degraded, the better and more safely to defraud him of his hard earnings. This argument never staggered me. The ballot in the hands of the Negro was necessary to open the door of the school-house and to unlock to him the treasures of its knowledge. Granting all that was said of his ignorance, I used to say, "if the Negro knows enough to fight for his country he knows enough to vote; if he knows enough to pay taxes for the support of the government, he knows enough to vote; if he knows as much when sober, as an Irishman knows when drunk, he knows enough to vote."[30]

Douglass never undervalued the importance of industry and economic independence among Negroes, yet he insisted that the cause of the Negro is not primarily industry but political freedom. "While the Constitution of the United States shall guarantee the colored man's right to vote, somebody in the South will want that vote and will offer the terms upon which that vote can be obtained."[31] Thus the Negro's economic welfare is made dependent upon his attainment of his Constitutional rights.

It was not until about 1910 that W. E. B. Du Bois emerged as a national protest leader comparable to Frederick Douglass. But even before this there was a significant continuity of the protest movement. The living politicians were still demanding civil rights for Negroes and by 1901 George Forbes and Monroe Trotter had begun the publication of the Boston *Guardian*, to counteract the conservative leadership of the race. Men like Charles W. Chesnutt were reacting strenuously against "Negro opportunists."

By 1905 a group of Negroes decided that the time had come for the organization of their protest activities. They met at Niagara Falls under the leadership of Monroe Trotter and W. E. B. Du Bois and pledged themselves to an unrelenting struggle for civil rights. They convened subsequently at Harpers Ferry as the Niagara Movement and issued a manifesto inspired by the martyrdom of John Brown.

[30] *Ibid.*, pp. 418-423.
[31] *Ibid.*, pp. 418-423.

With the incorporation of the NAACP in 1910, which comes down to date as the outstanding agency for the achievement of civil rights and which for a long time served practically as a medium for the fervid protestations of W. E. B. Du Bois, the Niagara Movement went out of existence. When Du Bois resigned from and left the NAACP in 1935, Walter White assumed the role of standard bearer of the Negro's struggle for political rights in the United States. Protest, therefore, has been a continuous attitude among Negroes; its effectiveness reached some sort of climax in the split of the Democratic Party at the 1948 national convention into a southern and northern wing over the issue of civil rights.

CONSERVATISM. The term conservatism is used here for want of a better one to describe this type of leadership. Perhaps the concept reaction or collaboration might have been employed, but there is the possibility that these terms might connote baseness to the mind of the general reader. For our immediate purpose, therefore, we shall describe and limit in a special way the more neutral concept, conservatism, and then employ it to characterize a certain type of leadership among Negroes. The conservative derives the principal source of his power from a ruling class whose dominant interest is opposed to the aspirations of the people whom he leads. The ruling class itself cannot approach the people directly because its interests would be too easily associated with its advocacy and the result would most likely be an aggravation of discontent among the people.

Since, however, the conservative is a person who has already established himself as a leader among his people, he is able to exploit his power in the interest of the ruling class. And yet, it should not be supposed that the conservative is an enemy of his people; he merely decides that in the given situation it is expedient to avoid the common cause and make peace with the enemy. Indeed, he may become personally convinced that the doctrines of the ruling class are the wisest ones for his people. *The essence of conservatism inheres in the fact that the leader identifies the enemy as the best friend of the people. He serves as a principal intermediary in securing advantages from this friend that will apparently outweigh those which may be secured by the people through their insistence upon ends embodied in their common cause.*

The ruling class, possessing the power, is able to endow the conservative leader with sufficient vicarious authority and control of material things to make it obvious to the people that his way is the correct one and that those who oppose him, because of the material emptiness of their leadership, are utopian dreamers. Ordinarily, what the ruling class desires most of the conservative leader is that he placate a restless and discontented people so that as *de facto* ruler it might be able to consolidate its position of conquest. Moreover, the conservative leader is intended to serve as a foil to outside criticism since he, being native to the soil and to the people, should naturally be presumed to be more sympathetic with the people's cause than the foreigner. It is similar to the familiar tactic of including a Socialist minister in an otherwise conservative cabinet.

With respect to leadership among Negroes, three leaders may be thought of as representative of this phenomenon of conservatism: W. H. Council, Booker T. Washington, and Joseph W. Holley. These three colored men were administrators of schools for Negroes. They were, therefore, in the peculiar position of being able to render fundamental service to Negroes. At the same time they had an unending need of funds to make their work a success. Horace Mann Bond in his *Negro Education in Alabama* discusses the early rivalry between Council and Washington and the nature of their appeal to the ruling class. Council, the principal of the A. and M. College at Huntsville, Alabama, went so far as to say: "When the old, grayhaired veterans who followed General Lee's tattered banners to Appomattox shall have passed away, the Negro's best friends shall have gone, for the Negro got more out of slavery than they did."[32] After 1895, however, Washington rose into prominence far above Council. Joseph W. Holley is a disciple of Washington. In 1903 he established the Albany Bible and Manual Training Institute, at Albany, Georgia, on his own initiative; from that time on his most pressing problem was that of developing techniques of approach to the rich for obtaining funds to operate and develop the school. In the process he evolved a philosophy of race relations and gradually became a conservative leader among Negroes.

As we have attempted to show in the previous section, there was and still is a definite need of the ruling class to discover Negroes with

---

[32] Horace M. Bond, *Negro Education in Alabama* (Washington, D. C., 1939), p. 205.

powers of leadership to counter the harassing attacks of white and Negro protest leaders. The opportunity was ripe in 1895 when Washington was selected, because at that time the reconquest by the southern ruling class of the politically awakened Negroes seemed practically assured. Therefore, to secure a Negro leader who could promulgate the virtues of the political *status quo* would be to have an effective means of fending off attacks from outside.

The conservative leader never makes a direct protest, and he always avoids the common cause of Negroes. As Booker T. Washington, in answer to a criticism of the southern press concerning a speech which he delivered in Chicago, and which appeared to carry protest elements, acknowledged: "I said that I made the same plea that I had made in my address at Atlanta, for the blotting out of race prejudice in 'commercial and civil relations.' I said that what is termed social recognition was a question which I never discussed."[33] Moreover, Jim Crow, a practice which sometimes makes a fanatic of the protest leader, is ordinarily explained away by the conservative leader. Says Washington in connection with a question about his dinner with Theodore Roosevelt: "In the South it is not the custom for colored and white people to be entertained at the same hotel; it is not the custom for black and white children to attend the same school. In most parts of the North a different custom prevails. I have never stopped to question or quarrel with the customs of the people in the part of the country in which I found myself."[34]

When complaint becomes necessary, it is usually made by way of a philosophy of human behavior and in apparent solicitude of the best interest of the oligarchy. This may be epitomized in Washington's famous epigram: "It is not possible for one man to hold another man

[33] Washington, *Up From Slavery*, p. 185.

[34] Emmett J. Scott and Lyman B. Stowe, *Booker T. Washington, Builder of Civilization* (New York, 1916), pp. 124-125. In order to distinguish the attitude of the protest leader compare that of Frederick Douglass, whose children were excluded from the public school in the district in which he lived in Rochester, N. Y. Says he: "I hardly need say I was not prepared to submit tamely to this proscription any more than I had been to submit to slavery, so I had them taught at home for a while. . . . Meanwhile I went to the people with the question and created considerable agitation. I sought to obtain a hearing before the Board of Education, and after repeated efforts with voice and pen the doors of the public schools were opened and Negro children were permitted to attend them in common with others." *Op. cit.*, p. 299.

down in the ditch without staying down there with him."[35] In limiting the Negroes' right to vote it is held characteristically that the white man injures not the Negro particularly, but rather himself: "The more I consider the subject, the more strongly I am convinced that the most harmful effect of the practice to which the people in certain sections of the South have felt themselves compelled to resort, in order to get rid of the force of the Negroes' ballot, is not wholly in the wrong done to the Negro, but in the permanent injury to the morals of the white man."[36]

On one occasion Washington called the attention of the "community" to the evil of lynching in this way: "It is unreasonable for any community to expect that it can permit Negroes to be lynched or burned in the winter, and then have *reliable Negro labor* to raise cotton in the summer."[37]

The conservative is always careful not to offend the ruling class and, though he expects to receive benefits, especially material benefits, for himself and his people, he never demands these as a right. This is so because it is the idea of "rights" which the oligarchy desires most of all to feel secure against. Indeed, this class will sometimes seem to go very much out of the way to demonstrate that the Negro can "get much more" if he approaches "the white man" in the proper manner. The Negro, the oligarchy feels, should not make a demand as if by public right. Therefore, the conservative perfects and advocates the suppliant approach. "My father taught me as a child," Joseph W. Holley relates, "never to go to a white man for a favor just before a meal and never go to his front door. Wait until the meal is over and he has had time to get his pipe or cigar, and then go to the kitchen and tell the cook you would like to speak to Mr. John Doe."[38] Speak-

[35] Booker T. Washington, *The Story of the Negro* (New York, 1940 [first published in 1909]), II, 124.

[36] Washington, *Up From Slavery*, pp. 119-120.

[37] Basil Mathews, *Booker T. Washington* (Cambridge, Mass., 1948), p. 223. (Italics added.)

[38] Joseph W. Holley, *You Can't Build a Chimney From The Top* (New York, 1948), p. 60. Says Holley further: "The truth is, we colored people can get what we want, if it is within reason, from a white man if we approach him in the right way. He is like the Negro in the minstrel show who says to his companion, 'Don't shove me! You may push me all you want to, but don't *shove* me!' You may push the white man in any reasonable direction you want him to go, but never shove him." *Ibid.*

ing of the Negro critics of his Atlanta address, Washington observes: "They seemed to feel that I had been too liberal in my remarks toward the Southern whites, and that I had not spoken out strongly enough for what they termed the 'rights' of the race . . . later these reactionary ones seemed to have been won over to my way of believing and acting."[39]

In the address itself Washington cautioned the Negro people that "It is important and right that all privileges of the law be ours, but it is vastly more important that we be prepared for the exercise of these privileges."

Probably no phase of the conservatives' activities so completely satisfies the motives of the ruling class as their teachings that the "southern white man" is the best friend of the Negro. The major struggle for civil rights for Negroes has always been led by white and black protest leaders from the North. Indeed, southern Negroes must continue to look to the North, just as the slaves did, for significant aid in their final liberation. Hence, the oligarchy's greatest fear is not of the relatively powerless Negroes in the South but of those freemen in the North who are able to come to their aid. Accordingly, when Washington admonished Negroes in his celebrated parable of the bucket to stop looking about for help and make friends with the white man, the ruling class immediately recognized the master. The force of this statement should be recalled: "A ship lost at sea for many days suddenly sighted a friendly vessel. From the mast of the unfortunate vessel was seen a signal, 'water, water; we die of thirst!' The answer from the friendly vessel at once came back, 'Cast down your bucket where you are.' . . . To those of my race, who . . . underestimate the importance of cultivating friendly relations with the southern white man . . . I would say: 'Cast down your bucket where you are' . . ."[40]

Any Negro of even the merest consequence who makes public utterances to the effect that Negroes and whites can solve their prob-

[39] *Up From Slavery*, p. 166. (Italics added.) In commenting upon the success of a group of Negro teachers in Georgia taking their case for the equalization of salaries to the courts, Holley says: "While salaries have been raised since, they are still not equal, and they are not likely to be, unless we change our tactics. You get anything within reason from the whites of the State by the *right approach*." *Op. cit.*, p. 170.

[40] *Ibid.*, p. 158.

lems in the South without "outside interference" will be certain to be acclaimed in the leading southern newspapers as a great oracle of his people.

Indeed, when Mr. Henry A. Wallace came to the South in 1948 to speak on civil rights in the interest of his campaign, he was met in Birmingham by a number of Negroes who were protected by the police and who carried signs which read in part: "We are progressing —leave us alone," and "Mr. Wallace we live in harmony with our fellowmen and are not rabble rousers." The eight or nine signs were to the effect that Negroes were satisfied with their condition and that they considered it an insult for Mr. Wallace to conceive of them as needing aid. One sign read "Down with FEPC"! In order to give the incident greater prestige among Negroes, the *Atlanta Constitution* (Sep. 2, 1948) reported that the Negroes said "They were students of the famed Tuskegee Institute. . . ." (To be sure, the sign-carriers were not students of Tuskegee Institute.) They were in fact, common laborers of Birmingham reportedly engaged for the occasion by a leading Birmingham newspaper.[41]

Another approach leading to the idea of friendship between the master class in the South and the Negroes is that of picturing the slave as being sympathetic with and eager to serve the master. Henry Grady, as we have seen, used it repeatedly as a foil against the charge of discontent in the South. Washington also agrees that "In order to defend and protect the women and children who were left on the plantation when the white males went to war, the slaves would have laid down their lives."[42] Moreover, it is in this same tenor that he made a solemn promise at Atlanta: "I pledge that in your effort to work out the great and intricate problem which God has laid at the doors of the South, you shall have at all times the patient, sympathetic help of my race. . . ."

On the crucial question of the Negro's right to assume the full political privileges of citizens, the conservatives ordinarily address their reservations and negative judgments to the Negroes themselves. The main argument seems to be that Negroes are not yet ready for the suffrage or, in any event, that the right to vote is not so important as they think. To seek the ballot now is like trying to "build a chimney

41 See the *Birmingham World* (Negro weekly), Sep. 10, 1948.
42 *Up From Slavery*, p. 9.

from the top." "It did not seem possible," Washington observes, "that a people who yesterday were slaves could be transformed within a few days into citizens capable of making laws for the government of the State or the government of the Nation."[43]

The method repeatedly employed of depreciating the political strivings of the people has been that of making an artificial dissociation of politics from economics and then concluding that the latter outweighs in importance the former. Thus, says Washington: "What our people most needed was to get a foundation in education, industry, and property, for this I felt that they could better afford to strive than for political preferment."[44]

But the conservatives tend to look at the political question in a more fundamental light. They argue that since the friendship of the southern oligarchy should be the dominant wish and aim of the Negro people and since to insist upon voting will clearly infuriate this class, the Negro should logically avoid political aspirations. "No greater injury has been done the colored people of this country than that which resulted from putting them in a position of political antagonism to their former masters."[45]

Since the conservative leader maintains that he does not "advocate that the Negro make politics or the holding of office an important thing in his life,"[46] the question arises as to the nature of his conception of the "race problem." The racial discriminations inherent in this problem constitute the dynamo behind the utterances of the protest leader. But the conservative, in his role of peacemaker among the Negroes, must minimize or explain away these discriminations. Accordingly, Washington relates: ". . . it is a pleasure for me to add that in all my contact with the white people of the South, I have never

[43] *The Story of the Negro*, II, 28. Recently in an argument that Negroes are not ready for Civil Rights, the abiding force of this contention was enunciated by Senator Allen J. Ellender from Louisiana: ". . . there has been an effort since the Civil War . . . to maintain white supremacy because of the fact that there were so many colored people in our midst who are uneducated and who are not far removed from savagery." University of Chicago Round Table, *Should We Adopt President Truman's Civil Rights Program?* Feb. 6, 1949, p. 11.

[44] *The Story of the Negro*, p. 66. To the same effect the author says: "Ignorant and inexperienced, it is not strange that in the first years of our new life we began at the top instead of at the bottom; that a seat in Congress or the State Legislature was more sought than real estate or industrial skill. . . ." *Ibid.*, p. 158.

[45] Booker T. Washington, *Frederick Douglass* (Philadelphia, 1907), p. 253.

[46] Scott and Stowe, *op. cit.*, p. 83.

received a single personal insult."[47] To be sure, the Negro cannot be "insulted" if he conceives of the system as worthy of respect—conceives of it in the following way, for example: "I was born in the South and I understand thoroughly the prejudices, the customs, the traditions of the South. . . . For that reason, if for no other, I will never willingly and knowingly do anything that, in my opinion, will provoke bitterness between the races. . . ."[48]

Therefore, since the "traditions" of the South are assumed to be sacred, the vital content of the Negroes' common cause is, by that very assumption, eliminated. It follows that the race problem itself may appear to be nonexistent even where it is most acute. "We have no race problem in Macon County, [Alabama]," Washington affirmed; "there is no friction between the races; agriculture is improving; the county is growing in wealth. . . ."[49] Neither is there any serious problem about voting because, says he: "During all the years that I have lived in Macon County, Ala., I have never had the slightest trouble in either registering or casting my vote at any election. Every white person in the county knows that I am going to vote in a way that will help the county. . . ."[50]

Moreover, when this definition of the political situation is accepted, the burden of the blame for the Negro's hardships is naturally made his own responsibility. "The most effective influence for race tolerance," Holley declares, "and the most powerful compulsion toward non-segregation, will come as we lift our mass intelligence, skill, and industry into responsible citizenship and Christian character."[51] As a corroboration of this Washington asserts: "One farm bought, one house built . . . these will tell more in our favor than all the abstract eloquence that can be summoned to plead our cause."[52] According to this theory, the Negro should prepare himself to do something that the community wants; if he prepares himself like the white boy in one of the great universities of the nation and finds it difficult, because of his race, to get an opportunity for the employment of his higher

[47] Up From Slavery, p. 122.

[48] Booker T. Washington, My Larger Education (New York, 1911), pp. 179-180.

[49] Ibid., p. 308. (See also Scott and Stowe, op. cit., pp. 34-36.)

[50] Ibid., p. 46.

[51] Op. cit., p. 222.

[52] Washington and Others, The Negro Problem, pp. 28-29.

preparation, then he is to blame for not educating himself to do what the "community wants."

The race problem thus emptied of its dynamic content, the conservative leader can then show the way by which it may be solved advantageously to Negroes. Accordingly, he illustrates:

> In Mississippi, for example, a coloured man and his wife had charge, a few years ago, of a post-office. In some way or other a great discussion was started in regard to this case, and before long the whole community was in a state of excitement because coloured people held that position. A little later the post-office was given up and the coloured man, Mr. W. W. Cox, started a bank in the same town. At the present time he is the president of the bank and his wife assists him. As bankers they receive three or four times as much pay as they received from the post-office. . . .[53]

Indeed, by way of this conception of the race problem, the meaning of racial antagonism and its "solution" may be made to appear so simple and even sanguinely exciting that one may consider himself fortunate for his social heritage as a Negro. Accordingly Washington observes: ". . . we [Negroes] should, as a race, thank God that we have a problem. As an individual I would rather belong to a race that has a great and difficult task to perform, than be a part of a race whose pathway is strewn with flowers."[54]

This philosophy of the inherent value of problems and difficulties is carried over into a principle of labor, which principle, it should be realized, is manual labor. This philosophy is exceedingly useful to the ruling class. To a great degree the race problem in the United States is a problem of labor exploitation. Slavery was a system for compelling Negroes to labor; Reconstruction involved crucially the problem of the oligarchy's regaining control of its black labor supply; and the contemporary problem centers about the striving of the black and white masses to win political rights to limit the exploitative freedom and power of the ruling class. Therefore, the views of the conservative on a program of action for black workers are pivotal in his complex of attitudes.

[53] Washington, *My Larger Education*, p. 161.

[54] *The Story of the Negro*, II, 401. Again: "Paradoxical as it may seem, the difficulties that the Negro has met since emancipation have . . . not always, but on the whole, helped him more than they have hindered him." *My Larger Education*, p. 4.

The protest leader ordinarily insists that, given the free prospects of American citizens, the Negro will not only work enthusiastically but also develop a demand for means of improving his efficiency and skill. The conservative leader, on the other hand, insists that the black worker must first learn how to work as a manual laborer so that he may be able particularly to instill in his being a love of labor for its own sake. By this means he will make himself reliable and indispensable to his employer; and thus achieve finally all the values of his higher aspirations virtually as a windfall. This philosophy of labor tends naturally to become the basis of the collaborator's conception of the proper educational course for Negroes. Washington illustrates these attitudes in saying: "No student [in Tuskegee Institute], no matter how much money he may be able to command, is permitted to go through school without doing manual labour."[55] This is evidently so because, says the leader ". . . I . . . learned to love labour not alone for its financial value, but for labour's own sake. . . ."[56]

Nevertheless, this conviction seems to have had a firmer utilitarian base, one closely associated with the exploitative demands of the ruling class. For education is conceived of not as a right of Negroes but rather as a privilege vouchsafed them by the oligarchy which has to be convinced of the value of this education to itself. Therefore, Washington points out that ". . . just so soon as the Southern white man can see for himself the effects of Negro education in the better service he receives from the labourer on the farm or in the shop; just so soon as the white merchant finds that education is giving the Negro not only more wants, but more money with which to satisfy these wants, thus making him a better customer . . . then the white taxpayer will not look upon the money spent for Negro education as a mere sop to the Negro race, or perhaps as money entirely thrown away."[57]

It is in this context, then, that the race conflict centering about industrial education has arisen. The white ruling class conceives of the entire Negro race as exploitable laborers; therefore it will concede industrial education, but considers higher education, just as it considered the slave's learning to read, a threat to the peace and order of

[55] *Up From Slavery,* p. 143.
[56] *Ibid.,* p. 52.
[57] *My Larger Education,* p. 304.

the community. In describing the attitude of whites in North Carolina in 1865, Henry L. Swint observes: "Some citizens felt that the Negroes should be educated as 'intelligent and useful free laborers,' but were unwilling to admit the possibility or desirability of higher education."[58] Indeed, Washington himself indicates the continuity of the exploitative interest in the tendency of the ruling class to limit the education of Negroes to that of improving his skill as a worker in saying: "In a certain way every slave plantation in the South was an industrial school. On these plantations young colored men and women were constantly being trained not only as farmers but as carpenters, blacksmiths, wheelrights, brick masons, engineers, cooks, laundresses, sewing women and housekeepers. . . ."[59] Therefore, to advocate that the Negroes ought to be primarily concerned in their schooling with industrial education is to win the wholehearted sympathy of the "best white people."

With respect to the Negro's exploiting his education after graduation, Washington becomes involved in a remarkable system of logic. To recognize the tremendous handicap of economic discriminations against Negroes would be to come face to face with the race problem. Therefore he relies upon the broad cultural assumption that merit will be recognized and rewarded regardless of race. But this seems not to have been convincing to Negroes for: "They replied that our case was entirely different. They said in effect, that because of our colour and because we carried in our faces the brand of a race . . . white people did not want us to succeed. In the end I usually wound up the discussion by recalling the life of Frederick Douglass, reminding them of the high position which he had reached. . . ."[60]

Color, then, as a bar to advancement is deflated; and as he concludes further, ". . . there is something in human nature which always makes an individual recognize and regard merit, no matter under what colour of skin merit is found."[61]

Indeed, this belief in an essentially capitalist philosophy of individualism leads Washington to take a consistently antilabor position in the continuing struggle between capital and labor. In condemning

[58] Op. cit., p. 117.
[59] Booker T. Washington, W. E. B. Du Bois, Paul Lawrence Dunbar, Charles W. Chesnutt, et al., The Negro Problem (New York, 1903), p. 11.
[60] My Larger Education, p. 103.
[61] Up From Slavery, p. 111.

strikes in the coal mines he relates his experience: ". . . my observation convinced me that the miners were worse off at the end of a
strike. Before the days of strikes in that section of the country, I know
miners who had considerable money in the bank, but as soon as the
professional labor agitators got control, the savings of even the more
thrifty ones began disappearing."[62]

This, then, is the character of the function of the coöperating
Negro leader; but what is the nature of the *quid pro quo?* The ruling
class assumes the dominant role of establishing the reputation of the
conservative leader and of defending him vigorously against any
attacks from protest leaders. It surrounds him with marks of distinction and honor and produces him as a victorious champion of his
people. Above all he is made an *intercessor* for his people in their
attempt to reach the ear or generosity of the ruling class. In short, he
is necessarily made a symbol of racial success, the apparent ideal of
Negroes' aspiration.

The ruling class, having divested the Negroes of power and excluded
them from the means of demanding public services and civil preferment by right, is now able to endow its conservative leader with power
capable of inspiring reverential fear and admiration in his people, and
this, at a cost incomparably smaller than that which would have been
involved had the full rights of citizens been available to them. For
example, it is very likely that the disadvantages which Negroes suffer
today in the South in one year due to the unequal distribution of
educational funds would outweigh in actual monetary value all the
philanthropy devoted to Negro education in the South since the Civil
War. Furthermore, this does not take into account the dollar value
of the range of civil limitations due to political impotence.

Of course, the people who own the wealth also have power. In
giving the leader control of funds, they also transmit their ideas and
philosophy. This was done principally through the system of paid
agents for the great philanthropic funds. These agents have been well
schooled, efficient men who have strong convictions as to what cultural direction is best for the Negro people. One protest leader called
them exaggeratedly the "evil geniuses of the Negro race." At any rate,
this rapprochement leads Washington to the conviction that ". . .
more and more, rich people are coming to regard men and women

[62] *Ibid.*, p. 49.

who apply to them for help for worthy objects, not as beggars, but as agents for doing their work."[63]

But the power of the conservative leader is not a simple one. Sometimes it can be made a frightfully intimidating force, especially to Negroes dependent upon it. Since the power is not derived essentially from Negroes but rather from the major antagonists of Negroes, the leader, like a vicar, can discipline with extraordinary impunity. Sometimes the nearest friends of the leader have been already publicly defined by Negroes in general as among their outstanding enemies. Moreover, the conservative leader may even come to the defense of the white antagonists of the Negroes' common cause. For example, Holley defends Governor Eugene Talmadge in this way:

The colored people's dislike for Mr. Talmadge was not on account of what he had done to them, but was largely due to the fact that he called them names. [Holley now illustrates the inconsequence of a name.] A white woman calls for her laundry, and the Negro laundress directs her daughter, Ferty, to fetch the laundry. Then the white woman inquires: "Liza, what is your little girl's name? You called her Ferty. Is that her full name?"

"No," said Liza, ". . . Me and my ole man didn't have but one child. He wanted it named after him, and I wanted it named for me, so rather than have a fuss we named her for both of us. His name is Ferdinand and by name is Liza, so we just named our little gal "Fertilizer."[64]

We have given some considerable attention to this type of leadership among Negroes not only because it is highly elusive but also because it continues to have a significant function and vitality. The pronouncements of Joseph W. Holley on race relations have been carried with approbation and praise in the outstanding southern newspapers. Many southern governors and politicians have been his friends, and he has addressed groups of conservative whites in the South. On February 4, 1949, for example, the Associated Press reported that he addressed "a white audience of Kiwanians" in Albany, Georgia, in this way: "Holley scored particularly the Rosenwald Foundation, the National Association for the Advancement of

[63] Up From Slavery, p. 133.
[64] Op cit., p. 140. Notice the almost disdainful social context of this story. Washington also points out that: "Mr. Vardaman and Mr. Tillman, it would seem, hate the Negro in the abstract, but they get along very well with the actual black man who is their neighbor." The Story of the Negro, I, 179.

Colored People and the CIO." Walter White, the Negro protest leader, has been criticizing Holley in the same manner as Chesnutt and Du Bois criticized Washington some decades ago. The white newspapers, of course, have taken up the challenge for Holley and have defended him most vigorously. On February 28, 1949, the *Atlanta Constitution*, in an editorial, said: "Before Walter White . . . makes any more disparaging remarks about Dr. J. W. Holley, Georgia Negro educator . . . he might ponder the words of another Negro educator . . . 'In all things that are purely social we can be as separate as the fingers, yet one as the hand in all things essential to mutual progress.'"

The editor merely completed his editorial with quotations from Washington, assuming that the latter has become canonized in the folklore of Negroes and that this should be sufficient to shield the modern conservative. At any rate, the comparatively insignificant progress of Holley appears to be indicative of the reduced ability of the oligarchy to impose a leader upon the Negro people.

COMPROMISE. Probably most, if not all, Negroes in the United States have reached some sort of compromise with the *status quo*. The characteristic of suspended conflict inherent in the Negroes' accommodation to the racial situation involves an attitude of compromise. Moreover, we could think of a leader who, after following some course of relatively radical action, becomes convinced that a more stable policy would be more productive of the goals desired. Perhaps most labor leaders, when they have achieved recognition for their union, tend to become less radical, preferring to "reach an understanding" with the employer rather than to use coercive measures. It is not exactly in this sense, however, that we wish to discuss this phenomenon.

We think of the Negro compromise leader as one who has become wedged in between protests and conservatism. *His fundamental attitudes are protest attitudes; yet, because of his dependent relationship to the ruling class, he has to act as if he were sympathetic with its interests.* However, unlike the conservative, he does not take the initiative in advocating the wishes of the oligarchy. He is conscious of those wishes and will exploit them only under pressing necessity. Indeed, he will most likely do what he can surreptitiously to frustrate them.

The compromise leader never becomes a great leader among

Negroes because he can seldom take an unequivocal position. The ruling class does not have complete confidence in him and the people do not know exactly in what social situations it will become convenient for him to champion their cause. Therefore he does not inspire courage and faith in himself among the people, though he may claim their respect and sympathy.

This type of leadership is found mainly among those men who hold official or semiofficial positions, such as those in the various "black cabinets" of the nation and among the Negro college presidents. The situation may be illustrated. During the opening years of this century, as a young man, John Hope became an ardent disciple and friend of W. E. B. Du Bois. He became, in fact, a convinced protest advocate. He went, even after he had become president of Atlanta Baptist College, to the meeting, in 1906, of the Niagara Movement at Harpers Ferry, a meeting consecrated to an unremitting struggle against conservatism. As Ridgley Torrence observes: "John Hope had taken a bold and courageous step in joining the Niagara Movement. . . . At that time it was the most radical activity of the race, in *direct opposition* to the theories best supported by financial supply."[65] Moreover, "He took its resolutions to his heart and kept them there for the rest of his days. He . . . was ever ready to 'sacrifice money, reputation, and life itself on the altar of right.' "[66]

And yet it was not long before Hope was presented with the inevitable dilemma. He wanted money to operate his school and every possible source seemed sterile save one: the funds of the great philanthropists. In the usual manner, therefore, he laid his case before them, but one by one the doors were closed to his plans. "Finally in desperation" he made contact with Booker T. Washington "to whom all the channels of northern philanthropy were at that time open. Then, as if by magic, things began to happen. Carnegie made a gift; the General Education Board made a gift; the society in New York voted a large sum, and the future of a new building . . . was assured."[67]

This done, however, Hope began to suffer pangs of conscience. He had been reduced to the point of having to admit fundamental obligation to the symbol of all that "he had detested" in a leader among

---

[65] *The Story of John Hope* (New York, 1948), p. 151. [Italics added.]
[66] *Ibid.*
[67] *Ibid.*, p. 159.

Negroes. How, now, could he face his colleagues of the Niagara Movement—especially Du Bois? As a catharsis, Hope sat down and bared his bruised soul to Du Bois in a long letter, a most remarkable document of personality conflict. He said that he expected to be verbally flailed for his apostasy, that he wanted Du Bois to understand his difficult position and above all not to withdraw his friendship. Thus he appealed: "I write to ask you whether you have me in your heart—not on your calling list or your mailing list but in your heart—on your list of friends. I am asking this question fearlessly as a strong man would ask his chieftain. I will receive the answer just as fearlessly. And however it may be, I shall be loyal to my chieftain still."[68] And so Du Bois answered in part:

You must not think that I have not known and appreciated your friendship for me or that I ever doubted or doubt now your loyalty to the principles which we both so sincerely believe. If I thought even that you were going back on those principles, my friendship is not of so slight a texture that I would easily give you up. Of course, I am sorry to see you or anyone in Washington's net. It's a dangerous place, old man, and you must keep your eye open. . . . In your position of responsibility your institution must stand foremost in your thoughts. One thing alone you must not, however, forget: Washington stands for Negro submission and slavery. Representing that, with unlimited funds, he can afford to be broad and generous and most of us must accept that generosity or starve. Having accepted it we are peculiarly placed and in a sense tongue-tied and bound. I may have to place myself in that position yet, but, by God, I'll fight hard before I do it.[69]

This, then, is the situation of the compromiser. He clings to his principles, but he submits to the ruling class at a price. There is another kind of Negro leader who may be confused with the true compromiser. He may be thought of particularly as the opportunist. He is, as such, unprincipled and attempts to exploit both the ruling class and the protest leaders in his own interest. He may be, for example, the president of a state-supported college. Knowing that the ruling class puts a very high dollar-value on the integrity of segregation, the opportunist encourages the protest leader to demand the lifting of the segregation barriers in the state university. At the same

[68] *Ibid.*, p. 162.
[69] *Ibid.*, p. 162.

time he makes certain that the oligarchy realizes the serious intent of the demand but he does this in the role of sympathizer with the whites. The expected result is that increased appropriations will be forthcoming to his use; with the condition, however, that he should advertise to the Negroes that the state has liberally satisfied the requirements of Negro education.

NATIONALISM. There is among Negroes, and indeed among modern peoples of color everywhere, a prepotent nationalistic attitude. This is so because they are confronted virtually in all parts of the world with highly nationalistic whites. In most parts of Asia and in Africa we may be sure that, in time, the counternationalism among the peoples of color will overcome the nationalism of the whites. But in the United States most leaders among Negroes have not been willing to exploit nationalism, at least to its logical intent, as a solution of the common cause of the people.

However, one celebrated black leader, Marcus Garvey, took up the challenge and planned to unloose and excite the timid nationalism among Negro Americans not as a final force in this nation but as one tributary to a great river of black nationalism flowing in Africa. He conceded "the white man's" right to be nationalistic in the United States; he thought that Negroes were unreasonable to expect the whites to be other than nationalistic; therefore he pleaded with Negroes to withdraw peacefully and go to Africa where their own nationalism could not be questioned. Thus he reasoned: "We must have a country and government of our own. We must make our own impression upon a world of injustice, and convince men by the same means or methods of reasoning as others by their strength do. Don't be deceived; there is no justice but strength. In other words, might is right; and if you must be heard and respected you have to accumulate nationally in Africa, those resources that will compel unjust man to think twice before he acts."[70]

To be sure, this national force would be used against whites in Africa since "there is but one alternative for ambitious and self-respecting Negroes, and that is to make it warm for all aliens in

[70] Amy Jacques-Garvey, op cit., p. 13. II, Moreover, ". . . the Negro can only arrest the attention of the rest of mankind in the quest for justice, for fair play, when we can produce to the world the 'real stuff' that makes man feel, if he doesn't hear." Ibid.

Africa. . . ."[71] Nationalism seemed so natural, even instinctual,[72] to
Garvey that he believed white people who championed any movement among Negroes for equal rights were deceiving them. "Don't
encourage [Negroes] to believe that they will become social equals
and leaders of the whites in America, without first on their own
account proving to the world that they are capable of evolving a
civilization of their own."[73]

But black nationalism needed more than the idea of a homeland.
It was necessary to produce among Negroes a new conception of
themselves, the counterpart of white race-pride. Therefore Garvey
went to the heart of the matter by avoiding the argument about biological equality and unreservedly insisting upon the purity and excellence of the black race. "We are told that God's throne is white,
although we believe it to be black."[74] And he said to the people:
"Negroes, teach your children that they are the direct descendants
of the greatest and proudest race who ever peopled the earth; . . .
it is because of the fear of our return to power, in a civilization of our
own, that may outshine others, [that] we are hated and kept down by
a jealous and prejudiced contemporary world."[75]

It followed, therefore, that the race ought to maintain its biological
purity. Accordingly, he declared: "The Universal Negro Improvement
Association . . . believes in and teaches the pride and purity of race.
We believe that the white race should uphold its racial pride and
perpetuate itself, and that the black race should do likewise."[76]

In the exploitation of this kind of thinking Garvey discovered, and
apparently with gratification, that he had become the natural friend
of the Ku Klux Klan. By a strange concourse of social logic the representatives of black and of white nationalism came to an understanding. Garvey, to be sure, was encountering considerable criticism from
a number of Negro leaders, especially from Du Bois. The conflict was
bitter. Thus Garvey said of Du Bois' type of leadership: "The gang
thought that they would have been able to build up in America a

[71] *Ibid.*, p. 46.
[72] Said he, ". . . we cannot do away with conditions that make America a
place of toil and trial and tribulation for you. People cannot help their in-
stincts. . . ." *Ibid.*, p. 348.
[73] *Ibid.*, p. 5.
[74] *Ibid.*, p. 108.
[75] *Ibid.*, p. 82.
[76] *Ibid.*, p. 38.

buffer class between whites and Negroes, and thus in another fifty years join with the powerful race and crush the blood of their mothers, as is being done in South Africa and the West Indies."[77]

In a brutal attack he charged that "Du Bois represents a group that hates the Negro Blood in its veins. . . ."[78] Moreover, he declared that although ". . . the educated Negro is making rightful constitutional demands, the great white majority will not grant them, and thus we march on to danger. . . ."[79]

The Klan thus appeared to Garvey not only as a means of increasing the discontent among Negroes but also as a tangible proof that his analysis was correct. In other words, he saw the activities of the Klan serving as a stimulus to the Negroes' reaching the conclusion that the United States should be abandoned for a homeland of their own in Africa. Therefore, although the majority of Negro leaders might have considered the Klan the Negroes' enemy, Garvey thought he saw in it a precious value ". . . because the Klan, through an honest expression of the white man's attitude toward the Negro, prepares him to help himself."[80]

In 1921 Garvey actually visited the Imperial Wizard of the Klan in Atlanta, Georgia, and came away with the impression that ". . . the Ku Klux Klan had [no] other desire than to preserve their race from suicide through miscegenation and to keep it pure, which to me is not a crime but a commendable desire and [does] not supply the reason why Negroes should attack them. . . . I believe in the purity, honor, and pride and integrity of each and every race."[81]

This, then, was the nature of Garvey's attempt to bring Negroes into national consciousness. The racial situation in his native country, Jamaica, could not have been approached in this way. It would have been, for example, rather meaningless to ask colored Jamaicans to go to Africa because over 90 percent of the Jamaicans are colored. Moreover, he could not have attacked the upper-class, assimilationist, light-colored people of Jamaica as he did the protest leaders in the United States because in achieving their higher status the upper-class Jamaicans never obligated themselves to the black masses.

[77] Ibid., p. 59.
[78] Ibid., p. 57.
[79] Ibid., p. 39.
[80] Ibid., p. 71.
[81] Ibid., p. 261.

Yet it is precisely at this point that Garvey, with his undoubted charisma, was able to drive home his thinking into the troubled hearts of the American black masses. He pointed out to them that the American mixed-bloods were really sorry for themselves, that fundamentally they did not like black people, that they would exploit their light color at the first opportunity even to the disadvantage of the masses; therefore their leadership was deceptive. In this way he ripped the plaster from the sore and put the protest leaders on the defensive. He brought the black masses up into a consciousness of power that they had never known. Indeed, he delivered them, for the moment at least, from racial shame; and, in his own words, "a new era of love, brotherhood and fraternity . . . dawned upon the race."[82] Claude McKay says of one of Garvey's meetings: "That night Liberty Hall was jammed with Negroes. Hundreds could not get in and the sidewalks overflowed with spectators. . . . Marcus Garvey transformed the great audience into a waving, shouting, frenzied host as he cried: 'Up, you mighty race, you can accomplish what you will.' "[83]

Probably Garvey, by his intense crusade against color exploitation, left American Negroes with a sense of greater identity. This has been an advantage to darker Negroes especially, and for this they were willing to contribute liberally to Garvey's fictitious, material symbols of nationalism. Moreover, he rapidly assumed a reputation of infallibility, and even such seemingly paradoxical acts as his sympathizing with the Klan did not shake the faith of his followers in him.

REVOLT. All through slavery, as we have seen, Negro leaders of more or less significance have arisen to attack the system by force. These insurrections, however, may be thought of as negative in intent. The slaves wanted to be free, but they were neither a powerful class nor the conscious determiners of a radically new social system. Although it may not be far-fetched to think of the slave uprisings as revolutionary, we should like in this section to limit our discussion to a brief review of the nature of the leadership which Communism offers Negroes in the United States. Thus far two books setting out the Communist plans for Negroes have been written.[84]

[82] *Ibid.*, p. 277.
[83] Claude McKay, *Harlem: Negro Metropolis* (New York, 1940), p. 154.
[84] James S. Allen, *The Negro Question in the United States* (New York, 1936); Harry Haywood, *Negro Liberation* (New York, 1948).

The theory is essentially this: that Negroes in the United States constitute a separate nation, that the heart of this nation is geographically located in the South in an irregular area composed of those counties in which Negroes comprise 50 percent and over of the population, and that Negroes should be given the right of self-determination in this interstate area, with an implied right to secede from the rest of the United States, thus assuming the responsibilities of a completely independent nation. James S. Allen states the Communist position as follows:

Historical, economic and social data substantiate the Communist view that the problem of the Negro is the problem of an oppressed nation. The Negro question in the United States is essentially of the same nature as that of retarded and oppressed peoples in Europe or in the colonies. Like these peoples, the American Negroes have been retarded in their social development by American imperialism. Like them, the Negro people have been repressed by a more powerful nation and have been prevented from emerging as a free and independent nation on an equal footing with the other peoples of the earth. Like many of these peoples, the American Negro is retarded by precapitalist forms of exploitation; a large sector of the Negro people is still bound by semi-feudalism in the South. Like other oppressed nations and colonial peoples, the Negroes—not as a class, not as a caste, but as a whole people—suffer from social and political oppression and from inequalities of all kinds. In addition to the problems of the various classes among the Negro people—problems which are shared with corresponding classes among other nations—the Negro people as a whole still face the problem of national liberation, of independence and freedom.[85]

The social situation among Negroes then is assumed to be similar to that among the smaller nationalities of Europe. Space does not permit us to examine this hypothesis critically; at any rate, two vital questions arise from this assumption: should leaders among Negroes begin forthwith to develop black nationalism with demands that the United States acknowledge the claim that the black belt is the legitimate home of the Negro nation, or should the Negroes wait until after the American socialist revolution to assert their national right? The Communists seem to hedge on these questions. They seem to say that black nationalism should develop hand in hand with the revo-

85 *Ibid.*, pp. 173-174.

lutionary movement. Thus, says Allen: "Today the struggle against the plantation system develops in the midst of a general struggle against capitalism. . . . Under present circumstances, a revolutionary proletariat finds its most important ally in the Negro people, who in their struggle against the relics of chattle slavery must at the same time strike a heavy blow at capitalism."[86]

It appears, then, that the revolution, led by the proletariat, is the dominant Communist cause; it is, however, assumed to be fundamentally the Negroes' cause also. But the Negroes' struggle against the southern oligarchy is immediate and continuing. Furthermore, any social action which weakens the power of the ruling class admittedly advances the revolutionary process; therefore, if the black masses are able to infuse their efforts with the vital emotions of an active nationalism and this with its locus in the heartland of the southern oligarchy, the cause of the final transformation of capitalism will, it is believed, be greatly enhanced. Harry Haywood indicates the deliberateness with which the Communist Party reached this conclusion: "In that year [1928], the Communist Party adopted a program which clearly placed the Negro problem as a question of an *oppressed nation*. . . . The program pointed out that in the Black Belt all the objective prerequisites exist for a national revolutionary movement of the Negro people against American imperialism. . . . Thus the new line of the Communist Party brought the issue of Negro equality out of the realm of bourgeois humanitarianism. . . ."[87]

Although there may be some potentialities in this program, it has not attracted any considerable following among Negroes. In fact, it may be very repulsive to most Negroes. It is essentially a somewhat artificial application of theories developed by Joseph Stalin in his study of "the National Question" with especial reference to Russian nationalities.[88]

Martyrdom. At a certain stage in the development of social conflict, an attack by the more powerful antagonist upon a leader of the weaker group is likely to produce a situation of martyrdom, a situation of heightened dysphoria and a crystallization of discontent about the injured leader as a symbol. The counterpart of martyrdom is the

[86] *Ibid.*, pp. 176-177.
[87] *Negro Liberation*, p. 205. (Italics added.)
[88] See his *Marxism and the National Question* (New York, 1942).

incident. The stronger group revenges the incident with a show of power. Martyrdom is not, however, always available to an "oppressed" group. If the struggle is in its early stages, the weaker group may see its leader destroyed and consider the event only as a misfortune—it may even gloat over his fate. In which case he becomes a *victim* rather than a martyr. But when the temper of the people has been excited to a certain point, a direct interference with its leader may serve to bring diffused unrest up to a crisis. Perhaps, for example, the deceptive capture of Toussaint l'Ouverture by the French during the revolutionary unrest in Haiti served more than anything else to provoke in the fighting blacks a determination and resoluteness to wipe out the whites. During the long struggle in India for national independence, Mahatma Gandhi used the threat of martyrdom repeatedly and effectively against the British. The execution of John Brown undoubtedly expedited the coming of the Civil War.

It appears that the possibility of martyrdom is again becoming available to Negro leaders in the United States. It may be observed in a readiness among Negroes in the South to put their employment and possibly their physical safety in jeopardy to carry on lawsuits against the state for civil rights: in education and for the suffrage.

Two significant instances of this situation occurred recently. Before a hearing of a Senate Judiciary subcommittee on the Mundt-Nixon bill, in May, 1948, Paul Robeson, in refusing to answer a question as to whether he is a Communist, declared: "Nineteen men are about to go to jail for refusing to answer that question. I am prepared to join them." The Committee did not take up his challenge. The Washington *Post* (June 1, 1948) reported that Senator Moore said after the hearing: "Robeson seems to want to be made a martyr. Maybe we ought to make him one." However, the ruling class does not think so lightly of the potentialities of the martyr as Senator Moore would imply, for the martyr is sometimes able to do for "the cause" what the leader in action cannot. It is clear that Robeson felt his imprisonment would act as a powerful excitant among the Negro people.

Again, on March 31, 1948, A. Phillip Randolph said before the Senate Armed Services Committee investigating racial discrimination in the Armed Services that "Negroes have reached the limit of their endurance when it comes to joining another Jim Crow Army to fight another war for democracy—a democracy they have never gotten."

Therefore he declared that if a draft law like that of World War II were enacted, he would call upon "all Negro veterans" to join him in a mass civil-disobedience movement. When Senator Wayne Morse retorted that such an act would probably be prosecuted as treason, he answered: "We would be willing to absorb the violence, absorb the terrorism, face the music, and take whatever comes."[89]

Randolph and his colleague, Grant Reynolds, then began to prepare for their campaign of civil disobedience. The attitudes of the Negro people were divided; yet they were deeply stirred, and there was considerable apprehension of a situation of martyrdom developing. Finally, however, the men called off the campaign because they said an executive order of July 26, 1948, gave them the assurance that segregation was "unequivocally banned" in the armed services. The Negro newspapers, generally, cried "coward" at this retreat. However, Grant Reynolds contended: "the response we received shows that Negroes are now ready in 1948, to go beyond the discussion, petition, and protest stage."[90]

VECTORS OF NEGRO LEADERSHIP

It is the habit among great leaders of Negroes to exclaim: "This is the way; and there is no other!" Each leader sees the road before him as the only right and proper one for Negroes to travel; the alternative avenues lead only to destruction and ruin. We may think, therefore, of this attribute of leadership as great lines of force which tend to sweep along incidental deviations and involve them in the major tendency. Thus, in the analysis of leadership trends, it may become confusing to accumulate every detail of the leader's life history and to give to each an equal weight. For example, there was undoubtedly greater agreement on the nature of the "good society" between Joseph Stalin and Leon Trotsky than between either of these two men and Winston Churchill. Yet, the disagreement in direction of leadership between the two Russians was so great as to make them think of each other as fundamentally opposed. It would seem, then, that for an understanding of leadership in the USSR, the disparate goals of these leaders

[89] See *Time*, LI, No. 15, April 12, 1948, p. 21.

[90] "A Triumph for Civil Disobedience," *The Nation*, August 28, 1948, pp. 28-29.

and not their incidental resemblances would be of determining significance.

Moreover, since different leaders in the same social context may take different roads leading to opposed goals, they cannot all be free from fault or mistake. Perhaps it may be possible to set up criteria to test the trueness of the course of action of leaders. There is, it appears, in western society at least, a social movement, amenable to socio-scientific analysis, which is powerful enough to invalidate the actions of leaders who misinterpret it. Therefore, we may assume that *genuine* leadership moves in the direction of the social movement, while *spurious* leadership moves in an opposite or erratic direction.

Let us illustrate this. In the latter part of the fifteenth century, Florence, one of the early cities of modern capitalism, was suffering from an essentially economic difficulty. The Italian monk, Girolamo Savonarola, one of the outstanding charismatic leaders of all time, entered the city and convinced the people that their trouble was religious. For a time he led them; at length, however, in 1498, events themselves closed in about him and his downfall was tragic. This leadership may be termed *spurious*; the society never turned back to it. On the other hand, the work of Oliver Cromwell, in leading an essentially bourgeois revolution, appeared to be undone with the advent of the Restoration; and yet, the Glorious Revolution corrected this reaction, leaving England free to continue to build upon Cromwellian gains. Thus, we may think of Cromwell's leadership as *genuine*.

And so also we may think of the "march toward democracy" as being a prepotent force in the United States.[91] This implies not only a rise toward full citizenship of all the people, but also a correlative change in the balance of power in the society. Moreover, the race problem is essentially a problem of democratic retardation. In this light, then, we may attempt to classify leadership among Negroes.

Of this leadership there seems to be four main lines of force: protest, conservatism, nationalism, and radicalism; and these appear to be negative and positive aspects of genuine and spurious leadership. The following scheme illustrates this:

[91] See Franklin D. Roosevelt Address at Los Angeles, Oct. 1, 1935; and *To Secure These Rights*, The Report of the President's Committee on Civil Rights, Washington, 1947, passim.

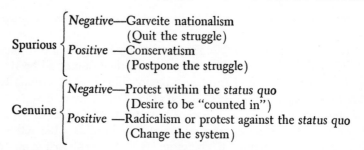

Spurious
- Negative—Garveite nationalism
  (Quit the struggle)
- Positive —Conservatism
  (Postpone the struggle)

Genuine
- Negative—Protest within the status quo
  (Desire to be "counted in")
- Positive —Radicalism or protest against the status quo
  (Change the system)

We may define Garveite nationalism as spurious because it is inconsistent with the modern democratic tendency, and negative because it desires peaceably to remove Negroes from the area of conflict, thus solving the problem by default. And this does not take into account the extreme unlikelihood of the accomplishment of such a plan. There seems to be no prospect of a return to Garveyianism among Negroes in the United States.

Conservatism, as Negro leadership, is spurious because it pretends to be aggressive whereas it actually facilitates the purposes of the anti-democratic class; and it is positive because, although it facilitates the wishes of the oligarchy, it yet expects that at a later date Negroes will, by sheer necessity, be granted all the well-being and civil rights that they now insist is due to them immediately. In its earlier manifestations also it provided Negroes with a symbol, superlatively honored by ruling-class whites, and therefore capable of being interpreted by the Negro masses as counteracting the debasing Negro stereotypes promulgated by this very class. Conservatism, which circumvented the Negro problem, has, in turn, been scrupulously avoided by the Negro people.

It is, of course, rather impossible to determine exactly the degree of retardation or obstruction to the people's cause, which is due to the activities of the conservative leader. This is so because some of the principal values involved cannot be measured. Of what value to Negroes is, say, the right to vote? And yet, we may think of the adverse effects of collaborating leadership as a direct function of its importance and urgency to the ruling class. Or, from another point of view, to the extent that the dominant power is able to impose such leadership upon the oppressed people, to that extent also the collaborator serves to limit the efforts of the people in the interest of their common cause. And it must follow that the greater the established acclamation and fame of the collaborator among his people, the greater the facility of the conqueror to realize its purpose through him.

Protest leadership, as we have described it, seeks the integration of the American Negro into the larger society. It seldom, if ever, questions the nature of the changing process of that society. Says Sterling A. Brown: "Negroes want to be counted in."[92] This type of leadership is genuine because it insists upon public rights equal to those of white citizens, thus integrating Negroes on a parity with the general citizenry; but it is negative because it is a clinging type of demand which does not look to the question of whether the social system, as it is, can grant its requests. Indeed, it is this apparent fault which probably caused Marcus Garvey to fulminate against the protest leaders. It has created a new crisis with the reformed thinking of such leaders as W. E. B. Du Bois.

Perhaps the radical leadership is both genuine and positive. It may be genuine because it demands here and now all the rights of unlimited citizenship for Negroes; and positive because it is not only conscious of the source of the limitation of these citizenship rights but also recognizes that the limitation itself is a function of the social system. Therefore, there is a demand for basic change. This leadership does not ask primarily to be "counted in" because it sees that the process of inclusion is a subordinate function of larger changes in the social system. In other words, this leadership thinks that the Negro protest alone would be of virtually no effect had it not been integrated in the larger and more powerful process of democratic transformation. Thus, it directs its strategy mainly to the larger problem of expediting the advent of democracy,[93] and it will employ the Negro protest and discontent as an auxiliary in seeking to expedite the democratic process. In this way Negroes do not ask to be included; they are in fact merged into the new society by their very involvement in the process of social change.

[92] "Count Us In" in *What the Negro Wants*, Rayford W. Logan, ed., Chapel Hill, 1944, pp. 308-344.

[93] "There are people," said President Truman on this point, "who are afraid of more democracy and greater freedom for all our citizens today." Address at St. Paul, Minnesota, Nov. 3, 1949.

Leadership in an Italian-American Community[1]

BY WILLIAM FOOTE WHYTE

THE TROUBLE with the slum district, some say, is that it is a disorganized community. In the case of Cornerville such a diagnosis is extremely misleading. Of course, there are conflicts within Cornerville. Corner boys and college boys have different standards of behavior and do not understand each other. There is a clash between generations, and, as one generation succeeds another, the society is in a state of flux—but even that flux is organized.

Cornerville's problem is not lack of organization but failure of its own social organization to mesh with the structure of the society around it. This accounts for the development of the local political and racket organizations and also for the loyalty people bear toward their group and toward Italy. This becomes apparent when one examines the channels through which the Cornerville man may gain advancement and recognition in his own district or in the society at large.

Our society places a high value upon social mobility. According to tradition, the workingman starts in at the bottom and by means of intelligence and hard work climbs the ladder of success. It is difficult for the Cornerville man to get onto the ladder, even on the bottom rung. His district has become popularly known as a disordered and lawless community. He is an Italian, and the Italians are looked upon by upper-class people as among the least desirable of the immigrant

---

[1] Reprinted from *Street Corner Society*, by William F. Whyte, The University of Chicago Press, 1937. Used by permission of the publishers.

272

peoples. This attitude has been accentuated by the war. Even if the man can get a grip on the bottom rung, he finds the same factors prejudicing his advancement. Consequently, one does not find Italian names among the leading officers of the old established business of Eastern City. The Italians have had to build up their own business hierarchies, and, when the prosperity of the twenties came to an end, it became increasingly difficult for the newcomer to advance in this way.

To get ahead, the Cornerville man must move either in the world of business and Republican politics or in the world of Democratic politics and the rackets. He cannot move in both worlds at once; they are so far apart that there is hardly any connection between them. If he advances in the first world, he is recognized by society at large as a successful man, but he is recognized in Cornerville only as an alien to the district. If he advances in the second world, he achieves recognition in Cornerville but becomes a social outcast to respectable people elsewhere. The entire course of the corner boy's training in the social life of his district prepares him for a career in the rackets or in Democratic politics. If he moves in the other direction, he must take pains to break away from most of the ties that hold him to Cornerville. In effect, the society at large puts a premium on disloyalty to Cornerville and penalizes those who are best adjusted to the life of the district. At the same time the society holds out attractive rewards in terms of money and material possessions to the "successful" man. For most Cornerville people these rewards are available only through advancement in the world of rackets and politics.

Similarly, society rewards those who can slough off all characteristics that are regarded as distinctively Italian and penalizes those who are not fully Americanized. Some ask, "Why can't those people stop being Italians and become Americans like the rest of us?" The answer is that they are blocked in two ways: by their own organized society and by the outside world. Cornerville people want to be good American citizens. I have never heard such moving expressions of love for this country as I have heard in Cornerville. Nevertheless, an organized way of life cannot be changed overnight. As the study of the corner gang shows, people become dependent upon certain routines of action. If they broke away abruptly from these routines, they would feel themselves disloyal and would be left helpless, without support.

And, if a man wants to forget that he is an Italian, the society around him does not let him forget it. He is marked as an inferior person— like all other Italians. To bolster his own self-respect he must tell himself and tell others that the Italians are a great people, that their culture is second to none, and that their great men are unsurpassed. It is in this connection that Mussolini became important to Corner- ville people. Chick Morelli expressed a very common sentiment when he addressed these words to his Italian Community Club:

> Whatever you fellows may think of Mussolini, you've got to admit one thing. He has done more to get respect for the Italian people than anybody else. The Italians get a lot more respect now than when I started going to school. And you can thank Mussolini for that.

It is a question whether Mussolini actually did cause native Americans to have more respect for Italians (before the war). However, in so far as Cornerville people felt that Mussolini had won them more respect, their own self-respect was increased. This was an important support to the morale of the people.

If the racket-political structure and the symbolic attachment to Italy are aspects of a fundamental lack of adjustment between Corner- ville and the larger American society, then it is evident that they cannot be changed by preaching. The adjustment must be made in terms of actions. Cornerville people will fit in better with the society around them when they gain more opportunities to participate in that society. This involves providing them greater economic opportunity and also giving them greater responsibility to guide their own destinies. The general economic situation of the Cornerville population is a subject so large that brief comment would be worse than useless.

One example, the Cornerville House recreation-center project, will suggest the possibilities in encouraging local responsibility. The center project constituted one of the rare attempts made by social workers to deal with Cornerville society in its own terms. It was aimed to reach the corner gangs as they were then constituted. The lesson which came out of the project was that it is possible to deal with the corner boys by recognizing their leaders and giving them responsibility for action.

The social workers frequently talk about leaders and leadership, but those words have a special meaning for them. "Leader" is simply a synonym for group worker. One of the main purposes of the group worker is to develop leadership among the people with whom he deals. As a matter of fact, every group, formal or informal, which has been associated together for any period of time, has developed its own leadership, but this is seldom recognized by the social workers. They do not see it because they are not looking for it. They do not think of what leadership is; instead they think of what it should be. To outsiders, the leading men of the community are the respectable business and professional men—people who have attained middle-class standing. These men, who have been moving up and out of Cornerville, actually have little local influence. The community cannot be moved through such "leaders." Not until outsiders are prepared to recognize some of the same men that Cornerville people recognize as leaders will they be able to deal with the actual social structure and bring about significant changes in Cornerville life.

So far this discussion sounds much like the anthropologist's prescription to the colonial administrator: respect the native culture and deal with the society through its leaders. That is certainly a minimum requirement for dealing effectively with Cornerville, but is it a sufficient requirement? Can any program be effective if all the top positions of formal authority are held by people who are aliens to Cornerville? What is the effect upon the individual when he has to subordinate himself to people that he recognizes are different from his own?

Doc once said to me:

You don't know how it feels to grow up in a district like this. You go to the first grade—Miss O'Rourke. Second grade—Miss Casey. Third grade—Miss Chalmers. Fourth grade—Miss Mooney. And so on. At the fire station it is the same. None of them are Italians. The police lieutenant is an Italian, and there are a couple of Italian sergeants, but they have never made an Italian captain in Cornerville. In the settlement houses, none of the people with authority are Italians.

Now you must know that the old-timers here have a great respect for schoolteachers and anybody like that. When the Italian boy sees that none of his own people have the good jobs, why should he think he is as good as the Irish or the Yankees? It makes him feel inferior.

If I had my way, I would have half the schoolteachers Italians and three-quarters of the people in the settlement. Let the other quarter be there just to show that we're in America.

Bill, those settlement houses were necessary at first. When our parents landed here, they didn't know where to go or what to do. They needed the social workers for intermediaries. They did a fine job then, but now the second generation is growing up, and we're beginning to sprout wings. They should take that net off and let us fly.

What Has Happened to the Feminist Movement?[1]

BY ARNOLD W. GREEN AND ELEANOR MELNICK

IF ANY movement can be said to have a determinable point of origin in time, the feminist movement in the United States is a hundred years old. It was formally declared at Seneca Falls, New York, in 1848, when the first Woman's Rights Convention was held. Tied as this early agitation was to the antislavery cause, it affirmed the equalitarian rights of a sexual minority deprived of political franchise and control of property. Subsidiary demands were soon introduced: equal education, access to jobs at all levels of the occupational scale, a single moral and marital standard.

The public statements and tracts issued by the early leaders of the movement—Lucretia Mott, Susan B. Anthony, Elizabeth Cady Stanton, Mrs. Emmeline Pankhurst, to name a motley few—indicated that its early dynamic was essentially a unilateral demand for historically preëmpted right and privilege. The heat of battle, and the overwhelming opposition of Victorian society generally, forced a disregard by these doughty female warriors of biological and social-functional differences between the sexes.

What, in essence, did they want? Equality in all things: equal right to divorce; in politics, to vote and lead affairs; in the economic realm, to achieve anything they desired and for which they exhibited individual capability; to receive equal educational advantages and rights in property; and to strike all sexual differentiation from law. What they believed would result from their proposed freedoms was not so

[1] This is a previously unpublished paper.

277

much a coöperative achievement as a unilateral one, because men had historically botched the job of governing, making a living, establishing peace and justice.

VICTORY AND DEFEAT

In the century that has elapsed, the feminist movement and all that aided its forward movement have chalked up almost all the *formal* gains which these determined women demanded of a sullen male society. As to whether all the claimed beneficent results have followed in the path of these gains, the negative answer is almost too easy. The observation that the claims of the feminists have not been fulfilled has become commonplace. The woman's vote did not destroy machine politics. The right of divorce, it might at least be argued, has not brought about happy sexual adjustment for women. The right to equal education and to strive in the job world have neither made leadership an equal accomplishment of women nor revolutionized business practices. While it is generally conceded that women own about two-thirds of all wealth in the United States, it must also be conceded that they neither control nor manage the organizations maintaining and producing that wealth.

In short, women have neither attained to the general level of leadership that the pioneers of the feminist movement insisted they would attain once the legal framework was provided, nor has the female invasion of strange pastures transformed those pastures into the Promised Land. In fact, the very fervor of the pioneers has become somewhat ludicrous in modern eyes, nowhere more in evidence than among groups of so-called emancipated women. The concerted demand by women's groups for more rights and privileges mounts apace, but the belief that a brave new world was a-borning, as a specific result, has waned.

Yet it can hardly be said that the feminist movement was a failure, if by that is meant that all that the prophets of reform promised would result from women's rights has not eventuated. The same could very probably be said for virtually every reform movement in history. All *large-scale* reform movements "fail," for two reasons: first, the proponents of reform assume a static set of conditions into which only a certain number of controlled desirable changes will be introduced, and that the new balance of forces can be predicted on the basis of those changes alone. Besides the original upsetting of the old balance effected by the reform itself, the desired changes combine in unpredictable ways with other concurrent changes. Second, reformers universally fail to consider that one generation can never guarantee the indefinite projection into the future of present-day values—a battle once won, even indeterminately in many cases, is often forgotten, at least by the descendants of the victors, and new goals, interests, and gods emerge.

It was equality in politics and equality in making a living which were the key demands of the feminists. These two areas are central to the power structure of all modern societies; an examination of what has happened to American women in these two areas should afford an answer to the question, what has happened to the feminist movement?

The first and primary political goal of the feminist movement was the franchise, attained in 1920 through the ratification of the Nineteenth Amendment. In that year for the first time women in all states of the union had the vote. The extent to which this right has been put to use is still a matter for debate. Unfortunately, we do not have in this country nation-wide registration of voters by sex. Information on certain states, for limited periods of time, indicate that there has been some increase in the proportion of women voters since 1920. Nevertheless, women consistently fail to exercise the franchise as often as men, in terms of the proportionate representation of both sexes in the population. One of the few intensive studies available indicates that in Erie County, Ohio, in the 1940 national election, about twice as many women failed to vote as men did.[2]

WOMEN AND POLITICS

Although the claim of the antisuffragists that women would not use the vote once it was given to them has proved to be in error, no clearly defined "woman's vote" has emerged. The woman's vote is tied to the man's. Married women vote much more frequently than the unmarried (in part, this may be due to the younger ages of unmarried women); but gainfully occupied women vote *less* than do leisured women. Most important of all, however, married women's voting behavior fluctuates with that of their husbands. Married

[2] Paul F. Lazarsfeld et al., *The People's Choice* (New York, 1944).

couples tend to vote together, or to abstain together. And while husbands frequently vote who have abstaining wives, the reverse occurs much less frequently.[3] Since women now comprise over one-half of the electorate, there would appear to be, here, a considerable gap between potential and achieved accomplishment.

As for the patterning of what women vote for, there are distinctive differences along sex lines. It remains true that social class differences among women are diagnostic of their political loyalties (further reference is made to this below), and that they tend to follow the lead of husbands and other male relatives in exercising the franchise. In general, however, they do tend to be more conservative than men, and to stress programs and platforms which extend the traditional female function of protection and nurture. Separate records for men's and women's voting were kept in the state of Illinois for the Harding-Cox election. Use of a "sex index" (the percentage of the male vote which the female vote amounted to) revealed insignificant differences for the Republican and Democratic parties; yet the sex indices for the Socialist and Prohibition parties, respectively, were 58.3 and 246.7.[4]

Women were the backbone of the prohibition movement. The repeal of the Eighteenth Amendment was sparked by the then Mrs. Charles H. Sabin, the now Mrs. Dwight W. Davis, who organized the Women's Organization for National Prohibition Reform. Protection of women on the job has interested many women's groups, and such legislation has always had the support of the Women's Bureau of the Department of Labor. Social problem issues such as child labor and pure food and drug measures have consistently interested various women's groups.

As one example of unilateral sex action, the Women's Conference on International Affairs, composed of fifty national women's organizations, met in Washington on October 20, 1944, to set up a program on United Nations Relief and Rehabilitation. Problems of international peace and international organization, in the vanguard of which will be found the politically potent League of Women Voters, can

[3] Harold F. Gosnell, Democracy the Threshold of Freedom (New York, 1948), p. 60.
Ruth M. Leach, Jobs and the Woman, National Association of Manufacturers, 1945.
[4] Harold F. Gosnell, op. cit., p. 71.

be said to have interested women in recent years at least equally with men. Women's groups sponsored the present United Nation's Charter provision that eligibility to serve shall not be prejudiced by sex, anywhere in the world, but this has remained an advisory measure, the separate nations deeming this a matter for individual sovereignties alone.

Women's demonstrated special political interests are consistent with the findings of various psychological tests. Statistically significant tests show that women are more in favor of greater privileges for women than are men. In attitude, they are more politically conservative: on labor, changes in government, religious, domestic, and moral issues; yet they are more antiwar and more in favor of governmental intervention and governmental ownership. They favor "economic equality," but are against "dutch treats."[5]

OFFICEHOLDING

The picture is much clearer in the area of officeholding. It cannot be said that the hopes of the suffragists in this regard have seen fruition. Women have gained auxiliary but not key posts within the major parties. They have, as a matter of fact, virtually preëmpted the bottom of the political ladder. Particularly in urban communities, a clear majority of women function as election clerks and inspectors, assisting precinct captains in checking lists of voters or registrants, running errands, and knocking on the doors of indifferent voters. The major parties are coming around to the idea that women function better in this last capacity than men—women especially are more unlikely to be prepared to resist political appeals addressed to them by other women. In the polling places women increasingly perform the routine tasks.

The formal opportunity to assume responsible tasks is theirs: in 1920 the Democratic party, and in 1924 the Republican party, provided for an equal representation of women with men in their respective national committees. But a questionnaire sent out in 1944 to all national committeewomen of both parties indicated a considerable disenchantment regarding their own influence—one-third of

[5] Catherine C. Miles, "Sex in Social Psychology," in *A Handbook of Social Psychology*, Carl Murchison, ed. (Worcester, Mass., 1935), pp. 683-797.

those polled stated they possessed no real power nor control over patronage.[6] On the other hand, the "fifty-fifty" plan has in many states been extended to State, District, County, or Precinct Committees—the plan requires that each committee have a chairman and vice-chairman of opposite sex, with equal voting power. By state law in some cases, by party regulation in others, many states have established a partial fifty-fifty plan, extending equality of representation to some but not to all of the party committees within the state. In only eight states has no effort been made to secure this goal either completely or in part.

There has been no discernible trend in the representation of women on the national nominating conventions. For the Republican party, the figures for 1920, 1932, and 1944 were 27, 87, and 99, respectively; for the Democratic, 93, 208, and 174. This was a disappointment to many, owing to the fact that the War and other conditions gave women in 1944 a clear majority of the eligible voters.

As for direct participation in government, discernible gains have been made in recent years. In 1928 there were 119 women state representatives, 12 state senators, and 7 members of Congress. In 1946, 234 women in state legislatures served in 39 states (16 of them senators and 218 in the lower houses), and 9 women in Congress. At the present time, the Eighty-first Congress also contains 9 women, including one Senator, Margaret Chase Smith, Maine Republican.

And there has been an increasing proportion of women's executive appointments. One has served in the Cabinet in recent years, although none serve at present. Women from time to time have held Ministerial posts, been Director of the Mint, served as Assistant Secretary of the Treasury. But for the most part women's appointments have been in "protective" capacities, reflecting in some measure the traditional female role: in education, social welfare, hospitals, training schools, food distribution and area rehabilitation, domestic relations and juvenile court judgeships[7] (for comparative figures, see note 7).

Attempting to assess women's political gains over the last century is a somewhat gratuitous task. In the first place, the values of the

    [6] Marguerite J. Fisher, "Women in the Political Parties," *Annals of the American Academy*, 1947, pp. 87-93.
    [7] Florence E. Allen, "Participation of Women in Government," *Annals of the American Academy*, 1947, pp. 94-103.

observer are virtually impossible to discount, for these will largely determine whether a measure of increased female political activity will constitute *gain* or *loss*. An indeterminate number of American women (apart from a perhaps more determinate number of men) appear cynical, indifferent, or contemptuous over the political gains of their own sex. Dr. Marynia F. Farnham, possibly the most frequently quoted writer on the modern woman, has sounded the call back to nursery and kitchen as the primal requirement for rescuing civilization.

And, assuming the value-premise that the obvious increase in this activity is a good thing, there is available no standard of comparison for judging what that increase should be, or might have been, contrasted with what is. A radical trend occurring in the short span of ten decades has created, among other results, hundreds of assessments of the women's movement, a few of which deplore the gain as loss but the majority of which are about evenly split between eulogies to accomplishment and diatribes against failure.

But without putting too fine a point on the matter, it would appear that palpable gains *have* been made: a closer approximation to the ideal of equal rights was secured, and many new occupational as well as political opportunities were opened up for women. The greatest general change effected by the women's movement, and one to which little attention has been paid, was the impetus given the steady nurturing of the philosophy of the service state, as it surely displaces the doctrine of definitively limited state action.

Nevertheless, the modern women's movement has become a failure if success must echo the battle cry of the nineteenth century feminist —"political equality"—for the split along sex lines in political activity which these early warriors envisioned has, if anything, been modified by the years. Significantly enough, the majority of women who might be considered the legitimate heirs to leadership in the movement— writers, national women's organization heads, elected and appointed political figures of prominence—are currently stressing a shoulder-to-shoulder stand with American men in a common enterprise and hope of the future. All are agreed that no specifically "woman's bloc" has been maintained, and most of them view this with a complaisance of which the late nineteenth century ax-wielder and hunger-striker were perhaps fortunately spared a foreknowledge.

VITALITY OF TRADITIONAL FEMALE ROLES

There are several reasons for this. Most important, perhaps, is the fact that the extremest demands of the feminists could only bubble at the surface of history. The minority of headstrong revolutionaries remained ignorant of the fundamental changes in social structure which must precede women's assuming positions of leadership generally, rather than over other women. The age-old division of labor between the sexes, however modified in recent decades, has remained more powerfully sanctioned than sexual revolution. The evidence clearly indicates that the majority of modern women make some semblance of the old housewife and mother role their supreme end. More accurately phrased, new rights and liberties striven for by the sex remain for the majority subsumed under the expectation of marriage and a home, the securing of which perpetuate by habit and functional necessity, if not by modern values, some degree of subservience to the husband's job, choice of associates, place of residence. In other words, the majority of modern women still regard themselves as followers, rather than leaders. Or, as one unreconstructed feminist phrases it:[8] "This is the major task—to shake these women out of the tradition that they are followers, and not leaders; that each individual must operate for herself, as an independent person working with other free spirits, and not as sheep blindly following the first one to jump over any particular stile."

Politically active women continue to complain that men still regard women as unfit for organizational work and hesitate to accord them responsible assignments. *And, as has been noted in the behavior of certain minority ethnic groups, oftentimes an ambivalence toward the success of one of their own is manifested:* the group tends to be proud of the individual's success, but concerned lest he take upon himself an attitude of superiority toward those he has left behind. Women leaders frequently complain of the "jealousy" of their followers.

Another lack of political realism shown by the founders of the movement was their belief that sex, in and of itself, could serve as something more than an insubstantial line about which to draw the

[8] Kathleen McLaughlin, "Women's Impact on Public Opinion," *Annals of the American Academy*, 1947, pp. 104-112.

variformed interests of women—those married and those single, employed women and homemakers, the rich and the poor. Time has shown sex to be an inferior means of organizing political interests when compared with social class, occupation, region, religious affiliation, and so on.

This can most clearly be seen in the dilemma presented the National Woman's Party, the direct descendant of the nineteenth-century suffragist movement. This group is small in relation to other national women's organizations and is made up for the most part of wealthy, educated women in late middle age—veterans who are still fighting the war of a hundred years ago: equality in a strictly literal sense. Each year since 1923 this party has introduced in Congress a constitutional amendment, H.R. 49, which would establish equality of all rights, regardless of sex, including equal property rights and the right to administer estates.

CLASS CLEAVAGES IN THE WOMEN'S MOVEMENT

The modern women's movement is now fractured along the planes of occupation and social class, dramatically demonstrated in the 1948 hearings on H.R. 49.[9] The women's groups representing women of property, and those holding high-prestige positions which bring them into direct competition with them, supported the bill. These included, besides the National Woman's Party, the General Federation of Women's Clubs and the National Federation of Business and Professional Women's Clubs, Inc. The main interest involved, however, would appear to be the disposition of family property. At the present time, in thirty-six states and the District of Columbia, where the common-law background holds as apart from the civil-law tradition, property accumulated during the marriage by the coöperative efforts of both husband and wife belongs to the husband and is under his control, except where the rule's effect is overcome by private agreement. However, in most of these States by express provision of law, and in others by interpretation, policy, and practice, the wife's earnings in outside employment are her separate property. The husband's earnings are primarily liable for support of his family, as those of the

[9] Hearings on the amendment relative to equal rights for men and women, Serial No. 16, Washintgon, D.C.: U.S. G.P.O., 1948.

wife are not (nor any of her separate property) unless she voluntarily makes them so by her personal contract.[10]

The opponents of the bill are members of organizations representing, for the most part, proletarian and "middle-class" women: the League of Women Voters; the American Association of University Women; the Congress of Women's Auxiliaries of the CIO; the United Office and Professional Workers of America, CIO; the National Council of Catholic Women; the National Consumers' League; and the A. F. L., including its women's affiliates. Representatives of these various groups pointed out at the hearings that women must have special protection on minimum wages and maximum hours and occupational hazards; protection for widows, wives, and minor children; protection against sex crimes; and alimony provisions in case of divorce. Critical questions were raised, such as what should "equality" mean with regards to military service? Should women be "equal" to men in seniority rights to industrial jobs, when only one sex requires special maternity-leave provisions in labor contracts? The Hon. Helen Gahagan Douglas pointed out that the wives and children of deceased male civil servants are presently protected by annuity and income provisions under retirement law, but women civil servants are not so covered: the equal-rights amendment might inadvertently hit the widow and children of the male civil servant.

The matter was brought to a head in a statement submitted by the United Office and Professional Workers of America, CIO:[11] "The sole benefit of the 'equal-rights' amendment is to women of property and large means who do not face the double burden of earning a living and providing for the care of children and a home. It is our opinion that discriminatory laws now existing against women of property can be wiped out without at the same time depriving women of the middle- and lower-income groups of the gains which they have won with such difficulty in the past." The opponents of H.R. 49 have submitted an alternative bill, H.R. 2007, the key provision of which states that there shall be no distinctions on the basis of sex in U.S. policy, "except such as are reasonably justified by differences in physical structure, biological, or social function."

William Blake pointed out long ago that the same law for different

10 *Ibid.*, p. 110.
11 *Ibid.*, pp. 208-209.

species represents not justice but tyranny. Apparently biology, no less than the well-nigh universal demand for special restrictive legislation to protect vested interest, presents arbitrary limits to the ardor of the equalitarian. The importance of this controversy could scarcely be exaggerated, indicating as it does that the original philosophy of the feminist movement is moribund, that the majority of politically active women are now prepared to effect some compromise with differential biological function and the remnants of traditional social structure which show no immediate signs of dissolvement.

H.R. 49 was decisively defeated in 1946, mainly through the intervention of women organized in opposition to it. At the present time it is in committee again, and it would appear fairly safe to hazard the prediction that it will not be passed unless so qualified that it appear indistinguishable from H.R. 2007, even though President Truman has continued to register his support of the bill.

OBSTACLES TO FEMININE POLITICAL ACTION

Divided though organized women may be on questions directly concerning power and its redistribution, one of the general handicaps facing such one-sex groups has been the rather academic atmosphere surrounding political action not devoted to specifically one-sex interests. On the whole, women stand apart from the center controls of power in our culture, and this is reflected in the way political action is approached. Until 1944 the League of Women Voters, powerful beyond its relatively few numbers though it is (a membership of approximately 83,000), maintained the practice of studying questions of policy for a minimum of two years before voting on them, prior to taking action.

And the complaint has frequently been registered that the General Federation of Women's Clubs, the largest overall women's organization, made up of several suborganizations, containing a fluctuating membership of about a million and a half, has devoted most of its time to listening to speeches and voting on issues about which the majority remain uninformed. Here, as elsewhere, the two main blocks to consistent and speedy forward motion remain the uncertain loyalty to one-sex political action on the part of a membership still primarily involved in traditional roles and goals, and a membership incorporating a diversity of interests and purposes as women. The genteel cultural and self-improvement emphases of so many of these groups interferes with the reality of political struggle.

One trend is particularly worth noting: in the past few years the number of women writers on the subjects of women's rights, and women in politics, who have come to espouse the doctrine of the sexes working together for common ends, has steadily increased. The notion that much of the old argument over equality in ability and rights was pointless is gaining currency. Women may be the "equal" of men in ability, but of a kind of ability which remains functionally differentiated according to biological characteristics and social usages, not to the extent argued by traditionalists, perhaps, but still within certain outside limits. Yet what lends an air of unreality even to the plea that men and women work together is the tacit assumption that women comprise some kind of bloc and that the individuals making it up can equally "coöperate" with men—a mistake in some ways as grievous as the feminist's idea that women could equally be made to organize against men.

On the political side, the "women's movement" today is made up of organizations which have divided to grasp either horn of the dilemma. Some demand working with men for common objectives; others demand unilateral action to achieve one-sex goals and purposes. Both tend to overlook that some women have maintained the traditional housewife-and-mother role virtually historically intact; and that other women are on their own on the job, as leisured *rentiers*, as professionals, as businesswomen and politicians, all of whom must compete in some way in a man-dominated world and are thus led to seek protective and restrictive rights and legislation. Certainly the advice of the doctrinaire is likely to be gratuitous. There may be some point in Dr. Marynia Farnham's exhortation to her sex to go back to the kitchen, raise babies and make their husbands happy, and cease caterwauling about an "equality" which has no functional significance. Such advice, however, blinks the fact that most jurisdictions have modified their alimony laws on the assumption that the modern divorced woman can find the means of earning her own living. *A system of duties can hardly be maintained intact when its concomitant rights are being undermined.*

Since in a culture increasingly characterized by specialized function and diversity of interest there is no male counterpart of the League of

Women Voters, it may be that in the not too distant future women will increasingly align themselves politically with men, but along the lines of specialized interests which transcend the lines of sex differences in some cases, but not in others. This would already appear to be happening.

COMBINING CAREER WITH FAMILY ROLES

If the expressed hope of the feminists that women should find a place for themselves in doing the world's work outside the home be applied to the present situation, then it might be said that they read the future correctly. On the other hand, no universal formula has been discovered for combining traditional and work roles (a course followed by the majority of modern women at some period in their lives), and it is also true that the sex has no more attained preëminence in the job world than in politics.

There has been a steady, although slow, increase in women's gainful employment. In 1940, 22.4 percent of the female population was so characterized; in 1900, only 20.4 percent. World War II, like World War I, was responsible for a tremendous spurt (possibly not so ephemeral in the later case): the peak was reached in August of 1945, when 36 percent of the female population fourteen years of age or older was gainfully employed; in absolute numbers, eighteen and one-half million, comprising 30 percent of the nation's total working force. The expected trend downward can scarcely be said to have commenced: in October of 1948, women comprised 29 percent of the total labor force.[12] Barring economic cataclysm, it seems likely that the long-time trend, starting in 1870, will recommence from an unprecedented high level.

The fact remains, however, that home and marriage still constitute the real as well as indeterminately ideal state of America's women. From 1900 to 1940, the number of full-time homemakers for every 100 males and females in the labor force fell only from 59 to 55; this surprisingly small decrease, however, is partly attributable to the steady rise in the number and proportion of women attending high school, which withdraws most women in that appropriate age-group, today, from outside work rather than from marriage.

[12] Women's Bureau, U.S. Department of Labor, lithographed release of November 30, 1948.

On the other hand, married women made up over one-third of the female labor force in 1940; the trend in absolute numbers being from 800,000 in 1900 to 4,500,000 in 1940. This trend is much more striking than that of employment for all women: in April of 1947 there were more married than single women working! Only 5,900,000 single girls were on payrolls, while 8,300,000 married women held jobs (about 7,600,000 of the latter were living with their husbands). This trend is not quite so startling when it is noted that only 22 percent of all married women were working in 1947, compared with 15 percent in 1940.

As to *why* women work, in contradistinction to the expectations of the feminists, the hypothetical average working woman's job is tied to marriage in some way. If married, she works from felt economic necessity or to maintain a higher familial standard of living than would otherwise be possible. If unmarried, she tends to regard her job as a stopgap until such time as she will be married.

The majority of married women who work do so from necessity. In 1940, in metropolitan districts of 100,000 or more, over 25 percent of wives whose husbands earned one to two thousand dollars a year were working; while less than 6 percent of those whose husbands earned three thousand dollars or more were employed (remunerative employment is for women a characteristically urban rather than rural phenomenon). Among married Negro women in the same districts, 33 percent worked, as compared with the figure for white married women of 14 percent. Various opinion surveys show that over 90 percent of employed women state either economic necessity or maintenance of a higher family standard of living as their motive for working, rather than interest in their jobs (unfortunately, we do not have comparable data for men!). Other studies show that women who are part of a family unit (either the family of orientation or procreation) contribute most of their take-home pay to the family.

The vast majority of single women do not prepare wholeheartedly for a career. This generalization can best be tested among college undergraduates, who could legitimately be inferred to be more career-oriented than any other comparable group within their age range. One such typical investigation, of an entering class of freshman girls in a women's college located near New York City, disclosed that only one-third had chosen their "major" with "preparation for vocation" in

mind. And although 39 percent expressed a deep interest in a vocation, 90 percent hoped to marry within five or ten years after graduation. For this group, on the Strong Vocational Interest Blank for
Women, "wife" headed the list of occupations, being chosen by over
70 percent, and there was little feeling expressed for any job as a
"career."[13]

It is certainly safe to say that the career woman is a statistical
abnormality. Most modern American women do, have, or will work
outside the home at some time during their lives, but they work
discontinuously, and that work is geared in some way to marriage
and/or family. A more or less typical cycle of work and non-work
appears to be emerging. Most women, particularly urban women, work
after leaving school and prior to marriage. With marriage, or soon
after, most will leave. After the birth of the first child, very few remain
in remunerative employment. Some never work again; others do, after
long or short periods of time. Those who are still young when
widowed or divorced tend to return to the job market. "Others during their marriage will return for continuous or discontinuous employment if conditions facilitate and job opportunities attract or if
economic necessity compels. For only a few women is gainful employment continuous as it is for men. For most, it is followed by withdrawal or discontinuous employment."[14]

As for what women do, modern technology's virtual elimination
of the strong back, plus the impetus of the War, have opened up
almost every job classification imaginable to some women. The U.S.
Employment Service lists only a few job classifications (about 5 percent) as unsuitable for women owing to physical disqualifications.[15]
The recent war-production program was responsible for women's
making deep inroads on conventionally defined "unsuitable" jobs.
For example, the number of women employed on Class I Steam
Railroads nearly doubled, to almost 116,000 in April, 1945, from
63,000, in January, 1943. Although most of the new workers swelled
the "professional, clerical, and general" ranks, in 1945 almost 2 per-

[13] Irene M. Wightwick, Vocational Interest Patterns (New York, 1945), pp.
29-30.
[14] Hazel Kyrk, "Who Works and Why," Annals of the American Academy,
1947, p. 51.
[15] Occupations Suitable for Women, U.S. Employment Service, Occupational Analysis Section, Washington, D.C.: U.S. G.P.O., 1942.

cent of all "yardmasters, switch tenders, and hostlers" employed by these railroads were women.

And not only in industry are women to be found in unaccustomed places. The Association of Bank Women, a national organization of women bank executives, possesses a membership of 358, including three women who are chairman of the board of directors of their banks, five who are president, as well as a quota of vice-presidents, cashiers, trust officers, managers of women's departments, and other executive offices.[16]

Nevertheless, although new fields have opened up to many women, the majority continue to be employed either in "women's jobs" or in new fields which pay little and do not confer prestige of a high order. According to the 1940 Census, three-fourths of all working women were concentrated in only twenty-three occupations, in most of which they comprised a clear majority of the total employed. Almost half worked in service industries, such as domestic service, laundries, hotels, and beauty shops (the number of "cosmeticians" doubled from 1930 to 1940); one-fifth were in manufacturing industries; almost one-fifth in trade industries (typists, stenographers, clerks, etc.); and a much smaller proportion in professional service fields such as nurse, teacher, librarian, and social worker. But women practically preëmpt these latter fields—women comprised over 90 percent of all librarians and 75.7 percent of all teachers. The greatest single gain for women since 1940 has been established in the "clerical and kindred workers" category: in that year women comprised 52.6 percent of all workers; by October of 1948, 60.2 percent.[17]

Most significantly, recent decades have not seen a steady gain in the high-ranking professions or in business administration. While in 1902, 8.45 percent of the Who's Who in America listings were women, there were only 6.24 percent in 1930-31.[18] From 1928 to 1945-46, the proportion of women in the total of superintendents of education at state or local levels dropped from 15 to 13 percent. There were only eight thousand medical doctors in 1940, and the proportion of women so classified has hovered about 5 percent of the total for

[16] Dorcas Campbell, Careers for Women in Banking and Finance (New York, 1944).

[17] Women's Bureau, U.S. Department of Labor, op. cit.

[18] Catherine C. Miles, "Sex in Social Psychology," op. cit.

the past forty years. The proportion of women law students declined during the War (in 1940, women comprised a little more than 2 percent of all lawyers in the country). In engineering, architecture, and chemistry, the number of women is infinitesimal, and no marked trends are evidenced. While women preponderate in social work, library work, and home economics, in spite of increased demands for trained workers in these fields the professional schools serving the latter two have recently been experiencing a decrease in enrollments.

While the proportion of all working women employed as professional and semi-professional workers dropped from 13.3 percent to 9.2 percent from April of 1940 to October of 1948, the proportion employed as operatives, laborers, craftsmen, and foremen rose from 20.1 to 22.1 percent. Women now comprise 16 percent of all industrial workers. The gains made during the War, at least in this area, are apparently in process of being solidified.

This is in part attributable to a decreasing prejudice against women on the part of organized labor, in turn fostered by the wartime demands for labor. In 1910 women were 3.6 percent of all union members; in 1940, 9.4 percent; and in 1944, 21.8 percent. There are no recent surveys on female officeholding in unions, but it is commonly conceded that these are not in proportion to women's membership in unions. Two probable reasons are the smaller proportion of women who hold higher skilled jobs in factories and the fact that, because of family commitments, they have less time to devote to union activities. There has, however, been an increasing tendency to use them as organizers since the War.[19]

And their increased membership has had a great deal to do with organized labor's backing of "equal pay for equal work" legislation. During the thirties, a buyer's market in labor, the demand for equality made by many male union heads had as its purpose keeping women off the job. But this could not have been the case over the last decade. The increased number of women working in industry, but, most important of all, the partial breakdown of segregated "women's work" in industry, has fostered the movement. Among the large unions presently advocating such legislation are the United Automobile, Aircraft, and Agricultural Implement Workers of America, and the

[19] Gladys Dickason, "Women in Labor Unions," *Annals of the American Academy*, 1947, pp. 87-93.

United Electrical, Radio and Machine Workers of America. Many States have enacted "equal pay" legislation, and a federal law to that effect is pending in Congress. This will merely extend present federal legislation. The Walsh-Healy Act of 1936 covering conditions of employment in the production of supplies for government contract makes no distinction between men and women with regard to the establishment of a minimum wage rate. And the Fair Labor Standards Act of 1938 provides for the fixing of minimum wage rates irrespective of sex; although the principle underlying this law is entirely different from that of "rate for the job," the law does establish as national policy the payment of the sexes with equally mandatory rates by private enterprisers engaged in interstate commerce.[20] For twenty-five years the federal civil service has strictly enforced the "equal pay" principle.

EDUCATION AND ASCENDANCY

Formal education is a primary channel of vertical mobility in our society, and no discussion of woman and the job world would be complete without some reference to it. Since Oberlin College first opened its doors to women on anything resembling an equalitarian basis, women have succeeded in gaining an ever-closer proportional representation in our institutions of higher learning. In 1939-40, according to the U.S. Office of Education, there were roughly two women to every three men students in colleges, universities, professional schools, normal schools, and teachers' colleges. During the war years the proportion of women increased to 65 percent, but in 1947 it had dropped to about 32 percent. This differential is even more striking with respect to training beyond college graduation. "Masters or second professional degrees were awarded to 8317 men and 3840 women, and doctorates or third professional degrees were granted to 1244 men and 123 women in 1939-40."[21]

For the employed college graduate, there is apparently a greater gap between the sexes in opportunity than between relatively uneducated men and women. Based on a stratified sample of almost 13,000, it was discovered that the median income for all working female

20 *Monthly Labor Review*, September, 1946, pp. 380-385.
21 *Higher Education for American Democracy*, Report of the President's Commission on Higher Education (New York, 1948), II, 40.

college graduates the country over in 1941 was $1590; for the men, $2620. And 95 percent of these women were working for others, while this was true of only 72 percent of the men. The occupational clustering was even more significant: 60 percent of all working female college graduates were schoolteachers.[22]

The training of women in school parallels that of men up to and including, roughly, high school. Women's education beyond that point tends to be more circumscribed in the differentiation of training for adult roles than is education for men. While there is a great deal of dissatisfaction with higher education being voiced generally today, comment upon women's education is particularly acidulous. It has been argued that women's vocational interests are almost as diversified as men's, but women's colleges, and even coeducational institutions, do not afford them equal opportunity for vocational preparation. A somewhat contrary position has been maintained: that women's collegiate training should prepare them for the statistically normal cycle of work, home-and-mother role, work, which a constantly increasing proportion of women of all levels of educational attainment are following. The argument runs that a masculine-dominated curriculum, mainly in terms of vocational training, is inappropriate for most women for whom the career has only interim value until marriage, or secondary value after marriage. Or, particularly in the case of the women's colleges, the woman who must go to work after marriage has received a "cultural" training which has prepared her in no real way for any specific field of endeavor.[23] Women's higher education, in other words, has failed to encompass the diversified after-school life experience of the educated woman. In the defense of college faculties and administrations, nevertheless, it might be pointed out that even at the present time men have preserved a more monolithic and determined vocational purpose than women, and that women's adult roles have been shifting ground so rapidly and confusedly in recent decades that the colleges are at least in part excusable for their failure to overcome this specific example of "cultural lag."

[22] Florence F. Babcock, *The U.S. College Graduate* (New York, 1941).
[23] Robert G. Foster and Pauline P. Wilson, *Women After College* (New York, 1942).

THE INDETERMINACY OF WOMAN'S ROLE

It is the present thesis that the measure of "equality" originally envisioned by the feminists has failed of accomplishment, that about thirty years ago, in both politics and the job world, a fairly stable level was reached which the further passage of time has only indeterminately altered. "Equality" is here being used in a functionless sense, as the same plane of achievement defined in traditional masculine terms. In coöperative situations defined by both sexes in terms of biological and social differentiation, it may be that a greater measure of "equality" is possible. Many available studies of Chinese peasant life have insisted on the strong, secure status-position of women in a milieu which is officially defined as dominated by the male.

The "failure," if failure it is, must have a multiplicity of explanations, only the most obvious of which will receive attention. Sheer biological terms alone can be enlisted only with great caution. In the case of general intelligence, the striking inconsistency of several findings would indicate that in all probability there is very little, if any, sex difference in intelligence, at least as now measured. In fact women's school grades, taken over the entire range of subjects, appear to rank somewhat higher than men's. Strenuous physical activity has been virtually eliminated from the industrial scene. It is believed by an increasing number of industrial employers that women have an advantage over men in jobs requiring detailed, fine, manual dexterity. In the middle range of skilled and subprofessional employments, employers have shown an unwillingness to hire women on the grounds that imminence of marriage, or primary concern with home, husband, and children, with the constant likelihood of leaving the job to complete a pregnancy, make it inadvisable to "waste time" in training women for jobs for which trained replacements are not immediately available. But this factor is not separable from women's sex role.

It is the indeterminacy of women's general role in modern society which has as much to do with their "failure" as anything else, both from the point of view of women themselves and that of their supervisors and colleagues on the job. Various studies have shown that the vast majority of women so consistently place marriage first as a career that little would be served by citing some of them. This tends to lend a certain lack of enthusiasm and drive to vocational goals on the part of at least the younger single woman. And the married woman has on the average neither the singleness of purpose nor the fund of energy to devote to furthering a career that the man, single or married, possesses. While it remains true that the majority of middle-class women, after marriage, never cease an eternal debate over whether or not they should attempt to "do something better than housework," this remains more a matter of vacillation than a purpose held above all other values—a purpose characteristic of males of their own class.

There remains another consideration, the residue of prejudice against, not so much the working woman per se, as the ambitious woman qualified by capability and temperament to compete with her male job associates. It is women in supervisory and administrative posts who arouse the ire of men and the jealousy of their sisters. In the case of men, the loud insistence "I wouldn't work for any woman" has a universal ring.

This is something which goes beyond prejudice against the working woman. Very infrequently are women doing "women's work"—librarians, nurses, schoolteachers, social workers, stenographers, waitresses, cosmeticians—ever verbally scorned. But the tacit assumption that there is a job ceiling for women is widely accepted, so much so that while there were eight women's services in operation during the late War, and the urgency of national crisis was smashing many long-preserved icons, there was little progress reported in accustoming "either men or women to the idea that women should be placed in positions of command over men, even when the relative natures of jobs indicated it."[24]

Interestingly enough, Elmo Roper reports in a survey made of professional men and executives on the one hand (those who have had personal experience in working with, and training, women), and "all men" on the other that while the former group felt that women were more tolerant of handling details than were the latter, they also felt women had less ability to handle people well and make decisions than did the latter![25] Roper opines that while prejudice may be in evidence here, the professional-executive group may be right in general that

[24] Dorothy Schaffter, "Educational Implications of Women's Military Training," Annals of the American Academy, 1947, p. 161.
[25] Elmo Roper, "How Do Women Rate With the Boss," Fortune Magazine, September, 1946, pp. 5-6.

girls, while competent bookkeepers or painstaking research assistants, may lack the decisiveness and the ability to "handle" people that characterizes leaders in most present-day fields.

Does the prejudice have any "real" basis? Several direct and indirect measurements have shown that men, on the average, are less subjectively sensitive and reactive in anger, fear, and the underlying sense of personal security.[26] This is not the place to enter the still-hot controversy over whether socially expressed sex differences are biological or cultural, or both, in origin. But to whatever extent women's administrative disabilities may be culturally explainable, there is virtual unanimity of opinion, based upon considerable life-history and attitude-testing evidence, as to their origin.

LEADERSHIP POTENTIALITIES INHIBITED

In our culture, especially in middle-class circles, a girl's primary social training early deviates from her brother's in the direction of playing passive, placatory, and personally wheedling roles with all male associates in order to gain personal ends. This had unitary functional importance in Victorian society for establishing rapport first with the dominant-protective male parent, and later with the dominant-protective husband. But today, parents, teachers, friends, and even herself, as she reaches the threshold of maturity, tend to vacillate in their expectations of both her conduct and her ultimate goal. She may marry, she probably considers marriage her primary purpose, but she remains convinced that "housewife" does not measure up to "career woman" in a society which increasingly fails to integrate the home with the career of its chief financial supporter—the husband and father.

She receives contradictory advice and experiences contradictory impulses to "play up" to men, be a good listener, flatter the male ego; and at the same time to establish forthright independent behavior, to compete on equal terms, to lead. Mirra Komarofsky has reported several Barnard girls being advised by male and female relatives to strive for a Phi Beta Kappa key, but to keep it hidden in the bureau drawer when going out on dates. This is one manifestation of the general split between love and achievement so characteristic of mod-

[26] Catherine C. Miles, *op. cit.*

ern society, experienced by males primarily in childhood, by females in maturity.

Tending to feel uncertain of herself if she launches out on a career, feeling somewhat "unsexed" indeed if she goes into anything other than a "woman's job," her insecurity is further increased by the abundant hostility expressed by her job associates, of both sexes, if she seeks to go beyond herself, and particularly if she gains a supervisory post. Owing to this general background of factors, the woman who does succeed in becoming a supervisor has a tendency both to "go by the book" in making decisions and issuing directions, and to attach greater importance to personal loyalty to herself on the part of associates and subordinates than to impersonal devotion to getting a common job done. She does both for the same reason—a feeling of insecurity and not quite belonging. There are "vicious circles" in more areas than Negro-white relations.

On the other hand, it appears unlikely that this sort of problem is experienced in extreme degree by an appreciable number of women. Very few women experience severe difficulties in high status positions because so very few ever attain them. And we do not know exactly how many women, in what degree, are frustrated in attempts or yearning to do so. In fact, if Bell's data have any general application, it would appear that males probably experience more career frustration than females. In his notably extensive study of Maryland youth during the depression, Bell found no overlap between any of the ten most frequently preferred occupations, and the ten most frequently followed, in the case of his male informants (they preferred aviator, physician, lawyer, engineer, musician; and got farm laborer, truck driver, industrial worker, store clerk, WPA helper, and so on). In the case of the girls interviewed, there was an overlap of six occupational classifications in preference and actual attainment: housewife, stenographer, teacher, secretary, domestic, sales clerk. Bell concludes:[27] "These comparisons suggest, among other things, that there is either less vaulting ambition among the young women, or else there is a good deal more realism in their understanding of themselves and the kind of world they are living in."

[27] Howard M. Bell, Youth Tell Their Story, Washington, D.C.: American Council on Education, 1938, p. 134.

NEW EMPHASES

Apart from the consideration of whether or no the women's move-ment has been successful, there is the more important matter of newly emerging emphases, new modifications of old feminist de-mands: this generalization is made on the assumption that the rather large army of women currently writing and discussing woman's place in the modern world accurately reflect the values and attitudes of their less vocal sisters. At one pole stands Dr. Marynia F. Farnham, exhorting a return to traditional role, value, and practice. At the other is the equally embattled Edith M. Stern, who calls housewifery a "brain-dribbling, spirit-stifling vocation." Perhaps significantly, how-ever, she issues no new call to arms, resigning herself to women's conservatism—there is little prospect for a Housewife's Rebellion, she says.[28]

But prevailing opinion assumes a middle ground, of which Mar-garet Mead now represents an exemplar: women must cease attempt-ing to win a foothold for themselves in a man's world, and should turn their attention to "fashioning a kind of woman and a kind of man who can work together in a human world, to which both sexes contribute equally." Supported by prevailing social reality, the opinion appears to be growing that both sexes are headed toward a common appreciation of *both* traditional and new women's roles, the latter representing real, but secondary, contributions to the world's work outside the home. This would seem to be indicated for as society is presently organized the majority of women will not, or cannot, follow either pattern to ideal extremity. They thus are being advised to get both society and home life in a balanced perspective.[29]

One thing is certain: so many structural changes have taken place that it would be impossible, by act of will or legislative fiat, to return to the balance of the sexes of a few decades ago. Men themselves are attuning to the work-housewife-work cycle. As specialization speeds apace, many of the traditional woman's home functions of nurture and protection are being taken over by organized agencies, a trend which, in turn, opens up new social service functions to the job-

[28] Edith M. Stern, "Women Are Household Slaves," *American Mercury,* January, 1949, pp. 71-76.

[29] Charlotte Luetkens, *Women and a New Society* (New York, 1946).

seeking woman in fields peculiarly her own and in which competition with males is minimal.[30]

Four million women between forty-five and sixty-four years of age held paying jobs during the week of February 8, 1947, and John Durand, of the U.S. Bureau of the Census, has predicted that there will be 5,500,000 by 1950.[31] The majority of these women are supporting dependents. In fact, at the present time almost three-fourths of all working women who live with their families contribute half or more of their take-home pay to their support. The cry of getting women off the job which is heard in some quarters[32] will result in little more than impassioned rhetoric, for by now there are more men who benefit from women's working than who suffer competition from the sex.

Traditional prejudice against the working woman, and the politically active woman, will in all probability continue to be voiced by men, but, provided that the recurrence of such an economic debacle as that of the thirties be successfully circumvented, it appears likely that such prejudice will wane. Prejudice against the working woman per se has definitely abated, and it is possible that prejudice against women in high-status and even supervisory posts will begin a long decline if so many men continue to benefit from women's general employment.

With much truth it might be said that the feminist movement is not dead, nor even moribund, but quietly goes about its modified aims with no visible lessening of strength or purpose. A minority of women have scaled the economic and political heights, oftentimes (and this is no mere figure of speech) against almost superhuman odds. Such women tend to be definite in their belief that the ground gained should be held, and further campaigns charted.

But the majority of modern feminists, if the term has not lost most of its historical connotation, and women leaders tend to be married women, with one or two children, who are more and more insisting on the combination of modified career and modified traditional role, at the same or different periods of the woman's life-cycle. This hope,

---

[30] Ruth M. Leach, *op. cit.*

[31] Julietta K. Arthur, *Jobs For Women Over Thirty-Five* (New York, 1947).

[32] A. G. Mezerik, "Getting Rid of the Women," *Atlantic Monthly*, June, 1945, pp. 79-83.

in conjunction with the plea to work alongside men rather than organize against them, was the keynote of the Women's Bureau Conference of 1948:[33] "Let's have a new crusade, not to knock men off their perch but to get a seat beside them."

And ". . . let us also start looking ahead and see if we can't work as men and women, as American people, to a world as a whole, rather than women against men, men against women."[34]

[33] Report on the 1948 Women's Bureau Conference, Washington, D.C.: U.S. Department of Labor, 1948, p. 173.
[34] Ibid., p. 172.

Contexts: Political Leadership

DURING THE last century, American political leadership has undergone vast and sweeping changes. Among many changes, the decline in personalized forms of persuasion and leadership seems one of the most crucial. The day of great orators and memorable debates, the period of face-to-face agitation, lives on only in the interstitial areas of the culture where minor parties grapple for a foothold. The politician of today barely addresses himself to his opponent, or to his opponent's arguments—and thereby to the electorate—but, rather, appeals directly to the voters, often in blithe disregard of his opponent's announced position. In part, because of the use of mass communication media, the political leader can no longer posit a select, homogeneous audience to whom he can pin-point his message. The politician can no longer take for granted that he and his audience will share a detailed set of common assumptions. The era of the "glittering generalization" marks a transition from a politics with large doses of rational clarification to a politics nucleated with impersonal techniques of persuasion.

Unlike former periods, where questions of "principle" and "interest" were customary contents of political polemic, the modern politico seeks and seizes upon "issues." "Issues" seem to be devices of a multi-group politics with its shifting realignments, while "interests" and "principles" tend to be the devices of a class-rooted politics, reflecting concern about more enduring aspects of significant statuses in the culture.

These changes find their expression primarily in the national and state political arenas. For the present, as shall be noted below, political relationships in the neighborhood and local communities remain highly personalized.

303

But the process is still in flux. Though the dominant parties' structures have an air of fixity and self-confidence about them, this stability may be more apparent than real. For these parties are experiencing silent metamorphoses more profound than the loud public clashes of political factions.

The last national election witnessed two such clashes: first, the cleavage between Southern and Northern Democrats bringing the open formation of the "Dixiecrats," and, second, the establishment of the "Progressive Party." Neither of these events has yet resulted in major political realignments and they are likely to be better understood as portents and symptoms than as important in their own right.

By 1952 the Progressive Party may have shriveled to a historian's footnote, yet in the winter of 1948 there were many able political observers who prophesied that this party would receive eight to ten million votes. The Progressive Party's failure to show anywhere near that total cannot be taken as evidence of the immutability of American political structures. The decisive rejection of the Progressive Party was not born of an abiding loyalty for either major party. More probably, it was attributable to motives of the most expedient nature: a desire not to "waste a vote," and a belief that the devil we knew was better than the one untried. The Progressive Party's defeat, too, was an outgrowth of its association with the Communist Party—an association which was fortuitous in the sense that it was not organically compelled by the Progressive Party's formal ideology. These indications, along with the steady increase in the "Independent Vote," suggest that a political mass exists which could at any time act as a lightning rod, attracting and catalyzing new political movements.

The only new political movement in North America to take party form and to obtain electoral successes, in the past two decades, was the Canadian Coöperative Commonwealth Federation (C.C.F.). In his study of "Leadership and New Social Movements" Seymour Lipset examines the social conditions from which this new socialist party emerged, considering in particular the social strata from which its leadership was recruited. It does not seem beyond the realm of possibility that should conditions comparable to those which Lipset indicates brought forth the C.C.F. come into existence in the United States, parallel political forms will also be brought into existence.

In the final article of this section the investigation of democratic forms of socialist leadership is continued by Lewis Feuer who reports on "Leadership and Democracy in the Collective Settlements of Israel," a study based in part on his own field studies in Israel. A sharp contrast is drawn between the patterns of leadership which were found in Israel and those in the Soviet Union. Though wide sectors of the Israeli economy are collectivized, Feuer found that modes of leadership there differed fundamentally from Lenin's conception, being highly democratic in both theory and practice. While recognizing that it is difficult to generalize about the problems of a socialist society in general from a study of Israel, Feuer believes that investigation of the Israeli communal settlements can provide much knowledge about the necessary conditions for maintenance of democratic leadership. As is indicated, Israel's forms of leadership and social organization are still in transition—at the time of this writing there are definite tendencies toward increased bureaucratization—but withal, Israel still provides a unique laboratory for the study of democratic forms of leadership in a socialist setting.

In the meanwhile, the major political parties continue to be transformed. William Foote Whyte's article on "The Changing Nature of Political Leadership" analyzes some of the forms and sources of these changes. Two major themes run through Whyte's study:

1. First, that the political leadership on the local level is still very largely a matter of personalized relations of a highly informal type.

2. The second theme woven through Whyte's analysis concerns the changes in the leadership pattern of local politics wrought by the depression. Whyte emphasizes that federal efforts to mitigate depression effects (e.g., the WPA) facilitated the ascent of patronage-powers into the higher regions of the political hierarchy. In this way one of the major controls usually available to the local leader was weakened.

It is doubtful whether this process was "brought about" by the depression and consequent governmentally initiated public works. It is probably true that the depression acted as a catalyst precipitating the clear-cut emergence of the trend toward smaller powers for local leaders. The public-works program was, however, only one crisis manifestation of a larger trend toward the assumption of governmental responsibility for economic stability and welfare.

For a long while now the federal government has expanded the number of its personnel. Through its market operations as well as its legislative program, the federal government has come to have a major role in the economy. These are long-term trends giving no suggestion of a return to a laissez-faire economy, regardless of the political party in power. In consequence, increasing attention is given to the national political level by businessmen, which tends to bring about a persisting reallocation of their political funds from local to higher levels. Even as expanding media of communication make political campaigning more expensive, local politicians find themselves in narrowing financial straits. Underlying this process is the perceptible maturation of the economy with a tendency for the number of local marketable favors needed by businessmen to dry up.

The fuller implications of the weakening of the local politician may be explored if one attends to the question of what has formerly kept local political machines together and maintained the loyalty of followers to local leaders. Several elements comprised the typical motivations which once cemented followers to the local politicians: (1) *expedient motivations:* these were of two kinds, anticipation of rewards or fear of punishments—for example, a follower's desire to get a political job, a recommendation for a job in private industry, a city contract, direct cash payment, or possible withdrawal of these; (2) *traditionalistic motivations:* e.g., belonging to and supporting a party because one's family always did; (3) *affectual motivations:* personal knowledge of and liking for a leader; (4) *legitimacy motivations:* believing in the moral qualification of a given leader, usually because of his personal qualities or because he has been *successful* and has proven himself in political battles.

With the transition to a mobile urban society and the beginning of cleavages between generations, traditionalistic motives for loyalty begin to wane, though they are still potent. Thus the proportion of independent voters seems greatest in urban communities and among younger voters. Simultaneously, the ties of expediency binding followers to local leaders are being worn away by the growth of civil service, the tightening of businessmen's local campaign funds, and by the rise of professional social work and public welfare agencies. The local political leader's ability either to indulge or to deprive his followers has been seriously curtailed by these developments. Since the former's *legitimacy* is connected with patronage-creating electoral successes, this too has suffered some impairment with the desiccation of patronage sources.

As Whyte indicates, affectual bonds between leaders and followers also tend to unravel as the leader moves upward. As he becomes obligated to other groups, he interacts less intensively with his original group and perhaps more superficially with varied other groups. In addition, as the political party structure becomes more closely intertwined with the complex legal apparatus of state and federal governments, it is possible that higher educational qualifications will be necessary for successful political leadership. Political leadership would tend to begin on higher levels in the organization and to involve an educational background at variance with those in the neighborhood, in both cases short-circuiting personal ties with local followers. There is some evidence that these factors are beginning to manifest themselves.

In brief, the ties once binding local leaders and followers in the major political parties are no longer as stable as they once were. Current observations on the decline of the old-fashioned city boss and on the Democratic Party's growing dependence on the CIO-P.A.C. are two indications of this. These changes constitute threats to the integrity of the local political machines. Among the measures which are in part defenses against these challenges are:

1. *Closer alliances with the rackets.* This is a pattern which Whyte unfolds with rich detail. Unlike the legitimate business which needs irregular favors, the racketeer is a steady customer, ever in need of political protection. He is therefore a regular source of much needed income. This alliance between local politicians and the racketeers, the "internal imperialists," is so common that it is now rarely a source of moral indignation.

2. *Bureaucratization of party structure.* In his coyly titled book "You're the Boss," Edward J. Flynn, Democratic boss of the Bronx, provides a clinically fascinating document on the bureaucratization of the Democratic Party. Flynn, for example, instituted a filing system in which all requests for patronage were recorded and regularly checked upon. He deliberately diminished personalized contacts between himself and his lieutenants, demanded that lines of communication be heeded, insisted upon regularized office hours, and explicitly modeled

his party after the organization of a business. (Flynn, incidentally, is a political leader who began his career on a relatively high level in the machine.) In part, the bureaucratization of the political party involves an effort to compensate for deteriorating personalized ties between leaders and followers.

3. *Alliances with charismatic leaders.* Of the several adaptations mentioned here, this seems the least probable of occurrence. The support rendered Huey Long by the Democratic machine of Louisiana, and without which his rise to national prominence would have been problematical, is an illustration of this possibility. Such alliances provide the party with new instruments of face-to-face persuasion and with new modes of legitimation. Nevertheless, they seem to be unpopular with most machine politicians, perhaps because of reasons similar to those underlying the general hostility between charismatic and bureaucratic leaders.

As local political leadership loosens its grip, it becomes important to secure reliable knowledge about the character of top-level leadership and of the elements binding it to its followers. One article in this section is designed to provide some limited knowledge of this area. In his article "Who Are the Government Bureaucrats?" Reinhard Bendix explores the social characteristics of "middle-bureaucrats," contrasting popular beliefs about government bureaucracy with his own findings. Bendix, it will be noticed, examines these bureaucrats not so much in terms of the organizational structure in which they operate—a task largely fulfilled by Robert K. Merton in his chapter in this volume—as in terms of their career and personal histories, and the groups from which they have been recruited. Bendix suggests that much of the public fear of and hostility toward government bureaucrats is unwarranted and, in turn, disposes the bureaucrats to behave in ways that are disapproved. Compared with business bureaucrats, the government bureaucrats probably have less in-group solidarity and are more carefully circumscribed by legal institutions; it is therefore improper, Bendix indicates, to conclude that they are either more "dangerous" or inefficient than bureaucrats in private industry.

The Changing Nature of
Political Leadership[1]

BY WILLIAM FOOTE WHYTE

When Boss Joseph Maloney lost his campaign for alderman in 1939, his Cleveland Club lost its last hold upon Cornerville, the South Side, and Welport. The power of the organization had been wasting away for years, and, when the final collapse came, there was nothing that Maloney could do except look back upon the happier days from the 1890's through the 1920's, when the Cleveland Club, under its founder, Matt Kelliher, had dominated Ward 4. He told me the story of the club in this way:

We had a captain in every precinct. He was a man who knew everybody in his precinct and could tell how just about all of them would vote. We had quite a variety of precincts. Over beyond —— Street was a pretty highclass precinct. You had to have an educated man in charge there. Then we had another precinct where most of the freight handlers lived. That was a different kind of job.

When people wanted help from the organization, they would come right up here to the office [of the club]. Matt would be in here every morning from nine to eleven, and if you couldn't see him then, you could find him in the ward almost any other time. If a man came in to ask Matt for a job, Matt would listen to him and then tell him he'd see what he could do; he should come back in a couple of days. That would give Matt time to get in touch with the precinct captain and find out all about the man. If he didn't vote in the last election, he was out. Matt wouldn't do anything for him—that is, unless he could show that he was so sick he

[1] Reprinted from *Street Corner Society*, by William F. Whyte, The University of Chicago Press, 1937. Used by permission of the publishers.

couldn't get to the polls. When Matt heard what kind of a fellow the man was, he could make up his mind about trying to do something for him.

When a man got a job through our influence, he would keep on paying his dues, and around election time we would expect him to make some kind of contribution to support the campaign. We never accepted money to indorse any candidate. In that way we kept our independence. . . . When I first ran for representative—I didn't want to run; I was selected by the organization—I contributed $150 toward the expenses, and the organization paid the rest.

In those days we held political office in order to be of service to the people. Of course, if Kelliher thought the city was going to buy a certain piece of property, and he had a chance to get it first, all well and good. He was in the real estate business, and there was a lot of money in that business when the city was expanding. But, with him, service to the people always came first. He never took a cent for the favors he was able to do. Matt and I never sold our jobs or charged for a favor.

In those days we really controlled. We could tell within fifty votes how the ward would go in any election. One time we changed the ward from Democratic to Republican overnight. That was in the mayoralty contest of 1905. There was a meeting in the club till three in the morning right before the election. We printed the slate we were backing and circulated it around as much as we had time for. When the people came to the polls, the captain would ask them, "Do you have the slate?" If they didn't, he would give it to them, and they would go in and vote it. When the votes were counted, we had carried the ward for the Republicans just like we carried it for the Democrats. One time a fellow says to Matt, "I'm not going to vote the ticket this time." There were thirteen votes against us in his precinct, and Matt would have given anything to know who the other twelve were.

Maloney explained the breakdown of the organization in terms of the shifting population, the New Deal, and the rise of "the racket element":

Today everything has changed. We've got a floating population in the South Side now. People are moving out all the time. You can't expect a precinct captain to know everybody any more. It's only in Cornerville that people stay in the same place.

Then the Italians will always vote for one of their own. We recognized them when we didn't need to. They didn't have many votes, and we could have licked them every time, but we gave them Italian representatives. We did it for the sake of the organization. But they wouldn't stick by us. The Italian people are very undependable. You can't trust them at all. They play a dirty game too. I estimate that now there are between eight hundred and a thousand repeaters in Cornerville every election. I've tried to stop that, but you can't do it. You can't tell one Italian from another.

In speaking of the disloyalty of the Italians, Maloney referred actually to a conflict of loyalties. From the time that the Italian immigrants got into street fights with their Irish predecessors, there was bitter feeling between the groups. Since the Irish controlled the ward politically, the Italians, as long as they were in the minority, had to follow the Cleveland Club in order to gain any political benefits. In recent years Italians who had the political support of the club were looked upon by Cornerville people as disloyal—traitors to the cause of Italian unity. As the proportion of Italian votes in the ward grew steadily, it was to be expected that the Italians would break away from the Cleveland Club.

To Maloney's charge about "repeating" in Cornerville, which is exaggerated but not otherwise untrue, Cornerville people reply with charges that the Cleveland Club would have fallen years earlier if it had permitted honest elections. My own observations and the unanimous testimony of Cornerville people indicate that the club used repeaters whenever needed. Maloney freely admitted that many of his voters lived outside the ward. "A man has a constitutional right to choose his own domicile. As long as he isn't registered in two places, it's all right." He continued his story:

In the old days it was different. The New Deal has changed politics altogether. With home relief and the W.P.A., the politician isn't needed any more in a district like this. Years ago a man out of work would come to us to see what we could do for him. Now he goes on home relief and then he can get on the W.P.A. That's all he wants. This relief is a terrible racket.

I asked whether a man did not need political backing to get on the W.P.A., and Maloney said it could be accomplished without such aid. I took this question up with Carrie Ravello, the wife of the state senator, and she gave me this answer:

That's right. If you're qualified, you can get on without going to a politician. But it will be four weeks before you get certified, and I can push things through so that you get on in a week. And I can see that you get a better job—if you're qualified. If you want to be a supervisor on a contracting job, I can't tell them, "Make Billy Whyte a supervisor," because you're not qualified for that job. You don't have the experience. I can only do something for you if you're qualified.

The corner boys corroborated some of these statements but added that many unqualified men with strong political backing had been able to get good W.P.A. jobs.

There were many politicians in Eastern City. The important question is: Whose political support was important in dealing with the W.P.A.? I asked Mrs. Ravello how she was able to help her constituents in this field. She explained:

I know Dave Collins. He is the state administrator, head of all the projects in the state. I can go right into his office. He knows my connections with [United States] Senator Corcoran.

I asked how Collins had attained his position.

He was appointed six months ago by the regional administrator. The regional administrator appointed him because he had the support of Senator Corcoran. Billy, I don't care what you say, these days it isn't what you know, it's who you know that counts.

She added that the most important connection one could have for the W.P.A. was the one with Senator Corcoran. Next in importance were connections with Representatives in Congress.

There were important changes in the federal administration of relief after the early days of the New Deal. In the beginning there was a tremendous demand for jobs, and there was no recognized means of distributing them except through the usual political channels. Paul Ferrante, the state senator's secretary, told me that the Ravellos obtained a number of work-assignment slips from a high state official so that, whenever they wished to place a man on a project, they had simply to fill out a slip. As the federal relief setup developed and became established on a permanent basis, the powers of local politicians in dealing with relief were progressively curtailed.

This does not mean that relief was taken out of politics. It means that the pressure had to come from higher up in the political hierarchy. As Carrie Ravello pointed out, she was able to deal effectively with the W.P.A. administration because of her connection with United States Senator Corcoran. If she had not such connections, she could have accomplished very little. This was substantiated by the stories of many other Cornerville people. They did not speak of going to see Senator Corcoran. From the view of the corner boys, his position was so high as to be out of sight. They did speak of soliciting the aid of Congressman Branagan. The congressman had several secretaries, one of whom was a young Italian who lived in the ward. Through him many Cornerville people were able to get W.P.A. work assignments.

There was no state boss to whom Senator Corcoran was responsible. On a smaller scale, Branagan had a similar standing. He had his own organization, and, since he represented several wards in Congress, he was not subject to any one politician in any one of the wards. There was no longer a ward boss in the Matt Kelliher sense in any of these wards. This did not mean that Corcoran and Branagan were independent of all other politicians. They had to perform services for and make informal alliances with other politicians in order to perpetuate their power. The important point is that they dealt with other politicians in their own right and were not subject to dictation from anyone in the areas they represented. With the immense power of federal patronage in their hands, they had achieved such a commanding position that other politicians had to come to them in order to secure their constituents a share in the benefits of the New Deal. With only his own organization behind him, the ward politician had scant power, as the story of Joseph Maloney indicates. He had to subordinate himself to his congressman or United States senator in order to meet the demands of his constituents.

Thus it appears that the New Deal helped to bring about a political reorganization whereby the localized organizations of ward bosses were to a great extent supplanted by a more centralized political organization headed by the United States senator, with the congressman next in line, and the ward politicians assuming more subordinate positions.

Maloney concluded his story with a discussion of the racket element:

Kelliher would never have anything to do with prostitution or with them fellows. . . . During prohibition, the bootleggers didn't mix in politics so much. Yes, they had to have protection, but they minded their own business more. Then, after repeal, the same people that had been bootlegging got the liquor licenses and when legalized horse- and dog-racing came along, they got into that. They've been spreading out all the time, and they've been trying to take over political control. It was in 1933 that I first realized how strong they really were. They got a lot of votes against me at that time. You see, men like Bob Madigan and Red O'Donnell can buy a lot of votes. Madigan runs that liquor place on —— Street, and O'Donnell controls a lot of horse rooms in this ward and has some liquor places too. They have a lot of fellows hanging around them, and they pass out a lot of free liquor, especially around election time. Then those number-pool fellows go right into people's houses, and they get quite a hold on the people. They've been spreading propaganda about me. Say an agent keeps his numbers and doesn't want to pay off on a hit. He tells the person, "I'm sorry, Joe Maloney had me pinched and the cops took all the slips off me, so I can't pay you." The people hold it against me, but it isn't true. I keep my hands off their business.

That crowd has been after me for a long time. They've been keeping their liquor places open after hours, and I didn't like that. And I don't think it's right to have them open on the Lord's Day either. And I knew that people were getting robbed in the —— Cafe, and I complained to the police about it. You see, the heart of the city is right in this ward. You'll find everything going on at night right down here.

They want to get me out of here. I've been threatened with a gun three times right in this office, and once a fellow pulled a knife on me. T. S. wanted to run me out of politics.

We might still be strong today if we hadn't picked up the wrong men. We elected Art Porcella representative, and he turned against us and went in with that racket crowd. Mike Kelly—he was my mistake. I really took him in against the majority of the organization. He had run for office three times, and he didn't get anywhere. Sometimes when a man ran against us, we recognized him and took him into the organization. Some-times that policy worked out and sometimes it didn't. Mulrooney [a club member] was friendly with Kelly, and he says to me, "Why don't you give Kelly a chance?" So we talked to Kelly, and he promised he would be faithful to the organization. We indorsed him, but then when the cam-paign got under way, we began to hear disturbing reports that he was a weak candidate. We sent out our men to investigate, and we found that the reports were true. It looked like two Italian candidates were going to be elected. To prevent that, we had to do something we never did before, indorse just one candidate. That's the way we put Kelly across, and he just made it.

When he went to the legislature, Kelly didn't want to have anything to do with committees dealing especially with the affairs of the city. He wanted to get on the legal affairs committee, and through my influence I got him there. That was at a time when all this new legislation on liquor licenses and horse- and dog-racing was coming through before that committee. Through that position he built up his law practice and got himself made counsel for the Liquor Dealers' Association. He caught me napping. While the racket element was fighting us from the outside, he was boring from within, and he did a lot of damage to the organization. . . .

Kelly fits right in with that element. That's why I had the police all against me in this last fight.

ECONOMIC TRENDS AND CYCLES

The Cleveland Club was organized primarily to provide political jobs and favors for its members, but its success depended also upon its relations with legitimate business interests and upon the business activities of its leading figures. Both Matt Kelliher and Joseph Maloney supported themselves through real estate transactions. This meant that neither man was financially dependent upon any group of constituents or any local business interest. When the city ceased to grow and the depression came, this source of income dried up. Maloney was not immediately threatened, since he had made himself a wealthy man in the earlier period, but the change in the situation meant that it would no longer be possible to build or maintain a political organization upon the same foundations that had served the Cleveland Club.

When Matt Kelliher was at the height of his power, industries in the state were expanding rapidly. The public utilities were particularly dependent upon franchises and other grants of power from the city and the state. When Kelliher sought to place some of his constituents in the employ of the railroads or the telephone company, they could not afford to turn him down. The old ward boss owed much of his power to his ability to place men in private industry as well as in government jobs.

The situation then completely changed. Business was no longer seeking new privileges; it was concerned primarily with holding its position. When politicians introduced legislation to deprive business of certain privileges, the businessmen had to defend their interests; but they could offer more money when new opportunities for profit were to be won than when an established position was to be maintained, and in a time of depression few jobs were available for any purpose. George Ravello was elected to the state senate in 1932. His wife told me that neither she nor her husband had ever obtained jobs for their constituents with the public utilities or with other large businesses. She said, "They are not obligated to me. Why should they do me a favor?" The businessman is no longer so intimately concerned with state and local politics. Today when he speaks of government he means the federal government.

The racketeers made money right through the depression and expanded their activities while business was retrenching. In the prohibition era the bootleggers had needed political and police connections, but their problems were relatively simple. A bootleg liquor shipment either went through or was stopped. It was not subject to all sorts of regulations. When a large part of their activities had been legalized, the racketeers needed to apply to the state and city governments for the privilege of carrying on and expanding their operations, just as the legitimate businessmen had done, and they developed an efficient monopoly organization to promote their interests. The rackets took the place of legitimate business in relation to politics.

The Cleveland Club was unable to make an adjustment to the substitution. Joseph Maloney had no scruples against gambling or racketeers as such. Speaking before his club on the eve of the 1939 aldermanic election, he said:

Politics is a business. You have to maintain the organization. Whenever a man has been friendly with the organization, I try to help him. I don't care if he sells numbers or lottery tickets as long as he pays the people when they win. Nobody can say they ever paid tribute to me to do business in this ward. As long as you mind your own business and keep your nose clean, I won't bother you. Of course, if they are friendly with the organization, we will try to help them out. But we don't believe in violence, stickups, and that kind of thing. We want law and order in the ward.

The Cleveland Club was organized to serve its members and could not cater primarily to the interests of another local organization without destroying its own foundations. Consequently, Maloney fought against the extending political power of the racketeers. And he fought in vain.

THE ALLIANCE BETWEEN THE RACKETS
AND LOCAL POLITICIANS

The young Cornervile politician has grown up along with the expansion of racket activity. The Cornerville lawyer who goes into politics has not been able to afford the best legal education and has not made the social connections required for the practice of corporation law. He finds criminal law the most profitable field in Cornerville and the racket cases the most profitable sector of that field. Even the racket cases do not provide a lucrative income, for a small politician is given only small cases. To finance his campaigns, he needs the help of his business clients, and, among these, the racketeers are most willing to help.

If the young politician had a profitable business, he might be able to support his own campaigns, but success in most businesses seems to draw a man away from a political career. There appears to be only one business which fits well with politics in Eastern City. That is the undertaking business. Senator Ravello and Alderman Fiumara were undertakers.

In the Italian community people generally have an undertaker of "their own kind," a man from the same part of Italy. In and around Cornerville there is at least one undertaker for each section from which many have emigrated. The undertaker must maintain active social relations and establish himself as a prominent figure especially among his paesani. The Italian funeral is an elaborate pageant participated in by all relatives and friends of the family. The undertaker's part in arranging and handling this occasion strengthens his position in the society.

If he has an established funeral business, the undertaker will be well known and well supplied with personal contacts before he enters politics. He counts on his own kind as a nucleus for political support. As undertaker and as politician, he wants to broaden his contacts, and the two activities reinforce each other. A political campaign advertises the funeral business, and the funeral business widens political contacts. Those who are not committed to a particular undertaker are inclined to give a family funeral to a politician in order to establish a connection with him. Having done the politician a favor by bringing him business, a man is in a position to ask a favor in return. If some people cannot afford his charges, the politician may bury their relatives for nothing. The dead man does not vote, but his relatives and friends do.

While some politicians are more dependent upon him, even the undertaker-politician must make an adjustment to the power of the racketeer. There is no one way in which this adjustment must be made. In Cornerville there is a wide variety in the relations between politicians and racketeers, as several examples will indicate.

Tom Marino, boss of the Taylor Club, was a 50 percent man in the numbers long before he entered politics. He ran for representative twice and continued his numbers business in his corner store at the same time. He was a figure of moderate importance both in politics and in the rackets. Marino was the only racketeer in Cornerville who had actually run for office, until Sully Defeo entered politics.

One local politician was known as the racketeer's candidate, since he owed his election to their support. He served the racketeers loyally in connection with all liquor and racing legislation and was rewarded with financial support and a number of jobs at the race track for his constituents. I have heard corner boys complain that the only way to get anything out of this politician was to approach him with the support of some prominent member of the T. S. racket organization, and in one campaign I had an opportunity to observe him taking his orders from the racket boss.

Eastern City newspaper stories about George Ravello presented the picture of a politician completely identified with racket interests. That was inaccurate, and yet it is easy to see how the impression arose. When Joe Kenney, a prominent and colorful Welport racketeer, was shot, Ravello rushed to his deathbed. The newspapers headlined his visit. Two days later Carrie Ravello had this to say to me about Kenney and her husband:

I like Joe Kenney because he was so regular. There was a lot of class to him. He was always helping out the poor people in his district. If you were down and out, you could go up to him and say, "Are you Joe Kenney? I hear you're a regular fellow." And he would give you something and tell you not to worry. He was very popular down in Welport. He could get all them bums and drunks out any time. You just go up to a house and knock on the door and say, "Joe Kenney sent me," and the man will get dressed and come with you to vote and repeat for Joe Kenney. There was a lot of class to Joe Kenney. He was a regular fellow. He knew his place in society. It was a great shock to me when I heard he was killed. I really liked him. I won't deny it. When he was dying, George was the only politician that was with him. . . . They [several prominent politicians] all ought to have gone to him in his hour of need. But they was all afraid to except George. George says to me, "I don't care what they say about him, he was always all right with me."

Shortly after the repeal of prohibition, Kenney had asked Ravello to try to secure for him a night-club liquor license. Ravello was new in office and was unable to do it. Kenney managed to get his license through someone who had better connections, but he knew that Ravello had done his best, and they were friends from that time on. Kenney supported Ravello in his political campaigns. Ravello enjoyed the company of tough guys, and he appreciated their political support.

While Ravello had done favors for Cornerville racketeers, he was never known as their particular candidate. With one exception, T. S. opposed Ravello in all his campaigns. Ravello was on a level with the racket boss and did not take his orders. He had nothing against racketeers, but he was not dependent upon them for financial support, and he refused to accept money from them or from anybody else in payment for favors.

Andy Cotillo had to fight against the influence of the racketeers in order to get his start in politics. Art Porcella was his strongest Italian rival and once defeated him in a very close election by means of racketeer support and the votes of repeaters. Cotillo set out to organize the district against this control at the same time that he fought against the Cleveland Club. He and his organization endorsed a dark-horse candidate for mayor when all other political organizations in Cornerville were supporting other men. On the day of that election Cotillo got into an argument with Len Cardullo, a prominent racketeer who was a close friend of Porcella. Cotillo said that if his candidate for mayor was elected, he would put the Cornerville racketeers right out of business. Cardullo answered him with a slap in the face. Cotillo was much bigger and stronger than Cardullo, but he was discreet enough to refrain from returning the blow. The story of this encounter was all over the district within a few hours after it took place.

Cotillo's candidate won the election, and Cotillo became the only Cornerville politician who had a connection with the new mayor. Immediately new members began to join his Victory Club, and within a few months Cotillo had the largest political organization in Cornerville. He himself got a job in the mayor's office. Just a year after his clash with Cardullo, he had his club indorse one of its members, Al Macarella, for representative, and he managed to secure the candidate's indorsement from a number of other clubs, so that he had an excellent chance of winning. Up until this time, Cotillo had complained about the elections that had been stolen from him. Now he let it be known that, through his connections with the mayor and the board of elections, he would have his men in control inside the Cornerville polling places. Still he needed more votes. He got together with Len Cardullo and made a deal. Cardullo's men were instructed to vote for Macarella for representative, and Cotillo's men were instructed to vote for Cardullo's candidate for the state senate.

Although Cotillo started his campaigns with the explicit purpose of overthrowing the political power of the racketeers and of the Cleveland Club, he had to make an agreement with one group in order to defeat the other. The agreement was a matter of temporary mutual advantage and did not necessarily mean that Cotillo would be unable to maintain a position of relative independence.

I have never heard of any Cornerville politician, except Andy Cotillo, delivering a direct challenge to the racketeers. Cotillo has never repeated his challenge. Whether he likes it or not, the politician must take into account the social position of the racketeer, which is in many respects similar to his own. The politician and the racketeer grow up in similar environments, have influence over the same groups or the same sorts of groups, are expected to perform some of the same functions, and have many interests in common. Between them, coöperative relations, of varying degrees of intimacy, are bound to develop. Carrie Ravello summed it up in this way: "Let's not kid ourselves, Bill; when we want to win, we go to the racketeers—all of us." Here she mentioned three of the most prominent and respected politicians in the state. "They do it, and the rest of them—we all do it."

THE POLITICAL CAREER

A Cornerville man can get ahead either in Republican or in Democratic politics. The nature of his activity will depend upon which route he chooses, for there is a fundamental difference between the two careers.

The Republican politician gets ahead by drawing himself to the attention of the upper-class people who control the party in the state, and, in so doing, he draws himself away from Cornerville. The career of Judge Gennelli provides an outstanding example of such behavior. He was born in Cornerville of a poor Italian family. He sold papers and shined shoes when he was a boy. He put himself through law school, became active in Republican politics, and won a minor judiciary appointment. Becoming more successful in his law business, he set up offices in the center of the Eastern City business district and hired girls of native American background as secretaries. Some time later he was given a better appointment on the bench. Quite early in his career he had moved out of Cornerville to a fashionable suburb. He won his party's nomination for attorney-general and waged a vigorous campaign to win the Italian vote. In this he failed. The Republicans lost and Gennelli ran behind his ticket. He fared little better in Cornerville than the other Republican candidates. Upperclass people looked upon him as an excellent judge and felt that his career testified to the vitality of American democracy. Cornerville people looked upon him as a high-class lawyer who was not concerned with helping them out of trouble. However, his inability to swing the Italian vote did not prevent Gennelli from rising. A later Republican administration promoted him to the highest court in the state.

Chick Morelli may never rise so high, but he is proceeding step by step along the route taken by Judge Gennelli—and every step takes him further away from Cornerville.

The Democratic politician gains his strength from the support of Cornerville people. His success depends upon his ability to deal with groups of people inside his district. Therefore, in order to understand his career, it is necessary to have some general knowledge of the nature of these groupings.

Corner gangs, such as the Nortons, or corner boys' clubs, such as the Cornerville S. and A., are to be found throughout the district.

They function as independent units, and at the same time some of the smaller ones fit in as parts of larger organizations.

In Cornerville there are a number of political clubs, each one started by a politician and built around him. Such a club is organized for the purpose of electing its boss (or one selected by him) to public office and of providing him with the voting strength necessary in order to make good political connections. In return, the boss is expected to advance the interests of the members. The members are pledged to support all candidates indorsed by the club. In practice, the boss decides which candidates are to be indorsed. When the club boss runs for office, he can generally count on the active support of most of his members; but often the club is united only nominally in other contests. The political club is made up of a number of corner gangs. (The boss and some members may be above the corner-boy level, but the bulk of the members consider themselves corner boys and are so looked upon by others.) The boss's own clique, with which he started his club, can be relied upon to support his decisions, but the other cliques maintain their informal associations and a considerable independence of action. Unless the boss takes pains to tie the cliques in closely with the nucleus of the club through consulting their leaders on matters of policy and giving recognition to the informal clique organization in prestige and favors, the club may break up. This has happened in a number of instances.

Each of the Italian Catholic churches has a large and active Holy Name Society. Officially, they have nothing to do with politics and do not indorse candidates, but in them one can readily observe certain major divisions in terms of political allegiance. For example, one of the societies was divided fairly evenly between supporters of Art Porcella's Washington Club and Andy Cotillo's Victory Club. Within these major divisions were various corner-boy cliques. Doc of the Nortons told me this story:

Joe wanted me to join the Holy Name Society. I stalled him off. I said, "I hear you've got a lot of cliques in there."

Joe said, "No, there's no cliques. Why don't you come in some night and see for yourself?"

So I did. I had to laugh when I came in that night. There were ten tables in that big room, and there were ten cliques. At one table was the A Street crowd. At another I saw the boys from X corner. It was

that way all around the room. One fellow called me over to sit with his
boys. Then Joe called me over to sit with his clique. . . . I said to him,
"What do you mean, there are no cliques here?"
He said, "Well, we get along pretty good just the same."

The mutual aid societies of the first-generation Italians participate
in politics, and each politician seeks to gain the support of his *paesani*.
However, the societies are not so influential in politics as the number
of their members would indicate, for many of the members are aliens.
It is the young men who are most active in politics, and it is generally they who mobilize the support of the older groups.

The local divisions of the Knights of Columbus and the Sons of
Italy are important to the politician primarily for providing opportunities for making valuable contacts. Since these organizations include men from all parts of the district, a number of whom have
considerable influence over groups of Cornerville people, it is advan-
tageous for the politician to become prominent in their activities.
While the local council of the Knights of Columbus is wholly Italian
in membership, the prominent council official has opportunities to
make contacts with Irish Knights of Columbus leaders, who have
important political positions or connections.

It is commonly assumed that the family is the most important
social unit in ward politics. Since the first and second generations
have drifted apart in Cornerville, the family seems to be less significant for politics than the informal clique, and yet its importance
should not be underestimated. In spite of the weakening of his family
ties, the Italian's network of family obligations extends far beyond
that which is experienced by the middle-class native American. Relatives are expected to help one another and to act in concert when it
is in the interest of the family. Thus the politician must reckon with
the family group in his campaigns. The women, who have no equivalent to the corner gang, tend to be particularly influenced by their
family connections.

A man who is part of a large family and can "swing" its vote to
one candidate or another becomes thereby a political figure of some
consequence. Such a man will probably be a leader or close to the
top in his informal group associations, in which case the groupings
will all support the same politician. It is the man who is not a leader
in one or both groups who faces a possible conflict. If his family sup-

ports one candidate and "the boys" support another, he must choose between his loyalties. That situation accounts for the defection of many men from either the family policy or the policy of the informal group.

Another break in the united group front results when the group is committed to Politician A but one of its members is committed to Politician B because he has received some specific favor. In this case the other members will recognize that this man is "doing the right thing" in discharging his obligations, and they will not put pressure on him to support Politician A.

The paesani tend to settle in one area, and those who are members of the same family usually live close together. The informal corner groups are also strictly localized. And each Cornerville politician has an area, generally where he grew up, which he considers his stronghold. Thus, if a man lives with his family on A Street, hangs on a corner of A Street, and A Street comes within the orbit of one particular politician, no conflict is likely to arise.

The politician does not build his organization out of an undifferentiated mass of people. He grows up in a society which is complexly organized. To be successful in his career, he must be familiar with its ramifications and know how to win the support of the groups which make it up.

No politician in Cornerville can be successful without the support of corner boys, and many corner-boy leaders enter politics. The corner-boy leader performs some of the politician's functions for his followers. He looks after their interests and speaks for them in contacts with outsiders. Yet there are a number of things he cannot do. He cannot get them political jobs or favors unless he subordinates himself and his group to some politician. It frequently occurs to him and his followers to ask themselves why the leader should have to subordinate himself. He feels that the politicians have neglected the people's interests. His friends try to persuade him to enter the contest. If he has any capacity for public speaking, their urgings will be hard to resist. He will begin to extend his contacts so that he moves in wider and more influential social circles.

In his first campaign he simply tries to prove that he has enough support to be taken seriously. When he has shown his strength, he is in a position to stage a more vigorous campaign or to make terms with his rivals. If he becomes an important figure, he will be offered money or perhaps even a political job if he will drop out of the contest and support another politician. If he accepts, his followers feel that he has "sold out," and it is difficult for him to continue as a political figure of any prominence. He may be able to retain some personal following if he is able to do favors for the boys, but he will no longer have a chance to win an election.

If he refuses to compromise himself and continues to run for office, the politician must find a way of financing his campaigns. Furthermore, he is required by the nature of his position to spend a great deal of money that he need not spend as a private citizen. Whenever a local organization gives any sort of entertainment, he is expected to contribute an advertisement for the program book or to buy a number of tickets. People know that the politician cannot afford to turn them down, and they put him at the top of the "sucker list." He is also expected to be a free spender in entertaining his friends and acquaintances. His corner boys can contribute little to help finance such political activity. If the politician has built up his own political club, he may obtain a campaign contribution from its treasury, but it is a rare club which has much to spare even for this purpose in the first few years of its existence. Since a man becomes obligated to those who contribute money to his campaign, the high cost of political activity tends to draw Cornerville politicians away from their original group ties.

At every stage in his career, the Cornerville politician is confronted with an actual or potential conflict of loyalties. The conflict develops as he attempts to advance himself politically and at the same time to maintain the support of the friends who were with him at the start of his career.

AFTER ELECTION

When the politician is elected—to the office of representative in the state legislature, for example—he carries on his activities at a higher level in the social structure. If he wants simply to make money and jockey himself into a political sinecure when his term is finished, he may do so by making the proper connections; but let us assume that he has a genuine desire to help his constituents and discharge his political obligations to them. He cannot do many favors for them at the beginning of his term. Under a Democratic governor, he will find that he is given one or two jobs to pass out to his constituents. Each representative of the controlling party receives a small share of patronage in return for supporting the governor's policies. If the Republican party is in power, the Democratic representative has little chance of getting any jobs from the administration. When I last inquired, jobs at the tracks for the racing season were handled through political channels under the supervision of the governor. The politician who supported legislation favored by the racing interests was rewarded by a share in this patronage. To get favors for his constituents, the legislator must make connections with the politicians who have power. In order to obtain their help, he must try to do favors in return. As a new man, he has little power to reciprocate and, consequently, has difficulty in obtaining favors.

It is frequently difficult for the politician to reconcile his loyalty to his constituents with the conduct required of him by his political superiors. In explaining why he had not done more for Cornerville, Joseph Maloney spoke in this way to a club of corner boys:

Sometimes you try to get a man a job through the mayor, and then some issue comes up between you and the mayor. Should you fight him or should you keep quiet? You have to weigh that question carefully. If you fight, you might lose a man a life-job, and he'll always say, "If Joe didn't pick that fight, I would have my job today."

On the other hand, if the politician never fights, his superiors conclude that he is easily brought into line and need be given only the crumbs of political patronage.

The Italian politician faces another difficulty. He wages his campaign locally against the Irish domination of the ward. When he goes up to the capital, he finds the Irish in control there. If they are to help his friends, he must help their friends, so he finds himself doing favors for the Irish. If his Italian constituents discover this, they are likely to conclude that he is betraying their trust.

It has been the experience of certain Italian politicians that the Italians are less appreciative of favors done them by Italians than are the Irish. Italians feel that the group bond obligates other Italians to help them. Therefore, they expect and demand help. Irishmen do not feel that Italians are obligated to them and therefore make an effort to show their appreciation for every favor received. The Italian politician starts his career with bitter feeling against the Irish. When he gets to know some Irish and has political dealings with them, he finds that they are really quite nice people—in this respect, nicer than his own. If he does not watch his step, his associations with the Irish and his regard for them will cut him off from his Italian constituents.

The ward politician is expected to maintain his position by doing favors, but that alone is not enough. The number of large and small favors within his power is limited, and the manner of distribution has important effects upon his career.

Generally speaking, the importance of the favors done for constituents varies with the importance of their positions in the social structure of the community. That is, the "big shot" who has influence over a number of groups receives more than the corner-boy leader who only influences one, and the corner-boy leader receives more than his followers. Thus, in order to get the maximum results, the man at the bottom level must try to have a man above him take his request to the politician. He then becomes obligated to his superior, and the superior becomes obligated to the politician who does the favor.

Late in the day of the Fiumara-Kelly-Maloney election, I met Mike Giovanni's brother Terry. He was wearing a Fiumara button and had been walking around to see what was going on in the various Cornerville precincts. I asked him who had done the really effective work for Fiumara. He said:

What do you mean? I don't want to favor nobody on that. You might as well say I'm doing the work. I was with the man three years ago when he started—before anybody around here knew him. [Fiumara's home was on the South Side.] If he wins, I'll be in. We'll show them cheap racketeers something. I was offered a lot of money to get out of town during this fight. I refused. Then I heard that I was gonna get beat up election day. Well, here I am, and they ain't touched me yet.

I asked what the racketeers would do if Fiumara were elected. "They'll try to make connections with him. They'll have to come and see me."

Six months later I again met Terry, and I asked him how his friend Fiumara was getting along. He answered, "What friend? To hell with him. Bill, the only good politician is a dead politician." He was uncommunicative about the reasons for his break with Fiumara, but it is clear that his earlier expectations had been bitterly disappointed.

Terry Giovanni had been state middleweight champion, and he was well known and popular on the street corner. He had the most influence around a corner where he had grown up, but he had many contacts among the corner boys throughout Cornerville and in other parts of the ward. He had been making a precarious living conducting a crap game and taking bets on horses. As his words indicate, he was an independent in action and did not consider himself part of the racket organization. I learned from other sources that he had given me a fairly accurate account of his services to Fiumara. He supported the politician at the very outset and was always a tireless and loyal worker. He persuaded his friends to take an active part in the campaign, but after all, he was just a corner boy. He did not have a position in the community which would have made it natural for the racketeers to come to see him when they wished to approach the politician. Since his conception of the size of the favors owed him by Fiumara was much bigger than his position in the social structure warranted, he was disappointed.

The politician must take the social organization of the neighborhood into account. Within the limitations it imposes, he may do favors for his old friends and for the rank and file of the people, and, if he refrains from taking all the cream for himself and his family, he may satisfy some of the corner boys. Yet there will always be a large number of the boys who will consider him disloyal because he gives the more important things to the more important people. The corner boys look upon politics as "a racket" and consider politicians double-crossers.

If an important man who influences many votes feels that a politician is untrustworthy, the politician is gravely handicapped. If some of the corner boys feel that he is untrustworthy, the handicap is not nearly so great. It is therefore not necessary for the politician to be trusted by people at all levels in his society. In fact, it is almost impossible for him to enjoy such general confidence. When he begins his career, his closest friends are little people like himself. Naturally, he promises them that they will receive the major benefits of his political activity. If he concentrates upon serving his own group, he will never win widespread support. In order to win support, he must deal with important people who influence other groups. When he has to make a choice, he must keep his promises to the big shots even at the expense of breaking those made to his friends. As long as he keeps his promises to the important people and they allow some political benefits to filter down to the men below them and so retain their positions in the social structure, the politician can be confident of retaining his popular support. Some corner boys will turn against him, but other groups of corner boys can be brought into line to take their places.

SUMMARY

The process whereby the politician moves up in his career can be described in terms of frequency of interaction with groups at different levels in society. As leader of a corner-boy group, the future politician has a high rate of interaction with his followers. He interacts more frequently with members of other groups than do his followers, but his corner gang is the center of his activities. When he enters politics, he increases his rate of interaction with other corner groups and, necessarily, decreases his rate of interaction with his original group. As he advances further, he begins interacting with men higher in the social structure. As he increases his rate of interaction with his "connections" and interacts with higher and higher connections, the frequency of his contacts with his original group is still further diminished. If some of the members of this group have been able to move up with him and mix in the same circles, the politician can maintain a high rate of interaction with them, but, as he rises in position, he loses touch with the day-to-day activities of the boys. He is no longer the leader of a corner-boy group in the sense that he once was. As the politician ceases to participate actively in the group, someone else must become its leader and take over the direction of its activities—assuming that the group remains a unit. In order to hold the support of his original group, the politician must maintain cordial relations with the new leader (involving a higher rate of interaction with him than with his followers). If, in the opinion of the leader and his group, the politician does not meet his obligations to them, the breakdown of their social relations may be observed in the sudden or gradual diminishing of the rate of interaction between the politician and the corner-boy leader.

Who Are the Government Bureaucrats?[1]

BY REINHARD BENDIX

A MAJORITY of the American people—in keeping with a tradition of long standing—are opposed to bureaucracy and in favor of good government. Many are reluctant to take a good look at the acknowledged evil of bureaucracy and only a few would admit to its necessity.

What can this business of the government be compared with? If we compare it, for instance, with any single enterprise, we would find that the government exceeds each one of them in its number of employees, in the diversity of its activities, and in the money value of its operations. But is it appropriate to make that kind of a comparison? It is more revealing to compare a large enterprise with the activities of one government agency, or the government as a whole with the total of enterprises clustering around highway transportation. In 1939 one out of every eight employees worked for the government, and in 1946 one out of every seven worked in highway transportation.

In 1913, 1,900,000 people were employed by the government, federal, state and local. By 1941 that figure had risen to 6,000,000. To enable these people to work for Uncle Sam, the American people paid on the average $13.64 per year in 1913, and $48.31 per year in 1941. When these figures are cited, we should try to bear in mind that this growth in government employment is not the same as the "growth of bureaucracy in Washington." Out of the 6,000,000 who worked for the government in 1941, only 1,358,150 worked for the federal government, and out of these, in turn, only a small minority worked in

[1] This is a previously unpublished paper.

Washington. The bulk of government employees is, therefore, to be found in the municipalities, county seats, and state capitols throughout the forty-eight states—not in Washington, D.C. Yet when bureaucrats are denounced people immediately think of Washington, not of the rest of the country.

Suppose we look, next, at the expenditures of government. In 1941 the American people could spend $88,700,000,000 (according to a report by the Twentieth Century Fund). This was the amount the people had available for saving and consumer's goods. Government expenditure during the same year of 1941 amounted to $23,100,000, which included an expenditure of $7,100,000 billion for the war. If we disregard this last item, we find that of the remaining $16,000,-000,000 of government expenditure, the federal government spent 36.9 percent (or $5,900,000,000), while 63.1 percent (or $10,100,-000,000) was spent by state and local governments.

PRIVATE ENTERPRISE AND GOVERNMENT BUREAUCRACY

Ordinarily, we do not think of the teacher, the clerk in the City Hall, or the engineer on a highway construction project or in the city water works when we get aroused over the "bureaucrats." Yet it is people of this kind who make up the bulk of government employees. If these are not the "bureaucrats" who menace our cherished liberties, then who are? And how do we account for the fact that there are so many of them in view of the general opposition to bureaucracy?

To many Americans the vast "enterprise" of their government appears as a great menace, especially to the "free enterprise" system. It seems inconceivable to them that the development of private enterprise under capitalism has led to the growth of government agencies. It is much easier to believe that the "bureaucrats" are in some kind of conspiracy to increase the activities of government in order to hold on to their jobs. Is this explanation reasonable?

Our executive agencies are becoming larger and more complex all the time, but so are the social and economic institutions of American society. More air-travel will require additional facilities and services on the part of the Weather Bureau and the Civil Aeronautics Authority. Executive agencies will grow because many business firms will ask for specific services which they cannot provide themselves. Many of the agencies which provide statistical information are another case in point. Life insurance companies are dependent on the detailed population data which the Bureau of the Census publishes. But these data will be of little interest to the farmers. They will want to know about price trends of farm products or about the merits of new types of fertilizer, and they get such information from the Bureau of Agricultural Economics and other agencies in the Department of Agriculture. Such data, however, are of little interest to the life insurance companies.

In other words, the variety of demands coming from the public is very great. As often as not these demands are at cross-purposes with one another; at the least, they are unrelated. It is naturally convenient to demand government services for oneself, and to raise a hue and cry if they are discontinued. At the same time, it is very tempting to complain about the evils of bureaucracy, as long as this does not affect the government services, which "we have coming to us" for the taxes we pay. Honestly, but not always reasonably, we expect services, forget that others do the same, and as a result complain about bureaucracy and its cost, while we have in mind the services which the government renders to others. On March 15 of every year very few of us look at our tax bill and say with Justice Holmes: "When I pay taxes, I buy civilization."

The term "bureaucracy" is also convenient as a campaign slogan. The opposition—any opposition—will speak of an incumbent administration as bureaucratic. And the incumbents will speak of themselves as forever concerned with greater efficiency in government. A change of administration will reverse these roles. But it will not change the fact that modern society requires a large-scale executive branch. Since this is a fact, we are legitimately concerned with the question to what extent government officials tend to develop into a "closed corporation." We want to know whether or not they have become or are becoming a group of powerful men, remote from public control and a "law unto themselves." (Obviously, these same questions are just as pertinent with regard to corporations officials, union leaders, or any other group of people who hold strategic positions in the large scale organizations of modern society.)

JOB MOBILITY IN GOVERNMENT AGENCIES

Under the Spoils System the personnel of the executive agencies in the federal government changed with changes of the party in power. Such changes in personnel were relied upon to counteract any development of vested interest in public office. Some advocates of the spoils system have maintained that the American government was "truly representative" as long as we changed the elected representatives of the people, as well as the appointed officials of government, from time to time. Prior to World War II the proportion of patronage positions in federal employment (i.e., the positions whose personnel would change with a change in administration) has declined steadily with the exception of a few years during the Great Depression. However, government employees are not only hired or fired when there is a change of administration. Personnel policies in this respect are the same as in business, except for the special safeguards as to merit and loyalty which government imposes. A comparison between government and business shows that manual and clerical workers who are employed by the federal government have a slightly lower rate of turnover as compared with similar workers in private enterprise. On the other hand, business executives, on the average, stay on their jobs much longer than the average administrator in the higher federal service.

The problem of bureaucracy persists, however, regardless of whether public or private employees show great job-mobility. In between the Vice-President and the worker on the bench, in between an agency head and the clerical worker, there are employees who are equally needed in business and government for their technical expertness and administrative experience. Employees who have these qualifications are the "middle managers." In the government they receive salaries of from $5000 to $10,000 annually. By and large they are recruited on the basis of their qualifications rather than on the basis of service to the party in power. "Middle managers" like this have a strong interest in a professional career and they are likely to be concerned with security and steady advancement, whether they work for business or for the government.

HOW MANY MIDDLE BUREAUCRATS?

Available evidence confirms these inferences. Two independent studies of federal administrators of this type have both arrived at an average of fifteen years for government service, compared with an average service record of thirty years or more among a sample of executives in large corporations. It is evident that such a discrepancy will have a significant effect on the day-to-day working relationship between high federal officials and business executives. *As between these two groups of managers in high positions, the diversity of opinions on controversial issues is likely to be greater among government officials.* More important yet, if the executives in large corporations remain in their positions year after year, their opinions and suggestions will probably carry additional weight in high policy councils by virtue of their permanence of tenure and the solidity of their position. In a society in which the status of the administrator is far inferior to that of the businessman, it is to be expected that the instability of personnel in the managerial positions of the federal government enhances this inferiority still further. *Measured by this standard alone, the chances of an abuse of power by business executives are considerably greater than are the chances for high government officials.* But this is hardly sufficient to dispel our concern with the latter, since their importance will continue to be great regardless of the party in power. We have a right to know what manner of men makes up this core of government officials.

Our first question should be: can we obtain an estimate of their number? The bulk of federal employees are, of course, in subordinate positions. Even many of the higher-paid employees need not be considered here, since their work is predominantly technical. A weather-forecaster, let us say, is an expert in his field, his salary may be $5600 annually, but surely we have little to fear from him for our liberties. Even if there are many more forecasters today than ten or fifteen years ago, they are not the people we have in mind when we talk loosely about "bureaucrats." The "public managers" we are concerned with are agency lawyers, accountants, engineers, economists, personnel officers, investigators, and so on, insofar as they occupy high positions which carry heavy administrative responsibilities. In 1938,

110,950 officials, or 13.7 percent of all federal employees, were made up of technical, scientific, and professional as well as managerial and administrative personnel. If we then consider that responsibility will in a rough way correspond to salary level and if we stipulate $5600 as our arbitrary dividing line, we find that among the employees in these occupational categories, 5449 earned a salary of $5600 or more. This still includes a good many expert technicians who have little to do with deciding how the government should operate. We have then a group of perhaps 3000 persons in the federal government service, at least in peacetime years, who would fit the popular conception of "bureaucrats."

CHARACTERISTICS OF MIDDLE BUREAUCRATS

The group of higher federal administrators which has here been described was sampled in a recent study and the results of this study enable us to characterize this administrative elite of the service. Predominantly it consists of men in their forties and fifties. A majority has come from the rural areas and small towns of this country, and their family background is typically middle-class. About 75 percent of the group studied came from families in which the father had been a farmer, a professional, or a small businessman. In fact, federal administrators come closer than most other groups to the American ideal of the young man who comes from a modest family background and makes something of himself through his own efforts.

Out of 222 of these officials, 117 completed their postgraduate education after starting their careers. More than half of these men have, therefore, earned their education in the literal sense of that word. By earning a living while obtaining an education, they lived up to the American ideal of the "self-made man." Both family background and economic self-reliance indicate that our higher federal administrators as a group have experienced within their lifetime a good bit of that social mobility which many Americans imagine to be characteristic of the society as a whole. On the other hand, a large proportion of prominent businessmen come from families already engaged in business, and in this way differ significantly from the administrators.

Education, while it has grown in importance during recent years, does not set federal administrators apart as a group of special interest or privilege. Not only have many administrators acquired their education through their own efforts; there is also little indication that educational qualifications by themselves lead to promotion in the federal service. Most of the younger men who came into the government with the New Deal had on the average a more intensive educational training than men who had entered public employment in earlier years. But this only reflects the increasing role of education throughout American society. Experience seems to count as much as education, if not sometimes more. At any rate, experienced administrators, who had only a high-school education are as highly paid as administrators with higher degrees.

Out of 245 higher federal administrators who held high administrative positions in 1940, 24.9 percent had entered government service directly from high school or college. Of the remainder, 22 percent had been farmers or businessmen, 43.2 percent had worked as professionals, and 9.3 percent had been employed in the government service of the states and municipalities. Before they came to work for the federal government, 184 out of 245 had worked in other occupations. It is not true, therefore, that people who work for the government are without practical experience in the various ordinary occupations of John Q. Public. It is true, however, that most of them had not been active in political life before they entered the government.

Another, perhaps a more telling, argument on this score, is the apparent fact that the business community itself fully recognizes the conspicuous abilities of the men in the higher federal service. Out of 184 administrators who answered this question, 32 indicated that they had never received job offers from private business, while 152 had together received 248 such offers. Fully 56.1 percent of these offers came from business firms. It is reasonable to conclude that many administrators who had entered government directly from school or after experience in private employment or as independent professionals were now regarded as desirable candidates for responsible jobs in private enterprise. This desire to hire federal officials stands in striking contrast to the many statements of business spokesmen who denounce the government for the incompetence of its officials. Of course, that denunciation is only one among many, and perhaps it is not given much credence among businessmen themselves.

Often this and other criticisms, which in the heat of battle are made of federal administrators, are not really directed against them; rather, they are expedient slogans, which cover up some basic disagreement concerning the extent of government action in a specific case.

BUSINESS AND GOVERNMENT BUREAUCRATS

In 1947 the Washington *Post* carried a cartoon which illustrates this point well enough. It depicted a harassed Uncle Sam interviewing an applicant while around him various sorry specimens of government officials are oppressed by low salaries, political smears, loyalty probes, and lack of recognition for their work from all sides. The caption read: "It's sure hard to get help these days." What does such vilification of government "bureaucrats" have to do with the political questions at issue? What light does the preceding analysis of federal administration as a social group throw on the problems which confront the American body politic?

Two different themes prevail in the popular denunciations of bureaucracy. One is that bureaucrats are inefficient, the other that they abuse their power. The diversity of origin, experience, and education that characterizes American federal officials undoubtedly promotes inefficiency. At any rate, they lack that homogeneity of conviction and training which has sometimes promoted administrative efficiency in other countries. But it is difficult to see how such diversity would enhance the dangers of an abuse of power.

Nevertheless, denunciations of bureaucrats are directed simultaneously at their inefficiency and at the dangers of government "interference." The implication is that businessmen are efficient and that we must fear for our freedom only at the hands of government officials. *This should make it evident that the familiar antibureaucratic slogans are but a disguise for a particular view of the "proper" relations between government and business in the American economy.* Yet the slogans have made converts among many who sincerely question the free-enterprise dogma. It has wide appeal because it invokes the honored traditions of the American revolution.

This wide appeal obscures two important considerations. As we have seen, federal administrators lack both tradition and homogeneity, and an unthinking opposition to the Washington bureaucrats reenforces this trait. Conversely, the relative weight of the more traditionally-minded military establishments is increased. To be sure, unification efforts (1948-49) have brought into the open intense rivalries between the various branches of the service, but these rivalries are of little moment. The strong internal traditions of the military establishments makes them a formidable power in the councils of high administration policy. Indeed the rivalries among the military have in many instances increased rather than decreased the aggregate influence of the military on policy deliberation. It is possible that future historians may look at the persistent weakness of the American civil service as one important reason for the growing strength of the military in our society.

This leads to a second consideration. In the American tradition, suspicion of the administrator is juxtaposed to the idea that he must render services to the public. Since everybody pays taxes, everybody feels entitled to receive such services. Whatever the logical contradiction in this tradition is, in practice it has led to a close tie between the various agencies of the federal government and the particular interest groups whom the agencies serve. Certainly the institutions and informal legacies of the American civil service have not stood in the way of such a development. And, therefore, if we look for homogeneity and tradition, we should look for it in the personnel and the practices of particular government agencies in conjunction with their "affiliated" interest groups. It is common knowledge that the close and often picayune supervision of administrative agencies by the Congress helps to strengthen the tie between agency and public. The stronger this tie is, the more problematic the like-mindedness within the executive branch becomes, which in turn jeopardizes the agreement necessary for successful policy formulation. The absence of homogeneity and tradition which this condition of the executive branch illustrates indirectly helps to give greater weight to the military, whose tradition and single-mindedness does not depend on public support in the same sense.

It is important to recognize the dangers inherent in an unqualified opposition to government bureaucracy. It is as important to understand the dangers of all bureaucracy, public and private. Inefficiency, red tape—the temptation to transgress authority can be found among government officials and among private employees. If there is less notoriety in business bureaucracy than in government bureaucracy, it is partly because businessmen are inclined to advertise only their successes, not their problems and failures. Administrators, to say the least, have less control over the publicity which their actions will receive. There are, moreover, some differences between a factory and a government agency, which obscure the fact that both are "bureaucratic organizations." One of these differences is the necessity of clearing any proposed action with other agencies, with the public, and within the agency so as to insure both legality and coördination. Less of this is necessary in business, although it is of importance there as well.

Another, and perhaps a more important, difference may be a difference in purpose. However complicated the largest private corporation may be, it is in the end concerned with the production or distribution of commodities. There are many different ways of making or distributing a given commodity, but these differences are limited in number and they are debated among a small number of executives. Government, on the other hand, is concerned with promoting the common welfare. And since the whole nation is engaged in a continuous discussion over what constitutes that common welfare, the actions of government are necessarily more complex than those of business. The more private enterprise is built into an "industrial empire" with its production of diverse commodities, its complex financial dealings, and its various attempts at extending its economic power, the more it will resemble an agency of the government. Under these conditions the decisions and actions of such an enterprise would be affected by considerations of overall economic policy, which involve as much attention to political as to economic chances.

The fact that business and government are both bureaucratic organizations, albeit different in some respects, gives little consolation to those who fear inefficiency less than they fear the abuse of power. They fear the small number of men who sit high in the councils of industry and of the federal executive branch. These men have powerful organizations at their disposal, which can do both great good and great harm in American society.

The preceding discussion suggests, however, that as a group, business executives show far more similarity in background and experience

than federal administrators. Thus, if a business is less subject to legal
controls than a government agency, it may be said also that the first
is likely to be under more effective leadership than the second. In
view of the further increase in the concentration of economic power
which has accompanied World War II, leadership is hardly evidence
for the inherent superiority of businessmen as some writers maintain.
If business executives are more effective leaders of their organizations
(as contrasted with government officials), then it is appropriate to
seek the reason in the unparalleled acclaim and the extraordinary opportunities for expansion which these leaders have enjoyed ever since
the Civil War. (It might be inferred that the problems of bureaucracy
in industrial enterprises have become more serious in proportion to
their increase in size and to their cumulative concentration of economic power.)

Trust in the business leader and distrust of the government official
is an important part of the American tradition. In *The American
Commonwealth* James Bryce called attention to it some sixty years
ago: "Since the people, being too numerous, cannot directly manage
their affairs, but must commit them to agents, they have resolved to
prevent abuses by trusting each agent as little as possible. . . . There
is no reliance on ethical forces to help the government to work. . . .
The aim of the Constitution seems to be not so much to attain great
common ends by securing a good government, as to avert the evils
which will flow, not merely from bad government, but from any
government strong enough to threaten the pre-existing communities
or the individual citizen." Yet, unlike sixty years ago, a large federal
government is here to stay, and this traditional attitude, which finds
expression in the common denunciation of bureaucracy, was harmless
only as long as the activities of the federal government were of little
significance in American society.

The question which we should ask ourselves today is: what do we
gain by hiring government officials and suspecting every step that they
take to execute the laws Congress has enacted? There must be proper
controls. But many experienced observers agree that these controls
will be more effective if we appeal to the loyalty of the government
employee rather than engage in "character assassination." We should
expect that an official be concerned with the policy he administers,
and we should distrust an official who fails to show such concern and

finds a dozen legal reasons for not acting at all. But as long as distrust of officials predominates, some administrators will timidly adhere to rules in order to escape criticism. Others will become unyielding partisans in behalf of some agency's program, because this distrust makes them intransigent. If we could learn to be less suspicious of officials, there might be more administrators, and fewer bureaucrats.

Leadership and New Social Movements[1]

BY SEYMOUR M. LIPSET

THE EMERGENCE of an electorally successful socialist party, the Coöperative Commonwealth Federation (C.C.F.), in the province of Saskatchewan, Canada, presents the possibility of studying the leadership pattern of a new social movement in a contemporary North American setting.[2] Various people have suggested that the nucleus of the leadership of a social movement comes from the marginal groups in the population, i.e., the more economically, socially, or personally maladjusted sections.[3] It is these groups who should—the hypothesis

---

[1] The data for this previously unpublished paper were collected during 1945-46 on a pre-doctoral field fellowship of the Social Science Research Council.

[2] In Saskatchewan the C.C.F. won an electoral majority in 1944, just thirteen years after it was first organized. The party in that year secured 53 percent of the total popular vote, and had a total dues-paying membership of over 30,000, 8 percent of the electorate. It is a rural protest party with an agrarian socialist ideology, very similar to that of the Non Partisan League, which won power in North Dakota, Saskatchewan's southern neighbor, shortly after World War I. Like the earlier Non Partisan League, the C.C.F. developed as a response of prairie wheat farmers to the coercions of a fluctuating wheat economy. See S. M. Lipset, "The Rural Community and Political Leadership in Saskatchewan," *Canadian Journal of Economics and Political Science*, August, 1947, pp. 410-428; also S. M. Lipset, "Political Participation and the Organization of the Cooperative Commonwealth Federation in Saskatchewan," *Canadian Journal of Economics and Political Science*, May, 1948, pp. 191-208; and the forthcoming book by the author, on *The C.C.F. in Saskatchewan*.

[3] "By the very nature of their role reform leaders tended to be people devoid of 'respectable' attributes. . . . The influences which prompted people to break from established institutions and to take up the cause of reform often increased opposition against them. Desire to escape from the boredom of routine tasks, inability to secure a living or recognition in any other way, love of power which was experienced in swaying large audiences or large reading publics, and personal

342

goes—be most likely to accept a new radical program for social change, in a period of social disequilibrium such as a depression or drought, while the old community and class leaders attempt to maintain the status quo.[4] Actually, however, the research data on the nature of leadership in new social movements are quite scanty and inconclusive.

In Saskatchewan, it has been possible to find out what the social and economic backgrounds of the leaders of an organized protest movement are. Information was secured about the social, economic, and political backgrounds of the delegates attending the 1945 and 1946 C.C.F. provincial conventions. These delegates, who were elected from forty-five constituency conventions held throughout the province, represented the best large-scale cross section of C.C.F. secondary leaders. Six hundred and twenty-eight delegates, out of approximately eight hundred who attended these conventions, filled out the questionnaires given to them. Of these, 71.8 percent were farmers or farmers' wives; 11.0 percent were workers; 2.7 percent were teachers; 10.5 percent were business or professional people; and 4.0 percent were miscellaneous or unknown.

C.C.F. RURAL LEADERS

The backgrounds of the 431 rural C.C.F. convention delegates explain, in large measure, the reasons for the comparatively rapid growth of the C.C.F. in rural Saskatchewan. These active, secondary leaders of the party were also the rural community leaders. Three-quarters of them held some position in a local or provincial coöperative.

Official positions in the coöperative movement are a good index of general community leadership, as the coöperatives are the major rural organizations in Saskatchewan. At the end of 1944, the year in which the C.C.F. came to power, the coöperatives had 299,686 members.[5]

'grudges' against persons in authority, may have mingled, along with other motives, with the sincere conviction of doing good." S. D. Clark, *The Social Development of Canada* (Toronto, 1942), pp. 14-15.

[4] A study of the members and leaders of Communist organizations suggested that they come from marginal groups, i.e., they tend to be members of minority, foreign-born, or ethnic groups, or people who are personally insecure. Harold D. Lasswell and Dorothy Blumenstock, *World Revolutionary Propaganda* (New York, 1939), pp. 277-300.

[5] "Cooperative Organization in Saskatchewan" *Cooperative Development,* Feb., 1946, p. 2.

The interrelationship between C.C.F. and coöperative leaders suggests either that the coöperative leaders started the C.C.F. or that the C.C.F. supporters succeeded in replacing the old coöperative leadership, as a result of the radicals' winning influence in the rural community. From the fact that 58.9 percent of those C.C.F. delegates more than forty-five years of age in 1945 held posts in the coöperatives *before* the C.C.F. was organized, it is clear that the C.C.F. did not win control of the coöperative movement from the outside, but rather

TABLE 1.   Percentage of Rural Delegates to the 1946 C.C.F. Convention Holding Posts in the Coöperative Movement

Posts	*All Delegates*	*Delegates Over 45 Years Old*	*Delegates Under 45 Years Old*
Any coöperative post	73.6	77.9	66.1
Wheat Pool Committee	60.4	64.8	54.4
Chairman or secretary, Wheat Pool Committee	34.1	39.2	25.0
Wheat Pool delegate	10.4	13.7	3.6
Director consumer's coöperative	39.2	39.2	39.2
Director provincial coöperative	10.0	13.7	3.6
Director credit union	5.7	5.9	5.4

that the existing coöperative leaders organized the C.C.F. Further evidence in support of this conclusion can be found in the fact that the average number of years of membership of the older C.C.F. delegates in the Wheat Pool, the largest coöperative in the province, was 20.4 years, and the median period was 21.7 years. The majority of them joined the Pool in 1923 and 1924 when it was first organized, at the time that it was the major agrarian protest movement.

Another index of the community leadership role of the C.C.F. officials is their record of participation in the farmers' educational organizations, the Saskatchewan Grain Growers Association, the Farmers Union, and the United Farmers of Canada (U.F.C.). These organizations have been in the forefront of all the struggles of the farmers since 1901. They supported the formation of most of the coöperative ventures and the independent political efforts in the province. Since the organization of the C.C.F., the present farmers' educational organization, the U.F.C., has declined greatly in membership and influence because most of its supporters have become active in the C.C.F. This transfer of participation from the educational organization to the political party is clearly shown by the organizational backgrounds of the C.C.F. leaders who are old enough to have taken an active part in these educational associations before the organization of the C.C.F.

As in the case of the coöperatives, the C.C.F. leaders were active in the farmers' educational organizations before the formation of the C.C.F. The data reveal that 70.1 percent of the older group of C.C.F. delegates were in one or more of these organizations before 1931, the

TABLE 2.   Membership and Positions in the Farmers' Educational Organizations of C.C.F. Delegates over Forty-Five Years Old

Organization	Members Percent	Officials Percent
Saskatchewan Grain Growers Assn.	56.4	19.4
Farmers Union	33.7	11.8
United Farmers of Canada	78.9	30.5
None	18.8	59.1

year the C.C.F. was formed in Saskatchewan, and 55.1 percent of those who belonged before the organization of the C.C.F., held official positions in them.

LOCAL GOVERNMENT

The rural areas of Saskatchewan have their own nonpartisan governmental institutions, separate from those of the towns and villages. The C.C.F. delegates, as Table 3 indicates, are also leaders in this form of community activity.

GENERAL RURAL LEADERSHIP

The foregoing data indicate that the overwhelming majority of the rural C.C.F. officials are community leaders. It could not be concluded from this information alone that the C.C.F. rural leaders and the community leaders are the same. It is conceivable that the active people in all three provincial political parties are community leaders. To examine this possibility, information was gathered about the po-

TABLE 3. Public Posts Held by Delegates to C.C.F. Conventions

Public Posts	Percent of all Delegates	Percent of Delegates Over 45 Years Old	Percent of Delegates Under 45 Years Old
Reeves	10.5	17.8	3.5
Rural municipal councilors	19.5	33.9	5.3
Hospital board	9.5	9.9	7.0
School board	55.8	73.3	35.1
Telephone board	34.2	39.6	17.5
Any public post	67.4	84.2	51.8

litical backgrounds of the officials of the coöperatives of the province. Two sets of data were obtained. From persons active in the coöperative movement of the province, information was secured regarding the political affiliations of 113 out of the 165 subdirectors or delegates of the Saskatchewan Wheat Pool, the largest and most impor-

TABLE 4. Party Affiliation of the Delegates to the Wheat Pool and Two Other Coöperative Conventions in 1946

Parties	Wheat Pool Delegates Percent	Two Coöperative Convention Delegates Percent
C.C.F.	84.9	82.9
Liberals	10.6	10.6
Conservatives	1.8	1.6
Social Credit	1.8	0.8
Labor-Progressive	0.9	0.0

tant coöperative. In addition, questionnaires similar to those given to the C.C.F. delegates were filled out by 122 delegates to the conventions of two of the more important coöperative organizations. The two sets of data are strikingly similar as may be seen from Table 4.

Though the coöperative movement of the province is officially neutral in politics, there can be no doubt that its leaders are largely supporters of only one party, the C.C.F. These coöperative supporters are not recent adherents of the party. Of the 122 delegates who filled out questionnaires and indicated their support of the C.C.F., 87.8 percent backed the movement before 1936, and 64.6 percent in 1933 or earlier.

The close ties between C.C.F. and coöperative leaders are further indicated by the fact that most coöperative leaders have held some post in the C.C.F. party.

TABLE 5.   C.C.F. Party Positions Held by Delegates to Two Coöperative Conventions in 1946

C.C.F. Position	Coöperative Delegates Percent
Any C.C.F. post	69.1
Poll committee member	56.7
Secretary, Poll Committee	14.4
Chairman, Poll Committee	7.2
Zone organizer	14.4
Constituency committee member	38.1
President of constituency	7.2
Provincial council member	7.2

These C.C.F. coöperative leaders, like the delegates to the C.C.F. convention, were also active in the three farmers' educational organizations. About three-quarters of them, 75.3 percent, belonged to, and 52.0 percent have held official positions in, one or more of these organizations.

ECONOMIC STATUS

Other studies of rural social organization suggest that rural leadership is correlated with higher economic status and farm ownership.[6] The C.C.F. officials, though leaders of a socialist political movement, also reflect this pattern, as Table 6 indicates.

[6] See Dwight Sanderson, Rural Sociology and Rural Social Organization (New York, 1942), pp. 598-600; and J. H. Kolb and Erde S. Brunner, A Study of Rural Society (New York, 1935), p. 353.

TABLE 6. Economic Status of Delegates to C.C.F. Conventions and of
Delegates to Two Coöperative Conventions Who Are C.C.F.
Supporters Compared with Total Rural Population[a]

	Saskatchewan 1941 Total Population[a]	C.C.F. Delegates	Coöperative Delegates
Size of farm (acres)	433.2	673.7	689.4
Value of farm	$6,435.7	$12,983.4	$14,189.9

[a] Farms and Farmers in Canada: Facts from the Census 1941 and 1931
(W. Sanford Evans Statistical Service, 1944), pp. 3, 10.

ETHNIC BACKGROUND

More than 50 percent of Saskatchewan farmers are members of
minority ethnic groups. Studies of radical movements have indicated
that a disproportionate number of leading elements come from minority ethnic groups. In terms of our earlier data concerning the
C.C.F., one would expect to find, however, that the C.C.F. rural
leaders come from the groups which have superior status in the community. This expectation is confirmed by the data in Table 7.

Scandinavians, who are the social equals of Britishers in the West,

TABLE 7. Ethnic Origin of the Delegates to the C.C.F. Conventions
and to Two Coöperative Conventions Compared with
Distribution of Total Rural Population[a]

Nationalities	Rural Population 1941[a] Percent	All C.C.F. Delegates Percent	C.C.F. Delegates Over 45 Years Old Percent	C.C.F. Delegates Under 45 Years Old Percent	Coöperative Delegates Percent
Anglo-Saxon ..	41.9	59.8	63.0	52.8	75.3
German	15.1	10.3	9.6	11.1	5.6
Ukrainian	10.3	2.5	0.9	4.4	0.0
Scandinavian .	10.1	16.3	16.4	16.1	11.2
French	5.0	2.0	1.8	2.2	1.1
Dutch	3.8	1.8	2.2	1.1	3.3
Polish	3.2	0.5	0.0	1.1	0.0
Others	10.6	6.8	6.0	8.3	3.5

[a] Farms and Farmers in Canada, p. 10.

and Anglo-Saxons are disproportionately represented in the C.C.F. rural leadership. In an Anglo-Saxon-dominated culture, persons of British descent tend to be chosen for leading position. Prejudice against "foreigners" makes those of other origins shy away from exposing themselves to criticism by becoming leaders. The same tendency holds true if country of birth is considered. Although in the census year 1941, 36.0 percent of Saskatchewan farmers forty years of age and over were born in non-English-speaking countries, this was true of only 17.8 percent of the C.C.F. delegates forty-five years of age or over in 1945.

It is interesting to note that the ethnic cleavages seem to be disappearing among the younger generation of C.C.F. leaders. There are 10.2 percent more non-Anglo-Saxons among the group under forty-five years old than among those above that age. The younger ethnics, who were born in Canada and speak English well, are coming more and more to assume their proportionate place in the rural social structure. The increase in non-Anglo-Saxons among the younger and more recent C.C.F. leaders may also be a reflection of the increased electoral support for the C.C.F. in the minority ethnic groups.

RELIGION

The C.C.F. leaders, as a group, differ significantly from the general rural population in religious affiliations. Here again, the minority groups are underrepresented.

TABLE 8.   Religious Affiliation of the Delegates to the C.C.F. Conventions and to Two Coöperative Conventions Compared with the Total Rural Population

Religion	Total Rural Population 1941* Percent	All C.C.F. Delegates Percent	C.C.F. Delegates Over 45 Years Old Percent	C.C.F. Delegates Under 45 Years Old Percent	Coöperative Delegates Percent
Protestant	64.2	86.8	90.2	78.9	90.8
Roman Catholic .	30.3	11.7	7.9	17.7	9.2
Greek Orthodox .	5.0	2.3	1.5	3.4	1.1

* Eighth Census of Canada, 1941, Population Bulletin No. A-5, Saskatchewan, Religion.

The relative absence of Catholics among the C.C.F. leaders is due to a number of factors. In the early period of the movement, the traditional hostility of the Church to socialism was explicitly directed against the C.C.F. in Saskatchewan. This undoubtedly prevented many Catholic supporters of the C.C.F. from openly aligning themselves with the party. Secondly, Saskatchewan Catholics tend largely to come from minority ethnic groups—Ukrainians, French, Polish— and therefore are likely to be underrepresented in rural leadership because of their ethnic background.[7] Protestant prejudice against Catholics also accounts for the lack of Catholic C.C.F. leaders. The C.C.F. as a movement is not anti-Catholic, but anti-Catholicism has deep roots among many Protestants in Saskatchewan. This religious prejudice has served to keep Catholics out of leading positions in many community institutions. But these varied resistances to the participation of Catholics in the C.C.F. and community institutions in general may be decreasing. As indicated in Table 8, there are over twice as many Catholics in the group of C.C.F. leaders below forty-five years of age as in the older group.

It is significant that the social and economic characteristics of the coöperative leaders differ from those of the general rural population in the same way as do those of the C.C.F. officials. The coöperative officials and the C.C.F. party leaders are predominantly well-to-do, Anglo-Saxon, Protestant farmers.[8] They are the "normal" rural community leaders. Wealth, Anglo-Saxon origin, and Protestantism are the main objective social factors that would be expected to be associated with status in our culture.

The sample collected of non-C.C.F. coöperative officials was not large enough to justify any conclusions about the backgrounds of those farm leaders who do not support the C.C.F. Only 21, or 17.7 percent, of the coöperative delegates who filled out questionnaires were not C.C.F. supporters. One difference between them and those backing the C.C.F. does stand out, however; 38.1 percent of the non-

---

[7] Ethnic influences in the United States are also similar to those in Saskatchewan. Segregated ethnic colonies participate much less in organizations such as the Farm Bureau and Coöperatives than the Anglo-Saxons. Farmers of Scandinavian and Teutonic origin participate more than those coming from the Slavic or Latin countries. See E. de S. Brunner, *Immigrant Farmers and Their Children* (New York, 1929), Chapter V.

[8] See data for coöperative delegates in Tables 6 and 7.

C.C.F.-ers were Roman Catholics, compared with 8.0 percent of the C.C.F. coöperators. This suggests anew that the opposition of the Church to socialism has been a major factor in deterring Catholic farmers from backing the C.C.F.

URBAN LEADERS

Election data analyzed elsewhere indicate that the C.C.F. support in the urban districts of Saskatchewan is largely working class. The working-class base of the urban C.C.F. is reflected in the backgrounds of the party's leaders, as indicated in Table 9.

TABLE 9. Occupational Backgrounds of Urban C.C.F. Leaders

	Convention Delegates	Constit- uency Executives	Prov. Council and Constituency Presidents	Total
Workers	45.9	63.6	52.2	50.0
Business and Professionals	43.4	24.7	38.1	34.3
Teachers	11.2	11.7	9.6	11.3

WORKING-CLASS LEADERS

The working-class leaders of the C.C.F. are largely skilled workers as evidenced by the fact that 84.0 percent of the worker delegates to the 1945 and 1946 C.C.F. conventions were members of the skilled trades, and that 89.5 percent of the working-class members of the C.C.F. Constituency Executives and Provincial Council were also skilled. These working-class leaders of the C.C.F. were among the higher paid labor groups in the province, earning an average of $2454 a year in 1945.

The higher economic status of the C.C.F.-ers becomes even clearer if the specific occupations of the working-class leaders are examined. More than half, 51.3 percent of all the C.C.F. labor leaders about whom there are data, were railroad workers. The six C.C.F. labor members of the 1944 Legislature were all employees of the railroads.

Skilled railroaders in western Canada have a special status position. They are among the highest paid workers in the community, often earning as much as many small businessmen. Their trade unions are the oldest and strongest unions in the nonindustrial agricultural West. For a long time the westerners' only direct contact with organized labor was with the unions of the railroad workers.

Many of the railroad workers entered the C.C.F. at a fairly early date as representatives of "Labor." The depression had reduced their income greatly, and the new Farmer-Labor Party gave them an opportunity to join up with the organized agrarians in a political bloc which would give them added strength. The urban areas were, therefore, won to the C.C.F. in the same way as were the rural districts. The upper strata of the working class, the organized skilled workers, joined the movement first, and became its leaders. This is confirmed by the organizational affiliations of the group. Sixty percent of the working-class leaders of the C.C.F. were members of trade unions, and 40.0 percent of them have held official posts in their union locals.

TABLE 10. Ethnic Origins and Religious Affiliations of Working-Class Leaders of the C.C.F.

Ethnic Origins	Percent	Religious Affiliations	Percent
Anglo-Saxon	77.8	United Church	53.8
Scandinavian	11.1	Anglican	15.4
French-Canadian	2.2	Lutheran	11.5
German	4.4	Baptist	3.8
Ukrainian	3.3	Presbyterian	3.8
		Roman Catholic	3.8
		Greek Orthodox	7.7

C.C.F. working-class leaders are similar to the rural leaders in other personal background characteristics. They belong to the culturally dominant group of Anglo-Saxon Protestants. Their religious affiliations also indicate the negative influence of the Catholic Church on the movement.

BUSINESS AND PROFESSIONAL LEADERS

The urban business and professional groups overwhelmingly support the Liberal and Conservative Parties, though a growing number of them have been voting C.C.F. in recent years. The contrast in the class electoral support of the three main parties in Saskatchewan is also reflected in the economic backgrounds of their leaders, as indicated in Table 13. The majority of the leaders of the old parties belong to the urban middle class, while the leaders of the C.C.F. are predominantly farmers and, to a lesser extent, workers.

The C.C.F. has made overtures in recent years to the small businessmen, urging them to support the new party to protect themselves from the monopolists. This appeal has not been very successful. The rural C.C.F.-ers regard the small merchants as part of the exploitative profit system which they would like to eliminate through coöperatives. The small town merchant, in turn, looks upon the coöperatives as a major threat to his security, at least as great a threat as the chain stores and the mail-order houses. This identification between the C.C.F. and the coöperative movement prevents the party from successfully appealing to small businessmen.

TABLE 11. Ethnic Origins of C.C.F. Leaders

	Farmers	Workers	Business and Professional
Anglo-Saxon	59.8%	77.8%	36.7%
German	10.3	4.4	10.0
Ukrainian	2.5	3.3	20.0
Scandinavian	16.3	11.1	13.3
French	2.0	2.2	3.3
Dutch	1.8	....	6.7
Polish	0.5	....	3.3
Others	6.8	....	6.7

The fact remains, however, that a minority of the business and professional groups do actively support the C.C.F. The data available about the backgrounds of these people are scanty, but they do suggest certain interesting hypotheses about the causes of this deviant class behavior. The urban middle-class leaders of the C.C.F. differ significantly from the farming- and working-class leaders in one essential respect, ethnic origins.

The data are suggestive of the relationship between a marginal social position, and radical political behavior on the part of members of an upper economic class. The C.C.F. in Saskatchewan is the party of the workers and farmers of the province. Economic constraints on these two groups led them to accept the need for widespread social reform designed to better their economic positions. *They were led into the new social movement by those individuals in their class who had both status and organizational experience.* The business and professional groups, on the other hand, decisively rejected the new party. In large part, as we have seen, the new C.C.F. movement was directed against them as the local representatives of the capitalist system, which the party desired to eliminate. To support the anti-private-business C.C.F. openly was, therefore, abnormal class behavior for a member of the urban middle class. Those who did so were regarded as "crackpots" by other businessmen. Most of the social and economic coercions on middle-class individuals tended to keep them supporting the old parties, which were controlled by individuals with the same class background as themselves.

The middle-class people who became C.C.F.-ers were, however, precisely those who were not accepted socially as members of the urban business community, before they joined the C.C.F. *They belonged, predominantly, to minority ethnic groups, which were not part of the Anglo-Saxon "upper class" of the towns and cities.* The urban upper-middle class in Saskatchewan is largely Anglo-Saxon. This is true even in areas where the population of the surrounding countryside is overwhelmingly composed of members of minority ethnic groups. The non-Anglo-Saxon businessmen are often newcomers to the business life of the towns—the children of farmers or once farmers themselves. They tend to retain their ties with the ethnic minority of the surrounding countryside, and remain socially marginal to the business community of the town in which they live. This was clearly brought out in a study of a small, predominantly Anglo-Saxon town in a Ukrainian farming district. One young Ukrainian merchant said to the writer: "The Anglo-Saxons made it plain that they were better than the Ukrainians and didn't want us, so the Ukrainians said, 'To hell with you; we can get along by ourselves.' "[9]

The two C.C.F. Ukrainian members of the Saskatchewan Legislature in 1944 were both small-town merchants who came from farm families. Both reported close ties with the Ukrainian rural community.

The data suggest that "deviant" class political behavior can be partially explained by other "deviant" sociological characteristics. Socially,

[9] See unpublished study by Jim Giffen.

the minority ethnic businessmen are part of the lower-class group of the Saskatchewan population. While they are not exploited economically, they are deprived socially by not receiving many of the attributes which usually go with business-class status. The cleavage between them and the Anglo-Saxon "upper class" is often as great as the split between the farmers and the business community. Subject to the cross-pressures of contradictory statuses, many members of the minority groups have seen fit to identify with the political party which is opposed by the "upper class," and which promises to strike at the community power-position of these dominant groups.

The acceptance by some C.C.F. agrarians of the minority ethnic members of the business community as leaders of the party is probably related to the fact that, in Saskatchewan, ethnic ties within groups which are rejected by the majority of the community outweigh economic class cleavages. The C.C.F. Ukrainian farmer will accept the guidance of an Ukrainian merchant, whereas the Anglo-Saxon farmer will not follow a businessman from his own national group.

Those members of a dominant economic class who belong to a minority cultural group, and are not socially accepted by the rest of their class, will tend to participate disproportionately in political movements whose programs appear to be inconsistent with upper-class economic interests. Such movements give minority group members of the upper class the possibility of assuming higher social status, or of striking at those who deny them the status which should be a concomitant of their economic positions. The contrast between the ethnic backgrounds of C.C.F. leaders and the urban middle-class leaders of the old parties leaves little room for doubt that this is true in Saskatchewan, as Table 12 indicates.

The Saskatchewan C.C.F. data on the backgrounds of "upper-class" radical leaders is similar to that found in European socialist movements. Robert Michels, the foremost analyst of the European Social-Democracy before World War I, reported that the Jews, who constituted the foremost minority group in the more ethnically homogeneous European countries, played a disproportionate role in the socialist movement. Middle- and upper-class Jews, who had an inferior social status, were attracted to a movement which promised to eliminate the causes of Jewish subordinate status.

TABLE 12. Ethnic Affiliations of Business and Professional Men Who Are Leaders of Saskatchewan Political Parties

	C.C.F.[a] Leaders	Liberal[b] Leaders	Conservative[c] Leaders
Anglo-Saxon	36.8%	84.7%	96.4%
Ukrainian	22.1	1.7	0.0
French Canadian	3.0	10.2	0.0
Scandinavian	13.2	1.7	1.2
German	10.8	0.0	2.4
Mennonite	6.0	1.7	0.0
Polish	3.0	0.0	0.0
Others	6.0	0.0	0.0

[a] 68 Convention Delegates, 1945 and 1946; Constituency Officials, 1946.
[b] 83 Members of the Legislature and Candidates in 1938 and 1944, and 1946 Constituency Officials.
[c] 59 Members of the Legislature in 1934, Candidates in 1944, and Constituency Officials in 1946.

Michels' explanation of the position of the Jew in the socialist movement also suggests that deviant economic-class behavior is related to marginal social status:

The origin of this predominant position [of the Jews in the European socialist movement] is to be found, as far at least as concerns Germany and the countries of Eastern Europe, in the peculiar position which the Jews have occupied and in many respects still occupy. The legal emancipation of the Jews has not been followed by their social and moral emancipation. In large sections of the German people a hatred of the Jews and the spirit of the Jew-baiter still prevail, and contempt for the Jew is a permanent feeling. The Jew's chances in public life are adversely affected; he is practically excluded from the judicial profession, from a military career, and from official employment. . . .

Even when they are rich, the Jews constitute, at least in eastern Europe, a category of persons who are excluded from the social advantages which the prevailing political, economic, and intellectual system ensures for the corresponding portion of the Gentile population: Society in the narrower sense of the term is distrustful of them, and public opinion is unfavorable to them.[10]

[10] Robert Michels, *Political Parties* (New York, 1919), pp. 260-261.

OLD-PARTY LEADERSHIP

The question will naturally be raised, that if the C.C.F. is the party of the leaders of the Saskatchewan rural community, from where do the two old parties derive their leaders. Unfortunately, no data comparable to the material on the C.C.F. could be obtained as neither of the old parties held a convention during the course of our field

TABLE 13.   Percentage Distribution of the Occupations of Different Groups of Leaders of Saskatchewan Political Parties[a]

Parties	Business and Professional	Farmers	Workers	Teachers
Liberal executive—1946	65.0	20.0	5.0	0.0
Liberal constituency presidents—1946	41.0	41.0	6.0	2.4
Liberal members of legislature—1934	46.5	46.5	2.3	2.3
Liberal members of legislature—1938	56.2	34.4	3.1	3.1
Conservative provincial council — 1946	63.9	26.7	5.3	2.7
Conservative members of legislature —1929	58.4	20.8	4.2	4.2
Conservative candidates—1938	54.2	20.8	4.2	16.7
Conservative candidates—1944	30.0	45.0	5.0	7.5
Social Credit candidates—1938	45.0	20.0	10.0	10.0
C.C.F. constituency executives—1946	5.1	75.1	13.1	2.4
C.C.F. provincial council and constituency presidents—1946	13.1	65.6	17.9	3.3
C.C.F. members of legislature—1944	6.4	59.6	12.8	14.9

[a] Data for table secured from *Canadian Parliamentary Guide* (Ottawa) for years 1930, 1935, 1939, 1945, and from interviews with various leaders of the Liberal, Conservative, and C.C.F. parties.

work. A statistical breakdown of data obtained in interviews with leaders of the Liberal and Conservative Parties suggests that the older parties secure their leaders from the business and professional groups of the province, even though Saskatchewan is preponderantly a rural area. The data in Table 13 help confirm the interpretation that the political cleavages in Saskatchewan life are closely related to economic class cleavages.

There are, however, large numbers of Saskatchewan farmers who did not support the C.C.F. in 1944. Obviously this large anti-C.C.F. rural minority must have a leadership structure. We can, however, do little more than suggest some tentative hypotheses as to the nature of this structure. Many of the non-C.C.F. rural leaders may be comparable to the C.C.F. urban middle-class leaders; that is, they are individuals who, for a variety of reasons, are not as well integrated in the total rural community as their C.C.F. neighbors, and are therefore exposed to a larger number of noneconomic cross-pressures. Since the old parties are predominantly urban middle-class organizations, the farmers who are active in those parties may be individuals who have stronger social or economic ties with urban life than do the C.C.F.-ers. This may come about in a number of ways—through active membership in a church such as the Anglican and Catholic churches, where religious ties outweigh class cleavages, or through membership in lodges and fraternal orders such as the Orange Order.

Secondly, there are a large number of cultural subgroups within the Saskatchewan rural community which, for reasons discussed elsewhere, are not supporters of the C.C.F.[11] The Mennonites, the French-Canadians, the Catholic population as a whole, and other minority groups have never been completely integrated into the general rural-community structure of the province. They therefore have an independent leadership structure which reacts differently to external social and economic pressures than do the dominant cultural groups.

A third possible source of anti-C.C.F. rural leadership may come from the large group of farmers who have had personal ties with, or received favors from, the Liberal Party, which dominated the political life of the province and of the nation for most of the twentieth century. The well-organized provincial Liberal machine placed many farmers under personal obligation as a result of its effective distribution of patronage and "Tammany Hall" type of service work.[12] Until the C.C.F. came on the scene in the thirties, most of the officials of the rural municipalities were connected with the Liberal Party, and many of them probably remained loyal to the party. These personal

[11] See S. M. Lipset, op. cit. (forthcoming study).
[12] See Escott Reid, "The Saskatchewan Liberal Machine Before 1929," *Canadian Journal of Economics and Political Science*, February, 1936, pp. 27-40.

relations with the Liberals undoubtedly constituted one of the effective cross-pressures working against the C.C.F. in the rural community.

The suggestions about the sources of Liberal leadership, however, must remain in the category of unproven hypotheses until further research is done on the Saskatchewan political scene in particular, and on the effect of cross-pressures on political behavior generally. We know that group affiliations determine the social behavior of individuals, but we know little about the strength of different group affiliations, especially those related to class actions in cross-pressure situations. Marxists assume that class position always takes priority over other statuses. This may be true in terms of long-run historical analysis, but we have no systematic information of what happens in concrete situations in different societies.

Conclusion. The growth of the C.C.F. was a result of a drastic shift in the political loyalties and attitudes of two economic classes, the farmers and the workers. This change can largely be explained in terms of the economic constraints on these classes.

Anyone who is required to change his habits of life and his habitual relations to his fellow-men will feel the discrepancy between the method of life required of him by the newly arisen exigencies, and the traditional scheme of life to which he is accustomed. It is the individuals placed in this position who have the liveliest incentive to reconstruct the received scheme of life and are most readily persuaded to accept new standards; and it is through the need of the means of livelihood that men are placed in such a position. The pressure exerted by the environment upon the group, and making for a readjustment of the group's scheme of life, impinges upon the members of the group in the form of pecuniary exigencies; and it is owing to this fact—that external forces are in great part translated into the form of pecuniary or economic exigencies—it is owing to this fact that we can say that the forces which count toward a readjustment of institutions in any modern industrial community are chiefly economic forces; or more specifically, these forces take the form of pecuniary pressure.[13]

It is obvious that social change is not a simple reflex action. Economic pressures, like all other social forces, operate through individuals. The extent to which any given individual or group is affected

[13] Thorstein Veblen, *Theory of the Leisure Class* (New York, 1934), pp. 195-196.

by such pressures varies according to his position in the social structure. The problem of who is most affected by changing social pressures, who leads the members of a group or class to accept a change, has never been successfully answered. As was indicated earlier, various theorists have suggested that receptivity to new ideas is largely related to marginal social status.

As acute an observer as Karl Mannheim has stated that "psychopathological types" are the innovators, the leaders of change. There can be little doubt that individuals who are socially or personally maladjusted are prone to accept the need for change before the rest of society. It is highly dubious, however, whether such individuals are the people who actually are the informal molders of new opinions at the "grass-roots" level. The statistical data on the backgrounds of the C.C.F. leaders demonstrate that in Saskatchewan a radical movement for economic reform was led at the "grass roots" by the people with status within the farming and working classes. *The local leaders of the party were not the marginal or deviant members of the society, but rather were the "old" class leaders.* This process was highly visible in the rural communities of Saskatchewan, since the class and community leaders were largely the same people. A class or community will not accept the leadership of its deviant members. The C.C.F. was able to grow rapidly in Saskatchewan because the "normal" class leaders were the first to become C.C.F.-ers.

Recent sociological researches have cast some light on the social forces which determine public opinion. Studies of voting behavior indicate that "group membership" is the foremost factor in affecting people's vote decision, i.e., individuals in the same religious group or social class tend to vote similarly. Paul Lazarsfeld, in his study, *The People's Choice,* suggests that individuals who belong to formal organizations, composed of persons with the same social and economic background as themselves, will be more likely to vote as the majority of their socio-economic group does than will individuals who are not integrated in their class through formal organizational affiliations.[14]

Concretely, this meant, in the United States, that the proportion of Republicans was higher among those with high socio-economic status, who belonged to various high-status organizations, than it was

[14] See Paul Lazarsfeld, Bernard Berelson, Hazel Gaudet, *The People's Choice* (New York, 1948), pp. 145-147.

among those with the same class background who were not members of such associations. Among the working class, those who belonged to organizations were more likely to be Democrats than the nonjoiners. These facts are explained by Lazarsfeld as follows: ". . . people who live together under similar external conditions are likely to develop similar needs and interests. They tend to see the world through the same colored glasses; they tend to apply to common experiences common interpretations. They will approve of a political candidate who has achieved success in their own walk of life; they will approve of programs which are couched in terms taken from their own occupations and adapted to the moral standards of the groups in which they have a common 'belonging.' "[15] The research findings on the effect of group structure in reinforcing the political attitudes of the group members are based on analyses of comparatively static electoral situations in the United States. The basic core of Democratic and Republican strength has not changed while under the observation of social scientists. In Saskatchewan, however, where fundamental shifts have taken place within a comparatively short period of time, the data on C.C.F. electoral support and leaders would appear to contradict the findings reported in *The People's Choice*. In 1934 in Saskatchewan, the C.C.F. was a minority party among all social classes. On the basis of Lazarsfeld's static analysis, those who belonged to class organizations such as coöperatives and trade unions would have behaved as the majority of the class did, by voting for the old parties. In fact, the members of these organizations were the leaders and first supporters of the C.C.F.

Our data indicate that when a class's attitudes are in a process of flux because of changing social and economic pressures, those individuals, who are most integrated in the class through formal organizations are the first to change. In Saskatchewan, it was the local leaders of the Wheat Pool, of the trade unions, who were the first to become C.C.F.-ers. The local class leaders were the first individuals to become cognizant of the need for change. Their position made it incumbent on them to make decisions and set new patterns of behavior for the rest of the class, in a situation in which the traditional methods were no longer adequate. These leaders were in the best position to realize the long-range implications for people in their own economic posi-

[15] *Ibid.*, pp. 148-149.

tion. The unorganized mass only became C.C.F.-ers gradually, following the organizationally active members of their class.

A study of Saskatchewan voting behavior *today*, however, would probably result in findings similar to those which Lazarsfeld secured in the 1940 elections in the U.S. The political situation in Saskatchewan is now relatively "static." It is "normal" class behavior for the workers and farmers to vote C.C.F. An unpublished study of cooperative members in Saskatchewan indicates that about 75 percent of the members of the Wheat Pool and other coöperatives voted C.C.F. in 1944, though only about 58 percent of the total farming population did so. Those who now belong to formal organizations among the farmers are more prone to vote as the majority of the class does than are those who are isolated. Among the urban middle-class groups, however, the isolated individuals are more likely to be C.C.F.-ers than those who are integrated in organized group activity.

It is necessary, therefore, to modify the assumptions about the marginality of the leaders of new social movements. When a large social class or group is changing its attitudes, the "normal" integrated leaders of the class are the first to change. They are more exposed to the social pressures on the class than are the marginal deviant or apathetic members. The relationship between marginal social position and radical political behavior only holds true for those radicals who come from the upper classes.

In small, isolated political parties such as the Communist Parties of the United States and Canada and the Socialist Party of the U.S., one would probably find, as Harold Lasswell did in his study of the Communist Party of Chicago, that the members and the leaders of these groups are disproportionately maladjusted socially. Such a situation, however, is only present in small parties, which are not genuine expressions of large-scale social pressures. These small parties are themselves marginal to the total society. If a small radical party succeeds in becoming the political voice of a large group in society, it will necessarily attract the "normal" integrated members of the class. The C.C.F., starting as a large movement, was therefore led from the beginning by the "normal" class leaders.

Leadership and Democracy in the Collective Settlements of Israel[1]

BY LEWIS S. FEUER

THE COLLECTIVE settlements of Israel, the so-called *kibbutzim*, are a laboratory for the study of the problems of a democratic socialist society. Until now, most of our sociology of socialist life has been limited to the data of Soviet experience. The Israeli collectives, however, have been a going concern for some time; indeed, several of them were founded prior to the Soviet revolution. The Jewish settlements were founded under material conditions which were less favorable than those afforded by the Russian soil. Nevertheless, the dominant patterns of human relations as they have evolved on the kibbutzim lead one to envisage socialist life more hopefully.

The Webbs have noted that the directive functions of Soviet socialism are concentrated in what they call the "vocation of leadership." A group of "super-citizens" are selected whose lives are dedicated to the unswerving adherence to and execution of the "General Line."[2] It is characteristic of this theory that it tends to produce what might be called a "doctrinal aristocracy," one which regards the people as its raw material for social reconstruction. Lenin's conception of the communist party was that of a vanguard which would bring socialist consciousness to the masses; he held that left to themselves the masses would not possess the creative resources adequate to an envisagement of socialism.[3] The vanguard, however, in its developed

[1] This is a previously unpublished paper.
[2] Sidney and Beatrice Webb, *Soviet Communism: A New Civilization?* (New York, 1936), I, p. 339.
[3] V. I. Lenin, *What Is to Be Done?* (New York, 1929), pp. 32-33.

form, acquires an identity and special personality structure which separate it from the people. The language of communist leadership is replete with phrases like the "need to activate" and "involve the masses." The terminology is one of calculations of "forces at our disposal." Leadership becomes less the democratic expression of the communal will than a series of external imposed directives.

A "HERESY" TAKES ROOT

Socialism in Palestine has developed in ways contrary to the Marxian scheme of things, and its unique conditions have produced a pattern of leadership which differs basically from Lenin's. In the first place, whereas Marx spoke of the peasantry as a "reactionary" class, and looked with approval upon the development of big cities as the means for rescuing the populations from the "idiocy of rural life," socialism in Israel, on the contrary, regards its farmers as its most progressive class and the mainstay of the socialist spirit. The redemption of the soil is the first task of Zionist colonizations, and the pioneers of the land are its first citizens. The collective form of economy, moreover, was not imposed from without by a directive bureaucracy. It sprang from the needs and consciousness of the Jewish settlers themselves. A founder-member of the first collective in 1911, Degania, writes: "Individuals were apt to give way under the strain of the hardships peculiar to Palestine; but cooperative life and work would triumph over everything. . . . This was the basis of the collective village, the Kvutsa. . . . There was nothing dogmatic about their ideal of the Kvutsa. It had not been borrowed from other lands or other peoples. It had not been dug out of musty volumes. It was an original Palestinian creation deriving from the sources of the national and ethical idea which the pioneer movement brought to the Jewish homeland."[4] There were settlers who came to Palestine with values which rejected agriculture as the occupation of a "reactionary peasantry." The realities of Palestinian life and the significance of the problem of the landlessness of the Jewish people led, however, to a "transvaluation of values," and the political ideology of the progressive farming class came to prevail.[5] If Jewish settlement was

[4] Joseph Baratz, Degania: The Story of Palestine's First Collective Settlement (Tel-Aviv, 1944), p. 12.

[5] Lionel Feitelberg, Afikim: The Story of a Kibbutz (Tel-Aviv, 1947), pp. 8, 13.

to be permanently planted in the soil, it was necessary to avoid the pattern of capitalist plantations managed by Jews and cultivated by a native Arab peasantry. The ideal of *Kibbush Ha 'avoda*, "the conquest of work," was born, and it summoned the Jewish pioneer to redeem the land with his own hands.[6] The alternative to capitalist plantations based on the exploitation of cheap native labor was the foundation of the communal farms, the kibbutzim.

Socialism in Palestine, in the second place, has not had to destroy or transform a previously existing capitalist system. Capitalist investment has not flourished in a land whose soil and resources are largely submarginal.[7] It is noteworthy that capitalist agriculture is concentrated in the orange plantations, the one agricultural sector which enjoys a favorable export market and rate of profit. The collectives are almost all based on mixed farming, not on monoculture, and they produce for the domestic market. They are creating an agricultural industry, not changing a received system of ownership.

Likewise, Palestine socialism has in large measure had to build an industrial technology *de novo*, and its pattern has evolved in a unique, syndicalist manner. To begin with, Britain, the mandatory power, was not interested in promoting industrial development in Palestine. There was, moreover, no inducement to capitalist investment in a country with a negative rate of profit. If colonization was to be pursued with vigor, it was essential that the trade union movement itself should fill the gap, create industries and job opportunities for immigrants. Where state initiative and capitalist enterprise were lacking, the Histadrut, the General Federation of Jewish Labor in Palestine, was obliged to develop its creativity to the maximum.

The socialist form of industry which Histadrut is evolving is free from the bureaucratic regimentation which often accompanies state control of industry. Through the *Hevrath Ovdim*, its central holding company, the Histadrut owns and operates the *Solel Boneh*, the country's great building undertaking; Phoenicia Glass Works, the

---

[6] Shlomo Zemach, *An Introduction to the History of Labour Settlement in Palestine* (Tel-Aviv, 1946), tr. Sylvia Satten, pp. 36, 40.

[7] The Kibbutz Dalya submitted a description of its land and soil structure to the United States Department of Agriculture and asked for technical advice. They were told that in America such land would be regarded suitable only for afforestation. Cf., *Glimpses of Jewish Settlement History*, Ed. B. Lurie (Jerusalem, 1948), Part IV, p. 9.

only plant of its kind in the Middle East; and *Hamegaper*, the rubber and tire factory. The Vulcan Foundry, Israel's only iron and steel works, is likewise owned by Histadrut; in addition, the Federation owns the Workers' Bank, the country's third largest financial institution, and it has a controlling interest in a large number of factories of diverse kinds.[8] The Histadrut enterprises are not administered in accordance with a central plan; each enterprise has its autonomous management, and must prove its competitive efficiency in a capitalist environment. "These institutions are also immersed in a constant state of commercial strife or competition, and have to dispense with the comfortable protection of State socialism. But perhaps the absence of State protection is one of the reasons for their success."[9] About one-third of the economy of Israel is socialist in form, a socialism of trade union ownership and communal farms.

INDIVIDUALISTIC SOCIALISM

The communal farms are, to a large extent, influenced by Marxian ideas. At Ein Hashofet, one of the children's project notebooks in school was entitled "A History of May Day"; it was a dramatized summary of recent class struggles and labor movements. Nevertheless, the communal farms have found the philosophy of Marxism wanting in those respects which involve the relations of men and their leaders within a community. One prominent leader, I. Shutzberg, of the Merhavia kibbutz, and now working with the Audit Union of the Workers' Agricultural Coöperative Societies, stated succinctly: "One can be a Marxist, but one must not cease to be a man." This emphasis on individuality, on the value and freedom of each person, this revolt against any tendency to treat persons as ciphers, has led to an intermixture of the Marxian doctrine with a variety of other components. As the Israelis see it, Marxism has stated a valid truth in its notion of the struggle of classes. But they do not regard this doctrine as the last word in the science of human relations.

Even in the earliest days of settlement, the Jews looked for some

[8] Samuel Kurland, *Cooperative Palestine: The Story of Histadrut* (New York, 1947), p. 213ff. Gerhard Muenzner, *Labor Enterprise in Palestine* (New York, 1947). This book has the most complete enumeration of Histadrut economic institutions. Also, cf. *25 Years of the Workers' Bank* (Tel-Aviv, 1947).

[9] G. Muenzner, *Jewish Labour Economy in Palestine* (London, 1945), p. 213.

philosophy which would attach more importance to the creative role of the individual. Among the immigrants of the 1904 Aliyah, there were those who had drawn sustenance from Nietzsche's philosophy, which had spread "an intoxicating incense in the darkness of the Jewish ghettos," and aroused a yearning for the world "in which every man holds his life in his own hands to make or re-make it according to his will."[10] A man's spirit could thus transcend the ugliness of the ghetto by which his body was circumscribed. The philosopher of Kibbutz Degania, A. D. Gordon, likewise criticized any socialism which in basing itself on the masses has lost sight of the individual, and his "religion of labor" had a strong kinship with Tolstoyan ideas.

The Zionist philosophy necessarily had to part company with the orthodox Marxian ideology. Lenin had denied that the Jews were a nation, and had said that "Marxism is irreconcilable with nationalism, be it ever so 'just,' 'clean,' refined, and civilised."[11] He had opposed the development of Jewish national culture and had urged Jewish Marxists to accept assimilation. Stalin, in the same vein, had called the Jews a "paper nation" which did not need to enter into political reckonings. Stalin had queried "what sort of nation, for instance, is a Jewish nation that consists of Georgian, Daghestanian, Russian, American, and other Jews, the members of which do not understand each other. . . ."[12] It was a mistake, said Stalin, to stress the psychological aspects of Jewish existence as against their socio-economic environment; to do so was to take the path toward mysticism and idealism.

REVOLUTIONARY CONSTRUCTIVISM

To give reality to the "paper nation," Israeli leaders have had to challenge the authority of Marxist passages over Jews' thinking. In Palestine this was the task of Berl Katznelson, whose life provides us with a case study in the leadership type of Israeli collectivism. Born in Russia in 1886, Katznelson, like so many Zionist leaders, passed through a Marxian phase, and was active in the Social Revo-

[10] Zemach, op. cit., p. 18.
[11] Lenin on the Jewish Question (New York, 1934), p. 15.
[12] Joseph Stalin, Marxism and the National Question (New York, 1942), pp. 14-16.

lutionary Party. He migrated to Palestine in 1908 and worked in various kibbutzim. In later years he helped found the Hamashbir, the coöperative purchasing agency of the communal farms, and also the Workers' Bank. Katznelson was regarded as the spiritual leader of the Palestine Labor Party. He edited the Histadrut newspaper, Davar, and organized the labor publishing house, Am Oved. His many-sided intellectual enterprises included publications on scientific vegetable growing. When he died in 1944, he asked to be buried at the communal farm beside Kinnereth.

Katznelson called his philosophy of leadership "revolutionary constructivism." The thinking of too many persons, he said, was determined by a "fashion-dictator whose design is law everywhere. Intellectually too many people are governed by the dictates of a 'Paris tailor.'" Socialist Zionism to exist must break with Marxian orthodoxy; thus a "deviationist" heritage was passed to the Israeli collectives, the demand that each person think for himself, that no rule of a "leader" or "party line" be accepted.[13]

Katznelson rejected Lenin's theory of "professional revolutionaries" as the bearers of leadership. "'Professional revolutionaries,'" Katznelson said, "who measure everything with the yardstick of their profession, impoverish the spirit of the movement. This is the bureaucratic degeneration which menaces revolution no less than religion—desecrating both."[14] Only full-time revolutionaries, according to Lenin, should be admitted into the revolutionary party; they would be the privileged harbingers of "socialist consciousness." Latent in this doctrine, from Katznelson's standpoint, is the separation between the party and the people.

Katznelson also stressed a type of education which would make for democratic, nonauthoritarian relations of leadership. In his essay, "Law and Legend in Youth Movements," he warned against indoctrination of "the military type where there exists complete harmony between the aim and the educational methods. Everything is centralized, everything leads to the given aim. In the center stands the commander. The rest need not think too much, but receive commands and to obey! There are periods when men flee from them-

13 Berl Katznelson, Revolutionary Constructivism, Habonim translation (New York, 1946), p. 2.
14 Ibid., p. 9.

selves, are content to have others think for them, decide for them, to depend upon someone else's strength and responsibility. In such periods, people are lured by the attraction of militarism and servility."

No party monolithic or militaristic in its conception of men's relations could thus fulfill the aspirations of Socialist Zionism. It idealized no leader or party committee; it idealized instead a new type of Jew—the "pioneer." "A movement in the center of which stands not the commander and the soldier, but the pioneer, who thinks and works, a man of culture and freedom and responsibility. . . ."[15]

UNITY BETWEEN LEADERS AND PEOPLE

The avoidance of a political professional class is achieved by the close linkage between political leaders and the communal farms of which they are members. Many of the Histadrut executives are on leave from their respective kibbutzim. Within the Cabinet, the Minister of Labor, Mordechai Bentov, is a member in good standing of Kibbutz Mishmar Haemek, a collective which has achieved remarkable results in applying progressive methods to secondary education. The Minister of Agriculture, Aharon Zisling, holds membership in Kibbutz Ein Harod, where he participated in large-scale projects of scientific agriculture. His chief assistant for the field of fisheries was naturally chosen from the fishing collective at Caesarea.

Israel's second strongest political party, the United Workers' Party (Mapam), is especially closely connected with the communal settlements. Indeed, this party may be regarded as the political expression of the agricultural collectives. Its executive secretary, Ben-Aharon, is a member of Givath Hayim, on temporary assignment to political work. The party daily newspaper, *Al-Hamishmar*, is edited by persons assigned by their respective collectives to work on "detached service" for their central organ. On the work-schedule of Ein Hashofet, I saw recorded the names of three persons assigned to such editorial work. Journalists, politicians, and statesmen still retain their ties with the communal settlements. They return to them for week ends, and I found two of Ein Hashofet's assignees eager to be recalled from Tel-Aviv so that they could resume their lives on the kibbutz, as teachers, agriculturists, or cattlemen. The families of the political representatives usually remain on the communal settlements,

15 *Ibid.*, p. 3.

and the representatives regard themselves as full members who, for the collective's sake and out of regard for the movement as a whole, have been sent on external duty.

A psychological unity is thus preserved between political leaders and the people. The motivations of the political leader tend not to be those of our politicians—there is less personal ambition, no motive of private pecuniary gain, and no cultivation of impulses to dominate others. On the collective, the political leader is regarded as an expert in political affairs, and as such no more exceptional than an expert in agricultural methods. Such persons are expected to impart their special information to their *chaverim* (comrades), and on their week ends at the kibbutzim, they generally give talks on the latest political developments. I heard Yirmiyahu Haggai, night editor of *Al-Hamishmar*, give one such talk at Ein Hashofet, and the following week a shliah (delegate) just returned from the United States lectured on his impressions of that country. Political leadership is a function which is exercised on behalf of the communal group; it is not characterized by the personal advertising, ego-enhancement, and antics of vote-getting which are typical of American political activity. The communal settlement chooses its representatives in the fullness of knowledge gained from years of coöperative work.

The leaders of the communal settlements are men conspicuous as the possessors of constructive talents. Whereas Marxian doctrine has tended to emphasize the values of destruction, the eliminations of an outmoded society, the whole spirit of Zionist socialism is by contrast an emphasis on creative construction. Revolutionary constructivism thus held that "revolutionary changes are worthless unless accompanied by earnest and socially regenerate 'constructive' efforts." There is likewise the philosophic insistence that the "creative potentialities of destruction" are limited. All this might seem to be commonplace, but it is the philosophy of construction which accounts for the fact that the leaders of the communal settlements have not been enlisted within the school of violence and terrorism. That the latter ideology has acquired no following on the kibbutzim despite the intense provocation is a testimony to their sound psychologic health. Yehuda, a leader of Kfar Menahem, explained their rejection of terrorist policy: "We ask: what has the Irgun built? What have they created? Have they founded any *kibbutzim?* Have they sent men into the Negeb? Have they brought grass to the desert?"

The men of the communal settlements do not regard the terrorists as men of action. Real action, they affirm, comes in the day-by-day redemption of the soil, in the construction of irrigation projects, and the development of new crops. The momentary act of violence is only a neurotic substitute, an irrational outlet—an attempt to build a Jewish state through a short cut rather than the road of arduous labor. When one recalls that Israel's 150 communal settlements became unyielding fortresses which withstood the Arab invasion, one must acknowledge that the constructivists had chosen the most fundamental path of action.[16]

MILITARY LEADERSHIP

A military force reflects the structure and tensions of the society from which it is organized. The *Palmach*, the Striking Force, was recruited primarily from the young men of the communal farms. Indeed, it is sometimes called the *Kibbutz* in arms. It was the *Palmach* which held the lines in May and June 1948 when the first onrush of Arab armies took place, and it was this force likewise which was called on to disperse the dissident terrorist groups. The military mores of the Palmach are unlike those of the American Army. There is no trace of the "caste system." The officers wear no distinctive insignia; they live and eat with the men. There is no such thing as

[16] Arthur Koestler, in his novel concerning the collectives, *Thieves in the Night*, has his hero join one of the terrorist groups. Koestler stayed for two weeks at the Kibbutz Ein Hashofet to gather background for his novel. The diary of the kibbutz at that time records: "There's good reason to worry about what he's going to put into that new book. His behavior here indicated that he's more capable than serious . . . there's good reason to doubt whether an outsider, spending a few days each in one Kibbutz after another, can handle the most basic and cardinal aspects of our existence without messing it up, the more so since the 'nihilist' who wrote "The Yogi and the Commissar" is handicapped in any attempt to understand a system of social values based on a belief in creative, communal socialism." Yosef Welfand, *Ein Hashofet: A Decade of Pioneering* (Tel-Aviv, 1947), pp. 144-145.

Among the settlers to whom Koestler dedicated his novel was Jonah, from Ein Hashofet. Jonah's reply to Koestler is a memorable document in kibbutz philosophy. Cf. A Letter from one of the 'thieves in the night,' *Youth and Nation*, XV (1946), 17.

waiting on the tables for an officers' mess. Nobody thinks in those terms. Instead, all the men in a company address each other by their first names. The officer is a man with some special ability, training, or longer experience, but the democratic spirit is so pervasive that when I was challenged to identify the officer of a company I was visiting, I was quite unable to do so.

I met the commander in chief of the Palmach, Israel Galilee, now Assistant Minister of Defense. An economist friend of the *Hamashbir Hamerkazi* made the introduction at a restaurant in Tel-Aviv. I thought I was meeting a fellow social scientist, and conditioned to the signification of insignia, could scarce believe that the unbedecked man in shirt sleeves was an army's chief commanding officer. Then I was told that he had been a defense soldier on kibbutzim almost since childhood days.

SAFEGUARDS AGAINST TOTALITARIAN CONTROL

Every collective system has within it a potential for totalitarian control, and it is important to study the institutional safeguards against such tendencies. In the Israeli collectives, this problem has given rise to an intense discussion over what is called "ideological collectivism." This doctrine is held by the left-wing *Hashomer Hatzair* (Young Guard) which comprises a group of fifty communal farms, associated in the Kibbutz Artzi. According to their view, the kibbutz exists in a hostile capitalist environment, which would, if it could, destroy it. They doubt whether the collectives can make possible a peaceful evolution to socialism. The kibbutz, as a socialist pioneering cell, must therefore strengthen its internal unity, its social and ideological discipline. "Ideological collectivism is essential in a form of life that refuses to adjust itself to the realities of the existing regime and strives to change it."[17]

Against this tendency to ideological collectivism Katznelson directed powerful criticisms. It was alien to the conception of the kibbutz to force political and ideological uniformity upon its members. Such a course, he said, would lead to a patriarchal, tribal socialism. "The system of 'ideological collectivism' that prevails in our world is taking us back, in a new guise, to a state of patriarchalism.

[17] R. ben Nachum, *The Kibbutz Artzi from its Foundations to the Present Day*, mimeographed (New York, 1947), p. 3.

Instead of the father of the family or head of the tribe, we have the 'secretariat,' a collective body symbolizing the unity and authority of the tribe. Just as under the patriarchal system it was impossible (not merely forbidden, but actually impossible) to overstep the bounds of the accepted customs and conventions of the family, so, too, in our own day, the member of the Kibbutz that is based on ideological collectivism is resigned to existing as an individual without intellectual independence, and to being merely a limb of the collective organism, and no more than a limb."[18]

Ideological differences would thus congeal into petty tribalisms, said Katznelson, and he noted that the children of Givat Brenner were precluded by ideological discord from attendance at the school at Kvutza Schiller. One cannot fill all the space in a member's soul, he declared, with the pronouncements of the pundits of the Kvutza.

The arguments for "ideological collectivism" are, of course, analogous to those by which the Soviet leadership justifies the ideological unity which it imposes on its people. The concrete conditions of kibbutz life, however, have thus far discouraged any tendency toward totalitarian control.

A guarantee against authoritarian power is found in the wholly voluntary character of kibbutz membership. A person can leave, go to the cities, or join another kibbutz. Since the economy is an expanding one, the precondition of alternative employments is fulfilled for the maintenance of liberty. As against bureaucratic tendencies on the part of leaders, there is the fact that the General Meeting is the supreme governing body of the kibbutz, and all committee decisions may be appealed to the General Meeting. The latter is usually held once a week, with an average attendance of about two-thirds of the membership, and an active participation in debate. The General Meeting elects committee members, and votes the annual budget.

The committee of management, commonly known as the Secretariat, is composed of three or more members. It generally includes a secretary, an organizer for the labor schedule, and a representative for external relations. The members of the Secretariat have no special privileges. They continue to do their full day's work in field, factory, school, or kitchen. The only exception that is made is for secretarial

18 Berl Katznelson, *An Indictment of the Present Situation*, Habonim translation (New York, mimeographed, undated), p. 8.

work which may require full-time attention to bookkeeping. The secretaries are secretarial; they are not so much policy-making officials as administrators of information offices. There is no chairman of the committee, and if it elects one for convenience, he has no official status. There is every concern to prevent the establishment of a permanent bureaucracy. Since public service is a responsibility additional to ordinary work, it is often difficult to get qualified persons to accept office. At nominations and elections, desired candidates are always trying to decline office on diverse grounds. The two-thirds vote which is required to elect often becomes a draft of an unwwilling candidate who avers his own lack of qualifications. Persons are simply preëmpted to committee responsibilities.[19]

In actual practice, "ideological collectivism" on the left-wing kibbutzim of Hashomer Hatzair has not worked out in a totalitarian direction. The official platform of the United Workers' Party, with which they are affiliated, does indicate a predilection for Marxian orthodoxy; it speaks of "the Soviet Union, the first working-class state, which has been carrying out the great socialist work of our generation and is fulfilling the historic mission of the November Revolution."[20] In actual fact, however, the Marxism of Hashomer Hatzair is dyed deeply with heretical hues. To begin with, the Hashomer Hatzair groups were driven underground in Russia after the Soviet Government in 1921 declared Zionism counterrevolutionary and illegal. Leaders like Pinchas Dashefsky were imprisoned. The Russian and Polish immigrants of the Third Aliyah in the early 'twenties were, nonetheless, affected by the upsurge of revolutionary ideology, and the leftist Kibbutz Artzi was their creation; their Marxian emphasis was largely a protest against what they conceived as the opportunist methods of Palestinian labor leadership.

There is no dictated uniformity of thought on the Kibbutz Artzi settlements. At Ein Hashofet, there are even members who hold Trotskyist ideas, and regard the kibbutzim as petty-bourgeois agencies which withdraw their members from the class struggle. At Gan

[19] Edwin Samuel, *Handbook of the Jewish Communal Villages in Palestine* (2nd ed., Jerusalem, 1945), p. 9. Lionel Feitelberg, *op. cit.*, p. 71. Also, Maurice Pearlman, Abraham Yisraeli, Shalom Wurm, *Essays on the Collective Settlement: The Kvutza* (Tel-Aviv [undated]), p. 30.

[20] Cf. *Unity Platform Adopted by the United Workers' Party of Palestine* (Tel-Aviv, 1948), pp. 1-2.

Shmuel, I found Habonim adherents who thought the class struggle ideology was too much emphasized, especially in view of the concrete situation in Palestine. Among the membership of the kibbutzim there was outspoken dissent from the official policy of binationalism. The schools make extensive use of Freudian ideas in their educational practice, and writers on the kibbutzim reject the application of Marxian canons of criticism to art and literature. The "sicha," the discussion group, is the favorite avocation of kibbutz members, and I saw such groups break out into protest when an attempt was made to presume the common acceptance of editorials in Al-Hamishmar. Large segments of the kibbutz membership are extremely critical of aspects of Soviet society. They may vote with another of the labor parties. Kibbutz life does not require compulsion of conscience.[21]

EXPRESSION OF CRITICISM

The free character of artistic expression in Palestine indicates that there is no group-taboo which forbids criticism of the kibbutz idea. We may especially mention the discussion which was provoked by the publication of the novel, Maagalot (Circles), by a member of the Kibbutz Ein Harod, Maletz. The book was issued by Am Oved, the publishing house of Histadrut. The hero of the novel, Menahemke, is oppressed by the "interminable vacuity" of kibbutz life, a microcosm peopled by lost souls. His tent is his refuge, and for him and Chanke, his wife, it shuts out a world, "petty, noisy, full of shadows and darkness." With the passage of years, he sees his children rooted in the kibbutz, and he and Chanke think that perhaps their effort was worthwhile. This novel had a tremendous effect on kibbutz opinion. There were numerous debates, and the author defended his work at public gatherings; at this own collective, the debate lasted six days.[22] It may be added that the current best seller

21 In Koestler's novel, Thieves in the Night, the kibbutz secretary intervenes in the hero's personal affairs, and insists that he marry a girl whom he does not love. The secretary threatens otherwise to bring the whole matter up before the committee. On the collectives, I was told that no leadership would dare interfere this way in personal lives. A reviewer from one of the kibbutzim wrote: "Are we really this crude, Mr. Koestler? In which kibbutz did you encounter such a story? In which kibbutz were such intimate questions handled in open discussion?" Zvi Frish, "Thieves in the Night," Youth and Nation, XV (1946), 27.

22 Cf. Dov Vardi, "A New Novel about the Kibbutz," Youth and Nation, 1945, p. 37.

in Israel, *He Walked the Fields,* with its often critical delineation of the new generation, has also provoked a widespread discussion. The ability of the collectives to maintain an atmosphere in which such outspoken deep-seated criticism is possible will be the final test of their immunity to authoritarian pressures.

It may be that future generations on the communal farms will experience tribal identifications more fully, and that individual criticism will be frowned upon. A promising young painter, Ezra Mintzer, who was born of kibbutz parents, and killed in the defense of Mishmar Haemek, wrote in his creed: "I don't favor individual expression, understood only by the artist himself. We are comrades of a collective society and the artist, like the others, is obliged to try to serve that collective society in which he believes."[23] Whether agricultural collectivism will lead to a neotribalism, what the kibbutz' pattern of evolution will be, are questions that are often debated in Israel. Some argue that there should be greater freedom of consumers' choices, to be made possible by the introduction of a medium of exchange within the kibbutz. Then if you don't smoke, you might substitute for your issue of cigarettes the purchase of a book or gift for your parents.

Substitution of commodities is not possible in the moneyless kibbutz economy. The problem of private property is often debated in the evenings. Shall radios be rotated in the homes, or be concentrated in public halls? Shall private gifts be allowed to accumulate in one person's possession? The question of the family is always on the agenda. Would it be wiser to have larger homes, so that the children would live with their parents? Does close family life interfere with the collective spirit of the kibbutz? Would the children be more secure with a home upbringing? On this there is general agreement, that the kibbutz is not a final form of evolution, that its forms are developing as it overcomes its problems of material existence.

Perhaps the most accurate measure of the egalitarian outlook of the communal farms is found in the extreme labor theory of value which underlies their accounting. "The Kibbutz does not distinguish between one type of labour and another—each is equally necessary

---

[23] Ezra Mintzner, *Kibbutz Hashomer Hatzair Merhavia* (Hebrew). Also, *The Palestine Post,* June 25, 1948.

and therefore equally valuable. . . ."[24] In its cost calculations, all persons are equal with respect to the distribution of funds for maintenance. A "work-day" in some given branch of production may be more profitable than a "work-day" in some other branch. In that case, the kibbutz reallocates its assignments of labor toward the more profitable channel.[25] Equality in the distribution of communal goods and services remains the norm, however, and there is no conception that the different types of labor must be rewarded in accordance with their differing marginal productivities. The economy of the Israeli communal farms is in this respect at variance with Soviet practice. The Jewish collectives have adhered to egalitarian ideas which Soviet economy has abandoned.

The social expression of economic equality in the Kibbutz comes in the evenings when the members gather in their "Night Club" for tea and coffee. Whether you are a committee official, farmer, or kitchen assistant, what counts is whether you are a good "chaver," a good workman and a good comrade.

GROUP SIZE AND DEMOCRATIC LEADERSHIP

The question naturally arises: to what extent is the pattern of democratic leadership and communal participation which exists on the kibbutz inextricably bound up with the smallness of the social unit? Does Michels' law of oligarchy overshadow social relationships once the community exceeds the operational limits of affectional coöperative relations?

The leftist Hashomer Hatzair settlements, in their quest for truly organic social units, limit their respective numbers to about 150 adult members. The principal group of settlements, Hakibbutz Hameuchad, on the other hand, encourages the unlimited growth of its 53 associated communal farms, some of which have exceeded a population of one thousand.[26]

<hr/>

[24] Lionel Feitelberg, op. cit., p. 94. "The concept of 'wages' is non-existent in the Palestine workers' agricultural settlements since no hired labour is employed there. . . . Accounts of collective settlements operate with what is known as 'subsistence cost' instead of with 'wages.' . . ." "Audit Union of the Workers' Agricultural Cooperative Societies, Audit Activities and Problems (Tel-Aviv, 1948), p. 23.

[25] Cf. Edwin Samuel, pp. 31-32.

[26] Aron Gertz, The Social Structure of Jewish Settlement in Palestine (Jerusalem, 1947), p. 53.

The Hashomer Hatzair settlements maintain that limitation of numbers is essential to preserve the "organic character" of the kibbutz. This they define as "striving for the utmost democratisation, the fullest possible participation of the members in the economic and social life of the kibbutz, the possibility for the individual to embrace every phase of the settlement in order to enable him to be responsible for the kibbutz as a whole." The numerical growth of a settlement, says the Hashomer Hatzair, should not be allowed to exceed its "social absorptive capacity, i.e., its capacity to allow its new members to be active in its operation." Where members increase beyond the social absorptive capacity, bureaucratic leadership develops, and the individual loses his sense of direct participation in the organic life of the community. "In such a kibbutz it becomes inevitable to refer all important decisions from the authority of the social cell of the kibbutz as such to a guiding and directing nucleus, thus creating the danger of alienating the individual from his society to the detriment of both." Once the kibbutz is thus overgrown, the general meeting becomes perfunctory. Although formally it remains the supreme institution, its authority is appropriated by committees and a controlling minority. Hashomer Hatzair therefore emphatically favors small settlements.[27]

As between the different associations of collectives, the dispute concerning numbers has tended to become academic. The normal increase of population through births has brought the numerical levels toward a common average. Also, in the large settlements, the grown children often prefer to leave their parent collective to found a new kibbutz of their own. The pioneer experience is something which the younger generation does not like to miss.

DEMOCRATIC LEADERSHIP IN INDUSTRIAL ORGANIZATION

The kibbutz pattern of democratic leadership is also confronted by problems which arise from the development of industrial factories in their midst. A distinguished authority like Lowdermilk regards Israel's most unique achievement as the combination of decentralized industry with agriculture.[28] At Dalya, for instance, there

---

[27] Ben Nachum, op. cit., p. 3.
[28] "In my opinion, Palestine's most important social achievement in the

is a factory which manufactures water meters, irrigation switches, and precision equipment. It employs about twenty-five persons. At Ramath Hashofet, there is a furniture factory with a large output fashioned in modernistic styles. At Afikim, forty-seven workers are employed (on a daily average) in its box and plywood factory, called Kelet, the only one of its kind in the Middle East. Now, the conditions of industrial management tend to separate the managerial class from the workers. How did Afikim work out a pattern of kibbutz democracy for its industrial sector:

> In the case of "Kelet" for example, . . . it is obvious that a management is necessary and, unlike the general officialdom of the Kibbutz as a whole, the management must necessarily be permanent, for its qualifications are technical and specialised. Similarly, the various branches of the farm also have to be managed by specialists who 'direct' the labour employed in their particular branch. The agricultural 'manager,' however, works together with his workers, usually doing the same sort of job that they are doing and, since the numbers involved are normally small, the close control and intimacy during work obviates the danger of distinctions creeping in. In the case of "Kelet," however, the situation is quite different; for there the management is a real management and the workers, as in any other factory, each have their particular small job to do. Contact and intimacy during working hours between management and worker is technically, if not ideologically, impossible, but despite this there is no friction. The "Kelet" factory is divided by a road from the living quarters of the Kibbutz and when this road is crossed the distinction between "manager" and "worker" automatically disappears, for, as members of the Kibbutz, they share equal responsibilities and rights. The levelling process is achieved not through an ideological approach to the matter, but because outside the factory itself, identities are lost in the general picture—factory managers and workers, agricultural workers, transport drivers, secretariat and the household staff become one—members of the same society linked together for a common aim. Certainly, at the General Meeting of the whole Kibbutz there is no difference between the voice of the factory workers and that of its manager, even on the subject of the factory itself, except in purely technical matters where naturally expert opinion is not debated by laymen.[29]

---

industrial field is the introduction of industries into the co-operative settlements which were originally intended to be purely agricultural." Walter Clay Lowdermilk, *Palestine: Land of Promise* (London, 1945), p. 85.

[29] Lionel Feitelberg, *op. cit.*, pp. 83-84.

Leadership in the kibbutz is the natural status of those whose initiative can guide the communal settlement to new achievements. Take the story of the foundation of "Kelet":

> There is one characteristic of a Kibbutz which applies to all forms of society—nothing happens of its own accord. Every development in a Kibbutz is the result of the personal initiative and push of one of its members. It is obvious, for instance, that until some individual has mooted the idea, there can be no collective examination, much less decision, on the establishment of some new enterprise as, for example, fishponds. In Afikim the situation is no different—"Kelet" has its "prophet," who believed in it from the beginning, and who has always been one of the main initiators of every step forward taken by the factory. At an early stage, . . . he set about writing letters to all parts of the world in order to find out what could be done. Ultimately, the Kibbutz agreed to send him on a trip of investigation, and with authority to acquire equipment within agreed limits . . . a few months later he returned to Afikim bringing with him a mass of new knowledge and the most up-to-date machinery.[30]

The communal settlements have thus assimilated industrial management into the structure of kibbutz democracy. The Histadrut industrial sector is grappling with the same problem, but as yet, without any measure of definitive success. The Histadrut, through its central holding company, the *Hevrat Ovdim*, owns or controls a large number of plants. The trade union movement, as we saw, is the country's largest employer. But no pattern of workers' participation in management has been evolved in the Histadrut industries. Each factory is operated by its autonomous management on the familiar capitalistic lines. The Histadrut has taken action, however, to prevent the formation of a bureaucratic class. The monthly salaries of even its highest officials are limited according to a sliding scale based primarily on familial need.[31] The question of workers' participation in management remains, however, a live political issue. The United Workers' Party, the political organ of the collectives, charges that the dominant group, the Palestine Labor Party (Mapai), has allowed bureaucratic tendencies and bureaucratic leadership to develop within the socialized industrial segment of the country. They therefore demand the democratization of control, "that public-Histadruth con-

---

[30] *Ibid.*, pp. 25-26.
[31] Muenzer, *Jewish Labour Economy in Palestine*, p. 217.

trols be maintained over the economic institutions of the workers, . . . and that their workers participate in their administration." Thereby, they aver, "the principle of class proprietorship" would be preserved.[32] *What is indeed noteworthy in Israel is that the collective settlements can exert strong political pressure that democratic forms be evolved in the industrial sector as well.*

The transport coöperatives were a remarkable instance of the development of tendencies toward class lines, and a consequent departure from the ideal of coöperative participation. Organized as producers' coöperatives, the transport agencies prospered, the values of their shares increased, until a new member would have to pay about LP 2000 for admission. The transport coöperatives began to hire labor rather than admit new members, and in 1942, for instance, there were 831 hired laborers working for the 1033 members of the passenger transport coöperatives.[33] This situation gave rise to an intense debate in Histadruth, which makes adherence to the socialist ethic a condition for membership. In 1945, its convention resolved that it would "no longer tolerate the exploitation of hired labor by its members." If hired labor were essential by reason of industrial fluctuations, the increments of profit were to be used to initiate the hired workers into the coöperative.[34] The moral and economic influence of kibbutz democracy was a significant factor in this decision.

SOCIALISM BY CONSENT

When Ivan Maisky, Soviet Ambassador to Britain, made a brief wartime visit to some of the collective settlements, he characterized them as "Utopian," as communistic to an extent not yet practicable in the Soviet Union. Arthur Koestler regards the men of the kibbutz as a group of "backwoods pioneer romantics," "absorbed in a unique experiment of creating a Lilliputian Utopia at the cost of Brobdingnagian effort," "the most naïve sort of fellow travelers, with touching illusions and an exasperating ignorance of facts."[35] How then shall we classify the collective settlements from the standpoint of social theory?

[32] *Unity Platform*, p. 4.
[33] G. Muenzer, *op. cit.*, p. 114.
[34] Cf. Ben Halpern, "A Problem in Practical Socialism," *The Jewish Frontier*, XII (1945), 22.
[35] Arthur Koestler, *New York Herald Tribune*, August 30, 1948, p. 20.

The kibbutzim, in their social structure, come closest to a realization of communism as Lenin defined it. In his *State and Revolution*, Lenin envisaged an order in which "primitive democracy" would once more be revived, in which "the mass of the population rises to independent participation, not only in voting and elections, *but also in the every-day administration of affairs.*" With accounting simplified, it becomes possible for all to participate in the control of industry, the need for managers disappears, and the antagonism between mental and physical labor vanishes; the last principal source of social inequality is thus obliterated.[36] Such is Lenin's conception of communism, and it is in large measure approximated in the workings of kibbutz democracy. For the community does participate collectively in its accounting and administration, and there is no inequality arising from a managerial class.[37]

As a form of communism, however, it has evolved in a way which falls outside Lenin's theory of social development. The communal settlements were not set up by a group of men who seized control of the state apparatus, to destroy the old society and create a new. Rather, they grew from below, without coercion, a "socialism by consent."[38] Moreover, in their social and economic relations, the communal settlements are a close approximation to Kropotkin's model of society. There are the decentralized, autonomous communes, banded together voluntarily into free associations of collectives; there is the combination of industry and agriculture which Kropotkin always advocated, and the use of coöperative bodies as the selling and purchasing agencies of the kibbutz.[39]

That there is a strong admixture of the Utopian in the man of the kibbutz is undeniable. This is well illustrated in the autobiography of one of the settlers:

Against the decadence of society and the degeneration of Jewish life we set the goal of a New Man and a regenerated Jew. We sought for a vision. . . . When the first Shomrim left for Palestine, those in the Diaspora were dreaming of a Shomer society in Eretz Israel which should serve as an example of social justice and of a new morality. A model society from

[36] V. I. Lenin, State and Revolution (New York, 1932), pp. 97-98.
[37] Fritz Naftali, "Socialist Aspects of the Kibbutz," *Youth and Nation*, XII (1944), 14.
[38] Norman Bentwich, *Judaea Lives Again* (London, 1944), p. 68.
[39] Peter Kropotkin, *The Conquest of Bread* (New York, 1936).

which an influence should emanate to the outside world—this was the first socialist concept of Hashomer Hatzair. . . . I can still remember how at that time, I pictured to myself our future society: I saw the 'Shomer Colony' in Palestine in the form of a citadel set high up on a hill . . . in the eyes of the community we appeared as an idealistic sect that had been captivated by a fantastic dream and a Utopia. Today we, too, look back upon that time as the period of romanticism in our movement. The Shomer Kibbutzim today are far from socialist monasteries set high upon the hills. . . . But it is impossible today to understand Kibbutz Artzi —the federation of Hashomer Hatzair Collectives in Palestine—without bearing in mind the bond between it and that first Shomer dream of the new society in Palestine. Without the Shomer Utopia, there would never have been the Shomer reality.[40]

When the Utopian aspiration is acknowledged, there still remains the fact that the communal settlements were an answer to needs which spring deep from the socio-economic sources of our civilization. If there is an Achilles' heel to collective enterprise in Israel, it will be found primarily in the material limitations of the soil and the extensive dependence on American financing.[41]

GENERAL IMPLICATIONS

The chief difficulty in generalizing from kibbutz experience to the problems of collectivist economy generally arises from the fact that the men of the settlements are, by and large, of uncommon intellectual and moral stature.[42] This is especially the case in the Hashomer Hatzair settlements, whose members have often grown up in the Hashomer youth movement, and have been selected from the best. But the other settlements likewise have a cultural level which, I believe, would be matched by no farming class in the world. The pioneer Jewish farmers are often intellectuals who have chosen to return to the soil. Then again, almost all Jews in Israel have undergone in their lives a "crisis experience." They have seen their friends

[40] Avraham Ben-Shalom, *Deep Furrows* (New York, 1937). Also cf. the prophetic insight of Theodor Herzl's novel into the "mutualistic order" of the New Society: *Old-New Land*, tr. Lotta Levensohn (New York, 1941), pp. 85-86.
[41] The contributions of Palestine Histadrut Campaign in the United States in 1946 amounted to nearly LP 500,000. Cf. Muenzner, *Labor Enterprise in Palestine*, p. 17.
[42] Cf. especially Henrik F. Infield, *Cooperative Living in Palestine* (London, 1946), p. 42.

and families destroyed, they have seen the bottomless cruelty of men, and the kibbutz, for many, is a new family, a haven in which one can work peacefully and allow one's affections to revive, in which the individual draws common strength from those who have suffered as himself. It is difficult to judge how much the unique accomplishment of the Israeli collectives is inherently dependent upon such special intellectual and psychological circumstances.

Nevertheless, kibbutz democracy and socio-economic forms have much to teach the world, especially in the communal development of backward areas. Jorge Garcia Granados, the Chairman of the United Nations Commission on Palestine, saw in the kibbutz the socio-economic form which might enable his native Guatemala to solve its own problems of Indian life and economic development.[43]

It is doubtful, however, whether the tribal aspects of kibbutz life will seem attractive to Western peoples. Socialism, among Western nations, is solely an instrumentality for individualism. Economic security and advantages may be sought in collective ways, but the latter are regarded solely as methods for achieving a greater free area for individual decision. There is little tendency toward honorific attitudes with regard to "collective decision." Americans like to be on their own, and such conceptions as the independence of family units are strongly embedded in their culture.

We can learn much, however, from the Israeli communal settlements concerning the precondition for the maintenance of democratic leadership. We speak vaguely of a society in which the individual is valued. What is such a society? It is one in which the individual does not regard himself with feelings of inferiority and unworthiness. Totalitarian modes of leadership are always based on people's feelings of self-abnegation, of abasement, before state, party, or tribe.

A person's attitude toward himself is largely a reflection of the attitude of others toward him. In the kibbutz economy, everyone is needed; each person can find a place. This is the social condition for the high valuation of the individual. In such a society, a person does not hate himself; there is no internalized ambivalence as a result of society's hostility toward him. This is why the kibbutzim can take the tortured, mangled lives of the survivors of concentration camps

[43] Jorge Garcia Granados, *The Birth of Israel* (New York, 1948).

and crematoria and, in the new communal environment, enable them to grow into democratic free citizens.

And their leaders? They will tend to be a unique blend of men of thought and action. Like the Prime Minister, Ben-Gurion, they will be men who have known the life of labor and who understand that our social age is still one of power relations. But they will also be men who are inheritors of a philosophic tradition and love for the sciences. Perhaps even as Ben-Gurion they will affect a pride in something like knowledge of Greek and reading of Plato. Above all, the political leader who sees his name on the communal work-schedule as assigned to temporary external work is always aware of his own status as the people's representative. The communal settlements have evolved that strange phenomenon of Israel, the cabinet minister in shirt sleeves, who continues to have his meals with his *chaverim* at the workers' restaurants.

Part Three: AUTHORITARIAN AND
DEMOCRATIC LEADERS

Contexts: Manipulation and Authoritarian Leadership

IN THIS section, the challenge to democratic values and the concern for their defense—the practical and ethical core of the volume—comes into sharpest focus. Several major questions are reiterated throughout the articles presented here:

1. What are some of the characteristics of authoritarian and democratic leadership? It is vital to know the former for diagnostic purposes and for judging when some sort of therapy or remedy is required. It is equally necessary to begin to spell out in a positive way the characteristics of democratic leadership, not only that we may recognize deviations from them, but also that their influence as regulative ideals may be made more potent.

2. What are some of the sources of authoritarian leadership? This is an important question because it should lead to data that can guide our remedies, making them less of a trial-and-error procedure.

3. What are some of the consequences of authoritarian leadership? An answer to this has certain prognostic value. Knowledge of some of the directions which authoritarian leadership may take and, particularly, some of the resultants which may weaken or impair authoritarian leadership itself, is useful for therapeutic purposes.

4. How can authoritarian leaders be effectively opposed? And not only effectively opposed, but opposed in such a way that democratic values are not lost in the process.

Almost all of the articles of this group touch in one way or another on each of the problems raised above, though some concentrate on one or two of these. In his "Notes on Democratic and Authoritarian Leadership," Daniel Bell discusses some of the characteristics distinguishing authoritarian and democratic leadership, as well as those character traits rendering the individual susceptible to appeals from authoritarian leaders. The latter are, in turn, examined as products of specific institutional patterns, particularly family organization, an implication being that the disposition to accept authoritarian leadership derives from some of our most fundamental social patterns.

Kurt Lewin's "Consequences of Authoritarian and Democratic Leadership" is a brief summary of a trend-making experiment in social psychology, and attempts to ascertain the resultants of democratic and authoritarian leadership. In attempting to formulate the characteristics of democratic leadership, in order to establish the group "atmosphere" needed for the experiment, Lippett and White (whose experiments are those discussed) have made significant strides, also, in explicating the component elements of democratic leadership. These, however, are formulated in behavioristic terms, while Bell's parallel comments are couched in psychoanalytical concepts. Though, in historical situations, acceptance of authoritarian leaders is conditioned by mass anxiety, the experiment Lewin describes indicates that authoritarian leadership need not abate this anxiety and may, in fact, heighten it. This further suggests that the prevalent notion of leadership as satisfying the needs of the group members in a situation is a simplistic one requiring considerable refinement. This same finding suggests (as J. F. Wolpert notes later) that references to the stability of the authoritarian group—the "thousand year Reich"—are more compensatory in nature than actually descriptive of the stability of authoritarian groups.

Of the many democratic values violated by authoritarian leaders, perhaps none is more central than the Kantian principle that every man should be treated as an end. He is not to be viewed as a tool, as a means to the ends of someone else. "All actions," Kant further stated, "relating to the rights of other men are wrong, if the maxims from which they follow are inconsistent with publicity." Conversely, "all maxims which require publicity, in order that they may not fail to attain their end, are in agreement both with right and politics." Commenting on these last two principles which are fundamental to democratic values, Melvin Rader has remarked:

"Kant thus makes 'pitiless publicity' the test of fair dealing. Practices that cannot stand the light of day, that require secrecy, double-dealing, and falsehood, are in all probability unjust and immoral. On the other hand, practices that do demand the light, that depend upon open dealing and informed public opinion, are in all likelihood fair and right."[1]

In his previously referred to article, Daniel Bell has noted how widespread manipulative and contemptuous attitudes are among contemporary leaders, finding their way into the practices even of leaders who conceive of themselves as highly democratic. T. W. Adorno presents a highly original strategy for opposing these leaders and their manipulative practices. Adorno's study, based on recent psychoanalytical investigations of the susceptibility to authoritarian leadership, goes far beyond the usual proposals which attempt to "expose" or debunk authoritarian leaders as "tools" or "crackpots." Leonard W. Doob's "Propagandists vs. Propagandees" considers one of the most characteristic forms of mass manipulation, propaganda, and proposes and evaluates a number of other vaccines against authoritarian leadership. In the final article of this section, "Elements and Problems of Democratic Leadership," by Bernard Kutner, methods of coping with authoritarian leaders within an association are weighed.

In combating the authoritarian leader's manipulation of the masses, and in the more general activity of democratic groups, two pitfalls deserve close survey. The first of these, the "pseudorealistic" use of manipulation to combat manipulation is given incisive treatment by T. W. Adorno. The second, absolute rejection of all manipulation, may be called the "pseudoidealistic" pitfall.

The fuller implications of these problems may be approached in the following way: As social action becomes more and more sophisticated, as antagonists subject each other's political styles and tactics to careful analysis, and as political espionage grows in importance, the leaders of even a democratic group may feel constrained to conceal some of their goals or plans from their own membership and, generally, from the public to whom they appeal for support. They fear that unanticipated consequences will emerge if they completely reveal their goals or plans. Fearing defeat if "pitiless publicity" is brought to bear on their plans, not because their own membership

[1] Melvin Rader, No Compromise (New York, 1939), p. 187.

might reject a given goal or strategy, but because it may forewarn their opponents, they only partially reveal their intentions and to that extent engage in manipulation.

Democratic leaders in such a situation confront a problem almost tragic in its proportions. Theirs is a dilemma of the most poignant ethical and psychological character. It is a genuine dilemma because two competing values—to hold fast to "pitiless publicity," or to safeguard a concrete advantage for a democratic group and its goals— have to be weighed against each other.

Neither the "pseudorealists" nor the "pseudoidealists" experience this as a dilemma. The latter readily decides in favor of the norm of nonmanipulation. Such idealism is "pseudo" because the norm of nonmanipulation, if treated as an absolute ethic and unconditionally adhered to, can without much difficulty have consequences which destroy the democratic group—all the more readily as democratic groups encounter authoritarian leaders who have no qualms about the use of manipulation and duplicity.

The opposite type, the "pseudorealists," those who easily employ manipulation on behalf of a "good cause," may soon begin to corrode the very values that they strive to realize. After a while manipulation of the "out-group" is extended to the "in-group"—"for their own good," of course—and the most that a once democratic group may salvage from such a process is a "benevolent tyranny."

Thus neither attitude can preserve the democratic group and immunize it against manipulation. The "pseudorealists" say in effect with Oscar Wilde that the only way to resist temptation is to succumb to it. The "pseudoidealists" evidently believe it unimportant whether the patient dies or lives, as long as the operation was a success. Somehow, the injuries which manipulation does to democratic values, and the damage which absolute nonmanipulation does to a democratic group's chances for survival must both be avoided or minimized. Though this is a problem at the heart of current democratic action, it has received very little attention. All that can be done here is to propose some extremely tentative suggestions[2] which seek to tread a

---

[2] The following suggestions were worked out during the course of discussions with Frank Riessman, Jr., in July, 1947. The present formulation is my own and Mr. Riessman cannot, of course, be held responsible for it.

tenuous middle path between the "pseudorealistic" and "pseudo-idealistic" approaches, not because a middle path is inherently superior to any extreme but because it appears to be the only one that can preserve a democratic group's values and existence.
(1) The conditions under which manipulation may be used, the specific groups toward which it may be directed, and the conditions under which it may be employed should be explicitly worked out by the in-group—i.e., all the members of the group. The group should be made aware of the problem of manipulation, and normative attitudes governing its use should be fostered. (2) Periodic self-criticisms, such as those mentioned by Bernard Kutner, should pay special attention to the manipulation practiced by the group's own leaders. (3) Manipulation by leadership, in the sense of incomplete goal and strategy disclosure, may be evaluated during these self-criticisms in the following ways: First, what was the intention of the leader; was it to secure the group against a danger, or was it principally to enhance his own status? Second, was the leader's judgment concerning the danger sound or alarmist? Third, did the leader attempt to solve the problem with use of nonmanipulative techniques? If the leader's intention was to safeguard the group against a demonstrable danger, and only after exploring nonmanipulative methods, his manipulation may be judged as being occasioned by extenuating circumstances. (4) Whether or not extenuating circumstances are found to exist, manipulation should evoke an attitude of moral repugnance. (5) People who manifestly enjoy or take pleasure in manipulation should be retrained, closely controlled, or kept out of leadership positions. (6) The group's educational programs might focus on those aspects of their "heroes'" or "founding fathers'" activities or writings which are antimanipulative. In this way the members will have an extra-group "court of appeal" to be used against present leaders who manifest proscribed manipulative behavior. (7) The educational program should internalize the group's long-range goals and integrate these with the members' daily activities. These long-range goals provide a setting in terms of which each defeat or victory may be interpreted. Without these explicit long-term goals, minor victories may be mistaken for the war's end, and minor defeats may be interpreted as the world's end. Clear-cut long-range ends minimize frustrations which

may conduce to manipulation. (8) Group rewards should be bestowed primarily for attainments of group goals which most closely conform to nonmanipulative norms.

Clearly each of these suggestions is experimental and would require considerable amplification before attempted use. Though they are far from adequate for a problem as pervasive as the one they are intended to mitigate, they may serve nevertheless to suggest some of the possible modes of attack.

Notes on Authoritarian and Democratic Leadership[1]

BY DANIEL BELL

THE LITERATURE on the techniques of leadership is vast and discursive. Long ago, the means of wooing a mass audience and the arts of persuasion were detailed by Aristotle in his *Rhetoric*. Hitler's technique of the "big lie" was already described by Aristotle when he said, "Public and open injuries are the easiest to do, because nobody could at all suppose them possible, and therefore no precautions are taken. The same is true of crimes so great and terrible that no man living could be suspected of them." And any hometown orator debating with an outsider instinctively knows what Aristotle observed: that "speeches that rely on examples are as persuasive as the other kind, but those which rely on Enthymemes[2] excite the louder applause."

Nor has the craft of political leadership been elaborated much beyond the descriptions of Machiavelli in *The Prince* and *The Discourses*. In the handbook of the practicing politician one might probably find such copybook maxims as "Injuries should be done all together so that being less tasted they will give less offense. Benefits should be granted little by little so that they may be enjoyed." Or, "it is well to seem merciful, faithful, humane, sincere, religious and also to be so; but you must have the mind so disposed that when it is needful to be otherwise you may be able to change to the opposite qualities. . . . A Prince must take great care that nothing goes out of his mouth which is not full of the above-named five qualities."

---

[1] This is a previously unpublished paper.
[2] i.e., premises that are understood and shared but not stated.

Almost the entire literature on leadership stems in large measure from the writings of Aristotle and Machiavelli. And shot through this literature are two distinct images which have shaped the thinking of social and political theorists—the image of the mindless masses and the image of the strong-willed leader. Both pictures are the product of a tradition-bound, class-biased point of view which has its origin in the social struggles of the Greek city-states. Curiously, however, this aristocratic bias found adherents in such diverse thinkers as Augustine and Lenin; it is a point of view which fits neatly any doctrine that fears democracy and mass participation. As a result of its largely unquestioned acceptance throughout social theory, it has had the impact of a cumulatively self-confirming hypothesis; its oft-repeated declaration that this is what man *is* disposes people to act in that fashion and has further the effect of inhibiting consideration, by the policymaker, democratic leader and social theorist, of what man *can be*.

TRADITION OF THE "MINDLESS MASSES"

The dominant political tradition in western thought has been conservative. And in large measure its biases have shaped political and sociological categories. This is especially so of the theory of the relation between leaders and masses. The fear of mass rule and the picture of the mass as capable only of creating violence and excess finds root primarily in Aristotle's *Politics*, and the categories he employed in describing political forms. In his three-fold typology of Aristocracy, Oligarchy and Democracy, Aristotle characterized the latter as the mob rule of the ignorant, which, because it can be easily swayed emotionally, allows the demagogue to come to power and impose his tyranny upon society. Democracy, then, for Aristotle, is an unstable social system which must degenerate into tyranny. As Thuycidides pointed out, however, the determining cause of tyranny was the existence of a large landless proletariat and the wide discrepancies in wealth in the Greek city-states. Originally tyranny had not the invidious sense it now carries, but meant simply a direct way of assuming power other than by hereditary succession. The earliest tyrants, such as Pisistratus, were deeply interested in land reform and came to power upon the promise of the redistribution of wealth. "To humble the aristocracy and uplift the lower classes: such was the general principle which guided the tyrants," writes Glotz. As a revolutionary movement "tyranny" brought large masses into the political arena and upset the traditional beliefs of the old ruling class. Some of the tyrants were cruel, many were great public builders. The system could not last, however, because there was no institutional way for power to be limited and perpetuated, so in many cases it became corrupt and feared. The Greek "tyrants," however, did pave the way for a democracy of participation; they helped make the voice of the free masses dominant in the age of Pericles.

Out of these social struggles, and the consequent threat to the privileged groups, developed political fears and political myths. The privileged groups, possessing much leisure time, were able to devote themselves to the arts, literature, and philosophy. They saw the claims of the dispossessed masses as a threat to the traditional cultural values they had built. In a sense, this was true. The masses of people lacked the education of the wealthy, and bitter and nihilistic in mood, looked askance at the mode of life of the upper classes. Out of this tension developed the fear, which has run as a persistent thread throughout western history, that the mass society must mean a leveling of culture and the destruction of traditional cultural values.

The image of the mindless masses developed in Hellenistic times and deepened in the Gracchian political struggles of the Roman Republic. The image of the raw and insensate mob was deeply printed into history by the spectacles of *panem et circenses*, bread and circuses, created by the Roman emperors.

Early Christian theological doctrines rooted the fear of the masses in a theory of human nature, which, in the religious terms of an Augustine (as in the later, secularized version of a Hobbes), the earthly city bore an ineradicable stain of blood. In Paradise there was neither private property nor government. Property and police were the consequences of the fall of Man. Property and police are signs not of man's civilization but of his corruption.

It was the explosive impact of the French Revolution, however, that brought the image of the mindless masses to the fore. The destruction of the *ancien regime* and the revolutionary rallying cry of equality sharpened the fears of the conservative critics, particularly the Catholic apologists, that traditional values (for the latter, those associated with authority and religious dogmas) would be destroyed.

These fears have given rise to a virile body of criticism and some of the keenest insights into the weaknesses of modern society. For a de Tocqueville and an Acton, there was an irreducible conflict between liberty and equality. Liberty guaranteed each man the right to maintain his own culture, whereas equality meant the "leveling" of culture and of taste to the lowest common denominators. For a Max Scheler, as for an Ortega y Gasset, the mass society was a "democracy of the emotions" whose result could only lead to the unleashing of irrational forces. For the Catholic Joseph de Maistre as later for the Anglican T. S. Eliot, the equality of men meant the destruction of unity and authority, the necessary components of an integral society.

This conservative tradition was not a peculiarly European strain. The fear of the passions of the many had a strong hold on the thinking of the American founding fathers, most of whom had an intimate knowledge of classical political history and theory. The fear was strong at the time because the issue of property and the claims of the debtors and landless were crucial political issues at the time of the founding of the Constitution. "Symptoms of a levelling spirit . . . have sufficiently appeared in a certain quarter to give notice of the future danger," wrote Madison in 1787. What he meant was that in the near future, when the majority of people would become propertyless, they would, through their votes, subvert the rights of those with property. And for the same reasons John Adams proposed a regal republic rather than a democracy because the masses were turbulent, ignorant, and poverty-stricken.

From this aristocratic viewpoint, that some hierarchy is necessary for the stability of society, Nazism has been characterized by modern conservative and Catholic critics as the natural end-product of democracy. Hitler is seen as the replica of the classical demagogue swaying the mindless masses and leading them in nihilistic revolt against the traditional culture of European life.

The question whether the characterization of modern society as a culture debauched by the need to pander to popular tastes is a definition of democracy can be debated. The criticism, it should be pointed out, can be made equally from Marxist theory which sees the exchange process as turning all things of value, including culture, into commodities to be assessed and traded at market prices. However, what is of interest here is the indication of the historical roots and particular perspective of the concept of masses and leaders which has dominated so much of political thinking and finds expression today as "science" in the elite theories of Pareto, Mosca, and Michels and, obliquely, in the earlier writings of Lasswell.

The value biases of the conservative tradition are clear. It fears the mindless masses and also the charismatic leader who alone can manipulate them. Both are equally threatening to tradition and legitimacy, i.e., the accepted order of power succession, and to the hierarchical structure of society which these institutions buttress. Out of these biases has come the image of masses and leadership in which description and value judgment have become so intertwined as to warp, for scientific purposes, a large number of social studies.

ASSUMPTIONS OF EARLY SOCIAL SCIENCE

In many of the earlier analyses of mass psychology and leadership there runs the theme, most explicit in Rene Fülop-Miller, of basic atavisms in the human mind. This view sees man as ridden by inexplicable fears similar to our primitive ancestors: when the veneer of civilization is stripped, the savage, who responds most easily to magic, is revealed. The purposeful leader knows how to invoke this magical sense. There is, first, ritual and ceremonial; its purpose is to create a setting of awe in order to aid the invocation of suprahuman powers. Then follows rhythmic marching and singing, in order to envelop the individual in the herd and supply the "oceanic feeling" of security. The rhythm changes to mass incantation and chanting—the interminable Duce Duce Duce Duce—as a supplication of the charismatic leader. And finally, the appearance of the leader—always at a distance so as to invoke mystery about his presence—to act as the mediator between fearful men and the greater powers beyond. Such is the outline, as it occurs in dithyrambic form, of the role and function of leadership. The sociological descriptions, which assume a seeming neutrality because of the dull and heavy jargon, make the same assumptions.

Until recent times, much of the sociological writings drew heavily on the work of Gustave LeBon for its description of leadership. Freud's major essay on mass behavior, Group Psychology and the Analysis of the Ego, is based largely on LeBon; modern texts in social psychology still make obeisance to him. LeBon's theory, stated in his book "The Crowd," is that in the group or the mass, individual differences are lost and that the consequent leveling makes it possible for a strong leader to impose his will on the mass. This he does through affirmation, repetition, and contagion. "Affirmation, pure and simple, kept free of all reasoning and all proof is one of the surest means of making an idea enter the minds. . . . Affirmation, however, has no real influence unless it be constantly repeated, and so far as possible, in the same terms . . . when an affirmation has been sufficiently repeated and there is unanimity in this repetition . . . what is called a current of opinion is formed and the powerful mechanism of contagion intervenes . . . for individuals to succumb to contagion their simultaneous presence on the same spot is not indispensable. The action of contagion may be felt from a distance. . . ." (Such a process, described more vividly in *The Hucksters*, is essentially the technique of modern advertising while the powerful mass media of radio, film, and television easily united far-distant people into one like-minded group.)

LeBon's underlying assumption is clearly that of the drifting mob and the purposeful leader. "The majority of men," he writes, "do not possess clear and reasoned ideas on any subject whatever outside their own specialty. The leader serves them as guide . . . the arousing of faith—whether religious, political or social, whether faith in a work, in a person or an idea—has always been the function of great leaders of crowds . . . to endow a man with faith is to multiply his strength tenfold."

A parallel assumption on the need for the leader is made by V. I. Lenin in his classic formulation of the theory of the revolutionary vanguard. Writing in his manual of revolutionary tactics, *What Is To Be Done*, he says: ". . . without the 'dozen' tried and talented leaders (and talented men are not born by the hundred), professionally trained, schooled by long experience and working in perfect harmony, no class in modern society is capable of conducting a determined struggle. . . . I assert (1) that no movement can be durable without a stable organization of leaders to maintain continuity; (2) that the more widely the masses are spontaneously drawn into the struggle and form the basis of the movement and participate in it, the more necessary it is to have such an organization and the more stable it must be (for it is much easier for demagogues to sidetrack the more backward sections of the masses); (3) that the organization must consist chiefly of persons engaged in revolutionary activities as a profession."

THE CONTAGION OF CONTEMPT

So potent and widespread are these foregoing assumptions in our society that few are immune from this attempt to capture and manipulate irrational fears and emotions as a means of political identification. The Henry Wallace meetings, carefully staged and directed, form an excellent example of the application in America of the style of mass meetings to which Europe has become long accustomed in the last two decades. The following is an excerpted and woven-together description of a Henry Wallace meeting by Aaron Levenstein in *The Call*, Sept. 10, 1947:

Off-stage stands the director . . . at his command the audience has been plunged into utter night . . . in the darkness each of the thousands is all alone and waits . . . the expectant silence and the loneliness grows heavier. If this continues surely someone must cry out . . . the director gives his signal . . . the corsage of loudspeakers pinned to the roof of the Garden booms out a welcome. At this meeting no chairman presides; the audience is to be its own master—by following the script and responding to the cues. Two alternating voices are heard—out of the audience itself. A boy and a girl speak to each other of their devoted love. From the roof of the Garden two spotlights pinpoint the young couple sitting in the arena. The microphones eavesdrop as they talk to each other . . . with words they weave the pattern for the night. They tell of their youthful hopes; they linger on their fears. "If only Franklin Roosevelt were here," says the boy. "He would know the answer." Suddenly the twin spotlights go out and they are submerged in the same darkness and silence that have swallowed the thousands around them. Suddenly, up on the stage another spot rings the face of a well-built man. "No, I am not Franklin Roosevelt," he says. "I am only his son."

He pauses. The impact of the name catches the man-headed ear. The applause is a wave lashing through the Garden mounting to the far rows under the roof. . . .

And so it goes, each speaker brought carefully into the spotlight with introductions voiced by the girl or boy, speaking earnestly and tremulously of their fears of war. But now the climax. A voice booms out of the loudspeaker. It declares: "Franklin D. Roosevelt is no longer with us. But there is a man in our midst who wears his mantel." From every side of the great arena circles of light burst forth. The spotlights flash back and forth across the crowd, roaming, searching among the cluster of white faces. . . . The loudspeaker continues: "Do you want to hear from him? His name is—"

And from the audience comes the roar "Henry Wallace." The loudspeaker comes in, its volume rising, "Yes, his name is Henry Wallace, Henry Wallace." The spotlights move faster through the darkness, as if seeking to find and pinpoint the face of every man in the crowd. Faster and faster they turn, seeking out the sadly groping now twisting and turning mass. The chanted name grows louder, the scattered voices are reaching out toward each other, the threads of sound are merging till they are almost a visible blanket. The uproar crashes on the eardrums; the spotlights hammer on the retina. Louder and faster and brighter. The tension mounts and breaks suddenly as the beams retreat into the darkness and leave one strong light focussed on the lectern. Behind it is the man with the loose forelock, who smiles with difficulty, waves his hand, clears his throat, nervously riffles the pages. . . .

As Adolf Hitler wrote once in his own manual on rhetoric, mass demonstrations "must burn into the little man's soul the proud conviction that though a little worm he is nevertheless part of a great dragon."

If the technique of manipulation implies a mindless mass, it also suggests that the leader is a unique and mysterious individual whose lineaments cannot be traced and the source of whose power can only be ascribed, not described. Leadership, in that sense, is "charismatic" or literally from the Greek, a "gift of grace." Although originally a religious term used by Paul, it has been given a secular twist by Max Weber who uses it to denote those men who, on the basis of personal heroism, asceticism, personal magnetism, or any other distinctive qualities, are immediately and unqualifiedly recognized by the masses as a leader. The authority of these leaders is personal rather than traditional, its source is "magical" rather than rational. In that sense such diverse moderns as Hitler, Huey Long, Franklin D. Roosevelt were charismatic individuals.

For Freud (in *Group Psychology and the Analysis of the Ego*) such phenomena is explainable through the metaphor of "hypnotism" as the model of all authority. The follower submits to the leader because he hopes to recapture his dependence on the parent, who once supplied the all-sufficing love and protection during his earliest years. Through the mechanism of *identification*, the psychological bond is cemented; the image of the leader is put in the place of the individual's own ego. Fearful of his capacity to make judgments and afraid to act on the basis of his own decisions, filled with anxiety and helplessness, the individual takes over into his own personality the values, habits and even gestures of someone who seems stronger or who seems to supply the ideal elements he lacks in himself. A group, he says, can come into existence only through a leader.

The acceptance of a pure leadership type or the statement that leadership is a natural gift is sometimes made by theorists who do not probe its presumed magical or atavistic basis. Freud, for example, assumes such a truth based on a genetic factor. In his essay *Why War* he remarks casually that the difference between leader and led is inborn. The statistician Francis Galton, and following him the Yale sociologist William Graham Sumner, argue that men of leadership, genius, and talent *always* find their way up the social scale because of "their natural gifts."[3] Sumner went further and argued that "masses of men who are on a substantial equality with each other can never be anything but hopeless savages. . . . Organization, leadership and discipline are indispensable to any beneficial action by masses of men."

Modern sociology, positivist in tradition, narrows its scope by avoiding a generic definition of leadership. To do so would require a critical theory of society in which the basic power structures, as well as its credendas and miranda, i.e., its beliefs and symbols, are examined to see if man is manipulated or allowed to realize his freedom by developing a sense of "self." Man is free, Marx once wrote eloquently, in an early exposition of Hegel, "if nature is his work and reality," so that he "recognizes himself in a world he has himself made."

In its positivism, however, modern sociology sees leadership as a specific response to a specific group situation. Thus the emphasis is on the different kinds of leaders rather than an attempt to find what may be common to the idea of leadership. Leadership thus is seen as a complex social function in which different types of leadership

---

[3] Galton's estimate that the number of men of genius in all history was four hundred and that an important segment of these were related by blood is contested by Charles Horton Cooley and the English writer J. M. Robertson.

roles emerge as responses to different types of group needs. The basic orientation of this research is to study leadership, not in terms of a series of traits or attributes, e.g., the leader is one who is "decisive" or "courageous," etc., but in functional terms, as the product of a complex give-and-take among group members. In these terms a leader is not a person marked by destiny or a man with a distinguishable stamp, but one, who because of his own personality structure, may fit the needs of a particular group and emerge as a leader in that situation. A person may thus be a leader in one situation and play almost no role in another.

These studies have been largely of interpersonal relations in small "face-to-face" groups where the interaction of particular individuals can be watched.[4] Few attempts have been made to relate these problems to the larger political scene where the propositions, which are largely psychological, can be related to institutional theory.[5] Of these few attempts, the most suggestive has been made by Erich Fromm in his book *Escape from Freedom*. In this work, Fromm has sought to relate different character structures of individuals to *historically* patterned roles and to show how these character types react in crisis situations.

THE AUTHORITARIAN CHARACTER STRUCTURE

Erich Fromm draws attention to the different character types that exist among peoples which predispose them to accept or reject differ-

---

[4] A representative study of this sort is Helen Hall Jennings' *Leadership or Isolation* (New York, 1943). One of the most stimulating is "Group Emotions and Leadership," by Fritz Redl, *Psychiatry*, 1942, No. 4. Mention should also be made of the researches of Kurt Lewin and his students on democratic and authoritarian groups, in which the democratic bias is present. A survey of such studies has been made by the writer, "Screening Leaders in a Democracy," *Commentary* V, No. 4 (April, 1948).

[5] For the beginnings of such an attempt see "Morale in the German Wehrmacht," by Edward Shils and Morris Janowitz, *Public Opinion Quarterly* (X, 1946). The authors sought to answer the question why the German army held together so strongly, even in the last days of the war, and suggest that the "primary group" structure was quite strong. The article however, possibly because of space considerations, tends to slight political factors such as the intense hostility of the outside world and the lack of a consistent political attitude of the Allies to the German army. A more formal analysis is made by Talcott Parsons in "Controlled Institutional Change" (*Essays in Sociological Theory* [Glencoe, Ill., 1948]). Parsons, discussing the reëducation of Nazis, analyzes the value-systems of specific sectors of the German people, but does not relate these attitudes to concrete institutions.

ent kinds of leaders. His central thesis is that German bourgeois family structure produced a dominantly sado-masochistic character type. This individual admires authority and tends to submit to it but at the same time he wants to be an authority and have others submit to him. The emergence of this type is established on sociological and historical grounds. Bourgeois morality with its crabbed Protestant view of sensuality and emotion has emphasized strong patriarchal authority, a thriftiness of feeling as well as money, a harsh sense of duty and compulsive restraint, order and methodicalness enforced by a religious impulse which glorified work and an economic impulse for the rational pursuit of money—the Malthusian Man. During the days of the Empire, the authority of the monarchy provided a feeling of security, and traditional religion and morality were strongly rooted. The shattering effects of the war produced a deep shock in this German character type: the Army could be ridiculed, a stolid worker could be President, the inflation ripped out the economic basis of security of the middle class. The feelings of powerless, anxiety, and isolation were the psychological mainsprings of Nazism.

While Fromm sees the sado-masochistic character primarily among the German middle-class groups, the authoritarian character permeated large sections of the German working class (as it has many classes throughout the world). The German Socialist poet and writer Ernest Toller, once reflecting on the causes of the failure of the Bavarian Revolution of 1919 in which he had been a leader, remarked: "Alas, the German workmen had been too long accustomed to blind obedience; they wanted only to obey. They confused brutality with strength, bluster with leadership, suppression of freedom with discipline. They missed their accustomed atmosphere; they found their freedom chaos." It is Fromm's general thesis that in modern society the individual finds himself helpless and bewildered by the constant pressures upon him and the inability to orient himself in terms of being able to control his own life. This extends from such minor instances as not really knowing which piece of soap, or radio, is better than another, to his general insecurity in the economic and political realm. This leads to a desire for escape. The principal social avenue of escape is submission to a leader. Where the character type of the people involves a basic dependence upon authority, the wish to surrender oneself and lose oneself becomes strong. The masochistic urge often rationalizes itself as deep "loyalty" and "love"; the sadistic urge, as "knowing best" or "having done so much" for other persons. Fromm here is not talking about acts, but an integrated character structure. It is the expression of the inability of the individual to stand alone without dominating someone. While sado-masochistic traits may exist in every individual, they become a character structure when they assume the form of dominant drives.

An authoritarian character does not lack courage or even initiative. But his actions are rooted in basic feelings of powerlessness that have to be overcome. Strength is won by leaning on a superior power or a call or a sense of duty. Lack of power is an unmistakable sign of guilt and inferiority, and if the authority in which he believes shows signs of weakness, his love and respect change to contempt and hatred. In Hitler's oratory, in his bitter, vengeful speeches and their implicit sadism, lies his appeal.

Fromm's book, while generally discursive, is based on the solid ground of research into the German family character. A coöperative study of the Institute of Social Research under the leadership of Max Horkheimer, has presented a full-scale historical and sociological analysis of the German Family (*Autorität und Familie* [Paris, 1936]). In this study the patriarchal family is seen as the training ground for authority. It prepares the children for participation in the wider society by stressing obedience and respect. The father is the surrogate or representative of the wider society. The family generates respect for authority and in reciprocal fashion other institutions in society stress the importance of the family.

AUTHORITARIAN AND DEMOCRATIC LEADERS

Crucial to any discussion of leadership is the problem of loyalties and heroes. The process of identification with someone is basic to any individual's psychological and biological development and is implicit in the very notion of socialization. Does that mean acceptance of the mystique of leadership, the inevitable hero-worship of "great men"? An answer has been attempted by Kris and Leites. They draw a distinction in Freudian terminology between ego function and superego function. The superego is that part of the individual which represents the acceptance of basic mores, codes, the 'rights and wrongs,' the shoulds and shalt nots. The ego is the critical mechanism which emphasizes self-protection and evaluation of situations.

Kris and Leites seek to draw a distinction between the democratic leader and the totalitarian leader on the basis that one represents the critical function of analysis, the second the mission to obey. In a specific analysis of German and Allied propaganda, the authors seek to impress the difference. Totalitarian propaganda emphasizes activity; its setting is the visible leader talking to the masses in the fashion of the hypnotist. Democratic propaganda sought to give greater weight to insight. It was less emotional, even less moralistic. Churchill's speeches in the spring of 1940 are taken as the best example of democratic propaganda. They factually related the grim situation, outlined resources and dangers. "Everyone could understand how his own behavior was related to the total situation and how this situation was structured. His detailed analysis . . . also contributed to the prevention of an inexpediently large and rapid increase in anxiety: unknown danger was transformed into a danger known in kind and extent . . . at the same time Churchill offered his own courage as a model: 'If you behave as I do, you will behave right.' "

The democratic leader, then, functions as a model, implying that in identifying with the leader he will best serve the ideals he shares with him. But the understanding of the situation is a precondition for such moral participation. The totalitarian leader who emphasizes a charismatic role offers himself as an object that replaces the superego functions in the individual.

But how ready is an individual in our society to assume the maturity of choice in evaluating critically the claims of a democratic leader? The problem of democratic leadership is shaped by the fact that while we live in a society of political democracy, almost all basic social patterns are authoritarian and tend to instill feelings of helplessness and dependence. We begin as dependent beings in the family situation. The nature of middle-class morality drives parents to impose basic patterns of conformity which will be subsequently demanded in the schools and in the factory. Our schools, despite the long years of effort toward progressive education, still operate largely on authoritarian models. Our factories, hierarchical in structure, are still, for all the talk of human relations programs, places where certain men exercise arbitrary authority over others. And from these questions any inquiry inevitably turns to the problem of bureaucratization. How, within the framework of impersonality and alienation which is modern society, can we create areas of genuine spontaneity in which group participation can be satisfactorily obtained? Ultimately, the problem of bureaucratization has to be considered within the matrix of power and within that area as the problem of the conflict of interests. These interests are psychological, involving the most crucial problems of personality integration, as for example the deeply personal issues of dominance and submission in any intimate situation. Even more, they are class interests, because they are interwoven with the key problem of how our society distributes the rewards and privileges at its disposal.

The Consequences of an Authoritarian and Democratic Leadership[1]

BY KURT LEWIN

THE PSYCHOLOGIST of today recognizes that there are few problems more important for the development of the child and the problem of adolescence than a study of the processes by which a child takes over or becomes opposed to the ideology and the style of living predominant in his social climate, the forces which make him belong to certain groups, or which determine his social status and his security within those groups.

A genuine attempt to approach these problems experimentally— for instance, that of social status or leadership—implies technically that one has to create different types of groups and to set up experimentally a variety of social factors which might shift this status. The experimental social psychologist will have to acquaint himself with the task of experimentally creating groups, creating a social climate or style of living. The sociologist I hope will therefore forgive him when he cannot avoid handling also the so-called sociological problems of groups and group life. Perhaps the social psychologist might prove to be even of considerable help to the sociologist. Frequently the investigation on the border line between two sciences has proved to be particularly fruitful for the progress of both of them.

Take, for instance, the concept "social group." There has been

[1] Reprinted from *Resolving Social Conflicts*, by Kurt Lewin (edited by Gertrud Weiss), Harper & Brothers, 1948. Used by permission of the publishers.

much discussion about how to define a group. The group often has been considered as something more than the sum of the individuals, something better and higher. One has attributed to it a "group mind." The opponents of this opinion have declared the concept of "group mind" to be mere metaphysics and that in reality the group is nothing other than the sum of the individuals. To one who has watched the development of the concept of organism, whole or Gestalt, in psychology this argumentation sounds strangely familiar. In the beginning of Gestalt theory, at the time of Ehrenfels, one attributed to a psychological whole, such as a melody, a so-called Gestalt quality— that is, an additional entity like a group mind, which the whole was supposed to have in addition to the sum of its parts. Today we know that we do not need to assume a mystical Gestalt quality, but that any dynamical whole has properties of its own. The whole might be symmetric in spite of its parts being asymmetric, a whole might be unstable in spite of its parts being stable in themselves.

As far as I can see, the discussion regarding group versus individual in sociology follows a similar trend. Groups are sociological wholes; the unity of these sociological wholes can be defined operationally in the same way as a unity of any other dynamic whole, namely, by the interdependence of its parts. Such a definition takes mysticism out of the group conception and brings the problem down to a thoroughly empirical and testable basis. At the same time it means a full recognition of the fact that properties of a social group, such as its organization, its stability, its goals, are something different from the organization, the stability, and the goals of the individuals in it.

How, then, should one describe a group? Let us discuss the effect of democratic, autocratic and laissez-faire atmospheres or clubs which have been experimentally created by R. Lippitt, and by R. Lippitt and R. K. White, at the Iowa Child Welfare Research Station. Let us assume the club had five members and five observers were available. It might seem the simplest way always to assign one observer to one member of the club. However, the result at best would be five parallel micro-biographies of five individuals. This procedure would not yield a satisfactory record even of such simple facts of the group life as its organization, its sub-groups, and its leader-member relationship, not to speak of such important facts as the general atmosphere. Therefore, instead of assigning every observer to one individual, one observer was assigned to record from minute to minute the organization of the group into subgroups, another the social interactions, etc. In other words, instead of observing the properties of individuals, the properties of the group as such were observed.

In one additional point sociology may well profit from psychology. It is a commonplace that the behavior of individuals as well as groups depends upon their situation and their peculiar position in it. In my mind the last decade of psychology has shown that it is possible to give a clearly detailed description of the peculiar structure of a concrete situation and its dynamics in scientific terms. It can even be done in exact mathematical terms. The youngest discipline of geometry called "topology" is an excellent tool with which to determine the pattern of the life-space of an individual, and to determine within this life-space the relative positions which the different regions of activity or persons, or groups of persons, bear to each other. It has become possible to transform into mathematical terms such everyday statements as: "He is now closer to his goal of being a first-rate physician," "He has changed the direction of his actions," or "He has joined a group." In other words, it is possible to determine, in a geometrically precise manner, the position, direction, and distance within the life-space, even in such cases where the position of the person and the direction of his actions are not physical but social in nature. With this in mind let us return to the social experiment which was undertaken at the Iowa Child Welfare Research Station.

THE EXPERIMENTAL SETTING

It is well known that the amount of success a teacher has in the classroom depends not only on her *skill* but to a great extent on the *atmosphere* she creates. This atmosphere is something intangible; it is a property of the social situation as a whole, and might be measured scientifically if approached from this angle. As a beginning, therefore, Lippitt selected a comparison between a democratic and an autocratic atmosphere for his study. The purpose of his experiment was not to duplicate any given autocracy or democracy or to study an "ideal" autocracy or democracy, but to create set-ups which would give insight into the underlying group dynamics. Two groups of boys and girls, ten and eleven years of age, were chosen for a mask-making club from a group of eager volunteers of two different school classes.

With the help of the Moreno test both groups were equated as much as possible on such qualities as leadership and interpersonal relations. There were eleven meetings of the groups, the democratic group meeting always two days ahead of the autocratic one. The democratic group chose its activities freely. Whatever they chose the autocratic group was then ordered to do. In this way the activities of the group were equated. On the whole, then, everything was kept constant except the group atmosphere.

The leader in both groups was an adult student. He tried to create the different atmospheres by using the following technique:

Democratic	Authoritarian
1. All policies a matter of group determination, encouraged and drawn out by the leader.	1. All determination of policy by the strongest person (leader).
2. Activity perspective given by an explanation of the general steps of the process during discussion at first meeting (clay mould, plaster of Paris, papier-mache, etc.). Where technical advice was needed, the leader tried to point out two or three alternative procedures from which choice could be made.	2. Techniques and steps of attaining the goal (completed mask) dictated by the authority, one at a time, so that future direction was always uncertain to a large degree.
3. The members were free to work with whomever they chose and the division of tasks was left up to the group.	3. The authority usually determined autocratically what each member should do and with whom he should work.
4. The leader attempted to be a group member in spirit and in discussion but not to perform much of the actual work. He gave objective praise and criticism.	4. The dominator criticized and praised individual's activities *without giving objective reasons,* and remained aloof from active group participation. He was always impersonal rather than outwardly hostile or friendly (a necessary concession in method).

During the meetings of the two groups, the observers noted the number of incidents and actions per unit of time. It was observed that the autocratic leader put forth about twice as much action toward the members as the democratic leader, namely, 8.4 actions as against 4.5. This difference is even greater if one takes into account only the initiated social approach, namely, 5.2 as against 2.1. Still greater is this difference in relation to ascendant or initiated ascendant behavior: the ascendant actions of the autocratic leader were nearly three times as frequent as those of the democratic leader.

In regard to submissive actions, the proportion was opposite, namely, more frequent by the democratic leader, although in both groups submissive actions of the leader were relatively rare. A similar relation held for the objective, matter-of-fact actions. Here too the democratic leader showed a higher frequency.

On the whole, then, there existed a much greater impact on the members of the group by the leader in autocracy than in democracy, and the approach was much more ascendant and less matter-of-fact.

When we attempt to answer the question "How does the leader compare with the ordinary member in an autocracy and a democracy?" we must refer to an ideal average member who is a statistical representation of what would happen if all activities were distributed equally among the members of the group, including the leader. In Lippitt's experiment the figures showed two facts clearly: first, in both groups the leader was really leading. The autocratic leader showed 118 percent more initiated ascendant acts than the average ideal member, and the democratic leader 41 percent more. Both leaders were less submissive than the average member, namely, the autocrat 78 percent, the democrat 53 percent. It was interesting to note that both showed also more matter-of-fact action than the average ideal member.

However, the difference between the ordinary member and the leader was much less pronounced in democracy than in autocracy, both in ascendant and submissive action. The democratic leader distinguished himself, also relatively, more by his greater matter-of-factness.

What do these figures indicate about the situation in which the autocratic and democratic group members find themselves? I can only mention a few aspects: In the autocratic group it is the leader who sets the policy. For instance, a child says: "I thought we decided to do the other mask." The leader answers: "No, this is the one I decided last time would be the best one." In dynamical terms such an incident means that the child would have been able to reach his own goal but the leader puts up a barrier against this locomotion. Instead he induces another goal for the child and a force in this direction. We are calling such goals, set up by the power of another person, an *induced* goal.

A parallel example in the democratic group might be this: A child asks, "How big will we make the mask? Are they out of clay or what?" The leader answers: "Would you like me to give you a little idea of how people generally make masks?" In other words, the leader in the democratic group, instead of hindering the children in getting to their own goal, bridges over whatever regions of difficulty might exist. For the democratic group, many paths are open; for the autocratic only one, namely, that determined by the leader. In an autocracy the leader determines not only the kind of activity but also who should work with whom. In our experimental democracy all work co-operation was the result of spontaneous sub-grouping of the children. In the autocracy 32 percent of the work groups were initiated by the leader, as against 0 percent in the democracy.

On the whole, then, the autocratic atmosphere gives a much greater and more aggressive dominance of the leader, and a narrowing down of the free movement of the members, together with a weakening of their power fields.

EFFECTS ON THE GROUP

What is the effect of this atmosphere on the group life of the children? As measured by the observers the child-to-child relationship was rather different in the two atmospheres. There was about thirty times as much hostile domination in the autocracy as in the democracy, more demands for attention and much more hostile criticism; whereas in the democratic atmosphere co-operation and praise of the other fellow was much more frequent. In the democracy more constructive suggestions were made and a matter-of-fact or submissive behavior of member to member was more frequent.

In interpreting these data, we might say that the "style of living and thinking" initiated by the leader dominated the relations between the children. In the autocracy, instead of a co-operative attitude, a hostile and highly personal attitude became prevalent. This was strikingly brought out by the amount of group or "we" feeling as against "I" feeling: Statements which were "we-centered" occurred twice as often in the democracy as in the autocracy, whereas far more statements in the autocracy were "I-centered" than in the democracy.

So far as the relation of the children toward the leader was concerned, the statistical analysis revealed that the children in the autocratic group who were *less submissive* to each other were about *twice* as submissive to their leader, as the children in the democratic group. Initiated approaches to the leader in the democratic group were less frequent than in the autocratic group. In autocracy the action by the member toward the leader had more the character of a *response* to an approach of the leader. The approach to the leader in the autocracy was more submissive, or kept at least on a matter-of-fact basis.

On the whole, then, the style of living in both atmospheres governed the child-child relation as well as the child-leader relation. In the autocratic group the children were less matter-of-fact, less co-operative, and submissive toward their equals, but more submissive to their superior than in the democracy.

Behind this difference of behavior lie a number of factors. The tension is greater in the autocratic atmosphere, and the dynamic structure of both groups is rather different. In an autocratic group there are two clearly distinguished levels of social status: the leader is the only one having higher status, the others being on an equally low level. A strong barrier kept up by the leader prevents any one from increasing his status by acquiring leadership. In a democratic atmosphere the difference in social status is slight and there exists no barrier against acquiring leadership.

This has a rather clear effect on the amount of individuality. In our experiment every individual in the democracy showed a relatively greater individuality, having some field of his own in spite of the greater "we" feeling among them, or perhaps because of it. In the autocratic group on the contrary the children all had a low status without much individuality. The type of sub-grouping showed this difference even more clearly. In the autocracy, there was little "we" feeling and relatively little spontaneous sub-grouping among the children. If the work required the co-operation of four or five members, it was the leader who had to order the members to get together. In the democracy those groups came together spontaneously and they kept together about twice as long as in the autocracy. In the autocracy these larger units disintegrated much faster when left to themselves.

These group structures, in combination with the high tension in the autocracy, led in Lippitt's experiments to a *scapegoat* situation. The children in the autocratic group ganged together not against their leader, but against one of the children and treated him so badly that he ceased coming to the club. This happened to two different children during twelve sessions. Under autocratic rule any increase in status through leadership was blocked and the attempt to dominate was dictated by the style of living. In other words, every child became a potential enemy of every other one and the power fields of the children weakened each other, instead of strengthening each other by co-operation. Through combining in an attack against one individual the members who otherwise could not gain higher status were able to do so by violent suppression of one of their fellows.

One may ask whether these results are not due merely to individual differences. A number of facts rule out this explanation, although of course individual differences always play a role. Of particular interest was the transfer of one of the children from the autocratic to the democratic group, and of another from the democratic to the autocratic one. Before the transfer the difference between the two children was the same as between the two groups they belonged to, namely, the autocratic child was more dominating and less friendly and objective than the democratic one. However, after the transfer the behavior changed so that the previously autocratic child now became the less dominating and more friendly and objective child. In other words, the behavior of the children mirrored very quickly the atmosphere of the group in which they moved.

Later Lippitt and White studied four new clubs with other leaders. They included a third atmosphere, namely, that of laissez faire, and exposed the same children successively to a number of atmospheres. On the whole, the results bear out those of Lippitt. They show a striking difference between laissez faire and democracy very much in favor of democracy. They show further two types of reaction in the autocratic groups, one characterized by aggression, the second by apathy.

On the whole, I think there is ample proof that the difference in behavior in autocratic, democratic, and laissez-faire situations is not a result of individual differences. There have been few experiences for

me as impressive as seeing the expression in children's faces change
during the first day of autocracy. The friendly, open, and co-operative
group, full of life, became within a short half-hour a rather apathetic-
looking gathering without initiative. The change from autocracy to
democracy seemed to take somewhat more time than from democracy
to autocracy. Autocracy is imposed upon the individual. Democracy
he has to learn.

Democratic Leadership and Mass Manipulation[1]

BY T. W. ADORNO[2]

THE CONCEPTS of "leadership" and "democratic action" are so deeply involved in the dynamics of modern mass society that their meaning cannot be taken for granted in the present situation. The idea of the leader, as contrasted with that of princes or feudal lords, emerged with the rise of modern democracy. It was related to the political party electing those whom it entrusts with the authority to act and speak in its behalf and who are, at the same time, supposedly qualified to guide the rank and file through rational argumentation. Since Robert Michels' famous *Soziologie des Parteiwesens*, political science has clearly demonstrated that this classical, Rousseauistic conception no longer corresponds to the facts.

Through various processes such as the tremendous numerical increase of modern parties, their dependence on highly concentrated vested interests, and their institutionalization, the truly democratic functioning of leadership, as far as it had ever been achieved in reality, has vanished. The interaction between party and leadership has become more and more limited to abstract manifestations of the will of the majority through ballots, the mechanisms of which are largely subject to control by the established leadership, notwithstanding the fact that in decisive situations "grass-root" democracy, as opposed to official public opinion, shows amazing vitality. Leadership itself, fre-

---

[1] This is a previously unpublished paper.
[2] This article forms part of the author's continuing collaborative work with Max Horkheimer.

quently severed from the people, became increasingly rigid and autonomous. Concomitantly, the impact of leadership upon the masses
ceased to be entirely rational and plainly revealed some authoritarian
traits which are always latent where power is wielded by a few over
many.

Hollow and inflated leader figures such as Hitler and Mussolini,
invested with a phony "charisma," are the ultimate beneficiaries of
these societal changes within the structure of leadership. These
changes profoundly affect the masses themselves. When the people
feel that they are unable actually to determine their own fate, as
happened in Europe, when they are disillusioned about the authenticity and effectiveness of democratic political processes, they are
tempted to surrender the substance of democratic self-determination
and to cast their lot with those whom they consider at least powerful:
their leaders. The mechanisms of authoritarian identification and
introjection which have been described by Freud[3] in regard to hierarchical organizations, e.g., churches and armies, may gain a hold
over large numbers of people, even within groups whose essence is
antiauthoritarian, such as, above all, the political parties. This danger,
though apparently remote for the time being, is counterpart of the
self-perpetuating entrenchment of leadership. The often-made observation that, today, democracy breeds antidemocratic forces and movements denotes the most obvious manifestation of this danger.

THE CONTENT OF DEMOCRACY

Hence, the ideas of democracy and leadership have to be given a
more concrete meaning so as to prevent them from becoming mere
phrases which may finally cover the very opposite of their intrinsic
meaning. It has been known throughout the ages—long before Ibsen
made it the thesis of his *Enemy of the People*, and in fact ever since
the problem of ochlocracy first arose in ancient Greece—that the
majority of the people frequently act blindly in accordance with the
will of powerful institutions or demagogic figures, and in opposition
both to the basic concepts of democratism and their own rational
interest. To apply the idea of democracy in a merely formalistic way,
to accept the will of the majority *per se*, without consideration for

[3] Sigmund Freud, *Group Psychology and the Analysis of the Ego* (London,
1922).

the *content* of democratic decisions, may lead to complete perversion of democracy itself and, ultimately, to its abolition. Today perhaps more than ever, it is the function of democratic leadership to make the subjects of democracy, the people, *conscious of their own wants and needs as against the ideologies which are hammered into their heads by the innumerable communications of vested interests.* They must come to understand those tenets of democracy which, if violated, logically impede the exercise of their own rights and reduce them from self-determining subjects to objects of opaque political maneuvers.

In an era like ours, when the spell of a thought-controlling mass culture has become almost universal, such a postulate, plain common sense though it may be, seems rather utopian. It would be naïvely idealistic to assume that it could be achieved through intellectual means alone. The consciousness, as well as the unconscious, of the masses has been conditioned by the powers that be to such an extent that it will not suffice simply to "give them the facts." At the same time, however, technological progress has made the people so "rational," alert, skeptical, and resistant against make-believes of all kinds—frequently they remain indifferent even to the highest pressure of propaganda, if important issues are at stake—that there can be no doubt about the existence of strong countertendencies against the all-pervasive ideological patterns of our cultural climate. Democratic enlightenment has to lean on these countertendencies which, in turn, should draw on all the resources of scientific knowledge available to us.

CONTRADICTION OF "DEMOCRATIC MANIPULATION"

Attempts in this direction, however, have a profound bearing on the idea of leadership itself. They would require a fearless debunking of the kind of leadership, promoted in modern mass society everywhere, which enhances an irrational transference or identification irreconcilable with intellectual autonomy, the very core of the democratic ideal. Simultaneously, democratic enlightenment imposes very definite demands upon democratic leadership. If such leadership has to take up certain objective, progressive tendencies within the mind of the masses, *this cannot mean, by any stretch of the imagination, that the democratic leader should "make use" of such tendencies;*

that for the sake of democratic aims he should manipulate the masses through shrewd exploitation of their mentality. What is needed is the emancipation of consciousness rather than its further enslavement.

A truly democratic leader, who is more than a mere exponent of political interests embracing a liberal ideology, would necessarily have to abstain from any "psychotechnical" calculation, from any attempt to influence masses or groups of people by irrational means. Under no circumstances should he treat the subjects of political and social action as mere objects to whom an idea is to be sold. This attitude would bring about an inconsistency between ends and means which would impair the sincerity of the whole approach and destroy its inherent conviction. Even on a purely pragmatic level such an attempt would inevitably fall short of the skill of those who think and act only in terms of power, who are largely indifferent to the objective validity of an idea, and who, unhampered by "humanitarian illusions," subscribe to the altogether cynical attitude of considering human beings as mere raw material to be molded at will.

For example, during the crisis of the Weimar Republic, the *Reichsbanner Schwarz-Rot-Gold*, a liberal progressive organization with considerable membership, tried to counteract the Nazi pattern of rational employment of irrational propagandistic stimuli through imitation, by introducing other symbols. Against the *Swastika* they set the three arrows, against the battle cry *Heil Hitler*, the *Frei Heil*, later modified to *Freiheit*. The fact that these awkwardly concocted symbols of German democracy are not even known in this country evidences their complete failure. It was easy enough for the Goebbels machinery to ridicule them. At least unconsciously the masses sensed very well that this type of counterpropaganda merely attempted to steal a leaf from the Nazi book; that it remained inferior within their own domain, and that, in a way, it conceded defeat through the very act of emulation.

TRUTH "PROPAGANDA"

It is hardly too bold to apply the lesson of this experience to our own scene. As far as the relationship of the masses to their own democracy is concerned, democratic leadership should not aim at better and more comprehensive propaganda but should strive to overcome the spirit of propaganda by strict adherence to the principle of truth. In its fight against Hitler, Allied leadership came to recognize this principle and countered German home propaganda with the exclusive statement of facts. This procedure proved not only to be morally superior to the technique of the German master-minds of propaganda, but also showed its effect by gaining the confidence of the German population.

To revert to this principle, however, involves a problem of utmost seriousness. If stated abstractly, the demand for uncompromising sincerity has an almost disarming ring of childlike innocence. Its very idea is torn to pieces by the exponents of *Realpolitik*, above all by Hitler himself, and their case is almost overwhelmingly strong. To enroll the support of the masses—thus the argument runs—one has to take them as they are and not as one wants them to be; in other words, one has to reckon with their psychology. It is useless to spread the objective truth without an evaluation of the subjects at which it is directed. This truth could never reach them and would remain completely powerless since it would always pass their understanding.

Propaganda, Hitler reasoned, has to adjust itself to the most stupid ones among those to whom it is addressed; it should not be rational but emotional. This formula proved to be so tremendously successful that to shun it seems to place one in a hopeless situation. Even the effectiveness of the truth principle of Allied war propaganda, it might be argued, could be ascribed to mere psychological conditions: only after Goebbels' system of the total lie and the Nazi promises of a short war and protection of the homeland against air attacks had broken down did truth fill a psychological want and become acceptable and enticing.

Neither can a sober appraisal of the American scene disregard the fact that propaganda itself is heavily libidinized. In a business culture in which advertising has become a public institution of frightening dimensions, people are indeed emotionally linked not only to the contents of advertising but also to the propagandistic mechanisms as such. Modern propaganda provides those who are exposed to it with some gratification of its own, vicarious or even spurious though it may be. The renunciation of propaganda would, therefore, require an instinctual renunciation on the part of the masses. This pertains not only to the bathing beauty which is associated with "Your Favorite Soap" but in a more subtle and deeply effective way to political propaganda.

The champions of fascist propaganda, in particular, have developed a ritual which, for their adherents, largely takes the place of any clear-cut political program. For the superficial observer the political sphere seems to be predestined to be monopolized by shrewd propagandists: politics are regarded by vast numbers of people as the realm of initiated politicians, if not of grafters and machine bosses. The less the people believe in political integrity, the more easily can they be taken in by politicians who rant against politics. Whereas the truth principle and its inherent rational processes demand a certain intellectual effort which is not likely to attract too many friends, propaganda in general, and fascist propaganda in particular, are thoroughly adapted to the line of the least resistance.

PROBLEMS OF TRUTH PROPAGANDA

Unless the truth principle is formulated more concretely, it will remain an unctuous phrase. The task would be two-fold. An approach must be found which does not make the slightest concession to those aberrations from truth which are almost inevitable if communications are adapted to their prospective consumers. At the same time it would have to break through the walls of inertia, resistance, and conditioned mental behavior-patterns. To those who prate about the immaturity of the masses this may seem to be a hopeless endeavor. However, the argument that people have to be taken as they are is only a half-truth; it overlooks the mass potential of autonomy and spontaneity which is very much alive. It is impossible to say whether an approach such as the one postulated here will eventually succeed, and the reason why it has never been attempted on a large scale must be sought in the prevailing system itself. Nevertheless, it is essential that it should be undertaken.

As a first step, communications would have to be developed which, while adhering to the truth, try to overcome the subjective factors which make truth unacceptable. *The psychological phase of the communication no less than its content should respect the truth principle.* While the irrational element is to be fully considered, it is not to be taken for granted but has to be attacked by enlightenment. Objective, factual reliability should be combined with the effort to promote insight into the irrational dispositions which make it hard for people to judge rationally and autonomously. The truth to be spread by democratic leadership pertains to facts which are clouded by arbitrary distortions and in many cases by the very spirit of our culture. It seeks to foster self-reflection in those whom we want to emancipate from the grip of all-powerful conditioning. This double desideratum seems to be the more justified since there can hardly be any doubt about the existence of an intimate interaction between both factors, the delusions of antidemocratic ideology and the absence of introspection (the latter fact being largely due to defense mechanisms).

In order to be effective, our approach presupposes a thorough knowledge of both content and nature of the antidemocratic stimuli to which the modern masses are exposed. It requires knowledge of the needs and urges among the masses which make them susceptible to such stimuli. Obviously, the main efforts of democratic leadership should be directed at those points where antidemocratic stimuli and subjective dispositions coincide. Since the problem is so complicated we content ourselves here with the discussion of a limited but highly critical area in which both stimuli and effects are heavily concentrated: that of race hatred in general, and present-day totalitarian anti-Semitism in particular.

ANTI-SEMITISM: SPEARHEAD OF FASCISM

It has been emphasized that the latter, as far as its political angle is concerned, is less a spontaneous manifestation, a phenomenon per se, than the spearhead of antidemocratism. There are few areas in which the manipulative aspect of antidemocratism is as unmistakable as here. At the same time it feeds on age-old traditions and strong emotional sources. Fascist demagogues regularly reach the high spots of their performance when they mention and deride the Jews. It is an indisputable fact that wherever and in whatever form anti-Semitism occurs, it is indicative of more or less articulate wishes for the destruction of democracy itself which is based on the inalienable principle of human equality.

A number of scientific investigations shed light on the relation between stimuli and susceptibility which marks the starting point of our approach. As to the stimuli, the techniques of American fascist agitators—defined by openly expressed sympathies for Hitler and German National Socialism—were scrutinized by the Institute of

Social Research.[4] These studies clearly show that American fascist agitators follow a rigid, highly standardized pattern which is based almost entirely on its *psychological* content. Positive programs are conspicuously absent. Only negative measures, mainly against minorities, are recommended, since they serve as an outlet for aggressiveness and pent-up fury. All the agitators' speeches, monotonously similar to each other, are primarily a performance with the immediate purpose of creating the desired atmosphere.

While the pseudopatriotic surface of these communications is a medley of pompous trivialities and absurd lies, its underlying meaning appeals to the secret urges of the audience: it spells destruction. The intelligence between the would-be Führer and his prospective followers rests upon the hidden meaning which is hammered into their heads through incessant repetition. The ideational contents of the agitators' speeches and pamphlets can be boiled down to a small number—not more than twenty—of mechanically applied devices. The agitator does not expect the audience to be bored by the endless repetition of these devices and hackneyed slogans. He believes that the very intellectual poverty of his frame of reference provides the halo of self-evidence, and even a peculiar attraction for those who know what to expect, just as children enjoy the endless literal repetition of the same story or ditty.

The problem of subjective susceptibility for antidemocratism and anti-Semitism was examined in the *Research Project on Social Discrimination*, a joint venture of the Berkeley Public Opinion Study Group and the Institute of Social Research.[5] The main theme of the study is the interconnection between psychological traits and motivations on the one hand, and social attitudes and political and economic

[4] Three monographic studies on the subject were written by T. W. Adorno, L. Lowenthal and P. Massing. A systematic presentation is contained in the volume *Prophets of Deceit* by L. Lowenthal and N. Guterman (New York, 1949). Cf. also T. W. Adorno, "Anti-Semitism and Fascist Propaganda" in: *Anti-Semitism. A Social Disease*, ed. Ernst Simmel (New York, 1946), pp. 125ff. Furthermore, mention should be made of the Coughlin study, *The Fine Art of Propaganda* by A. McClung Lee, which was undertaken independently by the Institute of Propaganda Analysis.

[5] The findings are presented in the book *The Authoritarian Personality* by T. W. Adorno, E. F. Brunswik, D. H. Levinson, and R. N. Sanford (New York, 1950).

ideologies, on the other. The findings amply support the assumption of a clear-cut separation between antidemocratic, authoritarian personalities and those whose psychological make-up is in harmony with democratic principles. Evidence of the existence of a "fascist character" is offered. Although very definite variations of this character can be found among its representatives in the population, there is nevertheless a concrete, tangible kernel, an overall syndrome common to all of them, which may best be defined as authoritarianism. It combines adulation of and submissiveness to strength, with sadistic punitiveness and aggressiveness against the weak. This fascist character syndrome is more strongly related to discriminatory, antiminority attitudes than to overt political ideologies; in other words, susceptibility to fascist stimuli is established on a psychological, characterological level rather than through the subjects' surface credo.

CONSENSUS OF AGITATION AND CHARACTER STRUCTURE

Comparison of the results of the two studies supports the theoretical hypothesis that a close affinity exists between the meaning of fascist politico-psychological devices and the characterological and ideological structure of those at whom the propaganda aims. The fascist agitator is, after all, likely to be also a fascist character. What has been observed in regard to Hitler—that he was a keen practical psychologist and despite his apparent lunacy very much aware of his followers' dispositions—holds true for his American imitators who, incidentally, are no doubt familiar with the recipes so cynically offered in Mein Kampf. A few illustrations of the harmony which exists between stimuli and susceptibility may suffice.

The agitators' overall technique of ceaselessly repeating rigid formulas chimes in with the fascist character's compulsive leaning toward stereotypical, rigid thinking. For the fascist character as well as his prospective leader the individual is a mere specimen of its kind. This accounts in part for the intransigent, congealed division between in- and out-group. In accord with Hitler's famous description, the agitator distinguishes mercilessly between sheep and buck, those who are to be saved, the chosen ones, "we," and those who are bad for badness's sake, who are a priori condemned and must perish, "they," the Jews. Similarly, the fascist character is convinced that all those who belong to his own clan or group, his friends and relatives, are the right kind of people, whereas everything strange is eyed with suspicion and moralistically rejected.

Thus, the moral yardstick of the agitator and his prospective follower is double-edged. Whereas both exalt conventional values and above all demand unquestioning loyalty to the in-group, they do not acknowledge moral duties toward the others. The agitator professes indignation against the governmental sentimentalists who want to send "eggs to Afghanistan," just as the prejudiced personality has no pity for the poor and is prone to consider the unemployed as naturally lazy, as a mere burden, and the Jew as a misfit, a parasite who might as well be exterminated. The desire to exterminate is connected with ideas of dirt and filth, and goes hand in hand with the exaggerated emphasis of external physical values, such as cleanliness and neatness. On his part, the agitator endlessly denounces Jews, foreigners, and refugees as bloodsuckers and vermin.

Finally, we might mention a consensus between fascist agitators and the fascist character that can be adequately explained only through depth psychology. The agitator poses as the savior of all established values and his country, but constantly dwells on dark, sinister forebodings, on "impending doom." Corresponding traits are to be found in the make-up of the prejudiced personality who always stresses the positive, the conservative order of things, and condemns critical attitudes as destructive. However, experiments with the Murray Thematic Apperception Test have clearly shown that he displays strong destructive tendencies in his own spontaneous fantasy life. He sees evil forces at work everywhere and easily falls for all kinds of superstitions and fears of world catastrophes. As a matter of fact, he seems to long for chaotic conditions rather than for the established order in which he pretends to believe. He calls himself a conservative, but his conservatism is a sham.

This correspondence between stimuli and patterns of reaction is of primary importance for a limited approach such as ours. It enables us to use the agitator's technique of lies as a guide for the realistic transformation of the truth principle into practice. By coping adequately with the agitator's devices, we would not merely reduce the effectiveness of his particular, and potentially highly dangerous, technique of mass manipulation; we may also come to grips with those psychological traits which prevent a large number of people from accepting the truth. On a rational level, the assertions of the agitator are so spurious, so absurd, that there must indeed be very powerful emotional reasons why he can get away with them. We may well presume that the audience somehow senses this absurdity. However, instead of being deterred by it, they seem to enjoy it. It is as though the energy of blind fury were ultimately directed against the idea of truth itself, as though the message actually relished by the audience were entirely different from its pseudofactual presentation. It is precisely this critical point at which our attack should aim.

The psychoanalytic connotations of our discussion are obvious. To carry the truth principle beyond the level of factual statements and rational refutation—which so far proved to be ineffective or at least insufficient in this area[6]—and to translate it into terms of the subjects' own personality, would be tantamount to psychoanalysis on a mass scale. Obviously this is not feasible. In addition to the economic considerations which exclude such a method and limit it to selected cases,[7] a more intrinsic reason should be mentioned. The fascist character is not a sick person. He does not show any symptoms in the ordinary clinical sense. As a matter of fact, the *Research Project on Social Discrimination* seems to indicate that he is in many respects less neurotic and, at least superficially, better adjusted than the non-prejudiced personality. The deformations which are no doubt at the root of the prejudiced character belong to the sphere of "character neuroses" which—as has been recognized by modern psychoanalysis—

---

[6] The most pertinent cases are the "Protocols of the Elders of Zion." Their falsity, which has been proven unambiguously, was widely publicized and officially sustained by independent courts, so that not even the Nazis could defend the authenticity of the forged document. Nevertheless they were used continuously for propaganda purposes and accepted by the people. The Protocols are like a hydra growing new heads as soon as an old one is cut off. Fascist pamphlets in this country still play them up. Characteristic is the statement of the late Alfred Rosenberg who, after the trial in Switzerland, declared that even if the Protocols were a forgery, they were still "genuine in spirit."

[7] Such a case has been described in detail by J. F. Brown in a monographic study undertaken within the framework of the *Research Project on Social Discrimination*, and published under the title, "Anxiety States" in *Case Histories in Abnormal and Clinical Psychology*, ed. Burton and Harris (New York, 1948). Further extensive psychoanalytic case studies of prejudiced personalities will be found in the forthcoming volume *Antisemitism, A Psychodynamic Interpretation*, by Nathan Ackerman and Marie Jahoda (New York, 1950).

are most difficult to cure and then only through treatment over a long period of time.

VACCINES AGAINST AUTHORITARIANISM

Under the prevailing conditions democratic leadership cannot hope to change basically the personalities of those on whose support anti-democratic propaganda depends. It has to concentrate on the enlightenment of attitudes, ideologies, and behaviors, making the best possible use of the insights of depth psychology, but it should not venture into pseudotherapeutic undertakings. Of course, such a program has something of the vicious circle, since a substantial piercing of the powerful defense mechanisms of the fascist character can actually be hoped for only through the full-fledged analysis which is out of the question. Nevertheless, attempts will have to be made. There are, to use Freud's phrase, "lever effects" in psychological dynamics. They occur seldom enough in the everyday life of the individual, but democratic leadership, which need not be content with psychological transference, but can rely on the resources of objective truth and rational interest, may be in a favorable position to induce them.

In this connection our knowledge of the agitators' devices may prove helpful. We might derive from them, as it were, vaccines against antidemocratic indoctrination which are more powerful than the mere reiteration of proofs of the falsity of various anti-Semitic allegations. A pamphlet, or manual, which was developed jointly by Max Horkheimer and the author, describes each one of the standard devices, the difference between their overt contentions and their hidden intentions, and the specific psychological mechanisms which foster the subjects' response to the standard stimuli. The manual is as yet in a preliminary stage and there still lies ahead the extremely difficult task of translating the objective findings on which it is based into a language that can be easily understood without diluting its substance. This task must be accomplished through trial and error, through the testing of the manual's understandability and effectiveness with various groups and by continuous improvements, before the manual can be distributed on a large scale. As a matter of fact, premature distribution may do harm rather than good. What is important for us here, however, is the approach as such, not its final elaboration. Its merits seem to lie in the fact that it combines the uncompromising truth principle with a real chance to reach some nerve points of anti-democratism. This it accomplishes through the elucidation of just those subjective factors which prevent the realization of truth. The least that can be said in favor of our approach is that it will induce people to reflect about their own attitudes and opinions, which they usually take for granted, without falling into a moralizing or sermon-izing attitude. Technically, the task is facilitated by the very limited number of the agitators' devices.

OBJECTIONS CONSIDERED

Our approach will doubtlessly call forth quite a few weighty objec-tions from both the political and the psychological direction. Politi-cally, it may be argued that the power interests behind contemporary reaction are much too strong as to be overcome by any "change of mind." It may also be said that modern political mass-movements seem to develop a sociological momentum of their own which is completely impervious to introspective methods. The first objection cannot be fully countered on the basis of leader-mass relations but has to be seen in connection with the constellations within the field of power-politics proper. The second political objection would not be valid under present-day circumstances, though it would be important in an *acute* prefascist situation. It tends to underestimate the sub-jective element in social developments and to make a fetish of the objective tendency. The sociological momentum can certainly not be hypostatized. The assumption of a group mentality is largely mythological. Freud has pointed out very convincingly that the forces which assume the function of an irrational cement of groups, as stressed by writers such as Gustave LeBon, are actually effective within each individual participating in the group and cannot be re-garded as entities, independent of individual psychological dynamics.

Since the emphasis of our approach lies mainly on the psycho-logical level, its psychological critique deserves a more detailed dis-cussion. The argument will be raised that we cannot anticipate any "depth-charge effect" of our vaccination. If our assumption of an underlying fascist character potential, which is in preëstablished harmony with the agitators' devices, is correct, we cannot expect the debunking of their devices to substantially alter attitudes which seem to be reproduced rather than engendered by the agitators' harangues. As long as we do not really touch upon the interplay of forces within our subjects' unconscious, our approach must remain rationalistic even if it makes irrational dispositions its subject matter. Abstract insight into one's own irrationalities, without going into their actual motivation, would not necessarily function in a cathartic way. In the course of our studies we have met numerous people who admit that they 'know they shouldn't be prejudiced,' who even display some knowledge of the sources of their prejudice, and yet maintain it stubbornly. Neither the role of prejudice in the prejudiced person's own psychological household nor the strength of his resistance should be underrated. However, while these objections denote a definite limitation of our approach, they should not discourage us altogether.

To start on a superficial level, the political naïveté of vast numbers of people—and by no means only the uneducated ones—is amazing. Programs, platforms, and slogans are taken at their face value. They are judged in terms of what appears to be their own immediate merit. Apart from a vague suspicion of the political rackets or the bureaucrats—a suspicion which, incidentally, is characteristic of the anti-democratic personality rather than of its opposite—the idea that political goals largely cover the interests of those who promote them is alien to many people. Even more alien, however, is the idea that one's own political decisions depend to a great extent on subjective factors of which one may not even be aware. The shock evinced by the dawning awareness of such a possibility may well help to bring about the aforementioned lever effect.

Though our approach will not reorganize the unconscious of those whom we hope to reach, it may nevertheless reveal to them that they themselves, as well as their ideology, represent a *problem*. The chances to achieve this are augmented by the fact that outspoken anti-Semitism is still deemed disreputable, that those who indulge in it do so with a somewhat bad conscience, and that they therefore find themselves to a certain extent in a conflict situation. There can hardly be any doubt, however, that the transition from a naïve to a reflective attitude brings about a certain weakening of its violence. The element of ego control is enhanced even if the id is not touched. A person who realizes that anti-Semitism is a problem, and that being an anti-Semite is even more of a problem, will in all probability be less fanatic than somebody who swallows the bait of prejudice, hook and line.

The possibility of revealing to the subjects their anti-Semitism for what it is: their own internal problem, is enhanced by the following psychological considerations. As has been mentioned, the prejudiced person externalizes all values, he stubbornly believes in the ultimate importance of categories such as nature, health, conformity to given patterns, etc. He displays definite reluctance against introspection and is incapable of finding fault with himself or those with whom he is identified. Clinical studies have no doubt that this attitude is largely a reaction formation. While being overadjusted to the external world, the prejudiced person feels insecure on a deeper level.[8] The unwillingness to search in oneself is first of all an expression of the fear of making unpleasant discoveries. In other words, it covers underlying conflicts. However, since these conflicts inevitably produce suffering, the defense against self-reflection is not unambiguous.

Though the prejudiced person loathes seeing his own "seamy side," he nevertheless expects some kind of relief from knowing himself better than he does. The dependence of many prejudiced persons on guidance from outside, their readiness to consult quacks of every description, from the astrologer to the human-relations columnist, are at least in part a distorted, externalized expression of their desire for self-awareness. Prejudiced persons, who are at first hostile to psychological interviews, very often seem to derive some kind of gratification from them once some rapport, however superficial it may be, has been established. This underlying wish which, in the last analysis, is the wish for truth itself, could be satisfied by explanations of the type we envisage. Such interviews might provide the prejudiced persons with a kind of relief and ignite what some psychologists call an "aha-experience." It should not be overlooked that the basis for such an effect would be prepared by the narcissistic

---

[8] The factor of insecurity as a motivation of prejudice has been stressed in various studies and is pointed out conclusively in the study, *The Anatomy of Prejudice*, by Bettelheim and Shils. It should be added that the economic insecurity that plays so large a role in the formation of antiminority ideologies seems to be inseparably interwoven with a psychological one, based upon the unresolved Oedipus complex, a repressed antagonism against the father. The interconnection between the economic and the psychological motivation still needs further clarification.

pleasure most people obtain from situations in which they feel important since interest is being focused on them.

The counterargument can point to the indisputable fact that these people have to defend their own prejudice since it fulfills numerous functions, ranging from the pseudointellectual one which provides easy, smooth formulas for the explanation of every evil in the world, to the creation of an object of negative cathexis, a catalyzer for aggressiveness. If the prejudiced person really has to be regarded as a character syndrome, it does not seem likely that he will relinquish a goal-persistence which is determined by his inner structure rather than by the goal. The last observation, however, contains an element which goes beyond the plausible critique of our approach. It is not so much the goal but the prejudiced person that matters in prejudice.

If, as has been said sometimes, anti-Semitism has very little to do with the Jews, the prejudiced person's fixation to the objects of his prejudice should not be emphasized. There is no doubt about the rigidity of prejudice, that is to say, the existence of certain blind spots in the prejudiced person's mind which are inaccessible to the dialectics of living experience. But this rigidity affects the relation between the subject and the object of hatred, rather than the choice of the object or even the obstinacy with which it is maintained. As a matter of fact, those who are rigidly prejudiced even show a certain mobility in regard to the choice of their object of hatred.[9] This was borne out by various cases studied in the Research Project on Social Discrimination. For instance, people who clearly belonged to the fascist character syndrome would—for some extraneous reasons such as being married to a Jewish woman—replace the Jews as objects of hatred by some other more or less surprising group, the Armenians or the Greeks. The instinctual urge is so strong in the prejudiced person and his relation to any object, his ability to form any real

[9] On the political level, this may be illustrated by some observations referring to Germany. Nazi propaganda always found it easy to turn the population's sentiments from one enemy to the other. The Poles were wooed for a number of years before Hitler unleashed his war machinery against them. The Russians, branded as the archenemy, became prospective allies in 1939, and regained their former status of Untermenschen in 1941. These sudden and mechanical changes from one rigid ideology to the other apparently did not meet with any considerable resistance on the part of the population. The relation between rigidity and mobility has been elaborated theoretically by Max Horkheimer and T. W. Adorno in "Elemente des Antisemitismus" in Dialektik der Aufklärung (Amsterdam 1947), pp. 235ff.

attachment, be the object loved or hated, is of such a problematic
nature, that he may not even remain faithful to his chosen foe.

The projective mechanism to which he is subject can be switched
around according to the principle of least resistance and the opportunities afforded by the situation in which he finds himself. It may
be expected that our manual will perhaps create a psychological situation in which the negative cathexis on the Jews is being shattered.
This, of course, should not be misunderstood in the manipulative
sense that one should replace the Jews by somebody else as targets of
hatred in the anti-Semite's mind. But the feebleness, arbitrariness,
and accidentality of the object choice per se may be turned into a
force which would make the subjects doubtful about their own ideology. When they learn how little it matters whom they hate as long
as they hate something, their ego might cease to side with hatred
and the intensity of aggressiveness might subsequently decrease.

OPERATION "BOOMERANG"

It is our intention to use the mobility of prejudice for its own conquest. Our approach might turn the indignation of the prejudiced
person against a truly adequate object: the agitator's devices and the
spuriousness of fascist manipulation proper. On the basis of our explanations it will not be too difficult to make the subjects aware of
the trickiness and insincerity of antidemocratic propaganda techniques. What matters in this respect is not so much the objective
falsity of anti-Jewish statements as the implicit contempt for those
at whom fascist propaganda aims, and whose weaknesses are systematically exploited. At this point, the forces of psychological resistance
may work against antidemocratism rather than against enlightenment.
Nobody, and least of all the potentially fascist character, wants to be
treated as a sucker, and this is precisely what the agitator does when
he tells his audience that they are the suckers of the Jews, bankers,
bureaucrats, and other 'sinister forces.' The American tradition of
common sense, of sales resistance, may be revitalized in this particular
field by our approach since the self-styled *Führer* is, in this country,
in many respects nothing but a glorified barker.

There is one specific area in which psychological exploitation, if
unveiled, will turn into a boomerang. The agitator generally poses as
a great little man, as a person who, in spite of his exalted idealism and

indefatigable vigilance, is one of the people, a neighbor, somebody close to the hearts of the simple folks; he comforts them through his condescending sympathy and creates an atmosphere of warmth and companionship. This technique, which, incidentally, is much more characteristic of the American scene than of the streamlined mass meetings of the Nazis, aims at a specific condition complementary to our highly industrialized society. It is the phenomenon which, in the sphere of mass culture, is known as "nostalgia." The more technification and specialization disrupt the immediate human relationships which were associated with the family, the workshop, the small entrepreneur, the more do the social atoms, which form the new collectivities, long for shelter, for economic security, and for what the psychoanalyst would call a restitution of the womb situation.

It seems that a considerable fraction of fanatic fascists—the so-called lunatic fringe—consists of those in whose psychology this nostalgia plays a particularly important role—the lonely, isolated, and, in many ways, frustrated people. The agitator shrewdly attempts to enroll their support by posing as their neighbor. A truly humane motive, the longing for spontaneous, genuine relationships, for love, is seized upon by the cold-blooded promoters of the inhuman. The very fact that people suffer from universal manipulation is used for manipulation. People's sincerest feelings are being perverted and gratified by swindle. Even if they fall for it momentarily, the desires involved are so profound that they cannot be satisfied by a sham. Treated like children, they will react like children who realize that the uncle who talks baby talk to them merely wants to ingratiate himself for ulterior reasons. Through such experiences the energy inherent in their longing may finally turn against its exploitation.

ILLUSTRATIONS OF MANUAL

THE MANUAL first describes the difference between the political orator and various kinds of agitators, and then gives a few criteria by which the agitator may be recognized. Furthermore, it discusses the devices to which the agitator's technique can be reduced, and explains how they work, and their specific appeal to the listeners.

Following are two examples of such discussions:

Martyr Hero. The main purpose of the agitator is to arouse our human interest in him. He tells us that he is a lonely, independent man who sacrifices everything to his cause and lives in modest circumstances. He repeats that he is not backed by big money or by any of the powers that be. He is particularly eager to make us believe that he is not a politician but aloof from and somehow above politics.

To pretend loneliness is an easy way to catch our sympathy. Today life is hard, cold, and complicated and everybody is somehow lonely. This is what he exploits. By stressing his isolation he appears to be one of us, suffering from the same causes from which we all suffer. Actually, however, he is not at all alone. He is the man with the good connections and he will boast about them whenever an opportunity presents itself. Then he will read to us the letter of that senator who praises his patriotic zeal.

He gives a sales talk all the time, but he wants us to believe that he is not selling anything. He is afraid of our sales resistance and, therefore, hammers into our heads the idea that he is a pure soul while others try to make suckers out of us. As a shrewd advertiser he exploits even our distrust of advertising.

He knows that we have heard about political racketeering and corruption and he utilizes our aversion to this sort of thing for his own political ends. For it is he who is a political racketeer with lieutenants, bodyguards, dark financial interests, and everything that is shady. He constantly shouts "Hold the thief."

There is one more reason why he plays the lone wolf. He poses as being needy so that we will do something for him and feel proud of it. In reality we are the poor sheep. While he attempts to flatter our vanity by suggesting that everything depends on our coming to his aid, he actually only wants us to become his followers, his yes-men who act automatically according to his orders.

If You Only Knew. The speeches of the demagogue are interspersed with hints of dark secrets, revolting scandals, unspeakable crimes. Instead of ever discussing a social or political question in a matter-of-fact way, he blames evil persons for all the ills from which we suffer. His accusations regularly refer to graft, corruption, or sex. He poses as the indignant citizen who wants to clean the house and he promises sensational revelations. This promise is sometimes followed up by hair-raising, fantastic stories. Just as frequently, however, he does not keep his promise but suggests that his secrets are too awful to be told in public, and that his listeners know anyway what he means. Both techniques, the performance as well as the withholding of revelations, work in his favor.

When he does tell the full story, he provides his listeners with the kind of gratifications they get from gossip columns and scandal sheets, only in much more glowing colors. Many people do not turn away when they smell bad odors but eagerly breathe the pested air, sniff the stench and pretend to find out where it comes from while complaining how awful it is. There is no doubt that these people, though they may not even know it, enjoy the bad smell. It is this widespread disposition to which the agitator's scandalmongering appeals. He moralizes about the vices and crimes of others and thus satisfies his listeners' curiosity and relieves the boredom of their drab lives. They often enough envy those whom they believe to do things which they secretly would like to do themselves. At the same time the demagogue gives them a feeling of superiority.

If he does not tell the story but simply teases the listeners with vague hints, he arouses their wildest imaginations. They can think up whatever they like. The agitator, however, appears as the one who knows, who has all the inside information, and who, one day, will come into the open with shattering evidence. Yet he also suggests that he does not even need to tell them. They know anyway—but it would be too dangerous to discuss things in public. They are always treated as though they were in his confidence, already members of his own group, and the unspoken secret ties them even more closely to him.

Of course, his listeners would never dare to commit any of the deeds which he ascribes to his foes. The less they can satisfy any extravagant wishes for luxury and pleasure, the more furious do they become against those who, as they fancy, enjoy the forbidden fruit. They want to "punish the bastards." This is the mood promoted by the agitator. While giving juicy descriptions of champagne orgies celebrated by Washington politicians and Wall Street bankers with Hollywood dancers, he promises the day of reckoning, when in the name of decency a good, honest blood-purge will be celebrated by him and his crowd.

Propagandists vs. Propagandees[1]

BY LEONARD W. DOOB

LEADERS IN civilized countries utilize mass media of communication to obtain and retain their positions of power. Propaganda with or without an accompanying display of force is flourishing. Since ordinary people are vulnerable to propaganda, prophylactic measures are being sought to protect them from propagandists. The problems provoked by each of these statements will be examined in the present chapter.

MODERN PROPAGANDISTS

The *Political Handbook of the World*, an annual publication of the Council on Foreign Relations,[2] gives a brief description of the governments in sixty-four countries. In 1948, all but nine of the nations and dominions had a cabinet or council officer whose title contained the word "education." The exceptions were: Australia, Canada, Germany, Liberia, Nicaragua, Switzerland, the United States, Vatican City, and Yugoslavia. Liberia and Nicaragua perhaps should be immediately eliminated from the list because information on their cabinets was lacking when the *Handbook* and also the *Statesman's Year-Book*[3] were published. Germany had no national government. Yugoslavia's governing body has officials with the titles of "Chairman of the Commission of Art and Culture" and "Chairman

---

[1] This is a previously unpublished paper.
[2] *Political Handbook of the World*, Walter H. Mallory, ed. (New York, 1948).
[3] *The Statesman's Year Book*, 1947, S. H. Steinberg, ed. (New York, 1947).

of the Cinema Committee." Vatican City is a very special kind of state. There remain only four democratic countries: the two members of the Commonwealth, Switzerland, and the United States. Even in these the federal government affects the educational system, although the top officials do not have cabinet rank.

The fact that virtually all countries of the world have a Ministry of Education gives some insight of a preliminary kind into the propaganda situation. Such tasks as the construction of schools, the selection of teachers, the allocation of federal funds to local school systems, etc., can or do have a bearing on propaganda. The teaching of the bare essentials of social living and of science, which may be influenced by the Minister of Education, is generally considered education, but simultaneously it helps shape the attitudes and philosophies of the new generation, a role which certainly has or can have propaganda implications.

Education usually refers to learning by children in the schools. Exactly which governmental official is charged with propagandizing adults in behalf of the regime and its values cannot be easily ascertained. In some countries it may be the Minister of the Interior. In others it may be the Minister of Communications who concerns himself not only with railroad repairs, postage rates, and the assignment of wave lengths to radio stations but also with the contents of the mass media.

In the United States, the propaganda and informational activities of federal officials are often disguised behind slightly deceptive titles, inasmuch as an act of 1913 states that "no money appropriated by this or any other act shall be used for the compensation of any publicity expert unless specifically appropriated for that purpose," and an act of 1919 prohibits the executive branch from using any part of an appropriation to influence Congressmen's attitudes toward legislation.[4] To ferret out the officials who send releases to the American press and radio requires an intimate knowledge of governmental functions which only a government servant or an investigating committee is able to secure. During World War II, the writer can vouch for the fact that the following titles obtained from the *United States Government Manual* were worn by men whose primary or secondary task was to influence the American people in behalf of the war effort, or

[4] James L. McCamy, *Government Publicity* (Chicago, 1939), pp. 6-8.

in behalf of the governmental organization or particular official who was their superior: Chief of Information Liaison; Assistant Coördinator; Associate Director; Special Assistant to the Secretary for Press Relations; Assistant to the Secretary; Director of Information.

In 1936 the services of the Brookings Institution were utilized by a Senate Committee investigating "the Executive Agencies of the Government" to determine exactly how much "publicity" those agencies were then disseminating.[5] It found that for the three months ending on September 30 of that year over seven million copies of almost five thousand releases had been distributed and that there were in existence in Washington over three thousand different mailing lists which contained, including duplications, approximately two and a quarter million names. The releases consisted of stories for the press and radio as well as motion pictures, film strips, exhibits, photographs, and posters. Incomplete figures showed that 146 government employees devoted all of their efforts to publicity and 124 did so on a part-time basis. Many if not all of the releases of the Forest Service, the Bureau of Standards, 'the Smithsonian Institution, and some of the other agencies contained "information" rather than "propaganda." Such releases also redounded to the credit of the administration producing them and certainly offered that or some other administration a propaganda vehicle to affect public opinion and even Congressional attitudes.

Government leaders, then, have at their disposal a propaganda machine which they may or may not employ to full degree. Under a totalitarian form of government, that machine is carefully constructed and utilized. In a democracy, it tends to be operated cautiously because of the widespread belief that the task of officials is to govern and not to defend a particular viewpoint. More important, no doubt, is the competition which the propaganda of a democratic government must face from the opposition, from pressure groups, and from the more or less independent mass media of communication. It is only during the crisis of a severe depression, a war, or some other "national emergency" that federal officials are encouraged to carry

[5] United States Senate, 75th Congress, 1st session, *Investigation of the executive agencies of the government: a preliminary report of the select committee to investigate the executive agencies of the government*, Senate Reports, 75th Congress, 1st session, 1937, pp. 531-553.

on propaganda. Even then the permission is granted reluctantly. During the last war, for example, the goal of the Office of Censorship in the United States was not to improve national morale but to safeguard military and naval security.[6] The Domestic Branch of the Office of War Information provided materials to the mass media, but no editor, program director, or motion-picture chain was compelled to disseminate them.

The citizen of every country is bombarded on all sides by propaganda. His government instructs and perhaps seeks to impress him. Commercial enterprises induce him to spend his earnings in ways they are eager to indicate. Groups and associations ask for his support. The mass media, intentionally or unintentionally, indoctrinate him with some not necessarily unbiased viewpoint. Childs[7] has traced this bewildering increase in propaganda to the extension of suffrage; the rise in the general educational level; the technical advances in the field of communication; the stepping-up of economic competition; and the growing need for coöperation in most phases of social and political life.

In democratic countries it is felt that ordinary citizens should be able to choose from among the competing propagandas or at least be in a position to evaluate the truth or falsity, the goodness or badness, of the appeals that are made to them. At the same time there is a growing realization that they are at a disadvantage when leaders confront them with propagandas. Too frequently they have neither the talent nor the time to make the sagacious decisions which will promote their own welfare. It is contended that their freedom of choice is only hypothetical and that, in fact, they are buffeted hither and yon by the forces in their society.

This picture of the poor propagandee is somewhat distorted. *Propagandas flourish not only because leaders are powerful but also because propagandees already possess impulses that can be touched off by propagandists.* People may be seduced by advertising into purchasing products, but in a real sense they themselves are in the market to be seduced: they have certain unsatisfied needs and ambitions which the advertiser manages to channel in his own rather than in some other

[6] Theodore F. Koop, *Weapon of Silence* (Chicago, 1946).

[7] Harwood L. Childs, "Propaganda and Society," *Education Against Propaganda*, Elmer Ellis, ed., *Seventh Yearbook*, National Council For The Social Studies, 1937, pp. 1-13.

direction. Some, many, or all of these needs and ambitions may have been stimulated by advertising in the past, which in turn has utilized other preëxisting impulses. There is, in short, a very complicated process of interaction at work: needs promote advertising, advertising promotes needs, and the spiral has a tendency to leap upwards. In different words, propagandists and propagandees have been socialized in a particular way; they affect or assist one another.

From this viewpoint, the same forces affect leaders and propagandees. Their common matrix is the society which has formed them and in which they function. They are both following their folkways and mores, leaders by seeking control and propagandees by following or obeying the commands that are thrust at them.

The foregoing statement of the problem, however, is not strictly applicable to a society undergoing change. At any given moment, the goal of the leader that is being achieved through propaganda may or may not be compatible with what is called the welfare of his followers. To say that the goal is or is not compatible requires an ethical judgment in broadest perspective. Through a smart advertising campaign, for example, the producer increases the sales of his product. Certainly he has been employing a legitimate medium in our society. Just as certainly the new consumers have coöperated because they have become convinced that some of their needs can thereby be satisfied. Is the particular mode of gratification promoted by the advertising the most satisfactory? What will be the short- and long-range effects upon them of this selection? Would it have been "better" for some other product to have succeeded in capturing the market?

In a democratic society the tendency still exists to reply to such questions by maintaining, in the manner of the eighteenth century, that truth and goodness will triumph in the long run. The increased sales are considered evidence of real needs and hence of the essential merit of the product. At the same time it is recognized that propagandees are handicapped and so often require protection, whether or not they themselves demand the protection. Advertisers are not permitted to operate with complete freedom. Their products and their advertising copy are regulated generally or specifically by the Federal Trade Commission and by varying laws in all of the forty-eight states.[8] Many newspapers, magazines, and radio stations have established

[8] Burt W. Roper, "State Advertising Legislation," Printers' Ink, 1945.

minimum standards to which they must conform. They themselves often have their own codes. The implicit or explicit assumption behind such restraints is this: truth and goodness can triumph in the propaganda arena only when propagandists and propagandees are more or less equally matched—and it is felt that the latter occasionally need some assistance.

There can be little doubt that propagandees are handicapped. Within limits they are most vulnerable to propaganda. Advertisers do increase the demand for their products. Public relations counsels do improve the reputation of their clients. Politicians plan and plot campaign strategy which successfully returns them to public office. Witch hunts can be made to boom. Morale and the conceptualization of the enemy are, indeed, affected by "psychological warfare." The teaching of any school or college subject, for example, may have an effect on students' attitudes which can be great or small.[9]

Unsensational attitude shifts, furthermore, have been shown to occur under somewhat artificial but more carefully controlled conditions.[10] In the regular classroom, the attitudes of students are measured by a standardized paper-and-pencil test. They then are exposed to the words of their instructor, a pamphlet, a motion picture, a debate, a radio program, a press release, a field trip, etc. Later their attitudes are measured again. Between the first and second measurement a shift in attitude scores occurs which is attributed to the propaganda in the interim. This attribution can occur with greater certainty if a comparable group is not exposed to the propaganda and if its scores remain substantially unchanged. Without this control, it is always possible to conclude that the change in the experimental group would have occurred in the absence of the propaganda.

VULNERABILITY TO PROPAGANDA

It is immediately important to note that not all individuals in real life or experimental situations are affected by propaganda. Observa-

[9] R. J. Longstreet, "An Experiment with the Thurstone Attitude Scales," *School Review*, 1935, pp. 202-208; Arthur J. Manske, "The Reflection of Teachers' Attitudes in the Attitudes of Their Pupils," *Teachers College, Columbia University Contributions to Education*, 1936, No. 702; Mapheus Smith, "Spontaneous Change of Attitude Toward War," *School and Society*, 1937, pp. 30-32; Margaret B. Sutherland, "A Study of the Effects of Learning French on Attitudes Toward the French," *British Journal of Educational Psychology*, 1946.

[10] Gardner Murphy, Lois Barclay Murphy, and Theodore M. Newcomb, *Experimental Social Psychology* (New York, 1937), pp. 946-980.

tions and quantified results are based on averages from which there are always variations. Who, then, is not vulnerable? The significant variables have not been isolated or weighted. On the basis of theoretical considerations and experimental findings, however, extremely tentative hypotheses can be formulated.

In the first place, those who do not perceive a piece of propaganda obviously cannot be affected. The hermit outside a society has established a kind of geographical immunity for himself; the moron in our midst is incapable of responding because he cannot grasp the forces that are supposed to affect him. Metaphorically the hermit and the moron represent extreme types with whom the propagandist must frequently reckon. He tries to reach the hermit by inundating the society with his propaganda and by repeating it endlessly until it almost literally is perceived in the wilderness. He affects the moron by simplifying that message—for example, by means of a Flesch formula for written prose[11]—until it is actually comprehensible to those on a low intellectual level. People who are neither hermits nor morons, moreover, are not automatically susceptible to perceiving propaganda. They have other, sufficiently absorbing interests with which the propaganda cannot compete. No radio program has a perfect Hooperating: the Americans not included in the listening audience have excluded themselves from hearing the commercials. The leaflets dropped to enemy troops in wartime may not be perceived when an unfriendly wind blows them askew or when commanding officers have them seized before they are read.

An individual's habitual predispositions, secondly, help determine whether he will learn the propagandist's message. Other things being equal, if the habits are favorable to the propagandist's cause, he will be more likely to learn the propaganda than if they are not—or the amount of effort required to convert him will be appreciably less. The adjective "favorable" in this generalization covers a multitude of phenomena. It may mean the propagandee's attitude toward the propagandist: a word from an accepted expert has more prestige in our society than one from a layman. It may mean his attitude toward a portion of the propagandist's message: a doctrine labeled "democratic" is more likely to seem acceptable in contemporary America than one called "communistic." It may mean the satisfied or unsatisfied needs within him: a hungry man will be affected to a greater degree by a restaurant sign or a revolutionary appeal than a satiated one. It may mean his past experience with similar propaganda: a glorious pledge in the platform of a political party will not impress an individual who once held high hopes for a similar promise in another campaign and who thereafter had been disappointed. Any one of these preëxisting habits does not inevitably facilitate or inhibit the learning of the propaganda. It has been shown, for example, that the ability to label one film "propaganda" diminished its influence[12] but that other individuals who saw a different film were affected even when they applied the label.[13]

The intellectual capacities of the propagandees also have an effect on his susceptibility to propaganda. Intellectual capacities include native intelligence, intelligence-as-measured-by-intelligence-tests, amount of schooling, school grades, and general or specific knowledge on a subject related to the propaganda in question. Many if not all of these factors are obviously interrelated. There is a most tentative, but statistically insignificant, suggestion in one experiment that more intelligent subjects were slightly less vulnerable to propaganda;[14] in other experiments it has been shown that the less intelligent ones were more immune[15] or that there was no relation between intelligence and vulnerability.[16] In short, the effect of intellectual abilities can be most varied—perhaps it depends upon the difficulty and reasonableness of the propaganda to be learned as well as on other habits of the propagandees. An individual of low intelligence learns with greater

---

[12] Carl I. Hovland, Arthur A. Lumsdaine, and Fred D. Sheffield, *Experiments on Mass Communications*, Volume 3 of *Social-psychological studies in the army during World War II* (Princeton, 1949).

[13] Barbara Bode, "An Experiment in Propaganda," *Journal of Adult Education*, 1941, pp. 310-312.

[14] Franklin H. Knower, "Experimental Studies of Changes in Attitude: Some Incidences of Attitude Changes," *Journal of Applied Psychology*, 1936, pp. 114-127.

[15] Solomon P. Rosenthal, "Change of Socio-Economic Attitudes Under Radical Motion Picture Propaganda," *Archives of Psychology*, 1934, No. 166.

Carl I. Hovland, A. A. Lumsdaine and F. D. Sheffield, *Experiments on Mass Communications, op. cit.*

[16] Arthur W. Kornhauser, "Changes in the Information and Attitudes of Students in an Economics Course," *Journal of Educational Research*, 1930, pp. 288-298; Arthur J. Manske, "The Reflection of Teachers' Attitudes in the Attitudes of Their Pupils," *op. cit.*

difficulty; at the same time, since almost by definition he possesses fewer of those habits equivalent to critical abilities, he is less able to appreciate the truth or falsity of the propagandist's claims. A more intelligent person can learn with greater dispatch but may be more critical.

In addition to the factors of perception, habitual predispositions, and intellect, a fourth variable must be taken into account: the actual surroundings of the propagandee at the moment he perceives the propaganda. Some but certainly not all of the active members of a highly organized group are more likely to respond favorably to the leader's propaganda and to the group's own intercommunications when they are in the face-to-face situation of the group itself than when they are alone. The mere presence of other people in the individual's surroundings, be it noted, is not necessarily efficacious, although it may be so. The other people must be reacted to as fellow members of the same group, as casual strangers, as relatives at a radio broadcast, as hostile out-groupers, etc. Other people constitute stimuli which evoke responses at the same time as the propaganda itself does; and these responses can affect the learning process.

COUNTERACTING PROPAGANDA

The leaders of a society frequently employ measures not to diminish the susceptibility of their followers to propaganda in general but to inoculate them against "wrong" or "bad" propaganda in particular. The local brand of patriotism is automatically safeguarded during the period of socialization and usually by the society's formal and informal communications media. Propagandees are thus given a strong system of habits which prevent them from succumbing to outside influences. When such habits do not exist—as is true for a few decades or more after a country has undergone a revolution—they must be constructed and then reinforced. The mass media extol certain themes and not others; rigid censorship is established to filter out the opposing ideas or forces; the regime seeks to win respect by deeds which lead to basic satisfactions. The same processes function in less dramatic form within all organized groups. They are also visible in segments of a society at any time. The curriculum of a school system may be broad but some subjects are always excluded. The mass media are not permitted nor do they permit themselves to disseminate material

considered to be immoral or corrupting. The most democratic country or institution limits freedom of speech in some manner if only, for
example, in the fields of morals, libel, and sedition.

Protection by official regulation is often but not always difficult to
achieve. Even Propaganda Minister Goebbels, who certainly employed
almost every conceivable word and deed to secure the loyalty and
coöperation of all Germans, continually feared outside forces like
foreign radio stations which he never did effectively or completely
counteract.[17] The leaders of a society or a group therein, however,
have one means at their disposal which can guarantee success: their
followers will be less corruptible if they have been provided with
basic satisfactions. Happy people are not in the market to go to war
or to be swayed by out-groupers. This is truly a panacea in theory; in
practice it malfunctions simply because people are neither easily nor
completely satisfied. Its success, consequently, is generally a relative
matter.

In a democratic society the question of prophylaxis is usually
phrased in modest and personal terms. How, the individual asks, can
he protect himself, his family, or his friends from propaganda? Or
what minor reforms can be introduced so that people by and large
will be able more successfully to analyze and evaluate the propagandas that engulf them? The lofty aim here is to diminish susceptibility to all propaganda.

Several attempts have been made to determine whether or not
instruction in the techniques of propaganda can achieve such an aim.
Biddle[18] wrote a series of nine lessons which he called "Manipulating
the Public." They explained in some detail how propaganda campaigns in the past had been staged. They were given to and studied
by eleventh- and twelfth-grade children in five different schools and
some freshmen in a college course. Before and after the instructions
in propaganda, these subjects took "a test of gullibility," which was
a questionnaire on the relations between the United States and the
Orient. In contrast with comparable control groups of students who
had the before-and-after-test but not the lessons, the experimental
subjects on the average were made significantly less gullible. In this

[17] Louis P. Lochner, ed., The Goebbels Diaries (New York, 1948).
[18] William W. Biddle, "Propaganda and Education," Teachers College,
Columbia University Contributions to Education, 1932, No. 531.

experiment, it appears that the development of "skepticism" concerning propaganda in general could be transferred to propaganda of a particular kind, even when that propaganda itself had not been analyzed in developing the skepticism.

Collier,[19] on the other hand, obtained quite a different result. In April of 1941 he lectured to a group of college students on Nazi propaganda techniques and required them to examine certain Nazi propaganda in great detail. As measured by an appropriate before-and-after questionnaire, this group on the average became more favorably disposed toward Nazi propaganda themes, whereas a comparable control group which did not receive the enlightenment grew more anti-Nazi during the same time period. Collier himself believes that his results were different because the Nazi propaganda was subtler than Biddle's materials and because his own subjects "were repeatedly exposed to the propaganda literature" in contrast with Biddle's students, who saw the propaganda concerning the Orient only as they took the gullibility tests. He thinks that classroom experiences with the Nazi propaganda are weak counteragents because of previously established tendencies which were, consciously or unconsciously, in harmony with Nazi propaganda. In this connection, bear in mind T. W. Adorno's thesis regarding the consensus of fascist propaganda and character structure.

It was the principal function of the now defunct Institute for Propaganda Analysis to stimulate the growth of courses in propaganda analysis in American high schools. Such courses, when they were established, were provided with a Manual and materials illustrating "the devices of propaganda." The technique consisted of explaining that propagandists, for example, employ a "plain folks" appeal which was somewhat superfluously defined as "the method by which a speaker attempts to convince his audience that he and his ideas are good because they are 'of the people,' the 'plain folks.' "[20] There were six other devices. Students were expected to be able to analyze all propaganda by labeling the propagandist's utterances with the appropriate device. The success of this approach, unfortunately, has never

[19] Rex Madison Collier, "The Effect of Propaganda on Attitude Following a Critical Examination of the Propaganda Itself," *Journal of Social Psychology*, 1944, pp. 3-17.

[20] Alfred McClung Lee and Elizabeth B. Lee, editors, *The Fine Art of Propaganda* (New York, 1939), p. 24.

been broadly and systematically assayed. Many students and teachers were enthusiastic, but their subjective testimonials constituted the only evidence in the organization's files. A sour note has been struck by Osborn.[21] In his experiment, high school students were taught to analyze propaganda in the manner of the Institute. These groups did not become more or less resistant to propaganda on capital punishment (a subject not mentioned during the instruction period) than comparable groups which had not received the instruction.

In spite of the fact that these three experiments were conducted at different times, employed different subjects, measured different attitudes, and utilized different materials, they lend themselves to certain generalizations. In the first place, instruction in propaganda analysis may increase resistance to propaganda (Biddle) and then again it may not (Collier, Osborn). Instruction alone cannot guarantee immunity or susceptibility to propaganda.

Then, secondly, the results of any one of the experiments necessarily are presented in the form of statistical averages. Each average conceals the fact of variability: there were always some students who were affected in a manner different from that of the majority. Biddle,[22] for example, reports that 27 percent of his experimental groups either were not affected by the lessons or else, in his language, became more gullible. Again a discrepancy between instruction and effects is apparent; this time it stems from variations not in the instructional technique but in the propagandees.

In the third place, these experiments raise the important problem of transfer: to what extent is new knowledge gained in one situation (the instruction period) employed in a different situation (the questionnaire administered after the instruction)? Many of Biddle's subjects did transfer their general ability to appraise propaganda to the test situation in which they were required to evaluate propaganda they had not previously studied. Osborn's were not so successful in doing so, even though the propaganda materials were very similar to those on the test. Similarity in materials, consequently, does not insure transfer; crucial is whether a similar attitude "set" is evoked in

[21] Wayland W. Osborn, "An Experiment in Teaching Resistance to Propaganda," *Journal of Experimental Education*, 1939, pp. 1-17.
[22] William W. Biddle, "Propaganda and Education," *op. cit.*

different situations. Propagandees who can analyze one kind of propaganda or, in theory, propaganda in general, will not necessarily exercise that ability in all situations.

A vast body of empirical suggestions on propaganda analysis comes from teachers who have actually attempted to deal with propaganda in their classrooms. Typical are the reports given in the *Seventh Yearbook* of the National Council for the Social Studies[23] and the very convenient summary by Dale and Vernon.[24] These reports do not contain verified information: they tend to be enthusiastically and naïvely impressionistic, as might be anticipated when no actual measurements have been taken, when no control group has been introduced, and when no follow-up study has been conducted. On theoretical grounds, however, the approach in its broadest outline can be called promising. The teachers, by and large, maintain that students in the classroom are not necessarily stimulated to learn to analyze propaganda through lectures on propaganda analysis or through an exposure of propaganda techniques. Their interest can be evoked by studying materials with which they are already familiar and which consequently intrigue them. It is claimed[25] that students are eager to discuss radio programs, motion pictures, newspapers, magazines, advertisements, etc., and that, if the discussion follows the procedural rules of the particular teacher who is writing the report on the "experiment," they will acquire a deeper appreciation of propaganda and their own responsibilities in a democratic society. Instead of confining this type of training to the mass media or to civics classes,[26] teachers often

[23] Elmer Ellis, ed., *Education Against Propaganda*, chap. 8, op. cit.

[24] Edgar Dale and Norma Vernon, "Propaganda Analysis: an Annotated Bibliography," *Bureau of Educational Research, Ohio State University*, 1940, No. 2.

[25] William W. Biddle, "Teaching Resistance to Propaganda," *Education Against Propaganda*, Elmer Ellis, ed., op. cit., pp. 115-126; William W. Biddle, "Propaganda and the Curriculum," *Curriculum Journal*, 1938, pp. 306-308; George C. Booth, "Can Propaganda Analysis be Taught?" *Junior College Journal*, 1940, pp. 310-312; Howard Cummings, "Teaching Propaganda Analysis," *Clearing House*, 1939, pp. 394-398; Caroline E. E. Hartwig, "Propaganda and the News in Grade VIII," *Education Against Propaganda*, Elmer Ellis, ed., op. cit., pp. 158-160; A. Jewett, "Detecting and Analyzing Propaganda," *English Journal*, 1940, pp. 105-115; Robert H. Lewis, "Propaganda and the News in Grade XI," *Education Against Propaganda*, Elmer Ellis, ed., op. cit., pp. 161-164.

[26] Roy A. Price, "Teaching Students in Socal-Studies Classes to Guard Against Propaganda," *Education Against Propaganda*, Elmer Ellis, ed., op. cit., pp. 127-133.

recommend that propaganda analysis be incorporated into, and enliven the presentation of, a regular school subject like history,[27] science,[28] or economics.[29] The idea of active participation is also advocated,[30] on the probably correct assumption that learning is facilitated when the individual is given opportunities to practice what he is being taught. For adults, the public forum in which a skillful leader draws almost every member of the audience into the discussion is said[31] to have its merits. At any rate, for those interested in pedagogical techniques and programs, there are suggestions galore.[32] In passing, it must be noted that the teacher himself must appreciate his own biases and the impact he has on his students before he can effectively provide them with insights into propaganda.[33]

Modern semantics seeks to interest people in their own language and hence, since almost all propaganda is expressed in language, this discipline can be considered a form of propaganda analysis worthy of a brief examination. Korzybski[34] constantly advocates what he calls conditional reactions in dealing with problems of unintelligibility and conduct. Thalamic or emotional responses should not occur automatically, he maintains, but should be inhibited by cerebral or intellectual

[27] Donald L. McMurray, "The Evaluation of Propaganda by the Historical Method," Education Against Propaganda, Elmer Ellis, ed., op. cit., pp. 134-146.

[28] Morris Meister, "What the Schools Are Doing to Further Intellectual Freedom and Democracy," High Points, March, 1939, pp. 14-17.

[29] A. S. Otis, "Educating For Democracy: Some Specific Suggestions," School and Society, 1939, pp. 532-534.

[30] Michael Levine, "The New York City High School Radio Experiment: 1935-36," Education Against Propaganda, Elmer Ellis, ed., op. cit., pp. 165-170.

[31] Carrol D. Champlin, "Forms and Subversive Propaganda," Educational Forum, 1939, pp. 181-184; John Brown Mason, "Public Forums Versus Propaganda," School and Society, 1937, pp. 311-313.

[32] Ralph D. Casey, "How to Read Domestic News," Education Against Propaganda, Elmer Ellis, ed., op. cit., pp. 27-41; Edgar Dale, "Movies and Propaganda," Education Against Propaganda, Elmer Ellis, ed., op. cit., pp. 71-86; Roscoe Ellard, "How to Read Editorials," Education Against Propaganda, Elmer Ellis, ed., op. cit., pp. 52-70; Clyde R. Miller, "Propaganda and Press Freedom," English Journal, 1939, pp. 821-827; O. W. Riegel, "How to Read Foreign News," Education Against Propaganda, Elmer Ellis, ed., op. cit., pp. 42-51; R. E. Wolseley, "Helping Pupils Read Newspapers Intelligently," School and Society, 1939, pp. 53-55.

[33] Ernest E. Bayles, "Obligations of Teaching in a Democracy," Educational Administration and Supervision, 1939, pp. 251-259; Helen I. Davis, "Propaganda for Preservation," High Points, June 1939, pp. 18-25; Annette Smith, "The Need For Tolerance," National Parent-Teacher, November 1939, pp. 5-8.

[34] Alfred Korzybski, Science and Sanity (Lancaster, Pa., 1941).

ones. His own technique consists in making the individual aware of the abstraction inherent in language. He does this by emphasizing that every object, every person, and every process in the external world is to a certain extent unique. Some attribute or, more probably, many attributes of that object, person, or process unavoidably are neglected or omitted when a word is employed to call attention to whatever it is the communicator has in mind. Words are not identical with their referents. To cause the individual to reflect on the inevitable abstract qualities of language, Korzybski suggests a number of simple mechanical devices. A subscript may be added to the word to indicate, for example, that $elephant_1$ and not $elephant_2$ is being discussed: both beasts have attributes in common but each is also different. Or the "same" animal may be called $elephant_{1929}$ at one time and then $elephant_{1949}$ to suggest that it has changed in twenty years. Quotation marks may be employed frequently to warn people that the word or phrase has been arbitrarily selected and hence must be evaluated. "Etc." may be a simple reminder that not everything has been included in a generalization and that everything never can be. Hyphens may be substituted for the conjunction "and" which often implies a dichotomy contrary to fact. The copulative verb "to be" is called dangerous because it suggests all-inclusiveness. For therapeutic or pedagogical purposes the nature of the abstraction process may be explained in detail, sometimes with the help of a little gadget called "the structural differential": by means of strings and disks the individual is made to realize that words can be employed on different levels of abstraction and that, regardless of the level, they cannot include all the attributes of the referent in question. Relaxation is the physiological and psychological goal that is sought.

Another principal school of semantics, that of Ogden and Richards,[35] also possesses a technique that can prove useful in propaganda analysis. Too frequently their system of Basic English is considered only as a proposed international language which non-English-speaking peoples can learn relatively easily. In addition, as they themselves have pointed out again and again,[36] it can serve as a rhetorical device for English-speaking individuals who wish to understand the meaning

[35] C. K. Ogden and I. A. Richards, The Meaning of Meaning (New York, 1927).
[36] C. K. Ogden, The System of Basic English (New York, 1934).

of their own words and of those which confront them. The task of following the small number of rules as a passage is "translated" into the 850-word vocabulary of Basic is most challenging. Skill is required, not to find the Basic equivalent of the expression being translated— a Basic Dictionary can solve this problem almost mechanically—but to discover the referents (if any) of the passage *before* it is rendered into Basic. The principles and vocabulary of Basic can be easily and quite painlessly learned, which is not true of most foreign languages.

OBJECTIVES OF PROPAGANDA ANALYSIS

Individuals differ: each person approaches a learning situation with different habits. In theory the teaching technique must be adapted to the individual. In practice, such an ideal method may not be feasible. For this reason, just as most educators cannot tutor their students individually—though they might prefer to do so—so the particular technique must be adapted as well as possible to the group being instructed. A technique suitable for grade-school students probably must be altered when it is applied to college students; a technique for bright children may not be effective with dull ones; one for the higher economic levels may be unsuited for the lower levels; one that is productive in New England may be sterile in the Southwest. Any technique has merit if it contributes to the objectives in view, but no one system should be considered the best under all conceivable circumstances.

If it is considered undesirable or impossible to prevent citizens in a democracy from being exposed to competing propaganda, the ultimate goal is to teach them to respond critically. (Riesman and Glazer, it will be noted later, use the critical response as an index of the degree of apathy.) But what is meant by "critically"? Tritely enough, it must signify deliberation, evaluation, and finally choice. This is an objective of western civilization which educators, clergymen, parents, and others have been attempting to attain for generations. How can steps be taken to attain immunity through the learning of habits that counteract whatever responses the propagandas evoke?

Negatively, it seems probable that an individual who responds rapidly to propaganda does not deliberate, evaluate, or choose wisely. He buys that beer, votes for that candidate, or obeys that propaganda impulse without considering adequately or at all the consequences of his action in the short or long run. What he does not do is to inhibit the learning process and whatever action results from learning the propaganda.

It is inhibition, therefore, which must first be cultivated if propaganda analysis is to be effective. Inhibition occurs when strong habits are elicited which prevent the learning of the propaganda until other habits have also been aroused. The inhibiting and the other habits must be evoked in all situations involving propaganda; they must be transferable.

It is futile to imagine that a lecture or a series of lectures, no matter how skillful or astute, can by itself effectively achieve such a goal. The lecturer is seeking to establish a new habit through verbal means, and this habit is expected to compete successfully either with responses evoked by the group to which the propagandees belong or with other habits which have been heavily reinforced during their lives. Words, whether they come from a preacher, a psychiatrist, a propagandist, or a propaganda analyst, cannot immediately overcome the heritage from the past, the pressures of the present, or the influences of the future.[37] Verbal truths do not set men free unless they themselves have already been actively seeking freedom; otherwise words merely help set them on the path toward truth—or falsehood. A patient suffering from a phobia is not cured by being told that his fear is irrational: he requires careful treatment.

Similarly, propagandees require careful treatment before they can appraise propaganda and appraise it correctly in terms of some value they possess. Epstein,[38] for example, found that a field trip tended to make students more "liberal" than did a conventional classroom discussion of contemporary issues. Eschen[39] has shown that a more realistic approach to current problems with opportunities to "form independent judgments" can produce different results from the customary lecture system.

In some manner, consequently, the teaching of propaganda analysis

[37] Cf. Elizabeth L. Billings, "The Influence of a Social-Studies Experiment on Student Attitudes," *School and Society*, 1942, pp. 557-560.

[38] Leon J. Epstein, "Attitudinal Changes Attendant Upon Variations in Experience," *Journal of Educational Research*, 1941, pp. 453-457.

[39] Clarence R. von Eschen, "An Evaluation of a Secondary School Course in 'Contemporary Problems' From Certain Stated Points of View," *Journal of Educational Research*, 1940, pp. 265-267.

must become a meaningful experience for the propagandees which thereafter will cause them to stop, to evaluate, and then to decide. An experience is more likely to be meaningful if it involves great rewards. Rewards are great when they satisfy numerous and important drives. Pedagogically it is imperative to absorb as much as possible of the propagandee's personalities and to demonstrate to them that deliberation, evaluation, and choice can bring satisfaction.

In this light it can be seen that the approach of the Institute for Propaganda Analysis, like any approach concentrating on the propaganda content itself, emphasized inhibition alone. It did not provide the additional responses which propagandees could make after they stated, "This is propaganda, and the propagandist is employing such-and-such devices." This limitation was actually appreciated by the Institute, and therefore it often proposed additional measures.[40] Likewise Korzybski and Ogden and Richards require more than inhibition from people who would learn semantics: they wish any linguistic stimulus to evoke a *variety* of responses. What are the responses which habitually must accompany inhibition and which, together with that inhibition, can constitute a transferable critical ability?

It is essential, firstly, for propagandees to learn that a piece of propaganda cannot be considered outside its *context*. Content analysis is only one of many steps in the dissemination or transmission of propaganda. The others include the propagandist, his motivation, his source of power, his position within society; the communications medium carrying the propaganda, its peculiarities, its prestige, its social role; the propaganda process within people which extends from the perception of the message and the evocation of previously learned responses to the learning of the new response and the spilling of that response into action; and the short- and long-range effects of the propaganda upon the propagandees.[41] To know all this about even a simple propaganda campaign is usually beyond the capability and interest of almost everyone, but to know that so much should be known before there can be a complete analysis is in itself inhibiting and conducive to further responses.

[40] Violet Edwards, "The School Executive and Propaganda Analysis," *School Management*, 1939, pp. 204-205; Clyde R. Miller, "Propaganda and Press Freedom," *op. cit.*

[41] Leonard W. Doob, *Public Opinion and Propaganda* (New York, 1948).

Then, secondly, the labeling of a communication "propaganda" and the identification of certain rhetorical devices therein itself may by itself bring pause without adequate evaluation. To evaluate—after the urge to evaluate is present—facts are required. In this sense the teaching of factual knowledge of any kind is a contribution to propaganda analysis, since thereby propagandees are rendered less suggestible.[42] Such knowledge must be utilized; for this reason students and citizens must learn to bring their knowledge to bear on all relevant situations. Here is another eternal problem that worries all educators, and no pat solution appears at hand. Fact-mindedness is not easy to teach in reference to propaganda situations because those situations are so diverse and are not fitted into the pigeonholes of conventional disciplines except, perhaps, for the social sciences. A competent engineer would laugh at a propagandist who tried to mislead him concerning certain technical details in the construction of a bridge, but he himself may be quite gullible in other fields (such as art or politics) to which he does not transfer the factual demands of his own profession. Fact-mindedness, moreover, must stimulate a quest for the significant facts, and many of these facts must be obtainable. Consumers, for example, can be taught to analyze advertising not only by becoming acquainted with advertising techniques but also by being given access to the facts concerning the advertised products.

At this point government in a democratic society can make a valuable contribution, perhaps without impairing what is considered to be freedom of speech. According to the Foreign Agents Registration Act and the Voorhis Act, persons and organizations in the United States who are engaging in propaganda on behalf of a foreign government or group, or who seek to overthrow any government through the threat or use of force or violence, must register with the federal government and—with certain exceptions—essentially reveal their identify in the propaganda they disseminate. These Acts, as Smith[43] has argued, do not interfere with the "right" to carry on propaganda. Propagandees are simply provided with some important facts on the basis of which they can evaluate the propaganda more "intelligently":

[42] Thomas E. Coffin, "Some Conditions of Suggestion and Suggestibility," *Psychological Monographs*, 1941, No. 241.

[43] Bruce Lannes Smith, "Democratic Control of Propaganda Through Registration and Disclosure," *Public Opinion Quarterly*, 1942, pp. 27-40; 1943, pp. 707-719.

the identity, expenditures, and activities of the propagandists. In practice, this information may or may not reach or be noticed by them, but at least it is available. Such legislation appears to penalize those with extreme propaganda-objectives, which is no doubt its intention and is in accord with the wishes of most Americans. It is, moreover, difficult to visualize how regulations like these might be extended to other domestic propagandists, although—as Smith indicates—there are actually laws requiring that news and advertising be clearly separated, that advanced public notice be given when new securities are to be issued, that radio stations register with the Federal Communications Commission, that manufacturers of food and drugs make no misleading claims, etc.

Deliberation and evaluation, in the third place, must eventually lead to a decision. Propaganda analysis is not synonymous with negativism or withdrawal. "That's propaganda" heralds inhibition and may suggest that the propagandee is therefore less susceptible. Eventually, however, he must choose to do or not do as the propagandist commands—or to adopt a third course. Related to propaganda analysis at this point are the values of the individual as well as of the group and the society in which he finds himself. If those values are narrow, no amount of training and then deliberation and evaluation will lead to a choice very different from one he might or would have made without the training. Any simple experiment which seeks to show that a propaganda-analysis technique will or will not make subjects less vulnerable cannot succeed completely: it may make them halt, it may make them evaluate, but it is not too likely to affect them fundamentally since fundamental changes in values are seldom glibly achieved.

It is necessary, consequently, to refer again to a technique previously mentioned: that of developing less propaganda-prone people by aiding them in the solution of their basic insecurities. This is the radical approach. It is also the most difficult one. Any other method by itself is never completely adequate, although it may make some momentary and significant contribution in its own right. Leaders will use propaganda, and propagandees will succumb to propaganda, to the extent that such insecurities remain unresolved.

Elements and Problems of Democratic Leadership[1]

BY BERNARD KUTNER

SEVERAL ASSUMPTIONS are made by a group when it forms for democratic action. First, it is assumed that in organizing itself, the power and authority necessary to conduct the work of the group must be delegated to individual members or subgroups. Secondly, a leader in a democratic group is *ascribed* authority and *invested* with certain defined powers. Finally, it is deemed illegitimate for a leader to assume powers not specifically delegated by the group or its governing rules. The final authority in any democratic group thus rests ultimately with the membership. It does not merely derive from, but it is felt to *maintain residence in*, the group.

A group organized for action may select its leaders by democratic methods, through some form of referendum or group agreement. These may include a central organizational leader and other subleaders (e.g., committee chairman or special functionaries). However, even before leaders are selected, a group must decide upon its goals and its methods for achieving them. The leader would, in a democratic group, be an individual who serves the group in various ways but, primarily, represents the group's goals and interests. Democratic leaders, to be really democratic, would homologously reflect the group they serve and must set aside personal interests or those of some special subgroup.

[1] This is a previously unpublished paper.

BALANCING EFFICIENCY AND DEMOCRACY

Leaders need authority—on this there can be little disagreement, since without authority leaders cannot carry out their functions. But the delegation of authority in a democratic group is never a mandate for any leader to employ authority without the eventual approval of the group. Where responsibility for action is not subject to critical examination, a democratic organization no longer exists. Nevertheless, some freedom of action is almost always imperative lest leadership become a sterile and unimaginative position making for red tape and unending delays. *Thus, the democratic group has a two-fold responsibility in delegating authority or choosing leadership: to preserve for itself the final authority on any question and to allow a modicum of operational freedom to its leaders.*

It would appear that every democratic choice of a leader involves a compromise between jealous preservation of power by the group and active, efficient performance of the group's mandate. A vigorous democratic organization must, however, constantly check its operations to make certain that it is not becoming "efficient" at the expense of its democratic methods. It is important to recognize that there is a current tendency to move from democratic to undemocratic procedures in the name of efficiency. In present-day social organizations, power easily consolidates from the many to the few—from cumbersome groups to convenient individuals.

The drive "to get things done" rather than "to do things democratically" has brought many an organization to its end. Often we suppose that because we live in the Western world where democracy is widely practiced, that it will come of its own accord—that it is "second nature." If it shows anything, much of the available evidence demonstrates the contrary, that democracy must be taught and learned to be practicable.[2] Where it is not *self-consciously* practiced, the tendency to accept laissez faire as the equivalent of democracy easily leads to the monopolization of authority. The perception of group goals tends

[2] See for example A. Bavelas and K. Lewin, "Training in Democratic Leadership,"*Journal of Abnormal and Social Psychology*, 1942, 37, 115-119. Also L. P. Bradford and R. Lippitt, *Supervisory Training for Group Leadership* (Cambridge, Mass., Publ. Research Center Grp. Dynamics, 1945).

to change in time, so that a passive membership may soon find that its leaders are working toward ends which it may not yet have considered or which are antagonistic to agreed-upon goals. Pigors, for example, sees the shift from democratic leadership to despotism as arising from a crisis or emergency in which autocratic measures are assumed by the leader "to save the group."[3]

It is also true that the same sort of shift may occur simply by default of the membership's interest or concern over the activities of the leader even though these may deeply involve them. Because leaders are often left in a position where they alone may serve the group's interest, they are often also the only individuals who are acquainted intimately with all of the details of the group's functioning. The larger the organization, the greater does this tendency exist. This concentration of information may have the added effect of leaving him as the only individual capable of intelligent action. Passive groups may therefore jeopardize their democratic structure unknowingly, permitting the aggregation of power, influence, and information to its leaders. Commitments in the group's name made by a leader assuming authority may embarrass the organization and threaten its members. The fault lies in two places: the leader's failure to assess correctly the relation of his action to group goals, or the tyrannical assumption of power by him, and the group's failure actively to control the limits of its leader's functions. Thus, while we must rely upon leaders, we cannot forfeit our function as policeman, censor, and supreme court without, at the same time, forfeiting our position as a member of a democratic group.

LEADERSHIP REPLACEMENT

When a discrepancy occurs between the group's goals and the leader's behavior or intentions with regard to the group's activities, the time for changing leaders has arrived. The leaders, servants of the group, must be replaceable. To retain its democratic nature a group must have a conscious awareness of the functions of its leaders so that a diagnosis for the retention or change of leadership might be made. A knowledge of leadership functions thus becomes of primary importance in assessing the democratic health of a group.

[3] P. Pigors, *Leadership or Domination* (Boston, 1935), pp. 125-127.

It may first be emphasized that a primary function of leadership resides in a special type of group representation.[4] The leader should represent an organization through channels specifically designed and delimited by the group itself. Specifically in terms of this representation of group interest, the leader is delegated the functions of executive administration. This involves the coördination and integration of many activities, the crystallization of group policy, and the assessment of new and diverse occurrences bearing on the group's functions. The leader serves also as a liaison between his group and outside organizations or individuals.

While a leader in a democratic group is permitted a degree of initiative and imaginative interpretation of these functions, in the final analysis the effects of his actions are subject to the approbation of the group he represents. Though a leader may also serve as a dynamic element in keeping the group functioning efficiently and may even be the "inspiring" element in the group, *it is first and always the representative function of leadership which is to be considered in retaining a leader.* The delicate mechanism of authority must be retractable lest a changing or unscrupulous leader is left in power so long that his authority is assumed to be permanently endowed.

Effective leadership may be said to be lost when any one of the above functions becomes impaired. Leadership in a democratic group implies that members of a group rely upon a leader to carry out the minimal functions of leadership in the hope that, through the division of labor imperative in group operation, the leader and the membership will complement each others activities to the end of group success. Leadership is, in this sense, the vehicle through which authority may be used to integrate and express the interests of the group. When it becomes an end in itself, or the vested interest of a given individual, the need for a change of leadership is apparent. It is to the group that the job of diagnosing the needs of group leadership must fall. The group, to remain truly democratic, must be the watchdog of its own leadership.

---

[4] Pigors has attempted to analyze the functions of leadership and has reduced these to one general function: representation, and three specific functions: initiation, administration, and interpretation. The author has drawn heavily upon Pigors' work in the present analysis. *Op. cit.*, p. 354.

AUTHORITARIAN LEADERS

Implied in the above analysis of democratic leadership are the conditions for unhealthy organizations. Undemocratic groups are characterized by authoritarian leadership in which authority (or to be more accurate, power) is assumed by fiat. Autocratic leaders come into power in many ways: they may be chosen by the members in democratic fashion, they may seize power directly by forcing the withdrawal of previous leaders, or, as happens in many cases, they may change into autocratic leaders where previously they had been democratic. Whichever may be the case, authoritarianism is, in part, recognized by its one-sided allegiances: the side of special interest rather than group interest. Often, autocratic leaders attempt to conceal these allegiances by declaring their actions to be "for the good of the group— in the long run."

At best, most memberships are only moderately active in organized groups to which they belong. As indicated earlier, the functions of the group are most often carried on by a smaller subgroup of active leaders. Under autocratic domination there often occurs a schism of major proportions between leadership and membership. This gap between leaders and members is reinforced in many ways: through the concentration of information and the sources of communication in the hands of the leader, the divorce of interests and aims of leaders from members by the conducting the affairs of the group through arbitrary decision, and by coercion. This schismatic tendency further separates the group from any possibility of reacting to the actions of their leaders. There appears frequently an effort to induce apathy into membership if it is not already there. Oppression followed by apathetic response can only lead to further oppression since autocratic leaders often feel that silence means acceptance.

Autocratic leaders often tend to regard themselves, members of their own group, and people in general in rather special ways. After finding their positions strong they may assume that they alone, because of their forceful personalities, have made it so, little realizing that respect and honor for a leader may come from a prior history of democratic leadership. An autocratic leader may tend to extend his authority and to consolidate a "position" for himself. Gradually, one may see by action and attitude the expression of his underlying feelings. At the base of autocratic leadership is an utter contempt for group values if not for individuals as well. Autocrats tend to feel that the public is stupid and can be led easily. They seem almost instinctively to accept the early-twentieth-century view of the public, outlined by such writers as LeBon, Tarde, and Trotter.

Summarily, their views make of the public a mob of instinct-ridden and emotionally unstable beings, having a single homogenized mind, weak and without self-control. It is indeed significant that autocratic leaders should regard members in their own organization as fitting into this portrait of the crowd. Views of crowd behavior have perennially been concerned with the instability, emotionality, and lack of critical judgment with which crowds are allegedly endowed (e.g., LeBon's point of view).[5]

RESISTANCE TO AUTHORITARIAN LEADERS

When authoritarianism strikes a democratic organization, resistance movements tend to arise. The denial of group aspirations with their resultant frustrations makes reaction in some form inevitable. The French Revolution, the American Revolution, the European underground movement in the late war, and the Negro's hostility toward his white oppressor are illustrations of this point. Resistances and rejections of leadership, which through the misuse of vested authority have resulted in authoritarian rule, are varied in kind. They may take the form of direct hostility toward the leader, individually or group-wise; organized resistance to control or overthrow of an autocrat may result in intergroup hostility—e.g., factions in the organization fighting among themselves, or hostility directed outwardly upon some easily recognized scapegoat. But regardless of the road of reactivity against the leader, one thing is certain: there remains in the acceptance of the acts of authority of such leaders an area of reservation on the part of the membership.

It is obvious that to cope with an authoritarian one must first comprehend the fact of authoritarianism. A group nucleus, recognizing such leadership, is itself responsible for bringing the fact home to the membership. The inevitable discrepancy between leader-goals and group-goals in an authoritarian-led organization must be broadcast for

5 Cf. LeBon, G., *The Crowd* (London, 1929), pp. 239.

active resistance to arise. Thus, well-informed, the group may initiate action to oust the leader. Wherever possible, the group should attempt to regain its integrity by forcing the withdrawal of its autocratic leaders. But often this is impossible, since authoritarian leaders tend to solidify and entrench themselves in anticipation of such resistance. The healthiest reaction to such "leadership" is the strengthening and consolidation of democratic forces within the organization. Vigorous and vocal rejection backed by well-organized numbers is the best single response to oppression.

The use of autocratic measures to evict autocratic leaders, "fighting fire with fire," while it may "work" in some cases, may have the disadvantage of making the group members cynical and disheartened. A combination of "charismatic" and democratic leadership under such conditions will tend to restore high morale. A dynamic, democratic leader, establishing limited goals which have popular approval may revitalize a group recently disorganized by a revolt against an authoritarian leader. Hence a reaffirmation of the group's purposes and the reinforcement of their sense of worthiness is an excellent means of responding to authoritarianism.

Where leadership is merely obstructing the path to the goal with selfish pursuits, the group has other means of dealing with him. They may force his resignation or withdrawal by constitutional means. When this cannot be done, more drastic action may be required. The clearest response in many situations would be the unanimous withdrawal of the membership from the organization and its reëstablishment under new democratic leadership. While this solution may be the most difficult, circumstances may sometimes force such a decision. Strong inner organization and conviction of the righteousness of the group's goals are the key elements in effective reorganization.

Where drastic measures need not be resorted to, the method of retraining group leaders in the use of authority and position has been found successful. While this type of solution has been effective in industrial plants, play groups, and Boy Scout groups, it is doubtful whether such a method could be practicable in many leadership situations. But the most reliable measuring-rod should be the judgment and active participation of the whole group in making any decision on leadership change.

CONSEQUENCES OF AUTHORITARIAN LEADERSHIP

Looking inward upon the structure of authoritarian-led groups, one may find the answer to ineffective leadership and group breakdown. Effective groups must be flexible enough to meet the needs of changing circumstances. But authoritarian groups are generally inflexible—the working force being controlled from above even at the lowest levels of action. Effective groups must be able to reorganize themselves when their structure becomes cumbersome and inefficient, or when there is a need for additional subgroups with authority. But autocratic groups tend to be top-heavy with authority and extremely resistant to any structural changes. Authoritarian control is the very antithesis of change since alteration of the prevailing group structure may symbolize a threat to authoritarian control. Thus, one often finds extreme resistance, even to minor changes in structure or function of the organization, by the authoritarian leader. Power and prestige may be lost through change, hence the rigid adherence to the *status quo* is sought. Further, there is frequently the tendency to demand strict compliance with the letter of constitutions, bylaws, and other such documents even when the spirit of the latter are thereby violated. Having manipulated and interpreted these authority-giving instruments to serve his ends, the authoritarian leader would not tolerate any reinterpretations which might reduce his effective control.

More invidious than these results of the selfish arrogation of vested authority is another more destructive effect, briefly stated: when a democratic group fails to satisfy its members through the encouragement of deep psychological involvements, anxieties are likely to develop among group members. These insecurities may lead to a search for new leadership—often culminating in some form of authoritarian direction. Or one form of anxiety-producing authoritarianism may, in fact, give way to another.

SELF-EXAMINATION AND DEMOCRATIC LEADERSHIP

Organizations established to pursue democratic action through democratic means must be constantly aware of their obligations to group interest. To this end, some form of soul-searching procedure calculated to warn itself of impending dangers seems advisable.[6] Surveillance, self-survey, self-assessment, and self-criticism are some of the methods which might achieve the goal of democratic unity. Subgroups of an organization may be set up to examine self-consciously the directions in which the organization is moving. It must weigh the apportioning of authority, the tendency of power to accumulate, the tendency for schisms between leader and group to manifest themselves, and other signs of authoritarianism characteristic of undemocratic or antidemocratic groups.

In brief, the group, to remain democratic, must make certain guarantees concerning the control of authority and the functions of leadership. It must guarantee that the group itself dispenses authority and may withdraw it at will. It must guarantee that the extension of authority to an individual or subgroup does not become a mandate for the limitless use of such authority. It must guarantee that the leaders understand their responsibility to the group and to the employment of authority for group goals. It must guarantee initiative and creativity to leadership but must reserve to itself the final judgment of leader-effectiveness. It must, most importantly, guarantee that the functions of the organization, its structure, procedures, and executive personnel may be altered by democratic processes. With such flexibility and unity of purpose, the achieving of group goals, becomes more probable. It guarantees the continued active existence of the group which, while examining itself, is pursuing its ends. While some such procedure is not offered as a panacea for curing the ills of organized groups, it may be expected at least to diagnose the sources of disorganization and autocracy.

[6] One such attempt, although arranged for somewhat different purposes, which might be usefully adapted by democratic-action groups may be found in H. Lasswell, *Psychopathology and Politics* (Chicago, 1930), Appendix B, pp. 277-282.

Part Four: THE ETHICS AND
            TECHNICS OF LEADERSHIP

Contexts: Some Pointed Problems
of Leadership

THE PRECEDING articles were devoted principally to ways of coping with authoritarian leaders and of fostering democratic leadership. In this section, instead of conceiving of the leaders as constituting a problem, our major emphasis will be on the problems which leaders face and to which they have to find solutions.

APATHY

The success or failure of democratic action depends often on the degree and extent of participation which can be evoked on its behalf. For this reason, the problem of apathy—whether we define it behaviorally or attitudinally—is a practical problem. Insofar, also, as democratic principles insist that men are both sovereigns and subjects, having both the right and the responsibility of participating in the decisions which affect their lives, the existence of apathy becomes a challenge to this principle, and implies that men have abdicated their decision—making prerogatives and duties. These, once forfeited, are easily pocketed as "proxies" by self-appointed oligarchs. Apathy is thereby a further problem for democrats, insofar as it sets the scene for manipulation by oligarchs. Finally, apathy is a problem because it keeps apart individuals who have similar frustrations or interests which could otherwise be coöperatively solved or examined. Separated from each other, individuals cannot contribute to the solution of their common difficulties and are thrown back upon necessarily limited individual resources.

The two articles which explore this subject approach it from contrasting perspectives and with differing emphases. The first, "Participation and Mass Apathy in Associations," by Bernard Barber, makes a structural-functional analysis of apathy with a view to determining which of our institutions exert pressure to withdraw the individual from participation in voluntary associations. In Barber's analysis, apathy is largely defined in a behavioristic way.

David Riesman and Nathan Glazer's "Criteria of Political Apathy" is concerned with the more affective components of apathy. Tracing the differences between nineteenth- and twentieth-century political action, they emphasize apathy as a *historical* problem which may have distinctive forms and conditions in our own era. Aside from acknowledged difficulties in defining apathy, an even more complex labor is the definition of its opposite—participation. Riesman and Glazer convincingly demonstrate that activity alone is an inadequate criterion of participation. Their extensive proposals for fuller criteria of apathy and participation comprise a thoroughgoing excavation of this subject.

To conceive of these criteria as useful solely for scientific research would be, however, to use them wastefully, for they are in actuality susceptible to other uses as well. Placing these criteria in a political context and viewing them as potential, regulative ideals, they may be seen as an unusually rich body of norms by which democratic action may be guided and evaluated. In this sense, what Riesman and Glazer have constructed is a model of how a follower in a democracy should behave. It is as such a unique contribution to political literature. For more than anything else, democratic action is in painful need of standards and norms which, though tentatively advanced, are spelled out and provide a framework for further discussion and development. Apart from such a body of norms, democratic action will have nothing but a menu of banalities upon which to diet. And by virtue of their almost infinite plasticity, these banalities can at best serve to cloak expediency, manipulation, and ineptitude in the raiments of righteousness and pathos.

PLANNING

The once popular arguments about "plan vs. no plan" seem to have lost the genuine ring, and the choice—if there ever was one— becomes less of a living option. The disputes over the desirability of planning have spent themselves because they posed sterile questions.

The thoroughly bogus dichotomy between "planning" and "freedom" is being appreciated for what it is: namely, an ideological slogan reflecting the fear of vested interests that specific kinds of planning, injurious to their traditional prerogatives, will take place.

It seems futile to argue whether there should be planning or no planning when in all segments of our society plans are every day created and implemented. If giant business corporations may—as they do—plan their complex operations down to the finest detail without evoking public hostility, there seems no reason to deny government a similar opportunity. If this conclusion is permissible, then the question of whether freedom and planning are compatible is a profitless exercise in dialectic. What is necessary instead is the sharpening of our sights so that questions are formulated about the specific conditions under which planning occasions loss or growth of democratic liberties. There are indeed many questions about planning which deserve an answer; for example: Who formulates the plan? What ends and standards are to be used in its establishment? Who implements the plan? What specific kinds of difficulties hinder efforts at democratic planning? How may these be overcome? What peculiar problems must leadership be prepared to handle when a group operates under a highly articulated plan?

The time is long past when our understanding of planning and its problems needs to be derived from armchair speculations. There are now many examples of large-scale plans available for scientific scrutiny. One of the most well known of these is the Tennessee Valley Authority. The TVA is a planned public enterprise of unusual relevance to this volume because it legitimated its operations in terms of a democratic, "grass-roots" doctrine. How this doctrine functioned in a planned organization and what some of its consequences were, are, among other problems of planning, subjected to analysis in Philip Selznick's study of the TVA, "Dilemmas of Leadership and Doctrine in Democratic Planning."

INNOVATION

How planning is to be extended into other segments of the culture in which it might be needed or how, for that matter, any innovation can be most painlessly introduced is a problem which continually besets leadership. (Some sociologists have, in fact, considered that innovation and leadership are synonymous.) Though leaders are often not the creators of innovations, they are frequently responsible for their successful introduction. Here again, as so often throughout our volume, current knowledge is a junior if not a silent partner to our needs.

Lewis A. Dexter's "Some Strategic Considerations in Innovating Leadership"—with addenda by Chester Barnard, Basil Liddell—Hart and Kenneth Burke—attempts to stake out the broad boundaries of a sociology of innovation. Dexter advances a number of hypotheses about the factors which impede acceptance of innovations and which hinder this aspect of leadership-functioning.

REMEDIAL CHANGE

The problem of innovation may be conceived of as inducing one type of change. Another important kind of change is that involved in the application of remedies. In the succeeding article, "Leadership in a Stress Situation," Alexander Leighton summarizes the conclusions he derived from a study of the Japanese-American Relocation Camp at Poston, Arizona, established by the government during World War II.

This article is of special interest because it closely approximates, on a group or sociological level, the therapeutic efforts of psychiatrists and psychoanalysts. Along with many other studies in this volume, it seems to be a harbinger of a sociological equivalent of psychotherapy, in which the object of treatment is not the individual but the group or community. One of the major problems of such a "group therapy" will be, as it is in individual therapy, adequate criteria of a "cure." That is, what conditions must exist before the group can be considered better, improved, or cured? What, in short, should be the goals of the group therapist? In Leighton's analysis, the goals of the group-therapist are in part the maintenance of the established authority and power relationships. This, of course, is only one possible solution; others might with equal legitimacy postulate the very opposite goals.

In conclusion, it will be helpful to the reader if he compares Leighton's treatment of nonrational and irrational elements (his eighth postulate) with T. W. Adorno's earlier injunction that democratic leadership should attempt to make people aware of their unconscious drives, motives, wants, and needs.

THE SELECTION OF LEADERSHIP

Ever since Plato, philosophers and scientists of Western culture have given thought to the problems of leadership selection. Where Plato prescribed intensive courses in the sciences and dialectic, followed by the temptations of practical experience, as a means of leadership selection and training, modern social science has evolved a panorama of pencil and paper, sociometric, and situational tests. These are described in clear detail by Joseph Eaton in his "Is Scientific Leadership Selection Possible?" Though these tests are not highly reliable, an even more difficult problem, as Eaton notes, is that of deciding the values which are to guide such testing. In the main, Eaton's discussion focuses on the scientific selection of leadership for offices which are not ordinarily filled by democratic procedures.

The utility of scientific methods of leadership selection in democratic, voluntary associations—in which the leadership is elected—is yet to be demonstrated. These, moreover, may be injurious to democratic values should they be used to by-pass the decision—making powers or sovereignty of the group's membership. The "democratic sociometric" tests described by Eaton—in which the group members themselves participate in the scientific selection—obviate much of this threat and are, perhaps, those selection techniques most deserving of careful examination for use in democratic groups.

Leadership tests seem to emphasize selection of "effective" or "successful" personnel, rather than balancing this with an equal concern for the selection of individuals who will be disposed to respect democratic procedures. For example, it seems perfectly feasible to devise and employ tests which will indicate the presence of authoritarian, manipulative, and contemptuous attitudes. These could be extremely useful if not employed in a manner that infringed upon the group's decision-making powers. Conceivably, tests of this sort might be required of those who sought to become candidates for leadership in a specific group. Their results need not disqualify any of the candidates; they might instead simply be publicly announced and viewed as part of the candidate's qualifications. The group membership must, however, be allowed to disregard "negative" findings, if it so chooses, and elect whomever it wishes. No matter how perfect, tests for leadership cannot infringe upon a group's right to make its own mistakes without at the same time subverting its democratic structure.

SUCCESSION

Regardless of their mode of selection, the leadership of a group changes. The contention of Alvin Gouldner's article on "The Problem of Succession and Bureaucracy" is that the period of leadership change is a crucial one in the life of all organizations and is deserving of special attention. Leadership succession is often attended by tension between the membership—or the subordinate leadership layer—and the successor. These tensions are, in turn, defined by the successor as problems and are customarily resolved by the use of a limited number of techniques. Gouldner's article attempts to outline some of the conditions giving rise to the stress of the succession period as well as those which conduce to the selection of the problem-solutions chosen.

Participation and Mass Apathy in Associations[1]

BY BERNARD BARBER

AMONG BOTH the citizens and the social scientists of American society there has been a continuous concern about what is very often called "mass apathy."[2] A journalist, for example, refers to apathy as "our fifth column."[3] A social reformer and quasi-social scientist sees "mass apathy" all about him: "What is this apathy that infects John Smith, American citizen, to the point where in utter frustration, despair, and hopelessness he exchanges life for existence?"[4] And the attitudes of the ordinary citizen, who regards "mass apathy" as a simple fact and a social problem, may be seen in the following typical letter-to-the-editor: "Most people are active for personal objects, but regarding public welfare they are passive. Rather than bestir themselves, they let such things go. Their apathy paves the way for bosses, and bossing protracts inertia."[5]

Always implicit and sometimes explicit in such judgments is the view that "mass apathy" refers to a state of affairs which is wholly bad for a democratic society. This view places an absolute emphasis

[1] This is a previously unpublished paper.

[2] The problem of "mass apathy" has lately been receiving more attention from academic social scientists, perhaps because of Professor Robert Lynd's remarks on apathy in his *Knowledge for What?* (Princeton, 1939). Professor Robert Merton of Columbia University will make the problem of "mass apathy" an important theme in his forthcoming study of a planned housing community.

[3] John M. Dumas, "Apathy—Our Fifth Column," *National Municipal Review*, xxxvi (1947), 494-496, 502.

[4] Saul D. Alinsky, *Reveille for Radicals* (Chicago, 1946), p. 66.

[5] John Daniels, "To Vitalize Democracy," *The Harvard Alumni Bulletin*, June 26, 1948.

on the democratic values which are involved. But such an absolute emphasis can lead to unrealistic, utterly utopian demands for "voluntary" participation by the individual citizen in the affairs of his society. The following is a typical expression of this utopian ideology: "Democracy does not exist unless each man is doing his part fully every minute, unless everyone is taking his part in building the state-to-be."[6] Now whatever the expressive and inspirational significance of the foregoing ideological statements may be, they cannot be accepted by the social scientist or the interested citizen as accurate scientific diagnosis. They are inadequate because they ignore certain facts about institutional structure in general, and certain fundamental features of American social structure in particular. The most general purpose of this essay is to demonstrate the necessity of putting the behavior to which the notion "mass apathy" refers, in the context of American social structure as well as of American democratic values. An enlarged understanding of this kind should contribute to the fuller realization of the democratic values themselves.

How, then, shall we particularize our general purpose? We shall do so by examining certain empirical, behavioral data on which the allegation of "mass apathy" in American society is often grounded. Since the democratic values call for full and voluntary participation by the individual, we shall take as our case participation in the voluntary associations which are so characteristic of, and numerous in, this country. This task requires, as a preliminary, a functional analysis of the place of the voluntary association in the American social structure. Then we can proceed, first, to a statement of the behavioral uniformities in this area, and, second, to their structural analysis. The analysis will demonstrate the relevancy to the problem of "mass apathy" of two aspects of social structure: first, the significance of the preëminence of occupational- and kinship-role obligations in American society and of their segregation from other role obligations; and, second, the exigencies of the type of large-scale formal organization which characterizes many voluntary associations. We shall, to anticipate, see the way in which these two structural factors are the source of what often seems, in the utopian perspective, to be irreducible alienation from the democratic values. Put more concretely, we shall see that the universal existence of active minorities and inactive majorities in

[6] Mary P. Follett, *The New State* (New York, 1918), p. 335.

voluntary associations does not emerge wholly out of psychological apathy and democratic despair.

For any given voluntary association, the stronger the ideological emphasis on the democratic values, the more apparent becomes the limitation on the full realization of these values imposed by the exigencies of formal organization. Hence the more frequent raising of the cry of "mass apathy" in and against the more democratic voluntary associations, even though inactive majorities exist in all voluntary associations. We shall therefore, finally, consider in detail the problem of "mass apathy" in these more democratic voluntary associations, especially insofar as executive functions are concerned.[7]

THE VOLUNTARY ASSOCIATION

The voluntary association is peculiarly characteristic of American social structure as over against other types of society.[8] In American society, kinship and occupational roles and their associated interests are, to a relatively large extent, segregated both from each other and from other interests. In the occupational and kinship spheres, members of our society achieve success and happiness by their own individual efforts and achievements. In other types of society, by contrast, kin, caste, and community groups determine many of these interests that are segregated in our society. It is for the organized accomplishment of these segregated interests, and for such of the interests related to occupation and kinship as cannot be achieved by the individual himself on the job or in his "isolated conjugal" family, that associations exist in great numbers in the United States.

The characteristics of the association as a sociological type derive from its functions for the American social structure. Since it pursues specific interests, it always has at least some explicit purpose. Usually, moreover, certain new purposes emerge, purposes which are important to the several members in different degree. The members are

[7] In a larger study, the author has analyzed, in addition to the case reported herein, two other cases of alleged "mass apathy." One is nonvoting in political elections and the other is voluntary participation in community and social welfare activities. See Bernard Barber, "Mass Apathy" and Voluntary Social Participation in the United States (Unpublished Ph.D. Dissertation, Harvard University, 1948).

[8] Much of what is said here about the United States applies equally to Great Britain and, in somewhat lesser degree, to the other countries of western Europe. Structural and behavioral similarities in Great Britain will be referred to in later footnote references.

also differentially aware of the existence of these emergent purposes. In a later part of this essay we shall see how this differential importance and awareness cause certain problems for the executives of democratic associations.

Since there is a multiplicity of discrete, relatively less important interests in our society which are not determined by kin or community groups, the individual has considerable choice in the matter of which he shall pursue. It is in this sense that membership in particular associations is voluntary. We must carefully note, however, that voluntary membership is never simply psychological willingness, but rather is always patterned by a complex of social, structural, and value considerations. For example, the increasing control by trade unions of access to jobs, manifested in "closed shop" practices, has altered the sense in which any individual worker's membership in a union is "voluntary."[9] The institutional factors which define the differential significance of voluntary membership have important consequences for participation behavior in the association.

A written constitution is typical of the association. This embodies a statement of the explicit purpose of the group and of the way in which the association will be organized to pursue this purpose. The chief feature of this type of organization is a set of offices defining the delimited obligations and responsibilities of those who fill the offices. These officeholders, these "officials," are chosen by the members. Sometimes only a few members, an oligarchy, choose the officials, but usually, in the voluntary association, all the members are given a vote in the election of officials since each and every member is assumed to have an equal interest. In principle, therefore, most voluntary associations are democratic. We shall examine, below, some of the conditions that limit the full realization of this democratic principle.

Although the association is characteristic of the United States, for the structural reasons which have been specified, it is not unique to our type of society. When similar structural conditions occur in small areas of societies which are, on the whole, structurally different from our society, voluntary associations emerge in those small areas.[10] It is only the vast proliferation of associations that is unique to our society.

[9] American Civil Liberties Unions, Democracy in Trade Unions (New York, November, 1943).

[10] See, for example, Louis D. Hartson, "A Study of Voluntary Associations, Educational and Social, in Europe during the Period from 1100 to 1700," Pedagogical Seminary, xviii (1911), pp. 10-31.

PARTICIPATION IN ASSOCIATIONS

Close investigation of the empirical data about participation in the voluntary association in the United States reveals three basic facts: (1) There is an almost countless number of associations in this country; (2) There is a large number of people who have no memberships in any associations at all; (3) There exists, in any given association, an active minority and an inactive majority among the members. Each of these facts requires some further comment and illustration.

1. The phenomenon that has been called "the proliferation of associations" in American society has been remarked upon countless times. Even after one hundred years, however, the *locus classicus* for the observation is still de Tocqueville, who was one of the first to be struck by the prevalence and significance of associations in the American Democracy. After his visit of 1831 he wrote: "In no country in the world has the principle of association been more successfully used, or applied to a greater multitude of objects than in America. Americans of all ages, all conditions, and all dispositions constantly form associations."[11]

Seventy-five years later, the most distinguished British observer of American life, Lord Bryce, was similarly impressed. "Associations," he said, "are created, extended, and worked in the United States more quickly and effectively than in any other country."[12] This from the inhabitant of a country which is not without its own multitude of voluntary associations![13] But American observers themselves were overwhelmed by what they did not fully understand: instance the following from Charles and Mary Beard's *The Rise of American Civilization*: "The tendency of Americans to unite with their fellows for varied purposes . . . now became a general mania. . . . It was a

---

For the "paucity" of associations in nonliterate societies, as he calls it, see R. M. MacIver, "Interests," *Encyclopedia of the Social Sciences* (New York, 1934). Also, on the lack of associations in the "folk society," see Robert Redfield, "The Folk Society," *American Journal of Sociology*, LII (1947), pp. 293-308.

[11] *Democracy in America* (1862), I, 216, as cited in Herbert Goldhamer and Noel P. Gist, "Social Clubs and Fraternities," *Development of Collective Enterprise*, Seba Eldridge, ed. (Lawrence, Kansas, 1943).

[12] *The American Commonwealth* (1911), II, 281, cited in Goldhamer and Gist, *op. cit.*

[13] See Crane Brinton, *The United States and Britain* (Cambridge, Mass., 1945), p. 72, for a comment on the proliferation of associations in Great Britain.

rare American who was not a member of four or five societies. . . . Any citizen who refused to affiliate with one or more associations became an object of curiosity, if not suspicion."[14] There is, almost literally, a countless number of voluntary associations in the United States. An endless variety of specific purposes does not begin to exhaust the possibilities for associations, for any two or more of these highly specific purposes may multiply themselves in several combinations. And to increase still further the possible number, there is always the fact of local and regional differentiation in a country so large as the United States. The following statistical data, therefore, are intended only to be illustrative.

Associations abound in cities and towns of all sizes. In 1924, there were almost 3000 local voluntary organizations in a group of 140 rural villages.[15] Yankee City, with a population of 17,000, had 357 associations when it was studied in the early thirties; Boulder, Colorado, a city of 12,000, has 245 associations.[16] In 1935, there were 200 associations for 7500 Negroes in Natchez; in Chicago, with 275,000 Negroes, there were 4000 associations.[17] The total number of associations in even a single major metropolitan area may be inferred from these figures.

Business and professional associations are large in number and usually are subdivided into many constituent parts. In the American Medical Association, for example, there are 2000 county, parish, and district societies. There are a great many welfare, charity, and reform associations, of which the so-called "youth-serving" organizations alone comprise 320 national organizations.[18] In 1928, the General Federation of Women's Clubs included 14,000 constituent clubs.[19]

[14] (New York, 1930), pp. 730-731.

[15] Edmund deS. Brunner and J. H. Kolb, Rural Social Trends (New York, 1933), pp. 102, 244, 372.

[16] W. Lloyd Warner and Paul S. Lunt, The Social Life of a Modern Community, Vol. I, Yankee City Series (New Haven, 1941); F. A. Bushee, "Social Organizations in a Small City," American Journal of Sociology, LI (1945), 217-226.

[17] Gunnar Myrdal, An American Dilemma, 2 vols. (New York, 1944), pp. 952-955.

[18] Merritt Chambers, Youth Serving Organizations (Washington, D. C.: American Youth Commission of the National Council on Education, 1941).

[19] Gladys Meyerand, "Women's Organizations," Encyclopedia of the Social Sciences (New York, 1935).

The "service clubs"—Rotary, Kiwanis, Lions, Exchange, Civitan, and Optimist—number more than 9000.[20]

2. Although in comparative perspective the United States may well be a "nation of joiners," a survey of the available data on the number of people with memberships in voluntary associations reveals the little-known fact that many have not even a single such affiliation.[21] This uniformity too holds for all types of areas in the United States, whether urban, suburban, small city, small town, or rural. The universality of this pattern indicates the pervasive effect of American kinship and occupational structures on urban and rural areas alike.

Two studies in metropolitan areas yield the same results. Among a sample of 5500 Chicago residents, Goldhamer found that approximately 30 percent of the men and 40 percent of the women had no memberships at all in associations.[22] Komarovsky reports for New York City that "in the bulk of the city's population, the unaffiliated persons constitute a majority."[23] In her sample, 60 percent of the working class and 53 percent of the white-collar men did not belong to a single association, with the possible exception of a church. Lundberg describes a similar participation situation in the suburban sections of the New York Metropolitan area.[24] In Erie County, Ohio, a medium-sized city with a surrounding rural area, a little less than 50 percent of the population belong to no associations at all.[25] In Yankee City, with only 17,000 population, only 41 percent of the total population are members of even one association.[26] The large

[20] C. F. Marden, Rotary and Its Brothers (Princeton, 1935).

[21] In England, the same is true. One study of two large urban areas in 1945 found that 59 percent of the whole sample belonged to no organization at all. Forty-one percent of the men and 79 percent of the women had no memberships at all in associations. See "Clubs, Societies, and Democracy," Planning, a Broadsheet issued by Political and Economic Planning, No. 263, March 21, 1947.

[22] Herbert Goldhamer, Some Factors Affecting Participation in Voluntary Associations (Unpublished Ph.D. Dissertation, University of Chicago, 1943), p. 19.

[23] Mirra Komarovsky, "The Voluntary Associations of Urban Dwellers," American Sociological Review, 11 (1946), 686-698.

[24] G. A. Lundberg, M. Komarovsky, and M. A. McInerny, Leisure, A Suburban Study (New York, 1934), p. 128, pp. 135ff.

[25] P. F. Lazarsfeld, B. Berelson, and H. Gaudet, The People's Choice: How the Voter Makes Up His Mind in a Presidential Campaign (New York, 1944), p. 145.

[26] Warner and Lunt, op. cit., p. 323, p. 339. See also Bushee, op. cit.

amount of nonjoining has been documented most extensively of all perhaps for the rural areas.[27]

3. "Who says organization, says oligarchy." Thus has Robert Michels stated in another form his "iron law of oligarchy."[28] Gaetano Mosca has also noted the tendency toward activity and control by a few in all organizations, governmental and nongovernmental alike.[29] Such large generalizations are really statements of the problem rather than adequate analyses, but they do indicate the extent to which the pattern of active minority and inactive majority occurs.

"Apathetic" memberships are not a new phenomenon in the United States, despite the widespread myth that voluntary participation was complete in a "golden age" of the town meeting in New England. It was writers of the nineteenth century, de Tocqueville, for example, who first "assigned to New England towns attributes they never possessed."[30] Present examples of both the direct and the representative types of town meeting are just like their prototypes in this respect.[31]

THE SCOPE OF OLIGARCHY

No matter what interest any particular association represents, we find the existence of an active minority in control. In the "service

[27] W. A. Anderson, Farm Women in the Home Bureau (Ithaca, N. Y.: Cornell University Agricultural Experiment Station, mimeo., 1941); W. A. Anderson, Farm Families in the Grange (Ithaca, N. Y.: Cornell University Agricultural Experiment Station, mimeo., 1943); W. A. Anderson and Dwight Sanderson, Membership Relations in Cooperative Organizations (Ithaca, N. Y.: Cornell University Agricultural Experiment Station, mimeo., 1943); W. A. Anderson and D. B. Fales, Farm Youth in the 4-H Club (Ithaca, N. Y.: Cornell University Agricultural Experiment Station, mimeo., 1944); and W. A. Anderson, "The Family and Individual Social Participation," American Sociological Review, 8 (1943), 420-425.

[28] Robert Michels, Political Parties, A Sociological Study of the Oligarchical Tendencies of Modern Democracy, trans. by Eden and Cedar Paul (New York, 1915), pp. 377, 401.

[29] Gaetano Mosca, The Ruling Class, trans. by Arthur Livingston (New York, 1939).

[30] John F. Sly, Town Government in Massachusetts (Unpublished Ph.D. Dissertation, Harvard University, 1925), pp. 166-167.

[31] L. L. Barber, Modifications of Town Government in New England (Unpublished Ph. D. Dissertation, Harvard University, 1941), Ch. X; and Lane W. Lancaster, Government in Rural America (New York, 1937), pp. 44ff.

clubs," for example, there is a very active nucleus and a large group who are "just members." Although each club has many committees and every member is expected to be active on at least one of them, many members are wholly inactive.[32] The American Legion was founded in 1919 by a small group and is run by a self-perpetuating oligarchy who have been called "kingmakers" by those who are critical of their power to name national commanders.[33] Goldhamer summarizes the situation for fraternal organizations as follows: "Though fraternal organizations are subject to democratic control, it appears that the actual formulation of policy . . . is largely the function of a few interested individuals, with the great bulk of the membership acquiescing so long as these policies do not interfere with their private lives."[34]

The Consumer Coöperative Movement, which stresses equal and active participation by all members more than most other associations do, is no exception to the active minority pattern. J. P. Warbasse, former President of the Coöperative League of America, says: "It is true that there is much indifference; usually a minority of the membership of local societies carry on the business."[35] Even in avowedly activist organizations, there is minimal participation. ". . . in the most powerful and deeply rooted People's Organizations known in this country the degree of popular participation reached a point varying between five and seven percent!"[36]

Figures for attendance at meetings of a wide variety of associations are another index of minority participation. In Boulder, Colorado, the average attendance for all types of organizations, including the churches, is only 51.4 percent.[37] In the organizations of the small town of Mineville in the Rockies, "usual attendance" consists of only a minority of the members.[38] Studies of local societies of the Coöpera-

[32] Marden, op. cit.
[33] William Gellerman, The American Legion as Educator (New York, 1938); Marcus Duffield, King Legion (New York, 1931), Ch. I.
[34] Goldhamer and Gist, op. cit., p. 175.
[35] James Peter Warbasse, Cooperative Democracy (New York, 1923), I, 21.
[36] Alinsky, op. cit., p. 198.
[37] Bushee, op. cit.
[38] Albert Blumenthal, Small Town Stuff (Chicago, 1932), Table XIII, p. 265.

tive Movement in different parts of the United States bear out the same facts.[39] Minority attendance in associations persists despite the frequent attempt to choose a time and place for meetings which least conflicts with the job and family obligations of the members. It persists also despite the enactment of bylaws imposing sanctions for nonattendance. Where they exist, such rules are more honored in the breach than in the observance.[40]

SOCIAL SOURCES OF PARTICIPATION PATTERNS

Can we account for these three uniformities of participation in voluntary associations simply by applying the value-laden term "mass apathy"? It is perhaps already apparent that a more adequate analysis requires consideration of certain features of the American social structure in which this behavior occurs.

We have already largely anticipated the explanation of the first uniformity, that of a vast proliferation of particular associations. American social structure, by segregating a large number of specific interests from kinship and occupational ties, with which they .are usually fused in other societies, creates the need for a corresponding number of voluntary associations to pursue these interests. This large number is in turn multiplied many times by the great social and geographical diversity of the United States.

But American social structure does more than segregate these other interests from family and job obligations. *It defines them as being of less importance than family and job obligations.* The relatively peripheral significance of the interests to which associations devote themselves explains in large measure the second and third uniformities: many people have no memberships at all; and, among those with memberships in any given association, the majority are inactive and participate minimally. Because of the individual's culturally prescribed preoccupation in the United States with obligations to his job and his "isolated conjugal family," there exists a socially structured pull away from membership in even those voluntary associations

---

[39] L. C. Kercher, V. W. Kebker, and W. C. Leland, Jr., *Consumers' Cooperatives in the North Central States* (Minneapolis, 1941), p. 44; and H. Haines Turner, *Case Studies of Consumers' Cooperatives* (New York, 1941), p. 267.

[40] Marden, *op. cit.*, p. 68.

relevant to his interests.[41] Further, even when he is a member of an association, the individual's interest is so limited that it leads to minimal participation. This definitely limited interest can be illustrated by the attitudes of members of such voluntary associations as farmers' coöperatives and trade unions.

But the general consensus among the farmers was that "as long as they give me good quality at low prices and a bonus besides, I do not care how or who runs the organization."[42]

The ordinary member sees no particular reason for "wasting" his time at meetings. "Let the officials run the union, that's what they're getting paid for," just about expresses his attitude. . . . As long as things go well, the average union member doesn't want self-government and is annoyed and resentful when an attempt is made to force its responsibilities on him.[43]

There is, in addition, another very important structural factor which contributes to the tendency toward inactive majorities in voluntary associations. The internal structure of the voluntary association itself, that is, with its formal organization and division of functions among members, makes it possible for a minority to achieve the interests of the association with the majority participating very little or not at all. This possibility, however, brings in its train certain consequences for the executives and the members of voluntary associations alike, consequences which are serious problems for both of them. Since these problems become especially acute in associations which stress democratic values, we shall examine both the sources and the consequences of these problems in such associations.

VALUES OF DEMOCRATIC ASSOCIATIONS

Practically all voluntary associations are democratic associations, that is to say, formal authority resides in the whole membership. Indeed, this is the typical pattern of organization throughout Ameri-

[41] Lack of space prevents our presenting here the detailed sketch of the American social structure which would provide a complete basis for this statement. For an indication of both the method and substance of such a sketch, see Talcott Parsons, *Essays in Social Theory* (Glencoe, Illinois, 1948).

[42] W. A. Anderson and D. Sanderson, *op. cit.*, p. 18.

[43] Will Herberg, *Bureaucracy and Democracy in Labor Unions*. Reprinted for Great Island Conference, New York City, 1947, from the *Antioch Review*, Fall, 1943, p. 18.

can society: the state itself, the major and minor political parties and groups, occupational associations—whether executive, professional, or labor—and special interest groups are democratic associations.

Note that this definition runs in terms of the nature of the internal structure of the association, not in terms of the nature of the interest it represents. Some "democratic" associations have particularistic criteria for membership, for example, interests relevant to kinship as such, religion, sex, nativity, or race—interests deriving from "ascribed" rather than "achieved" statuses. Other associations stress universalistic criteria; there is an almost "utopian" emphasis on such criteria in the Consumers' Coöperative Movement. Formulated in what are known as the Rochdale Principles, they include the ethical desirability of voluntary affiliation and membership rights open to all without regard to sex, race, occupation, nationality, social class, religious creed, or political attachment.[44] In an important sense, the associations with universalistic criteria are more democratic than those with particularistic criteria, but for our present purposes it is important only that both types have an internal structure based on the democratic authority of the membership.

What is the structure of procedures and instruments through which democratic authority is supposed to be realized? The constituents listed below compose an "ideal type" against which values and practice in any given association can be measured roughly as more or less democratic. The notion of a continuum, however crude, appears to be more realistic than some absolute standard in the examination of the democratic association. For, as will be seen, very few associations conform fully to the ideal type even in the expression of values, and practically none do so in practice.

By definition, then, the democratic association states the desirability of and makes provision for the active participation of all members, that is, for their regular and frequent attendance at meetings, their taking part in discussion, their working on committees and holding office at some time: in short, for their participation in the formulation and realization of policy. The fundamental democratic instrument is what Barnard calls "decision by vote."[45] Most democratic associations

[44] Kercher et al., op. cit., pp. 5ff.
[45] C. I. Barnard, Dilemmas of Leadership in the Democratic Process (Princeton: Published under the University Extension Fund, 1939).

implicitly guarantee this right. The Coöperative Movement states explicitly, as a cardinal principle, "one member, one vote," and even bans the use of proxies.[46] Where the membership of a democratic association is widely scattered, the referendum may be used to sound the will of the group.[47]

As a means to the distribution of responsibility and control, the democratic association is characterized by frequent and regular election of officers, short terms of office, and the rotation of any given official position among as large a number of members as possible. This value, we shall see, has a special relevance to the problem of security of tenure for executives in the democratic association. Where the association is large enough to be divided into many branches, it is considered desirable to have relatively large local autonomy, that is, a flow of power up from the local groups to the central coördinating group. In the large association, where national conventions are held, the democratic election of delegates to the convention is valued as a means of achieving total group influence on the policy of the association.

So that effective control over the executive may be guaranteed, the democratic association requires that the elected executive furnish regular, complete, and detailed reports on its implementation of policy and on all financial transactions. Members who are critical of the executive, or otherwise dissident, have a right to express their views, to communicate such criticism to fellow members, to organize groups within the association to foster their dissent, and, if these rights are denied by the executive, to inform the general public of their protest or to form a new association. The right of free speech in the national convention and in the official publication of the association gives the critical member the opportunity to transmit his opinion to the whole membership.

These are the several procedures for fulfilling the democratic values of participation. In practice, however, democratic associations typically fall considerably short of this fulfillment. It is our purpose here to analyze certain structural necessities in democratic associations which impede the full realization of the democratic values.

[46] Kercher et al., op. cit., pp. 5ff.
[47] Oliver Garceau, The Political Life of the American Medical Association (Cambridge, Mass., 1941), p. 19, discusses the use of the referendum in the A.M.A.

PROBLEMS OF THE EXECUTIVE IN
DEMOCRATIC ASSOCIATIONS

We can best achieve our purpose by considering some problems of the executive in the democratic association. These problems are commonly thought to arise simply out of "mass apathy" or out of the corruption and weakness of the particular men who are executives in democratic associations.[48] Corrupt men and indifferent members do aggravate these problems, perhaps, but they are due also to the nature of formal organization and to the functions of executives therein.[49]

There exists for every association, democratic or not, the necessity to take action in the interests of that association. An undifferentiated group of members is uncoördinated and cannot act effectively. Internal specialization of function and the coördination of differentiated functional roles are required both for efficient organizational effort and for adequate handling of changes in the external situation that affect the group purposes. Responsibility for the coördination of internal effort and for decision about external situations are among the necessary executive functions in any organized group. "Authority" is the attribute by virtue of which obedience to orders of the executive is granted and maintained. By definition, then, in every association there will be specialized functions; and authority to pursue those functions will be granted by members of the association to the occupants of executive roles.

"Taking action" is not in itself a simple matter. When an association is part of and adjusting to a relatively stable situation, it must maintain a relatively continuous and stable set of actions with respect to its purposes. When the association is expanding rapidly or when the external situation is changing, executives must make adequate diagnoses of organizational needs occasioned by the changes and must take prompt and firm action to meet these needs. Two kinds of knowledge are required for action by executives, in both stable and changing situations. These two kinds of knowledge may be called "general"

[48] Cf. Michels, op. cit., p. 205, "The desire to dominate, for good or evil, is universal."

[49] Some of the problems analyzed in this section arise in even the smallest democratic association, but they are present in their full number and clearest form in the large democratic association. The present discussion is, in effect, limited to the latter type.

and "special." "General" knowledge includes a high level of ability in the executive functions themselves and in the technical knowledge relevant to the purposes of the association. "Special" knowledge consists in acquaintance with the series of decisions that has constituted any particular association in its immediate and perhaps more distant past. Without the special knowledge of how his association has performed in the past, the executive cannot predict how it will act in the future. And on his ability to predict depends the possibility of competent executive decisions.[50]

The democratic association shares with other types of association the necessity for specialized executive functions and legitimate authority. But if executive functions in the democratic association are to be described adequately, we must keep in mind one of Barnard's dicta: "Executive processes are specialized functions in what we know as 'organizations.' If these functions are to be adequately described, the description must be in terms of the nature of the organization itself."[51] That is what we shall do here.

In the democratic association, it is the active minority that takes responsibility and becomes the executive. Barnard has also referred to the "persistent disposition to avoid responsibility" on the part of most men in the oligarchic type of organization he describes.[52] In the democratic association, members may also desire to avoid responsibility, but this is due at least in part to their preoccupation with other interests and to their willingness to have the active minority discharge the major concern for the interests of the association. In any case, the existence of an inactive majority often requires the active minority to take more power than is formally granted to it under a democratic constitution.

[50] This highly condensed statement of the nature of executive functions is introductory to the following discussion, in which it will be amplified. This statement derives chiefly from the following sources: Max Weber, *From Max Weber: Essays in Sociology*, trans. and ed. by H. H. Gerth and C. Wright Mills (New York, 1946); and Chester I. Barnard, *The Functions of the Executive* (Cambridge, Mass., 1938).

See also, for further abstract and concrete studies of the functions of the executive: H. C. Metcalf and L. Urwick, *Dynamic Administration: The Collected Papers of Mary Parker Follett* (New York, 1942); Grace Coyle, *Social Process in Organized Groups* (New York, 1930), Ch. V; and Marshall E. Dimock, *The Executive in Action* (New York, 1945).

[51] Barnard, *op. cit.*

[52] *Ibid.*, p. vii.

FULL-TIME OFFICIALS

Beyond a certain point, the size and interests of a democratic association compel it to have full-time officials. It is probably impossible to make any general statement for all associations about where this point may be fixed. It is determined by the peculiar needs of each group. However, when these needs require that at least one person devote so much of his time to the purposes of the association that he cannot continue in his regular occupational role, the association must appoint or elect a full-time executive. If the former part-time executive now becomes the paid, full-time official, he has changed his regular occupational role. A new career opens up for him.

In the democratic association, to conform with the value that equal participation requires rotation of officers, the formal rules provide for regular election of officials for short terms. It is, however, an empirical uniformity that at least a few of the officials serve continuously and for a long time. The long-tenure officials are the ones who have the requisite "special" knowledge of the history of the association. In some democratic associations, most of the long-tenure officials are elected; in some others, most of them are appointed; but in all democratic associations at least a few of them are elected. These few are responsible for the appointment of hired assistants, and in some cases this paid staff includes a large number of people. Where members of the association itself are not trained or available to fill the paid staff positions, outsiders are hired. These several uniformities in the term and tenure of executives may be found in many different democratic associations. For example, in the local and parent groups of the American Medical Association, the president, president-elect, and the vice-president have "almost universally short tenure." However, the secretary and treasurer are reëlected time after time.[53] In the American Legion, a National Commander is elected each year for one year and the constitution forbids reëlections. But the National Adjutant, once elected, becomes a permanent official, and in many ways the key official in the association.[54] In American trade unions, it is the pattern

[53] Garceau, op. cit., p. 48.

[54] Richard Seelye Jones, A History of the American Legion (Indianapolis, 1946), Ch. XXVI. Although the foreword claims this is not an "official" history, it would seem to be so.

for practically all elected executives to have long and continuous tenure.[55] Some of the special factors that influence the tenure of trade union executives will be analyzed below.

In any democratic association, the long-tenure elected officials become a center of power that may prevent democratic practices. Where these officials occupy the highest offices, they are often attacked by dissident members either for taking power inappropriate to their office or for continuing too long in that office in violation of democratic values. Both of these criticisms are made against trade union officials. Where the long-tenure officials occupy positions below the topmost ones, with the top ones being filled with rotating personnel, they are often criticized for usurpation of power. Such was the kind of criticism made of Dr. Fishbein, Secretary of the American Medical Association, and of the "kingmakers" in the American Legion who serve continuously on important standing committees.[56]

EMERGENCE OF CAREER INTERESTS

Any "career" may become a goal in itself, partially independent of the purposes of the organization in which the career is pursued. Careers in democratic associations are no exceptions to this tendency. Whereas the original interest of full-time and permanent officials were wholly like those of all other members, they soon develop additional, emergent interests in their "jobs." An elected official of a democratic association must of course be a member, and membership implies possession of the relevant interests. In many associations in the United States, these interests are based on professional and occupational skills. When a member is elected a full-time official, he may come to have a greater or more valuable skill as an executive than in his previous occupational role. Consequently, he has a great interest in maintaining his new skill and position. Moreover, occupational and professional skills that are not used are subject to a process of atrophy, the rate of which will vary with the type of skill and with the extent of change going on in the knowledge on which the skill is based. For example, the scientific knowledge on which medicine rests has been changing very rapidly, much more rapidly than the principles and

[55] American Civil Liberties Union, 1943, p. 52. See also, C. Wright Mills, *The New Men of Power* (New York, 1948).
[56] Garceau, *op. cit.*, and Jones, *op. cit.*

substantive content of the law. The professional skill of doctors-turned-executive will, accordingly, have a greater rate of atrophy than that of lawyers in the same position.

The atrophy of a former skill establishes new interests for the executives of the democratic association. So also does the higher general social status which comes with being the executive of a large and powerful group. For both reasons, there is a strain on the executive to preserve his new interests and advance them. *He has no formal protection for his position: hence the various informal ways in which he circumvents the formal prescriptions of rotation in office and actually secures extended tenure in an office in which he now has a great stake.* For many years past, John L. Lewis could not have returned to coal mining. No one would question that his present social status is in the upper middle class, not with the miners in the working class. Dr. Morris Fishbein probably cannot return to the active practice of medicine: it has changed too much since twenty-five years ago, when he was last engaged in active practice.

Thus, where there is no formal guarantee of security of tenure in an organization and where careers in that organization emerge, various informal devices for maintaining some security will be found. In many large democratic associations, the organization is "controlled" in such a way that officials are assured of reëlection. These control devices will be discussed later.

ROLE CONFLICTS

In the democratic association, since only members can be elected officers, the officials will have the appropriate symbols of the role and interest on which membership is based. As we have said, John L. Lewis *has* worked in the coal mines; and Dr. Fishbein *has* practiced medicine. It is implicit in the values of the democratic association that the officers should be "one of us." There exists a recognition, perhaps inarticulate, of the desirability that the executive be a man who through shared and common experiences, through a "style of life" even, has come to have and symbolically manifests the same values as the rest of the membership. The symbolic identification of the leader with the membership reassures the inactive majority that their interests are being safeguarded.

However, when he is the executive of a democratic association representing lower-class people, it is also necessary for the leader to have the established symbols of status and power, since in our society access to these symbols is granted to all men. When their executives have these symbols, the lower-class membership can feel that "our power" is adequate, for they know that these are the necessary instruments of achieving their interests. To this extent, therefore, it is useless for opposing interests to try to undermine the authority of leaders by exposing their possession of upper-class status and power. The members may even take a vicarious pleasure in the middle-class status, remuneration, and style of life of their leaders.

But such power and style of life may involve the executive of a working-class association in conflicts of roles. Such conflict, for example, occurs for what has been called the "progressive" type of union leader. This is the trade union executive who thinks of his work as a "calling," in which he works for "principles" and "humanity." He believes that there should be "rank and file" participation and that the officers should be of the same class origin as the members. Personal modesty, indifference to "getting ahead," dislike for "big shots" are among his ideals. When this type of executive marries, however, he accepts the middle-class "culturally normative definitions of the role of husband and father . . . [of] 'good provider' . . . [of] 'companion.' . . ." Because of his long hours on the job, he must often choose between job obligations and the expectations of his wife that he will conform to middle-class patterns. The conflict may be resolved by making the trade union office "just a job."[57]

Executives in democratic associations face still other problems. In the democratic association the membership grants authority to the executive to carry out the purposes of the group. But general statements of policy never cover all possible concrete cases. In a complex and changing situation especially, new and unforeseen cases arise continually. In these circumstances, the executives must act to adjust the purposes of the association to the external situation. In short, the executive must formulate the interests of the group to some extent, as well as realize them. Continuous, day-to-day, *ad hoc* decisions may cumulate into policy for the association. This process may be called "executive legislation," on the analogy of "judicial legislation" as

[57] Alvin W. Gouldner, "Attitudes of 'Progressive' Trade Union Leaders," *American Journal of Sociology*, LII (1947), 389-392.

analyzed by Cardozo.[58] This executive legislation may be approved *ex post facto* by the membership in convention or by referendum. But there is always the possibility that the executive will get out of touch with the wishes of the membership, as the judiciary may get out of touch with the wishes of the majority as expressed in legislation. The membership of an association often accepts a certain amount of executive legislation of which it mildly disapproves only because it considers the alternative course, abrogation, more costly or more harmful to the purposes of the association.

Where especially quick action is required, there are certain inherent difficulties in the democratic process of decision which causes strain for executives anxious to take appropriate action. There is, in short, what Barnard calls "the dilemma of the time-lag," that is, a conflict between the requirement of immediate action and the slowness of the democratic process of approval.[59] This dilemma adds to the need for executive legislation.

Still further, on technical matters especially, the members of a democratic association may not be able to judge what their interests are, and therefore the executives often have the task of formulating those interests. Moreover, insofar as there emerge new purposes in an association—purposes relating either directly to the original ones or arising from changes in the situation or in the needs of the organization—there may be a period in which these new interests are not manifest to the membership. In this period the executive may be more aware of the existence of these new purposes and of the need to take action than is the membership. The latter may complain that the executive is "wasting its time." They may not see the relevance and importance of the new problems. There may also be a difference of time-perspectives. The members may be taking the short-run view while the executive is taking the long-run view. Such differences about the nature and existence of purposes, about the relative importance of different purposes, and about time-perspectives create special problems in the democratic association, where the executive must justify its actions to the membership. Although these problems are often thought to arise simply out of the apathy of members, we can now

[58] Benjamin N. Cardozo, *The Nature of the Judicial Process* (New Haven, 1921).

[59] Barnard, *op. cit.*, pp. 8, 13.

see in what way they are inherent in the structure of the democratic association.

One final problem for the executives in the democratic association requires our attention. There are strains implicit in the executive role in all groups. For example, the decisions of the executive, although often considered simply technical decisions, are almost always moral decisions as well.[60] The executive must choose among values. Moreover, the strain on the executive is increased by the existence of uncontrollable and unpredictable elements in the situation in which he must act and by the limitations, sometimes very large, on the knowledge he can use in that situation. Such strains are great enough where authority is oligarchically structured. But they probably become greater in the democratic association, where actions must be justified to a membership ideologically confused about the nature of authority and attendant strains. It has been noted that there is, in modern Western society, "a certain 'utopianism' which tends to minimize the significance of authority, coercive power, and physical force in human affairs. . . ."[61] This is particularly characteristic of the "liberal" credo, and in the United States the democratic association has a strong "liberal" tradition. The consequent undermining of what the executive considers necessary power and authority can be destructive of effective action in particular cases.[62]

TECHNIQUES OF CONTROL

We have seen that there are special strains on the executive in the democratic association. It must formulate purposes and take "unauthorized" action, yet it must also justify these purposes and this action to the membership. It develops special interests of its own in job tenure within the association, yet this conflicts with the democratic requirement of rotation in office. We shall now consider some of the methods whereby the executive provides the necessary conditions for effective action and insures itself security of tenure. These techniques

[60] *Ibid.*, p. 281.

[61] See Introduction, pp. 56ff., to Max Weber, *The Theory of Social and Economic Organization*, trans. by A. R. Henderson and Talcott Parsons, ed. and with an introduction by Talcott Parsons (New York, 1947).

[62] C. Wright Mills, "Grass Roots Union with Ideas," *Commentary* 5 (1948), 240-247, describes a "grass roots" union the members of which "disrespect authority even when they have elected it."

of control are often criticized as "undemocratic" and "oligarchic." In any given association they may be "undemocratic" and nothing else. But we have seen that they may also have certain positive functions owing to the internal structure of the democratic association.

It is now a sociological truism that "informal" social organization is very important. This means that the scientific observer must always look at the actual behavior of a group as well as at the written rules governing the group. This is certainly true if one wants to understand the technique of control by the executive over the membership in the democratic association. Many of the formal instruments designed especially to secure control by the membership over the executive actually function in the opposite way. In practice they are employed by the executive to control the inactive majority.

For example, in the large democratic association, the regular convention is designated the supreme source of authority. It passes laws and determines policy for the executive. The executive is required to report on its actions since the last convention for the approval of the present convention. In practice, however, the convention is so much controlled by the executive that it is often merely a rubber-stamp approval mechanism.[63] Serious criticism of the incumbent executives is rare at conventions. In effect, for example, the permanent officials of the American Medical Association are "virtually free, in practice, of critical supervision."[64] Reports of past executive performance become empty formalities, glossed over by automatic acceptance.

There are techniques of control that operate after the convention has been held. The permanent executive may moderate its wishes or alter them in the resolutions that are presented to the convention for approval and then realize its actual purpose through subsequent "interpretation" of established policy. In most large democratic associations, the permanent executives publish an official journal which is the main medium of communication among the members. Once again, however, in practice, "the main purpose is to promote the policies of the national administration."[65] In the American Legion, for example, the official magazines are closed to dissident members.[66]

[63] American Civil Liberties Union, 1943; V. O. Key, Jr., Politics, Parties, and Pressure Groups (New York, 1947), pp. 70ff.; Garceau, op. cit.

[64] Garceau, op. cit., p. 84.

[65] American Civil Liberties Union, 1943, pp. 53-55.

[66] Gellerman, op. cit.

The influence of the *Journal of the American Medical Association,* in part because of its high quality and genuine usefulness, is particularly great. Dr. Fishbein, the editor of the *Journal,* is assiduous in "educating" the inactive majority of the membership in the views of the active minority, of which he is a key member. There is practically no chance for opposing views to be stated.[67] Control of the established instruments of protest and communication by the executive thus reinforces the inactivity of a majority which has other important interests.

THE PROBLEM OF DEMOCRACY IN TRADE UNIONS

The large trade union in the United States is essentially similar, in its democratic values and in its organizational structure, to other large democratic associations. Therefore it manifests the same divergence between democratic values and actual practice as other associations. This we have seen in examples cited in our analysis. However, since much of the criticism of the lack of democracy in trade unions has undoubtedly had ideological functions, this *similarity* has been ignored. There are legitimate differences of interest between management and labor in the United States. These differences of interest have caused numerous contests of strength, in which management and labor alike have used general appeals to democratic values. In these conflicts, management has often spoken as if only trade unions, among all associations, including its own interest groups, were undemocratic in practice. It has often spoken as if undemocratic practices were wholly due to the corruption of labor leaders and the "mass apathy" of workers. In their turn, labor leaders have often categorically denied their lack of democracy, or, implicitly admitting certain actual deficiencies, have pointed to the full democratic nature of their constitutions.[68]

Neither party to the conflict, nor yet the general public, has seen that it is dealing with some general problems of the democratic association. Such understanding might at least mitigate the conflict and might also lead to fuller implementation of democratic values in the trade union.

[67] Garceau, *op. cit.,* Ch. III.
[68] Such a defense was entered by the CIO in its pamphlet, *The Truth About the CIO,* 1945-46.

Let us note that the problem of democracy in trade unions takes on special significance from the size of the group involved and the vital nature of the interests affected. ". . . about seven million workers are employed in either closed shops or union shops and about four million more work under maintenance-of-membership clauses. This means that there are seven million jobs in the United States which can be held only by men who can satisfy the admission requirements of unions and eleven million which can be held only by men who are in good standing in their unions."[69] "Unions are, in fact," says one labor intellectual, "no longer purely voluntary private organizations to which the individual worker may or may not belong as he sees fit."[70] The internal government of trade unions is now affected with a kind of public interest.

However, there are two special aspects of the general problem in its application to trade unions and both of these warrant further discussion. These two special aspects are, first, the peculiarly important place of the democratic tradition in the trade union movement, and, second, the peculiar problems of status which confront executives of trade unions.

Among democratic associations, the trade unions as a group have a special connection with the democratic tradition. They represent a long history of protest against those elements in the established order which seek to deny to the common man his democratic rights, whether economic or political. Trade unions are part of what has been called "the leftist revolt" insofar as they have demanded the full and immediate realization of democratic values, sometimes even to a utopian degree. This is true even of the older, craft-type unions, the ones which have accepted the capitalist order and pursued cautious "business unionism." It is even more true of the socialist unions, whether of the craft or the industrial type. In the great industrial unions formed in the 1930's, there has been much emphasis on the importance of "rank and file" participation by the masses newly converted to economic democracy.[71] Many of the leaders of industrial unionism, whether they accept capitalism or desire a gradual intro-

[69] Sumner H. Slichter, *The Challenge of Industrial Relations* (Ithaca, New York, 1947), p. 101.

[70] Herberg, *op. cit.*, p. 23.

[71] Bruce Minton and John Stuart, *Men Who Lead Labor* (New York, 1937). Ch. VII.

duction of socialism, have felt themselves and their movement the instrument of a new democratic order.

Here, then, is the paradox. "Even in democratic unions, the effective power of top officials is greater, their grip tighter, their tenure more secure, their conduct in office less open to public criticism and control, than is commonly the case in our federal or state government in normal times. . . . [And yet the trade union movement] has always claimed to be the champion of a higher and fuller democracy than prevails in our capitalistic society generally and to provide an exemplification of such democracy within its own ranks."[72]

One source of this paradox lies in the exigencies of large-scale formal organization, as we have already seen. Another has its roots in the fact that family and job obligations have priority, for most members, over union activities. In our discussion of the Communists, we shall note a case which is interesting because it shows how the absence of this priority permits fuller participation. Still a third source are the peculiar status problems of executives in the trade union movement.

We have already noted that the pattern of officeholding by executives in trade unions is one of exceedingly long tenure, even of lifetime tenure, longer apparently than tenure in other democratic associations.[73] Is this difference due to a peculiar apathy among the members or corruption among the executives of trade unions? We shall point here to certain matters of the status and skill of union leaders that seem to be important causes of this pattern.

The trade union movement has provided an important channel of mobility for the working-class American. Chinoy's chapter in the present volume discusses this in some detail. Mills has made a study of the social origins of the trade union leaders that substantiates this. His sample included 50 percent of the presidents and secretaries of the A.F.L. and CIO national and international unions and the same proportion of the presidents and secretaries of the state federations of these two "houses of labor." About 60 percent of his sample were the sons of skilled laborers. Twenty-two percent had gone to college, the rest only to grammar and high school. The typical career pattern was for these men to start as workers, become officials of a

[72] Herberg, op. cit., p. 23.
[73] Michels, op. cit., p. 97, notes a similar pattern of tenure in the European working-class political parties.

local, and gradually work up to the top of a national or international union or a state federation. Their present salaries, reports Mills, are definitely "good" by middle-class standards.[74] In its report on thirty-six affiliated unions, the CIO found that eleven paid top salaries in 1946 of over $6000 and that the other twenty-five paid less than $6000, but with most of these around $5000.

Thus trade union leaders as a group have risen to enviable positions. Their general social status is good, their opportunities to aid the advance of their children great, and their effective influence on affairs large. Theirs is a situation which most Americans would like; they are successful men. And yet—and this is what is peculiar about their situation—they can, in general, maintain their position only by holding on to the *particular* positions they have. Career lines run pretty much within given unions. *There is very little possibility of moving from an executive position in one union to another position of equal or higher status in another union.* At best, an executive can move out of his own union into the state and national federation hierarchies. There is very little chance, moreover, that the trade union leader can transfer his ability to other job markets. He has been pretty much shut out of the government and business groups, partly because his very success may have rested on continual opposition to them. Thus the executive in the trade union is locked up in the labor movement, subject to very great pressure to maintain his general social status and to preserve his success by any means available. It is often to the detriment of the practice of democracy in trade unions that the best means available to the executive is to insure himself permanent tenure. In the effort to guarantee his tenure, the executive may abandon much that is essential in democratic values.

COMMUNISTS AND TRADE UNIONS

An analysis of the activities of Communists in trade unions can give us still further insight into the problem of democracy in these voluntary associations. At the same time it can show us, with particular clarity, the relevance of social structural considerations for understanding participation. Communists in the United States have joined trade unions for the same reason that they have joined other

[74] C. Wright Mills, "The Trade Union Leader: A Collective Portrait," *Public Opinion Quarterly*, 9 (1945), 158-175.

democratic associations of "the leftist revolt," to swell the chorus of protest against the existing capitalist order. And nowhere else have the possibilities for effective power of an organized active minority in the democratic association been more visible. "It seems inconceivable that several hundred Communists, all in key spots, can control a union like the UE with over half a million members, but it is a fact. They have organization and discipline and work around the clock to maintain their control with the aid of several thousand unidentified lesser Party members and fellow-travelers. They comprise less than one percent of the total membership but are such a well-organized minority that they control the unorganized majority."[75] A veteran trade unionist has said that the ordinary union member admires the Communists "because they do get things done."[76] They are not "apathetic." The great activity of Communists in trade unions does, of course, have basic motivational origins; they are devoted men, consecrated to their party. But there are structural considerations relevant to Communist activism, considerations which highlight the causes of "apathy" among the other members of trade unions. Most important of all, their role obligations are different from those of ordinary men.

Communists are men devoted to the purposes of their party. They differ from persons having conventional party affiliations in that anything else is second to those pervasive purposes, whether it be obligations to one's family, if one has a family, or earning a living. For the devoted Communist, the party is both his family and his job. If the party requires him to gain control of a trade union or some other democratic association, that becomes his job and a major obligation. He may devote his time to Communist purposes during the day when he is supposedly "on the job" for his employer. And he can work in the evenings and during the week ends, when other men are fulfilling their family obligations. Communists thus have the time as well as the energy "to get things done." Moreover, because they can be supported by their party, Communists can even afford to work without pay when a new trade union is being organized. Other men have to earn a living in a job which takes them away from the new organiza-

[75] Anderson, Franklin J., "Union Wreckers at the Switch," *Plain Talk*, I (1947), 31-34.

[76] Karl Baarslag, *Communist Trade Union Trickery Exposed* (Washington, D. C., 1947).

tion. When the organization has been successfully founded and requires full-time, paid officers, the Communists have a special claim on these powerful jobs.

IMPLICATIONS

In brief conclusion, it is desirable to bring out some implications of our analysis for democratic values and democratic action. The essential conclusion of our analysis has been that *both* democratic values and structural factors are relevant to the problem of "mass apathy" in the voluntary association. Both interact to create a certain kind of behavior. Perhaps the chief defect of those utopian views of participation which talk about "mass apathy" is that they look at the democratic values only. In this perspective, any discrepancy from full realization of the values seems to indicate alienation from those values. A great danger of the utopian attitude is that it sometimes, in its disappointment, becomes disillusioned or cynical rejection of the values themselves. A structural view of the whole of American society, such as we have taken here, can save us from this unwarranted pessimism. It is our hope that with this more adequate understanding of the problem of "mass apathy," democratic citizens and democratic administrators will be able to make concrete plans for enlarging participation in the democratic association.

Criteria for Political Apathy[1]

BY DAVID RIESMAN AND NATHAN GLAZER

AMONG THOUGHTFUL people today there is increasing discussion of political apathy. The discussion of apathy—and its converse, the "responsibility of the citizen"—has overflowed the boundaries of traditional political science and become the concern of the sociologist, the psychiatrist, the social psychologist, and, recently, the atomic scientists. From Gosnell's studies of nonvoting to the recent interest in the "no-opinion vote" in public opinion polls, from *Middletown* to recent studies of participation in voluntary associations, we have become increasingly aware that many millions of Americans remain aggressively unattached to the political events and discourse of their locality, their nation, and the world; that millions of others pay only casual attention; and that millions more only observe the game of politics as they would a horse race. Yet during recent decades politics has become increasingly important as a mode of conscious manipulation of the social environment; and complaints arise that people begin to flee from politics just when politics matters most for them.

It is not easy to separate from current complaints about political apathy those themes which represent old problems—for instance, traditional middle-class concern with lower-class indifference to politics

[1] The research project on character and political apathy in America of which this previously unpublished article is one outcome has been conducted by the senior author under the auspices of the Yale University Committee on National Policy. We are very much indebted to the Committee, and to the Carnegie Corporation which financed the work, for the opportunity to pursue these inquiries. This article has been read in an earlier version by a number of friends who made many helpful suggestions. We would like to express our appreciation particularly to Professors Reuel Denney and Herman Finer of the University of Chicago, and Dr. Henry M. Paechter of New York City, for their very careful and critical readings.

—and those which may represent perceptions of new types or meanings of apathy. The division between an active leadership and a passive multitude, in almost all spheres of life, has been almost universally observed; many social theories assume it is inevitable, and some that it is desirable. Yet such a generalization may obscure differences in the relative size of the passive multitude at different times; in the reasons for its passivity; in the intensity of its indifference; and in the subjective feelings which accompany the apathy. It is our thesis that, while the proportion of the passive may not have increased in recent decades, and even declined (Bryce commented on the passivity of the American multitude, and there is some evidence that participation, as contrasted with spectatorship, was low in the alleged heydey of the town meeting)—while, we say, the numbers of the apparently passive may not have increased, we do believe that there have been far-reaching changes in the reasons for passivity and in the types of apathy that have resulted.

CHANGING MEANINGS OF POLITICS

To make our point clear, we shall try to sketch out a contrast between the meanings of politics in the nineteenth century and in the twentieth in America, polarizing our discussion around two "ideal types" (in Max Weber's sense). Obviously, there were decisive differences between politics at the beginning of the nineteenth century and at the end of the century, and between the first decades of the present century and the fourth and fifth decades. Nevertheless, a century which began with Jefferson's victory and ended with Bryan's defeat, and saw in the intervening years Jacksonianism, the rise of the Republican Party, and the Greenback movement, can be handled—for our specific social-psychological purposes—as a unit. Similarly, our own century, since the first World War, shows certain common characteristics which can be very roughly contrasted with those of the nineteenth century.[2]

[2] A division of labor and of temperament exists between historians and social psychologists. The former, concerned with the past, tend to be wary of generalizations—a Spengler or Toynbee only proves the rule—and their knowledge furnishes them with event-ammunition to knock down generalizations made by others. The social psychologists are concerned with making generalizations; they often use "ideal types"; but increasingly in America they stick to the present time, or the short-run, and thus avoid what might be fruitful collisions with historians.

POLITICS IN THE EARLIER ERA. In our ideal-typical nineteenth century, politics was a limited sphere, clearly labeled, and distinct from religion, economics, sex, and other compartments. To be sure, the existence of politics in these nonpolitical spheres was recognized, and deplored, both when politics encroached from the side of the state and when it arose in the interpersonal and hierarchical relations of club, office, and home. Similarly, the intrusion of motives from the spheres of religion and economics into the realm of politics aroused violent protest. In general, the conventionally defined political problems, on local and national levels, were felt to be manageable by their customary devotees: a few professionals (the bosses) and full-time and part-time amateurs (statesmen and good-government people). In the latter part of the century particularly, some members of the instructed classes made a great effort to bring the masses out of what Marxists called their "age-old slumber," and thus apathy, as epithet and problem, became a middle-class concern. (Of course, for some middle-class people mass apathy remained an advantage, and the ward heelers who got out the ethnic vote were resented.) In general, however, the middle classes were optimistic in their belief that apathy (along with other social evils) would in good time be eliminated, as the franchise—the symbol of political involvement—was liberalized, as free education spread, and as ethnic assimilation proceeded.

People in the nineteenth century had little doubt as to the meaning of their political activity: like work, its value seemed self-evident, though, unlike work, it was an intermittent rather than an everyday concern; this state of affairs was not altered by the fact that political activity, for much of the period, was looked down upon as dirty or degrading work. Political viewpoints were relatively easily defined by one's class position and regional location; and so many local political tasks needed doing and were obvious that each active person could find satisfying political employment. This employment was satisfying because problems were indeed finally overcome by the reformer's zeal:

Since we ourselves believe that social science proceeds by generalization, and particularly by historical reconstructions and comparisons, we want this professional division of labor re-examined, on both sides. Thus, while our own further work since this article was written (in the winter of 1948-49) leads us to doubt the sharpness of some of the polarities set forth below, we feel it nevertheless makes sense to try, from our side as social psychologists, to deal with certain contemporary problems in their historical setting.

the franchise was extended, free education spread, conditions in the
prisons and asylums slightly cleaned up, factory legislation introduced, and so on. Perhaps it was only because these were, at least
when taken singly, relatively limited goals that reformers were so successful; the reformers operated within the changing climate of that
"capitalist civilization" which Professor Joseph Schumpeter has brilliantly described in *Capitalism, Socialism and Democracy*. In any
case, however, there was little, in England and America, to parallel
the enormous frustrations of the twentieth century. Moreover, the
mass media—that is, the press—were frankly partisan, fortifying the
reader, rather simply and in clear-cut fashion, in his political task and
role. Cynicism about the whole sphere of politics—as against cynicism about democracy, or monarchy, or some specific political form
or abuse—was scarcely known. Finally, though the ideology of political
participation was individualistic, with great emphasis on self-interest,
conscience, and personal responsibility, the *function* was largely social:
politics, like charity, served for its amateurs neither for insight nor
for the displacement of emotional energy but rather served to insti-
tutionalize social obligations and social satisfactions in carrying them
out, relating the individual to his community in occasional cere-
monies and action. (Today, we will suggest, the ideology of political
participation has become social, while the function has become
individual.)

In this period, of course, there were large groups of people who
continued to think of politics as someone else's job—the job of "my
husband"; the "wise, the good, and the rich" of Fisher Ames; the
"best people"; the English-speaking (including Irish) groups; the
white man (in the South); and so on. But, as we have said, it was
widely believed that the excluded groups were either adequately politicized by proxy (as in the case of women) or would in their own names
soon enter the political scene as responsible citizens. Consequently,
the excluded groups were not invaded by feelings of helplessness
toward politics, especially as politics was of little practical importance
in day-to-day living.

How do the many irrational political movements of the nineteenth
century fit into such a picture? There were the recurrent antiforeign
crusades and the fear of the mysterious secret orders, Catholic,
Masonic, even Phi Beta Kappa. These fears of, and fascination by,
the secret society are indeed an age-old theme in the West, and

beyond that in many other cultures, as Simmel has shown. Nevertheless, it is perplexing to think of the supposedly hard-headed state of Vermont being carried by the anti-Masonic ticket, or of John Quincy Adams fearing the Masons as today some people fear the "Jewish conspiracy" or the (domestic) Communists. Even allowing for opportunistic exploitation of the fears, they do seem indicative of a good deal of anxiety and distrust of people, and bewilderment about the social order. Likewise, the attack on the Bank of the United States had much of the magical quality of later money-crankery or of present-day exaggerations of the power of Wall Street or international bankers; the Bank became the symbol of a vague threat, with its technical role largely misunderstood. Some of these movements represented the fear of the (largely rural) population for the city slicker—or the wily European—a perennial theme in American fiction and politics. And of course, the slavery issue gave rise to exaggerated and reckless hopes and fears, both in the South and the North, until eventually fanatics could prevent any compromise solution. Thus, it appears that while the average citizen a hundred years ago grasped the local political scene (township, county, state) with little irrationality or displacement of affects, he frequently lashed out on national and international questions with disproportionate fear and hate.

It is, however, difficult to judge how much weight to give to these irrational nineteenth-century movements, as against the evidence of sober, limited, and responsible relationships to politics. There is always the danger of comparing a more or less realistic picture of the present with a nostalgic picture of a selectively-perceived past. Indeed, as we turn now to our ideal type of twentieth-century politics, we are aware of the difficulty in making comparisons inherent in the fact that we have less data available on the politically inarticulate in the nineteenth century than modern social science has provided for the twentieth century. For instance, we know very little about the readership of the highly politicized press of, say, the 1830's; perhaps the press reflected the preoccupations of the editors rather than the readers, and in any case we do not know what the latter made of what they read. Even today, in our opinion, the mass media give a false picture of political involvement by putting political news on the front page and—"every hour on the hour"—on the radio; while we can now perhaps correct this bias by intensive studies of listeners and readers, it is almost impossible to make such studies of the past.

POLITICS IN THE PRESENT ERA. Today, as we have indicated, politics refuses to fit into its nineteenth-century compartment; with the mass media behind it, it invades the citizen with its clamors and claims—it is no longer a take-it-or-leave-it affair. The invasion destroys the older, easy transition from local to national interests and plunges the individual directly into the complexities of world politics. At the same time, politics becomes more difficult to understand in a purely technical sense—partly because it invades previously independent spheres like economics, partly because of the growing scope and interdependence of political decisions. For instance, people must understand that higher taxes are necessary, not to meet government expenditures or even to redistribute wealth, but because the people must be kept from spending too much and adding to inflation.

Moreover, we suggest as a possible factor adding to the incomprehensibility of politics a drop in the general level of skills relevant to understanding what goes on in politics. While formal education has increased, the education provided by the effort to run a farm, an independent business, a shop, has decreased along with the relative decline in the importance of the lone entrepreneur, and a large proportion of the factors leading to success or failure are no longer in the hands of those remaining as entrepreneurs. No longer can one judge the work and competence of the politician or government administrator from the confident, often even overconfident, baseline of one's own work and competence. For one thing, work in the production-sphere is today simply less interesting for people than their leisure in the consumption sphere; the lowering of standards of competence applicable to the work of others reflects boredom with work as such. As Leo Lowenthal has pointed out in his article "Biographies in Popular Magazines" (in Lazarsfeld & Stanton, eds., *Radio Research 1942-43*, 1944, p. 507), the mass media reflect this shift in focus by reporting what the public figure has for breakfast or what night club he frequents, but in giving no picture of his day-to-day task. Indeed, this may be seen as part of a general drop in the level of connoisseurship of performance, as distinguished from mere consumption. Just as the nineteenth-century patron of theatre, vaudeville, or trotting races may have been a better and more active judge of the art than the modern patron of radio, movies, or races—where the talk is often horse-dope and not horses—so the cracker-barrel observers of Blaine

The Thrill That Comes Once in a Lifetime: BY H. T. WEBSTER

and McKinley may well have been closer and more competent judges of what actually happens in politics than their modern counterparts, spouting Winchell or, on a higher social level, Kiplinger or *Periscope*.

To be sure, one can still find plenty of businessmen who think themselves competent to judge any governmental job and who believe that they owe their own positions to their industry, ability, and flair. Such types are echoed, in the upper and upper-middle classes, by people who think their opinions about politics are based on their ability to discriminate and judge. But such people tend to deceive themselves—e.g., by the formula that what government needs is more businessmen-administrators—and their illusion that they are judging the actual job-performance of the politician is easily penetrated. The nineteenth-century businessman, who put a ward boss on his payroll, had a pretty good idea of where the money went, or at least had no doubt he could find out if he cared to. Likewise, Mark Hanna and some of those who backed him had a pretty clear idea of what would advance the interests of the business class. Today, however, the businessman who hires lawyers, fixers, and market researchers to deal with the government feels much more helpless in the hands of the specialists, and is less clear on where his interests lie.

Yet this very development, as we shall see, has an ambiguous bearing on competence. The businessman's increasing willingness to call in experts, and his growing doubt as to where his own interests lie—his loss (though often concealed in rhetoric) of the older cockiness and moral unequivocalness—are in a way recognitions of the need for greater and more specialized competence in politics, and therefore bespeak a growth of a certain kind of business competence. Moreover, the conditions of modern urban life produce many people who are forced into political awareness and out of political innocence by their jobs. A barkeep, handling cops, union business agents, and licensing authorities; an oil company economist, steeped in Middle-East politics; an atomic physicist negotiating a Navy research contract—the "knowingness" of such people must be weighed against the loss of competence of the older type of entrepreneur. Likewise, the millions who play "policy"—how ironic the name is!—or otherwise engage in illicit activity probably gain some political sophistication at what administrators call "the local level."

Perhaps we can sum up these contradictory tendencies by saying that people have, under the conditions of modern urban life, become somewhat more astute consumers of political news, while losing competence as producers of political events. But that involves the problem of deciding what events are to be compared in the two eras. What matters most is that we deal here with political competence and comprehensibility not only as abstract, intellectual matters, but also with the feelings of personal impotence which are in part the result of incompetence and incomprehensibility, in part its cause. Frequently, impotence rationalizes itself on the false ground of incomprehensibility. It is an open question whether, as Kris and Leites[3] maintain, people withdraw affects from a political scene which has become ungraspable and unmanageable, or whether it feels unmanageable because affects are withdrawn. In either case, the course of events, not understood, cannot be conceived of as under human control, despite its vastly greater importance for the individual's livelihood, well-being, and happiness.

On the face of it, this outlook resembles that of nineteenth-century political observers who insisted that man was limited in what he could do to effect far-reaching social changes, both by his own nature and by the organic nature of society, which followed its own laws of development. Edmund Burke and other conservative critics of the French Revolution at the beginning of the century, and the Social Darwinists at its end, represent two strands in this general line of thought. We believe, however, that these feelings of limitation were not accompanied by subjective feelings of impotence on the part of these thinkers or their audience, and that, at least in the case of the Social Darwinists and perhaps also in the case of Burke, a positively optimistic view was taken toward the course of society's organic development. If the world took care of itself—if reformers would only let it alone—one would not need to feel frustrated and helpless: one merely had to acknowledge this limitation, and devote oneself to less than apocalyptic changes. On the other hand, contemporary forms of social determinism tend to assume our civilization is running down, a view we find in the nineteenth century only in a few observers like Brooks Adams, who could hardly believe their own prophesies. Even the pessimists of the nineteenth century did not envisage how terrible politics actually became in the twentieth century. In fact, the Nazi and Soviet intellectuals could hardly imagine the mechanical brutali-

[3] Ernst Kris and Nathan Leites, "Trends in Twentieth Century Propaganda," in *Psychoanalysis and the Social Sciences*, G. Roheim, ed. (1947), pp. 400 et seq.

ties of totalitarianism in power; that is, their most vicious conceptions, prior to the seizure of power, could not keep pace with the later achievements of the SS or NKVD. Conversely, contemporary thinkers find it hard to construct imaginary good societies, or utopias, such as were bountifully conceived and experimented with in the nineteenth century.

Among people in the lower social strata, the belief persists today that the political world is a manageable one—but not by them: the "insiders," the "sixty families," or just plain "they" are in easy control of events. The feeling of impotence for these lower strata is based less on their own incompetence than on a fear of overcompetence on the side of the higher strata. This is a type of barbershop cynicism and "sophistication" which frequently turns up in replies to public opinion polls: "what do 'they' want to know for; they run their own show anyway." This impotence among the masses, however, is not matched by feelings of potency in the supposedly ruling groups: as the former feel mastered by vague personages, the latter feel mastered by vague events. Indeed, paradoxically enough, the leaders frequently rationalize inaction in a crisis on the ground that "public opinion" would not stand for any of the necessarily drastic alternatives—but the "public," whose opinion is allegedly deferred to, gains neither strength nor competence from this. Perhaps the very notion of a ruling class becomes ambiguous in such circumstances, when destiny is no longer manifest for leaders or led, and when leaders take refuge behind public opinion for their own inability to act. The full impact of this phenomenon has been delayed by the ability in crisis situations to call on still-extant specimens of nineteenth-century types (or those who can pose as such), personalities who create a feeling, frequently self-confirming, that they can control events. The important roles played by men like Henry Stimson, Grenville Clark, and Generals Marshall and Clay during and after the war suggest the hold of such types, and how much can be done by a few "key people" who, unlike most today, know what they want.

On the other side of the reckoning, and in contrast to all this, we can list certain more hopeful elements in modern approaches to politics. Does not the feeling of impotence itself testify to a more realistic awareness of the actual complexity of political decisions and developments, as compared to prevalent oversimplifications in the nineteenth century? Have we not built up a corps of specialists on different as-

pects of politics who know much more—though still not enough—
than the often narrowly partisan critics and lobbyists of the nineteenth
century? Are there not many people, and not only specialists, who
have become accustomed to thinking in world-political terms, and
cross-cultural terms, such as were hardly to be found amid the ethnocentrism of even a generation ago? Is there not a growth of the
"independent vote," both in municipal and national politics, no
longer to be bought either by a dollar or by "Pitchfork Ben" Tillman's brand of hokum? And can we not point to the growing use
of what are essentially political skills in certain areas outside of formal
political science—strikingly so in the field of labor-management relations? Can we not say that the responsible attitude toward politics
of many nineteenth-century figures was achieved at the cost of a narrow definition of politics? Several of these points require some
comment.

Undeniably, there has been a growth in a certain kind of realism
in recent decades. The mass media no longer discuss international
politics in terms of "national honor"[4] but in terms of strategic, including propaganda, considerations. The public is often asked to
support a policy because such support, in a kind of self-manipulative
balancing act, will influence public opinion; such arguments can only
be made because of the heightened popular understanding of psychological forces in politics. Thus, while affairs have become more complicated, there are many whose awareness of causes and interrelationships has kept pace with or even bettered the actual increase in
complexity. The results are two-fold. On the one hand, our awareness of complexity supports our feelings of impotence. On the other
hand, it leads to increasing reliance on experts. If we give up in
despair before the complexities of full employment or international
trade, we nevertheless have the faith that somewhere someone under-
stands this. On the whole, this faith is probably exaggerated—because
even if the matters are "understood" by technical experts in one
sense, too many factors outside their sphere of expertness prevent
them from being able really to put their competence into effect.

[4] Professor Finer suggests that current talk about "our way of life" is remi-
niscent of discussions of "national honor." But we think that the change is not
merely one in phrasing, but in breadth of content. Moreover, moral considerations tend today to be concealed under expediential and hedonistic ones: this
is a contemporary form of hypocrisy, as "national honor" calls to mind a Victorian
form.

To some extent, then, impotence before the growing complexity of social development is matched by certain realistic elements: by the very point of view which sees things as difficult to change, by dependence on experts, by an actual growth in competence among certain of the experts (who often manage to keep abreast of the changing course of events at the expense of time to think about them).

This growth of realism should be thought of in terms of a long historical perspective, in which a dialectic relationship between men's reason and their helplessness may be traced. At times, men have felt strong and secure because their ignorance of their society's workings was irrelevant to a stable social structure. Today, men tend to feel helpless because they know too much to be comfortable and too little to be of help. In the future, this balance may again change and understanding become a method of controlling the social environment; even in our time, a few exceptional people who enjoy thinking about politics—today's "dismal science"—anticipate this possible development. For many, perhaps most, people, however, what is called "realism" is merely a conventionally cynical and sophisticated but unperspectivistic way of viewing events—a rationalization for their surrender of intelligence in the field of politics.

The growth of the labor movement, and of the skill of certain elements in the working class in pursuing special interests, also raises the question whether we do not have a rise in political competence and potency outside of the traditional spheres of politics. This is unquestionably true: and one might point to other areas in which developments that were once left to fate and chance now become spheres for the exercise of intelligence and foresight: modern city planning may be mentioned as an example. Nevertheless, it is also necessary to point out that this growth of competence and the accompanying feelings of potency in certain limited spheres can go on while the context in which these developments occur deteriorates. Indeed, many people have observed how the virtues called "citizenship" may actually go into abeyance when people, on a number of segmental fronts, have handed over their detailed political affairs to specialists. Adam Smith was much concerned about this consequence of a division of labor from which, on its economic side, he hoped for national opulence and strength. His remedy—formal education—is still a favorite panacea.

Yet it sometimes appears that political good sense and courage survive more easily among urban working classes of little formal education. The Spanish workers, for instance, were more willing to fight against reaction than the German; the Germans placed more reliance in their trade-union and Social-Democratic "apparatus." But of course such national differences rest upon long historical developments—developments which, in the advanced industrial countries, have generated apathy by increasingly subjecting the workers to mobilities, decisions, and crises outside their own communal control.

Obviously the degree to which people feel impotent will depend on their class position, as well as their other group affiliations. We have described elsewhere the way in which political opinions become more and more detached from reality and from the self as one moves down the class ladder from the upper, through the middle, to the lower-middle class.[5] Moreover, many citizens, especially of the upper social strata as well as those in rural areas and small towns, try to escape being overwhelmed by the anxiety which flows from impotence by viewing politics as if they still lived in the nineteenth century, as if their political role, whether in direct action or in reaction to others' actions, was perfectly clear and unambiguous. But a much larger proportion of citizens attend to the political "news" only as spectators who watch the play, or watch others watching it, often repressing awareness that they are involved, perhaps fatally, with the doings on-stage.

Now of course, many Americans today might ask, why are the doings on-stage so dangerous or serious for us? Don't we have full employment or nearly so? Are we not entitled to sit back as long as things are going to our liking, since we will bestir ourselves when need arises? There is much force in these questions, especially as Americans often seem to get themselves better government than they "deserve" in terms of their respect for it, their interest in it, and their willingness to participate actively. Nevertheless, there would seem to be a good deal of evidence to back our own impression that Americans are not merely an amused audience for politics—an audience which feels it has the power to put on plays itself if it wanted to bother—but are exceedingly anxious about the political future. The last elec-

5 "The Meaning of Opinion," *Public Opinion Quarterly*, Vol. 12, Winter, 1948-1949, p. 633.

tion was for many, as poll data show, an unhappy choice between Truman, who was liked and trusted as a person but felt to be incompetent, and Dewey, who was disliked and feared for his "city-slicker" show of competence—a competence which, unlike Roosevelt's, was not mediated by an aristocratic air. While Truman's victory gave many people a feeling of potency, this was only a temporary surcease of the basic anxiety. That anxiety is testified to by many movies, by the many articles and stories that counsel troubled people on how to live, and by other evidence from popular culture; many foreign visitors have commented that Americans, with the atom bomb, are more frightened than the countries which lack it.

To sum up: there was a casual, hopeful quality both about participation and nonparticipation in nineteenth-century politics. Politics presented the citizen with a clear image, a clear call, and a clear task; and if he refused the call, or waited until his "betters" should address it to him, he still could understand the image and the task.[6] Though politics was an arena in which one might seek power, channels toward power were diffuse and motives for getting power were diluted. Today, on the other hand, both participation and nonparticipation in politics have become laden with new meanings in addition to the nineteenth-century ones which persist. Due to growing feelings of impotence, nonparticipation is no longer casual and hopeful. The spectators cannot relate themselves to what goes on because they have lost their own standards of performance, and have become dependent on experts not only for performance itself but for judging performance. The experts, in their specialization, learn to grapple successfully with various microspheres—and undoubtedly microspheric competence is increasing as political problems are recognized to exist in various types of planning and negotiation; but the experts themselves feel helpless in the macrosphere, and only the more disabused folk in the lower strata nourish the myth that there is an "inner circle" which knows how to manage them and to manage events.

APOLITICAL APPROACHES TO POLITICS.   On the whole, the situation we have described is now widely recognized. But it may be that the extent of the flight from politics is underestimated if we look only to

---

[6] Henry Adams found himself and some of his friends to be political unemployables in the post-Civil War period; there was no clear call or task for them. Of course, their focus was on the larger issues of national politics, though locally, too, they felt displaced by the Irish and by boss rule generally.

such indices as voting and opinion-holding on political questions, as measured by polls, as clues to political interest and participation today. For the indices reflect political action that may, in a greater measure than before, be apolitical. The influence of the nineteenth century is still strong, and many people, carrying on with an ideology of responsibility, continue to act as if politics were a meaningful sphere to them. We think such types decline in number and grow less effective. Partly owing to this ideological background, politics remains an area of group-conformity in certain circles; the college student or the successful businessman may "take up" politics as he takes up golf or any other acceptable hobby: it is good fun, good business, and a way to meet interesting people.

Moreover, paradoxically, the very fact that politics has become frightening makes it usable as a "phobic sector" for the needs of individual psycho-pathology: one may live one's life in fear of the fascists, the Jews, the Communists or the Negro vote, as one may live in fear of elevators or of microbes. All these approaches to politics are essentially *apolitical*—politics is not used for politics' sake, for the manifest ends politics is intended to serve. Now of course in all ages and among all people motives are mixed, and all institutions become diverted to other purposes than the formal ones they were designed to deal with. Moreover, people who enter politics for, let us say, hobby reasons may learn something and stay for quite other reasons. But throughout we speak of changes in matters of degree, and we think that much of what passes today for political concern is really an apolitical "agenda" of some sort—a way of filling up one's life; it is apathy in disguise.

However, if one is interested only in political behavior, one may ask whether this matters—whether motives matter at all so long as the institutional forces support political activity at its prevailing level? Motives do not matter if one's focus is the immediate future and if one assumes that, in general, things will go on as before. Moreover, many "apolitical" motives for engaging in political activity—such as the desire for conformity, or for a hobby—may be socially quite valuable; certainly not all such motives are "phobic." But the fact that political interest is sustained by so many forces whose linkage with politics is indirect or accidental implies that the present behavior of people is quite misleading as to their actual feelings about politics, and hence about their possible behavior in an altered future situation.

One can predict possible behavior in foreseeable contingencies only if one tries to understand the more permanent orientations of people toward politics. Well-worn political channels still carry affects, that is, emotional energies, which are labeled as political but which, if our guesses are right, increasingly spring from apolitical sources. Thus, the *mariage de convenance* between traditional politics and irrational psychological pressures may be quite unstable.

POLITICS: NEW MEANINGS FOR OLD. In the nineteenth century, two grounds were urged to justify popular participation in politics: self-interest and duty. Self-interest could be defined in narrowly individualistic terms or, more broadly, in class terms; it could be expanded to include the interests of the nation and even, at its ultimate extreme, the interests of all the peoples of the world. Whatever the ideology employed, duty and self-interest were largely seen as coincident. The present-day attack on apathy by organized labor and by some middle-class elements likewise assumes that duty and self-interest, still largely seen as coincident, are the legitimate bases for concern with politics. People should participate because they have at stake some definable interest or because they must look out for their weaker fellow's interest. Thus, both in the nineteenth century and today, the offensive against apathy rests on the assumption that participation in politics will be effective, that it will lead to improvement.

When, however, the incomprehensibility of politics makes self-interest obscure and when feelings of impotence make self-interest pointless even when clear, *we must ask whether self-interest alone, in its traditional senses, is enough to arouse people to concern or to action.* We think not. The operations people are called upon to engage in for their self-interest—getting out the vote, defending civil liberties, supporting the U.N., and so on—become more and more unrelated to directly realizable personal or even group goals, and seem less and less effective in reshaping the environment. As the spur of self-interest lags, the spur of duty is pushed—usually against that minority of already busy stalwarts who do most of the unpaid organizational work of the country. But this, too, is unavailing as these devoted few grow fatigued. We think that apolitical approaches to politics are in part the outcome of the failure of the older, "rational" stimuli; motives such as vanity, conformity, the desire for power, the need for projecting guilt, masochism and sadism—these now tend to replace the more traditional forms of self-interest on the part of the "political man."

Another way of looking at this same development is to see that the things people do that have a political meaning in the traditional sense —party activity, voting, following the political news—seem increasingly unrelated to their experience. Other things people do that seem to them more evidently related to their experience—joining a union and getting more pay, working with a PTA group to change certain school practices, combatting race tensions in a neighborhood—lose or conceal their political meaning; the people who do these things usually do not think of themselves as political. To be sure, a degree of divorce between the formal-political and the informal-political has always existed. But today the attempt to bridge the gap, and to inject meaning into the more traditional and formal political arena, seems increasingly to call on apolitical motivations.

Our own view is that new, legitimate motives can be called into play to support people's concern with politics. And we mean here the traditional types of politics as well as the newer types. But before we turn to discussion of our suggested new range of political self-interest, we must say something about the very large number of people for whom self-interest in politics can still have its nineteenth-century significance.

For one thing, there are of course increasing numbers of people who have to attend to politics because they are in it for a living, though indeed with the growth of civil service and such measures as the Hatch Act many of these become partially sterilized politically; politics for them is often a form of office gossip. Others who are in business for a living may be concerned with politics because of its effects on their business: if they have an "in" with one faction, they must fight to keep the other faction out. With the growing power of the government over economic life, this need has increased, and it no longer has the old, simple pork-barrel pattern. But as this operation becomes less crude and more specialized, businessmen, as we noted earlier, hire others to attend to politics for them, and these others have an interest in scaring businessmen and making them feel impotent. A much larger number of those who are concerned with politics are members of small or localized minorities who, because of their marginal position, may become the sport of contests between Republicans and Democrats. Thus, various groups of Jews and Negroes have been forced into contemporary American politics in self-defense, in turn forcing Dixiecrats in; other ethnic groups, too, may enter politics because of a locally or internationally precarious situation. Organized labor's participation in politics today has much of this character; as it becomes more entrenched and its leadership less vulnerable, it may well have less and less need to call on the rank and file for more than routine political action. (Of course, internal struggles within the unions remain, but in the older unions these, too, are a monopoly of a few.) On the other hand, independent farmers, concerned with crop loans, parity prices, and soil conservation work, are perhaps more active than ever.

The groups we have named add up to a sizable number; nevertheless, large numbers of people whose self-interest is less specific and direct—who want, let us say, peace, or whose wants are inarticulate—can be only very slightly affected by the victory of one or another of the major parties, or of the major political alternatives represented by the parties. Though people are of course crucially affected by war and peace, prosperity and depression—and, beyond that, by the styles of livelihood and living which go with preparation for each—they have almost no way of registering their concerns in these matters by way of the selection of meaningful alternatives.

For imagination in both the domestic and foreign policy spheres is crippled and the range of choices offered does not promise appreciably to add to the quality and security of life. Under such circumstances, people seem justified in not responding with emotional involvement to lesser issues which, however they are resolved, have little chance of making a real difference in their lives. Since the à la carte is unappetizing, they might as well eat table d'hôte.

It is sometimes assumed that with a different bill of fare people would become involved. But the experience of those countries with half-a-dozen or more political parties would seem to suggest that the difficulty does not lie solely in the variety of choice. The intractability of current democratic machinery and its way of presenting issues is one element in the problem, and public opinion polls on political issues may occasionally suggest methods of opening up a greater number of alternatives, permitting the recombination of expressed wants into a pattern closer to popular desire. The study of existing poll data, however, is not encouraging on this score: as we read the results, they show what socialists have called "the damned wantlessness of the poor" but beyond that, the wantlessness of the rich. The answer of the nineteenth-century radical was a simple one: only when we have a revolutionary crisis will we see the masses, no matter how ignorant or quiescent at the moment, rising to political competence and activity. So the radical asks people to be politically involved today that they may fill their role tomorrow. That is, the norm of political activity is given by the great revolutions of the past. We ourselves suspect that the concept of such an ultimate revolutionary crisis is still another leftover from the nineteenth century. It fails to take account of intervening changes in the meaning politics has for people. In any case, chiliastic hopes for a revolutionary situation, as a time when the politically dead shall rise, no longer supply any large number of people, outside of aging political splinter groups, with convincing reasons for political involvement.

In speaking thus, we are talking of America, though our remarks would also apply to much of Western Europe. For sections of the world in the early stages of industrialization, nineteenth-century concepts of politics (including revolutionary Marxism) are still appealing and relatively adequate. Likewise, nineteenth-century "good government" concepts still make sense for many local issues in America. However, national politics in America presents problems which have, it appears, outdistanced many fighting faiths and fighting formulae, often without a real confrontation of the older problems which gave rise to those faiths. For example, most American observers have concluded long since that nationalization of basic industry—still an issue in Europe—would solve neither our economic nor our political problems. This is partly because our techniques of social and economic manipulation have reached a degree of (at least potential) refinement which makes devices such as nationalization appear crude and even obsolete. Moreover, American intellectuals are in a position to see this partly because, unlike the British, they have very little influence to bring about such a change as nationalization; hence their concerns can run ahead of immediate action programs. Nevertheless, the more mature American political thinkers have hoped until recently that some European answer—Soviet Communism, Fabianism, Sweden's "Middle

Way," or whatnot—could be found applicable here, if only it could get a following. When they realize that even the attainment of many of the generous goals of European left-politics—social security, control of business, wealth redistribution, etc.—has not solved the problems of power and participation in America, these leaders of thought tend to withdraw, in despair and disgust, from politics. Hence, from the analysis of the actual programs proposed and their conceivable effects, it would appear that a program of political involvement for the United States which rests on the nineteenth-century experience with industrialism and the nineteenth-century faiths is doomed to disillusion its followers.

Thus, we conclude that self-interest, in its variety of traditional meanings, will not suffice to justify, from the standpoint of the individual, his concern with politics today. Is it, however, possible to see any new meanings which politics might have for people in America who do not have the kind of immediate stake in immediate political results that special groups have? At a time when current political demands seem to have less and less relation to fundamental changes in the quality of life, can we suggest convincing reasons why the now apathetic millions should become involved in politics? We have no "final" answer to this question, and certainly none that will hold for everybody. But we do suggest, as a possible partial replacement for nineteenth-century concepts and motivations, the notion that politics might again become, as it perhaps was for some of the Greeks and some eighteenth-century thinkers, one main clue to the meaning of human life, perhaps an "impractical" concern from the point of view of society and immediate action-programs, but an almost indispensable aspect of one's personal orientation in the world. As a mariner locates himself by knowledge of astronomy and the weather, so modern man might locate himself in the ramifying social world by grasping its political relations. By doing so, he could escape the confusions of ethnocentrism, and the dangers of depending on others for irrational guidance; he could secure a breathing space amid oppressive ideologies and anxious life-conditions. This "space" is small enough, and moreover it is filled with dangers, but as real dangers rather than ideological shadows, they can be handled, if not directly, then by a realistic psychological orientation. But the advantages of political understanding are not only these rather negative ones: like most of life's necessities, such as working for a living, the need for political orientation, when not too desperate, has a positive side: it aids the fuller realization of one's potentialities and, by curiosity and concern, relates one to his social surroundings. One can see politics, not only as a chore, but as an arena for the exercise of enjoyable skills of human understanding, companionship, and management; to be sure, elements of chore remain, as in any kind of work. Thus, political involvement, even where it does not immediately affect social behavior or succeed in controlling the social environment, may be a source of individual satisfaction on many different levels of experience.

The notion of continual change and progress has tended to become the principal means by which people, unwilling to commit their interests and their energies to relatively intractable situations, justify present-day involvement in politics. They do not dare face the possibility that the social environment is not going to be changed for the better very soon—that no leverage may be found to avoid, for example, war and rumors of war—that life will continue to be lived in a condition of crisis. Desperately, many people either persuade themselves that the political situation is more malleable than it is; or they withdraw from the frustrating "field," ignoring the minor but still worthwhile areas which are under their control. (Indeed, this is one mistake that the conservatives in the tradition of Burke or of Social Darwinism were less likely to make than progressives, since they started with minimal hopes anyway.) We think that the demand that political concern must produce visible and quick improvements limits the values such concern may serve. We think, moreover, that one may see the environment as relatively unchangeable by conscious human effort for the moment and perhaps for a long time to come—or, conceivably, as developing according to some immanent principle which we do not yet grasp—and still maintain that this presently uncontrollable or immanently developing social environment be a human concern. We must learn to relate ourselves to politics on two levels which may never meet: the level of "what might be done" and the level of "what is going on."

Indeed, is it not true that all life which is aware of itself can be lived on these two levels—one level on which we try to see and understand and imagine the world, without regard to the limits and necessities of an immediate here and now; and another level on which we must start from the given of our history and culture and work within it?[7] It is possible that the contradiction between these two levels strikes many people as greater today than ever before in history: for we live in the backwash of a vain effort to deny the two levels, and to insist that what we desire we can have, and what we cannot have we

[7] This two-level approach to politics and life is, of course, an oversimplified paradigm. It may clarify our outlook to restate it briefly here, in terms of a three-fold division of the timing and meaning of human activity generally. One part of life is lived on a moment-to-moment basis, close to sensuous detail, "private" or in the primary group. A second part of life is lived in terms of culturally-given time-spans—an hour, a workday, a workmonth, a social evening, a movie's hundred minutes, etc. The meaning of this part of life is largely provided by the culture in which the individual is caught up and wants to be caught up in: the individual acts as a participant in work or games or causes; he has little control over the rhythms, but is saved the task of furnishing his own. A third part of life is lived in terms of highly individuated time-spans: a lifetime, a career, a sojourn, a marriage, and beyond these, the lives of friends, children, pupils, countrymen. It is at this third stage that the individual transcends both his day-to-day life— eating, making love, going up and down stairs, bathing—and his culturally-taken-up life; here he sees his whole existence in the perspective of his personal time and the time of eternity.

Obviously, in any concrete person, these three spheres merge and overlap, and those are fortunate who are able to infuse their culturally-patterned tasks with daily and spontaneously enjoyable details, while seeing both in terms of a life-plan in which all spheres have their assigned roles. For many, perhaps most, people, however, the second sphere, that of the culturally-provided structures and motivations, usually succeeds in crowding out the spontaneous and idiosyncratic enjoyment of the first sphere—which is often felt as sheer "waste" or is made tolerable by being perceived as culturally-valued "experience"—and succeeds also in extinguishing the human recognition of the partial incommensurability between one's own life as a whole and the "life" of one's group or culture. In other words, such people put as much of their lives as they can into the culture's machinery, both for work and for play, and feel those parts of their lives which cannot be fitted into the culturally-given rhythms and perceptions as "not-life." A contrasting attitude would be that of many artists who regard as a total waste that part of life which consists of meeting inescapable social and political obligations. They see no way either to "spiritualize" these with trans-cending meanings or to "materialize" them with pleasant sensuous and human detail (the words in quotation marks are most awkward approximations of our meaning). Finally, there may be people—e.g., saints—who live as near as may be in the third sphere, aloof both from the primary group and its diurnal, ever-new and ever-old routines and from the tasks, recreations, and meanings which the culture provides to get its work done and to get most people through the day without their having to be saints. (This description has profited from reading The Multiformity of Man, by Eugen Rosenstock-Huessy, Norwich, Vt., 1948.)

We hope the reader can see the connection between our third, transcending sphere and the utopian-imaginative level of relatedness to politics, and between our second, culturally bound sphere and the level of lesser-evil "practical" politics.

must never desire: we refer, of course, to "scientific" Marxism and its Leninist heirs which, in its attack on utopian Socialism on the one hand, and on reformist Socialism on the other, denied that one had to or should divorce ultimate from immediate possibilities.

Rather than trying, then, as Marxism and other ideologies do, to bridge or deny the contradiction, we believe that political involvement today can be and needs to be attained by living, more or less simultaneously, on both levels: using our imaginative energies and our increasing knowledge of man to fashion better utopias, while not detaching ourselves from the lesser-evil choices and struggles of the immediate political milieu in which our bodies must live, suffer, and die. The great representatives of the tradition of utopian thinking, from Plato or More to William Morris and Bellamy, have plunged into at least occasional commitment in contemporary battles—without this, utopianism is in danger of becoming cold and unresourceful. (Of course, utopian thinkers have not always been clear that they were operating on two levels; one at the farthest reach of their thought, the other at the farthest reach of their practice.) Likewise, uninterrupted "as if" participation in contemporary crusades leads to the fanaticism which cloaks despair.

Does this ask too much of people? Will people retain the energy and courage necessary for commitment in current political turmoils if, on another level, they become aware of the probable futility, in long-run terms, of what they are doing? If they become detached enough from their situation to see it in perspective, will they not become contemptuous and withdraw from working with their fellow men? For many ex-radicals, of course, this is just what is happening, but these people are precisely the victims of ideological efforts to deny the two levels of awareness: they have projected onto the objective world the shock of their disillusion on discovering the contradiction. Perhaps, however, a greater number of people in America—as compared with Western Europe—suffer from the opposite difficulty: their imaginations are so dwarfed that they lack even enough detachment to refrain from such self-defeating action as selling out long-run ends for petty tactical gains. In other words, the "wantlessness" of which we spoke earlier leads many Americans to refuse to make utopian critiques of their self-styled "practical" political behavior: the petty gains loom large because no larger ends are envisaged. We find, for instance, city planners who cling to such easily attainable and easily demonstrable goals as better sanitation, fire protection, traffic flow, etc., while refusing to consider what their physical arrangements may do or fail to do for the human relations of the rehoused or relocated, in terms of the subtle factors which make for or against the creation of a lively and participative neighborhood. Another example can be found in the history of the New Deal. The aims of this movement were, on the whole, relatively limited: except for the TVA and a few other ventures, complete success would have done little to develop a more satisfying and less anxious American culture. The New Dealers were, for the most part, able to avoid this realization because they took the opposition of "Wall Street" and "the interests" as proof that their own agenda really promised radical change. Then the War came along further to obscure the fact that they had nothing more to ask of these convenient enemies than the program which ended in 1937.

We might speak, then, of a "frantic detachment" from politics on the part of people who were once involved and who have fled on discovering the intractability of any large-scale society—the gap between the better world they can envisage and the dreadful one they are committed to. And on the other hand, we might speak of a "frantic attachment" on the part of successful operators who, lacking what we call "the nerve of failure," constantly persuade themselves that their actions are meaningful, when in fact these actions may harm long-run goals if the operators dared spell these out.[8] Both frantic groups—the overdetached and the overattached—fear the loss of their respective certainties and hence seek to avoid the dilemmas of existence. Yet despite their example we think that living on two levels of relatedness to politics and facing its dilemmas is not as complex or difficult as it may sound: just such self-awareness is characteristic of some of the best traditions of Western—and even perhaps more widely human—thought and conduct. Only if we are psychologically

---

[8] See Riesman, "The Ethics of We Happy Few," *University Observer*, I (1947), 19. There is a *total* quality about these frantic attachments and detachments which makes us see them, under altered conditions, as possible sources of totalitarian politics, in which a symbiotic relationship may be formed between the groups who are totally politicized, with no saving grace of insight and detachment, and the groups who are totally unpoliticized, with no basis of judgment or experience of making lesser-evil, compromise choices.

crippled—apathetic—can we help responding to immediate situations which confront us, while, at the same time or another time, reflecting on what we are up to.

We may approach our conception of politics' contemporary role in another way by saying that, under the conditions of modern life, some degree of political involvement may become a "basic" human need, akin to the need for sex or for companionship, and one in which the question of "what for" will not be considered essential. For would not people be happier, would they not feel more vital and potent, if they recognized their political needs than if they ignored or displaced them? Conversely, are not political apathy and its concomitant feelings of political impotence sources of anxiety and frustration, no matter how narcotized under the conditions of modern life? In both cases, we think so; but our thinking is on a very tentative level. For one thing, it is not enough to give politics a psychic priority, to see it as a human need: there are many people who, choosing among their various needs on the basis of their temperament and gifts, can build a very satisfying life without the slightest attention to politics. Their gardens are enough, and their osmotic pressure against the news of the day, coupled with their intense activity in other fields, saves them from anxiety. Until conditions become far more desperate than they are—and perhaps especially if they should do so—it would seem ascetic, a kind of secularized Puritanism, to ask such people to be concerned with politics when it is evident that their lives are full and rich and adequately oriented without it. For no one can satisfy all his human needs, on all levels of living. And in these people there is choice to avoid politics, not flight from it.

The reader will observe that all the reasons we have suggested as to why people ought to take an interest in politics are seen from the point of view of the individual entirely; we have not suggested that he should be concerned with politics for any reason which transcends him. It will also be seen that our view of "self-interest" includes more than the self-defense or self-aggrandizement of the traditional nineteenth-century view; thus, we see it as a political interest of the self to live in a stimulating world of significant political happenings and horizons. This procedure differs from that of many who discuss apathy and whose focus, though they may speak in terms of self-interest, is on the needs of the society for a participating citizenry rather than on the needs of the individual. Sometimes, the existence of a possible contradiction between needs of individual and group is admitted, and political activity is put on the same basis as taxes and vaccination—a price one must pay for living in society; this, we think, is a tenable view. At other times an effort is made to deny the possible contradiction and to urge that the individual finds satisfaction in throwing himself into group political activity. A number of persons we have interviewed in connection with our study justify their own political concerns on just such a basis; they deny that they can be happy so long as political tasks which call them remain undone. As Marxism denies the contradiction between the two levels of what can be achieved and what can be imagined, so it serves, along with other ideologies, to deny the contradiction of interest between the individual and the group. Sometimes the fact that the individual has his being only in society—a genetic fact—is used to justify his surrender of claims at the behest of society—a moral *non sequitur*. Referring again to our interviews, we find that some of those respondents who cite only "altruistic" reasons for their interest in politics are actually rationalizing their use of politics as a phobic sector; they may, for instance, be fleeing from exigent problems of the self into the bottomless agenda which modern politics provides.

Again, we deal with two levels of existence. The road to political involvement today lies, we suggest, in awareness of the potential contradiction between one's own interest (and that of one's group, one's party, one's nation) and that of others, and in a search for those areas of joint advantage where sacrifice of the self or of the other is not necessarily in question. Yet we do not deny that extreme situations arise where the conflict cannot be solved short of martyrdom or murder; when this occurs, it is the most terrible tragedy, which no ideology can explain, conceal, or justify. For, though politics has often been called the art of the possible, there are times when it confronts man with impossible choices. Perhaps an increase in the proportion and intensity of these is one of the changes which distinguishes the modern era from the nineteenth century.

We propose, in what follows, to incorporate some of these notions on the changing meanings of modern politics, and of possible motivations for rational political interest, into our definitions of what is political apathy and its opposite, political involvement.

WHAT IS POLITICAL APATHY?

THE DEVELOPMENT OF INDICES FOR APATHY. While the preceding discussion is largely based on historical-philosophical reflections, we turn now to an account of our search for the proper criteria or indices for apathy and involvement to be used in analyzing our own interview material—some 150 long interviews—as well as data gathered by public opinion researchers largely for purposes other than the study of character and apathy. We can ask people today, as we cannot ask the dead, what politics means to them—though we do not have to take what they say at face value—and we can try to see, by careful analysis of their fully recorded responses, what role politics plays in their psychic economy at present, what role it plays in their group adjustment, and, within limits, what role it might play under changed social-psychological conditions.

Our investigation is only in its initial stage. We still do not fully grasp what apathy and involvement mean to people, let alone know how to detect these attitudes "operationally" in our interview material. Nevertheless, we feel that discussion of possible criteria may be advanced even by the report of inconclusive efforts.

Apathy in our usage refers to a fairly complex psychological orientation, closely related to historical developments both directly, through the impact of the changes we have touched on in the preceding section, and indirectly (by means of the character structures "created" or favored by a given historical setting). Faced with such complexity, the tendency in social science is to seek for a simple index or criterion which will stand for, or register, the complex phenomenon. Thus, industrial morale may be measured by absenteeism, anomie by suicide rates, the success of propaganda by bond purchases. The most apparent index for apathy is also some simple behavioral one such as voting, participation in certain political activities, attention to media transmitting political information, and so on. These behavioral indices are the first type of criterion for political apathy we will consider. As we shall see, the use of this type of index raises very sharply the danger of losing sight of the complexities of the problem to which the index points.

POLITICAL ACTIVITY AS AN INDEX OF APATHY. Four difficulties arise in equating apathy with inactivity, and in equating involvement with activity. The first is that an index based on activity does not help us to distinguish cases in which that activity is carried on for apolitical purposes. The second is the possible class bias of observation: stamping certain things the middle class does, or does more easily, as "activity." The third is the possible bias in favor of the more temperamentally energetic: the index will be an inadequate measure of varying social-psychological meanings if it is affected by physiologically-grounded factors. The fourth difficulty in using some form of activity as an index lies in the human meaninglessness of activity as such, apart from purpose: we could not infer purpose, which gives changing meaning to the activity, from the index alone.

   1. *Activity and apolitical uses.* While an apathy characterized by listlessness and lethargy may have its roots in neurosis, as in the case of a person whose energies are occupied with internal conflicts, individual and social neurosis might also lead to frantic political activity, as an escape from the self—an activity which we would also tend to label as "apathetic" in view of its quality and its origins, its use of politics as a "phobic screen" for the play of irrational affects. If one of the hypotheses one wishes to consider is that such "apolitical" political activity is on the increase, or widespread, an emphasis on formal political activities as the index to apathy will be of little use.

   2. *Activity and social class.* We sought for an index which would not be simply representative of middle-class judgments as to the political style of the lower class; and while we thought it altogether likely that, in any scale, the middle class would on the whole rank as less apathetic than the lower class, we wished to reduce class-relative factors to a minimum.[9]

   [9] While Gallup and other pollers occasionally ask questions such as "do you have a cold?" or "are you happy?" that are not class-typed, little has been done in public opinion research to develop and ask questions concerning politics in the widest sense that are not class-typed. To do this would require some knowledge of all political domains and interests in all social groups. How large this order is we can estimate from Kinsey's work. Sex is something we can be pretty sure exists in every human being, and its forms and meanings on the physical level to which Kinsey confined himself are not limitless. Yet the Indiana group found they had to learn the sex-lingo and sex-style of an enormous variety of people before they could ask questions which got home to their interviewees. Beyond that, they had to convince respondents that the interview was meaningful and that Kinsey and his coworkers understood what the respondents had to say. Kinsey, moreover, did not go beyond overt sex activity, whereas a questionnaire on politics would have to encompass all the intangibles which even quite limited definitions of politics imply.

We did not need evidence from our interviews to establish the obvious fact that political activity today is a matter very largely of clique affiliation and class position. At an urban progressive school where we had a group of interviews made, virtually everybody sent telegrams to congressmen, circulated petitions, and campaigned both in the presidential election and in the off-years. But our interviews seemed to us to show that most of these young people were nonetheless apathetic, in that their relationship to politics was apolitical—a matter of desperate need for group conformity and prestige and in some instances a phobic sphere as well. In many of these cases, we think that the individual, his adolescent fling in politics behind him, will settle into his business or professional life with a decreasing political interest unless there, too, it happens to be stimulated by group pressures. On the other hand, we had a group of interviews done among seniors in an urban trade school, where virtually no one had engaged in the slightest political activity, and where the level of political information was so abysmally low that one boy did not know to what party Truman belonged. Yet in a few of these cases the respondent indicated some awareness of those political developments which mattered for him personally: the draft, the chances for war, the outlook for labor unions. For these people, their adolescence is not, as so often with the middle class, a peak of political interest; when they enter the working force, they may be brought by their unions and their life-situations into some concern with politics.

Even then, however, the lower-class adult will find himself limited in his political activity by his class position, in subtle as well as obvious ways: he is apt to be more tired in the evening, and cannot take time off for meetings in the afternoon (unless he is a shop steward); he does not have a secretary, even if he is a leader in a local union, to type memoranda and make appointments; indeed, he is often ill at ease in handling such middle-class routines as telephone calls and memoranda; lower-class women with children find it of course still more difficult to be active politically. To be sure, the spread of education, the rise of unions and of other more or less formal associations, the increase in experience with government and corporate forms and routines—these developments are increasing the ability of the lower-class person to "act middle class," and to handle himself in the formalized aspects of political activity.

Studies of participation and nonparticipation in voluntary associations provide evidence that lower-class groups are in general more "privatized" than upper-class groups, no matter what forms of interest and participation are included in measuring lower-class participation. (So far as we know, however, no one has tried to see if lower-class men participate less in clique activity centering around sports, drink, and gambling; compare William F. Whyte's *Street Corner Society* and James West's *Plainville, U.S.A.*) Low-income people have very low participation in nonpolitical groups of any formal sort, and frequently have very little interest in matters that might be said to affect them directly. The experience of the Neighborhood Center for Block Organization in East Harlem is instructive in these matters: despite two years of active effort on the part of trained psychiatrists and social workers, it proved impossible to stimulate neighborhood groups in a slum area to deal even with the most pressing problems of daily life, such as housing-law violations, lack of playground space, and police protection. Although even slight coöperative efforts were impressively successful in improving neighborhood conditions, only about 2 percent of the residents—and these often the most psychologically disturbed—could be induced to participate in any group activity. Why this was the case is obscure—at the cordial invitation of the Center, we along with other social scientists have been trying to find out—but there would seem to be evidence that the conditions of lower-class life do not train people in the motivations and techniques, taken for granted in some sections of the middle class, which underlie coöperative activity. This is a point which converges with Ullmer and Mills' analysis of "Class Structure and Civic Leadership." Put another way, this brings us back to our earlier point, that activity, including political activity, in the lower class requires much more effort, and seems therefore much more fruitless, than in the middle class. With an index which simply measures gross activity, the lower class will simply disappear from consideration and the index will not do much to cast light on class differences in political apathy. Of course, it still remains desirable to explore further the relationships between class and clique position, on the one hand, and various types of political activity, on the other. (On class and clique determination of voting behavior, see Lazarsfeld, Berelson, and Gaudet, *The People's Choice*, excellent for its techniques and stimulating for its suggestiveness.)

3. *Activity and temperament.* Activity is relative not only to class and clique situations but also to temperament differences between individuals; we use "temperament" here to mean such things as native energy-level (apart from its directly psychic components), sanguinity, gregariousness, good health. The problem is that our focus of interest is not on apathy as a universal human phenomenon but on apathy as a social, a historical product. While the distribution of different kinds of temperament in different populations may well be connected with social and historical changes—see, for instance, the brilliant paper by Margaret Mead, "The Concept of Culture and the Psychosomatic Approach" (*Psychiatry*, 10, 1947, 57-76)—in the present state of psychosomatic knowledge, we prefer to get involved as little as possible in questions of temperament, limiting ourselves to those parts of personality and its expressions that are generally considered social in their determination. To isolate apathy as a product of social factors and history rather than of individual temperament is difficult in any case, but it would be even harder if we limited ourselves to the study of activity alone.

4. *Activity and purpose.* There is, finally, the consideration that political activity may be relative not only to a person's temperament and clique situation, but also to the context of his available political world of the moment. We can hardly call apathetic the behavior of someone who, fully aware of and completely involved emotionally in politics, yet decides not to be active, for want of meaningful activity at the time. Inevitably, we cannot survey political activity over a lifetime, much of it not yet lived, but must ask questions about the moment, the contiguous past, and the immediate future. Dipping in with an interview, our record of activity—as any behavioral index—must be incomplete and may be misleading. Since we view apathy as, among other things, a disproportionate relationship between means and ends—too much activity as well as too little—we cannot assume, because activity goes on, that it makes any human sense. For great numbers of people today, political activity is little more than an inherited ritual or routine, varying according to class demands and psychological needs.

5. *Activity as related to affect and competence.* We can sum up the foregoing paragraphs by saying that activity may conceal as much as it reveals about political apathy. Yet it would go much too far to

say that activity is irrelevant to an estimate of the political involvement of an individual. We cannot use it as an independent criterion without a great deal of further clarification. But we have found that we could use the record of activity, as it was revealed in an interview, as evidence in evaluating the individual's position on two other indices, those of affect and competence. It was these more "psychological" measures of apathy, rather than the "behavioral" one of activity, that seemed to give us a closer approximation to the quality of apathy itself, as our interviews revealed it. Certainly it is harder to work with such intangibles as (in our terminology) affect and competence, than with the (apparently) hard reality of activity. Yet the fact is that apathy itself is intangible: we cannot reduce it to an operational factor which we know does not include a good part of the meaning of our original object of study. We felt we must strive for criteria commensurate with our problem rather than shape our problem to the most readily available criteria.

If we are to understand apathy as "passionless existence"—one of the definitions given in the Oxford Dictionary—we need not explain why affectlessness (in the way the term is used by psychoanalysts) can be used as a criterion of political apathy. One might ask whether affectlessness is not a synonym for apathy. However, if we look at the pole opposite to political apathy, and consider the meaning and implications of political "concern" or "involvement," we will see immediately that affect or passionate existence is not a sufficient criterion to measure what we find. Concern and involvement imply awareness, appropriateness; yet passion may be blind, disproportionate. These considerations lead us to add to affect as an index of apathy another term: competence; and, as we shall see, to classify as "apathetic," according to our criteria those who, while ranking high in affect, are low in competence. Conversely, those who possess both affect and competence we term "involved," that is, nonapathetic.

We turn in the following two sections to a discussion of these criteria of affect and competence. Thereafter, we develop an additional set of criteria which, especially for the more politicized respondents, may be helpful in differentiating among affects, and hence among apathies.

POLITICAL AFFECT AS AN INDEX OF APATHY. These two dimensions, affect and competence, are obviously closely related. Just as the affect of the competent differs from the affect of the incompetent, so the competence of those of genuine affect differs from the competence of those who lack affect; the effort at distinction here faces problems similar to those of distinguishing between "cognitive" and "emotive" elements in intelligence.

At any rate, the use of these two indices simultaneously could give us four polar relationships: (1) those high in both dimensions; (2) those low in both; (3) and (4) those high in one and low in the other. Accordingly, we defined as (1) "involved" the person who combined high and genuine affect with competence; all others we classified as "apathetic." Thus we grouped in the apathetic category those (2) whose high affect and low competence indicated an "indignant" relationship to politics (it might also be an "enthusiastic" one); those (3) who were high in competence and affectless, and whom we termed "inside-dopesters"; and those low in both affect and competence, whom we called (4) the "indifferent."

These four types were, we suspected, related both to class position and to character structure; we expected, for instance, to find "inside-dopesters" in upper middle-class urban circles, "indignants" in rural and small-town Protestant areas. We do not yet have the sample that would permit us to test these hypotheses, though we have found interviews which illustrate them.

Affect is, of course, an intangible. It can be probed by projective tests such as the Rorschach, but these will not tell us very much about political affect, as distinguished from affect in other spheres of life. Specific answers to direct questions concerning political affect are, however, of more help than one might suppose. Thus, when we ask people what in politics gets them indignant or excited and how long they stay that way; what in politics makes them feel good or bad; whether they can get as worked up about politics as about other things in life; and so on—when we ask these direct questions, even rather non-commital answers, followed up by exploratory probes, are often quite revealing. A direct positive or negative answer to the first question bearing on affect, or to the whole series, may be belied by later answers in the series, or other parts of the interview.

For example, all the students in the progressive high school already referred to claim that politics makes a difference in the way they live, and that they get indignant about political happenings. However, the content of the answer gives us clues about the real nature of their alleged affect. We quote several responses to the question whether politics makes a difference:

> Not directly, but in a way I think it does; but in discussion with friends or parents I can usually take ideas or get facts from the discussion. In this way, these discussions make a difference.
>
> It makes no difference physically but it changes my mind—if I met someone who violently disagreed with me on an important issue it is bothersome for friendship. It affects me in this way.

Here politics is among other things a function of social intercourse in a group which makes "politics" obligatory. The first one quoted can "take ideas or get facts from the discussion"—for him politics is perhaps a means for self-improvement. The respondent who tells us that disagreement in political matters might be "bothersome for friendship" also volunteers that "if just two people were left in the world, they would still fight."

Working, then, both with what the interviewee tells us directly about his political affects and with what he "gives" of them without meaning to, we try to reconstruct the history of the individual's political affect, much as the archaeologist, working with fragments, tries to reconstruct a culture.

An individual may rate himself high, or low, in affect in contrast to his milieu. Hence, to understand what he tells us, we have to understand something of the milieu, if we are to make comparisons which transcend a limited group. Moreover, individuals differ very much in the style by which they express affect, or repress it. Possibly, we cannot avoid here the interjection of temperament factors, such as the distinction between choleric and sanguinic types—compare Jan Stapel, "The Convivial Respondent" (*Public Opinion Quarterly*, 11, 1947, p. 524). The popular folklore has it that "still waters run deep": people may feel deeply and yet not express this feeling by accepted patterns of gesture or speech. Contrariwise, the folklore would have it that easily surfaced affects are not genuine, but this, too, will vary, not only with individuals, but also according to the conventionalized mode of expression of affect in the particular group. So we must know something of what may be expected in the milieu to interpret the individual's idiosyncratic modification of group styles in vaunting affect or concealing it. It follows that we need a group portrait of political affect before we can draw the lineaments of the individual. But, of course, we learn of the group in part through the individuals who compose it, just as we learn of the individual in part from single answers to questions which then become interwoven with other answers. Thus, the method weaves back and forth, from the single answer to the whole interview, and from the single individual to the whole group of which he is a part. This is far from simple. Yet it is the kind of judgment which we constantly make in life—indeed, on which our lives and fortunes often depend—and which novelists and biographers must make when they tackle political subjects.

In this way, we try to arrive at a qualitative description of political affect, in all its subtleties and variations, as well as to judge whether it is, on the whole, high or low. The gamut of affects is wide: there is the affect of aggressive or sadistic types, who look for opportunities of releasing indignation onto politics; the affect of people who live in a slightly paranoid and autistic world; the affect of people with little staying power and the affect of those with great explosive power; the high affect of those whose roles as political leaders of certain groups require them to maintain a chronic political stance (which may feel "sincere" to them); the high, though repressed, affect of disillusioned folk who fear political affect and therefore deny it.

One crucial issue in all this is the source of the affect displayed in politics. Harold Lasswell, in *Psychopathology and Politics*, asserted that political behavior, if it is to be understood psychologically, must be understood in terms of affects arising in the personal ("primary") sphere and becoming displaced onto available ("secondary") political symbols. In a crude form, the notion that personal frustrations and tensions are displaced onto politics has become increasingly a part of our popular folklore and science; the personal experience of everyone offers examples. Professor Lasswell's more provocative question is rather whether *all* affect expressed in a political sphere must be considered as deriving from a personal tension or frustration. Perhaps in some ultimate or definitional sense there can be no other source for affect; and yet there is no question that we can distinguish between those in whom a clear link shows between the personal tension and its political expression, and those who seem to respond with emotion to the event itself. We may, that is, distinguish between an "idling" affect which seeks for justification or rationalization in politics, and an affect which is a reaction to specific political developments; the distinction here is analogous to the one Erich Fromm draws between idling and reactive hatred in *Man For Himself*. While such a phenomenological distinction does not answer the question as to the ultimate source of affect, it does indicate that there are different kinds of political affect, and we know from our experience of life that these different kinds may have different consequences.

This was, then, the first refinement we introduced in the use of affect as an index to apathy: where the affect expressed in politics is closely and directly linked to a personal tension—where the affect is "blind," so to speak, expressed on an available political object rather than directly aroused by the object—we did not consider that subject as showing affect in the political realm. Or, more precisely, we did not consider him politically "involved" if his affect was of this sort even if he might be considered politically competent—but, obviously, this very decision leads us away from any quantitative or quasi-quantitative use of either affect or competence as isolable criteria.

Finally, we found ourselves compelled to deal with still other elusive problems of the quality of affect. Our tendency had been to call those who show a great deal of affect without corresponding competence "indignant" types, but in some cases we felt that they were more properly called "enthusiasts." Moreover, "indignation" itself can be of different sorts: it can have the quality of an outlet for idling hatred and malaise which Svend Ranulf describes in his essay *Moral Indignation and Middle Class Psychology*; or it can represent a deeply human reaction to threat or atrocity. Often the presence or absence of competence would permit us to distinguish between these two types of indignation, but this is not always so.

POLITICAL COMPETENCE AS AN INDEX OF APATHY. In dealing with affect as an index we did not raise the question of how one defines politics, though obviously the problem of displacing affects which arise elsewhere onto politics implies a distinction of spheres between what is "politics" and what is "elsewhere." However, in establishing standards for political competence, it is even more necessary to define what we mean by politics.

1. What is "politics"? There is a great deal to be said for a "meteorological" definition—the term is that used by Kris and Leites

in the paper previously cited—perhaps an "entertainment" or "consumer's" definition: "interest in the world around one." In this sense, in terms of one's ability to react to events that do not affect one directly, but which are "interesting," one would be justified in testing for competence on the "politics" of the numbers game for the lower-class men, on tenement-house intrigues for lower-class women, and so on. In another sense, however, these things often do affect people in the lower class, at least immediately, more than a presidential election—in fact, we cannot speak of apathy, in its conventional use, in referring to someone who cannot affect the outcome of a political event, and who cannot be affected by its outcome.

An interest or consumer definition of politics would permit us to set up indices for political competence that would be relative to the interests of each social group; that is, each class or group would have a different index. As a practical matter, this would be exceedingly difficult—it would require determining what is important and interesting to a particular class, relative to that class, rather than in terms of what is important and interesting to another class. But apart from such considerations, such a definition of politics and hence of political competence would ignore our view that politics does determine the condition of people's lives today—including lower-class lives. And, as already stated, we believe that an awareness of those power-forces in the world which do matter for people, an awareness of the human potentialities for changing the social environment in the general interest—an awareness, that is, which transcends mere consumer's "interest," mere meteorology—is a human need whose satisfaction is important for individual psychic health. Of course there may be other, still more imperative needs.

One could also consider another type of judgment of competence which would be no less relativistic than a judgment in terms of local patterns of interest or consumption. By this test, one would be judged "competent" if one were able to perform the political tasks dictated by one's group milieu and party affiliation. Thus, the government official would be "competent" if he could handle the political news in the way demanded of him by his job, no matter how fragmentary his awareness of the long-run political forces in which his department, his class, and his country were caught. And the young Stalinist, knowledgeable on how to get Marcantonio reëlected, would be "competent" by the standards of his outfit—and even "incompetent" if he possessed the grasp of Marxist fundamentals demanded of an earlier generation of Communists and feared by the present generation. But, obviously, such complete relativism as this, which would equate the "functionally rationalized" with the rational (in Karl Mannheim's terms), would again be to deny our value premise: namely, that politics matters for people, irrespective of the ideology in which it is clothed in a particular culture and time and of the tasks or busywork demanded by that ideology. Our judgments of what is apathy, and of its subcomponents, must be based upon a standard which, while relative to long-term historical developments, does not fluctuate with party politics and anti-rationalist slogans; to that extent, our definitions of politics, hence of political competence, aim at a degree of universal validity, independent of culture and class.

Thus we are led to define politics, not in terms of mere passive interest nor in terms of roles demanded by one's station in life, but in terms of the human need for understanding the social environment and even of improving it. We define it, that is, in terms of our two levels of political awareness and action: the reflective and utopian and curious one, and the day-to-day struggle for the lesser as against the greater evil; to be judged competent one must have some grasp of both these levels.

2. *Distinguishing real from spurious competence.* Even when, for practical purposes, we limited our inquiries as to competence to the more traditional fields of politics, we still found it difficult to distinguish between an individual's awareness of real forces and superficial, atomistic consumption of political data. We had to distinguish between political reality and political illusion, even if that illusion was couched in conventionally "realistic" terms; inevitably, it is we who had to decide which is which, on the basis of our own political values and comprehension.

But in important respects we felt it necessary that our judgment of competence be relative. We could not judge everyone by the standard of a professor of political science; conversely, and perhaps unfairly, we expected more of the professor than of someone with (theoretically) less opportunity to acquire competence. We asked in each individual case: what could we expect, in terms of political awareness, in view of this individual's ability to deal with rather abstract matters, an ability partly native and partly learned? We also asked: what sort of awareness would this individual need in order to function in a satisfying way in "his" world? We asked a small-town person about rather more localized political matters than an urban person; we tried to discount, as far as possible, local and regional differences in distribution of the mass media. In every case, we tried to reduce, except for comparative purposes, questions of specific fact or opinion, such as are usually asked on polls, and to find questions which brought out the individual's ability to evaluate political forces. Since to some degree all of us live in the same world, these questions were identical for all people we interviewed, except insofar as we modified them to give the less articulate or intelligent a chance to respond.

This effort to allow for differences between rural and urban, and between articulate and inarticulate, raises many of the same complications as the effort to allow for class differences—ethnic differences also are important—and, of course, these various sets of differences overlap. In small-town and rural Vermont, where we had a group of interviews made, people are in easy contact with local and even state officials. Social distance between the politically influential and the noninfluential is small; indeed, many of the patterns of political meaning persist which we described above as typical for the nineteenth century. As against this, urban lower-class people, in our small number of interviews, seemed ordinarily to have no face-to-face contacts with officials; some of them, however, had a kind of taxi-driver wisdom and were more "knowing" than the Vermonters—less likely, for instance, to think that the interviewer must be a Communist because he asked questions about politics. Here, too, we do not have an adequate sample to permit comparisons; and in any case, we repeat, we have not solved the technical difficulties of developing a questionnaire to tap differential meanings of politics in the barely explored variety of American subcultures—what a political cosmology, for example, is wrapped up in the phrase: "Go fight city hall!"

In an effort to do this, however, we have asked people, for instance, what image they had of a political person, and of a nonpolitical person; whether they changed their minds about politics and when and why; whether they thought war or depression easier to avoid; whether they thought experts or the man in the street had better judgment; whether they trusted people, and whom they trusted on political questions.

We asked whether they thought their country, their school (for people in school), and their family was democratic, and how they could tell; what groups they felt had interests in common with themselves, and what groups antagonistic interests; and who they thought ran the country. Finally, we presented people with a series of political "dilemmas" and asked them what they would do if, for example, they came into possession of information which showed that "their" candidate in an election was corrupt, and if disclosure of such information would enable the other side to win; we said nothing about what their candidate stood for.

We did find, with our small haul of 150, that people in various social strata, urban and rural, young and old, felt they could take a crack at our questions and dilemmas. We did not have, as in the usual political questionnaire, a cluster of "don't knows" at the bottom of the socio-economic scale. Middle-class people, to be sure, had greater facility on some of the questions, but they were not likely to have thought in terms of all of them; for instance, they were usually challenged by the question as to their image or picture of a person very much interested in politics. This type of challenge is important, for it enabled us to use the interview as a sort of projective test, by seeing the kind of verbal and nonverbal (e.g., gestural) performance it elicited in sequence. It helped us, on the one hand, to get through the veneer of opinionatedness in the middle class and, on the other hand, to evoke what political competence there was in our lower-class respondents.

COMPETENCE AND AFFECT AS CRITERIA. We have worked intensively with some twenty interview protocols, and in each case made as complete a record as we could of all the grounds of our judgments, as we sought to determine apathy or involvement by the application of our criteria of competence and affect. (At the same time we made a judgment of character structure, on the basis of a typology which we do not touch on here, and compared character structure and political orientation.) We found in our use of these criteria that often we could not make separate judgments of each as easily as we could make a judgment of apathy or involvement directly. We found ourselves, moreover, moving away from primary attention to the specific questions which had been designed to reveal competence and affect respectively, and making instead judgments which treated the whole interview as a *Gestalt;* that is, all parts of our comprehensive questionnaire—covering popular culture, attitudes toward family and friends, philosophical values and many other things as well as politics—entered into and enriched our judgments.[10] Moreover, when we worked with the interviews, we discovered that in addition to employing our concepts of affect and competence, we were also tempted to smuggle in other criteria that were not explicit in our initial theoretical scheme. We were in the position, so frequent in social science, where our indices, despite our care to make them adequate to the complexities we were seeking to measure, turned out in many cases to be too mechanical to cover the whole range, the nuances and subtleties, of apathy and involvement. These difficulties arose, and our scheme of affect-competence seemed least illuminating, in the case of those who had fairly elaborate political ideologies, and who lived in politically saturated milieus. There ideology itself demanded that one be concerned with political events (just as in certain other environments ideology demanded the opposite), and a certain kind of competence could be avoided only by a remarkably high impermeability to the group.[11] Because general attitudes and orientations could be assumed, the range within a given orientation became exceedingly important.

In this situation, our recourse was to develop an additional set of criteria which, taken together with affect and competence rather than replacing them, would embrace more of the interview material and of our theoretical framework. This set of criteria was based on interview data we had originally planned virtually to disregard, namely, the detailed political ideology of the respondent. We had believed that in America—whatever might be found elsewhere—ideology is almost entirely a function of milieu, bearing little if any relation to individual character or to the psychological roots of apathy and involvement. Our view was, in other words, that party and ideological

10 Cf., e.g., Werner Wolff, *The Expression of Personality* (1943), p. 9: ". . . specific statements about personality items are often less accurate than free descriptions."

11 Rose Laub Coser has been engaged in analyzing for varieties of affect and competence a group of twenty-three interviews with the entire second-year class of students in a coeducational, progressive urban private school. Her preliminary analysis reveals that those who, on a series of questions, show competence and alertness vis-à-vis politics are those who also exhibit the least interpersonal tensions with their classmates.

positions in America do not bespeak a psychological choice: ordinarily the individual has no choice but to take the ideology offered him in his family, class, clique, and region.

Yet our interviews showed us that while this was on the whole true, there were crucial differences in the nuance and emphasis with which the ideology was expressed by each subject in our more highly political groups of respondents. We believed these differences to be significant both for revealing character structure and revealing apathy or involvement. We therefore developed, on the basis of our study of a variegated group of interviews, some general concepts of the way in which the coloring of one's ideology—more or less irrespective of its nominal content—may be related to an underlying apathy.

A set of criteria based on nuances of political statement inevitably will not be applicable to large numbers of people: first of all, to those who present virtually no political statements or opinions—and there are many of these—and then to those in whom these statements are very simple or primitive. However, our criteria, as will be seen in a moment, refer to such general categories that they might also be applied to views on family relations, education, and similar topics which have political bearing or implications, and we have often done this, though here, too, we run into some difficulty where views are not elaborated. Nevertheless, the main use of this set of categories was to serve as a refinement on the affect-competence scheme: for most people, the affect-competence scheme described the degree of political involvement or apathy sufficiently; but for those for whom politics is a focus of interest, the affect and competence categories were too gross, and a direct analysis of ideology permitted somewhat closer approximation. Moreover, these additional criteria directly introduced into our analysis of the interviews our judgments, set forth in the preceding section, on the need for a political orientation which combined elements of detachment and of attachment to one's time-bound and culture-bound milieu.

In what we have said, the reader may feel that our use of the term "apathy" is too idiosyncratic and complex, even in the light of scientific awareness that definition is an essentially arbitrary device. And, indeed, our choice of the term "apathy" rather than a word of less common use or of our own coinage is frankly polemical. It is a way of stating our conviction that current conceptions about apathy—seen in terms of failure to vote, to send telegrams, to inform oneself about politics, etc.—greatly oversimplify the problem of finding adequate ways for relating people to politics on its various levels. To seek an increase in formal political activity and information as such, without too much concern for the meaning of that activity or information, is self-deceiving. For it may blind one to the historical changes in the significance of politics for the individual which, in our opinion, have led to an increase in unconscious apathy, an apathy arising as a result of congruent changes in social structure and character structure, as well as in the political sphere alone. These changes are reflected in slight changes of ideology and of modes of expression of affect; these are possible clues to long-term developments whose consequences in political behavior have not yet become fully manifest—clues to the latent dynamics of politics.

To be sure, not all apathies are alike, and the "apathy" of the active is obviously different from the "apathy" of the quiescent. Nevertheless, in using the same term for both, we are seeking to emphasize functional similarities—primarily the inappropriateness of the political outlook or behavior of all the apathetic ones.

It is, moreover, not only apathy which is misconceived, but its opposite which we call "involvement." Here, too, we think that changes may be under way in those individuals and groups who are seeking for possible new modes of relatedness to politics. Our effort is to formulate criteria which will permit us to distinguish inappropriate and apolitical orientations, no matter how well rationalized and disguised, from orientations which might satisfy the need of modern men to meet their altered political situation with competence and fitting affect.

FURTHER CRITERIA FOR APATHY AND INVOLVEMENT

The criteria set forth below are meant to supplement, primarily for the more politicized respondents, the criteria of affect and competence. They are not yet exhaustive. Taken together, however, they help to differentiate apathetic, apolitical approaches to politics from involved and appropriate responses. They do not determine the correctness or misguidedness of an individual's political position: people can be mistaken without being judged apathetic, and conversely, they can be "right" despite a basic apathy. For any political position, then: (1) concern with human ends is less apathetic than concern with institutional means; (2) concern with what has been or potentially can be personally experienced is less apathetic than concern with remote items, access to which is gained through impersonal agencies of information diffusion; likewise, the ability to personalize and concretize distant events is less apathetic than the ability to report them; (3) concern with the welfare of self-and-others is less apathetic than concern exclusively with the self or exclusively with others; (4) concern with trends and elements that are not in the focus of attention of the mass media is less apathetic than exclusive concern with what is in their momentary focus; (5) ability to take a critical or independent view of authority[12]—its assertions of fact, and claims to special treatment or consideration—is less apathetic than unquestioning acceptance or rejection of these assertions and claims because of their authoritative source.

Obviously, these criteria overlap at a number of points. We have made no attempt to use them as a scale; to say, for instance, that we judge a person nonapathetic if he ranks high on three out of five. Rather, they constitute a check list of things to be looked for in characterizing the political style of a person. We say a few words in illustration and explanation of each.

HUMAN ENDS V. INSTITUTIONAL MEANS. When we ask people what could be done to make war less likely, some answer in terms of changing people, and some in terms of changing institutions; still others, of course, say that war is inevitable. But we cannot interpret such answers directly in terms of our criterion: it is the personal variant of a given ideological frame that tells us something about individual political orientation. Thus, if a politically sophisticated respondent emphasizes nationalization of industry, centralization of planning, control over industry, breakup of cartels, etc., with what seems to us a disproportionate emphasis on the specific institutional instrument rather than the human end, we become suspicious and wonder whether his interest in the human end may not be an excuse for his desire to institute a particular set of more or less belligerent

---

[12] "Authority" here must be taken in terms of the individual's group and not in any general sense; obviously, the authorities to which an obedient Stalinist, Zionist, Catholic, or Democrat submits are not the same.

means. We cannot tell this, we repeat, from the position itself. To be sure, some ideologies are so constricted that acceptance of them amounts to a virtual choice of totalitarian means; yet we can imagine a racist who puts more emphasis on freedom for the allegedly subject race than on means for destroying or controlling an oppressor race, and we can conceive of a Nazi who, before 1939, emphasized the strength-through-joy program, the end of unemployment, new motor roads and the *Volkswagen*, and who through all-too-human error, failed to see the necessary implications of other Nazi goals.

Conversely, acceptance of an ideology that exalts ends without reference to conceivable human means may tend toward apathy, as we think is the case with some current versions of pietism and quietism. For ends cannot be too serious when the problem of implementation is lightly regarded. We do not mean, of course, that one must always have means available before one can justify speculation about ends; it is again a question of the "two levels" of political relatedness we discussed above.

Though such questions seem highly theoretical,[13] the issue boils down to a fairly simple one: does the person possess, in the realm of politics, the "normal" human ability to differentiate ends from means? To take a common instance in everyday life, we are critical of the person who makes a compulsive ritual out of behavior that should serve convenience—keeping a house neat, for example. So, too, in political life, we find people whose aim of getting rid of "dirt"— municipal corruption, excess profits, un-American activities, etc.—has become a dangerous and compulsive ritual, blind to human priorities and consequences. Flight into politics typically uses political means without appropriate relationship to human ends.

THE PERSONALIZED AND CONCRETIZED V. THE IMPERSONAL AND REMOTE. The very nature of modern politics is such that we cannot form our political judgments on the basis of personal experience alone. If we try to do this, we will simply be applying "parataxic" frames of reference to the world. This misapplication is typical of the philistine, of the ethnocentric person who, in art, "knows what he likes," and in politics insists on judging everything that happens by the norms of his own morality, his own family, his own unquestioned

[13] For fuller discussion, see "Some Observations on Community Plans and Utopia" in *Yale Law Journal*, 57 (1947), 173.

way of life. Such a person is also one who makes the semantic error, discussed by S. I. Hayakawa,[14] of asserting firmly that "pigs is pigs" and can never be anything else: he knows a pig when he sees one. Probably the lower-class person, less sophisticated, is more likely than the upper-class person to fall prey to these fallacies.

Increasingly, however, people tend to make the opposite error, and it is with this that our second criterion deals. While the world that influences us is enormous, and while we must depend almost entirely on reports that we read or hear in order to evaluate it, we are inclined to apathy if we fail to measure these reports, wherever we can, by our personal identification with the described situation. When, for instance, we read that the Russian people have greeted with joy a decree lengthening hours of labor, because this permits them to do more for the beloved Stalin, we can use our own experience to discount the report as at least in part exaggerated. Of course, this personal reference may lead us into error: people are different; nevertheless, by means of this natural and widely used control, a large part of the political can be assimilated to personal experience.

We found in our interviews, however, a number of people—largely in the urban upper-middle class, young, and much concerned with politics—who did precisely the opposite: they were attracted by what was most abstract and remote; they parroted events and attitudes in the same forms and terms in which the mass media (for their class) present them; it never occurred to them to use their own experience, their own likes and dislikes, as a norm. We might suggest that this strand of apathy is a trained incapacity of the educated. These same people knew all about the disasters of the last years; they claimed great concern, great affect. Yet in many instances we found that the events which made an impression were those which the respondent could not possibly have assimilated in terms of personal experience. In such cases we were sometimes able to see that the reason for the apparent political concern lay in anxieties about group conformity patterns or in the use of politics as an escape from exigent and unconscious problems of the self.

It is in judging such cases that the problem of differential exposure to the mass media becomes important. The ability to react to the

[14] "The Revision of Vision," *ETC.: A Review of General Semantics,* IV (1947), 258.

remote may have been stimulated by, say, a vivid "March of Time" or CBS broadcast. Similarly, other sources, at school or elsewhere, might sensitize an individual to connections which will seem remote only to the less sensitive observer.

More typically, however, the mass media operate on a level of spurious personalization of events, which are made concrete and chummy by playing up personalities and local color. Thus it is apparent that this criterion is closely linked with the fourth one (see p. 553, below): concern with what is not in focus as against concern only with what is in the focus—and the conventional style of perception—of the relevant clique or media.

To avoid misunderstanding, we should emphasize that we are not equating political involvement with immediacy in time and space, and political apathy with physical or temporal remoteness. It is not apathy but its opposite to react strongly to Plato's *Apology*, for example, or to an account of misery on Okinawa. Rather, our point is simply that one's own experience, enriched by sensibility and imagination, is with all its weaknesses the only safe yardstick for judgment —paradoxically, it furnishes the only escape from solipsism. Indeed, we believe that many political disasters of our own time and of earlier times have resulted because of people's acceptance of political ideologies which their own experience might have disproved, had they trusted it or resorted to it. Programs of sacrifice and war can be put over just because people, failing to do this, act like "statesmen," applying *raison d'état*, and never, like kings, saying "*l'état: c'est moi.*"

Concern with Self-and-Others v. Concern with Self-or-Others. This criterion is closely linked to the one we have just discussed; it too demands that the individual see himself in the context of others and others in the context of himself. But by the use of this criterion we wish to make explicit our judgment, set forth above, that both selfishness and selflessness are obstacles to political involvement. As to the former, if we find an interview record which formulates the view that the respondent can achieve happiness for himself at whatever cost to others—or for his group or nation, at whatever cost to other groups or nations—we suspect first of all his political competence, since all experience suggest the interdependence of human beings and nations, and second, his humanity: otherwise, how could he be happy at the direct expense of others? In fact, these two judgments interlock: the respondent's lack of humanity will lead him to misjudge politics in long-run terms, no matter how effective he may be as an operator; he is apathetic because he does not penetrate to the real forces at work—certain forces, for example, which may tend after a time to reduce the power of the powerful and increase the power of the powerless—but sees politics only as the manipulable extension of his own ego and its group or territorial representatives.

If, on the other hand, we find an interview record of a person who thinks only of others, and never of himself or his group, we suspect a fear of facing or knowing the self (and the group), often coupled with a more or less unconscious desire to suffer.

One of our respondents, for instance, asked what he would do if he had six months to live and could do as he pleased, said he would use the "aura of reverence attached to one who has six months to live . . . to improve conditions." His whole interview is filled with references to the suffering of others, but he is oblivious to his own suffering, which leads to his inhuman willingness to make himself an instrument, even in his hypothetical last six months, for meeting unlimited obligations to a rather shadowy "humanity."

The case is extreme; while others among our group of interviews exhibit similar tendencies, selflessness is rationalized more typically in some hard-boiled vein. In all such instances, however, we feel there is something apathetic in a view of politics which fails to connect it with the speaker's own place in the world, and his own claims for happiness. As we all know, modern political leaders have become adept at exploiting the willingness of people to submit to intolerable conditions for some cause; the cause gives meaning to the followers' lives because these are completely lived in the "second sphere" of culturally-given tasks and motivations: there is insufficient attachment to life in the "first sphere" of day-to-day living, let alone sufficient detachment in the "third sphere" of transcending imagination. In much the same way, many leaders who make their careers on the basis of others' sacrifice are themselves "selfless," that is, ascetic; they, too, find meaning only in submission to a cause, though they may appear as highly egocentric.

If one thinks of earlier military heroes and their devoted followings, of earlier fanaticisms and crusades, it is not easy to see what is new in all this. Erich Fromm, in *Escape From Freedom*, pointed to resemblances between the social-psychological conditions which gave rise to the more virulent aspects of the Reformation and those which gave rise to modern fascism. If there are differences, they might be sought in the more limitless nature of modern totalitarian demands, and more effective techniques for their enforcement. Beyond that, we think there may be changes in individual psychology which have removed certain defenses people once had against the internalized voices of the peer-group; moreover, older barriers of property, theology, and class have been largely smashed. Whatever the degree of change, we can at least be sure that there is plenty of political dynamite available to those who can combine the apathy of the selfless and the apathy of the egocentric, sopping up into a political movement the affect of the incompetent and finding places for the technical but often cruel competence of the affectless.

CONCERN WITH WHAT IS NOT IN FOCUS V. CONCERN ONLY WITH WHAT IS IN FOCUS OF CLIQUE OR MEDIA. As throughout this discussion, here, too, our criteria shade into one another. Individuality of the focus of attention is related, on the one hand, to ability to put oneself (but not only oneself) into the figure-ground pattern of politics—our third criterion—and on the other hand, it is related to a critical attitude toward the (generally anonymous) authorities who tell people what their focus of attention should be, which is our fifth criterion. If we define politics in terms, *inter alia*, of efforts to change the social environment, we see that the ability to envisage such change involves originality. This can flow from the actual experiences people have, if they do experience them directly—that is, if they are able to look clear-sightedly at their own conditions and their own way of life. However, most people do not interpret their experience directly, but through the conventional, ideologized accounts of their life that are proffered them by the mass media and by other authorities. This passivity of perception, this permeability, is apathetic, no matter how frantic the concern with the flow of political news. Passivity suffocates the development of alternative and unexpected ways of handling political developments. In our culture, preoccupation with the stream of events as they are culturally perceived is praised as practical. Yet without utopian thought—thought which makes it worth while to apply human effort to the social environment rather than being overwhelmed by it—man's political inventiveness is stunted.

To be sure, not everyone can be a builder of utopias, nor do we expect originality in the sense in which the term is used in scholarship before we judge a person nonapathetic. Rather, our criterion is an effort to evaluate the mode of perception of the person—his ability, as a matter of degree, to criticize and judge pleasant and unpleasant, just and unjust, ways of social living. (Here, and generally, we have profited very much from the discussion in Erich Fromm's *Man For Himself.*) Where this ability is absent, people tend to become increasingly invaded in their individuality of judgment by what they are told, and by the stream of reportage furnished them through the mass media of communication. Increasingly, the mass media peddle the "inside dope," much like the Fascist agitator portrayed by Leo Lowenthal and Norbert Guterman in *Prophets of Deceit.* Like other opiates, it may make some people jumpy and other people quiescent, but both groups are functionally apathetic in the light of our criteria.

CRITICALNESS OF AUTHORITY V. SUBMISSIVENESS. We have already indicated, in preceding criteria, the sort of nonapathetic orientation a person may have who is able to criticize assertions and demands for attention from authoritative sources: such a person can concern himself with human ends, and can relate events to his own human experience and human desires; he can transcend, if only in slight degree, the way the mass media present political occurrences. And, on the contrary, we have spoken of the apathy indicated by an orientation to politics which is basically submissive, being concerned only with means, messages, and missions. Our fifth criterion deals explicitly with the relationship to authority. Of all our criteria, this one is probably most palpably linked to character structure; though conceivably submissiveness toward authorities of state, school, or religion may be the outcome of a rational, though mistaken, judgment, we usually expect to trace a basis in personality for the attitude.

Even so, it is necessary to distinguish various kinds of submissiveness. In one of our interviews, we came across a second-generation Italian youth, a trade school senior, who exhibited great docility to the middle-class interviewer, to the school officials, and to constituted authority generally. Yet there was nothing intense about this submission; it had the archaic quality of a fatalistic but upstanding and secure peasant, who had no characterological need to submit because he genuinely respected authority and took his humble place in the world for granted. Today, this attitude is rare in America, and when we find submissiveness it is usually rooted, not in respect for unquestioned authority, but in a sado-masochistic syndrome of incomplete rebellion and incomplete—and therefore all the more intense—submission. Through the examination of attitudes toward authority, we hope to be able to differentiate between rebelliousness as simply a highly critical attitude toward authority and rebelliousness as an irrational character orientation.

Intense cravings for submission, and irrational rebelliousness—these again are psychological constellations which invite the coming into power of people with destructive and harmful personalities, people who are themselves apathetic in their lack of concern for human ends and their ruthless egocentricity for self or group.

APPLICATIONS OF THE CRITERIA. Out of our 150 interviews, we have taken about 20 for intensive study in the light of our criteria of affect and competence, as well as the further criteria we have just now set forth. We have sought not only to classify the respondent as politically involved or apathetic as the case may be, but also to portray in detail his political orientation as it now appears and as we envisage its possible future courses—to give, so to speak, the political potential of the person. As is evident from the qualitative nature of the criteria, such work involves ransacking the entire interview for clues to the interpretation of the specifically political responses. Moreover, the responses are themselves qualified in meaning by our knowledge of the ideology of the group, perhaps a numerically very small group, to which the interviewee belongs; it would be absurd, for instance, to take at face value the remarks of a small child about killing people, but we would have to see where the child went beyond or gave an idiosyncratic twist to his current peer-group's lingo.[15] We must also, of course, take account of the respondent's age; where, for instance, we have worked with high school students, we must allow for the fact that the political style of adolescence is often not fully formed.

We have found for ourselves that the criteria, in all their elaboration, do permit us to encompass many of the nuances and subtleties of the interview material. To be sure, there are many cases where the

---

[15] For a fuller account of the method and its difficulties, see our discussion in "Social Structure, Character Structure, and Opinion," in *International Journal of Opinion and Attitude Research*, Vol. 2, Winter, 1948-1949, p. 512.

interview leaves us in doubt either because our questions and probes did not get beneath the surface or because politics for the individual is only surface—he cannot be said to have a political orientation, except embryonically, which is his. And of course we expect that people can fool us. We have found people who go through all the motions of affect so convincingly that, on first analysis, we have judged them nonapathetic, only to see on fuller scrutiny that this was a very smooth act. And conversely, we recall one instance of a returned veteran so cynical, so anxious to deny affect, that his interview was filled with brutal remarks; fuller examination revealed the very genuine affect which he was trying desperately, but quite unsuccessfully, to crush: it was apparent, for instance, that he was not submissive, not mass-media oriented, not as selfish as he claimed.

We wish it were possible to set forth here some of our material from our interviews and to show in detail how the protocol may reveal a syndrome of apathy—"indignant," "enthusiastic," "indifferent," etc., as the case may be—in terms of the criteria. However, even one of these discussions is apt to run the length of this article and space forbids including such an illustration. This is unsatisfactory because only through the details can the reader judge the validity of the research procedure. To be sure, this is not "validity" in the technical sense of proof of our results. In a few cases we have sought such proof—never fully adequate of course—by following a respondent up to see whether he fulfills predictions we have made on the basis of the interview. In other cases, we have tried to check our interpretation against the judgments of others who have had dealings with the subject: this may help test our methods but is hardly probative as to the individual, since all concerned may be deceived.

At the present stage of our work, however, we do not see the interview material as "proving" our criteria, let alone as proving something about the apathy of the Americans. For one thing, we have worked experimentally with some more or less homogeneous groups who were not meant to be representative. For another thing, we are still far from having a satisfactory instrument, in our interviews and methods of analyzing them, for the measurement of potentials for apathy and involvement in individuals; and then, as social scientists do not need to be told, it is a long step from what we call "handicraft" work with individuals to "assembly line" work with groups and social classes. A great deal of investigation by many social scientists will be necessary before we have such tools, and before the problem of using historical categories in social-psychological studies is pushed nearer to solution.

In the meantime, however, interview material can be fruitfully used, we think, to stimulate the development of hypotheses as to historical changes of the sort we have here proposed. We were struck, for instance, to find in a small community in southern Vermont a shading of difference between the way the young people and their elders expressed themselves about national and international political developments. The elders were many of them of the type we call "indignant"—high in affect, low in competence—and their indignation had a curdled quality, not an amiable one, which reminded us of similar folk as described in Granville Hicks' *Small Town*. Despite their actual lack of participation, these elders still felt some sense of relatedness to government, though this showed often only in grievance. Thus, they would tell the interviewer that they felt they ought to take part in politics, and felt guilt for not doing so. And in referring to events, they used the pronoun "I"—"I" think, "I" want, "I" hate, etc. The young people, the teen-agers, on the other hand, had less grievance and less sense of relatedness. They took whatever government gave them, including the draft, with an almost total passivity; it never occurred to them that they *ought* to do anything about it, except obey: they would certainly pass the current loyalty tests! Moreover, their interviews on politics are almost devoid of the pronoun "I"; sometimes the reference is to a group "we," and mostly to a group "they." Perhaps more "socialized," more coöperative than their parents, they do not even make use of the privilege of the underprivileged to gripe, to react—to feel strongly—about what happens to them. They have passed from "indignation" to "indifference," with low affect to match their low competence.

Our sample is much too small to be sure of this divergence. Nor are we sure whether we deal here with changed underlying attitudes, or with age-graded conventions for expressing or repressing affect, or with self-selection of the old who choose to live in small-town Vermont. Beyond that, we cannot be sure that any contemporary matching of old versus young can be taken as establishing historical changes, though it was just for the purpose of studying "older" political styles that we decided on a survey in Vermont. But we are trying to pin down and narrow possible sources of error of this sort as we work with the Vermont material.[16] And each such investigation may be viewed as a step toward the clarification and simplification of our criteria for apathy and involvement, with the hope of settling on some which are more "diagnostic" than others of the social and psychological complex which interests us. As ever, work on the problem weaves back and forth between the field and the study with, occasionally, mutual stimulation and, equally often, mutual discouragement.

One such discouragement lies in the fact, evident from the above discussion, that it is easier to define apathy than to define its opposite, easier to spot and describe negative political orientations and the reasons for them in individual psychology and social situation, than to describe what we feel to be *appropriate* political styles and to see where, if at all, these may be developed and encouraged. Even our few interviews make plain what many know: that there is no want of people to do the dirty work of totalitarian political movements in America; this is a potential in many who are now "indifferent" apathetic types. At the same time, we have come across, out of 150 interviewees, perhaps four or five who could be classified as actually or potentially nonapathetic, and we doubt if a more favorable picture would emerge from a more complete sampling job.

This is not surprising. Character and culture combine to generate apathy. At best, involvement becomes deviant behavior, rational and adaptive though it is in historical perspective. It is rational and adaptive for the individual because, as we have said, it helps to orient him in his world and to satisfy the human need to be political. It is rational and adaptive for the society because, ever since the disillusionments of the last decades, and ever since the discovery, made by many, that America under full employment is not a particularly happy or humanly lively land, we have needed to fire people's imaginations with the possibilities of a major leap to security and freedom. It is to the nonapathetic that we look for such utopian political inventions, and to

[16] The survey was made under the direction of Professor Martin Meyerson of the University of Chicago, and his wife, Marge Meyerson. The point about divergences between the young and the old was developed in discussions with them and with Rosalie Hankey, of the University of Chicago, who collaborated on the Vermont interviewing and analysis.

the recognition and support of those inventions when made by others. To be sure, inventions may be suppressed or ignored; all by themselves, they will not overcome apathy. But in the fate of an invention, as in the fate of a battle, there is often an element of chance. If we take the long historical view, we know that immense consequences have occasionally followed the inventiveness of a seemingly insignificant few. And if, on our other level of awareness, we take only the view of here-and-now, we can defend political involvement because, in our handful of instances, it seems to make the individual better able to face and enjoy life.

Dilemmas of Leadership and Doctrine in Democratic Planning[1]

BY PHILIP SELZNICK

As WE COME to face concretely and responsibly the problems of democratic planning, new dimensions of leadership confront us. Among these is the uneasy but indispensable union of statesman and administrator. In the process of creating and maintaining new instruments of control within the framework of democracy, the managerial expert is thrust upward to new and dangerous heights. The classic separation of administration and policy—perhaps never really meaningful—is now being speedily erased. New responsibilities, not always clearly defined, are generated by the ramifying consequences of decisions the administrator is called upon to make. He must increasingly take account of cultural values, of the distribution of power in the community, of public opinion—in short, he must share the primary qualities (and pitfalls) of statesmanship.

This coalescence of administrative and political leadership is not bought for nothing. We pay a price, measured in new sources of frustration. For the problem is not simply one of "educating the administrator to his new responsibilities," useful as such efforts may be; it is rather one of recognizing the special predicaments which accompany the emergence of the planner as leader. These predicaments become especially clear when the administrator identifies himself with an ideology.

In order to explore this problem as concretely as possible, we shall here focus attention upon one widely discussed instrument of demo-

[1] This is a previously unpublished paper.

560

cratic planning—the Tennessee Valley Authority.[2] The TVA provides useful case material in this connection. It represents in fact a substantial (though often exaggeratedly noted) effort to exercise unified, planful control over the development of a great river basin; its success has been hailed throughout the world as a portent of the future; but most important, it has been identified with a significant effort to democratize the administration of governmental functions. Indeed, when in 1942 the London Times reported on the Authority, it did so under the heading, "The Technique of Democratic Planning." The Times correspondent noted that he was impressed by the physical accomplishments of dam and power plant construction, but what interested him most was "the technique which the TVA had adopted with the deliberate aim of reconciling over-all planning with the values of democracy." Here the Times reflected what many feel to be the enduring significance of this much-heralded government agency. The theme of democracy in administration was also prominent in a widely distributed book, TVA: Democracy on the March, written by David E. Lilienthal, and in numerous speeches and pamphlets emanating from the Authority. In addition, much of the comment friendly to the agency has stressed its contribution to a new synthesis, one which would unite positive government—the welfare or service state—with a rigorous adherence to the principles of democracy.

TVA AS A SYMBOL

Both here and abroad, the TVA serves as a rallying point for those who favor a welfare state. The defense of the TVA—and the extension of its methods—is accepted among these groups as an elementary duty. What is known as the progressive movement in the United States (essentially the forces which mobilized the popular base of the New Deal) has treated the TVA as a symbol of its aspirations and has been quick to muster its forces behind the agency and its ideas whenever occasion demanded. This has been evident in the unequivocal defense of the TVA organization itself in controversies over finances and accountability; and especially in the vigorous espousal

[2] The following is adapted from the authors' TVA and the Grass Roots: A Study in the Sociology of Formal Organization (Berkeley and Los Angeles, 1949).

of the TVA as a model for regional development in other areas of the United States, and indeed, in China, the Philippines, Palestine, and central Europe. For these forces, support of the TVA is one of the ready touchstones of political acceptability.

This historic role of the TVA involves an interesting paradox. For it is primarily as a *symbol* that the Authority invites allegiance and denunciation. In its capacity as symbol, the organization derives meaning and significance from the interpretations which others place upon it. The halo thus eagerly proffered is a reflection of the needs and problems not of TVA but of the larger groups which require the symbol and use it. Hence controversy over the TVA may proceed irrespective of a close examination of the organization itself and the policies it pursues. When such inspections are undertaken, they are made with a view to exalting TVA or condemning it: on the one hand, as positive government liberating and advancing the people whom it serves, or, on the other, as a nefarious encroachment on free enterprise, with subversive intent. This need not surprise us, for the symbol is necessarily caught up in and manipulated by the broader issues and forces involved in social conflict. Since it is in the context of the larger struggle that basic political decisions are made, it is to be expected that the TVA should there lose its special identity and become merely a weapon in the battle and a focal point of attack and defense.

Yet however significant its symbolic character may be, TVA is and must be more than an idea. It is a living organization in a concrete social environment. From that obvious statement many things follow. The special leadership of such an organization (the group which must actually run it) is divided from the general leadership of its diffuse support (the labor leaders, the magazine editors, the liberal politicians) by the quality of *responsibility*. To those for whom the idea is primary, the symbol is enough and the actual organization which embodies it at any particular time may be somewhat irrelevant. But the symbol become apparatus generates its own problems for whose solution the administrative leadership is directly responsible. These new problems are concrete and pressing; they have a day-to-day urgency unlike political loyalty to an abstract ideal; they arise out of the need to weigh means and judge consequences in the context of practical action. The administrative leadership—of TVA, of a trade union, of a business corporation—is turned in upon itself, preoccupied with the tools at hand and with the concrete choices which must be made to implement the general policy it seeks to execute. Whatever the ultimate social implications of its choices, the organization in action must deal primarily with those who are immediately and directly affected by its intervention. In order to endure, it must find a way of adjusting itself to the institutions in the area of its operation—or pay the price of maladjustment. The administrative leadership cannot depend only or even primarily upon the diffuse support of elements not directly involved in its work; it must find support among local institutions, and develop smooth working relations with them. It must avoid a continuous atmosphere of crisis and conflict which may lead, in the first instance, to disorganization and frustration and, in the long run, to the upcropping of significant threats to the very existence of the organization itself. In short, the apparatus as an institution must seek some sort of equilibrium with the environment in which it lives.

To point to such an adjustment, or the need for it, is to speak of the normal course of events. Experienced participants in the administrative process are familiar with the continuous striving for adjustment, though few have spoken self-consciously of it. The management of its details is accepted as part of the ordinary common sense of administrative leadership. But it is often observable that where institutions have symbolic meaning beyond their own structure and behavior, a blindness to the organizational facts of life arises. Explicit statements which trace the history of the organization in terms of compromise and mediation are rejected out of hand, or at best, when accepted, are deemed shocking exposures.

We are not concerned here with exposures or revelations. But we are concerned with the problems which arise when a significant effort is made to combine democracy and planning. Obviously, this assumes that there are problems, that the road is not easy. Whatever our general commitment to the agency in question, we must take for granted that the TVA, like other human creations, is vulnerable to critical analysis.

We may approach this problem by considering in their relations (1) the democratic, "grass-roots" doctrine and policy of the TVA; (2) the inherent dilemmas posed by this or any similar doctrine when confronted by the need of the organization to adapt itself to the institutions of its area of operation; and (3) the consequences for policy and action which must follow upon any attempt to adjust to local centers of interest and power.

THE GRASS-ROOTS DOCTRINE

The responsible leaders of TVA have long recognized the indivisibility of policy and administration, have accepted without bashfulness or apology the role of statesmen. The interesting history of this statesmanship deserves to be fully recorded, but we are here concerned with but one aspect: the development and propagation of a set of beliefs by the Authority, on its own initiative, beliefs which serve to define the image of itself which the Authority's leadership would like to have accepted. These beliefs are to a large extent translated into policy, and they emphasize the democratic side of TVA's role as positive government. The essentials of this doctrine may be summarized as follows:

1. There is a great need to decentralize the administration of federal functions. While the continuing growth of the power of the federal government to intervene for the general welfare must be accepted, the method by which this power is exercised is of decisive importance for the future of democracy.

2. This decentralization can be made effective through such agencies as the TVA, which is permitted the freedom to make significant decisions on its own account. The TVA is a model of federal decentralization because, located in its area of operation and blessed with a large degree of managerial autonomy, it can make policy in the light of local needs. The content of this freedom can be spelled out very concretely: the right to set up its own personnel system, independently of the U. S. Civil Service Commission; the right to apply criteria of business efficiency and flexibility in making expenditures, free of the control of the General Accounting Office; and the right to apply revenues to current operating expenses, without itemized Congressional approval. These freedoms add up to a wide area of discretion concentrated in the hands of the TVA Board. In the terms of the grass-roots doctrine, all such decisions can thus be more democratic because decentralized to an agency located in the area of operation.

3. There should be active participation "by the people themselves" in the programs of the decentralized public enterprise. An additional

dimension of decentralization is introduced by the injunction that the services of state and local agencies are to be utilized, with the federal government providing a leadership that will strengthen rather than weaken or eliminate existing agencies. Further, management should devise means to enlist the active and conscious participation of the people through existing private associations as well as through ad hoc voluntary associations established in connection with the administration of the agency's program. This phase of grass-roots administration has played an important role in the TVA experience. It is exemplified on the one hand in the channeling of the Authority's agricultural program through the land-grant colleges of the Tennessee Valley states, and on the other in the creation of many farmer and citizen committees to participate in the administration of fertilizer distribution, rural electrification, urban planning, and land use programs.

4. The decentralized administrative agency of the TVA type should be given a key role in coördinating state, local, and federal programs in its area; and in the case of a regional development agency, it should be given primary responsibility to deal with the resources of the area as a unified whole. In this view, the place for the coördination of programs is in the field, away from the top offices which are preoccupied with jurisdictional disputes and organizational self-preservation. Coördination should be oriented to the job to be done, centering federal authority and its administrative skills and power upon the special needs and problems of the area. It follows from this requirement, as well as from the need for wide discretion in managerial matters noted above, that such agencies as TVA should not be made part of, say, the Department of the Interior.

Baldly stated, so runs the TVA doctrine. Those familiar with the bureaucratic shadowland will recognize here a strikingly ingenuous justification for maximizing the power of the TVA leadership. However that may be, surely any plea for decentralization must, by definition, call for an increase in the power of those to whom delegation of discretion is proposed. Nor need we shy from depending upon and utilizing the self-interest of leaders for achieving these purposes. The fact is that the doctrine as stated does introduce an effort to define the democratic dimension of planning. Taking it at its face value, what are some of the implications and difficulties of espousing such a view?

IMPLICATIONS AND DIFFICULTIES

This emphasis upon doctrine is relevant here because any attempt to introduce democratic planning will necessarily be partly a moral enterprise, an effort to qualify purely technical needs by bringing to bear criteria of value formulated as administrative principles. The problems of leadership become those of applying such principles within the context of practical action, which is to say, of expediency. This attempt to consciously inform administration with democratic values is one of the more obvious evidences of the convergence of administrative leadership and statesmanship.

We shall sharpen our insight into the problems raised by the application of the TVA's grass-roots doctrine if we pause to ask: Why has the Authority adopted these principles? It will not do, of course, to overlook the moral purpose; let us take that as granted. Yet the query persists. Why should the TVA, of all organizations, take up cudgels against Washington? Why should this vanguard agency embrace so warmly "existing institutions" and "the people?"

For a number of reasons, which we shall not detail here, there is a natural tendency for an organization to identify itself with an ideology, with a set of morally sustaining ideas which will lend support to decisions enforced by circumstance. This is merely a predisposition, however, and the quest it sets in motion is not necessarily uniform. Organizations established in a stable context, with assured futures, do not feel the same urgencies as those born of turmoil and set down to fend for themselves in undefined ways among institutions fearful and resistant. As in the case of individuals, insecurity summons ideological reinforcements.

The TVA was particularly susceptible to this kind of insecurity because it was not the spontaneous product of the local institutions. The TVA was not created as a response to pressure from the South. It was essentially an invasion and as such faced the task of weaning the attitudes of the people of the area from an initial hostility or suspicion. This task it has accomplished in very large measure. But the very fact that the task was there indicated the kind of special problem in statesmanship which the Authority faced. The TVA could not take its position in the Valley for granted. It had to feel its way. This was facilitated by the formulation of a policy which would reassure external elements and would so educate its own ranks in order to maximize the possibilities of social acceptance.

This interpretation gains strength as we recognize that the grass-roots doctrine filled what amounted to an ideological vacuum. The formulation of this doctrine did not precede the establishment of TVA, nor did its precepts materially influence the nature of the organization created by the TVA Act of 1933. The form of the TVA organization seems rather to have been an *ad hoc* development, related more to the specific political situation at the time of its inception than to any broad principles of public management. To be sure, the advantages were apparent of a corporate organization having the powers of government and the flexibility of private enterprise—a form already familiar in American government. But the key elements of the situation in 1933 which seemed to point to the need for an autonomous agency were (1) the struggle over public power, and (2) the experimental character of the TVA as a planning agency. Neither implied a self-conscious doctrine such as that developed by the Authority.

1. An autonomous agency, having broad powers of discretion, was an appropriate device for organizing a battle against the electric utility interests. A leadership could be chosen which understood its responsibilities in the national struggle undertaken by the Roosevelt administration. The autonomous directorate could muster its forces freely, in the light of the needs of the conflict, without being bound by rules formulated for extraneous ends and without being hampered by the customs and prior commitments of a federal department. This was part of the basis for the demand, supported by TVA's "founding father," Senator George W. Norris, that the Authority be free of U. S. Civil Service Commission control so that "spies" of the "power trust" might be prevented from infiltrating the organization. Again, the fact that TVA was permitted flexibility in the use of its funds was justified partly on the basis of the electric power controversy. This flexibility would make it possible for the agency to seize opportunities as they arose for advancing the cause of public power. For example, a local electric coöperative whose area was threatened with invasion by private utilities might receive emergency aid to fill gaps in its power lines.

2. The TVA Act, and more fully the message of President Roose-

velt requesting the legislation, represented a political challenge, even if it was not an entirely new departure in the exercise of federal authority for general welfare objectives. According to the President, the TVA was to be "charged with the broadest duty of planning for the proper use, conservation, and development of the natural resources of the Tennessee River drainage basin and its adjoining territory for the general social and economic welfare of the Nation." In the public mind, the meaning of TVA was bound up with the values of planning and social responsibility as corollaries of the public power controversy. This represented a model of positive government which could not be put forward for the federal government as a whole but rather, for reasons of strategy, as an "experiment" to be extended as conditions might warrant. In that capacity, and separated from the existing federal apparatus, the agency would remain in the national spotlight as a living example of what planning could accomplish. Moreover, the Authority still remains the receptacle of the hopes of those who stand for national planning; its autonomy is defended in political terms, on the basis of its program rather than of the grass-roots method.

It seems clear that in 1933 the implications of the managerial form of the TVA for the future of federal administration were not well understood. Certainly the problems of public power and planning were pressing, and no systematic doctrine, such as the grass-roots theory later put forward by the Authority, was envisaged. It is true that the Authority in its basic charter was authorized to coöperate with local and state institutions, but no positive program of strengthening existing institutions was outlined as part of the conception of the TVA. The Authority was also authorized to coöperate with federal agencies, but this has not been stressed by TVA as a basic objective; Mr. Lilienthal has suggested that regional agencies should be compelled to coöperate with state and local agencies but has not recommended a similar injunction with respect to organs of the federal departments.

THE FUNCTIONS OF DOCTRINE

If, as has been suggested, the special administrative form of TVA was derived from the circumstances of its inception rather than from general principles, it should be easy to see that an ideological vacuum would arise soon after the initial period of operation. After political and constitutional victory was assured, and it became clear that the TVA was to endure, it was necessary for the leadership to develop some notion of its place within the American political system. Somehow the question had to be answered: what now? Is the Authority a viable method of administering federal functions on a permanent basis, apart from the context of conflict and experiment?

It was natural—though perhaps not inevitable—that the leadership should look with pride at the organization which had won so much praise, and natural that it should feel that the TVA method had an enduring value as effective management in a democracy. To some extent, fondness for the grass-roots theory resulted from the fact that it was raised as a banner in the internal conflict which rocked the agency not long after its inception. A unified outlook was not known until the removal of Arthur E. Morgan by President Roosevelt. The struggle which led to that removal is often interpreted as having involved the question of whether the TVA would work with the people of the Valley or impose its program despite them. However that may be, it is clear that originally there was no unity, and that the special outlook of Harcourt A. Morgan and David E. Lilienthal was formulated in the course of controversy. The latter is always an effective environment for the crystallization of loyalties to a set of ideas.

The basic functions of this democratic TVA doctrine have been (1) internal, satisfying needs related to effective administrative communication, and (2) adjustment to the area of operation. The content of the doctrine is not, perhaps, of great significance for the former function, but it is decisive for the latter. Whatever the specific formulation, the idea of taking account of, or working with, or otherwise accepting the existing social institutions of the Valley is clearly consonant with the iron necessities of continuing to exist and work in that area. Whether or not the TVA had developed the grass-roots theory, it would have found it necessary in some way to get along with those forces which might wreck the program if moved to resistance. In relation to the states, counties, and other agencies of local government, the TVA could not have operated successfully without framing its program within the existing pattern of government, including the powers and traditional prerogatives of the local units. That must be taken for granted by any organization, public or private, which seeks to accomplish a large-scale operation within a populated area. The alternative is force—an alternative which even occupying armies in enemy lands are loath to use. In other fields, as in economics, the TVA must assume that the main industrial base in the Valley will be private industry. Its work must rest upon that fact, so that it may convince existing industry of the value of a good stewardship of the Valley's resources. Thus in one sense the grass-roots approach would seem simply to verbalize an administrative procedure which any agency would follow of necessity.

The flaw in that last statement is this: while existing centers of power must be taken into account, while compromise is assuredly essential to democratic policy, *expediency and compromise are not the same thing as capitulation.*

Why, then, has the TVA elected to espouse a doctrine which places a halo over procedures which might in any case be considered normal and necessary? One answer is that such a doctrine functions to clear away the suspicions and latent resistance with which an agency imposed from above might be greeted. It provides a vehicle for the justification of special efforts which may be made to placate the local leaderships and give them a stake in the fortunes of an organization not their own. Frontal appeals by local government to the TVA for favors may be avoided if the Authority itself systematically exploits opportunities to assist these units with advice and money. The doctrine serves also as a means of organizing a mass base for the Authority by formulating and justifying aid to labor unions, coöperatives, farmers, farm organizations, universities, and state governments. Such a base serves as protection if the agency is subject to attack. Indeed, it is clear from the record that the Authority expects support from those agencies with which it works. Thus when, in 1941, the President of the University of Tennessee publicly criticized the proposed construction of Douglas Dam, and seemed to call into question the general benefit of TVA for the Valley, the Authority was much displeased, and threatened to "reconsider" the method by which it carried on its agricultural program through the land-grant colleges. When it is understood that the method in question is offered as one of the prime examples of the grass-roots approach, the significance of this fact can easily be appreciated.

UNANALYZED TERMS IN THE DOCTRINE OF DEMOCRATIC ADMINISTRATION

TVA's espousal of the grass-roots doctrine places it squarely in the realm of statesmanship. We say statesmanship, not simply politics, because the Authority's leadership must take responsibility for the institutional consequences of the application of the ideology in action. The ascent to power is always marked by the need to qualify and chasten ideas in the light of commitments to the community. For the TVA, these commitments center upon the well-being of the Authority as an organization. We are not unfamiliar with the travail of ideologies when faced with the problems of responsible leadership in the total community, but it is important to recognize that a similar process takes place at the level of administrative leadership.

Language used for self-protection and exhortation develops terms which are unanalyzed, and persistently so, for their effectiveness derives from the diversity of meanings with which they may be invested. Carefully removed from operational tests, such symbols endure without hazard the shifting content of the behavior which they clothe. This is well understood in the field of frankly moral injunction, emotionally formulated, designed to persuade. But the continuity between the political harangue and the apparently technical devices of administrative relationship, while significant, is far less obvious.

This continuity derives in the first instance from the fact that all statements contain unanalyzed terms until and unless a specifiable context is at hand. Such ideas as "to achieve unity" or "lend assistance" assume meaning empirically only when we know how to answer the questions: with or to whom? under what circumstances? and for what? Very often, when methods are essentially routine, the selection implicit in such questions is understood by the participants, so that what seem to be unanalyzed abstractions have contexts adequately specified in precedent and practice. But when formulations of procedure are elaborated into organizational doctrine, and come to have a value and function apart from technical goals, the doctrine as such may take on a definitive role. It becomes a vehicle of organizational self-consciousness, a tool for the education of the ranks, and may become progressively divorced from any definite subject-matter. In the process of being informed with an affective content, the special procedural doctrine may be linked to some commonly accepted symbol—such as, in America, "democracy"—in order to share a derived and conditioned aura. Increasingly, concrete analysis will be avoided, and since *unanalyzed abstractions cannot guide action*, actual behavior will be determined not so much by professed ideas as by immediate exigencies and specific pressures.

It has been suggested that the Tennessee Valley Authority grew to organizational maturity under a natural pressure to come forward with a theory which would justify the very nature as well as the existence of the organization. For TVA was from its inception a challenge not only to the "power trust" but also, among other things, to the theory of government which prevailed in the Valley area: the idea of local sovereignty and "states' rights." Objectively, perhaps not always explicitly understood, it became the task of the Authority's leadership to find a means of mitigating the opposition to an organization imposed upon the area by the central government. This task, as a social need, does not, of course, mechanically determine the flow of ideas; but it creates a framework of problems and possible consequences for the life of the organization which select and reinforce convenient formulations, and which subtly reject those which carry an implicit challenge or which may tend to undermine essential loyalties.

It need not be denied that the notion of a grass-roots administration is a product of the TVA's genuine concern for democracy; that concern may be associated with the fact that the specific doctrine produced has been shaped by the need to adapt the organization to its institutional environment—to come to terms, to make its peace with the existing social structure. These objectives can, in a limited sense, go hand in hand, the one fortifying the other. But the limits are soon reached. For the needs of maintaining the organization tend to drive it toward alliances and mechanisms of participation which are specific and immediately most effective. Commitments are made, traditions and habits laid down, which have an inevitably restrictive pressure on the exercise of democracy. *As a consequence, there is a strong tendency for the theory itself to contain unanalyzed elements, permitting covert adaptation in terms of practical necessities.*

The most obvious of the unanalyzed elements in the grass-roots theory of administration is the use of such terms as "the people" and "institutions close to the people." Thus, in one of many formulations by Mr. Lilienthal we may read:

> To administer national laws entirely from Washington . . . tends to exclude and ignore the local and State institutions the people have already set up. Usually these agencies are close to the people and understand their problems; they can often be of great value in helping to carry forward national policies. But in the nature of things an overcentralized, remote administration of Federal functions will be unable or unwilling to enlist the active partnership of those existing institutions, public and private agencies such as the universities and extension services, local and State planning commissions, State conservation boards, chambers of commerce, boards of health—the list is long and inclusive.

Here we see an attempt to adjust the new requirements of public policy to the traditional federal system. Without desiring or trying to reverse the trend toward increased federal authority, it is suggested that authority be so exercised that the existing state administrative structures may be fitted into the new pattern. In the above quotation we find specified not only the need for decentralized administration, but its avenues as well. The administration of federal authority is to use "existing" agencies "close to the people." The assumption is made that these institutions are in fact representative of the people, or that in the long run they will most closely approximate representativeness. In those circles in the Authority which defend the official viewpoint, the tendency is to speak in terms of the "long run" and to make little effort to defend the existing character of the local organizations on the basis of democratic criteria.

The fact is that the Authority has had to adapt itself not so much to the people in general as to the actually existing institutions which have the power to smooth or block its way. It therefore becomes ideologically convenient to fall in with the general practice in the area of identifying the existing agencies with "the people," and permitting de facto leadership in the region to be its own stamp of legitimacy. In this way the grass-roots approach permits the Authority to come to terms with one of the most important elements of potential resistance by approving the maintenance and strengthening of the existing administrative apparatus at the state level. Moreover, since it may be assumed that this apparatus and its control is a primary prize in the struggle against federal encroachment, it is easy to see that the grass-roots approach permits a vital concession to the "states' rights" forces. All this quite apart from the conscious sources of the official doctrine.

OTHER AMBIGUITIES IN TVA DOCTRINE

Aside from the general problem of who are "the people," and the need to make explicit the criteria of selection, there are other ambiguities in the terms of the TVA doctrine:

1. There is a vagueness about the mechanics by which local influence may be brought to bear upon a decentralized agency. It is well known that where administrative control from the center is weak, the field officers of an organization may tend to become representatives of their area. As such, they are subject to the informal influence of close association with local problems, including the pressure of a public which must be dealt with on a day-to-day basis. An independent agency may indeed identify itself with the welfare of its region, and shape its techniques of administration in local terms. But it is not clear that the people of the Tennessee Valley have been afforded any significant control over the operations of TVA beyond the normal channels of congressional appeal. The responsibility for review of decisions of serious consequence lies with the Congress. The Tennessee Valley, as a region, does not make decisions on such important matters as the construction of dams or the expenditures of the regional authority.

2. It may be questioned whether the location of the central office of an agency is of itself decisive for the quality of being "close to the people." Long association, involving acquaintance with field personnel as well as with the habits, customs, and outlook of an agency, may be of equal importance. This is especially true if "the people" is identified with its organized expressions in the form of existing local governments and private associations. These institutions may build up a stable set of relationships with agencies controlled from afar, and yet feel that they are "close." The defense of the Bureau of Reclamation and the Corps of Engineers by many local groups from the Missouri Valley, and their fear of some new agency which, though decentralized to the area, might be alien, is a good example of such "closeness." The issue here is not the defense of one approach against the other, but simply to point out that the meaning of "close to the people" is unanalyzed.

3. The significance of "working through established agencies" may vary, depending, for example, on the relative strength of the local organizations. There may be effective coöperation between equals, or dominance by one side or the other. Much may depend on the extent of discretion and the degree of common agreement on general approach. The development of administrative constituencies[3] may significantly shape the concrete meaning of the method.

4. "Coördination" is another term whose meaning will be derived from the procedures it identifies. Like "unity," this is a word which is often used vaguely in order to avoid making real objectives explicit. It is an honorific, which must grace all administrative programs. But coördination involves control; and it is precisely the concrete lines of authority implied in any given system of coördination which constitute its meaning. Coördination may range from the mere circularization of ideas through the definition of jurisdiction all the way to the most thoroughgoing Gleichschaltung. In the TVA, one leading official has made a distinction between the "coördination of agencies" as the function of a regional authority and the "coördination of programs," the latter considered as proper. But of course if this involves the elimination of other agencies, whose programs are taken over by the regional authority, it will not be highly valued, as coördination, by the agencies in question.

5. "Participation of the people" is rated highly, but here again its significance depends upon such factors as the meaning of the program to the individuals concerned, the level of education, the actual locus of decision, and the nature of the organizations through which participation is achieved. Participation may range from mere involvement by means of devices established and controlled by the administrative apparatus to spontaneous organization based on and integrated with existing community patterns of coöperation.[4]

ADMINISTRATIVE DISCRETION

The propaganda of the "outs," of those who need not take responsibility for a definite course of action, may retain its unanalyzed

---

[3] See ibid., Chaps. IV and V, "TVA and the Farm Leadership: The Construction of an Administrative Constituency."
[4] See ibid., Part III, "The Formal Cooptation of 'Grass Roots' Elements—Ambiguities of Participation."

elements with impunity; but those who govern (in organizations large or small, private or public) are forced to act, and to assume responsibility for the consequences of events. As a leadership exercises its discretion in action, it generates a history. This history will, not always happily make concrete the unanalyzed abstractions of its doctrine.

Discretion is a process of selection—above all, the selection of tools for the execution of policy. But these tools are social facts: they have lives of their own, they have needs and predispositions which do not permit an easy manipulation for alien or indifferent ends. Human tools are recalcitrant; they ask a price, the price of commitment. He who would induce coöperation must agree to be shaped in turn, to submit to pressure upon policy and action. This give-and-take may not appear in its most significant forms in a contract or agreement. It may never be verbalized.

The influence of recalcitrant tools upon policy may not be readily apparent. It may not be directed to the specific program which prompted coöperation. Since the consequences of coöperation ramify widely, a coöperating group may execute a policy initiated by another without substantial deviation, but at the same time it may make demands in another field as the price of continued collaboration. The meaning of the relationship of author and agent, of initiator and tool, will not be understood until the consequences of coöperation for decision-making can be traced. Nor can an understanding of the act of discretion be divorced from its effect upon the position of the organization among its contemporaries, and upon its nature in the light of long-run objectives.

Management strives for discretion; a leadership seeks freedom of movement, a range of choice, so that it may more ably invest its day-to-day behavior with a long-run meaning. Prestige and survival are not normally accepted as legitimate ends of administrative activity, especially in government and among the subordinate units of a larger organization. But prestige and survival, even for the smallest unit—so long as there are those who have a stake in it—are real factors in decision, as participants know. *Lacking formal channels through which these barely hidden motives may operate, management requires enlarged discretion as a means of introducing the factors of prestige and survival into its choices among alternative methods for the execution of formal policy.*

This striving for discretion is reinforced as the role of the managerial expert grows in importance. Professionalization in management, providing ideals of method and loyalty to managerial objectives, creates a "responsible management." But, as the price of responsibility, the expert insists upon an enlargement of discretionary powers. He joins the ranks of other experts in denying to the layman the right to judge among alternatives when these lie within the province of specialized experience.

Discretion is selection, and it is also intervention. It enters upon an existing social situation, creating disequilibrium and anxiety until some new adjustment restores order and security. Intervention involves consequences for (1) enduring factors always present where prior social organization exists; and (2) conditions of imbalance or conflict which happen to exist at the time of intervention.

1. Administrative intervention cannot escape the force of precedent. Normally, the attempt to institute a program will run up against a network of prerogative and privilege which will have to be dealt with in some manner before operations proceed very far. (Aspects of this problem are analyzed by Gouldner in his article on "Succession.") Except in extreme cases, these interests will not be liquidated or even absorbed, but will remain as nuclei of power which the organization must take into account. This situation soon creates the problem, among others, of the representation of interests. This may take explicit form or, when the real pressures are strong and no formal avenues are permitted, representation may be informal and sometimes covert. Indeed, where the selective process implicit in discretion may invite criticism, the process itself may become informal and covert. When there is a serious uneasiness about informal representation, an ideology may be developed, or an existing doctrine, perhaps otherwise neutral, may be reinforced. A doctrine of legitimacy may be elaborated, justifying a specific selection of representatives when alternative possibilities are apparent. Where a program is broad, and representation of a general interest group or class (farmers, labor) is at issue, choice by the agency often signifies intervention among the competitors for leadership within the client group itself. This is a decisive act of discretion, and may often commit an organization to a faction with which it has no sympathy and a conflict it does not desire; or such discretion, when its consequences are recognized, may

be a means of modifying the social structure with which the organization has to deal.

2. Discretion may take place within a context of contending social forces. The loyalties of an administrative leader may be weaned away from exclusive attention to the organization with which he is identified when the interests of a social class or group are at stake in a general struggle. In such a context, administrative decisions may be made in terms of consequences for the overall contest, with the needs of the particular organization subordinated. An extreme case is the role of Communists in labor unions, in particular their tendency to subordinate the interests of a union to the needs of the general defense and extension of the policies of the regime in Soviet Russia. But the pattern is more general: In a period of anticlerical struggle, it will be expected that a devout Catholic administrator will devote some attention to the consequences of his actions for the welfare of the Church; in a period of considerable ethnic tension, the decisions of a Negro or a Jew might be expected to be shaped by considerations tangential to the special program of his organization; when sectional feeling runs high, an administrator in a federal agency might subordinate his loyalty to the agency as such to the struggle for the advancement of sectional goals.

The problem of administrative discretion is customarily raised in terms of the potentially arbitrary action of quasi-legislative or quasi-judicial regulatory bodies. This is of great importance as the practice of delegating authority to the executive power is extended. But from the point of view of organizational analysis it is the *internal relevance* of discretion which is especially significant. Administrators commonly develop commitments to methods and to specific organizations with which convenient relationships have been established. These in turn are related to client groups with ends and commitments of their own. As a consequence, a system of mutual dependence and aspiration develops which cuts across organizational lines. Hence the exercise of discretion must be analyzed with reference to the structure of the governmental system as a whole, as well as to the evolution of the particular organization itself. The execution of a program may be materially affected, in the long run, by the managerial structures which are built and sustained in connection with it. Insofar as discretion is permitted in the determination of the forms and interconnections of any given apparatus and its related organizations, a measure of control over policy itself will in effect have been delegated. The TVA's grass-roots doctrine seeks to maximize discretion. Depending upon the objectives of public management, this may be an unimpeachable program. It is not our concern to offer an appraisal. What is significant here is that the exercise of discretion in a concrete social context, under the pressure of organizational needs, created a problem of interest-representation, emphasized by action within a situation marked by controversy among groups and agencies.[5] In addition, the elaboration of a doctrine justifying the maximization of discretion poses significant alternatives for the federal structure unanticipated by the founders of the Authority.

The wide measure of corporate freedom afforded the TVA was related to its business function and justified by the experimental character of the projects, as well as by the exigencies of the electric power controversy. This has been extended by the TVA itself to a program for the decentralized administration of regular federal functions. On this view, the straightforward alternatives implicitly posed by the Authority for the future of the federal government are (1) no independent regional agencies; or (2) the subordination of departmental prerogatives to the discretion of the regional agencies. Since it is unlikely that the federal departments or their organized clienteles will willingly abandon structures and precedents established after considerable effort, it is possible that the concrete interpretation of grass-roots administration evidenced in the discretion exercised by TVA may endanger the general idea of decentralization itself.

Some of the "old-line" agencies have interpreted their experience with TVA to mean that an independent regional agency cannot effectively coördinate federal agencies in the field. For its part, the TVA leadership has felt that it need not be concerned about the consequences of its version of decentralization for the federal departments, for, it has contended, a democratic perspective is concerned not with the prerogatives of officials but with the needs and desires of the people. But this view encounters serious difficulties as we note that the special relation of these federal agencies to client publics which have a stake in their continued existence makes of them something

[5] See *ibid.*, Chap. VI, "Unanticipated Consequences, 1: The Struggle in Agriculture and the Role of TVA."

more than merely "bureaucratic domains." Hence the problem of discretion assumes its full significance only as we see its consequences for the role and character of the organization.

The organizational consequences of discretion are not often made explicit. However, one TVA official, discussing the future of the Authority's financing, made the following comment:

> The most obvious result of comprehensive revenue-financing power is to give the Authority largely independent discretion in the expenditure of funds on "development activities." The miscellaneous activities falling within this category are the ones spoken of in the statute with the least clarity. At the same time, they constitute the integrating cement of the Authority's 'regionalism.' Also, they are the activities most subject to conflict with the various activities of the various line departments of the federal government, and of the Valley states. The content of this development activities program has expanded and changed markedly in conjunction with the evolution of the Authority's concept of an integrated regionalism. With the completion of the major construction phase, the real character of the Authority will depend upon the character of its development activities program.

The TVA does not have and has not actively sought the measure of discretion involved here, but it is clear that a consideration of the implications of discretion raises problems significantly related to the emergent character of the organization itself.[6]

INHERENT DILEMMAS

Tension and dilemma are normal and anticipated corollaries of the attempt to manipulate events in the light of an abstract doctrine. Social structures are precipitants of behavior undertaken in many directions and for many purposes. Mutual adaptation establishes only an uneasy equilibrium. This in turn is continuously modified and disturbed as the consequences of action ramify in unanticipated ways. Practical leadership cannot long ignore the resistance of social structure, and is often moved thereby to abandon concern for abstract goals or ideals. But those who cannot take this road, who must continue to be identified with a doctrine and profess to use it in action, are con-

---

[6] See *ibid.*, Chap. VII, "Unanticipated Consequences, 2: Land-Use Policy and the Character of TVA."

tinually harassed by tensions between the idea and the act. Abstractions may fulfill useful functions in communication and defense, and may be long sustained as meaningful even when effective criteria of judgment are lacking. But an act entails responsibility, establishing alliances and commitments which demand attention and deference.

This is not to suggest that ideals are futile and abstractions useless. Tension does not mean defeat, nor does dilemma enforce paralysis. It is precisely the problem of leadership to find a means, through compromise, restraint, and persuasion, to resolve tensions and escape dilemmas. But in doing so, attention must be directed to the real forces which underlie its difficulties. This is the constructive function of analysis which seeks to take account of structural rigidities and the indirect consequences of executive action. Where such analysis is considered destructive, it is usually because doctrine, assuming an ideological role, is not meant to be analyzed. In extreme cases, unanalyzed doctrine ceases to operate in action at all, and the real criteria of decision are hidden in a shadowland of unrecognized discretion determined opportunistically by immediate exigency.

The TVA, in relation to its policy of grass-roots administration, is not immune to such difficulties. Though seldom made explicit, there are sources of tension which are recognized by members of the staff, and which have entered into the process of administrative decision. Among these may be noted:

1. *Doctrine and commitment.*[7] "Between the Idea and the Act Falls the Shadow." This is the most general, perhaps also the most banal, of the dilemmas inherent in the attempt to apply democratic principles in action. Doctrine is abstract, hence can be judiciously selective. In formulating the doctrine, qualifications may be introduced which condition its acceptance. But action is concrete, generating consequences which define a sphere of interest and responsibility, together with a corresponding chain of commitments. Fundamentally, this initial and inevitable discrepancy between doctrine and commitment derives from the essential distinction between the *interrelation of ideas* and the *interaction of phenomena*. The former is involved in doctrine, the latter in action. We can revise our formula-

---

[7] Cf. C. I. Barnard, *Dilemmas of Leadership in the Democratic Process*, Stafford Little Lectures (Princeton, 1939), p. 11.

tions but we cannot so readily call back our acts. In its most obvious sense, this discrepancy creates the normal necessity to revise decisions and even overall doctrine in the light of events.

Less obvious are the consequences of another type of commitment, that to the doctrine itself. When policy is institutionalized, executive decision is not readily reversible. Policy, which ostensibly should be determined on the basis of a scientific appraisal of practical means for the achievement of stated ends, becomes invested with prestige-survival value and may persist as official doctrine despite a weakening of its instrumental power. Whatever instrumental effectiveness the policy does have tends to be related to informal rather than professed goals. This may occur, for example, when a leadership becomes identified with a given policy. Or commitment to a doctrine may be preserved because of the pressure of public opinion or of important centers of power in the community. Hence such a commitment hampers scientific adaptation, though it may be necessary in fulfilling the needs of statesmanship. In this context, the British Labour Party's doctrinal commitment to socialism may be a burden to the leadership now that it is in power.

2. *Commitment to a doctrine may result in emphasis upon one type of adjustment at the cost of others.* While, as has been suggested, the TVA's grass-roots doctrine may be understood as reflecting the organizational need to come to terms with its institutional environment, the official doctrine does not appear to fill all of the Authority's needs for adjustment. Among the most important of the gaps is the need to adjust to the existing structure of the federal government. That, too, is part of the Authority's environment, though during the tenure of President Roosevelt the need to adjust to the federal structure may not have been as important for the survival of the organization as adjustment to local institutions. In any case, as reflected in the TVA doctrine, the need to adjust to the area of operation has been taken as basic. For the TVA has failed to develop a formulation which would be acceptable to the administrators in Washington, and in a practical sense there have been areas of serious maladjustment. It appears, indeed, that TVA has not faced up to the need to accept the federal structure as given, and has taken an "all or none" attitude whose revolutionary implications for the structure of the national government are accepted, though seldom made explicit. This ap-

proach is irresponsible in the nonderogatory sense of a single-minded pursuit of special goals which leaves consequences to be handled by those directly affected and by the compromises of history.

There are few organizations which can afford the luxury of a neat correlation of ideas and action. This is especially true when the doctrine is administrative, and commits the organization to a certain way of doing things. The needs which lead to or reinforce the formulation of an official doctrine do not ordinarily exhaust the demands made upon an organization. To be sure, there must be some warrant in action for the general ideas propounded by the leadership, but the latter is free to select from its program a set of objectives which will reflect its primary aspirations. This fragment may become the receptacle of meaning and significance and—on the level of doctrine, of verbalization—may infuse the organization as a whole with a special outlook. But only in those cases where a leadership is reckless of the fate of its charge may it drive toward complete consistency. The TVA has been no exception. Its needs are not simple and are certainly not exhausted by those which have generated the grass-roots theory. Apart from the problem just mentioned of adaptation to the federal structure, we may mention:

a) In the light of its commitments to press the struggle for public power, the TVA could not permit its electricity program to be channeled through any of the existing agencies of the state government in the area. Although TVA has acted primarily as a power wholesaler, it is fair to say, speaking realistically, that the power program has been one of "direct action." It is true that the power distributors are local municipalities and electric power coöperatives, and this is counted a grass-roots approach, but the difference between the operation of this program and the agricultural program is too great to be framed under the same procedural rubric. In power, the TVA has carried forward its own program, with stringent contractual controls. In agriculture, the TVA has shaped its program in terms of the existing framework of agricultural leadership. The power coöperatives have been built (though based on local response) with the direct and forceful intervention of the TVA itself. Such an approach has been ruled out in the agricultural field.

b) In 1942, during the wartime emergency, the TVA went ahead with the construction of Douglas Dam despite considerable protest from the area. Whatever the merits of the case, it is evident that in this important matter opportunities for local decision were not available. While the decision to build the dam was made in conjunction with the leaders of the national government, there is no evidence that the TVA Board opposed the development. In this matter, as in many others, the TVA represents national policy and executes that policy in other than local terms. Despite the consequent difficulties for adjustment to the area of operation, it would appear to have been consonant with the broad interests of TVA to produce the maximum possible power during wartime as a means of bolstering its position on a national scale.

Beyond the fact that an official doctrine, however sincerely held, is not usually operative in all phases of an organization's activities, it is worthy of note that ideas may serve multiple needs. The multiplication of the functions it serves may strongly bolster the doctrine because of the ease with which it comes to hand as repetitive problems are faced. For it is little more than a truism that the utility of an idea —not so much in inquiry as in smoothing the path of a predetermined course of action—may easily invest it with a specious cogency, drawing attention away from objective tests and evidence. Thus the idea of "unified resource development" may (1) aid in breaking down the barriers which separate technicians within the regional authority, and (2) serve as a justification for control of resource development by a single agency. Again, "water control on the land" is an effective formula which ties general welfare objectives such as the improvement of agriculture and soil conservation to the constitutional pegs of navigation and flood control; but the concomitant idea of carrying on soil conservation in order to protect the investment of the government in dams and reservoirs also serves to justify exercise of those functions by TVA rather than some other agency.

3. *Selective decision and total involvement.*[8] Democracy as method, and the grass-roots policy as method, represent modes of decision. Decision, however, demands only the partial consent of the participants, who are involved only obliquely in their capacity as voters or choosers. But the execution of decisions is a matter of action, and action tends to involve the participants as wholes. Hence coöp-

[8] Cf. *ibid.*, p. 10.

erative action, as Barnard says, "requires substantially complete conformance."

In other words, while the choice of a given course of action may involve the individual or group only to a limited degree, in fact there is a tendency for circumstances to demand more extensive involvement. Organizational action, once initiated, tends to push onward, so that the initiator may find himself enmeshed in new relationships and demands beyond his original intention. Here again the key word is "commitment." Every executive knows that the initiation of a new course of action is a serious matter precisely because of the risk involved that the establishment of precedents, of new machinery and new relationships—the generation of new and complex interests—may make greater demands upon his organization than he can presently foresee. The problem is not one of inner impulse, but rather of the structural forces which summon action and constrain decision.

Conformance, indispensable to the completion of the movement begun by decision, has therefore a qualifying effect and creates an inescapable tension. This means, in respect to the TVA, that while its decentralist policy may be instituted for special reasons (referable in part to the ideals of the leadership as well as to other factors), nevertheless there will be a tendency for the organization as a whole to be shaped by the process of conformance. It has had to go further in carrying out the policy than it may originally have intended; the formal process of consent has been transformed into concrete institutional relationships, generating new and unlooked-for demands.

4. *Insofar as discretion is delegated, bifurcation of policy and administration is reinforced.* It is basic policy inside the Authority that planning and execution should be united in a single administrative arm. But the delegation of functions involved in the grass-roots formula makes insistence upon this principle of unity somewhat anomalous. The channeling of programs through independent agencies necessarily delegates discretion, with the consequence that programs thus delegated may be extensively modified in execution. The dilemma is only made more explicit if controls are instituted which operate objectively to transform the independent local agency into an administrative adjunct of the Authority; execution may be brought into line with policy, but the grass-roots objective will have been

undermined. In the Authority, an attempt has been made to escape this dilemma, notably in the agricultural program, by denying in principle the possibility of a difference in objective between the initiating and the executing agency. A heavy price in the delegation of policy-making itself is paid for this relief, however.

5. *Theories about government become preëmpted by social forces.* It is unrealistic to weigh the implications of a theory of government on the basis of its abstract formulation. The propagation of a point of view carries with it an often unwished-for alliance with others who, for their own reasons, are espousing the same or a convergent doctrine. A theory about method may at any given time be linked with a special set of goals; support for the method, for some view of how to proceed, may imply a position on what to do, and conversely. Thus TVA finds itself in the camp of the supporters of "states' rights" in respect to both its criticism of overcentralization in government and its support of the state governments as "regional resources." But at the same time, in respect to the complex of political issues summed up in the extension of positive government, the Authority is very far in point of view from the general run of supporters of local sovereignty. TVA is therefore in the continuously ambivalent position of choosing between an emphasis on method and an emphasis on program—more accurately, of assigning a priority to one or the other. The tendency of the TVA leadership has been to emphasize method as basic and cut itself off from the general welfare movement. But it cannot divorce itself completely from its antecedents, and the ambivalence persists.

6. *Emphasis on existing institutions as democratic instruments may wed the agency to the status quo.* A procedure which channels the administration of a program through established local institutions, governmental or private, tends to reinforce the legitimacy of the existing elite. This is especially true when a settled pattern claims the exclusive attention of the agency, so that other groups striving for leadership may find their position relatively weakened after the new relationships have been defined. In strengthening the land-grant colleges in its area, the TVA has bolstered the position of the existing farm leadership. There is some evidence that in the process of establishing its pattern of coöperation, TVA refrained from strengthening independent colleges in the area not associated with the land-grant system; and, more important, that the TVA capitulated to the cul-

tural predispositions of the land-grant institutions, especially in relation to Negroes and tenant farmers. Again, the relatively dominant role of the American Federation of Labor unions in TVA labor relations has been objectively a hindrance to the development of labor groups having other affiliations. In general, to the extent that the agency selects one set of institutions within a given field as the group through which it will work, the possibility of freezing existing social relations is enhanced. This dilemma has been made most explicit in the TVA agricultural program; the latter, moreover, is perhaps the most important instance within TVA of the use of the grass-roots approach.

7. *Decision "at the grass roots" may be inhibited by the system of national pressure groups.* When important issues become crystallized in the programs of groups organized on a broad scale with a national leadership, local decisions may be influenced primarily by their effect on the outcome of overall controversy. The local problem is appraised not on its merits but in the light of the influence of a local decision on the general bargaining position of the leadership. Thus a local branch of the American Farm Bureau Federation or of a CIO union may have its attitudes framed for it by a long-run national strategy—a pending bill in Congress for the transfer of functions from one agricultural agency to another, or an impending organizing drive, or a national election. To the extent that a decentralized governmental agency is influenced by decisions made by local groups in national terms, it would appear that the grass-roots approach becomes the victim of the growing centralization of political decision.

8. *Commitment to existing agencies may shape and inhibit policy in unanticipated ways.* When the channels of action are restricted, programs may be elabrated only within the limits set by the coöperating organizations. The traditions and outlook of an established institution will resist goals which appear to be alien, and the initiating agency will tend to avoid difficulties by restricting its own proposals to such as can be feasibly carried out by the grass-roots organization. Where the grass-roots method is ignored, new structures may be built and shaped initially so as to be consistent with the desired program. An attempt to carry forward a policy of nondiscrimination (as against Negroes) will not proceed very far when the instrument for carrying out this policy—usually as an adjunct of some broader program—has

traditions of its own of a contrary bent. Moreover, the grass-roots policy voluntarily creates nuclei of power which may be used for the furtherance of interests outside the system of coöperation originally established. Thus the TVA distributes electric power through electric power boards which are creatures of municipalities, with the contractual reservation that surplus income shall be used only for the improvement of the system or for the reduction of rates. But the question has been raised: What if pressure arises to use surpluses for general purposes, that is, to finance nonpower functions of the municipal governments? And what if state governments undertake to tax these surpluses? The logic of the grass-roots policy might force the Authority to acquiesce. However, it is perhaps more likely that the Authority's commitment to function as a successful power project would take precedence over the grass-roots method.

9. *Existing agencies inhibit a direct approach to the local citizenry.* The participation of local people always takes place through some organizational mechanism, notably voluntary associations established to involve a public in some measure of decision at the end-point of operation. But such associations are commonly adjuncts of an administrative apparatus, which jealously guards all approaches to its clientele. If, therefore, a federal agency establishes coöperative relations with such an apparatus, it will be committed as well to the system of voluntary associations which has been established. Hence the channels of participation of local people in the federal program will be shaped by the intermediary agency. In respect to its "closeness to the people," the status of the federal government may not, in such circumstances, be materially altered. Viewed from this perspective, the grass-roots method becomes an effective device whereby an intrenched apparatus protects its clientele, and also itself, from the "encroachments" of the federal government.

THE TVA: SOME EMPIRICAL CONCLUSIONS

In stating these sources of tension, we have hinted at their application to the TVA experience. But in fact these problems are general. They represent one way of putting relevant questions about an organization which identifies itself with a grass-roots doctrine such as the TVA has espoused. It may be useful, therefore, to state briefly the

empirical conclusions which a study of the TVA experience in applying this doctrine has reached.

1. *The grass-roots theory as ideology.* The high self-consciousness
of the TVA in putting forth its special doctrine may be explained by
the function of that doctrine in facilitating acceptance of the Authority in its area of operation, and in fulfilling the need for some general
justification of its existence as a unique type of governmental agency.
The TVA was revolutionary both in respect to the attitudes of the
local people and institutions and in respect to the federal governmental system. By adopting the grass-roots doctrine the Authority was
able to stand as the champion of local institutions and at the same
time to devise a point of view which could be utilized in general
justification of its managerial autonomy within the federal system.
However, allegiance to this doctrine, and translation of it into policy
commitments, have from time to time created serious disaffection
between TVA and other branches of the federal government, including the Department of Agriculture and the Department of the Interior. As a result, on the basis of the TVA experience, these
departments have been moved to oppose the extension of the TVA
form of organization to other areas, a fact which is consequential for
the future of the Authority itself.

2. *Delegation of the agricultural program to an organized administrative constituency.* In the major example within TVA of grass-
roots procedure—the Authority's fertilizer distribution program—
there was constructed a strong constituency-relation involving the
land-grant college system on the one hand and the Agricultural Relations Department of TVA on the other. This constituency-relation
may be viewed as a case of informal coöptation, wherein strong centers
of influence in the Valley were absorbed covertly into the policy-
determining structure of the TVA. The TVA's Agricultural Relations
Department assumed a definite character, including a set of sentiments valuing the land-grant college system as such and accepting
the mission of defending that system within the Authority. In effecting this representation, the TVA agriculturists have been able to
take advantage of the special prerogatives accruing to them from their
formal status as an integral part of the Authority, including the exercise of discretion within their own assigned jurisdiction and the exer-

tion of pressure upon the evolution of general policy within the Authority as a whole. The special role and character of the TVA agricultural group limited its outlook with respect to the participation of Negro institutions as grass-roots resources and created a special relation to the American Farm Bureau Federation. At the same time, the operation of this coöptative process probably did much to enhance the stability of the TVA within its area and especially to make possible the mobilization of support in an hour of need. In this sense, one cannot speak of the decisions which led to this situation as "mistakes."

3. *In a context of controversy, the TVA's commitments to its agricultural constituency resulted in a factional alignment involving unanticipated consequences for its role on the national scene.* In the exercise of discretion in agriculture, the TVA entered a situation charged with organizational and political conflict. The "New Deal" agricultural agencies, such as Farm Security Administration and Soil Conservation Service, came under the attack of the powerful American Farm Bureau Federation, which thought of them as threats to its special avenue of access to the farm population, the extension services of the land-grant colleges. Under the pressure of its agriculturists, the Authority did not "recognize" Farm Security Administration and sought to exclude Soil Conservation Service from operation within the Valley area. This resulted in the politically paradoxical situation that the eminently New Deal TVA failed to support agencies with which it shared a political communion, and aligned itself with the enemies of those agencies.

4. *Under the pressure of its agriculturists, the TVA gradually altered a significant aspect of its character as a conservation agency.* The TVA agricultural group, reflecting local attitudes and interests, fought against the policy of utilizing public ownership of land as a conservation measure and thus effectively contributed to the alteration of the initial policy of the Authority in this respect. The issue of public ownership is taken as character-defining in the sense that it is a focal point of division and controversy, and it was such within the TVA for an extended period. The single-minded pursuit of its ideological and constituency interests led the agricultural group to involve the Authority in a controversy with the U. S. Department of the Interior over the management of TVA-owned lands.

5. *The grass-roots utilization of voluntary associations represents a sharing of the burdens of and responsibility for power, rather than of power itself.* The voluntary association device is interpreted as a case of formal coöptation, primarily for promoting organized access to the public but also as a means of supporting the legitimacy of the TVA program. Typically, this has meant that actual authority, and to a large extent the organizational machinery, has been retained in the hands of the administering agency. After nine years of operation, the county soil associations handling TVA fertilizer were found to be still tools of the county agent system, to which the TVA-test-demonstration program was delegated.

These conclusions confirm the relevance of the foregoing analysis, much of which—the scrutiny of unanalyzed abstractions and the diagnosis of inherent dilemmas—may be made prior to extensive field research. The results of such research, so cursorily stated here, suggest that the idea of free-floating independent agencies as instruments of democratic planning requires careful scrutiny, whatever the ultimate judgment may be. They suggest further that the statesmanship exhibited by the newly emerging managerial elites, while real, is circumscribed by the requirements of responsibility to particular organizations.

Some Strategic Considerations in Innovating Leadership[1]

BY LEWIS A. DEXTER

THE MOST important instrument with which the leader has to work is himself—his own personality and the impression which he creates on other people. Consciously or unconsciously, many politicians are aware of this, although generally speaking politicians are selected because they are by temperament already adapted to a situation and a social milieu; hence they do not have consciously to adapt themselves to the demands of the times. However, the innovator, the prophet, the reformer, the originator, are rarely essentially well-adapted to society. For people who think of new and different ideas are not likely to be people who conform readily, graciously, and with ease to the social pressures and directives upon them. Sociologists, for example, despite their wealth of propositional knowledge about society, are not usually distinguished for social "savoir-faire" at the inarticulate level of immediate response; any high school girl with a really good "line" is far more effective than most of them at making people feel at ease, and at making people "like" her.

For a professional sociologist, who is concerned with teaching students to get outside their own culture, to look at events free of the custom-based assumptions which ordinarily lead to misinterpretation and misevaluation, a general attitude of skepticism and criticism may be defensible and desirable. For the professional sociologist *as such*

---

[1] Reprinted with modifications and with a previously unpublished appendix from *The Journal of Liberal Religion*, 1944, by permission of the editors. Copyright, 1944, by *The Journal of Liberal Religion*.

is not concerned with bringing about any *particular* results except insofar as changing attitudes may be regarded as a particular result. For any one, however, who is concerned with assuming leadership toward greater social adjustment, there are more far-reaching responsibilities. Such a person will discover that his behavior, gestures, mannerisms, styles of clothing, all may enter into his effectiveness or ineffectiveness—and that in selling his ideas he must also be concerned with the impression he himself makes. This does not necessarily mean that the innovator must study how to be always pleasant and agreeable; indeed, there are messages which probably can be more effectively presented at first in the manner of the Old Testament Prophets. But it does mean that the innovator must study, to achieve maximum effectiveness, what role he ought to play and within the limits of the possible adapt himself to that role, *realizing always that changing situations may call for a change in roles.*

There is relatively little certain knowledge in this area as yet, even among anthropological field-workers; but certain examples will be obvious enough to common sense. Many a Harvard man or Englishman has lost friends and alienated people in the Middle West by a "decent reserve" which happens to be regarded west of Chicago as downright coldness; one of the hardest things some Yankees have to do in coming to the West is to learn to smile on occasions when they would merely nod at home. Vice versa, some Westerners in both New and Old England have found their "friendliness" and kindliness regarded as effusiveness or presumption. The problem of the leader is to realize which, if any, of his own eccentricities, due either to cultural difference in training or to individual variation, help him in getting a respectful hearing and which hurt. Since we all tend to cherish our own way of doing things, our tendency will be to magnify the use and minimize the harm of our own peculiarities. In fact, however, to continue with the preceding example, a New Englander in the Midwest, engaged in social reform, should, if he can, learn to smile more frequently, just as a Yankee in Santo Domingo should learn to give the *embrazo* readily. (One proviso should be added; the person who is obviously, painfully, imitating something not at all natural to him perhaps had better stick to his own customs; but he probably will not be an effective leader.) Similarly, an academic man, accustomed to the bantering wit of his fellows, must learn to modify his humor in dealing with other groups. On the other hand, a Southern or Spanish accent in many sections of the North is a helpful peculiarity; and some eccentricities in dress serve to "personalize" a man and his ideas, rather than hurt him.

There are many barriers to the acceptance of the viewpoint here put forward. Most of us like to think of ourselves and our traits as autonomous, integral, unchangeable units. To regard the seeming core of our personality itself as modifiable is to many shocking; yet, in principle, there is no more reason why a man should not put on and put off a set of gestures than there is to prevent his talking now in one language, now in another. Probably, those who successfully control gestures or mannerisms do not regard gestures and mannerisms as being a basic part of their personalities at all. (In David Riesman's and Nathan Glazer's chapter you will find a point of view which, by implication at least, appears to contradict almost entirely what has just been said.)

It should be stressed that even a relatively small amount of success in adapting oneself to the needs and demands of the situation is a triumph; clearly, in the present state of knowledge, complete or anywhere near complete adaptation would be impossible of achievement. Clearly, too, there will be many times and occasions for most leaders when considerations other than their role as leader will bulk large; presumably, however, it is possible to make a rational analysis of when it is most dangerous to yield to impulse and when it is most desirable to undertake a rational analysis of the situation.

"BLOOD OF THE MARTYRS"

Spoonfuls of salt should always be poured on one of the favorite beliefs of the folklorists of self-help. It is simply not true that ingenuity, inventiveness, and a perception of new needs smooth the way to promotion and pay. In fact, a readiness to recommend reforms is one of the greatest handicaps under which an ambitious apprentice can labor.[2]

[2] The major theme of this article might be stated somewhat differently. It could read: Statesmen, ministers, scholars, and citizens are continually faced with the problem of compromise. This does not mean that they must resolve a general abstract dilemma: To compromise or not to compromise? On the contrary, in any concrete instance the question which they must answer is: What is the optimum degree of compromise in this particular situation?

The sophist might argue that, though false, the belief is socially beneficial. Taking the thesis that the "blood of the martyrs is the seed of the church" as his text, he would point out that, although those who first introduce innovations usually succumb to the slings and arrows of outraged public opinion, sooner or later the more desirable new departures are, in fact, adopted, precisely as a consequence of the sufferings of their early advocates; and, since no man deliberately chooses to be a martyr, it is fortunate indeed that the superstition about the rewards of originality exists, for it causes men to become martyrs in spite of themselves.

However, in fact, the most that one can say with accuracy is that the blood of *some* martyrs may have been the seed from which *some* churches have sprung. By the world's standards, at least, such martyrs as the Albigenses of Languedoc, who fell before the orthodox and covetous crusaders of Northern France, during the era of St. Louis, died in vain; and it is open to grave doubt whether the ultimate suc-

---

When confronted with practical problems, political theorists, church social action leaders, scientific administrators, etc., tend to analyze them casuistically; but when they discuss social action theoretically, they are apt to be dogmatic. Note, for example, the scholar who asserts that he will let *nothing* interfere with complete freedom of research, publication, and teaching. Among political theorists, in particular, there has been a continuing tradition of revolt against the futility of such absolutism.

Among the outstanding critics of conventional political theory, one might name Machiavelli, Hobbes, and Lord Halifax, the author of *Character of a Trimmer* (fl. 1690). An outstanding modern example is E. Pendleton Herring in his *Politics of Democracy*. As a student of Herring's, the writer found himself forced into a position where James A. Farley became more admirable than Senator Norris, or Governor Bricker then Wendell Willkie. This means that one sacrifices moral considerations in evaluating political realities, or that one relies with Herring upon some unformulated limitation which enables the honest man to distinguish between legitimate compromise and illegitimate opportunism. The present article attempts rather to synthesize the sense of reality, which is to be found in the works of Halifax and Herring, with the vivid awareness of such moralists as William Lloyd Garrison and John Haynes Holmes that compromise can all too often be used simply as an excuse to avoid trouble and to let evil flourish unchecked.

This article arose too out of the writer's concern with a related problem, well illustrated in David Lindsay Watson's *Scientists Are Human*. Watson demonstrates that the original thinker—the scholar who looks for new methods or utilizes new techniques—is likely to handicap himself in terms of his own career as compared with his conventionally-minded brethren. But science taken as a whole will grow precisely of unorthodox discoveries.

What then is the obligation of the young scientist if he finds himself interested in borderline topics or unfamiliar methods?

cess of Quakerism is attributable to the willingness of early Quakers to suffer the stake.

Pure logic, on the other hand, will demonstrate the fallacy as a general counsel for everybody all of the time, of the old rhyme:

> Be not the first by whom the new is tried
> Nor yet the last by whom the old is laid aside.

But, under what circumstances is it wise to try the new first? As things go, it is often the most intelligent young people who see something that needs to be done and try to do it. They find themselves thrown against stone walls; and, according to temperament and experience, become cynical or embittered.

Perhaps some instruction in the sociology of reform might lessen their sufferings and benefit society through making possible more ready acceptance of new contributions. On the principle "Forewarned is forearmed," potential reformers would study the history of inventors and innovators. They would be told of Semmelweiss who valiantly tried to explain to fellow-physicians how "elementary" hygiene would reduce deaths at child-birth; and they would be shown how as a consequence, he was ostracized to the point where he sacrificed career, sanity, and life itself. They would study the case of Jonas Hanway, who first introduced the umbrella into England, and have it explained to them why he was mobbed. They would hear of eminent scientists who joined with the lay public in deriding the pioneers of aviation. They would see Servetus, the forerunner of Unitarianism, burned at the stake and Priestly, scientist and religious thinker, in effect, exiled two centuries later by public opposition. They would learn to understand why Roger Williams' "inconvenient questioning of land titles and his views on the Massachusetts charter" led to his banishment into the wilderness where he was "sorely tossed . . . in a bitter winter season not knowing what bread or bed did mean."

CURRICULUM FOR INNOVATORS

And, lest they gather the impression that these are matters of far away and long ago, there would be those to instruct them in the cost of unorthodoxy today. It would be explained that although in the western democracies resort to physical coercion is *relatively* rare, the pressures to conformity are still intense. Case studies to document this generalization would be made from the experience of men who are trying to advance the cause of human decency and efficiency today. These case studies would permit answers to such questions as: What happens to the Negro dentist in some backward area who tries to dissuade his patients from getting gold teeth if they do not need them? What is the fate of the worker who complains that his trade union's leadership is autocratic? What happens to the little street vendor who sells a magazine which influences, close to the Commissioner of Licenses, distrust?

Tables might be prepared of the average number of articles accepted by the more reputable academic journals from persons using orthodox scientific methods and terminologies and of the average number accepted from those who utilize a new (and afterward accepted) method or style; similar tables might be made of the salaries of the former group, as compared with the latter, at the same ages. Studies might be made of certain organizations to see who is promoted when and why; and these will demonstrate that those who accept the accustomed methods of doing business on the whole rise to the top. The careers of physicians who adopt *new and soundly based* treatments might be examined to see whether they lag behind less progressive men in income; it will be shown that poets who write in a new idiom are retarded in winning recognition.

If these facts are accepted simply as facts, the curriculum just outlined might serve only to discourage potential innovators; but wisely handled, the insistent question will be: *Why did these new ideas meet with so much opposition? How could that opposition have been avoided?* That is: *What changes in the method of presentation might have helped "sell" the basic idea?*

In each case, presumably, the answer will be somewhat different; but certain general conclusions will probably emerge from a study directed toward answering such questions.

INNOVATOR AS A PERSON

For example there is a motive, frequently present in resistance to change, of which the typical innovator is unaware. Schiller has expressed it thus:

> For, of the wholly common is man made
> And custom is his nurse. Woe then to them

That lay irreverent hands upon his old
House furniture, the dear inheritance
From his forefathers, for time consecrates
And what is gray with age becomes the sacred.

The typical innovator has no sympathy with such sentiments. Accordingly, to those who have grown up in some old-fashioned way of doing things, reform seems to be (and in fact sometimes is so handled that it really is) nothing but an excuse for more or less refined sadism. Anthony Trollope in *The Warden* presents an extremely touching picture of the sufferings which a reform may impose upon those who have grown into the old order of things.

Few innovators see, either, that frequently they suffer not so much because of their *good ideas* as because of their *total personalities*. That is to say, the kind of man who develops something new is apt to be relatively insensitive to customary courtesies in many respects. For personalities tend to be more or less integrated: and unorthodoxy in one field may well be accompanied by unorthodoxies in others. Veblen was not only a scoffer at classical economics; he was personally sarcastic. It is characteristic that several potential donors to a project for reducing the chances of war were unwilling to give anything when they observed that the leading advocate of the idea had dirty fingernails. He himself was not aware of this; he does not care about appearance. But they could not judge his ideas; they could judge his cleanliness. And so they refused to support his plan. So, in larger matters too, the man with a new vision is often unconventional. Priestley was both an original scientist and a deviant religious thinker; had he confined himself to one occupation or the other he might have been safer than in fact he was.

NEEDED: A SOCIOLOGY OF INNOVATION

It is imperative that embryo innovators realize that the chances are that they are wrong in any original suggestion which they advance. This does not mean that original suggestions should not be advanced. *It does mean, however, that men should make sure they know why things are done the way they are done before they propose different procedure.* Amateur strategists who ignore problems of supply and transport can always evolve paper-brilliant plans because they do not recognize that effective planning must be *organismic*. That is to say, a new proposal or innovation must fit into the limitations imposed by the attitudes and values of those who have to adopt it. Military critics, like Winston Churchill and Liddell Hart, have justly pointed out that the Allied commanders in the last war made a great mistake in not using the tank intelligently; but there had to be a change in the cautious, cavalry-minded thinking of the high command, before they could use the tank properly. It is, in fact, almost axiomatic that no genuinely new weapon will be used effectively because it takes time for generals to readjust their conceptions of military propriety to its possibilities.

Similarly, it might be abstractly desirable in the United States to adopt many features of Russian or German military organization; but, in fact, such adoption would presuppose a change in the attitudes and values of American officers and men. Or, in every congregation, and in every university, one may notice needed changes; but the man who first tries to introduce such changes "fails," because he tries to *impose* them upon persons whose attitudes and values are adjusted to the previous situation. Sometimes a leader who recognizes the necessity for a democratic educational process can, more or less slowly, get people to alter their attitudes and values. Corey, in a brilliant article on the nature of educational leadership,[3] which should be carefully considered by all would-be innovators, has shown how this may be done; but in other cases it is probably necessary to admit that, without a total reorganization of society, it is inconceivable in a measurable period of time, that one's proposals can be effectuated.

Finally, there should be emphasis upon the fact that no new approach can stand on its own merits. The use of influence and pressure are just as important in getting inventions and reforms accepted as in anything else. Kelvin started his academic career by trying to obtain publication for a paper which offended one of the leaders of his pro-

[3] Stephen Corey, "Cooperative Staff Work," *School Review* (1944), 336-345. See also Marshall Dimock, "Bureaucracy Self-Examined," *Public Administration Review* (1944), 197-207, for an analysis of the way in which the executive is limited by his subordinates' preconceptions and preferences. It should not be concluded from the above statement that it is necessarily an error to try to impose a new arrangement upon a group or institution. It may be that this is sometimes the best way to educate, but the innovator should undertake an advance analysis of the different possible ways of proceeding, and decide whether it is likely to be more effective to go so far as to have to retreat, or to proceed more slowly and comprehensively along the line suggested by Corey.

fession; but Kelvin's father, himself a well-known scholar, succeeded in smoothing the matter over. Mendel, on the other hand, undertook experiments which are basic to the whole science of genetics; but, published as they were, obscurely, they lay unnoticed until his methods were rediscovered about thirty years later.

This suggests that the apprentice innovator should learn not to come forth with proposals until he has undertaken an analysis of the situation and prepared a plan of campaign. An isolated article or act will either be ignored or considered scandalous, according to its nature, and will but rarely lead to any wider understanding. The innovator must know—after the first shot is fired—*what is to be done next;* who in relevant professions or organizations can be expected or persuaded, *for whatever motives,* to support the new departure. Who can understand what is actually being attempted? What alternative means of winning a livelihood are open to those who take risks? What friendships may be lost, what temptations to unhappiness and bitterness must be abjured?

Were such insight into the sociology of innovation widely provided, there might be fewer mute, inglorious Mendels, fewer potential Semmelweisses, hindered so completely by popular or professional disapproval that they make no effective contribution to human progress at all.

ADDENDUM

THIS ARTICLE in its original form provoked a number of letters of comment. By permission, I select excerpts from three of them.

Comments by Chester Barnard:

I have been reflecting on "Be Not the First." There seemed to me at first reading to be a bit of Veblenesque cynicism or sarcasm in it but it ends up all right. I have been thinking of the subject in connection with my experience with it and its application, for example, to the affairs of a telephone company. I think in addition to the obstruction that sometime comes from selfish interests and from the inertia involved in the reluctance of individuals to change habits; there are several other factors on which I would put a good deal of stress.

One thing I think has to be understood in considering the matter and that is that a distorted view is apt to come from emphasizing the difficulties encountered in getting those new inventions and innovations adopted which *subsequently* have proved to be of great value or importance. There are many varieties of inventors and innovators and most varieties are useless. Inasmuch as usually one cannot tell from mere inspection of ideas or devices whether they will work, the species proves to be a very burdensome nuisance sometimes. I suppose most people of experience have learned from it that in practical affairs, as in science, it does not make much difference how good a thing looks, you do not know it is good until you have tried it out. The practical facilities for trying many new things are rather limited, at least in a short period, and there is a great deal of labor involved in reviewing and refusing to adopt even the ideas of devices which are clearly not good for one reason or another. In other words, I think the limitations of time alone of responsible people just simply compel a conservative attitude if they are to live or function at all. What I am talking about here might be labeled the factor of time and effort in the selection of inventions and innovations for trial.

There is a resistance of groups to innovations that perhaps primarily grows out of fear of disruption of organization communication which they impose. Wherever there is organized cooperation there is certainly involved a complexity of subtle habits, attitudes, standardized expressions and so forth, whose smooth and more or less unconscious employment is essential to effective and comfortable collaboration. A new method, gadget, or idea of policy disrupts all this, increases the difficulty of collaboration, causes an increase in misunderstandings and increases the extent to which behavior has to be deliberate and conscious. This seems to me to be a fact of observation and induction of experience that most inventors and innovators will have difficulty in believing to be true but which the administrator will forget at his peril. In other words, the overcoming of such difficulties usually involves a cost or a risk of cost either in money or in some other value which may far offset the value of an otherwise good innovation.

This leads to the factor of the limits to the capacity of organized groups to accept innovations in a given period of time. I suspect that nearly all executives, though perhaps not many are explicit about it, are thoroughly aware of the practical impossibility of introducing more than a very limited number of innovations in a given period of time. Thus if I have five innovations in process of active adoption and five more admitted to be equally as good or even better are proposed, I am nevertheless likely to reject them for what may be a considerable period of time because the organization "cannot take it." Not only habitual methods and fixed attitudes are involved, but morale is also. Standards of performance are also in jeopardy.

There is also a somewhat analogous factor of the effect of new inventions and innovations in the increasing of complexity. This is a difficult thing to state in general terms. It suggests the importance of distinguishing between inventions and innovations which are *substitutes* for old devices or practices and those which are *additional* to such old devices or practices. The latter increase complexity. Thus for many years we have had to be most careful about, and to resist the addition of, gadgets on telephone sets for the increased complexity not only tends to increase the original cost out of proportion but it greatly increases the cost of maintenance and also the skill required. Thus there are only a limited number of gadgets that I want on my automobile; there are, no doubt, a number of others which could be demonstrated to be just as useful as those I have, but if I add them the contraption gets too complicated for easy operation and it also gets into trouble much more easily. The analogous thing can be observed in the operation of people in an organization. Thus an increase in the number of functions to be performed by a group increases the difficulty of their collaboration as well as the required capacities of the individuals.

Perhaps something should also be said about the irresponsibility of the inventor or innovator from the standpoint of those who have to accept or reject the new thing. The latter have to accept all the consequences if it is a short-time matter, and think they do if it is a long-time matter. The inventor or innovator usually has a limited personal responsibility and interest and perhaps usually almost no appreciation of the burdens, particularly in organizational and political matters, that an innovation involves. I have heard it said and I believe it to be broadly true that the skill and brains involved in putting most successful inventions into practical use are very much greater than that required in making the inventions themselves.

I think perhaps all of this is implicit in your paper and perhaps some of it at least is explicit. I have found that many scholars and the physical scientists have considerable difficulty in understanding these things.

Chester Barnard

Comments by Capt. Basil Henry Liddell-Hart:

Your dissertation on the sociology of innovation, and the drawbacks of being an innovator is very apt. I have had plenty of opportunity to observe the truth of your reflections in the course of studying history, as well as personal reason to note the effects. For example, when the Nazi danger arose, and the question of rearmament come to the fore, it was proposed that I should be appointed deputy to Hankey (Secretary of the Cabinet and of the Committee of Imperial Defence) in order to replan our defence system. After the Prime Minister of the time had considered it for a while, the proposal was shelved on the ground that I was too much of an innovator, and might not conform to pattern. Again, at the outbreak of war in 1939, Hore-Belisha proposed to the Army Council that I should be called in as an official adviser, and this time the opposition prevailed on the score of the innovations I had made when I had been his unofficial adviser, in the two years before the war—which still rankled in conservative minds. Then, early in 1942, following the disasters we had suffered, the plan of creating an Operational Research Department in the War Office, with myself at the head of it, was proposed by certain people in high quarters who valued my work and ideas. While the project was under discussion, I was called in to do a good deal of preparatory work, but when in the end the department was properly constituted, I was left out and a more conventional man appointed. The same thing happened in the case of the eminent scientist who was intended to be my colleague. He was regarded as too radical, in the light of previous work he had done as a consultant in the defence sphere, so a less distinguished but "safer" man was appointed instead.

That little bit of personal experience provides amusing confirmation of your conclusions—and is only a fraction of what might be cited.

B. H. Liddell-Hart

Comments by Kenneth Burke:

It seems to me as though "Be Not the First" should be quite a good "first approximation" to this aspect of suasion.

The only tinkering I would want to do would arise when you discuss the matter of gauging the situation. Particularly where some literary product is involved, among the things to consider there is also the responsibility to the *material itself*. That is: after one has worked on something for a certain length of time, even though he is working with nothing but a medium of communication (hence has a communicative motive implicit in his work), the perception of new possibilities, new relevancies, may come out of this very inquiry. And though the sort of considerations you mention are always good as admonitions, a 'morality of production' may quite properly induce one to pursue his inquiry until his manipulation of the communicative medium has impaired communication (so far as easy availability to many is concerned). If this sense of loyalty to the nature of one's materials (as disclosed by one's concentration upon them) is not stressed as a desirable motive, I think many can encourage themselves to think that communication means cajolery, compromise, finagling with extrinsic factors such as hungry egos, etc. I know you have no such equation in mind. *But there are many who are always so eager to have it said, that they'll say it for you unless you explicitly deny it.* At least, that's been my experience.

Kenneth Burke

Leadership in a Stress Situation[1]

BY ALEXANDER H. LEIGHTON

1. The problem which faces the administration of a community under stress is the problem of introducing remedial change. Before such change can be decided upon successfully, there must be understanding of the nature of the stress, the reactions of individuals to it, the effect on systems of belief and the effect on social organization.

This does not mean that great change is always necessary, but only that great understanding is. The slight, deft touch is often better than major alterations which—by upsetting total equilibrium—produce quite unexpected and unwanted results. Not infrequently the natural reactions of self-healing in the community are adequate. The point to be stressed is that when an administration decides to do little, it should do so on the basis of comprehension and not a blanket policy of laissez-faire.

2. In producing its elected changes, an administration should select means that are readily workable, not only in terms of the causes of the stress, but also in terms of the way the people are reacting, in terms of their habitual attitudes and beliefs and in terms of their customary forms for dealing with each other. It is never possible to ignore successfully these matters because in human society the cultural slate is never found wiped clean.

It is a common error of idealists and reformers to forget this fact, as was well illustrated at Poston. The people in charge of the schools and adult education brought to the Center a program of a progressive character that seemed to be excellent in itself, and possibly better than anything many of the evacuees had experienced previously. How-

---

[1] Reprinted from *The Governing of Men*, by Alexander Leighton, Princeton University Press, 1945. Used by permission of the publishers.

ever, in their planning these educators talked as if the physical removal of the evacuees had caused them to leave behind all their previous habits, notions and expectations in education. Attempts to put the progressive program into practice soon made it clear that the evacuees had brought to Poston their former ideas, and they were vocal in demanding that to which they had been accustomed. The education program ran into other difficulties besides this one (such as inability to get the kind of teachers who could carry it out), but the false assumption of a clean slate and a clear field in evacuee education was one of the principal pitfalls.

3. The remedial changes elected by the administration of a community under stress should be planned in successive stages stretched over a period of time. The results of each stage should be thoroughly examined and the plans for subsequent stages modified accordingly.

This suggestion concerns one of the basic differences between human engineering and other types. With a bridge or a building the entire structure can be laid out in advance in the form of a blueprint. For a community this may not be, because the foundation on which the structure is raised and the materials used in the building (that is, the individual people, their needs, reactions, beliefs, and social organization) are in a state of equilibrium that alters as the work progresses. Only by frequent checking for results and for changes in the material can human society be guided in a desired direction by an administration.

Clinical medicine is the common example of the same kind of problem. It is not possible to examine a patient once and then prescribe the whole course of treatment. Instead, the sick one has to be examined again and again so that both the effects of spontaneous alterations and the results of treatment can be taken into account.

The introduction of advisable alterations in general plans raises the problem of the effect of inconsistency. There can be no doubt that if people under stress feel that the administration is a ship without a rudder, it greatly adds to their uncertainties and consequently increases their stress. How can an administration change its course without appearing inconsistent?

Two things are needful: First, no alteration of policy should be arbitrary, and second, those alterations which are decided upon should be carefully communicated to the people concerned in such a manner that they will see the advisability. The role of communication and education will be discussed later in this chapter under heading 9.

With the best of conditions, some arbitrary alterations will be forced upon an administration through outside pressures, changes in personnel, and other circumstances. One can only advise the administrator to keep these to a minimum and to make them as reasonable as possible and to avoid attempting to protect himself with silence which, of all the courses open in a difficult situation, is usually the most tempting and least profitable.

Finally, in proposing alterations in policy and in other connections, it is well for administrator not to be too afraid of admitting they have been in error. It is more worthwhile to endeavor to have the people believe that the administration is honest than to try to convince them that it is infallible. No matter what happens, they will never believe the latter.

4. Wherever possible, plans for social change should be tried out on a small scale in a segment of the community and then, after the indicated modifications have been made, applied to the whole.

By this method, ponderous errors may be avoided, for administrative practice often suffers from the kind of limitation that is imposed on mass production. When an article is being manufactured by mass production methods, any change in form is likely to require that the whole assembly belt be stopped and tools and dies remodelled. Since the administrative machinery, with its formal memoranda, printed regulations and habits of the operators, is in many ways just as inflexible, it is wise for administrators to do what the manufacturer does, experiment with models before altering the plant. Not only does the model provide the administrator with an opportunity to try out various possibilities without any of them becoming irrevocable, but also, when the model is in good working order, it can, by serving as a demonstration, become both a vehicle for communicating the idea and an illustration of its usefulness. Furthermore, since the model will be possessed by only one part of the community, it may stimulate rivalry in other parts so that the administration may find itself impatiently besieged with requests to set into operation measures which otherwise would have been coldly received.

5. In producing changes in communities, the administration must identify and deal with the basic social units of the communities.

A basic social unit is a group of people who feel they belong together. In many places, particularly rural areas, these are neighborhood groups, but they may also be defined by kinship, religion, occupation, social caste and class, or minority status, etc., depending on the community concerned. The essential thing is that they have systems of belief in common that promote solidarity and have well-established habits of acting together as a group. The particular form and pattern varies in different parts of the world, and in complex societies there may be a number of overlapping basic social units, sometimes with considerable conflict. Successful administrative planning is dependent upon a knowledge of these units, of the organization of their leadership and of how they work together. With such information, an administration can employ the basic units as bricks in its over-all operations, as demonstrated in the extension work of the Department of Agriculture for which much care has gone into defining rural neighborhood units. The administration which attempts to put large plans into operation in complex societies without regard to the basic social units is like a man trying to put up a circus tent all alone in a high wind.

Poston, in the early days, was notable for having few stable social units with which the Administration could deal, but in the course of time the block emerged as the preëminently important segment for administrative purposes.

6. Communities under stress, with their labile but intense emotions and shifting systems of belief, are ripe for change. While this is a situation fraught with danger because of trends which may make the stress become worse before it gets better, there is also an opportunity for administrative action that is not likely to be found in more secure times. Skillful administration may be able to seize the moment not only to guide spontaneous shifts in constructive directions but even to achieve extensive changes that would otherwise be impossible or extremely difficult.

It is fairly well recognized in psychology that at periods of great emotional stir the individual human being can undergo far-reaching and permanent changes in his personality. It is as if the bony structure of his systems of belief and of his habitual patterns of behavior becomes soft, is pushed into new shapes and hardens there when the period of tension is over. There is probably always some slipping back toward the previous status, but there is often much retention of the new religious conversion and the effects of serious illness; and in some cases the results of intensive psychotherapy are probably of this character.

Possibly the same can be true of whole groups of people, and there are historical examples of social changes and movements occurring when there was widespread emotional tension, usually some form of anxiety. The Crusades, parts of the Reformation, the French Revolution, the change in Zulu life in the reign of Chaca, the Meiji Restoration, the Mormon movement, the Russian Revolution, the rise of Fascism, and alterations in the social sentiments of the United States going on at present are all to some extent examples.

However, when attempting to take advantage of a plastic condition in a community and introduce radical change, action must be well timed and based on adequate knowledge of the immediate situation. Administrations new to the community must be particularly cautious because an early blunder may make more impression than several blunders of greater magnitude committed later on after the people have come to accept and have some trust in the administrative leaders. It is much easier to avoid a bad impression at the start than to correct it later after people have developed convictions.

7. When an administration introduces change into a community, such change takes the form of alterations both in systems of belief and in social organization. New patterns in the social organization, such as self-governing bodies, or systems for education or the promotion of public health can be created in communities that previously did not have these things.

The most important points to keep in mind are that the people must feel motives for these innovations and that time is required for growth and establishment. It is very dangerous for administrators to assume that because they desire a certain pattern, such as self-government, and have decreed it and got the people to go through the forms, it therefore exists. Given time and an opportunity to function, what is in the beginning only a hollow shell will gradually develop solidity, but the weight and reliance placed on it by the administration should be commensurate with its stage of growth.

At the same time, too little responsibility and too little opportunity to function will cause the shell to crumble and vanish.

8. In producing remedial changes in a community, it is necessary to take into consideration the fact that people are more moved by appeals to the feeling man than to the rational man.

This point has long been known to practical men of trade, of politics, of advertising and of showmanship. Applied social science in industry has repeatedly shown that wage-incentive schemes and other plans based on a narrow assumption that man is a logical animal motivated by economic considerations, may yield poor results. Such schemes were usually based on the systems of belief of the top business executives and not on those of the workers.

Most people use their intelligence to attain ends dictated by their feelings and convictions and not as a matter of their basic motivations. With ourselves, no less than with foreign or "primitive" people, the choice of a career, of a marital partner, of religion, of friends, of political candidates, of place to reside, of food, of a doctor, of a lawyer, and many other crucial steps in life are carried out far more on the basis of feeling than on the basis of reasoning—and feeling means systems of belief and related patterns of sentiment in varying combinations, powered by needs, drives, aspirations and insecurities.

Societies move on the feelings of the individuals who compose them, and so do countries and nations. Very few internal policies and almost no international policies are predominantly the product of reason. To be sure, reason and thought are components, but they take the form either of rationalization to justify or of scheming to attain ends already decided upon at the dictates of feeling. Such thinking is not of the same order as that employed by the scientist who studies the biochemistry of muscle action. It should be noted, however, that even the scientist who reasons critically and with self-discipline in his approach to the muscle is just as much a creature of his feelings as anybody else when it comes to his relations with other people and to achieving his aspirations and securities. The chances are that the origin of his interest in the muscle is the result of feelings that have their roots in his systems of belief and his desire to be admired, to support his family, to prove his ability to himself and others and similar matters, conscious and unconscious.

To blame people for being moved more by feeling than by thought is like blaming land for being covered by the sea or rivers for running down hill. The administrator's job is to accept these things as they are and to take them into consideration, turn them to advantage if possible, but never to ignore them.

9. Communication and education are tools of major importance at the disposal of an administration engaged in producing change in a community under stress.

In the first place, the creation of adequate communication in itself constitutes a remedial measure. When communities are suffering from adverse influences, imaginations are busy with conjured images of hopes and fears that pass for reality, systems of belief become more than ever recalcitrant to reasoning, and with the general breaks in social organization there is often extensive damage to the routes by which reliable information was formerly spread.

While information and education are not cure-alls, they are powerful antidotes. There was hardly a phase of activity in the Center from agriculture to self-government that did not suffer as much or more from lack of information as it did from lack of supplies. This not only produced uncoöperative attitudes in evacuees, but also clogged the workings of the Administration itself, and promoted bad relations between the Center and the newspapers and public of the surrounding regions.

It is true that, because of the national emergency and the speed with which evacuation was accomplished, there were many important questions concerning which it was impossible to secure answers until much later. The whole situation was charged with inevitable uncertainty. However, this made it all the more important to make sure that those facts which were available were disseminated so that no avoidable uncertainties would be added to those which could not be helped. It was here that the absence of channels for adequate information distribution made itself felt and contributed a considerable additional load to the stresses the community was bearing. Many months passed before either the local Administration or the War Relocation Authority became aware of the magnitude of the problem.

This is an old story in government. Ignorance was an important factor in permitting the evils of the reconstruction after the Civil War, and one of the most significant forces making for later improvement was the appearance of better reporting in the North regarding the South. Students of industrial psychology have noted again and again that men cannot do good work when uninformed concerning its significance. Reports regarding morale in the armed forces stress time and time again the need of keeping men informed regarding what is happening to them and the meaning of what they are doing. T. E. Lawrence observed concerning his experiences in Arabia, "Morale, if built on knowledge, was broken by ignorance."

However, in addition to being remedial measures in themselves, communication and education are means whereby other remedial measures may be introduced into the community and made a part of its life. No matter how good a plan or an idea hatched by an administration may be, it is of little value until it becomes part of the consciousness and activity of the people. The history of government and industry is littered with schemes that have been labeled failure, but which in reality were never tried because they were never understood by those who had to grasp them before they could become action.

For all these reasons, the administration that gives special attention to communication with and education of the people will find itself properly repaid. Special attention means giving the matter first-order importance in plans and organization, comparable with that accorded public health, the police system and the provision of supplies and food. Where the people being administered speak a different language from the administering group, there is need for particular emphasis on the selection and training of interpreters, with reference both to their language skill and to their individual acceptability to the people. This is a matter far too often left to chance.

10. Communication from the people to the administration is no less important than the stream in the opposite direction, although it is even more often neglected. "I know just how these people think and feel" should be classed among "famous last words" of administrators.

The more formal and informal channels the administration sets up for the flow of complaints, observations and recommendations from the people the better. These are inherent in elective forms of self-government, but the process should not be limited to political mechanisms. Other techniques such as prizes for suggestions, boxes where anonymous complaints may be deposited and a number of agencies where people may come to discuss their problems without fear of reprisal should be instituted. Such measures not only serve to keep the administration aware of what is going on, but they also provide a means through which aggressions can be harmlessly discharged, whereby people can talk things out of their systems and whereby they can arrive at new perspective through a thorough airing of their feelings. The office of "Counselor" that has been created for workers in a number of large industries serves such purposes.

The direct flow of ideas from the people to the administration in one or another form, is not, however, sufficient. The people, while able to tell the administrators many things of value, do not know the whole story and frequently have far from adequate perspective concerning what they do perceive.

There is thus a gap in the total knowledge and insight of both people and administration—a gap which involves a broad view and interpretation of constantly changing complex relationships between people and their needs, stresses, beliefs and social organization. Such knowledge is required not only for retrospective understanding but also for the active tackling of current problems. The modern developments in applied social science show some promise of being able to fulfill these requirements.

The greatest promise, however, for men and their government, in stress and out of it, is in a fusion of administration and science to form a common body of thought and action which is not only realistic in the immediate sense of dealing with everyday needs, but also in the ultimate sense of moving forward in discovery and improved practice. This requires more than hiring social scientists to make reports. It requires an administration with a scientific philosophy which employs as its frame of reference our culture's accumulated knowledge regarding the nature of man and his society. Such an administration would have stated principles of operation thoroughly familiar to all its members and generally available for others to see. These principles would, however, be subject to revision on the basis of systematic and critical observation in which the members of the administration participated. Thus, hypotheses and supposed constants would be tested as in natural history by multiple, careful observations. The administration would be geared, not to exploitive or irresponsible experimentation, but to utilizing to the full the experiments constantly being performed by nature—by changing circumstances and the actions in relation to them which have to be taken.

This may seem visionary, and yet such a union exists to some extent between science and practice in other spheres of human activity. In medicine, for example, there is a scientific philosophy and a body of accumulated knowledge, and in addition, a set of principles which are continually receiving accumulations and modifications as a result of experience and practice. This does not mean, of course, to minimize the role of laboratory and controlled experiment in medical advance, but only to emphasize that clinical practice itself when carefully observed, recorded and analyzed is also a tremendous force for progress. Closely related to clinical practice is autopsy which the physician approaches, not to justify his diagnosis, but to learn how things really were and to improve his judgment.

It may be argued that administration cannot afford to be scientific because of the pressure it is usually under from the urgings or attacks of well-meaning enthusiasts, vested interests and political forces. Granting this to be a serious problem because of the emotions and conflicting, often hidden, motives that suffuse social issues, one may still insist that narrow expediency and secretiveness do not seem to be very effective means for solution, even temporarily.

No administration can avoid some errors and none can avoid misrepresentation. Truth, on the other hand, makes an exceedingly strong appeal for fair judgment. There is more hope for progress if the fear of leaving a mistake on the record is replaced by the desire to record improvement.

However, it is evident that the responsibility for such a development rests as much with the public as with the administrators, because in the long run it is the governed who determine the governing of men.

Is Scientific Leadership Selection Possible?[1]

BY JOSEPH W. EATON

THE SELECTION of qualified leaders is an important problem in any social order. Little is known about the processes that occur. What measurable qualities of personality and mechanisms of social engineering placed the American presidents into their positions of leadership, in spirited struggles against their contenders? How did Hitler evolve as "The Fuehrer" from the conglomeration of equally ambitious and often better educated charter members of the Nazi Party? We are no more enlightened about the ways through which lesser leaders reach their positions. We are at loss to predict their rise in a ladies' sewing circle, criminal gang, business corporation, or sport club on the basis of any measurable indexes.

We have some very interesting accounts on the descriptive level[2] but they do not combine into any integrated body of data on the subject of leadership. While they contain some useful hypotheses, with a promise of showing some degree of validity and reliability, the area of scientific description of leadership is largely virgin soil. The application of scientific methods to find persons who will live up to specified normative or value expectations has not progressed very far. Science has been of little help in measuring the stuff a good mayor, an honest judge or an effective labor organizer are made of; and if

---

[1] Reprinted with modifications from American Journal of Sociology, 1947, by permission of the editors. Copyright, 1947, by The University of Chicago Press.

[2] Paul Pigors, Leadership or Domination (New York, 1935); Ordway Tead, The Art of Leadership (New York, 1935); Fritz Redl, "Group Emotion and Leadership," in Psychiatry, V, No. 4 (November, 1942), 573-596.

some agreement concerning the ideal qualifications of these men could be reached, scientific methods for selecting men to meet these standards are not well developed.

This is not to deny the great strides which have been made in the field of psychometric measurement. Psychological tests are used widely to fill posts requiring a definite minimum level of intelligence of technical skill. Industrial and civil service employers make frequent and effective use of tests to fill subordinate jobs. But they generally shy away from them in choosing men for leadership and policy-making positions. There they turn to hunches, common sense, interviews, and other non-objective devices to make the selection. There are rigid standards for the appointment of a stenographer, but not for her boss. There are no standardized civil service examinations at higher levels. Whenever leadership is involved in a job, science abstains from voting in the selection process.

LEADERSHIP IS A GROUP VALUE

The difficulties in selecting leaders scientifically have much to do with the fact that leadership is not a standardizable objective behavior pattern, common to many situations. It is a group value judgment, varying with each group and the circumstances in which it operates. Leadership is a product of the social situation, the unique interactions of the participating members and the person attempting to assume leadership. Jennings concludes quite correctly that "the why of leadership appears not to reside in any personality trait considered singly, not even in a constellation of related traits, but in inter-personal contributions of which the individual becomes capable, in a specific setting eliciting such contributions from him."[3]

The very suggestion that leaders might be chosen scientifically involves a value judgment. The supporters of the autocratic "Fuehrerprinzip" need no scientific justification for their position. Claiming their post as the reward of ruthless competitive struggle on the principle of the "survival of the fittest," their leadership needs no other justification. According to this philosophy, leaders are chosen in charismatic fashion, by their inner conviction and their ability to force recognition from the public, which is not qualified to select them. In this approach to leadership, perhaps more appropriately called domi-

[3] Helen Hall Jennings, op. cit., p. 205.

nation,[4] scientific selection methods have no place. Success to rise from the masses is in itself sufficient proof of fitness.[5]

THE POWER BIAS. Leadership selection involves a power bias. Before any scientific choice process can be worked on, an arbitrary decision must be made on whose values are to guide it. Two possible alternatives exist:

1. Leadership is considered to be a constellation of qualities defined by an individual or a group of superiors in a hierarchy. They do the selecting of leaders in terms of their standards. This is how positions of leadership are filled in a bureaucracy, an army, or a business firm. Opportunity for the exercise of leadership is awarded by appointment from above.

2. Leadership is considered to be a constellation of qualities defined by prevailing sentiments in the entire group to be led. Through formal election, informal consensus or sympathetic inter-stimulation, members of the group find someone whom they are willing to follow. Provisional findings of a study of group contagion initiation, conducted by Polansky, Lippitt and Redl, show that this type of leadership is shown by the child who rates high in those qualities that also stand high in the value system of the group. This may be success with the opposite sex in adolescent social affairs or athletic ability in a summer camp group.[6] These democratic, group-value-reflective processes of leadership choosing are quite common in elections for local government officials, or officers of social groups and professional societies.

The hierarchical and democratic value determination in leadership are not necessarily exclusive. These two power biases are ideal types,

[4] Paul Pigors in his already quoted book, Leadership or Domination, develops this concept. He defines domination as a "process of control in which the forcible assumption of authority and the accumulation of prestige by a person through a hierarchy of functionaries, regulates the activities of others for purposes of his own choosing." (p. 74)

[5] For an excellent discussion of the different rationalizations for legitimizing self-assumed group leadership see Max Weber, The Theory of Social and Economic Organization, tr. A. M. Henderson and Talcott Parsons (New York, 1947), pp. 126-132.

[6] This study of the mechanisms of group emotional contagion has headquarters at the School of Public Affairs and Social Work, Wayne University, Detroit, Michigan. An article, containing some preliminary findings, is scheduled in Sociometry, Summer, 1949. Norman Polansky, Ronald Lippitt, Fritz Redl, "The Use of Sociometric Data in Research on Group Treatment Processes."

which rarely occur in their pure state. In any actual selection process, components of both are likely to be found, differences being largely a matter of degree. A bureaucrat who appoints a new department chief will often include the candidate's acceptability to his future subordinates among the factors determining his choice of a leader. In the election of a Speaker of the House of Representatives, his acceptability to the President, who yields independent power, is likely to be a factor. It has been shown that leadership involves basic value judgment. There must be a clear agreement on which members of a group—the few in a hierarchy or the many in a majority—should exercise the power of selecting. This value judgment must be included in the criterion of validity of the test.

American and British Army Selection tests suffered from the failure to face this fact. These Army tests, with which this article is largely concerned, did not reconcile the conflicting attitudes on leadership. Military leaders of the traditional type view the quality as equivalent to domination. Like the Colonel Edward L. Munson quoted in Daniel Bell's excellent article on leadership testing,[7] they define it in almost mechanical terms such as a leader is a man who "looks his men straight in the eye rather than shiftily."[8] Others want to encourage the coming into prominence of persons who can inspire subordinates to follow them, not as a matter of compulsion, but as an expression of confidence. Here the emphasis is, as it was in the Office of Strategic Services, on "social initiative, ability to evoke coöperation, organizing and administrative ability and acceptance of responsibility."[9] It is therefore not surprising that the Army tests, lacking a clear value criterion, could not be validated effectively.

SITUATIONAL DEFINITION OF LEADERSHIP

Few will disagree with Kimball Young in his conclusion that the "trait" or "type" concept of leadership has no selective or predictive utility.[10] There is no evidence as to what these traits are or how they

[7] Daniel Bell, "Screening Leaders in a Democracy" in Commentary, V, No. 4 (April, 1948), 368-375.

[8] Edward L. Munson, "Leadership for American Army Leaders," quoted by Bell. According to the latter, this manual was distributed widely during World War II by the U. S. Army and the Infantry Journal.

[9] The OSS Assessment Staff, Assessment of Men (New York, 1948), p. 31.

[10] Kimball Young, Social Psychology (New York, 1930), pp. 228-229.

might be measured. The view that there is a "leadership type of personality" neglects the fact that qualifications for leadership vary greatly for different positions. The individual behavior patterns that will be given recognition as indexes of leadership ability are not the same in a church, an army, a golf club and a girl scout troop, nor for the varied positions of leadership within each group. Leadership is a situationally defined capacity. Murphy's review of psychological leadership and other trait measurements emphasizes this point.[11]

The relativity of leadership to the social situation does not imply that there is no similarity in the aptitudes that make for leadership under different circumstances. If that were the case, leadership selection tests would be useless, since no leader ever functions only under one set of conditions. The potential value of leadership testing is enhanced by the observation that there appears to be some degree of persistence of leadership, despite changes in social circumstances. Courtenay[12] studied a group of 100 women high school graduates, who had demonstrated leadership through being elected to the Senior Girls Council. This group of girls was paired with a control sample of non-leaders of the same socio-economic background, ethnic heritage, scholarship record and age at graduation. Seventy-two of the leaders as against twenty-nine of the non-leaders sought higher education. The leaders also attended college for longer average periods of time, held more professional jobs, earned higher salaries and took a more active part in community activities. Zeleny,[13] after an exhaustive review of leadership studies, also comes to the conclusion that "outstanding leaders have demonstrated considerable ability to make adjustments." The possibility seems to exist that leadership selection tests that are valid for one particular group position will also have some validity for other, somewhat related positions.

The situational differences for leadership are particularly apparent when the qualities most likely to be emphasized in primary and in secondary groups are compared. In a relatively primary group, such as a platoon of the army or the sisterhood of a small church, leaders are

---

[11] Murphy, Murphy and Newcomb, op. cit., Chap. XIV, pp. 769-888, esp. 830-835.

[12] Ethel Courtenay, "Persistence of Leadership" in School Review, XLVI (February, 1938), No. 2, 97-107.

[13] Leslie Day Zeleny, "Leadership" in Encyclopedia of Educational Research, Walter S. Monroe, ed. (New York, 1941), p. 662.

likely to have frequent personal contact with those who are being led. The emphasis here is on actual personality traits, which can be demonstrated to the membership. Leaders must be able to get along with people at close range, be responsive to their feelings, and inspire them to common action.

In more secondary groups, the emphasis shifts toward symbolic character traits rather than real ones. The Army Division Chief or the President of a Federation of Church Sisterhoods has only occasional and formal contact with most of those who are being led. The leader's ability to influence others depends as much on his reputation as on actual performance. Love of humanity can be demonstrated by shaking hands with little girls, carrying flowers, in the presence of press photographers who will flash the picture all over the country. Courage need not involve the risk of death, but can be documented by a medal. Wisdom may consist of a speech, written by a ghost writer. This is not to imply that most secondary group leaders hold their posts only by virtue of such fictions. In the long run, the myths are likely to be exposed if they are without some reality basis. However, the fact remains that leadership in secondary groups emphasizes formal and symbolic relationships, as against the more intimate human contacts at the primary level. The type of personality best qualified for leadership in each kind of association is therefore likely to be somewhat different.

MEASURABLE FACTORS IN LEADERSHIP

Most leadership positions require specific technical skills. A superintendent of schools needs to know a good deal about teacher training, curriculum organization, state laws relating to education, etc. A general should know something about the weapons used by his troops and the things they can and cannot do. Most of these technical skills are to some extent measurable. Psychometric tests have made great strides in giving us fairly valid indexes to a person's technical capacity to type letters, fix electrical equipment, and work in a chemical laboratory. Classification tests, as used by the U. S. military services, the Civil Service Commission, and the Personnel Departments of many business firms have undoubtedly done much to eliminate erratic guesswork, favoritism, and pure chance in the selecting of minor leaders. These tests give those with superior technical qualifications a more than even chance of being selected.

But these psychometric tests are no measure of the personality traits, which make for acceptance of a leader because he fits the value expectation of those who select him or are placed under his charge. They do not measure specific social situations in which, as a leader, the candidate must operate.[14] Many employers try to remedy this shortcoming by supplementing written tests with oral interviews. Such interviews, however, have important methodological shortcomings, particularly if used to screen a large number of applicants:

1. The nature, content, and length of the interview varies widely with each interviewer and his ability to draw out different candidates.

2. The interviewer who does the rating of candidates is himself part of the oral test. He is occupied with thinking of responses to and asking new questions of the candidate. He is emotionally influenced by the candidate's reaction to him.

3. Individual interviews are not a good measure of a man's social behavior. The capacity to function well in the relaxing intimacy of most interview situations is not necessarily the same as the capacity to handle more complex social situations involving many people, in conflict or coöperation with them.

Both psychometric tests and oral interviews have little validity for the social personality qualities involved in leadership. In an effort to fill this gap, sociological tests are being tried out. These tests involve samples of the social circumstances and values required in a specific leadership situation. Two types of sociological tests—sociodramatic and sociometric—will be discussed.[15]

SOCIODRAMATIC TESTS. Sociodramatic performance tests involve activity by an individual or group in a social situation of simulated reality. The tests usually include an audience of observers and participants, who provide the simulated social environment. Sociometric ratings of the performance of the person tested, by the other partic-

[14] For an excellent discussion of these social factors see Delbert C. Miller, "The Social Factors of the Work Situation," in *American Sociological Review*, XI, no. 3 (June, 1946), 301-314.

[15] Most of the examples used in this section of the article have been published in a previous article by the writer. See "Experiments In Testing For Leadership," in *American Journal of Sociology*, LII, No. 6 (May, 1947), 523-535.

ipants, are often included. Sociodramatic tests are constructed so that they require proficiency in as many components as possible of the capacity under test, such as technical skills, muscular abilities, and social adaptations. They are tests of the total personality of the subject, designed to evaluate his over-all performance. Briefly, they are performance tests in a social setting.

Sociodramatic methods were used widely under such names as "maneuvers," "performance tests," or "simulated-action" tests in the American Army. Few of the officers responsible for their use in the training and classification of personnel ever heard of sociodrama or were acquainted with its literature.[16] Their motivation was nontheoretical and pragmatic: they were often neither psychologists, sociologists, nor psychometricians. They looked upon these tests as common-sense hunches, "a good way" to make a qualitative evaluation of training and personnel.

SOCIOMETRIC TESTS. Sociodramatic tests of leadership and social behavior have often been combined with sociometric measurements—ratings of individuals by their co-workers, inferiors, and superiors.[17] The United States Army used such ratings in its Officers Candidate Schools, officer efficiency ratings, and in its selection program of officers.

Many of the examples cited were experienced personally by the writer as a test-subject during his service in the American Army. The test procedures and methods of scoring were highly subjective. The data often raise more questions than they answer. However, the focus of this article is on methodology. These pragmatic testing devices are discussed to encourage research in developing more valid test instruments in the field of personality evaluation, the complexity of which has hitherto prevented the successful application of traditional paper-pencil and simple performance tests.[18]

16 See Psychodrama (New York, 1946); "The Advantages of the Sociometric Approach to Problems of National Defense," in Sociometry, IV, No. 3 (1941), 384-391; "Testing in Typical Life Situations," in Sociometry, III, No. 4 (1940), 320-327; "Group Methods and Group Psychotherapy," Sociometry (Mono. 5)—all written by J. L. Moreno.

17 See J. L. Moreno, Who Shall Survive? (New York, 1934).

18 See Kurt Lewin's experiments in democratic leadership: "Training in Democratic Leadership," by Alex Bavelas and Kurt Lewin in Journal of Social and Abnormal Psychology, XXXVII, No. 37 (January, 1942), 115-119; Leadership and Isolation by Helen Jennings (New York, 1943), p. 240; "Social Factors of the

MILITARY MANEUVERS

Military maneuvers are one of the earliest sociological testing devices.

Ever since the development of modern standing armies, maneuvers have been held to train and evaluate the performance of individuals and military units. Teams of inspectors would roam the maneuver area to rate the quality of performances. These ratings were highly subjective, with unknown validity or reliability. The maneuvers were also often planned so haphazardly that it was difficult to estimate their relevance to situations likely to arise in future combat. Some of the rating officers used superficial indexes of efficiency such as "cleanliness of uniform," "snappiness of drill," "sociability of officers," or gave undue considerations to spectacular actions which would be unlikely to take place under real combat conditions.

The erroneousness of this formalistic evaluation is underlined by a study of Measurement and Prediction of Leadership at the U. S. Military Academy at West Point.[19] There "leadership" ratings are given to all cadets by the members of the graduating senior class (a combined weight of 80) and the platoon commander (a weight of 20). Both are superior in rank to the lower cadets. There is a high degree of consistency from year to year, although a different group of seniors does the rating (r 847 between 3rd and 4th year ratings; r 677 between 1st and 4th year ratings). But they correlate most highly with ratings of military bearing, appearance, tactics, and athletics! Yet, the fact must be faced that a list of outstanding graduates, who actually made their mark in military or civilian life, did not show consistent high ratings in what was thought to be "leadership" at West Point. Instead, they were fairly representative of the whole class.

Efforts to objectify maneuvers were begun previous to World War II. Precautions for military security make much of the relevant data inaccessible. However, it is known that the Command and Staff College at Fort Leavenworth, Kansas, developed certain map-and-field

Work Situation," by Delbert C. Miller in *American Sociological Review*, XI, No. 3 (June, 1946), 300-314; "A Method for Evaluating Supervisory Personnel," by Eliot D. Chapple and Gordon Donald, Jr., in *Harvard Business Review*, XXIV, No. 2 (Winter, 1946), 197-214.

[19] David D. Page, "Measurement and Prediction of Leadership," in *American Journal of Sociology*, XLI (July, 1935), No. 1, 31-43.

problems which were repeated frequently so that the performance of one class of students could be compared to another. Every effort was made to have these tests correspond to situations likely to arise in a future war. The test results were considered in the evaluation of the training course, the level of individual achievement, and the selection of individuals for advanced training and promotion.

The sociodramatic performance tests used later by the Army Ground Forces, particularly at the Military Intelligence Training Center, were partly based on these experiences. It also appears that the performance tests of the German Army and the British Army War Office Selection Boards played a part in the development of American sociodramatic testing and will therefore be considered briefly in this article.

PERFORMANCE TESTING IN THE GERMAN ARMY

Reports from Germany available in 1941[20] indicated that the qualitative evaluation of performance tests played an important role in the selection of officer candidates. Ansbacher reports that applicants for commissions spent two days at a testing center, operated by a board of two military officers, one physician, and three psychologists. They were given paper-pencil intelligence tests and a battery of performance tests, some of which were sociodramatic. They included the following:

1. A Choice-Reaction Test, in which the subject had to operate a number of levers and pedals to produce lights on a screen, according to frequently changing directions.

2. A Command Test (Fuehrerprobe) in which the soldier had to instruct a group of soldiers in performing a mechanical task, such as making wire coat hangers.

3. Analysis of facial expression, handwriting, and speech quality.

4. Individual performance tests in carrying out difficult commands under strain—to evaluate bodily agility, intellectual efficiency, reaction to tension, etc.

5. Analysis of applicant's life history, and a personal interview.

On the basis of observations by the board, recommendations were made to a military commander concerning the suitability of candidates for training as officers in the Wehrmacht. These judgments

20 H. L. Ansbacher, "German Military Psychology," *Psychological Bulletin*, XXXVIII (1941), 370-392. Includes excellent bibliography.

were highly subjective. Although an attempt was made to score some of these tests, the scores were incidental. No findings concerning their validity or reliability have been reported. However, it appears that American military psychologists were influenced by these procedures.

TESTS OF THE BRITISH ARMY WAR OFFICE SELECTION BOARDS

When England was faced with the sudden need in 1939 to expand her army, it was necessary to make a rapid selection of qualified officer candidates. The task was intrusted to a psychiatrist with the rank of brigadier general, who was assisted by a staff of qualified psychologists and psychiatrists. They established the army War Office Selection Boards (W.O.S.B.) for making personality assessments of officers or officer candidates, to determine their suitability for various officer roles in the army.[21] Australia set up similar selection procedures for its services.[22]

Each board had one or more teams of three officers: a senior army officer with wide military combat experience, a military testing officer of regimental rank and with combat experience, and a psychiatric officer. Each team observed a group of seven or eight men during their stay of three to five days at the selection center and made recommendations concerning their utilization by the army.

An informal atmosphere prevailed at each board. Military restrictions were reduced to a minimum, and comfortable living quarters were furnished. The officer-observers mixed freely with their group of candidates. At the beginning, a battery of intelligence-and-knowledge tests was administered. Other tests involved visual patterns, first reaction to words, questionnaires about personal interest, and a request to spend fifteen minutes each in writing what the candidate thought his "best friend" and "worst enemy" would say about him. At the end of the program, the men were given interviews by members of

[21] J. D. Sutherland and G. A. Fitzpatrick, "Some Approaches to Group Problems in the British Army," *Group Psychotherapy* (New York, 1945), pp. 205-217. The writer took part in a five-day screening program conducted by one of the W.O.S.B. for psychological warfare units of the American Army. The description of individual tests in this section is based on this experience. Reports from England indicate that a full account of the work done at W.O.S.B. is in preparation. It is scheduled for release by H.M. Stationary Office.

[22] Cecil A. Gibb, "The Principles and Traits of Leadership" in *Journal of Abnormal and Social Psychology*, XLII (1947), 267-284.

their board. Much of the time was devoted to the administration of sociodramatic performance tests, including the following:

1. THE LEADERLESS-GROUP TESTS.   Several of the tests of the army W.O.S.B. were based on the leaderless-group technique developed by Major W. R. Bion of the Royal Army Medical Corps. A psychiatrist by training, Bion claims that this test gives a good indication of the capacity for mature and independent social relationships. In each test, a group of seven or eight individuals were given a common task. No indication was given as to whether individual or group performance was being judged. Each member was thus faced with a conflict between his desire to show his own ability and to get along with the other members of the group. He could work well only through others.

In one test the group was taken to a ravine. They were to build a bridge within a specified time without anyone's falling in. Boards and ropes of certain lengths could be found lying about nearby. The building of the bridge required considerable ingenuity. The group had to formulate plans as to where to start building, what methods to use, and who was most qualified for the different tasks. The problem was simple enough and used a definite enough number of implements to lend itself to standardization.

In another test the group was asked to discuss a current problem. The contributions of each person and his manner of expression during the discussion were noted. After a certain period of time the group was asked to select one man to summarize the result of its findings.

The final test evaluation was qualitative and based on what was called "empirical intuition." Ranking of candidates in order of their merit, ratings on a five-point scale, and the recording of certain objective test achievements were probably used in the initial stages of the interpretation of test results.

2. GROUP-LEADERSHIP TESTS.   There were several tests of the W.O.S.B. in which a leader was appointed for the group, although each member was given an opportunity to serve as leader in the same or a very similar situation.

One test involved a sand table, on which details of a tactical terrain were portrayed—roads, houses, railroads, rivers, woods, hills, etc. One of the officer-observers gave each leader a specific assignment, such as: "You are in charge of a patrol of seven men. You are at A. You have the job of blowing up the bridge at B by 12:00 p.m. The enemy positions are here. Your intelligence tells you the following facts about his equipment and plans. It is now 11:00 a.m. and raining, etc., etc." Each leader had to: (a) make a general plan of attack or defense; (b) assign definite tasks to each member of his patrol, giving each of them a briefing for contingencies which might arise.

Here, too, it is not known what method of rating was used. The performance of each applicant may have been rated in such terms as "leadership," "self-confidence," "ability to formulate plans," "ability to delegate authority," etc.

THE BLIND WAR GAME

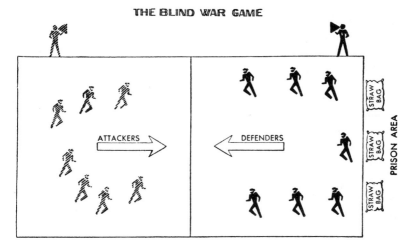

Another test of this type involved a group game of "blind war." The test took place on a level grass field, about fifty by one hundred yards (see diagram). Each half of the field was assigned to a team. Six or seven members were completely blindfolded. They could move only at the direction of their leader, who was not blindfolded. He would command each man to move so many steps forward, backward, right, left, etc. The object of the attacking team was to pick up three straw bags at the extreme of the defending team's territory and bring these bags into their area without being touched by a member of the defending team. The defenders could move only in their own area. Members of the attacking team who were touched by them were put into a "prison cage" behind the border of the defending team. They could be liberated there if touched by a member of their own team and if they succeeded in returning to their own territory without again being touched by a defender.

In this test applicants might have been rated on such bases as: ability to respond to instruction of leader; ability of leader to formulate a plan of attack or defense; ability of leader to command and direct his six or seven men in a co-ordinated manner; or the score of each game in terms of the number of prisoners taken by defenders and number of straw bags captured by attackers.

No validity or reliability data are available for any of these tests. This writer was, however, impressed by the fact that men in his group known to be very good or very bad leaders showed roughly similar behavior during these tests.

3. TESTS OF INDIVIDUAL COURAGE. The W.O.S.B. also had several individual performance tests, apparently designed to test physical courage of applicants in the presence of others.

In one test, applicants were asked to climb a big oak tree. At a height of fifteen or twenty feet they had to jump from one of the branches two or three feet in the air to catch a suspended rope on which they could slide down.

In another test a narrow board or a rope was suspended over a ravine. Applicants were asked to walk or swing along at a height of about fifteen feet and then jump down into a heap of dry leaves.

These and other tests, similar to those used in the familiar United States Army obstacle courses, involved slight elements of danger as well as a minimum of physical dexterity. Their method of evaluation is not known to the writer. Performance at different stages of the tests as well as total time required might lend themselves to standardization.

4. DEMOCRATIC SOCIOMETRICS. The routine method of selecting officers of the British Army, through direct commissions from civilian life or from the enlisted ranks by nomination by their commanding officers ("autocratic" sociometrics), did not produce a sufficiently large number of qualified applicants. Early during World War II the following experiment was therefore instituted in several military units, ranging in size from an infantry regiment to a platoon.[23]

All enlisted men, noncommissioned officers, and field grade officers

[23] Sutherland and Fitzpatrick, "Some Approaches to Group Problems in the British Army," *op. cit.*

were asked, separately, to make anonymous nomination of members of their unit who would make good officers. In order to provide a strong motivation to participate in these sociometric ratings, all groups were informed that some of the men selected by them might be returned to their units as officers.

All soldiers who received strong support from one or more of the three rating groups were selected for screening by an army war office selection board. However, no study was made to determine the relative validity of recommendations by the three groups—officers, noncommissioned officers, and enlisted men. Sutherland and Fitzpatrick report only that many qualified officers were discovered by this method. Its fairness also had a strong appeal in all ranks and helped to raise morale. The experiment was not repeated because the subsequent supply of officer candidates through normal channels of selection was adequate to meet existing needs.[24] The fear of some rank conscious officers of setting too many precedents of democratic influence in the selection process may also have been a factor.

5. VALIDATION. Military and administrative considerations prevented effective investigations of the validity of the W.O.S.B. procedures. Gibb, in his report on British and Australian Army leadership selection techniques, uses the training results from officer cadet units as an interim criterion of validity for the test procedures which chose the cadets.[25] In England, a sample of 1200 cadets chosen by W.O.S.B. methods during one period showed an increase of 12.5% (from 22.0 to 34.5) in the proportion of all cadets rated above average by their training officers and a decrease of 11.6% (from 36.6 to 25.0) in the proportion rated below average. In Australia, a group of 175 selectees had a failure rate of 9% in the officer training courses, instead of 36% for approximately 1000 cadets who had previously been chosen without benefit of Selection Board screening. Twenty-eight cadets, who were not recommended by the board and were allowed to enter officers training anyhow, showed a failure rate of 40%. While it must be recognized that success as defined by training supervisors is of

24 The American Army has made plans to use ratings by enlisted and civilian acquaintances among the selection procedures of enlisted men for attendance at Officers Candidate Schools. The new procedures come into effect in 1947. See Army-Navy Journal, LXXXIV, No. 12 (Nov. 23, 1946), 281-284 and 301-302.
25 Cecil A. Gibb, "The Principles and Traits of Leadership," op. cit., pp. 278-279.

course no guarantee that leadership success will be shown in action, it is reasonable to assume that may be some positive correlation. The samples used for these comparisons were not entirely comparable, but the comparisons give weight to the hunch that the sociological selection techniques give some degree of improvement over the methods that were used in the past.

ASSESSMENT OF PERSONNEL OF THE OFFICE OF STRATEGIC SERVICES

Murray and MacKinnon[26] report that sociodramatic and sociometric techniques were used in the screening of approximately five thousand and five hundred agents of the Office of Strategic Services during World War II, which borrowed heavily from methods developed by the British W.O.S.B. The most intensive testing was done on a one-hundred-and-eighteen-acre estate near Fairfax, Virginia. The soldiers had to hide their real identity and live under the strain of adopting a fake one. During the testing period of three days they formed a classless society without rank. A staff of psychologists, psychiatrists, and sociologists administered the tests and made a qualitative evaluation of all candidates on a five-point scale on the basis of the following ten personality traits:

1. Motivation for O.S.S. service overseas
2. Energy and zest
3. Emotional stability
4. Social relations
5. Leadership
6. Ability to keep secret information
7. Power of observation
8. Physical abilities
9. Practical intelligence in dealing with people, ideas, and things
10. Ability to do effective propaganda

The testing procedure included many conventional paper-pencil tests, interviews, projective tests, and sociometric buddy ratings by

26 Henry A. Murray and Donald W. MacKinnon, "Assessment of O.S.S. Personnel," *Journal of Consulting Psychology* (March-April, 1946), pp. 76-80. Also see "A Good Man Is Hard to Find," in *Fortune Magazine*, XXXIV (March, 1946), 92 and 217-224. A full and highly stimulating report on the entire O.S.S. testing program has been published by the O.S.S. Assessment Staff "Assessment of Men" (New York, 1948).

members of the class of one another. Thirty-five lifelike sociodramatic tests were administered to discover something about the personality structure of each soldier—his loves, his hates, his reaction to pressure and failure, his ability to make friends, his aspirations, fears, and psychological weaknesses. They included the following types of test:

1. STRESS INTERVIEW. The idea of using a stress test for selection purposes was first applied to the rating of police officers.[27] Several psychologists developed a mechanical apparatus at which two muscular operations had to be performed at the same time. The candidates were first given a chance to learn to operate the apparatus. Then suddenly the trained raters started to reprimand and make confusing suggestions. A numerical score was developed for rating characteristics such as emotionality; dominance; demeanor; inventiveness; speed of adjustment; memory of relevant details; and ego-orientation. The reliability coefficients reported were low, but the psychologists expressed the conviction that further experimentation with this technique seemed justified.

The O.S.S. used a different version: the applicant was told that he had just been caught in the secret files of a government department without authorization. He was given ten minutes to think of a good way to explain and justify his behavior. He was then subjected to a grilling cross-examination under a blinding eye-level spotlight to break his defensive story and observe his behavior when he told that he had failed.[28]

2. TEST OF FRUSTRATION TOLERANCE. In this test[29] the applicant was given an impossible task. He was asked to construct a five-foot cube with seven diagonals by means of a glorified "tinker-toy." Two trained staff members of the O.S.S. board, whose identity were not known to the soldier, were assigned to him to assist in the completion of the complicated task. They frequently made mistakes to thwart the person under test. One man would play the role of passive aide who

---

27 G. L. Freeman, G. E. Manson, E. T. Katzoff and J. H. Pathman, "The Stress Interview," *Journal of Abnormal and Social Psychology*, XXXVII, No. 4 (Oct., 1942), 427-447. Also see G. L. Freeman, "Suggestions for a Standardized Stress Test," *Journal of General Psychology*, XXXII (1945), 3-11.

28 O.S.S. Assessment Staff, "Assessment of Men," *op. cit.*, pp. 133-142.

29 Much experimental work has been done with nonsocial frustration tests. See Alvin F. Zander, "A Study of Experimental Frustration," *Psychological Monograph*, LVI, No. 3 (1944). Includes excellent bibliography.

was a bit slow and dull in following directions. The other aide showed impatience, lost his temper, was arrogant, and attacked the soldier's personal weaknesses. The behavior of the applicant in this frustrating situation was observed carefully.[30]

3. OBSERVATION OF DETAIL TESTS. In these tests candidates were given a map of an area and the opportunity to observe the terrain depicted by it. Later their memory for details was tested, without reference to the map or any notes the candidate may have made during his scouting tour. In another version, the candidates were given a map which could be studied carefully for eight minutes. Afterward they were asked to answer thirty specific multiple choice questions, which were scored objectively. Similar tests were used after observation of short moving picture reels.[31]

Other sociological tests included in the O.S.S. procedures were an observed interrogation of an escaped prisoner of war, preparation of a technical lecture for teaching purposes, debating, a court trial, athletic games, and physical obstacle courses. Check lists filled out by the observing staff members often lent themselves to objective comparisons. A detailed sociometric rating of the candidates by their fellows also was included. Scores of leadership, acceptance, and rejection were worked out. Diagrams were drawn to show the relative standing of the members of each class on acceptance, rejection, and leadership. "Considerable weight was given to the sociometric findings in deciding the final rating on social relations, since it was felt that the ultimate test was the man's cathexis (valuation) in the minds of his associates.[32]

TESTS OF THE ARMY GROUND FORCES

Sociodramatic tests were used by many units of the Army Ground Forces, although they often were not consciously recognized as tests. This article will limit itself to a brief discussion of two test situations which were used throughout the Army. No systematic studies were undertaken to test their validity or reliability. One of them, the Infantry infiltration course, was given to every soldier in basic train-

[30] O.S.S. Assessment Staff, "Assessment of Men," op. cit., pp. 102-112.
[31] Ibid., pp. 94, 124-128.
[32] Ibid., p. 187.

ing. The other, the Officers Candidate Schools, formed the basis for the selection of most officers.

1. THE INFANTRY INFILTRATION COURSE. This test was administered to most soldiers serving in the United States Army during World War II, as part of the battle-conditioning process. Each soldier had to crawl a distance of several hundred yards through mud, wire entanglements, and ditches. A "cover" of live machine-gun bullets was fired constantly a few inches above the crouching soldiers. Explosive charges were detonated at close proximity, covering the soldiers with mud and slush. A highly realistic simulation of battle conditions was achieved, both physically and socially. No time limit was specified. It was generally considered to be a test of "courage" and the ability to "take it." Soldiers who failed were often transferred into noncombat units. A general presumption prevailed that many soldiers who were likely to function poorly or break down under combat conditions could be detected with this type of test.

2. OFFICER-CANDIDATE-SCHOOL SITUATIONS. The Officers candidate training course (O.C.S.), which lasted for three or four months, included large numbers of sociodramatic exercises. Every student was called upon to practice duties which he would have to perform as an officer, including the command of troops, planning of action, personnel administration, etc. The behavior of officer candidates during and after school hours was under close scrutiny of the school staff and fellow-students. Reactions to the difficulties, disappointments, and strains of school life were carefully observed.

Sociometric ratings, called "buddy ratings," were solicited from each student about all other students in his training company to supplement the ratings of the school staff.[33] These ratings played an important part in the decision of many school commandants on who should or should not be allowed to graduate.

The United States Marine Corps sponsored a study to determine the extent to which success in combat could be predicted by grades received at its O.C.S. Combat-proficiency rating sheets were sent to commanding officers of recent O.C.S. graduates. Complete returns

---

[33] The methodology used in the construction of such ratings is presented in "Personnel Classification Tests," *War Department Technical Manual TM 12-260*, April, 1946, pp. 51-56.

were received on one hundred and eighty-five second lieutenants who had been in actual combat. It was found that success in O.C.S. as measured by paper-pencil tests, such as a Personal Inventory Sheet, General Classification and Mechanical Aptitude Test grades, and final composite numerical O.C.S. grades were not significantly related to success in combat, as measured by the combat-proficiency report of commanding officers. However, the buddy-rating scores were found to be the best predictor of the opinion held by senior combat officers in the field, with a tetrachoric correlation of .42. The report states:[34] "The evidence thus far presented points strongly to the conclusion that the men themselves are more capable of picking their own leaders than are their instructors and training officers." For example, if the buddy ratings had been used exclusively in the preselection of these O.C.S. graduates, the two lowest groups in combat ratings could have been eliminated by requiring a minimum score of 70. On the surface, this fact may seem to stand contradicted by the previously mentioned study at West Point,[35] where there was no correlation between the ratings of leadership by senior cadets of lower ranking cadets. However, the relations between different classes at West Point are very formal. Rank differences are carefully nurtured and maintained. In view of this, there is some justified doubt that they can be compared to the O.C.S. "buddy ratings," where all candidates are on the same rank level and therefore have more informal and intimate contact with each other.

MILITARY INTELLIGENCE TEST

At the Military Intelligence Center at Camp Ritchie, Md., as in the other Army schools, many sociodramatic performance tests were used to train soldiers and select the most qualified graduates for special assignments and promotions. The writer attended this school as a student. For purposes of illustration, two tests are described in detail.

1. THE NIGHT-ORIENTATION PROBLEM. Each soldier was given a compass, a flashlight, and a map. Soldiers were taken in pairs by truck at night to a point unknown to them, with instructions to make

---

[34] "Validation of Officer Selection Tests by Means of Combat Proficiency Ratings" (Medical Field Research Laboratory, Camp Lejeune, N.C.), M. & S. Research Project No. X-620. (Sub. No. 135), Progress Reports Nos. 1 and 2.

[35] David D. Page, "Measurement and Prediction of Leadership," op. cit.

their way to a point described by coördinates on their map. This test involved the solution of the following tasks:

(a) Identification of their location by night, by association of the terrain features with their map. The map might be in American, German, French, or English symbols, depending upon the type of test desired.

(b) Use of the map and a compass to find the way through difficult terrain to the coördinates designated as the meeting point. Avoidance of swamps, rivers, and cliffs had to be planned for.

(c) Precautions of combat patrolling had to be observed. No open light could be used. Major roads had to be circumvented, and noises reduced to a minimum. Patrols sometimes roamed in the area to check on strict adherence to these test conditions.

On arrival at the designated coördinates, soldiers were apparently scored on the following:

(a) Time required for completion of the test.

(b) Method used to reach the objective, the route taken, and the manner in which difficulties were overcome.

This test involved a knowledge of map-reading, use of compass, and certain elements of "leadership" and "courage" (dogs, barbed-wire fences, the darkness of night, cliffs, swamps, and rivers introduced a slight element of danger). The scoring was in rough qualitative terms. The fact that two soldiers worked together also reduced the value of the test for rating each student separately.

2. INTERROGATION OF PRISONERS OF WAR. This test took place in a tent containing a chair and a table. Documents taken from a German prisoner of war were handed to the student. An observer, who was seated inconspicuously in a corner of the tent throughout the test, briefed the student. For example: "You are a prisoner-of-war interrogator for the 247th Infantry Regiment. We are planning to attack tonight. Find out what the enemy can do to us when we attack. What are his plans, his resources, and where are his positions."

At the command of the student, after he had familiarized himself with the documents available, the prisoner was brought in. Prisoners were carefully trained soldier-actors. Most of them were anti-Nazi refugees who had been in Germany recently and who could portray their roles with unusual realism. Each "prisoner" had memorized his general role, which was in accord with the documents of which he was the supposed carrier. He had the kind of military information likely to be had by a German soldier of his rank and unit. This test required the following skills in the interrogator:

(a) Knowledge of the organization of the German army and the functions generally performed by different units and individuals of different ranks.

(b) Interpretation of actual captured enemy documents.

(c) Ability to do effective interviewing by "sizing up" the prisoner to determine the most effective method of approach—threats, promises, straightforward questioning, camouflaged probing, etc.

(d) Effective interrogation of the prisoner for information he would be likely to have in view of his assignment, rank, and general intelligence.

(e) Evaluation and reporting of his findings by the student.

Each student took several practice interrogations at different levels of difficulty. The ratings were largely qualitative but played an important part in determining the promotion and future assignment of the graduates.

ARMY OFFICER INTEGRATION

Sociometric and sociodramatic devices are part of the selection procedure in current use by the War Department for picking officers who will receive commissions in the Regular United States Army. An extensive research program is now in progress.[36] For reasons of military security many important details cannot be disclosed at this stage of the selection program, under which about fifty thousand new Regular Army officers are being chosen.

The criterion of selection was based on a sociometric rating device. To find out what an *outstanding* officer is like, officers of many different units were asked to rate one another as to the value of their services. All in all, over thirteen thousand were rated by several others who knew them well and had often served with them in combat. Ratings by officers of superior, equal, and inferior rank were included. Among the thirteen thousand there were approximately one thousand officers on whom all raters agreed that they were *outstanding*, one thousand were agreed to be *average*, and one thousand were

[36] Joseph W. Eaton, "The Army's Personnel Research Laboratory" in *Personnel*, March, 1947, pp. 326-331.

agreed to be *inferior*. The remaining ten thousand officers were not rated clearly and consistently by all raters and were not used in the study.[37]

The next step in the research was to discover the attributes of *outstanding*, *average*, and *inferior* officers. Four readily administered tools of classification were developed, each of which was found to differentiate reliably between the three categories of competence. The tests have a combined multiple correlation with the criterion of .67.

Three of the classification tools, a General Survey Test, a Biographical Information Blank, and Superior Officers Evaluation Reports are paper-pencil instruments. The fourth is a standardized sociodramatic interview of each applicant by a board of trained officers to test a candidate's ability in dealing with people.[38]

There are plans to follow up the careers of the officers selected with the help of these selection instruments in order to validate both the tests and the sociometric criterion on which they are based.

WHO SHOULD DO THE RATING?

It should be noted that a relatively democratic type of sociometric rating was employed, as officers of superior, equal, and inferior rank took part in the rating process. The possibility of including the ratings of enlisted men, particularly noncommissioned officers, in the criterion was considered by the research staff. Administrative difficulties prevented the collection of such ratings on a big scale. It is not yet known to what extent the lack of enlisted-men ratings decreases its validity. There are some indications that such ratings would not differ greatly from ratings by officers. On the other hand, the possibility exists that the limitation of the exclusive use of officer-raters allowed too much emphasis on "officers' club popularity." Enlisted men who work under an officer often have closer contact with him to evaluate his work than those of equal or superior rank, who have only superficial contact with him. Bonney's study of agreement between teacher's judgments and student choices certainly lends support to the view

[37] James Clarke, "Picking the 9000," *Infantry Journal*, LVIII (July, 1946), 7-12. Presents an interesting detailed account of the research work.

[38] E. Donald Sisson, "What War Department Psychologists Do," *Army Information Digest*, I (December, 1946), 46-51.

that superiors are strongly misled in their choices by their personal relation to those who are rated. She noted fairly consistent errors in rating of the students whom teachers judged to have many or few intimate friends and the actual social pattern of the classroom.[39]

The value of democratic sociometric rating is a disputed matter, not only in armies, but in businesses, schools, and governments as well. Admittedly, little factual data is available on the relative merits of autocratic, aristocratic, and democratic sociometric selection. "Good" and "bad" leaders of government have developed under all three systems. Even in democracies like the United States, technical experts, such as judges, city-managers, and civil servants, are selected by autocratic or aristocratic processes.

However, it should be noted that inferiors always rate their superiors.[40] In industry the tension created when managers rate a supervisor in one way, while men under him make the opposite evaluation, can end in resignations or strikes. In the Army there are no such simple sanctioned outlets for tensions. Periodic democratic sociometric ratings would give commanding officers an opportunity to discover these tensions before they can result in a dangerous decline in morale. Such ratings would not lead to a breakdown of military command, as sociometric ratings in the Army are not mandatory and finally decisive. They have never been more than one of several sources of information, of value to a commanding officer in arriving at a judgment. Combined ratings of superiors, equals, and men from all inferior ranks appear to have more validity. Men of all ranks are more likely to have confidence in the judgment of a commander if it is known than in the selection of leaders he took into consideration the views of all concerned.

CIVILIAN APPLICATIONS

There have been several interesting reports on the attempted use of sociological tests for selecting personnel for industrial and civil service positions involving leadership. The British Foreign Service uses the general methods developed by the War Office Selection

[39] Merl E. Bonney, "Sociometric Study of Agreement Between Teacher Judgment and Student Choices" in *Sociometry*, X (May, 1947), 133-146.

[40] I. J. Melscher and I. Weinstock, "Ratings of Supervisors by Subordinates," *Personnel Journal* XIX, No. 1 (May, 1940), 37-40.

Boards in screening candidates for junior posts. Mandell reports an exploratory trial by the United States Civil Service Commission with an "Oral Group Performance Test."[41] Barnard and Brody used this technique in selecting Public Health Officers for their in-service training program in New York City.[42]

In the Group Oral Performance test, six to nine candidates are invited to sit around a table and discuss a technical question, such as "What control measures should be taken to protect New York City from rabies." Four examiners are seated in the background and rate each candidate on the basis of the following six factors:[43]

1. *Appearance and Manner*—Poise, physical alertness, nervousness, restlessness, attentiveness, mannerisms.
2. *Speech*—Power of expression, vocabulary, diction, modulation.
3. *Attitude Toward Group*—Tact, coöperation, ability to mix, flexibility.
4. *Leadership*—Ability to assume lead without giving offense, acceptance by group.
5. *Contribution to Group Performance*—Team worker or prima donna, awareness of objectives of group discussion, ability to reconcile differences.
6. *Scientific Approach*—Ability to marshal data, awareness of implications, ability to reason, ingenuity, mental alertness, judgment.

Bernard and Brody suggest that the group oral performance test may well have the following advantages over the ordinary oral interview:

1. More time to observe each candidate. In a three-hour interview nine candidates can be studied during the entire period. If individual interviews were given, only twenty minutes could be devoted to each of them.
2. Examiner can devote full time to observing, listening, and taking notes.
3. Eliminates the examiner from the content of the test. There is no

41 Milton M. Mandell, "The Group Oral Performance Test" in *Public Personnel Review*, VII, No. 4 (October, 1946), 209-212.
42 Margaret W. Barnard and William Brody, "A New Method of Selecting Health Officers-in-Training" in *American Journal of Public Health*, XXXVII, No. 6 (June, 1947), 715-720.
43 *Ibid.*, p. 719.

temptation to use the oral interview to show what the examiner knows rather than to evaluate the candidate.

4. Reduces loss of reliability of the oral interview, which might result from the use of different questions to different candidates, or by information given to later candidates by those examined earlier.

5. Provides a more natural social setting than the usual question-and-answer contest between the candidate and his examiners.

6. Eliminates suspicion by candidates that others were shown favoritism by getting easier questions.

7. Shows each candidate in a social situation, particularly one in which he must assert himself in a group of professional colleagues.

8. The test requires no special interviewing skill on the part of the examiners.

9. Participants in the test, both candidates and examiners, find this method of interviewing more enjoyable and relaxing.

Sociometric ratings by the candidates of each other's performance were not included in these experiments. So far, too little experience with this technique has been gained to permit a more valid comparison with the standard examiner-candidate oral interview.

CONCLUSION

It is apparent that many efforts have been and are being made to put the selection of leaders on a scientific basis. So far, this goal is far from being achieved. The agencies which have been most concerned with the problem have been, for the most part, of a governmental nature—armies and civil service commissions. They have made some challenging experiments in their efforts to fill junior positions of leadership, but have produced no data that would permit an evaluation of their results. Few follow-up studies to test the results were even attempted. There is enthusiastic agreement among most of those who have initiated and executed sociological tests that they add a considerable degree of insight and accuracy to the results achieved through the more conventional selection procedures—psychological tests and oral interviews. The judgments of these experts should be respected; their hunches might well encourage further research, but they remain to be validated.

Many of the experiments had to be undertaken under great pressure. There was no time for adequate preparation and often little for reflection about what was being done. It must also be recognized that this kind of research is expensive. Only large organizations have the resources to experiment with specific sociometric and sociodramatic test procedures, suited to their special needs, and even there, budgetary limitations often precluded any serious analysis of results. Neither the U.S. Army nor the O.S.S. sponsored an evaluation study of their procedures.

Most of the sociological tests were developed without a clear definition of the criterion against which the test can be validated. The sociometric definition of an *outstanding, average,* and *inferior* officer underlying the Officers Integration Program of the United States Army, despite its shortcomings, is a good beginning. It specifically defines leadership in terms of the social values of a large sample of officers functioning in the organization. Basic to the development of a well-validated test is an agreement of what kind of leadership is wanted, directed toward what kind of goals, and within the framework of what kind of values.

The specific skills to be tested have been analyzed into many components. They involved the application of specific and typical technical, muscular, and social skills and were often conducted in a social situation of simulated reality, with trained assistants and observer-raters. Considerable degree of refinement was achieved in this direction by the O.S.S. and the War Office Selection Boards.

For some of the tests scoring devices with a high degree of reliability may have been worked out. But in general, much work remains to be done in developing refined scoring methods and even more in the objectification of interpretation of the observers. Most of the scoring and interpretation was done on the "hunch level," on the basis of the insight of the observer. One potentially fruitful direction might be the increased use of sociometric ratings by all participants of a test. The experience of Officer Candidate Schools with "buddy ratings" indicates that they may be among the most valid indexes of leadership.

It is doubtful that leadership selection can ever become as refined as the measurement of temperature or calories. "Leadership" is too complex and composite a quality to lend itself to fine numerical grading. Expression of final test results in rough gradations, such as deciles or quartiles of the total test population, may well be the direction of investigation. No test can hope to fully measure the unique qualities of each personality—those unknown and perhaps unknowable factors which provide an exception to any social regularity. Science is not ready to reduce man to a formula, from which he can be synthesized. Until such a day comes, any measurement of human qualities is likely to have a validity far below the point of certainty. Leadership selection is a form of prediction. In that field, science, as the harassed weather forecaster and public opinion pollster will testify, has not been able to measure and control enough of the multitude of factors to permit a crystal-ball prediction with more than a moderate degree of probability. However, leadership tests which could separate the extreme cases—those very likely to succeed or fail as leaders— would be an important scientific achievement.

The introduction of more refined processes of leadership selection may well have one important social consequence that cannot be taken lightly. Tests, rules, and procedures are hostile to all deviants, the exceptional persons who do not quite fit into the average stereotype. Puny Napoleon I of France might never have been able to meet American Officer Candidate School standards and certainly lacked the height to become a policeman in any of our larger cities. What test could be made flexible enough to have given a passing grade to the invalid Franklin D. Roosevelt, whose position of leadership required of him the utmost mobility? Psychiatrists have called attention to the operation of compensation mechanisms. The development of a tight automatic testing program for the selection of leaders must leave room for the unconventional case, who fits no mold, and perhaps because of this, has a strong motivation which makes him outstanding. This applies particularly to the *charismatic leader.*[44] The scoring machine must never be allowed to rule out human judgment.

Sociological tests, together with the more conventional psychological tests and oral interviews, have been useful in reducing the risk of selection of leaders. They may well have been more valid in picking the extreme cases—those most likely to be failures or successes—than the average, although definite evidence for this hunch is lacking. Improvement in the validity of the techniques discussed in this paper would result in important social savings. In our complex society, there

[44] H. H. Gerth and C. Wright Mills, *From Max Weber* (New York, 1946), pp 245-264.

are frequent occasions when potential leaders must be selected quickly from large numbers of applicants, to hold important positions or to take training courses leading to them. The improvement of sociodramatic and sociometric testing devices may provide additional degrees of refinement to efforts to put leadership selection on a more scientific basis by supplementing human judgment with objective tests.

The Problem of Succession
and Bureaucracy[1]

BY ALVIN W. GOULDNER

INTRODUCTION

CLASSICAL POLITICAL scientists, attuned to the vicissitudes of crowns and courts, have, in their concept of succession, left a residue of observation and analysis that bears reëxamination by modern social scientists. Limiting their attention to the *highest* authorities of government, they have noted that replacement of a new for an old ruler was often attended by intense public crises. "Such periods have frequently been characterized by bitter conflicts occasionally developing into full-fledged wars, of which the Spanish, Polish and Austrian wars of succession are outstanding examples."[2] Political scientists have conceived of the method of succession as "one of the principal factors determining the stability of any given form of government" and have therefore used it as an attribute for the classification of types of governments.

It is interesting, however, that modern sociologists, far from being influenced by these judgments, have almost entirely ignored the phenomenon of succession. It is possible that the political scientists' association of the concept of succession with problems of the most supreme authorities may partially account for this, for modern sociology is largely secular in outlook and, carrying the stamp of dis-

[1] This is a previously unpublished paper.
[2] Frederick M. Watkins, "Political Succession," *Encyclopedia of the Social Sciences.*

enchantment common to our age, looks to "pedestrian" things for enlightenment.

While reserving fuller treatment of this question for later discussion, it may be observed that the sociologists' neglect of the concept of succession becomes acutely problematical if account is taken of the pivotal role it acquired in the work of Max Weber. Insofar as Weber had a theory of historical change, his major analytical categories posited an alternation of charismatic and bureaucratic or traditional modes of authority. These rotations were conceived of as cyclical fluctuations within a trend which moved toward increasing rationalization of social action.[3]

Charismatic authority, involving the acceptance of a ruler because of his singular personal attributes, was held to disrupt the process of rationalization when existent routines proved inadequate to growing problems. Hostile to workaday procedures, a charismatic movement is alienated from economic and familial institutions and supports itself irregularly. Charismatic authority is, then, ephemeral to the extreme. Ordinarily, its instability provokes insecurity among the charismatic leader's staff and followers—who seek to safeguard their material and ideal interests. Their anxiety, Weber states, is brought to a climax by the problem of succession.

Weber proposes that the methods used to secure a successor result in routinizations which, depending mainly on the economic context, move in either a traditionalistic or bureaucratic direction. *To Weber, then, the problem of succession is the umbilical cord which connects charisma to its heir.* Succession is the key concept which in his analysis bridges the polarized modes of authority. Yet despite this concept's analytically strategic role, Weber fails to give a coherent picture of its content and its function in his system of theory. Exactly how succession leads in the one case to bureaucratic, and in the other, to traditionalistic, authority is unclear.

More recently, some of the problems attendant upon succession in

[3] Cf. Introduction by H. H. Gerth and C. Wright Mills (editors), *From Max Weber: Essays in Sociology* (New York, 1947), for a similar interpretation. My colleague, Jeremiah Wolpert, has suggested that *continuing* rationalization increasingly delimits the possibility of traditionalistic authority and, also, radically modifies the nature of charismatic authority, so that the latter's traits may be deliberately manipulated. This type is, perhaps, more meaningfully characterized as pseudocharismatic, suggests Wolpert.

a bureaucracy have received comment from Arnold Brecht[4] and Marshall Dimock.[5] Both Brecht and Dimock have focused, in particular, on the problem of "bureaucratic sabotage," the resistance of the "permanent" staff of a bureaucracy to the policies of their superior, especially when he is new to office. Dimock attributes this sound-proofed conflict to a short circuit in communication between the successor and the old staff, who over the years of their association have developed subtly expressed understandings of which the successor is ignorant. Why the communication failure occurs, and in particular what its institutional conditions are, is not considered in any detail. While noting that the successor makes his entrance primed for change, Dimock gives no explanation of the circumstances which engender this attitude.

In actuality, empirical studies of the process of succession and its concomitant problems are practically nonexistent. In the following discussion observations will be drawn from a study of an absentee-owned factory near Buffalo, New York. This factory, which combines both mining and surface processing operations, is located in a rural community into which urban characteristics are only slowly seeping. These observations are offered with the following intentions:

1. To suggest and provide a warrant for certain hypotheses concerning the interrelations between succession and the development of bureaucracy.

2. To outline a theoretical context in which one commonly noted industrial phenomenon, "strategic replacements," may be usefully fitted.

3. To illustrate the potential utility of employing a "secularized" concept of succession in the study of organization. By a "secularized" concept of succession is meant the replacement (for any reason) of an individual in a strategic position in any formal or informal group, without prejudice as to whether this group is large or small, autocephalous or heterocephalous, of broad or narrow jurisdiction and composition. Such a concept of succession would, it seems, escape the Carlylean implications of that employed by political scientists.

[4] Arnold Brecht, "Bureaucratic Sabotage," *Annals of the American Academy of Political and Social Science*, June, 1937.

[5] Marshall E. Dimock, "Bureaucracy Self-Examined," *Public Administration Review*, Summer, 1944.

CASE HISTORY OF A SUCCESSION[6]

At the time we began our study two things were at the center of the plant personnel's attention: first, an accelerating degree of bureaucratization and, second, a series of replacements among foremen and supervisors.

Among many evidences of growing bureaucratization[7] was an increasing separation between the company's and workers' property; the company having begun a stricter control over its machinery, raw material, and finished product, making these less accessible to workers for personal use than formerly. The old personnel manager, an informal, community-conscious man with little formal education and a "dislike of paperwork," was replaced by a rule-sensitive, company-conscious man with some college education.

The number of paper reports required from supervisors was being increased; a formal, printed "warning" notice used for disciplinary purposes was introduced. The no-absenteeism rule was being strictly enforced; new modes of punching in and out were promulgated; the supervisory staff was being extended and divided into two groups—"know-how" and "do-how" foremen. The characteristic impersonalized "atmosphere" of bureaucratic structures began to pervade the plant.

These innovations, it is crucial to observe, began shortly after the arrival of a new plant manager, Vincent Peele.[8] The correlation between succession and crystallization of bureaucratic trends was, in this instance, striking.

Shortly after his arrival, Peele began to remove some of the old supervisors and foremen and to bring in new ones. Four replacements were made with men in the plant. The new personnel manager was brought in from the plant at which Peele had formerly been manager. (It had been a smaller and less important factory.) Several new foremen's positions were opened up and promotions made to these.

[6] I should like to record my deep appreciation to Maurice Stein, Paul Mahany, Joseph Davis, John Sommers, Cornelius Vodicka, Gunnar Hanson, George Amos, and Jo Ann Setel, students who assisted in the field work.

[7] Max Weber's ideal-type bureaucracy has been used as a heuristic guide and most of the variables mentioned below are stressed in his concept of bureaucracy.

[8] This name, like all others used, is fictitious in order that anonymity of the company, plant, and personnel will be preserved.

This rapid change of supervisory personnel following a succession is so familiar in an industrial situation that it deserves a distinctive name and, in this paper, has been called "strategic replacement."

What is there about the role of a successor that conduces to increased bureaucratization and strategic replacement? The problem may be separated into two parts: (1) The frame of reference of the successor and the definitions of his situation to which it disposes, and (2) the objective attributes of the factory situation.

THE SUCCESSOR'S FRAME OF REFERENCE. In this case, succession involved advancement for Peele, the new plant manager. The main office personnel, who determined his promotion, reminded Peele of his predecessor's inadequacies and expressed the feeling that things had been slipping at the plant for some while. They suggested that the old plant manager, Godfrey, was perhaps getting overindulgent in his old age and that he, Peele, would be expected to improve production quotas. As Peele put it, "Godfrey didn't force the machine. I had to watch it. Godfrey was satisfied with a certain production. But the company gave me orders to get production up." With the pressure of renewed postwar competition things would have to start humming; traditionalized production quotas were to be rationalized.[9]

Peele, grateful for his opportunity to ascend in the company hierarchy, of course heeded the main office counsels. It may be emphasized that a "briefing" does more than impart technical data; it also functions to structure attitudes toward an assignment. Peele, therefore, came to his new plant keenly sensitive to the impersonal, universalistic criteria which his superiors would use to judge his performance. He knew his progress would be watched; he desires also to express his gratitude and is, consequently, anxious to "make good." As a member of the main office administrative staff commented: "Peele is trying hard to arrive. He is paying more attention to the plant. But he lacks Godfrey's [the old plant manager's] personal

[9] Roethlisberger and Dickson have emphasized the tendency of informal cliques of workers to limit in a traditionalistic way their output, by their beliefs concerning a "fair day's work." Our comment indicates that restriction of output, or "sabotage" as Veblen referred to it, is not manifested solely by operatives but is found among managerial personnel as well. Veblen has, of course, long since noted this; he tended, however, to focus on the rational motives for "sabotage" among managers, neglecting the traditionalistic component.

touch. Peele will follow along organizational lines, while Godfrey handled things on the personal basis."

There is, however, a second and apparently conflicting element in the new plant manager's frame of reference. On his way up, he may have made friends whose loyalty and help expedited his ascent. Since the time of succession is often a time of promotion and enhanced power, it may be the moment of reckoning awaited by the friends when their past favors to the successor can be reciprocated. There seems little question, however, that this particularistic element in the new plant manager's frame of reference is a minor one.

For if worse comes to worst, he may evade the old obligations since he is now no longer among those to whom he owes them. Or, more likely perhaps, he may interpret fulfillment of old particularistic obligations as a *means of securing personnel* which would enable him to guarantee successful accomplishment of his new mission and of the abstract, impersonal goals to which he is mainly oriented. This need evoke no conflict of values within the successor, for one's friends are most often viewed as "competent" people, and in the case of a highly placed individual there are reasons why this is very probable.

Thus, even before setting foot into the plant, Peele had a notion of the kinds of things which needed "correction," and was tentatively shaping policies to bring about the requisite *changes*. He defined the situation as one calling for certain *changes*, changes oriented to the abstract, rational standards of efficiency. Because he is a successor, new to the plant, a stranger among strangers, as yet untied by bonds of friendship and informal solidarity with the people in his new plant, both his perceptive and executive capacities may be relatively devoid of nonrational considerations.

THE FACTORY SITUATION. Oriented toward efficiency and the minimization of nonrational aspects of the factory organization which would impede it, the new plant manager entered the factory. He found that to which his frame of reference has been sensitized. Inevitably a factory, like any other social organization, reflects a compromise between formal and informal organization, between rational and nonrational norms. Peele found that workers "borrowed" tools from the plant for their own personal use, that they have customarily helped themselves to raw materials and even finished products for use about their homes, workshops, and farms. He found that some workers preferred to "punch in" early and accumulate a little overtime, or "punch out" early on special occasions. The miners, far from eager to conform with Protestant norms of regular work, believed that a certain amount of absenteeism was one of their traditional prerogatives and a normative way of manifesting that "down here, we are our own bosses." The new plant manager's expectations were confirmed: the plant was in "evident" need of specific changes to heighten its efficiency.

Whom could Peele hold responsible for this "lax" state of affairs? Oriented to formal and individualistic diagnoses, he tended to place responsibility on the old supervisory staff, and indicated that he considered it their duty to remedy the situation along lines he suggested. At this point he encountered his first sharp resistance. "Every foreman had set ways," explained Peele. "When I wanted to make some changes the supervisors told me, Godfrey used to do this and that. . . . I didn't make many changes and I'm satisfied with the changes I've made. The foremen are getting smoothed off now. [You had some difficulty with the supervisors . . . ?—interviewer] Yes, I had some trouble in straightening out shirkers. Some of them thought they were going to get fired. I could work on *these* guys. But others, who didn't expect to get fired, were. Each foreman is just a little bit on edge now. They don't know whether they're doing right. . . . A new plant manager is going to make some changes—to suit my own way. *I had to watch them.* I made those changes."

Thus among the things the new plant manager resolves to change, when he encounters their resistance, are the old supervisory personnel. But why is it that the old supervisory staff resists the new manager's plans?

A new manager is faced with a heritage of promises and obligations that his predecessor has not had an opportunity to fulfill. These old obligations are most important when made to the old supervisory staff, or to others constituting the old plant manager's informal social circle. For placed as they often are in powerful positions, they may be able to mobilize sentiment against him, or use dilatory tactics to impede his efforts, unless he fulfills his "inherited" obligations.

An interesting illustration of this at the plant involves the present union president, Ralph Byta. Byta was a neighbor of Godfrey and had been induced by him to come to work at the plant. Godfrey had made Byta some promises which he was unable to meet, due to his sudden death.

Some four months after Peele's arrival, Byta ran for and was elected president of the local union. Byta's new position was now much more invulnerable than those of the other "old lieutenants" who held supervisory positions. He could not be replaced or fired and had to be "dealt with." As Byta put it: "The good men know that a union's the best way to get ahead. You can't walk into the company and ask them for a raise for yourself. It's different though if you represent 150 men. *Then, too, if the company sees you're a leader (and the company sees it!) well, maybe you can get yourself a raise.*"

Nor was Byta's expectation a fanciful one; it had solid justification in the company's previous actions. As a member of the main office administrative staff told an interviewer: "Some of our foremen are ex-union presidents. . . . The union can pick out a good man for president. If you want a good man pick the president of the union. If you have good morale, the men elect responsible people to the union leadership."

At first Byta played the role of a "militant" and was characterized by management as "bitter." Months after his election, the new plant manager had a "man to man" talk with him, and Byta is now viewed by management as much more "reasonable" than when newly elected. Byta's case is an example of the problems with which a new manager is confronted through the old lieutenants and members of the old informal group.

Resistance to a new plant manager by the old group of lieutenants may be provoked for reasons other than the former's reluctance to acknowledge the old manager's obligations. The new manager, for example, may not be viewed as a *legitimate* successor by the old lieutenants; they may consider one of their own group as the legitimate heir. In this company, the supervisor of ——— building is *customarily* viewed as "next in line" for promotion to manager. It seems significant, then, that Peele was most hostile to the supervisor of ——— building, considering him to be the "least strict" of all the supervisors.

On one occasion Peele had to be hospitalized during a siege of heated wage negotiations. The supervisor of ——— building became acting plant manager. From management's point of view, he played an extremely ineffectual role in the negotiations, not attempting to "handle" or "control" the situation when it headed toward a strike.

In general, the annoyance of the old lieutenants is sharpened when they find their once-favored status incompletely understood or deferred to and perhaps ignored by the successor. The old lieutenants' resistance to the new manager finds its counterpart among the rank-and-file operatives when measures planned to foster efficiency are initiated. The operatives resist because they resent the infringements that these make on their established prerogatives. That an increase in efficiency often means greater work effort on their part, without compensatory rewards, is viewed as unjust.

They may also, like the supervisors, question the legitimacy of the new manager. Whether or not this occurs depends, in part, on the specific yardsticks used by a particular group of workers to evaluate a manager's "right" to hold his job. The point to be underscored is that succession provides an occasion when questions about the legitimacy of a manager will be elicited and considered most permissible.

The manner in which a manager gets his position may be one of the criteria of legitimacy. For example, "coming up from the ranks" may be a criterion of legitimate authority among workers in present-day industry. The way in which the manager exercises his authority may be another measure of his legitimacy. If, for example, he recognizes workers' traditional rights and "does not act superior," the workers in this plant are likely to consider his authority legitimate. These workers, also, think a manager should "stand on his own feet" and not be meticulous about clearing problems through the company's main office.

Sensitized, however, as the manager has been by his main office briefing, the successor is quick to define some of the workers' customary rights as impediments to efficiency. He will, too, again influenced by his status as a successor, tend to await main office dispositions of problems, thus irking operatives who still think of a manager very much as an independent entrepreneur. As a main office staff member recognized, "A new plant manager is more prone to lean on the top administration than is a more experienced one."

An index of the degree of rank-and-file resistance to a new manager is the prevalence of what may be called the "Rebecca Myth."[10] Some while ago, Daphne DuMaurier wrote a book about a young woman who married a widower, only to be plagued by the memory of his first wife, Rebecca, whose virtues were widely extolled. The idealization of the absent is a well-known phenomenon. One may suspect that almost every former plant manager is, to some extent, idealized by the workers, even though he may have been disliked while present.

It was precisely such a situation that confronted Peele. In fact, workers' reminiscences about the regime of "Old Godfrey" are scarcely less than a modern version of "Paradise Lost." The workers' comments spontaneously contrast and compare, playing the old manager off against the new. The social function of the Rebecca Myth seems plain enough. By attaching themselves to Godfrey's memory, the workers can, in his name, *legitimate* their resistance to changes planned or implemented by Peele.

The new manager was, therefore, faced with two interrelated problems. First, how to implement the efficiency goals he had set himself. Second, how, as a necessary condition for solution of the first problem, to eliminate the resistance to his plans by workers and supervisors. In addition, Peele was enmeshed in a problem on a totally different, a psychological, level. This is the problem of coping with his own mounting anxiety which, situationally aroused by the definition of his promotion as a "test," is further accentuated by the resistance he meets. He has, broadly, two major tactics of solution available to him: (a) the technique of informal solidarity and/or (b) the technique of impersonal routinization or other changes in the formal organization.

BUREAUCRATIZATION AND STRATEGIC REPLACEMENT AS PROBLEM SOLUTIONS

The successor can attempt to arouse informal solidarity and group sentiment, harnessing them to his goals. Such an approach might be

---

[10] In another connection, the Lynds have commented on this phenomena. "Middletown is wont to invoke old leaders against new leaders who threaten to leave the 'safe and tried middle of the road.' " Robert S. Lynd and Helen Merrell Lynd, *Middletown in Transition* (New York, 1937), p. 413. Cf. also Chap. VIII, "Managers and Owners, Then and Now," in W. Lloyd Warner and J. O. Low, *The Social System of the Modern Factory* (New Haven, 1947), for a pithy account of the functioning of the Rebecca Myth during a strike. Sections of this chapter are reproduced earlier in this volume.

exemplified by the appeal: "Let's all pitch in and do a job!" The use of gemeinschaft or, more properly, pseudo-gemeinschaft[11] as a tactic for promoting his ends is employed by Peele, within the limits permitted by his personality. He has, for example, taken pains to get to know the men. "I talk with them," he says, "I congratulate them about births and things like that, *if I can only get an inkling of it*. Personal touches here and there help." But pseudo-gemeinschaft is an inadequate means to the manager's ends because it premises two things not always available.

1. It requires, firstly, a greater consensus of ends and sentiments between management and workers than exists. As an obvious example, Peele (like most managers) was primarily concerned about meeting his production quota and keeping costs down. The workers are, however, much less interested in these. It is difficult to maintain, to say nothing of creating, informal solidarity in pursuit of ends which are differentially valued by group members.

2. Secondly, the successor wise to the ways of pseudo-gemeinschaft would require *knowledge* of the informal networks and the private sentiments they transmit, if he were to manipulate them successfully. But *because he is a successor*, and has little "inkling" of the subtle arrangements and understandings comprising the informal structure, these are inaccessible for his purposes. As already indicated, he even has difficulty with the informal group nearest his own level, the old lieutenants.

The successor is, therefore, impelled by these circumstances to respond to his problems by resort to tactics more congruent with his role: impersonal techniques or formalized controls and the use of strategic replacements.

The problem of disposing of the old lieutenants is one which takes *time*. A new manager cannot, and often will not, act too hastily for fear of precipitating a conflict for which he is not yet prepared. He does not wish to be accused of failing to give the old lieutenants a "chance," nor of seeking to install his favorites with indecent haste. He spends some time "sizing up" the situation, looking for possible allies and lining up replacements.

---

[11] Cf. Robert K. Merton with the assistance of Marjorie Fiske and Alberta Curtis, *Mass Persuasion* (New York, 1946), pp. 142-144, for a general discussion of the concept of pseudo-gemeinschaft.

In the meanwhile, however, the manager has no social "connective tissue," that is, no informal group structure, between himself and the lower echelons. Relatively isolated at this point, he receives mainly formal and technical communications. His anxiety is channeled into suspicion of what is happening below. One worker sized up the situation as follows: "When Godfrey was here, it was like one big happy family. Peele is all business. Why, Godfrey could get on that phone, call up the foreman and have the situation well in hand. *Peele has to come around and make sure things are all right.* Maybe that's why he's bringing in his own men."

One of the familiar ways Peele used to relieve his anxiety was by being omnipresent. His practice of always being in the plant and walking all around drew universal comment, always hostile. This is not enough, however, because the manager is well aware that the men modify their behavior on seeing him approach.

In the absence of a position in a well-developed system of informal relations within the plant, and because he cannot be everywhere at once, personally checking up, the new manager begins to introduce and emphasize adherence to the rules. He elaborates a system of "paper reports" which enable him to "keep his finger on things." Observing informal gatherings of workers chatting, he is somewhat upset not merely because of what they are *not* doing, but also by what they may be saying and doing and is attracted to a "make work" policy. He seeks to keep the men busy, perhaps acting on the Protestant precept that the "devil finds work for idle hands."

When he considers the moment judicious he begins to make the strategic replacements, spinning out a new informal group that will conform to his needs, support his status, and through whose network he can guarantee that the meaning or "spirit" of his orders will be communicated. This last point deserves emphasis, for no matter how model a bureaucratic structure he may mold, its formal rules will be enmeshed in and in need of reinforcement by a framework of non-rational values.[12]

The technique of strategic replacements obligates the new lieutenants to the successor, establishing extra-formal ties between the two, which the manager may draw upon to implement his goals. The

[12] Cf. Reinhard Bendix, "Bureaucracy: The Problem and Its Setting," *American Sociological Review*, October, 1947, for a discussion of this problem.

degree to which this technique does obligate the new lieutenant to the successor was observed in an interview with a newly appointed foreman. Unlike his references to the preceding managers, this foreman called the new manager by his first name, was very reluctant to give voice to near-universal references to Peele's strictness, and fantasies that Peele is better liked than Godfrey. Thus strategic replacement—changing the occupants of certain formal statuses—is, by way of its consequences upon informal organization, functional to the status security of a successor.

To summarize this discussion of the interplay of succession, bureaucratization, and strategic replacements: It should be clear that, as this was a plant with a history of some twenty-five years, and part of a large expanding company, it was far from innocent of bureaucratic procedures. Nor was Peele devoid of bureaucratic intentions prior to his arrival. There was no such pure case available for study. On the contrary, the plant had experienced a degree of bureaucratization, and the new manager was oriented to values which might have lead him in a bureaucratic direction, regardless of the circumstances of succession.

The point here, however, is that the role of a successor apparently involves the occupant with certain problems which, from his viewpoint, are *conditions* of his action. *These conditions conduce to the same process of bureaucratization as do the new manager's company-structured values.* The existence of the conditions concurrent with succession make bureaucratization *functional* to the successor. Put in another way, it is the emergence of the problems of succession which require that the successor *learn* and use bureaucratic methods. The presence of these conditions exerts pressure on the successor to organize bureaucratically. He organizes bureaucratically, not only because he wants to or because he *values* these above other methods, but because he is *compelled* to by the conditions of succession—if he wishes to maintain his status.

In this plant there were about six managers from the time of its inception: an average of about one for every five years of its existence. This suggests that it is necessary to consider another specific dimension of succession, the *rate* of succession. When contrasted with comparable institutions of societies antecedent to our own, the rate of succession in the modern factory seems "high." The modern corporation, one of whose manifest functions is to enable business organizations to persist beyond the life of their founders, is an institutional condition for this high rate. Another institutional condition for the high rate of succession is, in one of its facets, absentee ownership or, more fundamentally, private ownership of large-scale means of production.

In such a situation authority becomes something of a commodity handed back and forth under certain general conditions. Like a commodity, it can then be only rarely custom-tailored, fitted to size, and tends to be standardized to facilitate its transference. Where authority may have to be transferred frequently, personalized loyalty to those who wield it may impede its mobility. It is therefore functional to the mobility of authority to attach workers' loyalty to the rules, not the plant manager. Thus bureaucratization is functional to an institutionally conditioned high rate of succession while, in turn, a high rate of succession operates as a selecting mechanism sifting out a bureaucratic mode of organization.

Reference to authority as a "commodity," while somewhat inexact in the above paragraph, nevertheless serves to call attention to some distinctive dynamics of certain modern forms of social control. In modern business-industrial societies, as in all their Western European predecessors back to the epoch of tribal disintegration, property is a basis for the acquisition of authority, prestige, influence, and power. In itself, "property" connotes the *superiority* of those who have specific rights in a valuable object as against those who do not—at least, insofar as these valuable objects are concerned. Thus the factory owner, by virtue of his ownership of a specific property form, is simultaneously endowed with *authority* over his employees. In current business societies, authority is a customary concomitant of ownership of means of production.

Insofar, then, as production property is involved in a market, and can be bought and sold for cash and credit, so, too, is the correlate authority. If modern property forms are distinguished by the extent of their involvement in a market so, also, are modern means of social control, including authority.[13] The high rate of succession in the

[13] Nor, of course, is authority the only means of social control involved in market transactions in modern society. A recent New York Court decision awarded J. Moffett $1,150,000 from the Arabian-American Oil Co. for using his Washington "influence" to obtain Saudi Arabian concessions for the company. "Influence isn't illegal; it's a salable commodity. . . ." T. R. B., *The New Republic*, March 7,

economy has, therefore, as a further institutional condition, a market for production property. If the problem of succession is translated into the economist's terms, "labor turnover" among strategic personnel, another of the institutional conditions of a high rate of succession emerges: a free labor market. There seems reason to believe that a high labor turnover, on any level, would disrupt informal group systems, deteriorate nonrational consensus, and impede integration of worker and job. The careful specification and delimitation of functions, an emphasis on rule-oriented behavior, crucial aspects of bureaucratic organization, may serve as functional equivalents for disorganized informal patterns.

Informal organization and consensus is not, of course, disrupted solely by succession or labor turnover. Other crucial sources of their disorganization, which cannot be developed here, would include cleavage along status lines. Moreover, it seems uncertain whether the conclusions tentatively presented here would apply, on the same level of abstraction, to other institutional spheres such as political parties and governmental organization. It may, however, prove fruitful to examine the differential degrees of bureaucratization manifested by the Democratic and Republican parties on the one hand and small radical parties on the other. Despite the greater size of the former (and this should seem crucial to those who account size a compelling determinant of bureaucratization), they have only recently begun to develop in a decidedly bureaucratic way.[14]

The tiny groups of the left, however, are far more advanced in this respect. Whether the persevering traditionalistic loyalties to the larger parties, creating a low degree of succession and turnover, and the much-remarked-upon high turnover among radical groups, is a mechanism related to their differential degree of bureaucratization is a hypothesis worth investigation. In a similar area, the history of the Russian Bolshevik party is rich with data suggestive of the role played by rapid succession in fostering bureaucratization. Lenin's definitive defense of his bureaucratic conception of party organization (*What*

1949. Similarly, the Lafollette Committee on "Education and Labor" revealed, by its study of labor spies, that violence was purchasable for use by established institutions. As the availability of the modern public-relations counselors or "press agents" indicates, prestige is also purchaseable.

[14] Cf. Edward J. Flynn, *You're the Boss* (New York, 1947).

Is to Be Done?) is largely oriented to the problem of maintaining "continuity of organization," and the need to cope with repeated police arrests of "leading comrades." The history of the development of civil service in the United States (or elsewhere) would, on the face of it, also appear to contain data for evaluating the hypothesis presented here. Two aspects of succession in this area apparently deserve close study: (1) the high rate of succession among elected or appointed departmental heads, which is institutionally conditioned by periodical elections; (2) the "spoils system" with its rapid "rotation in office," as the historical antecedent of American civil service.

It may be well to close this section with a caution: *No systematic theory of bureaucracy is here intended.* All that has been suggested is that a *high rate of succession is one mechanism*, among others, apparently functional to the development of bureaucratic organization.

Deserving of more positive emphasis, however, is this: Since groups possess forms of stratification, it cannot be tacitly assumed that all individuals, or all positions, in the system of stratification exert equal influence on those decisions from which bureaucratization emerges as planned, or unanticipated consequence. Pedestrian as this point is, Weber's analysis of bureaucracy largely ignores it. Bureaucratic behavior in a factory must be either initiated by the manager, or in any event finally ratified by him or his superiors. What has here been essayed is an analysis of some institutionally derived pressures convergent on certain strategic positions compelling their occupants to behave in ways which make them accept or initiate bureaucratic patterns.

THEORETICAL ADDENDUM

IF THE concept of succession is to be fruitfully articulated with current theory, it seems necessary to reëxamine the question raised in the opening discussion: namely, why has so little attention been afforded the concept of succession by modern sociologists? Insofar as this neglect is an outcome of the structure of existent theory, careful specification of the sources of inattention may provide programmatic directives hastening organic integration of the concept. The following propositions are tentatively offered in explanation of the failure to develop and employ the concept of succession *insofar as structural-functional theories are concerned*.[15]

1. Modern structural-functional theory concentrates on problems of the *persistence and/or equilibrium* of social systems and the elements conditioning this. It has, therefore, tended to neglect *systematic* treatment of those variables, such as the rate of succession, which elicit transformations, change and/or disequilibrium.

2. Postulating a *social system* on a unique level of integration, it has intensively cultivated those variables which are construed as necessary for analysis of distinctive properties of social systems, e. g., roles, institutions, and scales of stratification. Relatively little attention has, therefore, been fixed upon those potentialities, e. g., death (which may occasion succession) of the units of the social systems analyzable in terms of other sciences such as biology. The theoretically derived pressure has led to focus on (a) the continuity and (b) the integrity of social systems. A possible result has been that the *transiency* of those units who occupy social positions and engage in patterned behavior has been neglected.

3. Structural-functional theory has tended to use the concept of "conditions" as a *residual* category, focusing in the "action schema" on means and ends. The problem of succession has, historically, been associated with an element, death, which would be treated as a "condition" in structural-functional theory. So, too, would the *rate* of succession.

4. Structural-functional theory uses a set of mechanisms or structures to provide an interpretive context of variable behavior. It employs these

[15] Our critical appreciation of structural-functionalism is greatly indebted to the work of Robert K. Merton. Cf. especially Merton's discussion of Talcott Parson's "The Position of Sociological Theory," *American Sociological Review*, April, 1948.

structures as if they were stable and unchanging. Thus the tendency is, in the case of concepts such as role and status, to assume that temporal considerations are irrelevant to the directives they contain for behavior. Focus on succession involves attention to the *genetic* dimension of a status. *The history of a man in a role* is here emphasized. Factors such as newness and unfamiliarity or long occupancy and experience become significant. Such time-oriented analyses of role playing are clearly of practical importance and are probably of more theoretical relevance than is assigned them in existent structural-theory.

5. In recent structural-functional theory the concept of *informal* structure has come to serve certain analytical purposes similar to that for which, in Max Weber's theory, the concept of *Charisma* was used. Thus, to Weber, Charisma punctured rationalization, while to certain recent structural-functionalists,[16] informal group structures reflect and generate deviations from formal systems of organization. There is, therefore, less theoretical tension to clarify and systematically develop the concept of succession, since it has, in terms of recent orientations, become less strategic than it was to Weber's sociology. The present effort may be regarded as a partial synthesis of these approaches.

In general, postulation of an isolable (social) system probably tends to minimize examination of problems, events, or processes involving *relations between* systems—e. g., the biological and social. Especially so when the science concerned with the system is relatively undeveloped and has much to occupy it *within* its field-boundaries. In one limiting case, which while logically limiting is of great practical import, the problem of succession involves intersection of two conceptually separable systems or causal series, the biological and social. This is the case of succession precipitated by the death of an occupant of a social position. There would seem a double sense in which modern social theory might heed Ruskin's sarcasms about a hypothetical science of gymnastics that postulated men had no skeletons. Internal consistency, and parsimony, are necessary but not likely to be *sufficient* criteria of postulate-sets for a social science oriented to ultimate secular responsibilities.

The fact is that people in strategic positions, as in others, do die. Sometimes suddenly and sometimes in a context in which their followers and lieutenants orient themselves to and anticipate their demise. It is, of course, not being suggested that death is the only, or even the most significant, circumstance of succession. Succession obviously occurs also under purely *social* conditions, e. g.; promotion, retirement, replacement, etc. Moreover, it is quite evident that the problems of succession would not be evoked

---

[16] Philip Selznick, "Foundations of the Theory of Organization." *American Sociological Review*, Feb., 1948.

unless some social positions tended to persist beyond the occupancy of an individual.

Nevertheless, it seems deserving of emphasis that even if there were no *socially* compelled occasions of succession, it would necessarily occur by virtue of man's biological structure and functioning. As some melancholy wit once remarked, the only thing that a man *must* do is die.

Insofar as organizations do react to threats to their security, succession may be conceived of as a universally "traumatic" experience of all social organizations, impairing lines of communication and authority, disrupting extant patterns of informal relations, and portending or resulting in alterations of policy. It is, surely, an aspect of social organization that "practical men" (at least) ignore only at their peril.

It seems possible that the concept of succession may be articulated with a "Theory of Organization," *methodologically* modeled, as Parsons and Selznick have suggested, along psychoanalytical lines. In this sense, succession would be a diagnostic concept potentially applicable in analyses of concrete organizations, but possibly irrelevant in any given case. It seems especially useful since its symptomatology has a high degree of visibility.

Following Selznick's approach to the theory of organization, it is tempting to consider succession, bureaucratization, strategic replacement (or charisma) as "an adaptive response of a coöperative system to a stable need, generating transformations which reflect constraints enforced by the recalcitrant tools of action."[17] Such a commitment, however, must await radical reconstruction of Selznick's theory of organization along lines implicit in Merton's general critique of structural-functionalism.[18]

Our own analysis has adopted a "general orientation" which conceives of bureaucratic behavior as a *problem-solving* type of social action—rather than as an "adaptive response of a coöperative system." We are thus led to ask *what* the problems were, that is, *how* they were conceived or formulated, *who*—in a given social structure—perceived a certain situation as problematical, how this person's status influenced their perception of this situation, and the kinds of *status-influenced solutions* proposed and implemented. Thus for an emphasis on "adaptive" responses is substituted an emphasis on status-generated perspectives which may lead to definitions of problems and proposals for solution which may easily be divergent from the "needs" of organizations. If organizations respond to stable or other needs, they do so influenced by powerful individuals who, having distinctive kinds of status-determined identifications with a group, perceive these needs as problems.

[17] Cf. *ibid.*
[18] Merton, *op. cit.*

Part Five: AFFIRMATIONS AND
RESOLUTIONS

Contexts: Summary Remarks

THE THINKING of social scientists today, as of intellectuals generally, cannot be neatly sewn together and presented as a logically airtight, smoothly integrated whole, except by those with either a malicious sense of humor or a regal disregard for the facts. Despite a growing core of agreement, conflicts of emphases or interpretations, variations in conceptual schemes, and divergence in ultimate ends represent the state of current social science. This dissonance finds its reflection within the individual scholar as well as the group. Out of this ferment there will come a new unity. But until it does, the actual state of affairs deserves to be portrayed in its complexity, without pretense of finality or complete agreement. Of necessity, this lack of harmony must be mirrored in a coöperative volume such as this.

As in earlier sections, and precisely because it is found there, our summing up has been deliberately designed to present contrasting perspectives and emphases. It cannot simulate complete accord and march, single-file, in utter certitude to a predestined end. Our summing up must, instead, give expression to the diversity, the uncertainties, the conflicts which exist implicitly, and, by "fanning out," at least encompass the major problem areas. Without attempting to summarize articles which are in a sense themselves summaries, the differential focuses of the concluding articles may be noted. Thus Alfred McClung Lee concentrates on the power manifestations of leadership, emphasizing their complex interconnections in political and economic institutions. Jeremiah Wolpert returns to the problems of the legitimation of leadership, developing them analytically and placing them in a broad historical perspective. In his concluding article, Robert Nisbet attends to the relations between mass anxiety and leadership patterns, noting, in particular, the condition of primary groups and their effects upon leadership.

But if there is diversity here, there are also, as again we may note throughout, the tangible contours of common concerns. The problems and concepts that Freud, Weber, Marx, Durkheim, and Mannheim bequeathed have an unmistakable and possibly disquieting influence pervading the volume. Significantly, too, no one of these is looked upon as the master, as the sole fountainhead of all sociological wisdom. Dissatisfaction with a formalistic social science runs through these pages, and there is a frequently voiced insistence on a social science which is historically and culturally oriented. Many of the articles exemplify the sense that social science has a social, problem-solving function which cannot be performed unless the feudal walls surrounding each discipline are pierced. The action orientation that is found is commonly predicated on an acute recognition that by no means all of the scientific returns are in, but that, nevertheless, perfectionist demands should not forestall use of the little that is known. In terms of social policy, there is a tendency to assume that the era of "free competition" and "laissez faire" is well behind us, that some form of planning is inevitable, but that this involves real dangers to democratic liberties for which new safeguards have to be invented, that the "nationalization" of industry is not identical with its "socialization."

In sum, we end, as we may be found throughout, in diversity and in unity.

Power-Seekers[1]

BY ALFRED McCLUNG LEE

SOME MEN and women serve, exploit, dominate, or lead their fellows more aggressively or at least more successfully than do the vast majority, the so-called common men. They do so for a complex of factors, somewhat different in detail at least in any given case. But regardless of motivation or rationalization, the drive for personal control of greater power is a most absorbing channel for energies of those who obtain and retain influence in society well beyond that of their fellows.

This is far from saying in an oversimplified manner with Nietzsche[2] that a "living thing seeks above all to *discharge* its strength—life itself is *Will to Power.*" Certainly aggression, as Freud[3] has pointed out, is a common human characteristic, but it can scarcely be equated with Nietzsche's *Will to Power.* Persons react as a whole to life situations, and their reactions are weighted by many interrelated drives and interests—such as self-preservation, sex, vanity, frustration, aggression, anxiety, self-destruction—which may or may not figure in the drives of a person for control over more social power. The contention here is simply to recognize that the acquisition of greater personal power is one of the common outlets for human aspirations and energies and that some become more absorbed in that outlet than do others.

The personal quest for social power takes a great many forms.

[1] This is a previously unpublished paper.
[2] F. W. Nietzsche, *Beyond Good and Evil* (1886), transl. by Helen Zimmern (New York, n.d.), p. 14.
[3] As, for example, in Sigmund Freud, *Civilization and Its Discontents,* transl. by Joan Riviere (New York, 1930), pp. 123-124. See also John Dollard and others, *Frustration and Aggression* (New Haven, 1939).

Politicians, businessmen, labor leaders, bureaucrats, statesmen, financiers, officers of the armed forces, educators, philanthropists, clergymen, public relations experts, lawyers, engineers, psychiatrists, "society" leaders, civic executives, and gangsters—to mention a range of types—are all more or less consciously and actively concerned with the quests of themselves and others for the control of more power. Power-seekers drive themselves to utilize their personal characteristics, their face-to-face associations, and their grasp of more broadly political, economic, and other social resources and techniques to multiply their power.

Political power consists basically of the profit from bartering actual or promised bits of special privilege ("representation"), including such matters as pride of identity and apparent security, for political support. When such support is convertible in job lots in the wholesale market, for something more desirable than the power cost to get it retail from supporters, the political power-seeker is on his way to bigger things. He may use or convert accumulated power in the job-lot market for a seat in a bigger "game" (a higher office or control over a larger machine), governmental honors, control of governmental structure, cash from graft, or the fruits of some degree of absolutism, possibly a dictatorship over a city, state, or country.

POLITICAL AND BUSINESS POWER

Business power derives basically from buying in quantities at less than wholesale and selling for more retail, the reverse of the general process from which political power arises. Business power is the profit from purchasing quantities of a product or service wholesale and bartering them retail for bits of economic power (money, credit, commodities, services, statuses). When the business power-seeker is "on the make," he is building up a reservoir of power in economic terms which can be paid out in graft to obtain political preferment, which can bring the honor of high office, titles, or other social distinctions, which can increase the "fun of the game" through ushering him into "bigger time operations," or which can yield eventually the fruits of absolutism, perhaps a dictatorship over a large corporation, a nationally ramified financial group, a political party, or a supernational cartel system.

As these brief and rough analyses indicate, the differences between the two types of social power mentioned are of technique and detail rather than of usefulness to their possessors. Moreover, *as the operations become larger few power-seekers can or want to remain exclusively in their original fields.* A military or business power-seeker cannot get very far without becoming adept at political strategies or hiring the services of a political expert. Atomic physicists seldom concerned themselves with social power problems until the atomic bomb was developed. They then found themselves, whether they liked it or not, forced to organize, to interpret their work for popular information, to protect their professional futures by making representations to government officials and deals with politicians, and in other ways to wield great social power and to protect their control of it, a struggle in which they have not been notably successful.

Regardless of whether one may have wanted originally to become a power-seeker or not, the bigger the operations in which one becomes involved, the more important in one's perspectives becomes the quest for and the manipulation of power. W. M. Kiplinger[4] puts it this way, "As a business man rises in the scale of material success he tends to work more and more for the sport of the thing. Business becomes a game. He wants to be a player in the next bigger league—up the scale. Money becomes more important to him for the pile of chips it will buy in the game of business. It isn't the money he's after; it's the power, influence, prestige, standing, rank." Just as accurately, a parallel statement could be made with regard to powerful politicians, top labor leaders, responsible generals, and even those who are moving into the higher reaches of educational and religious hierarchies and certainly of social movements.

The traditional European pattern for many centuries was for power-seekers to dominate more and more of the business, political, and social life of a locality and then of more than one locality. But the development of modern transportation, communication, and other organizational facilities made possible mass-propaganda and mass-exploitation techniques and resources. In the United States during the nineteenth century, a general geographical approach gave way before an approach through special fields, such specialties as finance, steel manufacturing, electric utility operation, and air lines. The tra-

[4] W. M. Kiplinger, "The Business Man: What He Is and Why," *New York Times Magazine*, January 23, 1938, p. 2.

dition of localism "ended in America before the cities were finished.
. . . Before their crude booming and boosting could mellow into a
burgher-spirit, the age of business adventure on a national scale had
opened, with the conclusion of the Civil War. Business men neglected
the cities they had made, for a whole continent lay before them, waiting development.' "[5] Why waste time with local politicians who over-
charge for "service"? The big game lies ahead. Pay the overcharging
local politician and perhaps pay some other politician to destroy his
power, but get on with the game. "I would just as soon buy that kind
of alderman," said a businessman,[6] "as a pound of beef. If the people
will elect such men, the blame is theirs; and they must pay the bill!
So pay the rascal his blackmail; and spread the cost over *their* gas
bills. That is democracy!" And that, too, was a far cry from the
expediency-reinforced and thus fairly operative *noblesse oblige* of
those who successfully controlled power in a more localized economy.

Mass propaganda and mass organization—mass social action—have
made possible scrambles for power in tremendous national and international arenas undreamed of by a mere Queen Elizabeth or Napoleon, a Metternich or Bismarck. An air transportation or fruit or
chemical colossus can dominate a large segment of a specialty
throughout the globe and have power transcending that of a great
many national states. "If propaganda has imbued a whole people with
an idea," a Hitler can scheme, "the organization can draw the consequences with a handful of men."[7] The propaganda can be for a candidate, a commodity, an idea, or an all-embracing program, as in Hitler's
case. The method of assent can be a vote or a purchase or a nod. The
organization can be a political party, a corporation, or a social movement. It all has as a result—despite protestations to the contrary—at
least the potentiality of placing vast new mass power in the hands of a
diminishing group. Regardless of "free enterprise" and "democracy,"
too, Thurman W. Arnold can point to the fact that "no entrenched
bureaucracy, whether political or industrial, is ever willing to risk its
power on the gamble that it may be more efficient than new groups
which are beginning to rise in society."[8] As in war, so in the arts of

---

[5] Miriam Beard, A History of the Business Man (New York, 1938), p. 625.
[6] Quoted by Charles Norman Fay in *ibid.*
[7] Adolf Hitler, Mein Kampf, tr. Ralph Manheim (Boston, 1943), p. 582.
[8] Thurman W. Arnold, Cartels or Free Enterprise?, Public Affairs Pamphlet
No. 103, 1945, p. 8.

peace, after the propaganda and the other actionist phases of a power drive have quieted down, T. E. Lawrence can tell us how "the old men came out again, and took from us our victory, and re-made it in the likeness of the former world they knew. Youth could win, but had not learned to keep, and was pitiably weak against age. We stammered that we had worked for a new heaven and a new earth, and they thanked us kindly and made their peace. When we are their age no doubt we shall serve our children so."[9]

As the foregoing suggests, social power has sufficient in common to be subject to unified definition. Businessmen may not understand politics and may despise the politicians from whom they purchase, wangle, or force special privileges. Politicians may not understand business and may despise the businessmen with whom they have traditionally had to "do business." *But what they deal in are two different manifestations of social power, differently derived but transferable from one area or form to the other with or without the formality of reduction first to the common denominator of money.*

The personal control of social power should not be confused with the mere formality of ownership. The control of social power is the ability to supply or to deprive something to someone. Social power itself is any of the types of human, other animal, botanical, and other mechanical energy now or potentially usable for social purposes. It is manifested in the spading of a garden, the delivery of a speech, the use of a horse to pull a wagon, the nourishment of animals by energy-giving plants, the purposeful burning of a lump of coal, and the turning of an electric generator by water power. Social power is, within limits and through channels defined by culture and current expediencies, convertible from one form to another. Bertrand Russell points out that the "attempt to isolate any one form of power, more especially, in our day, the economic form, has been, and still is, a source of errors of great practical importance."[10] He discerns that the "laws of social dynamics are laws which can only be stated in terms of power, not in terms of this or that form of power." The power vested

[9] *The Letters of T. E. Lawrence*, ed., by David Garnett (New York, 1939), p. 262. This is a piece that appeared in the introduction to the privately circulated Oxford Text of Lawrence's *Seven Pillars of Wisdom* (1926). According to Garnett, *ibid.*, "It was omitted, on the advice of Bernard Shaw, from the Subscribers' edition [1938]."

[10] Bertrand Russell, *Power* (New York, 1938), pp. 14, 13.

in an aristocratic status may derive from military prowess, gangsterism or piracy, commercial or industrial activities, or a lucky discovery. Such insights apparently led Lincoln Steffens to state that political corruption, for example, "is not a temporary evil, not an accidental wickedness, not a passing symptom of the youth of a people. It is a natural process by which a democracy is made gradually over into a plutocracy."[11]

The growing realization of the similarity of social power, regardless of its manifestations, has come with the rise of big business and big government. As a spokesman for gas and electric utility corporations observed in 1924, "When you affect the economic thought of the people, you automatically affect their political thought."[12] Upon the basis of similar evidence, the public relations director of the National Association of Manufacturers put it this way in 1937, "Now, more than ever before, strikes are being won or lost in the newspapers and over the radio. The swing of public opinion has always been a major factor in labor disputes, but with the settlement of strikes being thrown more and more into the laps of public officials, the question of public opinion becomes of greater importance."[13] With the total war of 1939-1945 ushering in a new period of business mergers in the United States, financed by the boom in war materials, the permeations of business-derived and politics-derived power into each other and into the rest of our social life have become even more apparent.

Because of Bertrand Russell's speculative rather than objective approach to the study of power, he attributes greater influence in societal causation to those possessing power than is warranted. "The men who cause social changes," Russell contends, "are, as a rule, men who strongly desire to do so."[14] He even asserts that "love of power is the chief motive producing the changes which social science has to study."

[11] Lincoln Steffens, *Autobiography* (New York, 1931), p. 413.

[12] J. B. Sheridan, Director, Missouri Committee on Public Utility Information, as quoted in U.S. Federal Trade Commission, *Efforts by Associations and Agencies of Electric and Gas Utilities to Influence Public Opinion* (Government Printing Office, 1934), p. 52.

[13] James P. Selvage, "Memorandum on Community Public Information Programs to Combat Radical Tendencies and Present the Constructive Story of Industry, April 1937," reprinted in U.S. Senate Committee on Education and Labor, *The National Association of Manufacturers* (Report No. 6, Part 6, Government Printing Office, 1939), p. 280.

[14] Bertrand Russell, *op. cit.*, p. 15.

Russell thus embraces the position of popular folklore and propaganda on the great-man causation of social events. Hoover "caused" the Depression following 1929. Roosevelt "got us out of it." Hitler "created" the Nazi state. Russell fails to see that those who control social power have what amounts to a symbolic, instrumental, and manipulative, rather than a causative, relationship to the societal developments with which they are associated. One has only to recall the unionizing drives in certain major American industries, unsuccessfully fought against with tremendous resources and determination by employers, and the struggle culminating, for the time, in the 1945 British Labour victory to realize that there are societal forces and limitations which transcend any will-to-power of individuals. Especially illustrative are the efforts of the automotive titans during the middle 1930's and later to buck the tide of social change which brought about the unionization of their workers. In discussing such developments, Robert S. Lynd concludes "that industrial capitalism is an intensely coercive form of organization of society that cumulatively constrains men and all of their institutions to work the will of the minority who hold and wield economic power,"[15] but, he adds, even this minority are not "free" men. He notes that "this relentless warping of men's lives and forms of association becomes less and less the result of voluntary decisions by 'bad' or 'good' men and more and more an impersonal web of coercions dictated by the need to keep 'the system' running. These coercions cumulate themselves to ends that even the organizing leaders of big business may fail to foresee, as step by step they grapple with the next immediate issue, and the next, and the next." D. C. Blaisdell and Jane Greverus emphasize this impersonal and overwhelming operation of societal forces and processes in their *Economic Power and Political Pressures* when they observe, "The gradual expansion of suffrage, unionization, popular control of legislation, extension of social services—all these things are now in the realm of public policy and cannot be removed except by a violent revolution and the use of unexampled force. Even then, most of them would be retained."[16]

[15] Robert S. Lynd, "Foreword" to R. A. Brady, *Business as a System of Power* (New York, 1943), p. xii.

[16] D. C. Blaisdell and Jane Greverus, U.S. Temporary National Economic Committee Monograph No. 26 (Government Printing Office, 1941), p. 4.

Fundamental to all control of great social power—whether derived from physical, biological, or societal sources—is popular support or acquiescence. Such support or acquiescence may appear on the surface to be entered into rationally by numbers of people at a specific time. This interpretation of an event such as an election, however, merely reflects the "social contract" myths in our traditional thought patterns and is not borne out by detailed studies. Upon the basis of repeated samplings of voter opinions in selected areas, for example, Paul F. Lazarsfeld concludes that "elections are decided by the events occurring in the entire period between two Presidential elections and not by the campaign. . . . Only a very small percentage of people can be considered so truly undecided that propaganda can still convert them, and those are likely to be of a special kind."[17] Propaganda has, it should be added, a role in interpreting significant events "occurring in the entire period," in relating those events to popular attitudes and sentiments. It is part of what Kimball Young calls "the larger process of legend- and myth-making."[18]

Factors deciding an election or an advertising struggle antedate not only the campaigns but in many cases even the lives of the candidates or corporations and of those who go to the polls or to the retail outlets. Candidates for office and advertisers of retail commodities, like other power-seekers, relate themselves to preëxisting principles, slogans, struggles, needs, and aspirations. Their chief contributions to popular discourse consist of rewordings, reinterpretations, reidentifications. In other words, of repackagings or rebottlings of old materials in the light of current events, needs, interests, developments. Personal control over great aggregations of social power result from (1) the careful development and exploitation of personal assets; (2) the use of personal connections, face-to-face contacts; (3) the shrewd capture and manipulation of power-statuses in the evolving structures of society, the Horatio Alger type of course; or (3) the agitation of a movement, a social deviation, in which the chief power-status will be held and utilized, the reformist or radical course; and (4) the con-

[17] Paul F. Lazarsfeld, "The Election Is Over," *Public Opinion Quarterly,* 8 (1944), p. 330. See also Lazarsfeld, B. Berelson, and H. Gaudet, *The People's Choice,* 2nd ed. (New York, 1948).

[18] Kimball Young, *Social Psychology* (2nd ed.; New York, 1944), p. 505.

solidation and stabilization of control through institutionalizing instrumentalities.[19]

The relation of popular support to the power-seekers can also be stated in this wise: The common man purchases certain brands of commodities, sets aside a portion of his time for the radio, magazines, newspapers, and motion pictures, subscribes to the political positions of a party or clique, devotes a large share of his energy to a job, aspires to economic and social goals, maintains a fairly orderly relationship with his family and community, and serves as one of the instruments for recreating biologically and culturally similar human beings. All these attitudes, beliefs, and activities represent allocations of the common man's personal support to enterprises which—added to those of his fellows—furnish the bases for the great aggregations of social power now present and growing in society. Much of the manipulative effort of the great enterprisers therefore takes the form of propaganda (including paid advertising as well as other types of publicity) directed toward modifying the energy-allocation patterns of current and potential supporters.

When changes in energy-allocation patterns occur, for reasons that are not necessarily related to the manipulative efforts of power-seekers, enterprisers are swept into and out of control statuses or at least make gains or suffer losses. Popular patterns of thought and action are thus focal points of attack in the continuing struggle for great social power, the endless propaganda struggle, which pervades all the myriad communication mediums of modern society. Whether it be what we eat for breakfast, what we smoke or drink for relaxation, toward what we strive for ourselves or our families, how we express "personality," for whom we vote, even what or whom we might worship—all these patterns of belief and activity are under constant pressure from those who selfishly or idealistically have a stake in our energy-allocation patterns, our whole range of habitual attitudes and behavior patterns.

LIMITS OF POWER

The "rank and file" in the more complex societies and possibly in all societies apparently find a need for power-seekers. They at least

[19] See A. M. Lee, "El Poder Personal y la Acción Social," *Revista Mexicana de Sociología*, 9 (1947), pp. 341-351.

support and willingly utilize the services of those who dare to organize their fellows for great accomplishments in statecraft, city-making, education, science, religion, art, industry, and commerce and who usually find a part of their reward in speculative profits and/or the control of enterprises. This is not to suggest a bow to any Nazi *Führer* or other leadership principle, to any authoritarianism. Quite the contrary. With the rise of equalitarianism, except in cases of mass hysteria and subterfuge, the power the rank and file permit power-seekers to take in return for their services has been trimmed to more and more manageable limits. Democratic humanity is learning ways to permit the power-seekers to make their social contributions at the price of only temporary and limited power, as it were at a "more reasonable price." Democracy and concomitant popular education thus are serving as antidotes for some of the dangerous proclivities of the power-seekers. But the struggle has not been a decisive one. If democracy and popular education can become more realistic and func-tional, less ritualistic and nominal, they will be even more successful in this movement. But the forces making for the concentration rather than the diffusion of the control of social power are ever alert, and the trends toward bigness and integration throughout society aid such aggressive minority interests.

Just as humanity apparently needs the power-seekers to the extent that they serve and do not oppress, so the power-seekers are learning that they need some degree of popular good will or acceptance or, at least, acquiescence. The public no longer will be obviously damned and exploited and put up with it. William Hazlitt discerned this when he observed that the "only thing that can give stability or confidence to power, is that very will of the people, and public censure exercised upon public acts, of which legitimate Sovereigns are so disproportionately apprehensive."[20] Well-informed power-seekers who are not too frantic in their scramble have learned that there are limits and channels within which they must "play the game," whatever their specific game may be. Influential in maintaining the power of the British House of Lords, for example, has been the fact that "the leaders of the Conservative or Tory peers have been clever enough

[20] William Hazlitt, in his *Political Essays* (1819), reprinted in *The Collected Works of William Hazlitt*, ed. A. R. Waller and Arnold Glover (London, 1902), III, 305.

to avoid many really violent conflicts with the Commons."[21] Power-seekers, as a part of this situation, have also learned that rising lieutenants must be encouraged, utilized, and kept within manageable bounds. Such a vast system as the American Telephone & Telegraph Company, to illustrate, recognizes in its policies of management quite clearly this problem of power-seeking. As Chester I. Barnard, onetime president of the New Jersey Bell Telephone Company, writes, "The maintenance of incentives, particularly those relating to prestige, pride of association, and community satisfaction, calls for growth, enlargement, extension. . . . The overreaching which arises from this cause is the source of destruction of organizations otherwise successful."[22]

Even in countries with democratic pretensions, humanity manages only in noncrisis times to obtain the services of the power-seekers at not too great a price. It has yet to find ways to cope with the prolonged consequences of mass hysteria and self-sacrifice, anxiety and panacea-testing in times of war and depression. It is not enough to say offhand with Ralph Waldo Emerson that the "imbecility of men is always inviting the impudence of power."[23] In times of stress, men find themselves agreeing to courses of action, to grants of social power, that they would resist militantly in "normal" periods. The justifications of American foreign policies in the "cold war" following World War II are especially illuminating on this point. Even in noncrisis years, the power-seekers constantly push for better "prices," for more stable monopolistic structures within which to consolidate their gains, and for less possible interference from new and more representative (apparently less costly) enterprisers.

Power-seekers have inherited or seized upon many techniques to achieve, maintain, and extend their controls, and they have employed many specialists—military, religious, legal, medical, philosophical, historical, oratorical, scientific, educational, artistic, and literary. But behind all social power, more or less immediately, is popular influence, whether the influence takes the form of traditional culture patterns

---

[21] Lord Strabolgi, "Case Against the House of Lords," New York *Times Magazine*, July 28, 1946, p. 32.

[22] Chester I. Barnard, *The Functions of the Executive* (Cambridge, Mass., 1938), p. 159.

[23] Ralph Waldo Emerson, *Representative Men* (1850) (New & rev. ed.; Boston, 1883), p. 23.

defining the structure and working principles of society, the form of transient popular fads, or the form of ignorance, boredom, or neglect. The consequences of popular discontent may not be apparent or pressing for a long period. As a result of this delay and of the constant pressure toward reaction—toward the centralization of power in fewer hands—humanity has not yet learned enough about the control of enterprisers to avoid periodic violent redistributions of social power. In fact, as Lyford P. Edwards concludes, "We may take it for certain that revolutions, even violent revolutions, will occur periodically for a long time to come. We hear some talk about substituting peaceful evolution for violent revolution, but such talk is only what the theologians call 'pious opinion'—laudable, but imaginative. No technology is being developed for the purpose of translating this talk into action. Modern political science, so-called, is much like medieval physical science, largely a matter of incantations, exorcisms, and witch-hunting."[24] A revolution is naturally not always such a full-dress performance as the French Revolution of 1789 and the Soviet Revolution of 1917. There are many degrees of violence and reorganization between such revolutions and the so-called "peaceful evolution" and its necessary but difficult measures.

The foregoing are some observations, conclusions, and hypotheses on the nature and ramifications of social power. They are necessarily sketchy, because of space limitations, but they are perhaps suggestive to the growing number who realize that the problems associated with the control and manipulation of social power are a neglected area in sociology and in social science generally.

[24] Lyford P. Edwards, *Natural History of Revolution* (Chicago, 1927), p. 212.

Toward a Sociology
of Authority[1]

BY JEREMIAH F. WOLPERT

THE PROBLEM of authority is basic to the understanding of the variety of types of leadership. Over the span of historical development the character of leadership has been defined according to the conceptions of authority which dominate a given society. Since this development has not been uniform, different kinds of authority exist at the same time and can be understood only when referred to their cultural matrices. In every case, however, what distinguishes the character of authority is the fact that *it must find ethical sanctification.* Through the ethics of authority, whether flowing from the dominant groups or subgroups within a social order, leadership is carried out. Leaders in order to command a following must either appeal to the impersonal rightness of that for which they stand or carry within their persons a specific ethic which is recognized as such. The process by which allegiance to authority is engendered must be considered apart from its ethical content for more often than not in modern society it is a technical problem for leaders.

Before proceeding further, it should first be emphasized that the analysis of authority always calls up deep-seated sentiments outside the realm of inquiry on the part of the inquirer. He is directed toward the problem by interests which are certainly not purely intellectual ones. Moreover, the assumptions upon which his interpretation rests are an integral part of his value system. If this be true, the best approach to the problem would seem to lie in a frank recognition on

[1] This is a previously unpublished paper.

the part of the inquirer of the ethical standards by which he analyzes different types of authority. Allowance can then be made for particular affirmations or rejections of types of authority. Too often, "authority" has been confused with "authoritarian," which is merely a particular type of authority. If this is made clear it establishes the point that any social order has its form or forms of authority.

CHARISMA OR PSEUDO-CHARISMA?

Max Weber's sociology of authority has within it the materials which can give both methodological hints and insightful source-material for such an analysis.[2] Weber's reference to "the disenchantment of the world"[3] implies the existence of a kind of society opposite to that in which charismatic authority operates. Charismatic authority is vested in a leader to whom is imputed superhuman qualities. On the surface, it would appear that charismatic authority is a constant which returns time and again in periods of revolutionary transformation. This, however, is contradicted by the much greater weight Weber gives to the long-term effects of the rationalization of life which the "disenchantment of the world" implies.

These two interpretations of charismatic authority can be reconciled if a distinction is made between rationalization as an objective process and rationality as it informs the life of individuals. The effects of rationalization have been to breed personality malfunctions which cut the ground from under the guidance of individual behavior by the rationality which resides within the person. It has as a consequence the effect of pushing people toward actions over which they have no conscious control; actions which are compensatory for the frustrations which an impersonal, schematized order brings in its train. On the face of it, this seems to guarantee the continuance of charisma, but in reality it produces a most blatant counterfeit, for modern hero worship takes place within an objective context of total rationalization.

For charisma to be genuine, it must function in a social order which is free of bureaucracy as a value system. In earlier societies manifesting bureaucracy, there were always extra-bureaucratic value systems which

---

[2] Max Weber, *The Theory of Social and Economic Organization*, trans. by A. M. Henderson and Talcott Parsons, ed. (New York, 1947).

[3] Max Weber, "Science as a Vocation," *From Max Weber: Essays in Sociology*, transl., ed. by H. H. Gerth and C. Wright Mills (New York, 1946).

transcended it. In ancient Egypt, religious values stood above bureaucratic organization, and religious values also were a keystone of the Byzantine society. However, in the case of modern bureaucracy, there are no transcendent norms which are viewed unquestioningly and as superior to those which are functionally effective.

The pseudo-charisma of our time belies its earlier character by the way in which it can be fabricated through the manipulation of techniques of mass persuasion. The resultant hero worship is qualitatively different from that which Weber sets down as the charismatic type. It moves on the level of ideology, not that of myth. The ideological level results from the realization that ideas are weapons to be used in social struggle. It is the intellectual parallel to a functionally rational industrial order. The level of myth is that on which absolute value systems pervade the social order in all its parts and transcend in meaning any of the forms in which it is immanent.

Modern pseudo-charisma is a product of very conscious rationality. Only a society which assumes the legitimacy of reducing persons to commodities can produce it. It makes no difference whether the origins of such manipulation of persons be in a cutthroat competitive economic system, or can be traced to political sources in which the state power acts as the fulcrum of manipulation.

THE REDUCTION OF AUTHORITY

Forms of authority are to be understood in relation to the overall character of the social order in which they operate. This is especially relevant in marking off types of leadership which, if they are to be effective, must operate within the given context of authority. Not only is leadership limited objectively by given patterns of authority, but the will to lead of the leader is vitiated if what he stands for cannot command a following. The leader seeks to achieve ends through social action, but he as an individual is buoyed by his following. His effectiveness in no small measure derives from how much loyalty he can count upon. *When the core of authority suffers erosion, when its ethical justification dissolves, manipulative techniques become all the more necessary, and the stability of social relationships suffers accordingly.* Such has been the case in modern industrial society, with authority narrowing down more and more to its power base.

This situation coincides with our distinction between myth and ideology. When the nature of authority is clouded in myth, whether of the traditional type such as kingship or of the more impersonal kind represented by natural-law and natural-rights philosophy, the flow of response from rulers to ruled is much less ambiguous. The right to rule, its basis of legitimacy, is derived from a full blown cosmology. The hierarchy of control does not stand by itself, but draws strength from a shadowy background of assumptions which are accepted as valid. These assumptions also gave spiritual cohesion to the social order by establishing it upon a cosmological basis which was taken for granted. The works of man could always be expected to be subject to critical analysis but when ideas of authority rested upon a basis which was considered to be rooted in universal laws, authority had a stability which the ideological society lacks. Where myth prevailed, the idea of natural law, from which derived the conception of natural rights, was considered to be a legitimate transcription of Newtonian science to the social level.[4]

As it came under the scrutiny of the Utilitarians the nonrational basis of natural rights was revealed. It was shorn of its claim to scientific validity. The experience of the French Revolution which, while asserting the universal validity of its ideas, served to foster the special interests of the nascent middle class, made large groups receptive to the discredit which was heaped upon the natural-rights philosophy. The waning natural-rights philosophy suffered attack not only from the left but from the disinherited right which was on the counterattack. Natural rights was an effective foundation for authority as long as its nonrational basis was conceived to be derived from a universal harmony. As soon as its instrumental function in pushing forward the aims of specific groups was made explicit, it began to wither as a basis for authority.

Marx's intellectual bombshell,[5] which stripped the ethical character from modes of thought and revealed a class interest underlying them, marks the transition from myth to ideology, even though Marx himself claimed mythological validity for the claims of the proletariat. Henceforth the attempt to base authority upon extrarational cosmo-

---

[4] J. F. Wolpert, "The Myth of Revolution," *Ethics*, July, 1948, pp. 245-255.
[5] Karl Marx and Friedrich Engels, *The German Ideology* (New York, 1939).

logical assumptions was more often contrived than spontaneous.[6] Such meretricious myth-building reached its climax in the various fascist ideologies which flourished after the first World War.

Behind the current of intellectual transition, briefly described, were deep-going social changes. As more and more societies became industrialized, there was a drift toward bureaucratic norms in government. This was typified by the direction which the French Revolution took. The moral fervor of the Republic of 1794 gave way to the spoilsman's calculation of the Directory, and then the efficient bureaucracy of Bonaparte. The impact of the growing rationalization of life cut away the nonrational, extrapolitical assumptions of authority baring the naked force which lay in the background of state power. The autonomy of the political, once free of commonly held moral and metaphysical imperatives, sharpened the conflict between groups with divergent interests. The use of ideas as weapons upon the political battlefield was part of the same process. The consequence of an all-enveloping relativism, which both mirrored and gave impetus to institutional malfunctioning, left no permanent base for authority, shearing off one of its major prerequisites, that those who accept it do so in the expectation that it has continuity. Paradoxically, with the increased *instability* of authority, there was a corresponding emphasis, in grandiloquent terms, upon its *timelessness*. This was given full expression in Mussolini's evocation of a new Roman Empire and Hitler's boast of the thousand-year Reich.

SOCIAL SOURCES OF IRRATIONALITY

Karl Mannheim in his "Man and Society in an Age of Reconstruction" has contributed much to the analysis of this historical development.[7] By implication he has taken sharp issue with Veblen who, with his technocratic bent, conceived that the logic of industry would result in the growth of rational self-control and action by those who were involved in the machine process.[8] Erich Fromm as well, in his "Escape From Freedom," delineated the socio-psychological conse-

6 Georges Sorel, *Reflections on Violence*, trans. by T. E. Hulme (New York, 1941).

7 Karl Mannheim, *Man and Society in an Age of Reconstruction* (New York, 1940).

8 Thorstein Veblen, *The Theory of Business Enterprise* (New York, 1904).

quences of this development.[9] The implication to be drawn is that the objective rationalization of life has fostered subjective irrationality.

People suffer under the constrictions of a system over which they have neither control nor understanding, with the result that they come to view their lives as directionless. Pigeon-holed into a pattern, the ends of which they are ignorant, their sense of individual distinctiveness and self-insight suffer accordingly. They labor under tensions which demand release; compensations of an irrational character provide a way out. These are irrational solutions because they do not help to solve basic problems but rather exacerbate them. Such a situation has provided a livelihood for public relations men and other propagandists and agitators with similar febrile stimulants to purvey.

It might seem that, with such powerful sources of irrationality to draw upon, the bases of authority would be strengthened rather than weakened. This conclusion is possible, however, only if one confuses irrationality with nonrationality. The former is an unguided explosive reaction to frustration of a cramped institutional order. The nonrational type of attitude is the product of value systems which, whether traditional or set in the framework of absolute ends, provided both an explanation for how things worked and acted as ballast for emotional stability. Modern irrationalism is a mere means of blowing off steam with no awareness on the part of groups of any defined ends. It is the counterpart to "anomie" which Durkheim pointed out as a peculiarly modern disease.[10] When people are alienated from involvement in group values, when they are always on guard against manipulation, they become more susceptible to manipulation in areas which they conceive as legitimate outlets of expression. In contrast, the nonrational includes an awareness on the part of individuals that they hold certain ends in view as valid, even though their underpinning is not empirically verifiable or explicable.

Another contributing factor which has furthered irrationality has been termed "basic democratization" by Mannheim.[11] "Basic democratization" recognizes the right of participation by all in political activity, but frustrates genuine freedom of decision by all because the

---

[9] Erich Fromm, *Escape From Freedom* (New York, 1941).

[10] Emile Durkheim, . . . *Suicide; étude de sociologie* (Nouvelle édition; Paris, 1930).

[11] Karl Mannheim, *op. cit.*

power structure prevents the fulfillment of the formal promise of participation. The path to achievement of the most short-term ends through political action is so strewn with obstacles that the ordinary citizen is prone to wash his hands of the whole business. Consequently, in this area he encounters more frustrations to add to his already considerable sum. To the public, politics becomes either a dirty affair of exploitation, and hence to be shunned, or it becomes a metaphysics standing alone, to which all other activities are subordinated. There is little room in either case for rational authority to operate. From the perspective of the politician, who operates within the former pattern, authority withers before expediency. In the latter pattern, energy becomes concentrated upon the conquest of power, with politics dwarfing all other areas of human activity.

The former condition is prevalent in the United States, the latter in Europe. It may be that the dominant attitude in the United States is an earlier stage than that reached in Europe, for among the left-wing splinters in the U.S., there is a comparable attitude to that found in Europe. The pattern of authority in America, as it impinges upon political affairs, shares in the pervasive ideological individualism permeating a social structure which is still formally geared to the natural rights philosophy.

RELIGIOUS AUTHORITY

It is not surprising that when, as in the present day, authority is subject to extreme manipulation, which leads to its degradation, the specter of fear lurks ever in the background. The function of authority (as an ideal type) has been to minimize the scope and range of fear as a determinant of social relationships. In terms of historical priority, it was religious authority which most consciously filled this role. In the Western world, both the Protestant conception of authority which puts the burden of acceptance on the individual conscience, and Catholic universalism which conceives of the church as an instrument of social control operating on the basis of universally accepted dogma, screened the naked power which lies behind authority. Dostoevski, in the section on the grand inquisitor in "The Brothers Karamazov," drove home the lesson of the despotic core which is the ultimate basis of Roman Catholic authority. To maintain its myth in an age of ideology, Catholicism has had recourse to the same manipulative techniques found in the secular realm. What is more important, it has been able to achieve its aims only by alliances with state power, which it theologically condemns as sinful since the historical separation of church from state.[12]

The Protestant conception has undergone secularization and, as a mass society of monolithic corporate wealth has come into being, its original function has changed. Fromm has pointed out the dire socio-psychological consequences of Protestantism in reducing individuals to helpless pawns of overpowering impersonal forces. Religious authority, of whatever kind, is most deeply interwoven with myth, since it put the basis of its legitimation in revelation, an area least open to empirical refutation. Such authority has now become internally contradictory for it is only at the acquiescence of either economic or political power that any church is allowed scope. There is a tacit understanding, which churchmen deny at their peril, that one of the major functions of religious authority is to bolster the secular *status quo.*

The degradation of religious authority has contributed considerably toward calling into question authority as such. In both their generically religious sense and in their secular form, both major religious ideologies have had socio-psychological consequences which have fostered individual helplessness in the face of modern problems. The Catholic inculcation of norms has superficially given the individual a closer relatedness to group activity, but a more intensive analysis reveals its real failure. Though Catholic doctrine provided the basis for genuine authority in the Middle Ages, in our age it can only operate upon an *authoritarian* level. The church has tried to make the best of the secular and sacred worlds and has corrupted both in the process.

It cannot present its dogma as self-evident but must resort to subterfuge in order to make itself compatible with the modern situation. The rigid authoritarianism which the church enforces, if internalized, heavily burdens the personality, for the individual must at the same time assimilate conflicting secular values. The church cannot relieve him from this burden. The Catholic is forced to be searching continually for some *via media* to connect himself as Catholic with his other pursuits. The solidarity which the church as an insti-

[12] Salo Baron, *Modern Nationalism and Religion* (New York, 1948).

tution affords is being constantly challenged by the claims of the larger society so that there is no resolution of the resulting strain upon the personality.

We are much more familiar with the effects of Protestantism upon authority and personality.[13] The internalization of authority through conscience fosters rigidity of response and tremendous guilt since the individual has only himself to blame for the ills which befall him. All of this has been penetratingly described by Fromm. The explosiveness bred by such frustration and its intensification by frustrating social conditions, particularly among the lower middle class, has made this class most receptive to fascism. The nihilistic character of fascism, no matter how grandiose its ideology, is a consequence of the conditions which produce it. The mass backing which fascism demands is generated by a purely negative response on the part of the aimless thousands of petty bourgeoisie, who can no longer endure their suffocating position. They merge together and submit to escape a situation rather than to organize a new one. Their response is irrational, not non-rational, since fascism cannot offer any real solution to their problem. The emphasis which fascism places upon authority testifies to its absence. The bond of solidarity which fascism attempts to create is an uncreative way of surcease from unbearable conditions. It is not the condition for the pursuance of a new social order.[14]

In respect to the lower middle class, the effect of the component in Protestantism which emphasizes individualism leads to the annihilation of individuality. However it would be wrong to ignore the component in Protestantism, as a secular force, which may lead in a more fruitful direction. That is, its concentration upon the ethical aspect of religion. This ethical aspect has, when taken seriously and kept within formal religious boundaries, nourished the social gospel of the sects.

The stand of the recent world conference of Protestant churches in rejecting laissez-faire capitalism comes largely from the social gospel. However, by its hedging rejection of capitalist ethics *in toto*, the ambiguity of its position was revealed. When the ethical aspect of Protestantism is secularized it may provide the ground for overturn-

[13] Max Weber, *The Protestant Ethic and The Spirit of Capitalism*, trans. by Talcott Parsons (London, 1930).
[14] Franz Neumann, *Behemcth* (New York, 1942).

ing conformity to capitalist ethics. To those who have internalized the ethic of Protestantism, the disparity between lip service to it and contradictory behavior becomes glaring. The secular Protestant who is sincerely motivated strives to bring actual conduct into closer relation to ethical prescriptions. Santayana in "The Last Puritan," gives a picture of such motivation, in Oliver Alden. Collectively it is a modern form of return to the pristine character of the original image of true believers.

The plight of the modern liberal is similar in this regard. From an individualist orientation he is driven toward preoccupation with the moral basis of his actions. He implicitly seeks to shape a form of authority which will most closely conform with the "categorical imperative." Ironically, such deviant Protestantism breeds a rigid character structure which is the opposite of that needed for a spontaneous bridging of the gap between ethics and action.

In contradistinction, the Catholic conception of authority, in its theological roots, minimizes the ethical aspect of religion. This serves to bolster the stability and continuity of the church, since it cannot be called to account for the unethical actions of individual members of the hierarchy. Authority is placed beyond the reach of the secular world so that worldly actions cannot be a legitimate basis for criticism of the church. The Catholic attitude toward authority, internalized by members of the church, is lacking in both the ethical grounds and psychological dynamic for overturning such authority. The doctrine of papal infallibility is an ingenious bureaucratic device which leaves the office inviolate no matter who fills it. It is one of the many examples of the church's ability to adapt nonreligious means to bulwark its authority.

The powerlessness of religious authority as an independent force in our age reveals a general condition for the operation of authority. Where the attempt is made to base authority upon a set of moral or transcendental postulates, without any effective independent means of enforcing it, such authority inevitably loses its transcendental character. This has become increasingly clear in the case of the Catholic Church, if one considers its development since the Reformation. At the other extreme, when obedience can only be secured through naked power, authority loses its effectiveness. These are the polarities within which modern societies operate with both extremes leading to similar consequences. Only in cases in which power and authority are inextricably intertwined can authority have the chance of enduring.

BUREAUCRATIC AUTHORITY

Bureaucracy is the most rational form of authority since its criteria are operational.[15] Paradoxically, to be effective, the bureaucrats must be convinced of the "rightness" of the operations they perform, not merely of their effectiveness. Historically, bureaucracy has been most efficient in social orders which contain extrabureaucratic values, as we have noted. In such societies the canons of bureaucracy were viewed as derived from extrarational norms permeating the social structure. Though we recognize bureaucracy as effective in the large-scale industry of a capitalist order we should be aware that by itself it would be almost useless. The present concern of industrial sociology with the importance of the informal structure in understanding attitudes of the worker suggest that bureaucratic norms have not filtered down the lines of authority.

If the cultural and historical character of bureaucracy is recognized it tells us something important about the authority it is able to engender. The fact that the bureaucrat has as a dominant value administrative efficiency has allowed him to continue on in his position despite radical changes in the governing ideology of the state power. The German Beamten who began his career under the Empire continued through under the Weimar Republic and even under Hitler.

What we may reasonably infer from the foregoing discussion is that bureaucracy by its nature cannot act stably as an independent source of authority. Its canons are efficiency and regularity, which, taken by themselves, do not afford the necessary kind of cement for social solidarity. No modern social order can operate without bureaucracy but, contrariwise, no social order operates by bureaucracy alone. Bureaucracies are always instruments which take on the color of the ends to which they are put. Weber has stressed the impersonal character of bureaucratic authority. If this alone were its distinguishing point one would have to accept bureaucracy as self-sufficient. But in stressing this point Weber played down the nonrational overtones which breathe authority into any office held. The managerial executive of a large industry certainly has more authority than that which

[15] Max Weber, "Science as a Vocation," op. cit.

his office defines. He can, for example, draw on the legendary image which his type has in the American social structure, tapping non-rational sources which lie outside bureaucratic definition.

The very fact that bureaucratic organization is an integral part of every modern social structure has fostered the growth of ideologies which, in some sense, compensate for the sterility of bureaucracy in effecting social solidarity. If the period of the French Revolution can be taken as the dividing line after which the inroads of bureaucratic organization became the *sine qua non* of modern social organization, it is since that period that a variety of many-hued ideologies have flourished. These ideologies have all sought to command absolute allegiance in order to establish the bases of authority once and for all. Nevertheless, behind their glittering façades the knuckled fist of force has given the lie to their pretensions. To take each of these ideologies at their face value would be a fruitless task, because they are variations on the same theme. There are constants which stand behind the many-faced masks, constants which fit in with the objective conditions of modern society.

CAESARISM: THE MODERN PERENNIAL

Caesarism, which to some extent is the precursor of our century's fascism, is the most representative of ideologies which compensate for the rigors of objective rationalization of society. Napoleon I stands as its great exemplar[16] and, though Bonapartism is a dead issue in French politics, the dynamics behind it brought forth a Boulanger in the eighties and find current expression in the person of De Gaulle. Since the legitimacy of monarchy lingered on into the first part of the nineteenth century, the Napoleonic form of Caesarism sought to harness the monarchical principle to the emerging recognition of the masses as an active factor in politics. The military man, which Napoleon was *par excellence*, drew much of his attractiveness from the idea that he stood above politics. He stood forth boldly, at least in the eyes of the many, as one who would take account of no special interests but would act rather as a severe mediator of conflicting groups. The French situation was quite logically the sire of this type of authority, for during the revolutionary period the army had been thoroughly overhauled, its feudal trappings stripped away, and for a time it became

[16] Guglielmo Ferrero, *The Principles of Power*, trans. by Theodore Jaeckel (New York, 1942).

the most democratic of institutions within the French social structure.[17] Caesarism in other countries could not become an effective force until armies in general had accepted the principle of universal military training and the concept of the citizen soldier.

After Thermidor, the army pursued an autonomous course, building up its own form of routinization and aims which Napoleon capitalized upon. The upper bourgeoisie, seeing it as a guarantee of their security, and ideologically bankrupt, gave themselves over to the new Caesarism. They could garner their profits while the Caesar kept up the front of being above parties. Napoleon ordered the state upon an authoritarian principle which gave lip service to democratic aspirations.

Such perversion of the democratic principle brought about its debasement. It reflected the usage of democracy as an ideology, the first of a long series of calculated uses, which helped to bring into disrepute the generic democratic principle. The Thermidoreans had tried it before, but Napoleon manipulated it in a much more subtle and devastating fashion. That the monarchical principle was vestigial was made clear by the acceptance of Napoleon into the Hapsburg family. The legitimacy of monarchy died long before kings ceased to rule.

Again, in France, this was made most manifest in the latter part of the last century and in our own. The Action Française, which set forth sweeping claims for the return of the monarchy, could count among its adherents a handful of *ancien régime* devotees and disinherited intellectuals. Its chief ideologist, Maurras, bared its fraudulent base in his explicit reduction of Catholicism to expediency. Avowedly an atheist, he favored the Gallican form of Catholicism as the state religion, as a necessary adjunct to the reinstitution of the monarchy. Even his conception of the monarchy bore little relationship to that of the *ancien régime*, for it was compounded of a virulent nationalism which was the distinct product of post-1789 France. Both monarchy and Catholicism were therefore screens for a reactionary nationalism. This was the direct antithesis to the legitimate phase of monarchy when the political derived its claims from the religious sphere.[18]

Twentieth-century Caesarism, unlike its Napoleonic progenitor,

[17] Crane Brinton, *A Decade of Revolution* (New York, 1934).
[18] *Ibid.*

does not have to use the remnants of monarchy to bolster its claims. The effectiveness of the monarchical principle has vanished among the vast majority of Western states. Caesarism in its fascist twentieth-century form spurns any connection with monarchy. With the growing basic democratization the flavor of monarchy is a hindrance which smacks of the dead past. Fascism must present itself as "radical" in order to gain the impetus of a mass movement.

Superficially, Weber's criteria for charisma, the imputation of superhuman qualities to a leader and the spontaneous identification of the followers with the leader, would seem to apply to Caesarism. However, on closer examination there is only a surface resemblance. Charisma, generically, can operate only in a social order which moves on the level of myth. Modern society with its rational forms of organization fails to meet the criteria for the operation of a genuine charisma. The pseudo-charisma which is rife in modern society is much better understood if it is conceived as Caesarism, which is an independent type of authority.

Its first modern exponent, Napoleon, was not only a master of manipulation of other people but also of himself. He was a rationalist of the highest order who depended upon conscious control of the techniques of mass persuasion known to his age. In his flair for self-dramatization and striking verbalization he was a master political showman. The leaders of modern mass movements all depend upon techniques of manipulation. The allegiance of the masses to the leader, although seemingly the same as that found in a genuinely charismatic situation, derives from different sources.

The will to follow a leader functions within a totally different type of social structure from that which genuine charisma demands. Sociopsychologically, as we have noted, the dynamic of mass movements is a compensation for the overrationalization of formal social organization. This is a qualitatively different base from the kind of society which generates true charisma. In the latter case, charisma is the epitome of a society which has little formal organization, while in the former it is the antithesis. The true charismatic leader carries within himself the seeds of what can become objectively absolute ends. He states in highly personalized terms a set of values which after his death may become generalized.

Christ, who stands as the ideal type, carried a message which when routinized could find objective residence in the Church, even though there was a distortion of values in the process. The modern Caesarist, on the other hand, since he makes power the ultimate touchstone, cannot create values which are enduring. His ideology is a patchwork to fit the needs of the moment. The crumbling Nazi power structure had no fundamental value elements in it which could transcend its adaptability to a given situation. The forces which created it still exist but if they seek new objectification they will in all likelihood do so in different ideological colors. *The modern Caesarist leaves no precipitate of value behind him, only refinement of technique and social and psychological wreckage.*

POLITICAL POLICE

Perhaps the most characteristic instrument of Caesarism is the organization of a political police as an integral part of the state. Out of this institution comes the refinement of techniques of control and also the most devastating social psychological flotsam. *The existence of political police eloquently testifies to the illegitimate and hence basically authorityless content of Caesarism.* Political police operate outside the boundaries of any legal system, their function being defined in terms of naked force and their power existing autonomously. Their existence is an index of the illegitimacy of particular states. The workings of a political police serve to demoralize those who are its targets, making them impotent through stark fear. This is the antithesis of the form of control which seeks to generate allegiance to the state by setting it up as a moral agent above and beyond its punitive functions. The fear which the political police inspires is an animal fear, one calculated to paralyze the moral attributes of man, to wrest from him his humanity. It is a reduction to the Hobbesian state of nature in which man is *homo homini lupus*, or more lately glorified by Spengler when he defined man as a beast of prey. Both Bruno Bettelheim's[19] and David Rousset's[20] picture of the impact which the Nazi death camps had upon the disintegration of personality bear agonizing testimony. While there is no comprehensive documentation similar to that of the Nazi case, there is enough evidence to draw similar conclusions in the case of the Soviet state.

[19] Bruno Bettelheim, "Individual and Mass Behavior in Extreme Situations," *Journal of Abnormal and Social Psychology*, 1943, pp. 417-452.
[20] David Rousset, *The Other Kingdom* (New York, 1947).

In his pioneer study "Dictatorship and Political Police," E. K. Bramstedt[21] shows the origin of political police in the Napoleonic state. Every Caesarist regime since has resorted to this instrument of terror. From Fouche to Himmler the head of the political police has held a key position in the Caesarist state. Whereas Fouche's role was relatively modest, and his area of activity circumscribed, subsequent historical development has witnessed the vast expansion and refinement of techniques of torture by the political police.

AUTHORITY AND LEGITIMACY

It must not be thought that states which do not have a political police are merely, by that fact, legitimate. The concept of legitimacy as applied to a social order is greatly in need of redefinition. As used by Weber it was the touchstone of authority, but his definition was an operational one and in that sense incomplete, for he consciously sought to eliminate problems of value from his analysis. The value question is vital to a concept of legitimacy: otherwise there is no judgment by which one may be considered as fulfilling general needs more adequately than another. There is still a crying need for an objective theory of value by which different kinds of legitimacy may be compared with one another. Legitimacy of itself cannot answer the question posed by the problem of authority.

As we have conceived of it, authority must always contain a non-rational basis for its operation, while legitimacy need not. In the contractual societies of the Western world the idea of legitimacy has meaning in reference to Gesellschaft norms.[22] These norms are spelled out in largely legal terminology. The mode of orientation, as Weber called it, is zweckrational; that is, people cannot be held legitimately responsible for actions which contravene norms which are not explicitly stated. Legitimacy is consequently all too often swallowed up by legality. It is no wonder then that the basis of solidarity has been eroded.

The divisiveness which is endemic to the social structure of the present Western capitalist world is a function of the way legitimacy is defined. If people can be held together only by short-term needs,

---

[21] E. K. Bramstedt, Dictatorship and Political Police (London, 1945).

[22] Ferdinand Tönnies, Fundamental Concepts of Sociology, trans. by Charles P. Loomis (New York, 1940).

social bonds are constantly in dissolution. The effects of this condition upon personality structure have been to vitiate the spontaneous co-operativeness of individuals, producing in abundance such types as are represented in fiction by Weidman's Harry Bogen of "I Can Get It For You Wholesale" and Schulberg's mobile Sammy. Ironically, these types, who are pathetic offshoots of a process they do not comprehend, are consciously blatant in their self-assertion. On the French scene, Celine's nihilistic lost souls reflect an even more advanced stage of the dissolution of the bonds of authority. They are aware of their pulverization and pitifully attempt to make a virtue out of their demoralization.

It is evident that in the cases in which political police have been institutionalized the resulting obedience is an effect of directly manipulated fear. In the contractual society the lack of a base for authority produces the insulated, atomized individual who is driven to accumulate power and wealth to compensate for his precarious insecurity.[23] The lack of any genuinely recognized authority, whose place is taken by ersatz substitutes, is the condition for normlessness.

NATIONALISM AND CONSTITUTIONALISM

We have concentrated upon delineating the emergence of a specific substitute authority as represented by Caesarism. However, even in countries which have not succumbed to this type of despotism, one of its most important ingredients is dominant. Nationalism has come to be the final arbiter of conflicting social values,[24] and since it is a value which is devoid of specific ethical content, it has ravaged the very nation it glorifies. The close historical association of Protestantism with nationalism has worked to the disadvantage of the former. Nationalism has blotted out opposing standards even though inroads have been made into its dominance as the growth of fifth column warfare during the past two World Wars attests.

In contrast to Protestantism, Catholicism's strong theoretical dissociation from the authority of any particular nation or nationalism has allowed it to maintain much more autonomous authority. Even though Protestantism has largely lost its religious dynamic, the effect

[23] Harold Lasswell, World Politics and Personal Insecurity (New York, 1935).
[24] Hans Kohn, The Idea of Nationalism (New York, 1944).

of the Protestant ethic upon personality has nourished the authority of nationalism. For both nationalism and Protestantism are divisive by definition. The right of individual conscience, which teeters desperately through lack of relatedness to supraindividual tenets, is often replaced by the self-determination of the nation as a corporate personality. Insofar as Catholics have accepted this, they have departed from a Catholic conception of authority.

The emergence of nationalism and liberalism from the common matrix of the rising middle class was bridged in part by constitutionalism. The nineteenth century has justly been called the century of constitution worship. The *sine qua non* of formulating a constitution, as soon as a new nation emerged, represented the recognition given to the rationalist universalist cosmos of natural law. This is substantiated by the attitude and actions of the liberal nationalist who conceived the principles of nationality and universality to be complementary, not contradictory. It is most clearly borne out in the life and writings of Mazzini and to some extent by the German nationalists of 1848. The year 1848 marks the dividing line of this more bland type of nationalism from its strident successor. Constitutions in this phase of nationalist development were considered to be fruitful outlines of social systems.

The thrust from below which, beginning in 1848, sent tremors of anxiety through the middle classes was accompanied by the romantic deification of the nation, and broke apart the alliance of nationalism and left-wing forces. Nationalism became a principle which was self-justifying, requiring no legitimation by a transcendent universalism. It functioned as a lightning rod to make harmless the aspirations of the emergent proletariat. Nationalism was aptly dubbed the socialism of the stupid and its most telling victory was won in 1914 when the Second International was shattered by the allegiance of its members to claims of the nation.[25] Insofar as nationalism became a conscious ideological weapon in the hands of the ruling groups, the ruling groups grew less concerned with constitutional prescriptions which checked the full power of nationalism.

Constitutions nowadays are not constructed so as to be in accord with suprapolitical aims. Even in the U.S. and England, where con-

[25] Merle Fainsod, *International Socialism and The World War* (Cambridge, Mass., 1935).

stitutionalism has a long tradition, it has been subject to the uses of conflicting interests. Whereas in its heyday the constitution gave some insight into the governmental and social structure of a particular nation, today constitutions often serve as a mask to conceal the actual governmental and social processes. The last and most grievous failure of genuine constitutionalism was that of the ill-fated Weimar Republic.[26]

On the face of it, the Portuguese and Soviet constitutions stand as paragons of democracy; but one would be extremely naïve to think that they describe the actual functioning of government in these nations. Constitutions have thus become ad hoc formulations which screen and confuse. Even in the U.S. and England, whose governments operate through legal norms derived from constitutions, there are hidden powers in the constitution which can overturn it. The phrase "constitutional dictatorship"[27] is quite modern and there is no telling whether the modifier might be dropped when extreme situations arise. In all cases nationalism and the interests of particular groups have reduced the abstract authority of constitutions to a convenient fiction.

In a world which is organized in its workaday activities along bureaucratic lines, the intensity of nationalism as an emotional force commanding the highest authority gives some surcease from the loneliness and lack of relatedness felt between individuals. Carried to its logical extreme it leads to racism, which characteristically enough reached its highest pitch in Germany, a nation perhaps more highly bureaucratized than any other.

SCIENCE AS A BASIS OF AUTHORITY

Many who have recognized the dire effects of the erosion of the bases of authority in the modern age have looked to its rehabilitation through science. In some respects, the nature of science would seem to provide a basis for authority which would be comparable to prescientific bases. On closer examination it becomes clear that the use of science as authority faces dangers similar to those we have grown so used to in nonscientific ideologies. The values implicit in the scientific method are enough to provide the extrarational basis of

[26] Arnold Brecht, Prelude to Silence (New York, 1944).
[27] Clinton Rossiter, Constitutional Dictatorship (Princeton, 1948).

authority for the *scientist* if he assimilates them. To consider them adequate for great masses of people would, however, lead to a disregard of the differentiation of function involved. Insofar as people are moved to legitimize their actions by invoking science, without being familiar with the rigors of the method, they fall into scientism. Journalistic popularizations of scientific activity which draw Utopian conclusions and thus nourish false hopes are all too common. The myth of science has become in some cases an ideological tool used to sanctify attitudes and actions which bear small resemblance to what the working scientist would accept as scientific.

Compared with other myths of authority, modern science does not authorize any particular cosmology.[28] It fosters an agnosticism toward final questions, leaving such problems to metaphysics. Even though men like Eddington and Jeans have attempted to construct a cosmology drawn from modern science, they have been justly called to account by their fellow scientists for deriving unwarranted implications from scientific findings. The laymen may be persuaded to accept and assimilate a new conception of the universe, but scientists as such know differently. Moreover, the use of science as a basis of authority suggests an hierarchical social order, a "New Republic" in which scientists would play the role which Plato reserved for the philosopher-kings. In like manner would the propagation of "the noble lie," which Plato considered legitimate, lead to the concentration of power and knowledge in a few select hands. These chosen ones, from what we know of personality, might develop a self-assured arrogance which could lead to the Rousseauist conception that men can be forced to be free.

The universality which science possesses has been recognized as a quality which is sadly needed in our present predicament. The point has been made that in an era in which the divisiveness of group truths have multiplied, science is the only authority which can claim to be universal. It makes no distinctions between men who differ in national background and class position. This must be recognized as a strong claim, but the ideological divisiveness which plagues our age is more often an effect rather than a cause of basic social malfunctions. Certainly the means of science are universal, but the ends to which they are directed is a problem presently outside the range of scientific

[28] George H. Mead, *The Philosophy of The Act* (Chicago, 1938).

determination. The universality implicit in scientific method could become an effective social force if the social materials for a world society were at hand. Without these conditions the authority of science is used to bolster conflicting political authorities.

Nevertheless, the possibility of science giving impetus to universality should not be disregarded. In the social sciences the work of Kurt Lewin and his co-workers in group dynamics is of particular importance along this line. Though the stage of broad generalization has not been reached, the empirical demonstration of the functional superiority of a democratic form of organization, its ability to nurture a personality type which is more secure and hence less given to seeking a scapegoat, suggests that democracy can find rational grounds for asserting its worth. Even to a limited extent, it can be seen that science can bolster the claims of a democratic form of authority, and it would therefore seem that on scientific grounds it is the duty of the scientist to take the side of fostering democracy, if Lewin's suggestive studies are proved valid.[29]

Science *alone* cannot be considered as a basis for social authority. It tends to contradict itself when used in this manner by falling into scientism. It does not have the power base to enforce authority and so must turn to some form of political power to enforce its claims. However, when we realize the possibilities which studies in the social sciences afford toward the rational validation of a democratic social order, science can perform a positive social function. The ethical basis of the democratic ideology, given a social structure which harmonizes with it, can possess authority, the power to enforce it, and a rational basis upon which to reconstruct the tattered fabric of social solidarity.

STRATEGIES OF SOCIAL CHANGE

Even if the above be true, we are still faced with the most pressing and difficult problem of moving from the given social order, with its structural irrationalities, to the desired end which is posited. The attempt to bring the claims of democracy down into the pattern of everyday living, to make it a living force, instead of a tool to be manipulated, has tremendous obstacles to overcome. Most obvious,

[29] R. Lippitt and R. K. White, "An Experimental Study of Leadership and Group Life," *Readings in Social Psychology*, ed. Newcomb and Hartley (New York, 1947), pp. 315-330.

but nonetheless most important, is the necessity of shifting the power base from capitalist sources to one which will have communal goals, with sufficient checks upon those who represent the community. The fulfillment of this objective action alone, though necessary, is hardly sufficient, as attempts toward socialism which consider this approach as self-sufficient have so disastrously shown. Again, Kurt Lewin in his article, "Group Decision and Social Change,"[30] has provided suggestions as to how people may be mobilized along paths in pursuance of a common goal without being driven or deceived. His conclusions, which have an empirical basis, imply that there is a spontaneity of group identity, and willingness to push forward, which could be summoned up for crucial occasions.

As important as this direction is, it must be paralleled by a concerted effort at building the type of personality which will be secure, self-sufficient, and self-insightful. Since personality is nourished incipiently in the family situation, and the attitudes toward authority gain their contours from this processing, a family atmosphere and structure which would generate such attitudes would seem to be an important point of attack. It must be realized that particular family patterns and atmospheres reflect the larger social pattern and cannot be understood apart from them.[31] Nevertheless, the institution of the family provides much more promising results for enduring change than an isolated frontal attack upon given political and economic institutions.

The middle class is much more receptive to changes in child rearing than lower-income groups and can be persuaded to make changes in this area. The lower-income groups would be much more difficult in this respect, because they do not have the leeway to pay attention to such problems. The method of evoking willingness to change in this regard would have to come from members of their own group, who have gained a measure of authority. If sufficient numbers of individuals are raised in an atmosphere in which the ambivalent attitude toward authority, which expresses itself in the need for love and the fear of its withdrawal, is muted, while *constant efforts at changing*

[30] Kurt Lewin, "Group Decision and Social Change," *Readings in Social Psychology*, ed. Newcomb and Hartley (New York, 1947), pp. 330-344.

[31] Erich Fromm, "Individual and Social Origins of Neurosis," *Personality in Nature, Society and Culture*, ed. Kluckhohn and Murray (New York, 1948), pp. 407-413.

political and economic institutions are going on, there will be a nucleus from which the total social pattern may be changed. We are well aware that personality needs are functionally related to the given norms of a social order and this two-pronged attack seems to be the only positive way toward reshaping the bases of authority.

In his illuminating study "Power and Personality," Harold Lasswell, using clinical materials, describes the interacting processes of personality development and social background.[32] It is important to note that Lasswell has not allowed himself to be bound by the walls which artificially divide academic disciplines. Similarly, all other studies which have been concerned with these problems have had to break across barricaded academic walls. This suggests that the authority of separate disciplines, which operate institutionally in the pursuit of knowledge, must themselves be transcended and subordinated to the more rational authority which is immanent in the quest for knowledge itself. Only from the intellectually adventurous personality, rather than the rigid academician, can come the type of knowledge and understanding we are so much in need of in the social sciences.

It should not be concluded that what has been cursorily projected implies a sudden disappearance of the nonrational from the human make-up, or its role in the formation of authority. What is implied, however, is that the nonrational aspect of authority will be more nearly harmoniously geared to the rational requirements, rather than being constantly contradictory.[33] Nor must it be concluded that some sort of conflictless order is possible. Conflict in spheres of authority seems to be a given. We may, however, hold the not altogether unwarranted hope that methods of adjudication of such conflicts will be developed when the basic problems which dog our paths are moving toward provisional resolution. It would be naïve to expect that the power which lies behind authority will ever dissipate itself. Intimations of Utopian anarchism are more harmful than helpful. We may rather expect that naked power will be minimized by being set in a mold of both ethical and rational authority which is always vigilant to affirm that power is a means rather than an end. Our present existence has made us all too familiar with the disastrous results which ensue when authority is reduced to its power base.

[32] Harold Lasswell, *Power and Personality* (New York, 1948).
[33] Erich Fromm, "Individual and Social Origins of Neurosis," *op. cit.*

Leadership and Social Crisis[1]

BY ROBERT A. NISBET

MORAL CRISES in civilization are less often the consequence of right against wrong or truth against error than they are of right against right and truth against truth. The present crisis of freedom and order in Western society—and all that is implied in the problem of leadership—would be easier to resolve were it plainly the outcome of antagonistic forces of good and evil. But who can doubt that the present premonitions of disaster and the whole tragic sense of life so evident in modern literature arise from a cultural condition in which we see the things we value destroyed or weakened by elements we also value. Thus on the one hand we prize equalitarian democracy, individualism, secularism, science, and the liberating impersonalities of modern industrial life. On the other hand, however, we continue to venerate tradition, the corporate moralities of family, church, and community, close personal involvement in clear moral contexts, and secure social status. Conflicts between these values in the modern Western world symbolize our deepest social conflicts and make difficult the perspective of leadership.

To regard all evil as a persistence of the past has been until recently a favorite conceit of the progress-nurtured liberal. But the contemporary intellectual, without wholly losing his faith in the future and his distrust of the past, is nevertheless coming to see a more and more enigmatic shape to those elements of the present that point most clearly to the future.

In the literature of moral revaluation that has spread so widely in recent years one theme stands above all others: the glaring discrepancy between morality and power. It is this which has disillusioned and

[1] This is a previously unpublished paper.

alienated a generation of thinkers from cherished ideas of economic and political reform. If there is one inference to be drawn from this literature it is that *moral purpose has been sacrificed to technical excellence and power.* Heretofore valued norms of human uplift have become tragically irrelevant to the social and psychological demands of the time. A more subtle inference might be the perception of widespread failure to bridge the gulf between moral ends and institutional realities by intermediate norms and procedures based upon knowledge.

What is the social vision that gives meaning to the varied processes of contemporary society? Is it democracy that we in the West would sight as our guiding star? Russia, much like Hitler's Germany, stridently reiterates its popular and democratic foundations. Each nation has been able to document its reiterations by reference to many of the same revolutionary forces in nineteenth-century Europe that we in the West continue to celebrate. Is it the Common Man? There is no country in the modern world that does not defend its most despotic invasions of liberty or security by an appeal to the sanctity of the common man. Is it Reason? Only the naïve persist in treating either the Communist or Fascist Leviathan, with their far-flung and "progressive" schemes of scientific management, as mere irruptions of the irrational. Immoral, if we like, but not irrational. Nor would we dare claim, in painful memory of the superb assurance with which the Russian, the German, and the Japanese fought in the recent war, that spiritual faith alone is the touchstone of the cultural salvation that each of us continues to hope for.

Few moderns would reject any of these values—democracy, reason, faith, the individual—for they are clearly the heritage of all that is most distinctive and noble in the Western heritage. Yet few would deny that in each of them there is something for modern man that is elusive and curiously irrelevant. As symbols none of them seems to stand in clear relation to the actual problems of the culture we find ourselves in. It is not that either democracy or rationalism is obsolete. *It is rather that the embedded meanings of each lack that sharp relevance to immediate circumstances that is the condition of effective symbolism.* And the problem of symbolism is indeed at the very heart of the problem of leadership in the modern state.

"Now when we examine how a society bends its individual members to function in conformity with its needs, we discover that one important operative agency is our vast system of inherited symbolism. There is an intricate expressed symbolism of language and of act, which is spread throughout the community, and which evokes fluctuating apprehension of the basis of common purposes. The particular direction of individual action is directly correlated to the particular sharply defined symbols presented to him at the moment."[2]

But in our own time, as many observers have pointed out, more and more of this "vast system of inherited symbolism" has become dim to the vision and weak to the touch. Inherited symbolism does not now afford so secure a foothold to reason, nor to leadership. Two centuries of individualism in ethics, religion, economics, and politics have acted to weaken the symbolism upon which both reason and leadership have traditionally relied. In short, we are dealing with a difficulty that is social in the broadest sense.

Contemporary interest in the problem of leadership is closely related to inquiries into the nature of the social bond, to studies of group identification, social role, and other problems of interpersonal relations. All of these are, to a significant degree, theoretical reflections of the basic moral preoccupation in our age with the adjustment of the individual to a complex political and economic order. Future historians of Western society are not likely to miss in their intellectual inquiries the present compelling importance of the problem of insecurity. "The most obvious symptom of the spiritual disease of our civilization," an English scholar has written recently, "is the widespread feeling among men that they have lost all control of their destinies. . . . It is not new for men to be cogs in the machine; it is new for them to be frustrated by the fact."[3]

Not a few of the contemporary mass movements in politics are directed to the people for whom society has become cold and unapproachable, to the disinherited and the disenchanted. Those who professed wonder that the crude and fantastic doctrines of Hitler could have enlisted the intellectual support of millions of otherwise intelligent human beings missed, in the phenomenon, the deep urge of Germans to become morally identified, to escape from a world in which economic mechanism and caprice combined to create feelings

[2] A. N. Whitehead, *Symbolism, Its Meaning and Effect* (New York, 1927), p. 73.

[3] Robert Birley, *Burge Memorial Lecture for 1947*.

of frustration and insecurity. If moral security came with conversion to Nazism, the convert could agree perversely with Tertullian that intellectual absurdity might be the crowning appearance of truth.

In his classic account of the religion of ancient Greece, Sir Gilbert Murray has described the period following the Peloponnesian Wars as one "based on the consciousness of manifold failure, and consequently touched both with morbidity and with that spiritual exaltation which is so often the companion of morbidity. . . . This sense of failure, this progressive loss of hope in the world, threw the later Greek back upon his own soul, upon the pursuit of personal holiness, upon emotions, mysteries and revelations, upon the comparative neglect of this transitory and imperfect world for the sake of some dream world far off, which shall subsist without sin or corruption, the same yesterday, today, and forever."[4]

Murray uses the phrase "failure of nerve" to describe the collapse of the moral ties which had bound the individual to others and given him a warming sense of direction of his own destiny. A collapse which left the external world as something hostile, cold, and fortuitous. The failure of nerve in declining Athens was an intellectual transformation, but it accompanied the steady disintegration of the cementing bonds of the old community. The ties of family, community, and religion, the ancient conveyors of Athenian values, had grown weak under the incessant impact of war and economic tensions. Increasingly the outer world of society took on a harsh and formidable appearance; a world at best to tolerate, not to participate in. Out of social disintegration emerged the undifferentiated, atomized masses. Out of it, too, came the solitary, inward-turning ego.

In the present age, as many writers bear witness, signs abound that point to the spreading incidence of analogous conditions. It is not necessary to succumb to fatalism or sterile determinism to perceive that we, too, face a society, especially in Europe, composed in ever-increasing numbers of amorphous and incoherent masses of people who have seen spiritual meanings vanish with the forms of traditional society and who struggle vainly to find reassimilation. This is an age of the omnicompetent state and of economic interdependence, but it is also an age of bewildered masses and of solitary, obsessed individuals.

Anxiety, a contemporary novelist has written, is the natural state of

4 Gilbert Murray, *Five Stages of Greek Religion* (New York, 1930), p. 18.

twentieth-century man. At the very least, anxiety and frustration have become the natural state of the contemporary novel, and of much poetry and drama as well. The hero in the contemporary novel, it has been said, is not the man who does things, but the man to whom things are done. The morbid, normless being, twisted into passive neuroticism by the conflicting compulsions of an incomprehensible world, bids fair to become the reigning literary type of the age—a kind of inverted Tom Jones. In much contemporary fiction there is vagueness and indecisiveness of intent, accompanied by a belief that the exterior world is a vast scene of purposeless and inexplicable forces. The notion of the impersonality of society is a pervasive one; a society in which all actions and motives seem to have equal value and to be perversely detached from human direction. Widespread, too, is the vision of irresistible fate, before which the mind and spirit of the individual are helpless. Nor can one miss the ethical implications of those literary works in which the most intense individual spirituality is set in conditions of rotting social circumstances. The ancient quest for spiritual ecstasy through mortification of the flesh has been transposed, it would seem, into the same quest but through mortification of circumstances.

THE RISE OF "SOCIAL" MAN

It would be difficult to exaggerate the importance in contemporary writing of the problem of the individual in his relation to the social and moral world. The spectacle of the individual caught treacherously in a world of shifting norms is not merely a widespread theme in literature; it has become a basic theoretical problem of the humanities and the social sciences. The "lost individual," to use Dewey's phrase, is a creature of as much concern to the politics of a Lasswell, the anthropology of a Mead, and the psychology of a Horney, as to the theology of a Niebuhr or Demant.

The problem of the individual and his relation to society is an old one. Quite apart from the concern with the problem in the ancient and medieval worlds, it has been a continuous theme of the social sciences since the seventeenth century. Present concern with the bases of order is not wholly new. But it is important to observe some of the differences between present and earlier inquiries. From the seventeenth through the nineteenth centuries the dominant perspectives of order were essentially *political* and *economic*. The rise of the theory of secular sovereignty in the sixteenth century became the major response to the problem of stability and, indeed, has remained the most influential. From Bodin to Rousseau the chief objective of political theory was the reconciliation of man and the secular state. The rise of formal economics at the end of the eighteenth century did not significantly change this objective. The origins of political economy rested on the assumption of self-sufficient individuals bound together by the impersonal ties of a mechanical system. The main effort of economists went toward the ascertainment of the theoretical conditions under which a state based upon aggregates of free and discrete individuals could achieve economic stability.

But now it is the *social problem* that has come to the fore. What was in the first instance an exclusive interest of sociology has become a more and more influential and characteristic aspect of all the social sciences. The very shift in terminology is instructive. Concepts of sovereignty, contract, equilibrium, and instinct, to be sure, have not disappeared. But increasingly they are rivaled in theoretical interest and empirical inquiry by such terms as *status, identification, group, anomie, interpersonal relations, security, role,* and *leadership,* terms which reflect vividly the transfer of attention to an area of association that heretofore has been indifferently regarded if not neglected altogether. It is not necessary to describe in detail the separate lines of investigation associated with the names of such contemporary students as Mayo, Bakke, Lasswell, Fromm, Murphy, Warner, Moreno, Parsons, Merton, and many others in the front ranks of social science, to bring pointedly to attention the fact that in all of the social sciences at the present time *there is a gathering momentum in the whole study of social cohesion,* interpersonal relations, call it what we will. Where the solid fact of the individual was the basis of analysis and the unit upon which systems of theory were based a generation ago, it is now the primary *relationships* among men that are becoming central. They provide the guiding perspective of studies of industry, community, race, and nation. In these relationships is found the clue not only to cultural stability but to the stability of the individual himself. The "individual" has become for both conceptual and therapeutic purposes a kind of unity of social memberships and intensities of participation.

The scientific nature of many of these inquiries into the conditions of association and dissociation, and the relation of the individual to the group, is apparent. On all sides, particularly in sociology, applied anthropology, and social psychology, the basic elements of the associative process have become subjected to experimental and comparative studies. Controlled studies of the intensities of social relationships, the processes of leadership, depictions of social position in factory and community, measurements of tensions within and among groups—all of these are to be regarded as among the most hopeful signs on the horizon for the revitalization of human relations—in industry and community.

But there is a quickly reached limit to both the theoretical value and the practical utility of studies in human relations that lose sight of the historically given institutional realities of our time. Thus, an experimentally controlled study of the effects of varying kinds of leadership upon groups of children, or a study of associational spontaneity in an isolated workroom in a factory, has, in each case, a true value that can be perceived only when these contrived situations are interpreted in the light of their larger surroundings and in light of the historical position of these surroundings. In their efforts to uncover "natural" social relationships certain contemporary students are likely to wander into the same blind alley that the classical economists were led into—a blind alley that can be described most tersely as doctrinaire universalism.

To deal with problems of social structure and personal identification, however scientifically, without recognition of their historical background, without regard for their institutional setting, is at once to underestimate the complexity of these problems and to make almost impossible any practical utilization of the answers. It is not possible to regard problems in social relations in the same perspective in which the physicist or chemist regards his problems. Concepts such as function, structure, identification, dissociation, and leadership have theoretical and practical relevance only when their referents are regarded as the outcome of historical processes. Not that the narrative method of the academic historian points the way here. What is important is to see the present as a *historical* stratification of elements, some new, some old, all in varying patterns of interaction.

EFFICIENCY AND INSECURITY

Now all of this is related closely to the problem of leadership. For the interest in leadership, so pronounced at the present time, is a manifestation of the same intellectual pattern that contains the interest in problems of association and dissociation. And beneath this total pattern of ideas lie the psychologically and morally baffling institutional circumstances in which more and more individuals find themselves in contemporary society. These circumstances are in a real sense the very materials of the practical problem of leadership. It is important to remind ourselves continuously that leadership is inseparable from specific, environing conditions.

What Livingston Lowes has written on the creative process is relevant in a consideration of the relation between leadership and the materials of leadership. " 'Creation' like 'creative' is one of those hypnotic words which are prone to cast a spell upon the understanding and dissolve our thinking into haze. And out of this nebulous state of the intellect springs a strange but widely prevalent idea. The shaping spirit of Imagination sits aloof, like God, as He is commonly conceived, creating in some thaumaturgic fashion out of nothing its visionary world. . . . [But] we live, every one of us—the mutest and most inglorious with the rest—at the center of a world of images. . . . Intensified and sublimated and controlled though they be, the ways of the creative faculty are the universal ways of that streaming yet consciously directed something which we know (or think we know) as life. Creative genius, in plainer terms, works through processes which are common to our kind, but these processes are superlatively enhanced."[5]

In leadership there is something of the same combination of imagination and experience that goes into the creative process; Leadership indeed is one manifestation of the creative proclivity. To draw organization out of the raw materials of life is as much the objective of the leader as it is of the artist. *Structure or organization is the primary concern of the leader, as form is the concern of the artist.* Leadership is no more comprehensible than any other type of imaginative creation except in terms of the materials. "Every great imaginative conception is a vortex into which everything under the sun may be

[5] J. Livingston Lowes, *Road to Xanadu* (Boston, 1930), pp. 428, 429, 430.

swept. . . . For the imagination never operates in a vacuum. Its stuff is always fact of some order, somehow experienced; its product is that fact transmuted. . . . I am not forgetting that facts may swamp imagination, and remain unassimilated and untransformed."[6]

Whether we consider the leader as planner, policy maker, ideologist, or as exemplar, we are dealing essentially with an imaginative conception, a vortex, into which the materials of the environing culture are swept, assimilated, and expressed. And even as the creative urge in literature, art, drama, and religion expresses itself selectively, so to speak, in history, taking note now of one theme, now of another, forming thus distinguishable ages or periods, even so does leadership. For there are configurations of leadership, from age to age, even as there are historic configurations in the arts and sciences. It is difficult not to believe that leadership presents itself, as do poetry and painting, in historical types, each given form and illumination by some distinctive theme.

Now the theoretical problem of leadership in contemporary democracy must be seen in light of the conditions which have produced the widespread scientific interest in problems of social structure and function, identification, role, and status. All of these problems are intellectualizations of a social crisis created by certain changes in the relation of individuals to institutions. From these changes has come the obsessive problem of insecurity. And, more than anything else, it is insecurity that gives the unique color to leadership in our time.

The modern release of the individual from the traditional ties of religion, class, family, and community has made him free—free at least in the negative sense of disenchantment with, and aloofness from, the old moral certainties. But for many individuals this emancipation from the traditional fetters of custom and prejudice has resulted not in a creative sense of independence but in a stultifying feeling of aloneness and irresponsibility. For generations after the dissolution of the legal bonds of medievalism the social ties remained to bind individuals. But the same forces which led to the breaking of the legal bonds began to dissolve the psychological bonds and to smash the sense of lateral and vertical interdependence.

Our social crisis is essentially a crisis within the same order of social relationships that is undergoing disintegration in the civilizations

[6] Ibid., pp. 426-427.

peripheral to the West, societies indeed that have received the full impact of Western civilization. Even as the ancient loyalties and allegiances—to caste, family, village community—are weakening in such areas as India, China, and Burma, thus creating in almost painful intensity the problem of leadership, so have the analogous loyalties become weak in our own society. Basically, ours is also a crisis in transferred allegiances. In any society the concrete loyalties and devotions of individuals—and their typical personality structures—will tend to become oriented toward those institutions which in the long run have the greatest perceptible significance to the maintenance of life. In earlier times, the family, church, class, and local community drew and held the allegiances of men, not because of any indwelling instinct to associate, not because of greater impulses to love and befriend, but because these were the chief security-providing and authority-giving agencies in the personal lives of individuals.

Leadership—actual leadership—was so subtly and so delicately interwoven into the fabric of kinship, guild, class, and church that the conscious problem of leadership hardly existed. So far as the bulk of people were concerned leadership came not from distant political rulers but from the innumerable heads of families, villages, guilds, and parishes. Between the individual and the highest ruler in the land there lay a continuous hierarchy of intermediate orders and intermediate leaders. There was indeed a kind of chain of leadership in society even as in philosophic imagination there was a "great chain of Being" that connected the lowest inorganic substance to God.

Contemporary interest in leadership in mass society, like the related interest in social cohesion, has been precipitated by the growing irrelevance of traditional centers of association and authority. As modern events make plain, the older primary centers of association have been superseded in institutional importance by the great impersonal connections of property, function, and exchange in modern society. These connections have had a liberating influence upon the individual. Through them he has been able, not only in Europe but also in parts of India, China, and Latin America, to shake off the restraints of patriarchal and hierarchical servitude. But the impersonal relations have had an isolating influence, for they are in no broad sense social relationships. As Park has written: "Everywhere in the Great Society the relations of man, which were intimate and personal, have been more or less superseded by relations that are impersonal and formal. The result is that in the modern world, in contrast with earlier and simpler societies, every aspect of life seems mechanized and rationalized. This is particularly true in our modern cities, which are in consequence so largely inhabited by lonely men and women."[7]

The moral and social isolation, the increasing individual insecurities, the rash of tensions that characterize so many areas of modern life, should not be dismissed as merely urban phenomena. For, as recent studies have shown, the old stereotype of the rural area must be discarded and replaced, in the United States at least, by a picture which contains in an increasing number of localities these same phenomena. When agriculture becomes dominated by the principles of organization that have characterized industrialism, the social consequences are the same.[8]

The point that is crucial here is that the basic decisions in modern mass society have become vested increasingly in organizations and relationships that operate with technical and essentially nonsocial procedures. Vital activities have thus been removed from the competence of the older traditional areas of practical decision-making. In consequence, their sheer institutional importance has waned. Their growing economic and administrative irrelevance has been the basis of their decline in symbolic importance, a fact of the utmost significance to the social basis of leadership in modern society.

Thus in industry, as A. D. Lindsay has written, "the tendency is to specialize planning and organization in a few hands and to ask unskilled repetition work of the great mass of work-people. . . . The factory manager is primarily a technician. He has to contrive an organization of human effort which in conjunction with the operation of machinery will produce the most efficient results. He does not treat his factory as a real society, but as a collection of forces or powers. He is not a leader and does not consider the problem of leadership. A leader has power because he is trusted and believed in; no man can lead or govern without somehow winning the confidence of those whom he leads. Business management is a much more impersonal

[7] Robert Park, "Modern Society," cited by S. de Grazia, The Political Community (Chicago, 1948), p. 107.

[8] See the valuable study by Walter Goldschmidt, As You Sow (New York, 1947).

business. . . . The odd result is that 'the management'—whether employers or managing directors, do not lead the men they control. They have enormous power over men's lives but they are not their leaders. The men choose their own leaders to defend them against management."[9]

But even in trade unions, those at least which have also become large-scale organizations, the problem of social cohesion and leadership is a pressing one. For the forces of impersonality and rationalization have entered here also, even as they have entered into many of the larger political, charitable, and educational organizations in the contemporary world. Nor have these forces been absent in religion, especially Protestantism. There is in consequence a disinclination among many Protestants to stand now, as did their forefathers, on the primacy of individual faith to organization, of conscience to institutional membership. The widening implications of the problem of the lost individual in modern society have not been lost on those for whom the answer is to be found within Christianity. There is growing awareness that ecclesiastical leadership, if it is to be decisive, must be rooted in social structure, not merely in faith.

Much has been written about the gigantic Manhattan Project during the second World War, the extraordinary and unprecedented spectacle of tens of thousands of individuals working for several years upon a product the nature of which few of them knew or were permitted to discover, and who were forbidden even to look too closely into the identities of their fellow workers. Such an organization is manifestly extreme, but in retrospect the Manhattan Project may with some justice be viewed as a kind of extension of the scene in which more and more workers find themselves in modern industry. The impersonalism and mechanization of relationships in many areas of industry and government, the frustrations that come from noninvolvement in even minor decision-making, and the consequent feelings of anonymity, cannot help but react disastrously upon the almost universal desires of men for status and for intelligible leadership.

The impersonalization of social relationships in modern Western society can be seen also in the rise of formal public and private administration. We are most indebted to Max Weber for perceiving the

[9] A. D. Lindsay, The Modern Democratic State (New York, 1943), pp. 184-185.

historical importance of bureaucracy. Weber saw in the development of bureaucracy the same exclusion of qualitative social differences and the same reduction of cultural diversity to mechanical uniformity that distinguished philosophical rationalism of the seventeenth and eighteenth centuries. "It is decisive for the specific nature of modern loyalty to an office that in the pure type it does not establish a relationship to a person, like the vassal's or the disciple's faith in feudal or in patrimonial relations of authority. Modern loyalty is devoted to impersonal and functional purposes. . . . The fully developed bureaucratic mechanism compares with other organizations exactly as does the machine with the nonmechanical modes of production."

In bureaucracy, as Weber saw, there is created a kind of abstract regularity of authority which is at once the fulfillment of equalitarianism and of impersonality. "Its specific nature, which is welcomed by capitalism, develops the more perfectly the more bureaucracy is 'dehumanized,' the more completely it succeeds in eliminating from official business love, hatred, and all purely personal, irrational, and emotional elements which escape calculation."[10]

It is obvious that an extraordinary number of activities which in earlier times were the functions of smaller unities and their leaderships have undergone a transforming rationalization of procedure. There has been a transfer of responsibilities and custodianships from the vast plurality of primary, close relationships to a diminishing number of great, bureaucratically administered agencies which operate with a maximum of technical efficiency. The administration of such functions as charity, hospitalization, unemployment assistance is manifestly more dependable, more regular, and more pervasive when so organized. But the gains in technical efficiency and diffusion of service do not offset the resulting problems of identification and security among individuals.

SECURITY WITH FREEDOM

At bottom, social organization is a pattern of basic identifications in which feelings of reciprocity and intimacy are interwoven. Only thus does the individual have a sense of status. Only thus is communication established which makes effective leadership possible. But

[10] Max Weber, *Essays in Sociology*, ed. Gerth and Mills (New York, 1946), pp. 199, 216.

if social stability is rooted in personal identification and in groups and associations small enough to provide a sense of participation, then, plainly, there is a serious problem presented by the vast increase of forces of impersonality and anonymity; especially when in these forces there are lodged the basic economic and political decisions affecting the individual's existence.

It is a problem in security, but it is also a problem in the perspective of freedom. For there is evidence that people tend "to react favorably to authoritarian leadership when they are emotionally insecure or when they find themselves in an ambiguous and critical social position."[11] Leadership then becomes invested with a sacred significance that offers surcease from the frustrations and anxieties of society. Studies of the National Socialist movement in Germany suggest strongly that the greatest appeal of Hitler lay in those areas or spheres of society in which feelings of moral isolation and social anonymity were strong.[12] As Drucker has written: "The despair of the masses is the key to the understanding of fascism. No 'revolt of the mob,' no 'triumphs of unscrupulous propaganda,' but stark despair caused by the breakdown of the old order and the absence of a new one. . . . Society ceases to be a community of individuals bound together by a common purpose, and becomes a chaotic hubbub of purposeless isolated nomads. . . . The average individual cannot bear the utter atomization, the unreality and senselessness, the destruction of all order, of all society, of all rational individual existence through blind, incalculable, senseless forces created as result of rationalization and mechanization. To banish these new demons has become the paramount objective of European society."[13]

The leadership of Hitler was no simple revival of ancient forms of force, nor was it based upon any of the traditional ritualizations of remote mastery or domination. Kolnai has told us that the word *Führer* has the meaning, among others, of "guide." "The intimacy implied in modern '*Fuhrertum*' corresponds to the idea that the

11 Krech and Crutchfield, *Theory and Problems of Social Psychology* (New York, 1948), p. 429.

12 See, for example, H. Peak, "Observations on the characteristics and distribution of German Nazis," *Psychological Monographs*, 59, No. 276. Also, Loomis and Beegle, "The Spread of German Nazism in Rural Areas," *American Sociological Review*, 1946.

13 Peter Drucker, *The End of Economic Man* (New York, 1939), p. 67.

Leader is—in a particular sense—congenial to the People, linked to it by special bonds of affinity. . . . In an address delivered by Hitler at the Nürnberg Party Congress in 1934, we find the definition: 'Our leadership does not consider the people as a mere object of its activity; it lives in the people, feels with the people, and fights for the sake of the people! . . . It is even suggested, much in the spirit of Schmitt, that the *Führer* system guarantees the only real 'democracy,' for it alone secures an effective 'representation of the people.' "[14] We are deceiving ourselves if we refuse to see that behind the appearance of Nazism lay, on the one hand, widening areas of social disintegration produced by many of the individualistic forces that we ourselves celebrate, and, on the other the popularization of the State as a spiritual area of salvation for the disinherited.

The modern intellectual has been, on the whole, the political intellectual. In his eyes the apparatus of formal government has appeared the most desirable medium of social and moral reform. The result has been to throw the greater weight of attention upon the creation and utilization of *political* leadership, upon *political* administration, leaving other types of leadership in society—and their fate in modern history—unexamined. Only in the most recent years has the problem of leadership in industry, in trade unions, in all the essentially nongovernmental forms of association, come to assume respectable significance. This fact, to be sure, has various explanations, but not least among them is the suspicion that however crucial the State may be in modern civilization, political leadership is not enough. For political leadership plainly becomes capricious and inadequate to the demands of freedom and order unless it is rooted deeply in the variety of social and economic and cultural leaderships in society.

The historic significance of political democracy has resulted not so much from its insistence upon individual freedom as from its proffer of the State as an area of psychological participation and integration. Democracy arose at a time when the older social unities were undergoing a radical displacement caused by industrialism, urbanism, and the various other individualizing and secularizing forces of modern history. In the inspired utterances of its advocates, democratic free-

[14] Aurel Kolnai, *The War Against the West* (London, 1938), pp. 150, 153, 156.

dom came to be envisaged not as the preservation of immunity from the State but as full participation in the power of the State. Democracy popularized and in a significant sense sanctified the State relationship. The continuous expansion of political power and responsibility that has been inherent in the democratic state would be inexplicable were it not for the underlying, popular, emotional acceptance of the State as a haven and provider even as the Church held this role in earlier Europe.[15]

The socialist tradition which followed Marx accepted at its full value the theory of the omnicompetent state. It has, however, contributed little to an adequate conception of the management or the administration of the society envisaged by socialists. The naïveté which underlay Marx's own view of the state was expressed in his curious statement that "when, in the course of development, class distinctions have disappeared, and all production has been concentrated in the hands of a vast association of the whole nation, the public power will lose its political character."[16] A half a century later Lenin could write, in the same vein, of the "simple" transition to socialism. "The bookkeeping and control necessary for this have been simplified by capitalism to the utmost, till they have become the extraordinarily simple operations of watching, recording, and issuing receipts, within the reach of anybody who can read and write and knows the first four arithmetical rules. . . . When most of the functions of the State are reduced to this bookkeeping and control by the workers themselves, it ceases to be the 'political' State. Then the public functions are converted from political into simple administrative functions.' "[17]

As the result of an uncritical attitude toward political power and of a mechanistic view that organizational and leadership problems are settled by history itself, contemporary socialists have been found disastrously short in the kind of administrative knowledge that is needed in the planned state. It is a striking commentary on the history of modern socialism that nearly all of the actual techniques utilized in contemporary national planning—in England and the United

[15] Tocqueville, Ostrogorski, and Max Weber, among others, have dealt with this fully.

[16] *Communist Manifesto* (Chicago, Ill., Charles H. Kerr and Co., 1940), p. 42.

[17] *The State and Revolution* (New York, 1939), p. 205.

States, as well as in Soviet Russia—are the product chiefly of experience by capitalist nations in wartime.[18] The manifold problems of bureaucracy and leadership, of social incentives, of autonomous areas of responsibility, and of the preservation of group freedoms in the planned state have no readier answer in traditional socialist thought than they have in the orthodox theory of public administration.

The planned state we must have in one degree or another. The alternative in the economic, military, and political society that we have developed is simply chaos. But we need not assume, as many technicians have assumed, that planning merely with a view toward economic and political processes is sufficient. For our main problems are social—social in the exact sense that they pertain to the personal relationships among human beings and to the status of individuals. To refer to the social problem in any concrete sense is to refer to the actual groups and associations in which human beings live—to families, trade unions, local communities, churches, professions, and all the other forms of association in a complex civilization.

To suppose that these centers of leadership will remain vital and symbolically important when they have become institutionally irrelevant in our economic and political order is to indulge in fantasy. The decline of kinship as an important psychological sphere within Western society has been, at bottom, no more than the diminution or disappearance of those institutional functions which formerly gave the kinship group centrality in the life of the individual. It would be naïve not to see that the loss of institutional functions by other groups —groups now central in our industrial civilization—may have analogous consequences. Social groups thrive not upon moral fervor or ritual enchantment but upon what they can offer their members institutionally in the way of protection and well being. Thus, as more and more liberals have come to realize, there is a profound social difference between a State that seeks to provide a legal scene within which trade unions and coöperatives themselves can raise their members' standard of living, and a State that seeks, however benevolently, to make this its own direct and exclusive responsibility.

The demands of effective leadership, like the demands of freedom and security, necessitate a large amount of autonomy and functional

[18] This point has been stressed by E. H. Carr in *The Soviet Impact on the Western World* (New York, 1946).

significance in those spheres of society which are *intermediate* to the individual and the State. In one of his most perceptive passages Tocqueville wrote: "It must not be forgotten that it is especially dangerous to enslave men in the minor details of life. For my own part I should be inclined to think freedom less necessary in great things than in little things, if it were possible to be secure of the one without the other."[19] The implications of this statement are more relevant to our own age than they were a hundred years ago when Tocqueville wrote. For it is only in the present age that the technical command of communication and the psychological knowledge of attitudes have made it possible in any full sense to invade, politically, the private areas of existence.

The assumption that centralized power must carry with it centralized administration was tenable only in a day when the range of governmental activities was limited. It is no longer tenable. As government, in its expanding range of functions, comes ever closer to the spheres of primary social existence, the need is intensified for a theory of public administration that will be alive to social and psychological values and to the relationship between political power and cultural associations and groups. In this connection, Karl Mannheim has written that "It is obvious the modern nature of social techniques puts a premium on centralization, but this is only true if our sole criterion is to be technical efficiency. If, for various reasons, chiefly those concerned with the maintenance of personality, we deliberately wish to decentralize certain activities within certain limits, we can do so."[20]

We cannot be reminded too often that the stifling effects of centralization upon leadership are as evident in large scale private industry as in political government. Big government and big business have developed together in Western society, and each has depended upon the other. To these two has been added more recently a third force in society, big labor. In all three spheres there has been a strong tendency to organize administration in terms of ideas of power inherited from the seventeenth and eighteenth centuries. In all three spheres there are perplexing problems created by the widening gulf between, on the one hand, a technically trained and experienced

[19] *Democracy in America* (New York, 1945), II, 230.
[20] Karl Mannheim, *Man and Society in an Age of Reconstruction* (New York, 1940), p. 319.

managerial group who lead and, on the other, the rank-and-file membership.

"Centralization in administration," David Lilenthal has written, "promotes remote and absentee control, and thereby increasingly denies to the individual the opportunity to make decisions and to carry those responsibilities by which human personality is nourished and developed.

"I find it impossible to comprehend how democracy can be a living reality if people are remote from their government and in their daily lives are not made a part of it, or if the control and direction of making a living—in industry, farming, the distribution of goods—is far removed from the stream of life and from the local community. 'Centralization' is no mere technical matter of 'management,' of 'bigness versus smallness.' We are dealing here with those deep urgencies of the human spirit which are embodied in the faith we call 'democracy.' "[21]

The larger problem of society and leadership at the present time is not that of the devolution of administrative authority within formal political government. It is the division of powers and responsibilities between political authority, wherever lodged, and the whole plurality of autonomous social groups in our society. These are the areas of psychological security, as they are the areas within which practical freedom unfolds. They are also the primary spheres of leadership. So long as public opinion is confronted with the choice between insecure individualism in these areas of existence and political collectivism, the trend toward centralization will not be arrested, and the moral attraction of Leviathan will become irresistible.

[21] T. V. A. Democracy on the March (New York, 1944), p. 139.

INDEXES

Name Index

Subject Index

Agitator, aloofness of, 81-84
  as bullet-proof martyr, 87, 88
  as feeling the "inner-call," 87-89
  as great little man, 82-87
  as persecuted, 89-91
  as self with inside knowledge, 97-99
  as tough guy, 96-97
  charismatic, 60-63, 99
  fascist, 80 ff.
  intimations of, 80 ff.
  open display of, 81 ff.
  portrait of self of, 82 ff.
  sacred, 63
  secular, 63
  speeches of, 82 ff.
  techniques of, 81-99
        See also Leaders; Leadership
Alienation, Marx's view of, 57
  society and, 645 ff., 680 ff.
  Weber's view of, 57
        See also Crisis; Mastery
Apathy, activity and, 532
  affect and, 539, 545 ff.
  altruism and, 530
  apolitical approaches to politics and,
    518 ff.
  as fifth column, 477
  career interests and, 493 ff.
  changing means of politics and, 506
  character and culture with, 558-559
  class structure and, 534 ff.
  cliques and, 553-555
  communists and, 502-504
  constitutions and, 480 ff.
  control and, 487 ff.
  criteria for political, 505 ff.
  democracy and, 479 ff., 489 ff.
  democratic associations and, 490 ff.

Apathy—(Continued)
  formal organization and, 479
  frantic detachment and, 528
  full-time officials and, 492 ff.
  guilt and, 520
  impotence and, 529
  indices for, 531
  in trade unions, 499-502
  man as limited and, 513
  marginal position and, 521-523
  Marxism and, 531
  masochism and, 531
  oligarchy and, 484 ff.
  participation in associations and, 481-
    484
  passionless existence and, 536
  personalized and impersonalized, 549-
    553
  political competence and, 540
  political concern and, 525
  politics in the earlier era and, 507
  politics in the present era and, 510
  procedures for fulfilling democratic
    values and, 489 ff.
  projection and, 520-521
  purpose and, 535 ff.
  reactive hatred and, 540
  real and spurious, 542
  realism, growth of, and, 516
  role conflicts and, 494 ff.
  sadism and, 521
  scope of oligarchy and, 484
  social distance and, 543
  social intercourse and, 538
  social sources of participation and,
    486-489
  status and, 514 ff.
  temperament and, 535

730